TRENDS AND ISSUES IN INSTRUCTIONAL DESIGN AND TECHNOLOGY

Second Edition

Edited by

Robert A. Reiser
Florida State University

John V. Dempsey
University of South Alabama

Upper Saddle River, New Jersey
Columbus, Ohio

Library of Congress Cataloging in Publication Data

Trends and issues in instructional design and technology / edited by Robert A. Reiser, John V. Dempsey.—2nd ed.
p. cm.
Includes bibliographical references and index.
ISBN 0-13-170805-8
1. Instructional systems—Design. 2. Educational technology.

LB1028.38.T74 2007
371.33—dc22 2005058416

Vice President and Executive Publisher: Jeffery W. Johnston
Executive Editor: Debra A. Stollenwerk
Assistant Development Editor: Elisa Rogers
Editorial Assistant: Mary Morrill
Production Editor: Alexandrina Benedicto Wolf
Production Coordination: Carlisle Publishing Services
Coyeditor: Robert L. Marcum
Design Coordinator: Diane C. Lorenzo
Cover Designer: Terry Rohrbach
Cover Image: Corbis
Production Manager: Susan W. Hannahs
Director of Marketing: David Gesell
Senior Marketing Manager: Darcy Betts Prybella
Marketing Coordinator: Brian Mounts

This book was set in Times by Carlisle Publishing Services. It was printed and bound by Hamilton Printing. The cover was printed by Phoenix Color Corp.

Copyright © 2007, 2002 by Pearson Education, Inc., Upper Saddle River, New Jersey 07458. Pearson Prentice Hall. All rights reserved. Printed in the United States of America. This publication is protected by Copyright and permission should be obtained from the publisher prior to any prohibited reproduction, storage in a retrieval system, or transmission in any form or by any means, electronic, mechanical, photocopying, recording, or likewise. For information regarding permission(s), write to: Rights and Permissions Department.

Pearson Prentice Hall™ is a trademark of Pearson Education, Inc.
Pearson® is a registered trademark of Pearson plc
Prentice Hall® is a registered trademark of Pearson Education, Inc.
Merrill® is a registered trademark of Pearson Education, Inc.

Pearson Education Ltd.
Pearson Education Singapore Pte. Ltd.
Pearson Education Canada, Ltd.
Pearson Education—Japan
Pearson Education Australia Pty. Limited
Pearson Education North Asia Ltd.
Pearson Educación de Mexico, S.A. de C.V.
Pearson Education Malaysia Pte. Ltd.

10 9 8 7 6 5
ISBN 0-13-170805-8

Contents

Preface

This book provides readers with a clear picture of the field of instructional design and technology (IDT). Many textbooks in the IDT field focus on the skills needed by instructional designers and technologists. However, we believe that professionals in the field should be able to do more than just perform the skills associated with it. They should also be able to clearly describe the nature of the field, be familiar with the field's history and its current status, and be able to describe the trends and issues that have affected it and those likely to affect it in the future. This book will help readers attain these goals.

Strengths of the Book

As will be obvious when reading this book, the text is **written to capture and maintain reader interest**. A glance at the first chapter will also reveal that **information is presented in a manner that students should have no difficulty understanding**. As editors of this volume, we exhorted each of the chapter authors to write their chapters so that the information would be understandable to graduate students just entering the field, and we reviewed and edited each chapter with this goal clearly in mind.

The book **covers the latest trends in the field**, including such topics as knowledge management, learning science, Web-based instruction, and reusable learning objects. Moreover, the chapters that address these and other trends are **written by many of the leading figures in the field**.

The book not only covers recent trends, but also clearly **describes the historical and psychological foundations of the field**. By covering the field's past, present, and future, the book provides an excellent overview. Indeed, many students who read the first edition of this book late in their programs of study have indicated that it wasn't until they read it that they had a clear understanding of the field.

The book also contains a section (Section 5) that describes **what IDT professionals do in a variety of work settings**. As they read, students will see that IDT activities often differ from one setting to the next. Reading about the successes (and failures) of the field in each of these settings should pique student interest in working in one or more of them.

The book also offers **practical guidance on getting a job and succeeding at it**. Although there are many positions available for recent graduates of instructional design and technology programs, most students have very little knowledge of how to search for and obtain a good professional position. The chapters in Section 6 provide students with a variety of useful suggestions in these areas, including how to prepare a résumé, make contacts within an organization, prepare for an interview, develop a professional network of supporters, and succeed at their jobs.

Pedagogical Features

This book offers a variety of features designed to help readers learn about the nature of the field and the trends and issues affecting it. Each section begins with a **Section Overview** that focuses the reader's attention on the topics covered and shows the reader how the chapters within are related. The **Chapter Introduction** highlights key points and indicates how the chapter is related to other chapters and/or the section theme. Moreover, each chapter is also preceded and followed by what we think is one of the most effective instructional tools we have employed in our trends and issues courses—a series of **study questions** designed to facilitate learning.

Two types of study questions are provided for each chapter. In most cases, **Knowledge and Comprehension Questions** at the start of each chapter require students to identify the key ideas presented and demonstrate their understanding of those ideas. In contrast, most of the **Application Questions** at the end of each chapter require readers to go beyond the information provided and use other resources such as the Internet, print materials, fellow learners, and professionals in the field to generate answers/solutions to the questions/problems that are presented.

We have used questions as important features in our own Trends and Issues courses. First, we strongly encourage our students to use the questions to help them attend to, understand, and reflect on some of the key ideas presented in the materials we ask them to read. Second, we use questions as points of discussion when students meet in small collaborative groups (either in face-to-face sessions or online) to discuss the readings, and when we hold large-group sessions (again, either face-to-face or online), during which the small groups share and discuss their conclusions with the rest of the class. This combination of instructional strategies has proven to be a very effective learning tool and has been quite popular with our students. We strongly believe that instructors, students, and other readers will find the questions beneficial.

New in this Edition

The second edition of this book differs from the first edition in many ways, notably the inclusion of **13 new chapters**. Many of these chapters provide an in-depth look at topics that were not covered or just briefly touched on in the first edition:

- How constructivism has influenced instructional design
- The learning sciences
- The First Principles of Instruction
- Holistic design models, particularly the 4C/ID model
- Managing scarce resources on instructional design projects
- Knowledge management systems
- Informal learning
- Reusable learning objects
- Principles for designing multimedia instruction
- A debate on the future of instructional design

Several of the new chapters address topics discussed in the first edition, but are now written by new authors who provide different perspectives:

- Human performance technology
- Instructional design in the military
- Instructional design in international settings
- Instructional design in higher education

All of the 19 chapters that appeared in the first and second editions have been updated and, in many cases, expanded. For example:

- Chapter 1 defines the field and includes an extensive discussion of the new AECT definition.
- The history chapter (Chapter 3) describes the results of recent surveys examining the extent to which media have been used to deliver instruction in various settings.

Acknowledgments

This book would not have been possible were it not for all the hard work done by the contributing authors. As a group, they voluntarily spent hundreds of hours putting together a series of chapters that provides readers with what we consider to be an excellent overview of the IDT field, and of the trends and issues that affect it. We would like to express our deepest thanks and sincere appreciation to all of these authors for their outstanding efforts. They did an excellent job, and we are confident that after you read the chapters you will feel the same way.

Thanks also to our reviewers: Heng-Yu Ku, University of Northern Colorado; Linda L. Lohr, University of Northern Colorado; Francine Shuchat Shaw, New York University; Noelle Sweany, Ithaca College; and Dr. Elaine Traynelis-Yurek, Mary Baldwin College and Virginia Commonwealth University.

We would also like to express our sincere appreciation to Debbie Stollenwerk and Alex Wolf at Merrill/Prentice Hall, to Becky Barnhart at Carlisle Publishing Services, and to our excellent copyeditor, Robert L. Marcum at editorbob.com.

Robert A. Reiser
John V. Dempsey

Teacher Preparation Classroom

See a demo at
www.prenhall.com/teacherprep/demo

Your Class. Their Careers. Our Future. Will your students be prepared?

We invite you to explore our new, innovative and engaging website and all that it has to offer you, your course, and tomorrow's educators! Organized around the major courses pre-service teachers take, the Teacher Preparation site provides media, student/teacher artifacts, strategies, research articles, and other resources to equip your students with the quality tools needed to excel in their courses and prepare them for their first classroom.

This ultimate on-line education resource is available at no cost, when packaged with a Merrill text, and will provide you and your students access to:

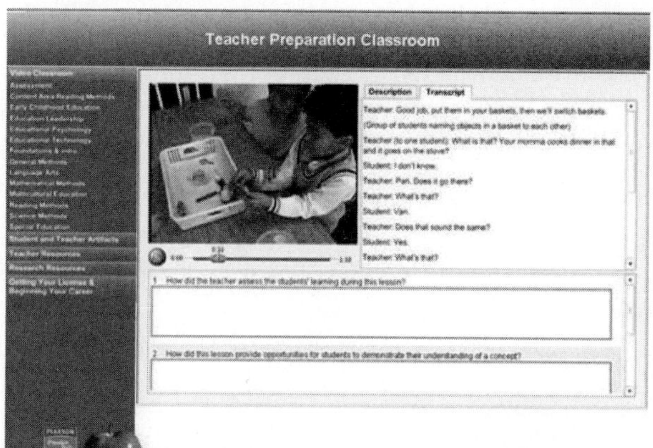

Online Video Library. More than 150 video clips—each tied to a course topic and framed by learning goals and Praxis-type questions—capture real teachers and students working in real classrooms, as well as in-depth interviews with both students and educators.

Student and Teacher Artifacts. More than 200 student and teacher classroom artifacts—each tied to a course topic and framed by learning goals and application questions—provide a wealth of materials and experiences to help make your study to become a professional teacher more concrete and hands-on.

Research Articles. Over 500 articles from ASCD's renowned journal *Educational Leadership*. The site also includes Research Navigator, a searchable database of additional educational journals.

Teaching Strategies. Over 500 strategies and lesson plans for you to use when you become a practicing professional.

Licensure and Career Tools. Resources devoted to helping you pass your licensure exam; learn standards, law, and public policies; plan a teaching portfolio; and succeed in your first year of teaching.

How to ORDER *Teacher Prep* for you and your students:
For students to receive a Teacher Prep Access Code with this text, instructors **must** provide a special value pack ISBN number on their textbook order form. To receive this special ISBN, please email **Merrill.marketing@pearsoned.com** and provide the following information:

- Name and Affiliation
- Author/Title/Edition of Merrill text

Upon ordering *Teacher Prep* for their students, instructors will be given a lifetime *Teacher Prep* Access Code.

Introduction

Robert A. Reiser
Florida State University

John V. Dempsey
University of South Alabama

Many of us who have been in this field for a while have had the experience of trying to explain our profession to our parents. Long explanations, short explanations—the end result is always the same. Our parents go cross-eyed and mumble something like, "That's nice, dear."

How about your parents? How much do they know about the field you are now studying, the field this book is about? They probably can't describe it very well; perhaps they can't even name it. But that puts them in some pretty good company. Many professionals in this field have trouble describing it. Indeed, many of them aren't sure exactly what to *call* it—instructional technology, educational technology, instructional design, instructional development, instructional systems, or instructional design and technology (IDT), the name we, the editors of this book, have decided to use. Just what is the nature of the field that practitioners call by so many names? This is the basic question that the contributing authors have attempted to answer.

This volume grew from each of our experiences in teaching a "Trends and Issues" course at our respective universities. For many years we used an ever-changing collection of readings from various sources. For all the differences between our two courses, there were greater similarities. (Dempsey was, after all, a student in Reiser's Trends & Issues course shortly after movable type was invented.) So, it was natural then that we spoke on several occasions about the kind of text we would like to have if we had our druthers.

When Debbie Stollenwerk at Merrill/Prentice Hall encouraged us in our delusions, our first idea was to produce a book of reprints from germane periodicals. As our discussions continued, however, we decided to invite a number of the most talented individuals we know in the field to contribute original manuscripts. The result was the first edition of *Trends and Issues in Instructional Design and Technology.*

Together, the two editors have a total of approximately 50 years of experience teaching Trends and Issues courses. Practically each time one of us has taught our course, we have revised it in some way to update the content and/or to improve the instructional methods we used. The result is a course that students are very enthusiastic about, both in terms of what they learn and the ways in which they go about learning. In this edition, we have tried to incorporate the content and instructional strategies that have made our own trends and issues courses successful.

Organization of the Book

This book is organized into seven sections. The first section of the book, "Defining the Field," focuses on **foundational issues**. Key terms in the field are defined and a history of the field is presented.

Section 2 focuses on **theories and models of learning and instruction**, with particular emphasis on those that serve as the central underpinnings of our field. This section also presents many of the key principles of instruction that are common across various instructional theories, and offers a variety of suggestions for those professionals in our field who are involved in designing instruction.

Section 3 focuses on **phases in the instructional design process**. The actual design of instruction is but one aspect of this process. This section focuses on trends related to other crucial parts: implementation; the use of models of evaluation; and recent approaches to the diffusion and institutionalization of instructional innovations. Key ideas related to the management of instructional design projects are also covered.

The fourth section focuses on **human performance technology** (HPT) and a series of related trends. The key ideas and practices associated with HPT are discussed. Noninstructional solutions to performance problems, such as electronic performance support systems and knowledge management systems, are described.

The fifth section describes **what IDT professionals do in a variety of work settings**. These settings include business and industry, the military, health care, public schools, higher education, and the international arena. As students read this section, they will see that the impact the IDT field has had on training and education varies greatly across these settings. The authors offer suggestions on how we might increase that impact in the future.

Section 6 focuses on **how to get an IDT position and succeed at it**. In addition to offering practical suggestions to job seekers, it describes some of the professional organizations, publications, and competencies that will foster the growth of IDT professionals.

Section 7 focuses on **new directions in the field**. For a variety of reasons (relating to the types of settings in which we tend to work), practitioners in the IDT field have been on "the bleeding edge" of technological changes in education and training. That technological role has accelerated in the last decade. Toward the later half of the 1990s and up through today, an interest in the Internet and networked instruction has flourished, and advances in multimedia, telecommunications, and other technologies have taken place. Topics discussed in this section include distributed learning, reusable learning objects, and multimedia. A debate regarding the future of instructional design ends this section.

There are a number of areas critical to our field that we purposely did not address. Chief among these is instructional and learning research. Likewise, we specifically encouraged the contributing authors to emphasize the key ideas and practices associated with the topic they were describing, as opposed to "how to do it." By doing so, we do not intend to give the impression that research and skill development are less important. We do feel, rather, that these areas are beyond the scope of this book.

The many talented authors and leaders in the field who have contributed to this book join us in the hope that by the time you finish reading it, you will have a clearer picture of the nature of the field of instructional design and technology and the trends and issues that have and will affect it. If we succeed in our efforts, then you may be able to clearly describe our field to your parents or anyone who will take the time to listen.

SECTION 1
Defining the Field

Overview

This section of the book is designed to give you a clear picture of the general nature, or characteristics, of the field we have chosen to call instructional design and technology. Over the years, a variety of different terms have been used as the label for the field and a variety of different definitions of the field have been put forth. Which label and which definition are best? It is unlikely that there will ever be a generally agreed-upon answer to this question. Nonetheless, we believe that a book that describes trends and issues in a particular field should begin by providing a clear picture of the nature of that field. That is what we hope to do in the first section of this book.

The three chapters in this section focus on definitions within our field, as well as on the history of the field. Chapter 1 discusses many of the prominent definitions of the field that have been put forth over the past century. Moreover, it presents our label for the field—*instructional design and technology*—and provides a definition for that term.

As you might expect from the label we have chosen, one of the key defining features of the field of instructional design and technology is the process known as instructional design. Chapter 2 discusses the major elements, or phases, that comprise the instructional design process, and discusses some of the distinguishing characteristics of that process.

The other key defining feature of the field of instructional design and technology is instructional technology, which many individuals both inside and outside of the profession equate with instructional media such as computers, videos, CD-ROMS, overhead and slide projectors, and many other types of devices (hardware) and materials (software). Chapter 3 provides a definition of the term *instructional media* and then discusses the history of instructional media and the history of instructional design. This history should provide you with further insights as to the nature of our field, and how those characteristics have evolved over time.

Robert A. Reiser[1]
Florida State University

CHAPTER 1

What Field Did You Say You Were In?
Defining and Naming Our Field

Knowledge and Comprehension Questions

1. From the early 1900s through the 1950s the field that some call instructional technology (or, as is the case in this book, instructional design and technology) was usually associated with instructional media. What instructional media were prominent during this period? What instructional media are prominent today?
2. Describe some of the similarities and differences among the three "process" definitions of instructional technology that were developed during the 1960s and 1970s.
3. Describe how each of the following definitions are different from previous definitions of the field:
   a. The 1994 AECT definition
   b. The new AECT definition
   c. The definition of instructional design and technology used in this text

Editors' Introduction

As the title of this book indicates, the focus of this volume is on trends and issues in the field of *instructional design and technology*. What is the nature of this field? What are its boundaries? How shall we define it? Unfortunately, there are no generally accepted answers to these questions. At any one point in time, different individuals within the field have used different terms as the label for the field and have defined the field differently. Furthermore, the labels and definitions that have been used have changed from one period of time to the next. In light of all the differences of opinion concerning labels and definitions, we feel it is important to begin this book by describing the general nature of the field and assigning a particular label to it.

Over the years, the term that has been used most frequently as the label for the field has been *instructional technology*. By focusing on some of the most prominent definitions of the past century, Bob Reiser describes how the meaning of that term has changed over time. He also presents and discusses two recent definitions and indicates why, in this book, we have chosen to use *instructional design and technology* as the label for our field.

---

[1] I would like thank Walter Dick, Don Ely, and Kent Gustafson, each of whom reviewed various portions of this manuscript and provided me with invaluable feedback. Portions of this chapter previously appeared in a journal article in *Educational Technology Research and Development* (Reiser & Ely, 1997).

What are the boundaries of the field we are in? How shall we define it? Indeed, what shall we call it? These are important questions that professionals in our field should be able to answer or, because there is no generally accepted "correct" answer, at least be able to discuss intelligently. This chapter is intended to provide you with information to help you formulate tentative answers to these questions. The chapter will examine how the definition of the field has changed over the years, present two new definitions, and discuss the term that we will use in this book as the label for our field.

Before beginning to examine the definitions of our field, it is important to point out that not only have the definitions changed, but the actual name of the field itself has often varied. Over the years, a variety of different labels have been used, including, among others, such terms as *audiovisual instruction, audiovisual communications,* and *educational technology.* However, the term that has been used most frequently has been *instructional technology*. This is the term that will be used in the next few sections of this chapter. However, the issue of the proper name for the field will be revisited near the end of the chapter.

What is the field of instructional technology? This is a difficult question to answer because the field is constantly changing. New ideas and innovations affect the practices of individuals in the field, changing, often broadening, the scope of their work. Moreover, as is the case with many professions, different individuals in the field focus their attention on different aspects of it, oftentimes thinking that the work they do is at the heart of the field, that their work is what instructional technology is "really all about."

Over the years, there have been many attempts to define the field. Several such efforts have resulted in definitions that were accepted by a large number of professionals in the field, or at least by the professional organizations to which they belonged. However, even when a leading organization in the field has endorsed a particular definition, professionals in the field have operated from a variety of different personal, as well as institutional, perspectives. This has held true among intellectual leaders as well as practitioners. Thus throughout the history of the field, the thinking and actions of a substantial number of professionals in the field have not been, and likely never will be, captured by a single definition.

Early Definitions: Instructional Technology Viewed as Media

Early definitions of the field of instructional technology focused on instructional media—the physical means via which instruction is presented to learners. The roots of the field have been traced back at least as far as the first decade of the twentieth century, when one of these media—educational film—was first being produced (Saettler, 1990). Beginning with this period and extending through the 1920s, there was a marked increase in the use of visual materials (such as films, pictures, and lantern slides) in the public schools. These activities were all part of what has become known as the visual instruction movement. Formal definitions of visual instruction focused on the media used to present that instruction. For example, one of the first textbooks on visual instruction defined it as "the enrichment of education through the 'seeing experience' [involving] the use of all types of visual aids such as the excursion, flat pictures, models, exhibits, charts, maps, graphs, stereographs, stereopticon slides, and motion pictures" (Dorris, 1928, p. 6).

During the late 1920s through the 1940s, as a result of advances in such media as sound recordings, radio broadcasting, and motion pictures with sound, the focus of the field shifted from visual instruction to audiovisual instruction. This interest in media continued through the 1950s with the growth of television. Thus during the first half of the twentieth century, most of those individuals involved in the field that we now call instructional technology were focusing most of their attention on instructional media.

Today many individuals who view themselves as members of the instructional technology profession still focus much, if not all, of their attention on the design, production, and use of instructional media. Moreover, many individuals both within and outside of the field of instructional technology equate the field with instructional media. Yet, although the view of instructional technology as media has persisted over the years, during the past 50 years other views of instructional technology have emerged and been subscribed to by many professionals in the field.

1960s and 1970s: Instructional Technology Viewed as a Process

Beginning in the 1950s, and particularly during the 1960s and 1970s, a number of leaders in the field of education started discussing instructional technology in a different way—rather than equating it with media, they discussed it as being a process. For example, Finn (1960) indicated that instructional technology should be viewed as a way of looking at instructional problems and examining feasible solutions to those problems. Lumsdaine (1964) indicated that educational technology could be thought of as the application of science to instructional practices. As you will see, most of the definitions of the 1960s and 1970s reflect this view of instructional technology as a process.

The 1963 Definition

In 1963, the first definition to be approved by the major professional organization within the field of educational technology was published, and it too indicated that the field was not simply about media. This definition (Ely, 1963), produced by a commission established by the Department of Audiovisual Instruction (now known as the Association for Educational Communications and Technology), was a departure from the "traditional" view of the field in several important respects. First, rather than focusing on media, the definition focused on "the design and use of messages which control the learning process" (p. 38). Moreover, the definition statement identified a series of steps that individuals should undertake in designing and using such messages. These steps, which included planning, production, selection, utilization, and management, are similar to several of the major steps often associated with what has become known as systematic instructional design (more often simply referred to as instructional design). In addition, the definition statement placed an emphasis on learning rather than on instruction. The differences identified here reflect how, at that time, some of the leaders in the field saw the nature of the field changing.

The 1970 Definitions

The changing nature of the field of instructional technology is even more apparent when you examine the next major definition statement, produced in 1970 by the Commission on Instructional Technology. The commission was established and funded by the United States government to examine the potential benefits and problems associated with increased use of instructional technology in schools. The commission's report, entitled *To Improve Learning* (Commission on Instructional Technology, 1970), provided *two* definitions of instructional technology. The first definition reflected the older view of instructional technology:

> In its more familiar sense, it [instructional technology] means the media born of the communications revolution which can be used for instructional purposes alongside the teacher, textbook, and blackboard. . . . The pieces that make up instructional technology [include]: television, films, overhead projectors, computers, and other items of "hardware" and "software" . . . (p. 21)

In contrast to this definition, the commission offered a second that described instructional technology as a process:

> The second and less familiar definition of instructional technology goes beyond any particular medium or device. In this sense, instructional technology is more than the sum of its parts. It is a systematic way of designing, carrying out, and evaluating the whole process of learning and teaching in terms of specific objectives, based on research on human learning and communication, and employing a combination of human and nonhuman resources to bring about more effective instruction. (p. 21)

Whereas the commission's first definition seems to reinforce old notions about the field of educational technology, the second definitely defines the field differently, introducing a variety of concepts that had not appeared in previous "official" definitions of the field. It is particularly important to note that this definition mentions a "systematic" process that includes the specification of objectives and the design, implementation, and evaluation of instruction, each term representing one of the steps in the systematic instructional design procedures that were beginning to be discussed in the professional literature of the field (e.g., Finn, 1960, Gagné, 1965; Hoban, 1977, Lumsdaine, 1964; Scriven, 1967). The definition also indicates that the field is based on research and that the goal of the field is to bring about more effective instruction and learning (echoing the 1963 emphasis on this concept). Finally, the definition discusses the use of both nonhuman and human resources for instructional purposes, seemingly downplaying the role of media.

The 1977 Definition

In 1977, the Association for Educational Communication and Technology (AECT) adopted a new definition of the field. This definition differed from the previous definitions in several ways. Perhaps most noteworthy was its length—it consisted of 16 statements spread over 7 pages of text, followed by 9 pages of tables elaborating on some of the concepts mentioned in the statements, as well as nine more chapters (more than 120 pages) that provided further elaboration. Although the authors clearly indicated that no one portion of the definition was adequate by itself, and that the 16 parts were to be taken as a whole, the first sentence of the definition statement provides a sense of its breadth:

> Educational technology is a complex, integrated process involving people, procedures, ideas, devices, and organization, for analyzing problems and devising, implementing, evaluating, and managing solutions to those problems, involved in all aspects of human learning. (p. 1)

Much like the second 1970 definition put forth by the Commission on Instructional Technology, the 1977 definition places a good deal of emphasis on a systematic ("complex, integrated") design process; the various parts of the definition mentioned many of the steps in most current-day systematic design processes (e.g., design, production, implementation, and evaluation). It is particularly interesting to note that the 1977 definition statement was the first such statement to mention the analysis phase of the planning process, which at that time was beginning to receive increasing attention among professionals in the field.

The 1977 definition also broke new ground by incorporating other terminology that, within a period of a few years, was to become commonplace in the profession. For example, it included the terms *human learning problems* and *solutions,* foreshadowing the frequent current-day use of these terms, especially in the context of performance technology.

The 1977 definition also included detailed tables describing the various learning resources associated with the field. This list gave equal emphasis to people, materials, and devices, reinforcing the notion that the work of instructional technologists was not limited to the development and use of media.

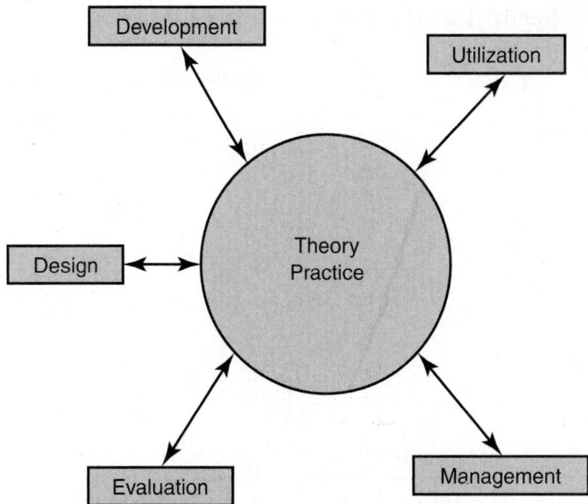

FIGURE 1.1 The five domains of instructional technology.
Source: From *Instructional Technology: The Definitions and Domains of the Field* (p. 10), by B. B. Seels and R. C. Richey, 1994, Washington, DC: Association for Educational Communications and Technology. Copyright 1994 by AECT. Reprinted by permission.

The 1994 Definition: Beyond Viewing Instructional Technology as a Process

During the period from 1977 to the mid 1990s, many developments affected the field of instructional technology.[2] Whereas behavioral learning theory had previously served as the basis for many of the instructional design practices employed by those in the field, cognitive and constructivist learning theories began to have a major influence on design practices. The profession was also greatly influenced by technological advances such as the microcomputer, interactive video, CD-ROM, and the Internet. The vast expansion of communications technologies led to burgeoning interest in distance learning, and "new" instructional strategies such as collaborative learning gained in popularity. As a result of these and many other influences, by the mid 1990s the field of instructional technology was very different from what it was in 1977, when the previous definition of the field had been published. Thus it was time to redefine the field.

Work on a new definition of the field officially commenced in 1990 and continued until 1994, when AECT published *Instructional Technology: The Definitions and Domains of the Field* (Seels & Richey, 1994). This book contains a detailed description of the field, as well as the following concise definition statement:

> Instructional Technology is the theory and practice of design, development, utilization, management, and evaluation of processes and resources for learning. (p. 1)

As is evident in the definition, the field is described in terms of five domains—design, development, utilization, management, and evaluation—five areas of study and practice within the field. The interrelationship between these domains is visually represented by a wheel-like graphic with each domain on the perimeter connected to a "theory and practice" hub (Figure 1.1). This representation scheme was designed in part to prevent readers from coming to the erroneous conclusion that these domains are linearly related (Richey & Seels, 1994).

Unlike the second 1970 definition and the 1977 AECT definition, the 1994 definition does not describe the field as process oriented. In fact, the authors of the 1994 definition state they purposely excluded the word *systematic* so as to reflect current interests in alternative design methodologies such as constructivist approaches (Richey & Seels, 1994). Nonetheless, the five domains identified in the definition are very similar to the steps that comprise the "systematic" processes described in the previous two definitions. Indeed, each of the five terms (design, development, utilization, management, and evaluation) or a synonym is used directly or indirectly in one or both of the previous two definitions.

The 1994 definition statement moves in some other new directions and revisits some old ones. For example, much like the 1963 definition statement, the 1994 statement describes the field in terms of theory and practice, emphasizing the notion that the field of instructional technology is not only an area of practice, but also an area of research and study. The documents in which the 1970 and 1977 definition statements appear also discuss theory and practice,

[2] Many of these developments will be discussed in detail in succeeding chapters in this book

but the definition statements themselves do not mention these terms.

In at least two respects the 1994 definition is similar to its two most recent predecessors. First, it does not separate teachers from media, incorporating both into the phrase "resources for learning." Second, it focuses on the improvement of learning as the goal of the field, with instruction being viewed as a means to that end.

Although the 1994 definition discusses instruction as a means to an end, a good deal of attention is devoted to instructional processes. The authors indicate that the "processes . . . for learning" (Seels & Richey, 1994, p. 1) mentioned in their definition refer to both design and delivery processes. Their discussion of the latter revolves around a variety of instructional strategies and reflects the profession's current interest in a variety of instructional techniques ranging from traditional lecture/discussion approaches to open-ended learning environments.

Two Recent Definitions

In the past few years, several new definitions have been published. In this section we will focus on two of these—one that an AECT committee has recently produced and one that we, the authors, have developed.

The Latest AECT Definition

At the beginning of 2006, just before the publication of this text, an AECT committee was finishing work on a book presenting a new definition of the *concept* of educational technology (Januszewski, in press).

The one-sentence definition statement that will appear in that book is as follows:

> Educational technology is the study and ethical practice of facilitating learning and improving performance by creating, using, and managing appropriate technological processes and resources. (n. p.)

One of the book's many useful features is a chapter devoted to explaining each of the key terms in the definition statement and discussing how the new definition differs from previous ones.[3] Some of the key terms that the authors discuss in that chapter are described here.

One key term in the new definition is the word *ethical*. This term focuses attention on the fact that those in the profession must maintain a high level of professional conduct. Many of the ethical standards professionals in the field are expected to adhere to are described in the AECT Code of Ethics (Welliver, 2001).

[3] Michael Molenda and Rhonda Robinson are the primary authors of this chapter.

The new definition also focuses on the notion that the instructional interventions created by professionals in the field are intended to *facilitate* learning. The authors contrast this viewpoint with those expressed in earlier definitions, in which it was stated or implied that the instructional solutions that were produced would cause or control learning. The new perspective recognizes the important role that learners play in determining what they will learn, regardless of the instructional intervention they are exposed to.

The new definition also indicates that one of the goals of professionals in the field is to *improve performance*. The authors indicate that this term emphasizes that it is not sufficient to simply help learners acquire inert knowledge. Instead, the goal should be to help learners *apply* the new skills and knowledge they have acquired.

Unlike previous definitions, in which terms such as *design*, *development*, and *evaluation* were often used to denote major processes or domains within the field, the new definition uses the terms *creating*, *using*, and *managing* to describe the major functions performed by educational technology professionals. The *creation* function includes all of the steps involved in generating instructional interventions and learning environments, including analysis, design, development, implementation, and evaluation. The *utilization* function includes the selection, diffusion, and institutionalization of instructional methods and materials, and the *management* function incorporates project, delivery system, personnel, and information management. The authors point out that these three less technical terms are used to describe the major functions so as to convey a broader view of the processes used within the field.

The definition also uses the adjective *technological* to describe the types of processes professionals in the field engage in and the types of resources they often produce. The authors, drawing on the work of Galbraith (1967), indicate that technological processes are those that involve "the systematic application of scientific or other organized knowledge to accomplish practical tasks" (p. 12). The authors also indicate that *technological resources* refer to the hardware and software that is typically associated with the field, including such items as still pictures, videos, computer programs, DVD players, and so on.

The Definition Used in This Text

One of the many strengths of the new AECT definition of educational technology is that the definition clearly indicates that *a focus on systematic processes* and *the use of technological resources* are both integral parts of the field. The definition that we will use in this text emphasizes these two aspects of the field as well as the recent influence the human performance technology movement has had on the profession.

As will be pointed out in later chapters (e.g., Chapter 14), in recent years many professionals in the field of instructional design and technology (IDT), particularly those who have been primarily trained to design instruction, have been focusing their efforts on improving human performance in the workplace. Although such improvements may be brought about by employing instructional interventions, careful analysis of the nature of performance problems often leads to noninstructional solutions, such as instituting new reward structures, providing clearer feedback to workers, developing electronic performance support systems (Chapter 15), creating knowledge management systems (Chapter 16), and/or promoting and enhancing opportunities for informal learning (Chapter 17). This new emphasis on improving performance in the workplace via noninstructional as well as instructional methods has been dubbed the human performance technology, or performance improvement, movement. We believe that any definition of the field of instructional design and technology should reflect this emphasis. The definition that we have developed, and that we will use in this book, clearly does so. The definition is as follows:

> The field of instructional design and technology (also known as instructional technology) encompasses the analysis of learning and performance problems, and the design, development, implementation, evaluation, and management of instructional and noninstructional processes and resources intended to improve learning and performance in a variety of settings, particularly educational institutions and the workplace. Professionals in the field of instructional design and technology often use systematic instructional design procedures and employ instructional media to accomplish their goals. Moreover, in recent years, they have paid increasing attention to noninstructional solutions to some performance problems. Research and theory related to each of the aforementioned areas is also an important part of the field.

As noted earlier, this definition highlights two sets of practices that have, over the years, formed the core of the field. We believe that these two practices—the use of media for instructional purposes and the use of systematic instructional design procedures (often simply called *instructional design*)—are the key defining elements of the field of instructional design and technology. Individuals involved in the field are those who spend a significant portion of their time working with media and/or with tasks associated with systematic instructional design procedures. We believe that one of the strengths of this definition is the prominent recognition it gives to both aspects of the field. More importantly, we feel the proposed definition, unlike those that have preceded it, clearly points to the efforts that many professionals in the field are placing on improving human performance in the workplace through a variety of instructional and noninstructional means. There is no doubt that many of the concepts and practices associated with human performance technology have been integrated into both the training future ID&T professionals receive (Fox & Klein, 2003) and the activities those individuals undertake once they enter the profession (Van Tiem, 2004). The definition we put forward clearly reflects this reality.

Naming the Field: Why Should We Call it Instructional Design and Technology?

The definition proposed in this chapter also differs from most of the previous definitions in that it refers to the field as *instructional design and technology* rather than *instructional technology*. Why? Most individuals outside of our profession, as well as many inside of it, when asked to define the term *instructional technology*, will mention computers, videos, CD-ROMs, overhead and slide projectors, and the other types of hardware and software typically associated with the term *instructional media*. In other words, most individuals will equate the term *instructional technology* with the term *instructional media*. This is the case in spite of all the broadened definitions of instructional technology that have appeared over the past 30 to 40 years. In light of this fact, perhaps it is time to reconsider the label we use for the broad field that encompasses the areas of instructional media, instructional design and, more recently, human performance technology. Any of a number of terms come to mind, but one that seems particularly appropriate is *instructional design and technology*. This term, which has also been employed by one of the professional organizations in our field (Professors of Instructional Design and Technology), mentions both of the areas focused on in earlier definitions. Performance technology, the most recent area to have a major impact on the field, is not directly mentioned because adding it to the term *instructional design and technology* would make that term unwieldy, and because in recent years instructional design practices have broadened so that many of the concepts associated with the performance technology movement are now regularly employed by those individuals who call themselves instructional designers.

In this book our field will be referred to as *instructional design and technology*, and we will define this term as indicated here. However, regardless of the term used as the label for our field and the specific definition you prefer, it is important that you understand the ideas and practices that are associated with the field, and the trends and issues that are likely to affect it. The purpose of this book is to introduce you to many of those ideas, practices, trends, and issues. As you proceed through this book, we anticipate that your view of the field will evolve and we are confident that your understanding of the field will increase. Moreover, we expect that you will be able to add your reasoned opinion to the ongoing debate concerning the "proper" definition and label for the field we have called instructional design and technology.

Application Questions

1. Each of the two recent definitions of the field mention (1) systematic processes, (2) technology (or media), and (3) performance improvement. However, the authors of each definition seem to differ to some degree with regard to the way they define or view each term. Describe the differences in the ways these terms are defined (viewed) in each definition.
2. Identify which of the two recent definitions you prefer. Describe why.
3. Which of the two terms discussed in this chapter—*instructional design and technology* or *instructional technology*—do you think is a better one to use as a label for our field? Explain why you feel this way. In doing so, describe what you see as the advantages and disadvantages of using each term. If you believe another term is better than both of these, list the term you prefer, and explain why you prefer it.
4. Write your own definition of our field. This definition may either be one you create, one that was taken verbatim from this chapter or elsewhere, or one that is a modified version of an existing definition (all of the definitions discussed in this chapter still exist!). Also describe why you prefer this definition. After you have done this, interact with two other individuals in your class and compare your definitions. Decide on a definition the three of you are comfortable with. Share it, and the reasons why you like it, with the other members of your class.

References

Association for Educational Communications and Technology (1977). *Educational technology: Definition and glossary of terms*. Washington, DC: Association for Educational Communications and Technology.

Commission on Instructional Technology. (1970). *To improve learning: An evaluation of instructional technology*. Washington, DC: U.S. Government Printing Office.

Dorris, A. V. (1928). *Visual instruction in the public schools*. Boston: Ginn.

Ely, D. P. (Ed.). (1963). The changing role of the audiovisual process in education: A definition and a glossary of related terms [Special issue]. *AV Communication Review, 11*(1).

Finn, J. D. (1960). Technology and the instructional process. *AV Communication Review, 8*(1), 5–26.

Fox, E. J., & Klein, J. D. (2003). What should instructional designers and technologists know about human performance technology? *Performance Improvement Quarterly, 16*(3), 87–98.

Gagné, R. M. (1965). The analysis of instructional objectives for the design of instruction. In R. Glaser (Ed.), *Teaching machines and programmed learning, II: Data and directions*. Washington, DC: National Education Association.

Galbraith, J. K. (1967). *The new industrial state*. Boston: Houghton Mifflin.

Hoban, C. F., Jr. (1977). A systems approach to audiovisual communications: The Okoboji 1956 keynote address. In L. W. Cochran (Ed.), *Okoboji: A 20 year review of leadership 1955–1974*. Dubuque, IA: Kendall/Hunt, 67–72.

Januszewski, A. (Ed.). (in press). *Educational technology: An analysis and explanation of the concept*. Mahwah, NJ: Lawrence Erlbaum Associates/AECT.

Lumsdaine, A. A. (1964). Educational technology, programmed learning, and instructional science. In E. R. Hilgard (Ed.), *Theories of learning and instruction: The sixty-third yearbook of the National Society for the Study of Education, Part I*. Chicago: University of Chicago Press.

Reiser, R. A., & Ely, D. P. (1997). The field of educational technology as reflected in its definitions. *Educational Technology Research and Development, 45*(3), 63–72.

Richey, R. C., & Seels, B. B. (1994). Defining a field: A case study of the development of the 1994 definition of instructional technology. In D. P. Ely (Ed.), *Educational media and technology yearbook: 1994*. Englewood, CO: Libraries Unlimited.

Saettler, P. (1990). *The evolution of American educational technology.* Englewood, CO: Libraries Unlimited.

Scriven, M. (1967). The methodology of evaluation. In *Perspectives of curriculum evaluation* (American Educational Research Association Monograph Series on Curriculum Evaluation, No. 1). Chicago: Rand McNally.

Seels, B. B., & Richey, R. C. (1994). *Instructional technology: The definition and domains of the field.* Washington, DC: Association for Educational Communications and Technology.

Van Tiem, D. M. (2004). Interventions (solutions) usage and expertise in performance technology practice: An empirical investigation. *Performance Improvement Quarterly, 17*(3), 23–44.

Welliver, P. W. (Ed.). (2001). *A code of professional ethics: A guide to professional conduct in the field of educational communications and technology.* Bloomington, IN: Association for Educational Communications and Technology.

Kent L. Gustafson and Robert M. Branch
University of Georgia

CHAPTER 2

What Is Instructional Design?

Knowledge and Comprehension Questions

1. Describe the core elements (phases) of the instructional design process.
2. Describe the distinguishing characteristics of the instructional design process.
3. Examine the definition of instructional design that the authors provide in the conclusion section of the chapter. Do you think it is a satisfactory definition? If so, why? If not, either write your own definition, identify another definition of instructional design that you prefer, or indicate how you would revise this one.

Editors' Introduction

In the previous chapter, it was pointed out that systematic instructional design (more often simply referred to as instructional design) is one of the key defining elements of the field of instructional design and technology. What is instructional design? As Kent Gustafson and Rob Branch point out in this chapter, it is a systematic process that is employed to develop education and training programs. Although there are many instructional design models (i.e., many versions, or approaches, to the instructional design process), a key set of elements, or phases, are incorporated into most of the models. The authors describe each of these elements and then go on to describe some distinguishing features (characteristics) of instructional design. By focusing your attention on the phases and distinguishing features of the process, you should get a clear picture of what is meant by the term *instructional design*.

Instructional design (ID) is a systematic process that is employed to develop education and training programs in a consistent and reliable fashion. Instructional design is a complex process that is creative, active, and iterative. Although the exact origins of the instructional design process can be debated, the writings of Silvern (1965) represent an early attempt to apply general systems theory (Bertalanffy, 1968) and systems analysis as an approach to solving instructional problems. Silvern was particularly interested in how general systems theory (GST) could be used to create effective and efficient training for aerospace and military training and published what some consider the first ID model.

A *system* is an integrated set of elements that interact with each other (Banathy, 1987). Systems theory postulates that a system and its elements are interdependent, synergistic, dynamic, and cybernetic. *Interdependent* means no element can be separated from the system since all elements depend on each other to accomplish the system's goals. *Synergistic* means that together, all the elements can achieve more than the individual elements alone. Thus the whole is greater than the sum of its parts. *Dynamic* means that the system monitors its environment and that elements within the system can be adjusted in light of changes in that environment. *Cybernetic* means the elements efficiently communicate among themselves, an essential condition for a system to be interdependent, synergistic, and dynamic. These characteristics are essential to understanding the instructional design process and how its elements work together to achieve the system's goals and objectives.

In the 1960s, the ID process was applied in some higher education settings (Barson, 1967) but its use did not become widespread. By the early 1970s, the use of instructional systems design (another term for ID) had become common in all branches of the military (Branson, 1975) and had started to appear in industrial and commercial training applications. During the 1970s, ISD became accepted as a standard training methodology in many large organizations and is now used throughout the world.

Silvern's model, and practically all other early ID models, were based on *behaviorism*, broadly defined as the philosophy and values associated with the measurement and study of human behavior (Burton, Moore, & Magliaro, 1996). Although behaviorism is commonly associated with B. F. Skinner and stimulus-response theory, most of the early writers held far more encompassing theoretical and philosophical perspectives. Early behaviorists believed, as many ID practitioners believe today, that a variety of behaviors can be observed, measured, planned for, and evaluated in ways that are reasonably reliable and valid. Cognitive psychologists, particularly from the perspective of information processing (e.g., Gagné, Wager, Golas, & Keller, 2005), also have made major contributions to the underlying theory of instructional design.

Instructional designers believe that the use of systematic design procedures can make instruction more effective, efficient, and relevant than less rigorous approaches to planning instruction. The systems approach implies an analysis of how its components interact with each other and requires coordination of all design, development, implementation, and evaluation activities. Imagine the chaos that would result if three teachers who had been assigned to work on different parts of an instructional unit about computers did not coordinate their efforts. Teacher A might write objectives stressing facts about computer hardware and operating systems. Teacher B might design instruction focused on using application software. And teacher C might design a test emphasizing the role of computers in society. Although this example may seem extreme, even a single teacher can create major incongruities among objectives, strategies, and evaluation by not using systematic thinking. Many college students have had the experience of thinking they knew what the teacher was expecting only to find the exam focused on individual facts while they studied concepts or vice versa. Many learners in training programs in business, industry, government, and the military have experienced similar problems.

Although a variety of systematic instructional design processes have been described (e.g., Dick, Carey, & Carey, 2005; Gagné et al., 2005; Morrison, Ross, & Kemp, 2004; Smith & Ragan, 2005) all descriptions include the core elements (also referred to as *phases*) of analysis, design, development, implementation, and evaluation (ADDIE) to ensure congruence among goals, objectives, strategies, and evaluation and the effectiveness of the resulting instruction. Figure 2.1 represents one way to depict the relationship among these core elements/phases.

Analysis often includes conducting a needs assessment (Kaufman, 2000; Rossett, 1993), identifying a performance problem in a business setting, or some other environment (Gilbert, 1978; Harless, 1975; Mager & Pipe, 1997), and stating a goal (Mager, 1997a). *Design* includes writing objectives in measurable terms (Mager, 1997b; Dick et al., 2005; Smith & Ragan, 1999), classifying learning as to type (Gagné et al., 2005; Merrill, 1983), specifying learning activities (Briggs, Gustafson, & Tillman, 1991), and specifying media (Reiser & Gagné, 1983; Smaldino, Russell, Heinich, & Molenda, 2005). *Development* includes preparing student and instructor materials (both print and nonprint) as specified during design (Morrison et al., 2004). *Implementation* includes delivering the instruction in the settings for which it was designed (Greer, 1996). *Evaluation* includes both formative and summative evaluation, as well as revision (Dick et al., 2001). Formative evaluation involves collecting data

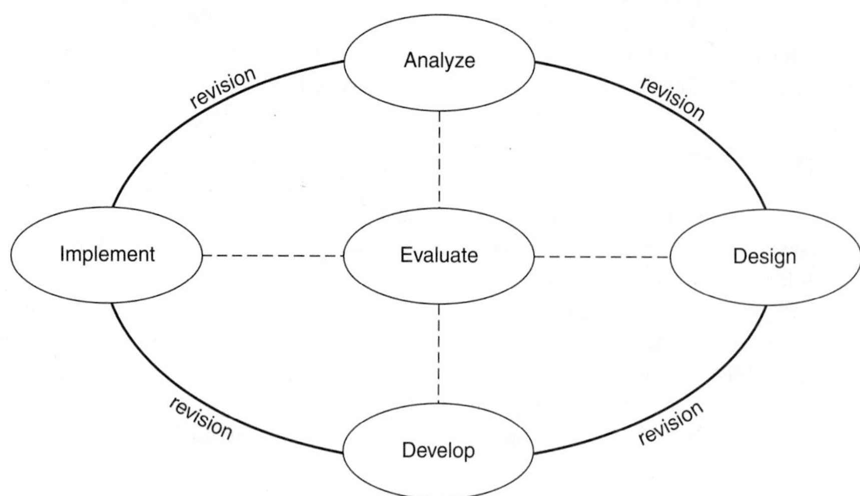

FIGURE 2.1 Core elements/phases of instructional design (ADDIE elements/phases).

to identify needed revisions to the instruction while summative evaluation involves collecting data to assess the overall effectiveness and worth of the instruction. Revision involves making needed changes based on the formative evaluation data.

It is important to note that the ADDIE activities typically are not completed in a linear step-by-step manner even though for convenience they may be presented that way by various authors. For example, during the life of a project, as data are collected and the development team gains insights, it is often necessary to move back and forth among the activities of analysis, design, and formative evaluation and revision. Thus, the iterative and self-correcting nature of the instructional design process emerges as one of its greatest strengths.

It also is important to note that there is some confusion in the literature on instructional design because the term *instructional development* also has been used to describe the entire process. In fact there is a Division of Design and Development of the Association for Educational Communications and Technology (AECT) that has as its focus the process we have been describing in this chapter as instructional design. When instructional development is used to describe the overall process, the term *instructional design* is often used to describe the ADDIE element we have labeled *design* in this chapter. Readers are advised to ask themselves how any given author is using these terms when reading the literature in the field.

Instructional Design Models

While ADDIE illustrates the conceptual components of ID, there remains a need to indicate *how to practice* the ID process. Instructional design models serve this purpose by describing how to conduct the various steps that comprise the process. Instructional design models also allow people to visualize the overall process, establish guidelines for its management, and communicate among team members and with clients. A variety of ID models have been created to describe how the process might be carried out in different settings (Gustafson & Branch, 1997, 2002). One of the most popular and influential ID models was created by Dick et al. (2005) and is depicted in Figure 2.2. Although their terminology does not align exactly with ADDIE and the number of elements is different, the five elements of analysis, design, development, implementation, and evaluation are all present. Examination of other ID models will produce similar findings. Although authors "slice and dice" the five core ADDIE elements in many different ways and use a variety of terminology, careful examination will reveal that all contain the core elements in one form or another.

Among the variations in models are the degree to which they make assumptions about the user setting and ultimate implementation of the instruction. Gustafson and Branch (2002) have suggested that models may be classified according to the primary type of instruction they are designed to produce. The three categories the authors describe are instruction that is likely to be delivered in a *classroom* by an instructor, instructional *products* such as computer-based modules designed for wide distribution, and large-scale instructional *systems* such as an entire distance learning course or degree program. There also are models dedicated to the activities of ID project managers (England & Finney, 1999; Greer, 1996).

Unfortunately, there is a relatively small amount of high-quality empirical literature to support the contribution

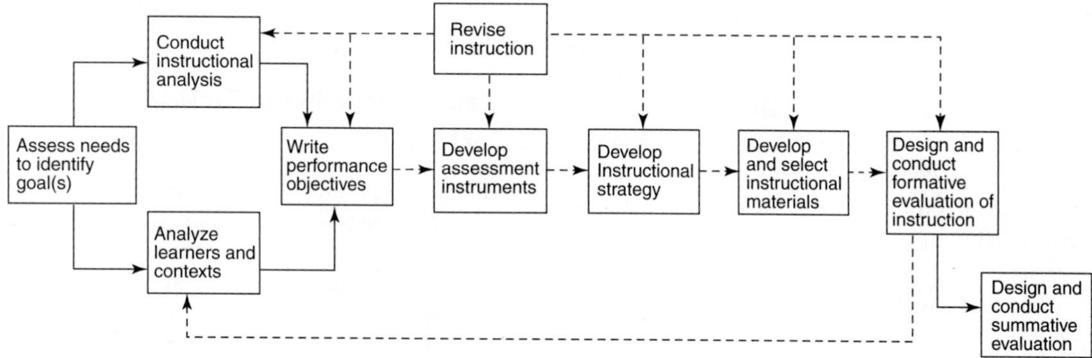

FIGURE 2.2 Example of a popular instructional design model.
Source: From The Systematic Design of Instruction (6th ed.), W. Dick, L. Carey, & J. Carey, 2005, Boston: Allyn & Bacon. Copyright © 2005 by Pearson Education. Reprinted by permission of the publisher.

of ID to designing effective and efficient instruction. Descriptions of highly successful ID efforts include reports written by Bowsher (1989), Mager (1977c), Markle (1991), and Morgan (1989). Ertmer and Quinn (2003) have published a useful set of abbreviated ID case studies from a variety of settings, but little empirical data on their effectiveness is provided.

Why haven't more success stories been published? It is likely due to practitioners not having the time or motivation to prepare scholarly articles to meet the requirements of research publications, whereas the models are generally designed by academics who have few opportunities to test them in authentic situations. Proprietary interests may also limit the amount of information made public by commercial developers about exactly how the ID process is conducted and its benefits to users. Nonetheless, the process is widely used in business, industry, and military training, and instructional designers and their clients clearly believe it results in improved learning and performance.

Characteristics of Instructional Design

Although the ADDIE activities mentioned earlier represent the fundamental concepts of the instructional design process, there are several characteristics that should be evident when the process is employed. These include the following:

1. Instructional design is learner centered.
2. Instructional design is goal oriented.
3. Instructional design focuses on meaningful performance.
4. Instructional design assumes outcomes can be measured in a reliable and valid way.
5. Instructional design is empirical, iterative, and self-correcting.
6. Instructional design typically is a team effort.

Instructional Design Is Learner Centered

Learner-centered instruction means that learners and their performance are the focal points of all teaching and learning activities. Teaching and other forms of instruction are simply means to the end of learner performance. Thus, there may be no initial assumption that a live teacher is even needed for the learner to achieve the stated objectives. Self- and group study, technology-based instruction, and teacher-based strategies are all options to be considered, with the result often being a mix of all these and other strategies. Learners may also be given opportunities to select their own objectives and/or learning methods in some circumstances. This change in perspective from teaching to learning represents a paradigm shift of immense power when planning for effective educational environments.

Instructional Design Is Goal Oriented

Establishing well-defined project goals is central to the ID process. Goals should reflect client expectations for the project and, if met, ensure its appropriate implementation. Unfortunately, many well-intended projects fail from lack of agreement on the goals or the decision to put off this important step in the false belief that this can be settled later. Identifying and managing client expectations is of particular importance to the project manager, but team members also need to share a common vision of the anticipated outcomes of the project. The ultimate question for an instructional system is "Have the goals of the project been attained?"

Instructional Design Focuses on Meaningful Performance

Rather than requiring learners to simply recall information or apply rules on a contrived task, instructional design focuses on preparing learners to *perform* meaningful and perhaps complex behaviors including solving authentic problems. Learner objectives are stated so as to reflect the environment in which students will be expected to apply the acquired knowledge or skill. Thus, there should be a high degree of congruence between the learning environment and the setting in which the actual behaviors are performed. While it is usually easier to identify performance settings for training programs (e.g., operating a drill press) than for school-based learning (e.g., a college biology course), instructional designers should strive to identify authentic performance measures for either setting.

Instructional Design Assumes Outcomes Can Be Measured in a Reliable and Valid Way

Related to the issue of performance is creating valid and reliable assessment instruments. For example, if the objective is to safely and efficiently operate a drill press, then a valid (authentic) assessment technique would likely involve both having an observer with a checklist observe the learner performing selected drilling operations and also examining the quality of the products created. In contrast, a multiple-choice, paper-and-pencil test would not be a valid measure of performance. In schools the issue of validity often is more complex, but nonetheless the instructional designer can still ask how the knowledge and skill might be applied or otherwise used to enhance the validity of the assessment. Reliability concerns the consistency of the assessment across time and individuals. Obviously, if the assessment is not stable, its validity is seriously compromised.

Instructional Design Is Empirical, Iterative, and Self-Correcting

Data are at the heart of the ID process. Data collection begins during the initial analysis and continues through implementation. For example, during the analysis phase, data may be collected so as to compare what learners already know to what they need to know. Guidance and feedback from subject matter experts ensures the accuracy and relevance of the skills and knowledge to be taught. Results of research and prior experience guide the selection of instructional strategies and media. Data collected during formative tryouts identify needed revisions, and data from the field after implementation indicate whether the instruction is effective. Although the data may not always bring good news, they are always "friendly" in that they provide a rational basis for decision making and a basis for successfully completing the project. Thus, the ID process usually is not as linear and sequential as most ID models imply.

Instructional Design Typically Is a Team Effort

Although it is possible for a single individual to complete an ID project, usually it is a team effort. Due to their size, scope, and technical complexity, most ID projects require the specialized skills of a variety of individuals. At a minimum, a team will typically consist of a subject matter expert, an instructional designer, one or more production personnel, clerical support, and a project manager. Sometimes a single individual may play more than one role on a team, but larger projects invariably require greater specialization. For example, high-tech projects may require computer programmers, videographers, editors, graphic artists, and interface designers. Demands for logistic support in the form of clerical staff, librarians, business managers, and system support expand as the size and duration of projects increase.

Conclusion

In recent years there have been many advances in learning theory, the technology of development and delivery systems, and in the training, skills, and sophistication of instructional designers. However, the unifying variables contained in most of the original ID models remain the same. These unifying variables are that instructional design is a *systematic process,* usually conducted by a team of professionals. It involves *analysis* of a performance problem, and the *design*, *development*, *implementation,* and *evaluation* of an instructional solution to the problem or need. Additionally, instructional design is an empirical process that is learner centered and goals oriented, geared toward reliable and valid measurement of meaningful skills and knowledge. We have no doubt that these elements and characteristics of the instructional design process will continue to hold true in the future as further advances in the field occur.

While instructional design is well accepted in business and industry, government, and the military, its use also is growing in colleges and schools, especially as they become involved in distance learning programs that require high-quality instruction, often without the benefit of live instructors. Proprietary schools and companies providing occupational skills or certification in technical areas also increasingly look to instructional design as the means of ensuring both the effectiveness and relevance of their offerings.

Instructional design as currently practiced has much to offer both now and in the future, but it does not meet all the needs for enhancing human performance in a complex and ever-changing world. Other chapters in this book describe alternative approaches to raising performance that already have assumed, or are likely to assume, important roles in complementing instructional design. Research on these alternatives, and the practical experience of instructional designers, will undoubtedly result in modifications in instructional design practices, but the underlying elements and characteristics of instructional design will remain the basis of its efficacy.

Application Questions

1. Gustafson and Branch contend that most early behaviorist writers held far more encompassing theoretical and philosophic perspectives on behaviorism than that of B. F. Skinner and stimulus-response theory. Using the library, the Internet, and other outside resources, investigate the theories of a well-known behaviorist other than Skinner (e.g., Thorndike or Tichner). Was Gustafson and Branch's contention correct regarding the theorist you investigated? Explain why or why not.
2. Study the Dick, Carey, and Carey model (Figure 2.2). There are 10 sequential components to the model as it is presented. Redesign the model three different ways. You may exclude components if you wish or add others you think are missing. Do you think any of the models you have constructed are an improvement over the Dick, Carey, and Carey model? Explain why or why not.
3. Gustafson and Branch have suggested that models may be classified according to the primary type of instruction they are designed to produce (in a classroom, instructional products, and large-scale systems). Discuss how each component of the ADDIE model would differ for each of these environments. Support your contention with concrete examples.

References

Banathy, B. H. (1987). Instructional systems design. In R. M. Gagné (Ed.), *Instructional technology: Foundations* (pp. 85–112). Hillsdale, NJ: Lawrence Earlbaum Associates.

Barson, J. (1967). *Instructional systems development: A demonstration and evaluation project*. East Lansing, MI: Michigan State University. (ERIC Document Reproduction Service No. ED 020 673)

Bertalanffy, L. (1968). *General systems theory*. New York: Braziller.

Bowsher, J. E. (1989). *Educating America: Lessons learned in the nation's corporations*. New York: John Wiley & Sons.

Branson, R. K. (1975). *Interservice procedures for instructional systems development: Executive summary and model*. Tallahassee, FL: Center for Educational Technology, Florida State University. (NTIS Nos. AD-A019 486 to AD-A019 490)

Briggs, L. J., Gustafson, K. L., & Tillman, M. H. (Eds.). (1991). *Instructional design: Principles and applications* (2nd ed.). Englewood Cliffs, NJ: Educational Technology Publications.

Burton, J., Moore, D., & Magliaro, S. (1996). Behaviorism and instructional technology. In D. Jonassen (Ed.), *Handbook of research for educational communications and technology*. New York: Macmillan.

Dick, W., Carey, L., & Carey, J. (2005). *The systematic design of instruction* (6th ed.). Boston: Allyn & Bacon.

England, E., & Finney, A. (1999). *Managing multimedia: Project management for interactive multimedia*. Reading, MA: Addison-Wesley.

Ertmer, P., & Quinn, J. (2003). *The ID casebook: Case studies in instructional design*. Upper Saddle River, NJ: Merrill/Prentice Hall.

Gagné, R. M., Wager, W. W., Golas, K. C., & Keller, J. M. (2005). *Principles of instructional design* (5th ed.). Belmont, CA: Wadsworth.

Gilbert, T. (1978) *Human competence: Engineering worthy performance*. New York: McGraw-Hill.

Greer, M. (1996). *The project manager's partner: A step-by-step guide to project management*. Amherst, MA: HRD Press.

Gustafson, K. L., & Branch, R. (1997). Revisioning models of instructional development. *Educational*

Technology Research and Development, 45(3), 73–89.

Gustafson, K. L., & Branch, R. (2002). *Survey of instructional development models.* (4th ed.). Syracuse University: ERIC Clearinghouse on Information Resources.

Harless, J. (1975). *An ounce of analysis is worth a pound of cure.* Newnan, GA: Harless Performance Guild.

Kaufman, R. (2000). *Mega planning: Practical tools for organizational success.* Thousand Oaks, CA: Sage.

Mager, R. (1997a). *Goal analysis: How to clarify your goals so you can actually achieve them* (3rd ed). Atlanta, GA: Center for Effective Performance.

Mager, R. (1997b). *Preparing instructional objectives* (3rd ed.). Atlanta, GA: Center for Effective Performance.

Mager, R. (1977c). The winds of change. *Training and Development, 31*(10), 13–16.

Mager, R., & Pipe, P. (1997). *Analyzing performance problems* (3rd ed.). Atlanta, GA: Center for Effective Performance.

Markle, D. G. (1991). First aid training. In L. J. Briggs, K. L. Gustafson, & M. H. Tillman (Eds.), *Instructional design: Principles and applications,* (2nd ed.). Englewood Cliffs, NJ: Educational Technology Publications.

Merrill, D. M. (1983). Component display theory. In C. M. Reigeluth (Ed.), *Instructional-design: Theories and models: An overview of their current status* (pp. 279–334). Hillsdale, NJ: Lawrence Erlbaum Associates.

Morgan, R. M. (1989). Instructional systems development in third world countries. *Educational Technology Research and Development, 37*(1), 47–56.

Morrison, G., Ross, S., & Kemp, J. (2004). *Designing effective instruction* (4th ed.). Hoboken, NJ: J. Wiley & Sons.

Reiser, R., & Gagné, R. (1983). *Selecting media for instruction.* Englewood Cliffs, NJ: Educational Technology Publications.

Rossett, A. (1993). Needs assessment. In G. J. Anglin (Ed.), *Instructional technology: Past, present, and future* (2nd ed.) (pp. 156–169). Englewood, CO: Libraries Unlimited.

Silvern, L. C. (1965). *Basic analysis.* Los Angeles: Education and Training Consultants Company.

Smaldino, S. E., Russell, J. D., Heinich, R., & Molenda, M. (2005). *Instructional technology and media for learning* (8th ed.). Upper Saddle River, NJ: Pearson Education.

Smith, P. L., & Ragan, T. J. (2005). *Instructional design* (3rd ed.). Hoboken, NJ: John Wiley & Sons.

CHAPTER 3

A History of Instructional Design and Technology

Robert A. Reiser[1]
Florida State University

Knowledge and Comprehension Questions

1. How is the term *instructional media* defined in this chapter? Why are teachers, chalkboards, and textbooks excluded from the definition?
2. Describe one way in which each of the following events or movements are related to current ideas or practices associated with *instructional media*:
   - School museums
   - Audiovisual instruction movement
   - World War II
   - Post–World War II developments
   - The communication theories movement
3. Many who have examined the history of instructional media have noted that as each new medium comes along, history repeats itself. Does this notion seem to apply to instructional films, instructional television, and computers? If so, in what way(s) does it apply?
4. Describe one way in which each of the following events or movements are related to current ideas or practices associated with the field of *instructional design*:
   - World War II
   - The programmed instruction movement
   - The behavioral objectives movement
   - The criterion-referenced testing movement
   - The work of Robert M. Gagné
   - The launching of Sputnik
5. During the 1970s and 1980s, interest in instructional design grew in some sectors and diminished or had little impact in others. Describe how interest in instructional design waxed and/or waned in the following sectors during the 1970s and 1980s:
   - Academia
   - Business and industry
   - The United States military
   - The international arena
   - Public education in the United States

Editors' Introduction

Inasmuch as you are reading this book, it is likely that you are, or will become, a professional in the field of instructional design and technology. We believe that a professional in any field should be knowledgeable about that field's history. This chapter is intended to provide you with that knowledge. As was pointed out in the first chapter of this book, over the years, two practices—the use of instructional media and the use of systematic instructional design procedures—have been at the center of the field. In this chapter, Bob Reiser discusses the history of instructional media and the history of instructional design.

In addition to describing past events, this chapter briefly discusses recent developments in the field's history. These events include the performance technology movement, the increasing interest in constructivism, and the rapidly growing use of online instruction (these recent trends are discussed in greater detail in other chapters in this book). Therefore, this chapter should provide you with a clear picture of where our field has come from as well as give you a brief introduction to some of the current trends that are affecting our field.

[1] I would like thank Walter Dick, Don Ely, and Kent Gustafson, each of whom reviewed various portions of this manuscript and provided me with invaluable feedback. Portions of this chapter previously appeared as a book chapter (Reiser, 1987).

In Chapter 1, the following definition of the field of instructional design and technology was put forth:

> The field of instructional design and technology encompasses the analysis of learning and performance problems, and the design, development, implementation, evaluation, and management of instructional and noninstructional processes and resources intended to improve learning and performance in a variety of settings, particularly educational institutions and the workplace. Professionals in the field of instructional design and technology often use systematic instructional design procedures and employ instructional media to accomplish their goals. Moreover, in recent years, they have paid increasing attention to noninstructional solutions to some learning and performance problems. Research and theory related to each of the aforementioned areas is also an important part of the field.

As is clear from this definition statement, over the years, two practices—the use of systematic instructional design procedures (often simply called *instructional design*) and the use of media for instructional purposes—have formed the core of the field of instructional design and technology. This chapter will review the history of the field by examining the history of instructional media and the history of instructional design. From a historical perspective, most of the practices related to instructional media have occurred independently of developments associated with instructional design. Therefore the history of each of these two sets of practices will be described separately. It should also be noted that although many important events in the history of the field of instructional design and technology have taken place in other countries, the emphasis in this chapter will be on events that have taken place in the United States.

History of Instructional Media

The term *instructional media* has been defined as the physical means via which instruction is presented to learners (Reiser & Gagné, 1983). Under this definition, every physical means of instructional delivery, from the live instructor to the textbook to the computer and so on, would be classified as an instructional medium. It may be wise for practitioners in the field to adopt this viewpoint; however, in most discussions of the history of instructional media, the three primary means of instruction prior to the twentieth century (and still the most common means today)—the teacher, the chalkboard, and the textbook—have been categorized separately from other media (cf. Commission on Instructional Technology, 1970). In order to clearly describe the history of media, this viewpoint will be employed in this chapter. Thus, instructional media will be defined as the physical means, other than the teacher, chalkboard, and textbook, via which instruction is presented to learners.

School Museums

In the United States, the use of media for instructional purposes has been traced back to at least as early as the first decade of the twentieth century (Saettler, 1990). It was at that time that school museums came into existence. As Saettler (1968) has indicated, these museums "served as the central administrative unit[s] for visual instruction by [their] distribution of portable museum exhibits, stereographs [three-dimensional photographs], slides, films, study prints, charts, and other instructional materials" (p. 89). The first school museum was opened in St. Louis in 1905, and shortly thereafter school museums were opened in Reading, Pennsylvania, and Cleveland, Ohio. Although few such museums have been established since the early 1900s, the districtwide media center may be considered a modern-day equivalent.

Saettler (1990) has also stated that the materials housed in school museums were viewed as supplementary curriculum materials. They were not intended to supplant the teacher or the textbook. Throughout the past hundred years, this early view of the role of instructional media has remained prevalent in the educational community at large. That is, during this time most educators have viewed instructional media as supplementary means of presenting instruction. In contrast, teachers and textbooks are generally viewed as the primary means of presenting instruction, and teachers are usually given the authority to decide what other instructional media they will employ. Over the years, a number of professionals in the field of instructional design and technology (e.g., Heinich, 1970) have argued against this notion, indicating that (1) teachers should be viewed on an equal footing with instructional media—as just one of many possible means of presenting instruction; and (2) teachers should not be given sole authority for deciding what instructional media will be employed in classrooms. However, in the broad educational community, these viewpoints have not prevailed.

The Visual Instruction Movement and Instructional Films

As Saettler (1990) has indicated, in the early part of the twentieth century, most of the media housed in school museums were visual media such as films, slides, and photographs. Thus, at the time, the increasing interest in using media in the school was referred to as the "visual instruction" or "visual education" movement. The latter term was used at least as far back as 1908, when the Keystone View Company published *Visual Education,* a teacher's guide to lantern slides and stereographs.

Besides magic lanterns (lantern slide projectors) and stereopticons (stereograph viewers), which were used in some schools during the second half of the nineteenth century (Anderson, 1962), the motion picture projector was one of the first media devices used in schools. In the United States, the first catalog of instructional films was published in 1910. Later that year, the public school system of Rochester, New York, became the first to adopt films for regular instructional use. In 1913, Thomas Edison proclaimed, "Books will soon be obsolete in the schools. . . . It is possible to teach every branch of human knowledge with the motion picture. Our school system will be completely changed in the next ten years" (cited in Saettler, 1968, p. 98).

Ten years after Edison made his forecast, the changes he had predicted had not come about. However, during this decade (1914–1923), the visual instruction movement did grow. Five national professional organizations for visual instruction were established, five journals focusing on visual instruction began publication, more than 20 teacher-training institutions began offering courses in visual instruction, and at least a dozen large-city school systems developed bureaus of visual education (Saettler, 1990).

The Audiovisual Instruction Movement and Instructional Radio

During the remainder of the 1920s and through much of the 1930s, technological advances in such areas as radio broadcasting, sound recordings, and sound motion pictures led to increased interest in instructional media. With the advent of media incorporating sound, the expanding visual instruction movement became known as the audiovisual instruction movement (Finn, 1972; McCluskey, 1981). However, McCluskey, who was one of the leaders in the field during this period, indicates that while the field continued to grow, the educational community at large was not greatly affected by that growth. He states that by 1930, commercial interests in the visual instruction movement had invested and lost more than $50 million, only part of which was due to the Great Depression, which began in 1929.

In spite of the adverse economic effects of the Great Depression, the audiovisual instruction movement continued to evolve. According to Saettler (1990), one of the most significant events in this evolution was the merging in 1932 of the three existing national professional organizations for visual instruction. As a result of this merger, leadership in the movement was consolidated within one organization, the Department of Visual Instruction (DVI), which at that time was part of the National Education Association. Over the years, this organization, which was created in 1923 and is now called the Association for Educational Communications and Technology (AECT), has maintained a leadership role in the field of instructional design and technology.

During the 1920s and 1930s, a number of textbooks on the topic of visual instruction were written. Perhaps the most important of these textbooks was *Visualizing the Curriculum,* written by Charles F. Hoban, Sr., Charles F. Hoban, Jr., and Stanley B. Zissman (1937). In this book, the authors stated that the value of audiovisual material was a function of their degree of realism. The authors also presented a hierarchy of media, ranging from those that could only present concepts in an abstract fashion to those that allowed for very concrete representations (Heinich, Molenda, Russell, & Smaldino, 1999). Some of these ideas had previously been discussed by others, but had not been dealt with as thoroughly. In 1946, Edgar Dale further elaborated upon these ideas when he developed his famous "Cone of Experience." Throughout the history of the audiovisual instruction movement, many have indicated that part of the value of audiovisual materials is their ability to present concepts in a concrete manner (Saettler, 1990).

A medium that gained a great deal of attention during this period was radio. By the early 1930s, many audiovisual enthusiasts were hailing radio as the medium that would revolutionize education. For example, in referring to the instructional potential of radio, films, and television, the editor of publications for the National Education Association stated that "tomorrow they will be as common as the book and powerful in their effect on learning and teaching" (Morgan, 1932, p. ix). However, contrary to these sorts of predictions, over the next 20 years radio had very little impact on instructional practices (Cuban, 1986).

World War II

With the onset of World War II, the growth of the audiovisual instruction movement in the schools slowed; however, audiovisual devices were used extensively in the military services and in industry. For example, during the war the United States Army Air Force produced more than 400 training films and 600 filmstrips, and during a two-year period (from mid 1943 to mid 1945) it was estimated that there were over four million showings of training films to United States military personnel. Although there was little time and opportunity to collect hard data regarding the effect of these films on the performance of military personnel, several surveys of military instructors revealed that they felt that the training films and filmstrips used during the war were effective training tools (Saettler, 1990). Apparently, at least some of the enemy agreed; in 1945, after the war ended, the German Chief of General Staff said, "We had everything calculated perfectly except the speed with which America was able to train its people. Our major miscalculation was in underestimating their quick and complete mastery of film education" (cited in Olsen & Bass, 1982, p. 33).

During the war, training films also played an important role in preparing civilians in the United States to work in industry. In 1941, the federal government established the Division of Visual Aids for War Training. From 1941 to 1945, this organization oversaw the production of 457 training films. Most training directors reported that the films reduced training time without having a negative impact on training effectiveness, and that the films were more interesting and resulted in less absenteeism than traditional training programs (Saettler, 1990).

In addition to training films and film projectors, a variety of other audiovisual materials and equipment were employed in the military forces and in industry during World War II. Devices that were used extensively included overhead projectors, which were first produced during the war; slide projectors, which were used in teaching aircraft and ship recognition; audio equipment, which was used in teaching foreign languages; and simulators and training devices, which were employed in flight training (Olsen & Bass, 1982; Saettler, 1990).

Post–World War II Developments and Media Research

The audiovisual devices used during World War II were generally perceived as successful in helping the United States solve a major training problem—namely, how to train effectively and efficiently large numbers of individuals with diverse backgrounds. As a result of this apparent success, after the war there was a renewed interest in using audiovisual devices in the schools (Finn, 1972; Olsen & Bass, 1982).

In the decade following the war, several intensive programs of audiovisual research were undertaken (e.g., Carpenter & Greenhill, 1956; Lumsdaine, 1961; May & Lumsdaine, 1958). The research studies conducted as part of these programs were designed to identify how various features, or attributes, of audiovisual materials affected learning; the goal being to identify those attributes that would facilitate learning in given situations. For example, one research program, conducted under the direction of Arthur A. Lumsdaine, focused on identifying how learning was affected by various techniques for eliciting overt student response during the viewing of instructional films (Lumsdaine, 1963).

The post–World War II audiovisual research programs were among the first concentrated efforts to identify principles of learning that could be used in the design of audiovisual materials. However, educational practices were not greatly affected by these research programs in that many practitioners either ignored, or were not made aware of, many of the research findings (Lumsdaine, 1963, 1964).

Most of the media research studies conducted over the years have compared how much students have learned after receiving a lesson presented via a particular medium, such as film, radio, television, or the computer, versus how much students have learned from live instruction on the same topic. Studies of this type, often called media comparison studies, have usually revealed that students learned equally well regardless of the means of presentation (Clark, 1983, 1994; Schramm, 1977). In light of these repeated findings, critics of such research have suggested that the focus of such studies should change. Some have argued that researchers should focus on the attributes (characteristics) of media (Levie & Dickie, 1973), others have suggested an examination of *how* media influence learning (Kozma, 1991, 1994), and still others have suggested that the research focus should be on instructional methods, rather than on the media that deliver those methods (Clark, 1983, 1994). In recent years, some of these types of studies have become more prevalent.

Theories of Communication

During the early 1950s, many leaders in the audiovisual instruction movement became interested in various theories or models of communication, such as the model put forth by Shannon and Weaver (1949). These models focused on the communication process, a process involving a sender and a receiver of a message and a channel, or medium, through which that message is sent. The authors of these models indicated that during planning for communication it was necessary to consider all the elements of the process, and not just focus on the medium, as many in the audiovisual field tended to do. As Berlo (1963) stated, "As a communication man I must argue strongly that it is the process that is central and that the media, though important, are secondary" (p. 378). Several leaders in the audiovisual movement, such as Dale (1953) and Finn (1954), also emphasized the importance of the communication process. Although at first audiovisual practitioners were not greatly influenced by this notion (Lumsdaine, 1964; Meierhenry, 1980), the expression of this point of view eventually helped expand the focus of the audiovisual movement (Ely, 1963, 1970; Silber, 1981).

Instructional Television

Perhaps the most important factor to affect the audiovisual movement in the 1950s was the increased interest in television as a medium for delivering instruction. Prior to the 1950s, there had been a number of instances in which television had been used for instructional purposes (Gumpert, 1967; Taylor, 1967). During the 1950s, however, there was a tremendous growth in the use of instructional television. This growth was stimulated by at least two major factors.

One factor that spurred the growth of instructional television was the 1952 decision by the Federal Communications Commission to set aside 242 television channels for educational purposes. This decision led to the rapid development of a large number of public (then called "educational") television stations. By 1955, there were 17 such stations in the United States, and by 1960 that number had increased to more than 50 (Blakely, 1979). One of the primary missions of these stations was the presentation of instructional programs. As Hezel (1980) indicates, "The teaching role has been ascribed to public broadcasting since its origins. Especially prior to the 1960s, educational broadcasting was seen as a quick, efficient, inexpensive means of satisfying the nation's instructional needs" (p. 173).

The growth of instructional television during the 1950s was also stimulated by funding provided by the Ford Foundation. It has been estimated that during the 1950s and 1960s the foundation and its agencies spent more than $170 million on educational television (Gordon, 1970). Those projects sponsored by the foundation included a closed-circuit television system that was used to deliver instruction in all major subject areas at all grade levels throughout the school system in Washington County (Hagerstown), Maryland; a junior-college curriculum presented via public television in Chicago; a large-scale experimental research program designed to assess the effectiveness of a series of college courses taught via closed circuit television at Pennsylvania State University; and the Midwest Program on Airborne Television Instruction, a program designed to simultaneously transmit televised lessons from an airplane to schools in six states.

By the mid 1960s, much of the interest in using television for instructional purposes had abated. Many of the instructional television projects developed during this period had short lives. This problem was due in part to the mediocre instructional quality of some of the programs that were produced; many of them did little more than present a teacher delivering a lecture. In 1963, the Ford Foundation decided to focus its support on public television in general, rather than on in-school applications of instructional television (Blakely, 1979). In many cases, school districts discontinued instructional television demonstration projects when the external funding for those projects was halted (Tyler, 1975b). Instructional programming was still an important part of the mission of public television, but that mission was now wider, encompassing other types of programming, such as cultural and informational presentations (Hezel, 1980). In light of these and other developments, in 1967 the Carnegie Commission on Educational Television concluded,

> The role played in formal education by instructional television has been on the whole a small one . . . nothing which approached the true potential of instructional television has been realized in practice. . . . With minor exceptions, the total disappearance of instructional television would leave the educational system fundamentally unchanged. (pp. 80–81)

Many reasons have been given as to why instructional television was not adopted to a greater extent. These include teacher resistance to the use of television in their classrooms, the expense of installing and maintaining television systems in schools, and the inability of television alone to adequately present the various conditions necessary for student learning (Gordon, 1970; Tyler, 1975b).

Shifting Terminology

By the early 1970s, the terms *educational technology* and *instructional technology* began to replace *audiovisual instruction* as the terms used to describe the application of media for instructional purposes. For example, in 1970 the name of the major professional organization within the field was changed from the Department of Audiovisual Instruction to the Association for Educational Communications and Technology (AECT). Later in the decade, the names of the two journals published by AECT were also changed—*Audiovisual Communication Review* became *Educational Communications and Technology Journal*, and *Audiovisual Instruction* became *Instructional Innovator*. Moreover, the group that the United States government established to examine the impact of media on instruction was called the Commission on Instructional Technology. Regardless of the terminology, however, most individuals in the field agree that up to that point, instructional media had had minimal impact on educational practices (Commission on Instructional Technology, 1970, Cuban, 1986).

Computers: From the 1950s to 1995

After the interest in instructional television faded, the next technological innovation to catch the attention of a large number of educators was the computer. Although widespread interest in the computer as an instructional tool did not occur until the 1980s, computers were first used in education and training at a much earlier date. Much of the early work in computer-assisted instruction (CAI) was done in the 1950s by researchers at IBM, who developed the first CAI author language and designed one of the first CAI programs to be used in the public schools. Other pioneers in this area included Gordon Pask, whose adaptive teaching machines made use of computer technology (Lewis & Pask; 1965; Pask, 1960; Stolorow & Davis, 1965), and Richard Atkinson and Patrick Suppes, whose work during the 1960s led to some of the earliest applications of CAI at both the public school and university levels (Atkinson & Hansen, 1966; Suppes & Macken, 1978). Other major efforts during the 1960s and early 1970s included the development of CAI systems such as PLATO and TICCIT. However, in spite of the work that had been done, by the end of the 1970s, CAI had had very little impact on education (Pagliaro, 1983).

By the early 1980s, a few years after microcomputers became available to the general public, the enthusiasm surrounding this tool led to increasing interest in using computers for instructional purposes. By January 1983, computers were being used for instructional purposes in more than 40% of all elementary schools and more than 75% of all secondary schools in the United States (Center for Social Organization of Schools, 1983).

Many educators were attracted to microcomputers because they were relatively inexpensive, were compact enough for desktop use, and could perform many of the functions performed by the large computers that had preceded them. As was the case when other new media were first introduced into the instructional arena, many expected that this medium would have a major impact on instructional practices. For example, in 1984, Papert indicated that the computer was going to be "a catalyst of very deep and radical change in the educational system" (p. 422) and that by 1990 one computer per child would be a very common state of affairs in schools in the United States.

Although computers may eventually have a major impact on instructional practices in schools, by the mid 1990s that impact had been rather small. Surveys revealed that by 1995, although schools in the United States possessed, on average, one computer for every nine students, the impact of computers on instructional practices was minimal, with a substantial number of teachers reporting little or no use of computers for instructional purposes. Moreover, in most cases, the use of computers was far from innovative. In elementary schools, teachers reported that computers were being primarily used for drill and practice, and at the secondary level, reports indicated that computers were mainly used for teaching computer-related skills such as word processing (Anderson & Ronnkvist, 1999; Becker, 1998; Office of Technology Assessment, 1995).

Recent Developments

In recent years, rapid advances in computer and other digital technology, including the Internet, have led to a rapidly increasing interest in, and use of, these media for instructional purposes, particularly in training in business and industry. For example, a recent survey by the American Society of Training and Development of over 340 companies in the United States (Sugrue & Kim, 2004) revealed that 24% of the total amount of training hours during 2003 was presented via technology, as compared to less than 10% in 1999. During the same period, the percentage of training hours delivered by instructors in classrooms decreased from 80% in 1999 to 68% in 2003.

The percentages reported for the year 2003 in the aforementioned survey are quite similar to the precentages reported in a survey of over 1,200 training organizations in the United States conducted by *Training magazine* in 2004 (Dolezalek, 2004). Results of that survey revealed that on average during 2004, 70% of all training in the participating organizations was delivered by instructors in classrooms, whereas 25% was presented by technology (8% by instructors via technology from remote locations and 17% via computers without the involvement of an instructor).

In the past few years, interest in using the Internet and computers for instructional purposes has also been rapidly growing in higher education. For example, a recent study (Market Data Retrieval, 2005) revealed that during the 2004–2005 academic year, nearly two thirds of all colleges and universities in the United States offered online courses as well as accredited online degree programs. Moreover, an earlier study (Phipps, 2004) revealed that during 2001–2002, more than 3 million students were enrolled in online courses. In addition, the use of technology-based course management systems, such as *Blackboard* and *WebCT*, in university courses has rapidly increased. During 2002, 83% of colleges and universities used these types of systems, whereas in 2004–2005, virtually all such institutions did so (Market Data Retrieval, 2005).

Technology is also playing a major role in the delivery of instruction in the various branches of the United States military. For example, the Navy currently offers more than 1,500 online courses, including at least 120 military-specific courses (Chisholm, 2003a). In addition, more than 50,000 students were recently enrolled in 32 online courses offered by the Air Force Institute for Advanced Distributed Learning (Fuhr, 2004). The Army and the Marine Corps are also investing heavily in technology-based training. For example, the Army currently operates approximately 250 digital training facilities that provide standalone computer-based training as well as Web-based instruction to military and civilian personnel worldwide (Chisholm, 2003b), and there are similar types of facilities at all major Marine Corps bases (Chisholm, 2003a).

In the past few years, the availability and use of technology in public schools in the United States has also increased significantly. For example, whereas in 1998 there was an average of 6 students for each computer in the public schools (Anderson & Ronnkvist, 1999), by 2004 that average had dropped to 3.8 students per computer (Market Data Retrieval, 2004). Furthermore, in recent years, within schools there has been significant growth in the number of computers with Internet access. Whereas in 1998, the ratio of students to Internet-accessible computers was greater than 12:1, by 2003 that ratio had declined to 4.4 students per computer (National Center for Educational Statistics, 2005).

The data in the preceding paragraph clearly indicates that the amount of technology available in schools has increased in recent years. However, the history of instructional media reveals that an increased presence of technology in the schools does not necessarily mean an increased use of that technology for instructional purposes. Is this still the case today? Data from a 1999 survey of public school teachers in the United States and a similar survey conducted in 2000–2001 shed some light on this issue.

Results from the aforementioned surveys reveal that the percentage of teachers using technology for instructional puproses seems to be increasing. In the 1999 survey, 53% of the teachers who had access to computers or the Internet at school reported that they used technology for classroom instruction (National Center for Educational Statistics, 2000). In contrast, 92% of teachers who responded to the 2000–2001 survey reported using some instructional activities requiring technology (SRI International, 2002).

How frequently do teachers use technology for classroom instruction? This question was not addresssed in the 1999 survey, but 55% of the teachers responding to the 2000–2001 survey indicated that they had students engage in some technology-based instructional activity frequently (once per week or more). However, the technology-based instructional activity that the largest percentage of teachers (33%) used on a frequent basis involved helping students improve their computer skills. In addition, 29% of the teachers indicated that they frequently used technology for drill-and-practice activities. In contrast, only 20% of the teachers indicated that they frequently used technology to have students solve problems or analyze data, and only 10% indicated that they had their students use the Internet to do research (SRI International, 2002). In short, the evidence indicates there has been growth in the use of technology for instructional purposes in schools, but at this point in time there appears to be little support for predictions that the introduction of computers and the Internet into schools will revolutionize instructional methods.

Most of the evidence presented in this section clearly indicates that in recent years there has been a significant increase in the use of instructional media in a variety of settings, ranging from business and industry to the military and higher education. What are some of the reasons for this increased usage? In business and industry and the military, the Internet has been viewed as a means of providing instruction and information to widely dispersed learners at a relatively low cost. Moreover, in many cases, the easy accessibility of computers makes it possible for learners to receive instruction and/or performance support (often in the form of an electronic performance support system or knowledge management system) when and where they need it, as they are performing particular job tasks.

In higher education, distance education via the Internet has been seen as a low-cost method of providing instruction to students who, due to a variety of factors (e.g., job and family responsibilities, geographic factors), might not otherwise have been able to receive it. However, questions regarding the cost effectiveness of such instruction remain unanswered (Hawkridge, 1999).

Another reason that the newer media are being used to a greater extent may be due to their increased interactive capabilities. Moore (1989) describes three types of interactions among the agents usually involved in an instructional activity. These interactions are between learners and instructional content, between learners and the instructor, and among learners themselves. Due to their attributes, the instructional media that were prevalent during some portion of the first two thirds of the past century (e.g., films and instructional television) were primarily employed as a means of having learners interact with instructional content. In contrast, through the use of such features as e-mail, chat rooms, and bulletin boards, the Internet is often used as a means of having learners interact with their instructor and with other learners, as well as with instructional content. This is one example of how some of the newer media make it easier to promote the various types of interactions described by Moore.

In addition, advances in computer technology, particularly with regard to the increasing multimedia capabilities of this medium, have made it easier for educators to design learning experiences that involve more complex interactions between learners and instructional content than has previously been the case. For example, as the amount and type of information (e.g., print, video, audio) that computers can present has increased, the type of feedback, as well as the type of problems, that can be presented to learners has greatly expanded. These increased instructional capabilities have attracted the attention of many educators. Moreover, the ability of computers to present information in a variety of forms, as well as to allow learners to easily link to various content, has attracted the interest of instructional designers having a constructivist perspective. They and others who are particularly concerned with presenting authentic (i.e. "real-world") problems in learning environments, in which learners have a great deal of control of the activities they engage in and the tools and resources they use, find the new digital technology more accommodating than its predecessors.

As some of the examples in the previous few paragraphs demonstrate, in the past few years computers, the Internet, and other digital technology have often been used to promote learning and performance via some "nontraditional" means. For instance, computer-assisted electronic performance support systems, knowledge management systems, and learner-centered learning environments often serve as alternatives to training or direct instruction. When the current-day impact of instructional media is being considered, these types of applications should not be overlooked.

Conclusions Regarding the History of Instructional Media

Of the many lessons we can learn by reviewing the history of instructional media, perhaps one of the most important involves a comparison between the anticipated and actual effects of media on instructional practices. As Cuban (1986) has pointed out, as you look back over the past century of media history, you are likely to note a recurrent pattern of expectations and outcomes. As a new medium enters the educational scene, there is a great deal of initial interest and much enthusiasm about the effects it is likely to have on instructional practices. However, enthusiasm and interest eventually fade, and an examination reveals that the medium has had a minimal impact on such practices. For example, Edison's optimistic prediction that films would revolutionize education proved to be incorrect, and the enthusiasm for instructional television that existed during the 1950s greatly abated by the mid 1960s, with little impact on instruction in the schools. Both of these examples involve the use of media in schools, the setting in which the use of instructional media has been most closely examined. However, data regarding the use of instructional media in business and industry supports a similar conclusion; namely that in spite of enthusiasm about the use of instructional media in business and industry, *until recently* media have had a minimal impact on instructional practices in that environment.

What about the predictions, first made in the 1980s, that computers would revolutionize instruction? As the data from schools reveal, by the mid 1990s that revolution had not occurred. However, data from the turn of the century reveals increases of computers and the Internet in schools. Moreover, during the past five years, these media have taken on an increasingly larger instructional and performance support role in other settings such as business, industry, and higher education.

Will the impact of media on instruction be greater in the future than it has been in the past? In light of the aforementioned reasons for the increasing use of the newer media, I think it is reasonable to predict that over the next three to five years, computers, the Internet, and other digital media will continue to bring about greater changes in instructional practices than the media that preceded them. The growth may be slow, but recent data leads me to believe it is likely to be steady.

History of Instructional Design

As mentioned earlier, in addition to being closely associated with instructional media, the field of instructional design and technology has also been closely associated with the use of systematic instructional design procedures. As was indicated in Chapter 2, a variety of sets of systematic instructional design procedures (or models) have been developed, and have been referred to by such terms as *the systems approach*, *instructional systems design* (*ISD*), *instructional development*, and *instructional design* (which is the term I will use in the remainder of this chapter). Although the specific combination of procedures often varies from one instructional design model to the next, most of the models include the analysis of instructional problems and the design, development, implementation, and evaluation of instruction procedures and materials intended to solve those problems. How did this instructional design process come into being? This portion of this chapter will focus on answering that question.

The Origins of Instructional Design: World War II

The origins of instructional design procedures have been traced to World War II (Dick, 1987). During the war, a large number of psychologists and educators who had training and experience in conducting experimental research were called on to conduct research and develop training materials for the military services. These individuals, including Robert Gagné, Leslie Briggs, John Flanagan, and many others, exerted considerable influence on the characteristics of the training materials that were developed, basing much of their work on instructional principles derived from research and theory on instruction, learning, and human behavior (Baker, 1973; Saettler, 1990).

Moreover, psychologists used their knowledge of evaluation and testing to help assess the skills of trainees and select the individuals who were most likely to benefit from particular training programs. For example, at one point in the war, the failure rate in a particular flight training program was unacceptably high. To overcome this problem, psychologists examined the general intellectual, psychomotor, and perceptual skills of individuals who were able to successfully perform the skills taught in the program, and then developed tests that measured these traits. These tests were used to screen candidates for the program, with those individuals who scored poorly being directed into other programs. As a result of using this examination of entry skills as a screening device, the military was able to significantly increase the percentage of personnel who successfully completed the program (Gagné, personal communication, 1985).

Immediately after the war, many of the psychologists responsible for the success of World War II military training programs continued to work on solving instructional problems. Organizations such as the American Institutes for Research were established for this purpose. During the late 1940s and throughout the 1950s, psychologists working for such organizations started viewing training as a system, and developed a number of innovative analysis, design, and evaluation procedures (Dick, 1987). For example, during this period, a detailed task analysis methodology was developed by Robert B. Miller while he worked on projects for the military (Miller, 1953, 1962). His work and those of other early pioneers in the instructional design field are summarized in *Psychological Principles in System Development*, edited by Gagné (1962b).

More Early Developments: The Programmed Instruction Movement

The programmed instruction movement, which ran from the mid 1950s through the mid 1960s, proved to be another major factor in the development of the systems approach. In 1954, B. F. Skinner's article, "The Science of Learning and the Art of Teaching," began what might be called a minor revolution in the field of education. In this article and later ones (e.g., Skinner, 1958), Skinner described his ideas regarding the requirements for increasing human learning and the desired characteristics of effective instructional materials. Skinner stated that such materials, called programmed instructional materials, should present instruction in small steps, require active responses to frequent questions, provide immediate feedback, and allow for learner self-pacing. Moreover, because each step was small, it was thought that learners would answer all questions correctly and thus be positively reinforced by the feedback they received.

The process Skinner and others (cf. Lumsdaine & Glaser, 1960) described for developing programmed instruction exemplified an empirical approach to solving educational problems: data regarding the effectiveness of the materials were collected, instructional weaknesses were identified, and the materials were revised accordingly. In addition to this trial and revision procedure, which today would be called formative evaluation, the process for developing programmed materials involved many of the steps found in current instructional design models. As Heinich (1970) indicates:

> Programmed instruction has been credited by some with introducing the systems approach to education. By analyzing and breaking down content into specific behavioral objectives, devising the necessary steps to achieve the objectives, setting up procedures to try out and revise the steps, and validating the program against attainment of the objectives, programmed instruction succeeded in creating a small but effective self-instructional system—a technology of instruction. (p. 123)

The Popularization of Behavioral Objectives

As indicated previously, those involved in designing programmed instructional materials often began by identifying the specific objectives learners who used the materials would be expected to attain. In the early 1960s, Robert Mager, recognizing the need to teach educators how to write objectives, wrote *Preparing Objectives for Programmed Instruction* (1962). This small, humorously written programmed book, now in its second edition (Mager, 1984), has proved to be very popular and has sold over 1.5 million copies. The book describes how to write objectives that include a description of desired learner behaviors, the conditions under which the behaviors are to be performed, and the standards (criteria) by which the behaviors are to be judged. Many current-day adherents of the instructional design process advocate the preparation of objectives that contain these three elements.

Although Mager popularized the use of objectives, the concept was discussed and used by educators at least as far back as the early 1900s. Among those early advocates of the use of clearly stated objectives were Bobbitt, Charters, and Burk (Gagné, 1965a). However, Ralph Tyler has often been considered the father of the behavioral objectives movement. In 1934, he wrote, "Each objective must be defined in terms which clarify the kind of behavior which the course should help to develop" (cited in Walbesser & Eisenberg, 1972). During the famous Eight-Year Study that Tyler directed, it was found that in those instances in which schools did specify objectives, those objectives were usually quite vague. By the end of the project, however, it was demonstrated that objectives could be clarified by stating them in behavioral terms, and those objectives could serve as the basis for evaluating the effectiveness of instruction (Borich, 1980; Tyler, 1975a).

In the 1950s, behavioral objectives were given another boost when Benjamin Bloom and his colleagues published *Taxonomy of Educational Objectives* (1956). The authors indicated that within the cognitive domain there were various types of learning outcomes, that objectives could be classified according to the type of learner behavior described therein, and that there was a hierarchical relationship among the various types of outcomes. Moreover, they indicated that tests should be designed to measure each of these types of outcomes. As we shall see in the next two sections of this chapter, similar notions described by other educators had significant implications for the systematic design of instruction.

The Criterion-Referenced Testing Movement

In the early 1960s, another important factor in the development of the instructional design process was the emergence of criterion-referenced testing. Until that time, most tests, called *norm-referenced* tests, were designed to spread out the performance of learners, resulting in some students doing well on a test and others doing poorly. In contrast, a *criterion-referenced* test is intended to measure how well an individual can perform a particular behavior or set of behaviors, irrespective of how well others perform. As early as 1932, Tyler had indicated that tests could be used for such purposes (Dale, 1967). And later, Flanagan (1951) and Ebel (1962) discussed the differences between such tests and the more familiar norm-referenced measures. However, Robert Glaser (1963; Glaser & Klaus, 1962) was the first to use the term *criterion-referenced measures.* In discussing such measures, Glaser (1963) indicated that they could be used to assess student entry-level behavior and to determine the extent to which students had acquired the behaviors an instructional program was designed to teach. The use of criterion-referenced tests for these two purposes is a central feature of instructional design procedures.

Robert M. Gagné: Domains of Learning, Events of Instruction, and Hierarchical Analysis

Another important event in the history of instructional design occurred in 1965, with the publication of the first edition of *The Conditions of Learning,* written by Robert Gagné (1965b). In this book, Gagné described five domains, or types, of learning outcomes—verbal information, intellectual skills, psychomotor skills, attitudes, and cognitive strategies—each of which required a different set of conditions to promote learning. Gagné also provided detailed descriptions of these conditions for each type of learning outcome.

In the same volume, Gagné also described nine *events of instruction*, or teaching activities, that he considered essential for promoting the attainment of any type of learning outcome. Gagné also described which instructional events were particularly crucial for which type of outcome, and discussed the circumstances under which particular events could be excluded. Now in its fourth edition (Gagné, 1985), Gagné's description of the various types of learning outcomes and the events of instruction remain cornerstones of instructional design practices.

Gagné's work in the area of learning hierarchies and hierarchical analysis also has had a significant impact on the instructional design field. In the early 1960s and later in his career (e.g., Gagné, 1962a, 1985; Gagné, Briggs, & Wager, 1992; Gagné & Medsker, 1996), Gagné indicated that skills within the intellectual skills domain have a hierarchical relationship to each other, so that to readily learn to perform a superordinate skill, one would first have to master the skills subordinate to it. This concept leads to the important notion that instruction should be designed to ensure that learners acquire subordinate skills before they attempt to acquire superordinate ones. Gagné went on to describe a hierarchical analysis process (also called *learning task analysis* or *instructional task analysis*) for identifying subordinate skills. This process remains a key feature in many instructional design models.

Sputnik: The Indirect Launching of Formative Evaluation

In 1957, when the Soviet Union launched Sputnik, the first orbiting space satellite, there began a series of events that would eventually have a major impact on the instructional design process. In response to the launching of Sputnik, the United States government, shocked by the success of the Soviet effort, poured millions of dollars into improving math and science education in the United States. The instructional materials developed with these funds were usually written by subject matter experts and produced without tryouts with learners. Years later, in the mid 1960s, when it was discovered that many of these materials were not particularly effective, Michael Scriven (1967) pointed to the need to try out drafts of instructional materials with learners prior to the time the materials were in their final form. This process would enable educators to examine the materials and, if necessary, revise them while the materials were still in their formative stages. Scriven coined the term *formative evaluation* for this tryout and revision process, and contrasted it with what he labeled *summative evaluation*, the testing of instructional materials after they are in their final form.

Although the terms *formative* and *summative evaluation* were coined by Scriven, the distinction between these two approaches was previously made by Lee Cronbach (1963). Moreover, during the 1940s and the 1950s, a number of educators, such as Arthur Lumsdaine, Mark May, and C. R. Carpenter, described procedures for evaluating instructional materials that were still in their formative stages (Cambre, 1981). However, in spite of the writings of such educators, very few of the instructional products developed in the 1940s and 1950s went through any sort of formative evaluation. This situation changed somewhat in the late 1950s and through the 1960s, as many of the programmed instructional materials developed during that period were tested while they were being developed. However, authors such as Susan Markle (1967) decried a lack of rigor in testing processes. In light of this problem, Markle prescribed detailed procedures for evaluating materials both during and after the design process. These procedures are much like the formative and summative evaluation techniques generally prescribed today.

Early Instructional Design Models

In the early and mid 1960s, the concepts that were being developed in such areas as task analysis, objective specification, and criterion-referenced testing were linked together to form a process, or model, for systematically designing instructional materials. Among the first individuals to describe such models were Gagné (1962b), Glaser (1962, 1965), and Silvern (1964). These individuals used terms such as *instructional design*, *system development*, *systematic instruction,* and *instructional system* to describe the models they created. Other instructional design models created and employed during this decade included those described by Banathy (1968), Barson (1967), and Hamerus (1968).

The 1970s: Burgeoning of Interest in the Systems Approach

During the 1970s, the number of instructional design models greatly increased. Building on the works of those who preceded them, many individuals created new models for systematically designing instruction (e.g., Dick & Carey, 1978; Gagné & Briggs, 1974; Gerlach & Ely, 1971; Kemp, 1971). Indeed, by the end of the decade, over 40 such models were identified (Andrews & Goodson, 1980). (A discussion of many of the instructional design models developed in the 1980s and 1990s is contained in Gustafson & Branch, 2002).

During the 1970s, interest in the instructional design process flourished in a variety of different sectors. In 1975, several branches of the United States military adopted an instructional design model (Branson et al., 1975) intended to guide the development of training materials within those branches. In academia, during the first half of the decade, many instructional improvement centers were created with the intent of helping faculty use media and instructional design procedures to improve the quality of their instruction (Gaff, 1975; Gustafson & Bratton, 1984). Moreover, many graduate programs in instructional design were created (Partridge & Tennyson, 1979; Redfield & Dick, 1984; Silber, 1982). In business and industry, many organizations, seeing the value of using instructional design to improve the quality of training, began adopting the approach (cf. Mager, 1977; Miles, 1983). Internationally, many nations, such as South Korea, Liberia, and Indonesia, saw the benefits of using instructional design to solve instructional problems in those countries (Chadwick, 1986; Morgan, 1989). These nations supported the design of new instructional programs, created organizations to support the use of instructional design, and provided support to individuals desiring training in this field. Many of these developments were chronicled in the *Journal of Instructional Development*, a journal first published during the 1970s.

The 1980s: Growth and Redirection

In many sectors, the interest in instructional design that burgeoned during the previous decade continued to grow during the 1980s. Interest in the instructional design process remained strong in business and industry (Bowsher, 1989; Galagan, 1989), in the military (Chevalier, 1990; Finch, 1987; McCombs, 1986;), and in the international arena (Ely & Plomp, 1986; Morgan, 1989).

In contrast to its influence in the aforementioned sectors, during the 1980s instructional design had minimal impact in other areas. In the public school arena, some curriculum development efforts involved the use of basic instructional design processes (e.g., Spady, 1988), and some instructional design textbooks for teachers were produced (e.g., Dick & Reiser, 1989; Gerlach & Ely, 1980; Sullivan & Higgins, 1983). However, in spite of these efforts, evidence indicated that instructional design was having little impact on instruction in the public schools (Branson & Grow, 1987; Burkman, 1987b; Rossett & Garbosky, 1987). In a similar vein, with a few exceptions (e.g., Diamond, 1989), instructional design practices had a minimal impact in higher education. Whereas instructional improvement centers in higher education were growing in number through the mid 1970s, by 1983 more than one fourth of these organizations were disbanded and there was a general downward trend in the budgets of the remaining centers (Gustafson & Bratton, 1984). Burkman (1987a, 1987b) provides an enlightening analysis of the reasons why instructional design efforts in schools and universities have not been successful, and contrasts these conditions with the more favorable conditions that exist in business and the military.

During the 1980s, there was a growing interest in how the principles of cognitive psychology could be applied in the instructional design process, and a number of publications outlining potential applications were described (e.g., Bonner, 1988; Divesta & Rieber, 1987; "Interview with R. M. Gagné", 1982; Low, 1980). However, several leading figures in the field have indicated that the actual effects of cognitive psychology on instructional design practices during this decade were rather small (Dick, 1987; Gustafson, 1993).

A factor that did have a major effect on instructional design practices in the 1980s was the increasing interest in the use of microcomputers for instructional purposes. With the advent of these devices, many professionals in the instructional design field turned their attention to producing computer-based instruction (Dick, 1987; Shrock, 1995). Others discussed the need to develop new models of instructional design to accommodate the interactive capabilities of this technology (Merrill, Li, & Jones, 1990a, 1990b). Moreover, computers began to be used as tools to automate some instructional design tasks (Merrill & Li, 1989).

Into the Twenty-First Century: Changing Views and Practices

During the 1990s and into the twenty-first century, a variety of developments have had a major impact on instructional design principles and practices. A major development has been the increasing influence of the human performance technology movement (see Section 4 of this book). This movement, with its emphasis on on-the-job performance (rather than on learning), business results, and noninstructional solutions to performance problems, has broadened the scope of the instructional design field. Indeed, in recent years many training organizations have adopted the practices those in the human performance technology field have been advocating. In fact, those organizations recently recognized by the American Society for Training and Development for their exceptional efforts in fostering and supporting workplace learning and performance were cited for their *use of noninstructional solutions* to learning and performance problems, as well as their *emphasis on business result*s, two key principles associated with the human performance technology field (Sugrue & Kim, 2004).

Another major factor that has affected the field since the 1990s has been the growing interest in constructivism. Constructivist views of learning and instruction have had a major impact on the thoughts and actions of many theorists and practitioners in the instructional design field. For example, the constructivist emphasis on designing "authentic" learning tasks—tasks that reflect the complexity of the real-world environment in which learners will be using the skills they are learning—has had an effect on how instructional design is being practiced and taught (e.g., Dick, 1996). Although some have argued that "traditional" instructional design practices and constructivist principles are antithetical, in recent years numerous authors have described how consideration of constructivist principles can enhance instructional design practices (see, for example, Chapters 5 and 6).

In addition to the aforementioned developments, many training organizations and similar types of organizations have used innovations such as electronic performance support systems (see Chapter 15), online learning (see Chapter 28), reusable learning objects (see Chapter 29), and knowledge management systems (see Chapter 16) to improve learning and performance. In recent years, these and other developments, such as the use of rapid prototyping (see Chapter 18) have changed the nature of the work done by instructional designers.

Conclusion

Although this chapter has provided separate accounts of the history of instructional media and the history of instructional design, there is an obvious overlapping between these two areas. Many instructional solutions arrived at through the use of instructional design processes require the employment of the instructional media discussed in the first half of this chapter. Moreover, many individuals (e.g., Clark, 1994, 2001; Kozma, 1994; Morrison, 1994; Reiser, 1994; Shrock, 1994) have argued that the effective use of media for instructional purposes requires careful instructional planning, such as that prescribed by models of instructional design. In the field of instructional design and technology, those whose work is influenced by the lessons learned from the history of media *and* the history of instructional design will be well positioned to have a positive influence on future developments within the field.

Application Questions

1a. As indicated in this chapter, today there is some optimism that the Internet and the World Wide Web will have a major influence on the way instruction is presented to learners. Based on what you know about these technological innovations, and what you read about the history of instructional films, television, and the computer, indicate whether you think the Internet and Web will have a major impact in one or more of the following areas:

a. Educational programs at grades K (kindergarten)–12
b. Higher education (community colleges, colleges, and universities)
c. Adult education (in businesses, government, and/or the military)

1b. Ask one of the faculty members in your program to discuss his or her views on this matter. Reexamine your initial beliefs by comparing them with those expressed by the faculty member. Then prepare a brief report comparing your views with those of the faculty member you interviewed.

2. Team up with a group of three or four other students in your class. Each of you should then identify an alumnus from your program whom you would like to interview, preferably in person or via telephone. Ask each alumnus to indicate which recent trends in our field have had the greatest effect on her or his work, and to describe the nature of that impact. Then summarize your group's findings and share those findings via an oral report delivered to the rest of the class. Some specific trends mentioned in this chapter that you might want to ask the alumni about include:

a. Performance technology
b. Electronic performance support
c. Distance learning
d. Constructivism
e. Rapid prototyping
f. Knowledge management

References

Anderson, C. (1962). Technology in American education: 1650–1900 (Report No. OE-34018). Washington, DC: Office of Education, U.S. Department of Health, Education, and Welfare.

Anderson, R. E., & Ronnkvist, A. (1999). *The presence of computers in American schools: Teaching, learning and computing: 1998 national survey* (Report #2). Irvine, CA: Center for Research on Information Technology and Organizations. (ERIC Document Reproduction Service No. ED 430 548)

Andrews, D. H., & Goodson, L. A. (1980). A comparative analysis of models' instructional design. *Journal of Instructional Development, 3*(4), 2–16.

Atkinson, R. C., & Hansen, D. N. (1966). Computer-assisted instruction in initial reading: The Stanford project. *Reading Research Quarterly, 2*, 5–25.

Baker, E. L. (1973). The technology of instructional development. In R. M. W. Travers (Ed.), *Second handbook of research on teaching.* Chicago: Rand McNally.

Banathy, B. H. (1968). *Instructional systems.* Belmont, CA: Fearon.

Barson, J. (1967). *Instructional systems development. A demonstration and evaluation project: Final report.* East Lansing, MI: Michigan State University. (ERIC Document Reproduction Service No. ED 020 673)

Becker, H. J. (1998). Running to catch a moving train: Schools and information technologies. *Theory into Practice, 37*(1), 20–30.

Berlo, D. K. (1963). "You are in the people business." *Audiovisual Instruction, 8*, 372–381.

Blakely, R. J. (1979). To *serve the public interest: Educational broadcasting in the United States.* Syracuse, NY: Syracuse University Press.

Bloom, B. S., Engelhart, M. D., Furst, E. J., Hill, W. H., & Krathwohl, D. R. (1956). *Taxonomy of educational objectives: The classification of educational goals. Handbook 1: Cognitive domain.* New York: David McKay.

Bonner, J. (1988). Implications of cognitive theory for instructional design. *Educational Communication and Technology Journal, 36*, 3–14.

Borich, G. D. (1980). *A state of the art assessment of educational evaluation.* Austin, TX: University of Texas. (ERIC Document Reproduction Service No. ED 187 717)

Bowsher, J. E. (1989). Educating America: Lessons learned in the nation's corporations. New York: Wiley.

Branson, R. K., & Grow, G. (1987). Instructional systems development. In R. M. Gagné (Ed.), *Instructional*

Technology: Foundations (pp. 397–428). Hillsdale, NJ: Lawrence Erlbaum Associates.

Branson, R. K., Rayner, G. I., Cox, J. L., Furman, J. P., King, F. J., & Hannum, W. H. (1975). *Inter-service procedures for instructional systems development.* Fort Monroe, VA: U.S. Army Training and Doctrine Command.

Burkman, E. (1987a). Factors affecting utilization. In R. M. Gagné (Ed.), *Instructional technology: Foundations* (pp. 429–456). Hillsdale, NJ: Lawrence Erlbaum Associates.

Burkman, E. (1987b). Prospects for instructional systems design in the public schools. *Journal of Instructional Development, 10*(4), 27–32.

Cambre, M. A. (1981). Historical overview of formative evaluation of instructional media products. *Educational Communication and Technology Journal, 29*, 3–25.

Carnegie Commission on Educational Television (1967). *Public television: A program for action.* New York: Harper & Row.

Carpenter, C. R., & Greenhill, L. P. (1956). *Instructional film research reports: Vol. 2* (Technical Report No. 269-7-61). Port Washington, NY: U.S. Navy Special Devices Center.

Center for Social Organization of Schools (1983). *School uses of microcomputers: Reports from a national survey* (Issue No. 1). Baltimore, MD: Johns Hopkins University, Center for Social Organization of Schools.

Chadwick, C. B. (1986). Instructional technology research in Latin America. *Educational Communication and Technology Journal, 34*, 247–254.

Chevalier, R.D. (1990). Improving efficiency and effectiveness of training: A six year case study of systematic change. *Performance and Instruction, 29*(5), 21–23.

Chisholm, P. (2003a). From ships to shore [Electronic version]. *Military Training Technology, 8*(6).

Chisholm, P. (2003b). Learning from a distance [Electronic version]. *Military Training Technology, 8*(4).

Clark, R. E. (1983). Reconsidering research on learning from media. *Review of Educational Research, 53*, 445–459.

Clark, R. E. (1994). Media will never influence learning. *Educational Technology Research and Development, 42*(2), 21–29.

Clark, R. E. (2001). What is next in the media and methods debate? In R. E. Clark (Ed.), *Learning from media.* Greenwich, CT: Information Age.

Commission on Instructional Technology (1970). *To improve learning: An evaluation of instructional technology* (Vol. 1). New York: Rowker.

Cronbach, L. J. (1963). Course improvement through evaluation. *Teachers' College Record, 64*, 672–683.

Cuban, L. (1986). *Teachers and machines: The classroom use of technology since 1920.* New York: Teachers College Press.

Dale, E. (1946). *Audio-visual methods in teaching.* New York: Holt, Rinehart & Winston.

Dale, E. (1953), What does it mean to communicate? *AV Communication Review, 1*, 3–5.

Dale, E. (1967). Historical setting of programmed instruction. In P. C. Lange (Ed.), *Programmed instruction: The sixty-sixth yearbook of the National Society for the Study of Education, Part 11.* Chicago: University of Chicago Press.

Diamond, R. M. (1989). *Designing and improving courses and curricula in higher education: A systematic approach.* San Francisco: Jossey-Bass.

Dick, W. (1987). A history of instructional design and its impact on educational psychology. In J. Glover & R. Roning (Eds.), *Historical foundations of educational psychology.* New York: Plenum.

Dick, W. (1996). The Dick and Carey model: Will it survive the decade? *Educational Technology Research and Development, 44*(3), 55–63.

Dick, W., & Carey, L. (1978). *The systematic design of instruction.* Glenview, IL: Scott, Foresman.

Dick W., & Reiser, R. A. (1989). *Planning effective instruction.* Englewood Cliffs, NJ: Prentice Hall.

Divesta, F. J., & Rieber, L. P. (1987). Characteristics of cognitive engineering: The next generation of instructional systems. *Educational Communication and Technology Journal, 35*, 213–230.

Dolezalek, H. (2004). Industry report 2004: *Training* magazine's 23rd annual comprehensive analysis of employer-sponsored training in the United States. *Training, 41*(10), 20–36.

Ebel, R. L. (1962). Content standard test scores. *Educational and Psychological Measurement, 22*, 15–25.

Ely, D. P. (Ed.). (1963). The changing role of the audiovisual process in education: A definition and glossary of related terms [Special issue]. *AV Communication Review, 11*(1).

Ely, D. P. (1970). Toward a philosophy of instructional technology. *British Journal of Educational Technology, 1*(2), 81–94.

Ely, D. P., & Plomp, T. (1986). The promises of educational technology: A reassessment. *International Review of Education, 32*, 231–249.

Finch, C. R. (1987). Instructional systems development in the military. *Journal of Industrial Teacher Education, 24*(4), 18–26.

Finn, J. D. (1954). Direction in AV communication research. *AV Communication Review, 2*, 83–102.

Finn, J. D. (1972). The emerging technology of education. In R. J. McBeath (Ed.), *Extending education through technology: Selected writings by James D. Finn.* Washington, DC: Association for Educational Communications and Technology.

Flanagan, J. C. (1951). Units, scores, and norms. In E. T. Lindquist (Ed.), *Educational measurement.* Washington, DC: American Council on Education.

Fuhr, J. (2004). Airmen educator: Interview with General Donald G. Cook [Electronic version]. *Military Training Technology, 9*(4).

Gaff, J. G. (1975). *Toward faculty renewal: Advances in faculty, instructional, and organizational development.* San Francisco: Jossey-Bass.

Gagné, R. M. (1962a). The acquisition of knowledge. *Psychological Review, 69*, 355–365.

Gagné, R. M. (1962b). Introduction. In R. M. Gagné (Ed.), *Psychological principles in system development*. New York: Holt, Rinehart & Winston.

Gagné, R. M. (1965a). The analysis of instructional objectives for the design of instruction. In R. Glaser (Ed.), *Teaching machines and programmed learning.* Vol. *II Data and directions*. Washington, DC: National Education Association.

Gagné, R. M. (1965b). *The conditions of learning.* New York: Holt, Rinehart & Winston.

Gagné, R. M. (1985). *The conditions of learning* (4th ed.). New York: Holt, Rinehart & Winston.

Gagné, R. M., & Briggs, L. J. (1974). *Principles of instructional design.* New York: Holt, Rinehart, & Winston.

Gagné, R. M., Briggs, L. J., & Wager, W. W. (1992). *Principles of instructional design* (4th ed.). New York: Holt, Rinehart & Winston.

Gagné, R. M., & Medsker, K. L. (1996). *The conditions of learning: Training applications.* Fort Worth, TX: Harcourt Brace.

Galagan, P. A. (1989). IBM gets its arms around education. *Training and Development Journal, 43*(1), 34–41.

Gerlach, V. S., & Ely, D. P. (1971). *Teaching and media: A systematic approach.* Englewood Cliffs, NJ: Prentice Hall.

Gerlach, V. S., & Ely, D. P. (1980). *Teaching and media: A systematic approach* (2nd ed.). Englewood Cliffs, NJ: Prentice Hall.

Glaser, R. (1962). Psychology and instructional technology. In R. Glaser (Ed.), *Training research and education.* Pittsburgh: University of Pittsburgh Press.

Glaser, R. (1963). Instructional technology and the measurement of learning outcomes: Some questions. *American Psychologist, 18*, 519–521.

Glaser, R. (1965). Toward a behavioral science base for instructional design. In R. Glaser (Ed.), *Teaching machines and programmed learning. Vol. II. Data and directions.* Washington, DC: National Education Association.

Glaser, R., & Klaus, D. J. (1962). Proficiency measurement: Assessing human performance. In R. M. Gagné (Ed.), *Psychological principles in system development.* New York: Holt, Rinehart & Winston.

Gordon. G. N. (1970). *Classroom television: New frontiers in ITV.* New York: Hastings House.

Gumpert, G. (1967). Closed-circuit television in training and education. In A. E. Koenig & R. B. Hill (Eds.), *The farther vision: Educational television today.* Madison, WI: University of Wisconsin Press.

Gustafson, K. L. (1993). Instructional design fundamentals: Clouds on the horizon. *Educational Technology, 33*(2), 27–32.

Gustafson, K. L., & Branch, R. M. (2002). *Survey of instructional development models* (4th ed.). Syracuse, NY: ERIC Clearinghouse on Information & Technology.

Gustafson, K., & Bratton, B. (1984). Instructional improvement centers in higher education: A status report. *Journal of Instructional Development, 7*(2), 2–7.

Hamerus, D. (1968). *The systems approach to instructional development: The contribution of behavioral science to instructional technology.* Monmouth: OR: Oregon State System of Higher Education, Teaching Research Division.

Hawkridge, D. (1999). Cost-effective support for university students via the Web? *Association for Learning Technology Journal, 6*(3), 24–29.

Heinich, R. (1970). Technology and the management *of* instruction (Association for Educational Communications and Technology Monograph No. 4). Washington, DC: Association for Educational Communications and Technology.

Heinich, R., Molenda, M., Russell, J. D., & Smaldino, S. E. (1999). *Instructional media and technologies for learning* (6th ed.). Upper Saddle River, NJ: Prentice Hall.

Hezel, R. T. (1980). Public broadcasting: Can it teach? *Journal of Communication, 30*, 173–178.

Hoban, C. F., Sr., Hoban, C. F., Jr., & Zissman, S. B. (1937). *Visualizing the curriculum.* New York: Dryden.

Interview with Robert M. Gagné: Developments in learning psychology: Implications for instructional design; and effects of computer technology on instructional design and development. (1982). *Educational Technology, 22*(6), 11–15.

Kemp, J. E. (1971). *Instructional design: A plan for unit and course development.* Belmont, CA: Fearon.

Kozma, R. B. (1991). Learning with media. *Review of Educational Research, 61*(2), 179–212.

Kozma, R. B. (1994). Will media influence learning: Reframing the debate. *Educational Technology Research and Development, 42*(2), 7–19.

Levie, W. H., & Dickie, K. E. (1973). The analysis and application of media. In R. M. W. Travers (Ed.), *Second handbook of research on teaching.* Chicago: Rand McNally.

Lewis, B. N., & Pask, G. (1965). The theory and practice of adaptive teaching systems. In R. Glaser (Ed.), *Teaching machines and programmed learning. Vol. II. Data and directions.* Washington, DC: National Education Association.

Low, W. C. (1980). Changes in instructional development: The aftermath of an information processing takeover in psychology. *Journal of Instructional Development, 4*(2), 10–18.

Lumsdaine, A. A. (Ed.). (1961). *Student response in programmed instruction.* Washington, DC: National Academy of Science, National Research Council.

Lumsdaine, A. A. (1963). Instruments and media of instruction. In N. L. Gage (Ed.), *Handbook of research on teaching.* Chicago: Rand McNally.

Lumsdaine, A. A. (1964). Educational technology, programmed learning, and instructional science. In E. R. Hilgard (Ed.), *Theories of learning and instruction: The sixty-third yearbook of the National Society for the Study of Education, Part 1.* Chicago: University of Chicago Press.

Lumsdaine, A. A., & Glaser, R. (Eds.). (1960). *Teaching machines and programmed learning: A source book.* Washington, DC: National Education Association.

Mager, R. F. (1962). *Preparing objectives for programmed instruction.*Belmont, CA: Fearon.

Mager, R. F. (1977). The "winds of change." *Training and Development Journal, 31*(10), 12–20.

Mager, R. F. (1984). *Preparing instructional objectives* (2nd ed.). Belmont, CA: Lake.

Market Data Retrieval (2004). *Technology in education 2004: A comprehensive report on the state of technology in the K–12 market.* Shelton, CT: Market Data Retrieval.

Market Data Retrieval. (2005). *The college technology review: 2004–2005 academic year.* Shelton, CT: Market Data Retrieval.

Markle, S. M. (1967). Empirical testing of programs. In P. C. Lange (Ed.), *Programmed instruction: The sixty-sixth yearbook of the National Society for the Study of Education, Part 2.* Chicago: University of Chicago Press.

May, M. A., & Lumsdaine, A. A. (1958). *Learning from films.* New Haven, CT: Yale University Press.

McCluskey, F. D. (1981). DVI, DAVI, AECT: A long view. In J. W. Brown & S. N. Brown *(Eds.), Educational media yearbook: 1981.* Littleton, CO: Libraries Unlimited.

McCombs, B. L. (1986). The instructional systems development (ISD) model: A review of those factors critical to its successful implementation. *Educational Communications and Technology Journal, 34*, 67–81.

Meierhenry, W. C. (1980). Instructional theory: From behaviorism to humanism to synergism. *Instructional Innovator, 25*(1), 16–18.

Merrill, M. D., & Li, Z. (1989). An instructional design expert system. *Journal of Computer-Based Instruction, 16*(3), 95–101.

Merrill, M. D., Li, Z., & Jones, M. K. (1990a). Limitations of first generation instructional design. *Educational Technology, 30*(1), 7–11.

Merrill, M. D., Li, Z., & Jones, M. K. (1990b). Second generation instructional design (ID2). *Educational Technology, 30*(2), 7–14.

Miles, G. D. (1983). Evaluating four years of ID experience. *Journal of Instructional Development, 6*(2), 9–14.

Miller, R. B. (1953). A method for man-machine task analysis (Tech. Rept. No. 53-137). Wright-Patterson Air Force Base, OH: Wright Air Development Center.

Miller, R. B. (1962). Analysis and specification of behavior for training. In R. Glaser (Ed.), *Training research and education.* Pittsburgh: University of Pittsburgh Press.

Moore, M. G. (1989, April). Three modes of interaction. In *Issues in instructional interactivity*. Forum conducted at the meeting of the National University Continuing Education Association, Salt Lake City, UT.

Morgan, J. E. (1932). Introduction. In B. H. Darrow, *Radio: The assistant teacher.* Columbus, OH: R. H. Adams.

Morgan, R. M. (1989). Instructional systems development in third world countries. *Educational Technology Research and Development, 37*(1), 47–56.

Morrison, G. R. (1994). The media effects question: "Unsolvable" or asking the right question. *Educational Technology Research and Development, 42*(2), 41–44.

National Center for Educational Statistics. (2000). *Teachers' tools for the 21st century: A report on teachers' use of technology.* Retrieved July 12, 2005, from http://nces.ed.gov/pubs2000/2000102A.pdf

National Center for Educational Statistics. (2005). *Internet access in U.S. public schools and classrooms: 1994–2003.* Retrieved July 12, 2005, from http://nces.ed.gov/pubs2005/2005015.pdf

Office of Technology Assessment. (1995). *Teachers & technology: making the connection.* Washington, DC: Office of Technology Assessment.

Olsen, J. R., & Bass, V. B. (1982). The application of performance technology in the military: 1960–1980. *Performance and Instruction, 21*(6), 32–36.

Pagliaro, L. A. (1983). The history and development of CAI: 1926–1981, an overview. *Alberta Journal of Educational Research, 29(1)*, 75–84.

Papert, S. (1984). New theories for new learnings. *School Psychology Review, 13*(4), 422–428.

Partridge, M. I., & Tennyson, R. D. (1979). Graduate programs in instructional systems: A review of selected programs. *Journal of Instructional Development, 2*(2), 18–26.

Pask, G. (1960). Electronic keyboard teaching machines. In A. A. Lumsdaine & R. Glaser (Eds.), *Teaching machines and programmed learning: A source book.* Washington, DC: National Education Association.

Phipps, R. A. (2004). *How does technology affect access in postsecondary education? What do we really know? Report of the National Postsecondary Education Cooperative Working Group on Access-Technology*. Retrieved July 12, 2005, from http://nces.ed.gov/pubs2004/2004831.pdf

Redfield, D. D., & Dick, W. (1984). An alumni-practitioner review of doctoral competencies in instructional systems. *Journal of Instructional Development, 7*(1), 10–13.

Reiser, R. A. (1987). Instructional technology: A history. In R. M. Gagné (Ed.), *Instructional technology: Foundations*. Hillsdale, NJ: Lawrence Erlbaum Associates.

Reiser, R. A. (1994). Clark's invitation to the dance: An instructional designer's response. *Educational Technology Research and Development, 42*(2), 45–48.

Reiser, R. A., & Gagné, R. M. (1983). *Selecting media for instruction.* Englewood Cliffs, NJ: Educational Technology Publications.

Rossett, A., & Garbosky, J. (1987). The use, misuse, and non-use of educational technologists in public education. *Educational Technology, 27*(9), 37–42.

Saettler, P. (1968). *A history of instructional technology.* New York: McGraw-Hill.

Saettler, P. (1990). *The evolution of American educational technology.* Englewood, CO: Libraries Unlimited.

Schramm, W. (1977). *Big media, little media.* Beverly Hills, CA: Sage.

Scriven, M. (1967). The methodology of evaluation. In *Perspectives of curriculum evaluation* (American Educational Research Association Monograph Series on Curriculum Evaluation, No. 1). Chicago: Rand McNally.

Shannon, C. E., & Weaver, W. (1949). *The mathematical theory of communication.* Urbana, IL: University of Illinois Press.

Shrock, S. A. (1994). The media influence debate: Read the fine print, but don't lose sight of the big picture. *Educational Technology Research and Development, 42*(2), 49–53.

Shrock, S. A. (1995). A brief history of instructional development. In G. J. Anglin (Ed.), *Instructional technology: Past, present, and future.* Englewood, CO: Libraries Unlimited.

Silber, K. H. (1981). Some implications of the history of educational technology: We're all in this together. In J. W. Brown & S. N. Brown (Eds.), *Educational media yearbook: 1981*. Littleton, CO: Libraries Unlimited.

Silber, K. H. (1982). An analysis of university training programs for instructional developers. *Journal of Instructional Development, 6*(1), 15–28.

Silvern, L. C. (1964). *Designing instructional systems.* Los Angeles: Education and Training Consultants.

Skinner, B. F. (1954). The science of learning and the art of teaching. *Harvard Educational Review, 24*, 86–97.

Skinner, B. F. (1958). Teaching machines. *Science, 128,* 969–977.

Spady, W. G. (1988). Organizing for results: The basis for authentic restructuring and reform. *Educational Leadership, 46*(2), 4–8.

SRI International (2002). *The integrated studies of educational technology: Professional development and teachers' use of technology.* Retrieved July 12, 2005, from http://www.sri.com/policy/cep/mst/SRI_Professional_Development Report_2002.pdf

Stolorow, L. M., & Davis, D. (1965). Teaching machines and computer-assisted systems. In R. Glaser (Ed.), *Teaching machines and programmed learning. Vol. II. Data and directions*. Washington, DC: National Education Association.

Sugrue, B., & Kim, K. H. (2004). *ASTD 2004 state of the industry report*. Alexandria,VA: American Society for Training and Development.

Sullivan, H. J., & Higgins, N. (1983). *Teaching for competence.* New York: Teachers College Press.

Suppes, P., & Macken, E. (1978). The historical path from research and development to operational use of CAI. *Educational Technology, 18*(4), 9–12.

Taylor, B. J. (1967). The development of instructional television. In A. E. Koenig & R. B. Hill (Eds.), *The farther vision: Educational television today.* Madison, WI: University of Wisconsin Press.

Tyler, R. W. (1975a). Educational benchmarks in retrospect: Educational change since 1915. *Viewpoints, 51*(2), 11–31.

Tyler, R. W. (1975b). Have educational reforms since 1950 created quality education? *Viewpoints, 51*(2), 35–57.

Walbesser, H. H., & Eisenberg, T. A. (1972). A *review of the research on behavioral objectives and learning hierarchies.* Columbus, OH: Ohio State University, Center for Science and Mathematics Education. (ERIC Document Reproduction Service No. ED 059 900)

SECTION 2

Theories and Models of Learning and Instruction

Overview

In recent years, the field of instructional design and technology has been greatly influenced by new theories and models of learning and instruction. This section of the book discusses some of these new theories and models. It also reviews some of the longstanding theories and models that continue to exert a powerful influence on the field.

Chapter 4 provides an overview of the psychological foundations of the field. It discusses the key ideas and principles associated with seven theories (behavioral learning theory, cognitive information processing theory, Gagné's theory of instruction, schema theory, cognitive load theory, situated learning theory, and constructivism), and discusses the ways in which these theories have influenced instructional design practices.

Chapter 5 provides an in-depth view of how constructivism has influenced the instructional design process and the nature of instructional activities. The chapter also discusses *learning science*, a new academic discipline closely associated with constructivist thinking, and *design research*, a research approach that those in the learning sciences community often employ.

Chapter 6 discusses two different epistemologies (perspectives on the nature of knowledge): the positivist perspective, which has long served as the basis for many practices in our field; and the relativist perspective, which in recent years has gained many adherents among instructional designers and technologists. The chapter goes on to describe how these two different perspectives affect our views about how people learn and how we should design instruction to support learning.

Rather than concentrating on the differences that exist between the various theories of learning and instruction that have affected our field, Chapter 7 focuses on commonalities. The chapter describes a set of prescriptive instructional principles, which the author terms *First Principles of Instruction*, that can be found in some form in almost all instructional design theories and models.

Chapter 8 focuses on holistic instructional design models. Such models are characterized as well suited for designing instruction that enables learners to perform complex learning tasks. The chapter describes the key features of holistic models of instructional design and contrasts them with traditional models.

In recent years, instructional designers have paid increasing attention to motivational issues, often focusing on instructional means of increasing the likelihood that learners will engage in a learning task and persist at it. Chapter 9 discusses a variety of issues related to learner motivation and presents a popular model for designing instruction that motivates learners.

Marcy P. Driscoll
Florida State University

CHAPTER 4

Psychological Foundations of Instructional Design

Knowledge and Comprehension Questions

1. What is meant by the term *learning*?
2. According to most psychological theories, how does learning occur?
3. Identify the key belief underlying Skinner's behavioral learning theory.
4. Describe how antecedents and consequences affect learning.
5. Describe four ways in which behavioral learning theory has influenced instructional design practices.
6. What is the key difference between behavioral learning theory and information processing theory?
7. What roles do attending, encoding, retrieval, and feedback play in the learning process?
8. How does prior knowledge influence learning?
9. Describe two ways in which information processing theory has influenced instructional design practices.
10. What functions do schemata serve in the learning process?
11. How is a learner's cognitive load affected by the presence (and by the absence) of appropriate schemata?
12. In general, how does the 4C/ID model attempt to facilitate learning?
13. Describe one way in which situated learning theory differs from behavioral learning theory and from information processing theory.
14. Describe how, from a situated learning theory perspective, learning occurs.
15. Describe what is meant by the terms *community of learners* and *anchored instruction*.
16. What is the primary reason for defining different categories of learning?
17. What is meant by the term *conditions of learning*?
18. In general, what is the purpose of Gagné's events of instruction?
19. Describe a key difference between the constructivist view of learning and the information processing theory view.
20. Describe two ways in which constructivism has influenced instructional design practices.

Editors' Introduction

Instructional design practices have been greatly influenced by a variety of different theories of learning and instruction. Over many years, three of these theories—behavioral learning theory, cognitive information processing theory, and Gagné's theory of instruction—have had a major influence on instructional design. In recent years, schema theory, cognitive load theory, situated learning theory, and constructivism have offered different views of learning and instruction, and have influenced the practices of many of those involved in the design of instruction. In this chapter, Marcy Driscoll describes the key ideas associated with each of these theories and discusses the ways in which these theories have influenced instructional design practices.

This chapter provides an overview of the major psychological concepts and principles of learning that are foundational to the field of instructional design (ID). The behavioral learning theory of B. F. Skinner, for example, contributed concepts such as reinforcement, feedback, behavioral objectives, and practice to the design of instruction. Cognitive theories such as information processing and schema theory shifted the focus of the ID field to attributes of learners and the role of prior knowledge in learning new knowledge and skills. Situated learning theory is also shifting the ID field toward consideration of sociocultural factors in learning. Finally, instructional theories such as Gagné's and recent constructivist approaches provide guidance for designing learning environments that facilitate the acquisition of desired skills, knowledge, and attitudes.

Regardless of the differences among psychological perspectives on learning, an underlying assumption of most is that instruction will bring about learning. This assumption is what is important to those in the ID field. As Gagné (1995/1996) put it, "There are, after all, some useful human activities that are acquired without instruction, and others that result from self-instruction. But most practical and purposeful activities, such as the pursuits involved in vocational and technical training, are learned in settings that employ instruction" (p. 17).

Learning Defined

Most people have an intuitive notion of what it means to learn—they can do something that they could not do before or they know something that they did not know before. But learning must be distinguished from physical growth, or maturation, which also leads to abilities that were not present before. For example, young children are soon able to grasp objects in both hands simultaneously as they develop muscular control and coordination. This change in ability, however, is not considered learning. Changes in ability that are only temporary are not considered learning either, because learning implies a kind of permanence. Thus, the increased abilities of an athlete taking a performance-enhancing drug would not be thought of as learning.

In most psychological theories, *learning* is defined as "a persisting change in human performance or performance potential" (Driscoll, 2005, p. 9), with *performance potential* referring to the fact that what is learned may not always be exhibited immediately. Indeed, you may remember many instances in which you were never asked to demonstrate what you had learned until a unit or final test was administered. It is important to note, however, that such demonstrations of learning are important for instructional designers to establish the effectiveness of instruction. How else can they determine the impact of instruction if they do not, in some way, ask learners to perform what was to be learned in the first place?

Learning is defined further by how it is thought to occur. In most psychological theories, learning comes about as a consequence of "the learner's experience and interaction with the world" (Driscoll, 2005, p. 9), and this interaction is understood as an individual process. That is, the individual interacts with the world surrounding her, and this experience leads to an increased ability to perform in a particular way. A focus on the individual learner is why there has been such historical interest in differences among individuals and why the performance of individual learners is assessed after instruction. What differs among particular learning theories is how they describe the observed outcomes of learning and how they explain the learning process. Some of these differences are described in later sections of the chapter.

Recently, however, a perspective is emerging that calls into question the individuality of learning. Adherents of this view believe that "[psychological] individuality can only be properly identified and analyzed after the levels of community have been factored out" (Lemke, 1997, p. 49). In other words, learning is to be understood in terms of the activities of people living within a particular sociocultural setting. In this view, learning is more than a change in performance of a single individual; it can encompass the performance of a group of individuals sharing a common purpose or intent or engaged in a common practice. Furthermore, learning is characterized not just by the processes within individual learners but also by the processes shared by and affecting the members of a defined group.

In the sections that follow, major psychological concepts and principles of learning are explored and their implications for ID discussed. In some cases, such implications have already been observed as influences on the field. In others, implications are being imagined and proposed as potential and future influences on the field.

Behavioral Learning Theory

B. F. Skinner, throughout his life and career, advocated an approach to the study of psychology and learning that is focused on behavior (see, e.g., Skinner, 1938, 1969, 1987). At the core of his radical behaviorism is Skinner's belief that learning can be understood, explained, and predicted entirely on the basis of observable events, namely, the behavior of the learner along with its environmental antecedents and consequences. *Antecedents* refer to the cues occurring in the environment that signal the appropriateness of a given behavior. A stop sign, for example, signals to the driver that the appropriate behavior is to apply the brakes. Likewise, a teacher's admonition to "Listen up!"

signals to learners that they should stop talking and pay attention. According to Skinner, the consequences of a behavior then determine whether it is repeated and thus considered to be learned. For instance, a learner who is rewarded with a teacher's smile for paying attention in class will be more likely to follow the teacher's direction at a later time than one whose behavior goes unnoticed. Similarly, a learner who tries a new strategy for finding information on the World Wide Web is more likely to keep using it if it proves to be successful (and is thus reinforced) than if the strategy does not yield the sought-for information.

The principles of behavior modification that Skinner and his disciples investigated in their research and tried out in instructional applications have had significant impact on the ID field. To begin with, behavioral learning theory is empirically based, which means that behavior is observed both before and after an intervention such as instruction has been implemented, and the observed changes in performance are related to what occurred during the intervention. If there is no change in behavior, then the intervention cannot be considered effective. In the ID field, these observations are part of formative evaluation, which is conducted to collect information about whether instruction resulted in learning and how it might be improved to result in even better learner performance.

The emphasis in this theory on the behavior of the learner also contributes to concepts such as behavioral objectives and the importance of practice in instruction. For example, prior to instruction, teachers and instructional designers can determine whether learners have already acquired a desired behavior by observing them. Desired behaviors that are not exhibited can be specified as objectives, or learning outcomes, to be addressed in the instruction that is being designed and developed. In a similar way, specifying desired behaviors as objectives points out the need to ensure that learners have sufficient opportunities to practice these behaviors as they learn.

Finally, behavioral theory influenced early conceptions of instructional feedback. That is, feedback was assumed to be essentially equivalent to reinforcement. When learners responded correctly during instruction, immediate feedback that the answer was correct was expected to reinforce the response. Likewise, feedback that an answer was wrong was expected to reduce the incidence of incorrect responding. Because of the anticipated reinforcing benefits of feedback, designers employed instructional strategies such as linear programmed instruction, which broke instruction into small steps and required learners to respond frequently (see, e.g., Holland & Skinner, 1961), thus virtually ensuring errorless performance. Unfortunately, these designs were boring to learners, who could also "peek" ahead at answers before they responded, which meant that the presumed benefits of feedback were rarely realized (Kulhavy, 1977).

Cognitive Information Processing Theory

The informational value of feedback became apparent when researchers and practitioners began to adopt the perspective of information processing theory. This view rose to prominence among psychologists in the 1970s, and variations of it continue to be investigated and articulated today. Like behavioral theory, information processing theory regards the environment as playing an important role in learning. Where it differs from behavioral theory, however, is in its assumption of internal processes within the learner that explain learning. "The birth of computers after World War II provided a concrete way of thinking about learning and a consistent framework for interpreting early work on memory, perception, and learning. Stimuli became inputs; behavior became outputs. And what happened in between was conceived of as information processing" (Driscoll, 2005, p. 74).

Atkinson and Shriffin (1968) proposed a multistage, multistore theory of memory that is generally regarded as the basis for information processing theory. Three memory systems in the learner (sensory, short-term, and long-term memory) are assumed to receive information from the environment and transform it for storage and use in memory and performance. With sensory memory, learners perceive organized patterns in the environment and begin the process of recognizing and coding these patterns. Short-term or working memory permits the learner to hold information briefly in mind to make further sense of it and to connect it with other information that is already in long-term memory. Finally, long-term memory enables the learner to remember and apply information long after it was originally learned.

In addition to stages through which information passes, processes such as attention, encoding, and retrieval are hypothesized to act on information as it is received, transformed, and stored for later recall and use. For instance, learners who fail to pay attention will never receive the information to be learned in the first place. To be most influential on learning, attention must often be directed so that learners heed specific aspects of the information they are being asked to learn. Similarly, the process of encoding provides a means for learners to make personally meaningful connections between new information and their prior knowledge. Finally, retrieval enables learners to recall information from memory so that it can be applied in an appropriate context.

Feedback from an information processing perspective, then, serves two functions during learning. First, it provides the learner with knowledge about the correctness of his response or the adequacy of his performance. While this knowledge is certainly important during learning, it is not sufficient for correcting misconceptions or other errors in performance. The second function of feedback, therefore, is to provide corrective information that the learner can use to modify performance. In essence, feedback completes a learning cycle where the feedback can be used to continually modify what is stored in memory and used to guide performance.

In addition to changing our conception of feedback, information processing theory shifted our focus to various attributes of instruction and how they can facilitate or impede information processing and thereby learning. It also put increased emphasis on the role of prior knowledge in learning new knowledge and skills. For instance, a learner who already knows a good deal about the topic of instruction can call to mind many cues that will be helpful in processing whatever information is new. A learner with little prior knowledge, however, can make few connections between what is already known and what she is being asked to learn.

To assist learners in processing information, practitioners have incorporated strategies into their instructional designs that direct attention, facilitate encoding and retrieval, and provide practice in a variety of contexts. The use of boldface and italic print in text materials, for example, can draw learners' attention to important information just as the use of color in diagrams or slides can help them distinguish important features of visual information. Graphical diagrams and imagery strategies can help learners make meaningful connections between their prior knowledge and the new information they are learning. Finally, providing many different kinds of examples or problems in different contexts can help learners apply the knowledge they are acquiring to situations where it is relevant.

Schema Theory and Cognitive Load Theory

What distinguishes experts from novices in the way they structure knowledge and in their ability to solve problems? Such questions have prompted developments in learning theory that, while still cognitive in orientation, diverge from information processing perspectives. According to schema theory, knowledge is represented in long-term memory as packets of information called schemata. Schemata organize information in categories that are related in systematic and predictable ways. For instance, my knowledge or schema of "farm" may encompass categories of information such as kinds of animals raised there, types of crops grown, implements used, and so on. Learners use existing schemata to interpret events and solve problems, and they develop new and more complex schemata through experience and learning.

Automation is important in the construction of schemata, because learners have only so much processing capacity. "Indeed, knowledge about working memory limitations suggest[s] humans are particularly poor at complex reasoning unless most of the elements with which we reason have previously been stored in long-term memory" (Sweller, van Merriënboer, & Paas, 1998, p. 254). More sophisticated and automatic schemata free a learner's working memory capacity, allowing processes such as comprehension and reasoning to occur. However, a high cognitive load is put on learners when they do not have appropriate or automated schemata to access, or when the learning task imposes a heavy demand on working memory processes.

From their investigations of cognitive load theory, Sweller et al. (1998) suggest instructional strategies designed to reduce extraneous cognitive load in instructional materials. These include providing worked examples and partially completed problems that learners review or finish solving. In multimedia instruction, Mayer and Moreno (2003) suggest that narration, rather than onscreen text, be used with animation or diagrams so that learners' attention is not split between two sources of visual input. The split-attention effect can also be reduced in text-based instruction by integrating explanations within diagrams instead of requiring learners to mentally integrate text and pictures (Sweller et al., 1998).

Finally, the evolution of cognitive load theory has focused increasing attention in the instructional design field on learning of complex, cognitive skills. Van Merriënboer and his colleagues have proposed the 4C/ID model for complex learning (described in Chapter 8), which calls for learning tasks to be sequenced in ways that reduce cognitive load (van Merriënboer, Kirschner, & Kester, 2003). That is, learners are gradually introduced to a series of task classes, each of which represents, on a simple to complex continuum, a version of the whole task. These are supplemented with just-in-time information and part-task practice, depending on the learner's growing expertise and the need for automaticity.

Situated Learning Theory

Whereas the context of learning is recognized as important in information processing theory, it takes on a more central and defining role in situated learning theory. As a currently emerging view, situated learning (also called *situated cognition*) theory is regarded by its proponents as "a work in progress" (Kirshner & Whitson, 1997), and there is little consensus yet of its positioning within modern learning theory (Driscoll, 2005). As such, the implications it may hold for the field have yet to be seen.

Unlike behavioral and information processing theory, situated learning theory relies more on social and cultural determinants of learning than it does on individual psychology. Specifically, knowledge is presumed to accrue in "meaningful actions, actions that have relations of meaning to one another in terms of some cultural system" (Lemke, 1997, p. 43). For example, children selling candy on the streets of Brazil developed techniques for manipulating numbers that are related to currency exchanges, whereas their age-mates in school learned standard number orthography (Saxe, 1990). To understand why the candy sellers acquired the particular mathematical knowledge that they did and why it was so different from what their age-mates learned requires reference, at least in part, to the "mathematical and economic problems linked to the practice" of candy selling (Saxe, p. 99).

Thus, learning from a situated perspective occurs through the learner's participation in the practices of a community, practices that are mutually constituted by the members of the community. Consider, for example, the profession as a community of practice. As a student, you are a newcomer to the community, engaged in learning its models and practices and becoming ever more competent as you gain experience in these practices. With increasing participation, newcomers become oldtimers in the community, individuals who control the resources and affect the practices of the community at large. Faculty members in programs, for example, change the practices of the field through their participation in research and development.

According to Wenger (1998), learning as participation can be defined:

- Individually; i.e., as members engage in the practices of a community
- Communitywide; i.e., as members refine the practices of a community and recruit new members
- Organizationally; i.e., as members sustain the interconnected communities of practice through which "an organization knows what it knows and thus becomes effective and valuable as an organization" (p. 8)

Organizations that hire instructional designers, for example, constitute their own communities of practice that embody the ways in which design is conducted in the context of their businesses. Yet their practices are influenced by the academic communities from which they recruit their instructional designers. It should also be obvious that the influence of interconnected communities of practice works in both directions; academic programs modify their practices from time to time based on what they learn from the organizations where they place their graduates.

Proponents of situated learning theory point to its strength as integrating knowing with doing. That is, one learns a subject matter by doing what experts in that subject matter do (Lave, 1997). As an emergent view or "work in progress," situated learning theory perhaps may not yet have yielded definite implications for the field, but several are indicated nonetheless.

For over 10 years, Scardamalia and Bereiter (1994, 1996a) have researched a community-of-learners approach to instruction called CSILE, or Computer-Supported Intentional Learning Environment. CSILE is a computer tool that enables students to engage in the discourse of a subject matter discipline in a scholarly way. They focus on a problem and build a communal database of information about the problem. With current Web technologies, CSILE has the capability now of linking experts in the field with students in the classroom in mutually constituted knowledge-building efforts (Scardamalia & Bereiter, 1996b).

The influence of situated learning theory is also being felt in designs for anchored instruction. The Cognition and Technology Group at Vanderbilt (1990) proposed anchored instruction as a means of providing a situated context for problem solving. Specifically, they developed video adventure programs containing a series of embedded problems that engage viewers in attempting to solve the problems. The video adventure story provides a realistic, situated "anchor" for activities such as identifying problems, making hypotheses, proposing multiple solutions, and so on. The expectation is that students will engage in authentic practices of the discipline in which a given set of problems is anchored, whether mathematics, science, or history, for example.

Anchored instruction has been criticized for providing a simulation of a community of practice, casting the learners as observers rather than participants (Tripp, 1993). But the Vanderbilt group has evolved an approach where students begin with a video-based problem but then move through cycles of learning where they consult various knowledge resources, share ideas, and revise their understandings (Schwartz, Lin, Brophy, & Bransford, 1999). Web-based software provides a visual representation of the learning cycle and facilitates students' action and reflection, as well as their interaction with others. As with CSILE, this affords an opportunity for learners to collaborate within a broader community and leave a legacy for others to use and build upon.

Gagné's Theory of Instruction

Although many learning theorists may be interested in what their work means for instruction, the explanation of learning is their primary concern. Robert M. Gagné, on the other hand, was primarily concerned with instruction and how what is known about learning can be systematically related to the design of instruction. He proposed an integrated and comprehensive theory of instruction that is based primarily on two foundations: cognitive information processing theory and Gagné's own observations of effective teachers in the classroom. A long-term collaborator of Gagné, Briggs (1980) wrote also that "I never asked Gagné about this, but I believe his early work in [designing training programs for] the Air Force must have been an important factor in his later derivation of his (a) taxonomy of learning outcomes, (b) concept of learning hierarchies, and (c) related concepts of instructional events and conditions of learning" (pp. 45–46).

As it evolved, then, Gagné's theory of instruction came to comprise three components:

- A taxonomy of learning outcomes that defined the types of capabilities humans can learn
- Internal and external learning conditions associated with the acquisition of each category of learning outcome
- Nine events of instruction that each facilitate a specific cognitive process during learning

Taxonomies of learning existed before and since Gagné's formulation of his, but none other besides his includes all three domains in which individuals are presumed to learn: cognitive, affective, and psychomotor. According to Gagné (1972, 1985; Gagné & Medsker, 1996), there are five major categories of learning:

- Verbal information; i.e., knowing "that" or "what"
- Intellectual skills; i.e., applying knowledge
- Cognitive strategies; i.e., employing effective ways of thinking and learning
- Attitudes; i.e., feelings and beliefs that govern choices of personal action
- Motor skills; i.e., executing precise, smooth, and accurately timed movements

The reason for defining different categories of learning outcomes stems from the assumption that they must all require different conditions for learning. For example, learning to ride a bicycle (a motor skill) is different in fundamental ways from learning the multiplication table (verbal information), which is different in fundamental ways from learning to solve scientific problems (intellectual skill).

The differences in conditions of learning across categories of learning outcomes provide guidelines for which conditions must be included in instruction for specifically defined instructional goals. For example, instruction on the goal of "perform CPR" (motor skill) is likely to include a demonstration of the procedure, individual practice on the procedure, and perhaps a job aid depicting each step. On the other hand, instruction on an attitudinal goal implicit in job training on an electronic support system (such as "choose to use the help function before seeking human assistance") is likely to provide a human model and focus on the benefits of making the desired choice.

In addition to conditions of learning that are unique to each learning outcome, there are conditions of learning that facilitate the process of learning in general. Gagné conceived of the nine events of instruction as learning conditions to support internal processes such as attention, encoding, and retrieval. The events of instruction are presented briefly as follows:

1. Gaining attention—a stimulus change to alert the learner and focus attention on desired features.
2. Informing the learner of the objective—a statement or demonstration to form an expectancy in the learner as to the goals of instruction.
3. Stimulating recall of prior learning—a question or activity to remind the learner of prerequisite knowledge.
4. Presenting the stimulus—an activity or information that presents the content of what is to be learned.
5. Providing learning guidance—a cue or strategy to promote encoding.
6. Eliciting performance—an opportunity to practice or otherwise perform what is being learned.
7. Providing feedback—information of a corrective nature that will help learners improve their performance.
8. Assessing performance—an opportunity to demonstrate what has been learned.
9. Enhancing retention and transfer—examples or activities that prompt the learner to go beyond the immediate context of instruction.

The application of Gagné's theory is often a highly analytical affair, and it is therefore possible to lose sight of the overall context for learning while dealing with all the details of instruction. As a means of helping instructional designers integrate multiple goals into instruction, Gagné and Merrill (1990) propose the notion of an enterprise schema. The enterprise schema defines the context for learning, the reason for learning a particular set of goals in the first place. For example, the enterprise schema of "managing a lemonade stand" provides a meaningful context for learning how to exchange currency, how to calculate needed supplies based on an anticipated volume of business, and so on.

Constructivism

The final theory to be considered in this chapter is not yet a single theory, but rather an epistemology, a collection of views sharing a fundamental assumption about learning that contrasts sharply with the assumptions underlying theories such as information processing. The contrast can be drawn this way. In information processing theory, learning is mostly a matter of going from the outside in. The learner receives information from the environment, transforms it in various ways, and acquires knowledge that is subsequently stored in memory. In constructivist approaches, on the other hand, learning is more a matter of going from the inside out. The learner actively imposes organization and meaning on the surrounding environment and constructs knowledge in the process. (This is discussed more fully in Chapter 5)

From a radical constructivist point of view, knowledge constructions do not have to correspond with reality to be meaningful, but most constructivist researchers agree that not all knowledge constructions are equally viable. To sort out which ideas are viable and which are not, learners must test their personal understandings against those of others, usually peers and teachers.

Constructivism has been keenly felt in the world, partly because it seems to contrast so starkly with the other foundations, such as information processing and Gagné's theories, that have influenced practices in our field. Some of the philosophical issues related to these views are taken up in Chapter 6 and so will not be repeated here. Rather, I have chosen to describe a few of what I perceive to be the greatest impacts of constructivism on the field.

To begin with, constructivist researchers focus attention on high-level, complex learning goals, such as "the ability to write persuasive essays, engage in informal reasoning, explain how data relate to theory in scientific investigations, and formulate and solve moderately complex problems that require mathematical reasoning" (Cognition & Technology Group at Vanderbilt, 1991, p. 34). While these kinds of goals are certainly definable using taxonomies such as Gagné's, under such approaches they do not necessarily assume the prominence that constructivists would assign to them. Addressing broad and complex learning goals is also consistent with constructivist beliefs that individuals do not all learn the same things from instruction.

Constructivism has also had a substantial impact on views pertaining to the learning conditions and instructional strategies believed to support constructivist learning goals. To engage learners in knowledge construction, facilitate tests of their understanding, and prompt reflection on the knowledge generation process itself, constructivist researchers have recommended the creation and use of complex learning environments. Such learning environments should:

- Engage learners in activities authentic to the discipline in which they are learning.
- Provide for collaboration and the opportunity to engage multiple perspectives on what is being learned.
- Support learners in setting their own goals and regulating their own learning.
- Encourage learners to reflect on what and how they are learning.

The rapid growth in computer technologies has assisted researchers in creating different kinds of technology-mediated learning environments that implement these strategies. It remains somewhat difficult to judge the effectiveness of these systems, however, because advances in assessment have not kept up well with advances in technology. Furthermore, constructivists argue that assessment of individual student learning should involve authentic practices observed during learning and would not necessarily reveal a uniform level of accomplishment across learners.

Conclusion

This chapter has presented a brief introduction to some of the major psychological principles and avenues of thought that have contributed (and continue to contribute) to professional practices in the field of instructional design. Behavioral and cognitive information processing theory came out of research programs dominating psychology in the 1960s and 1970s. Gagné's theory evolved through two decades of research from the 1960s to 1980s and integrates cognitive with behavioral views. These theories collectively form the bedrock on which the field of instructional design was founded and initially developed. They provided, and continue to provide, useful and reliable guidance for designing effective instruction.

Schema theory, cognitive load theory, situated learning theory, and constructivism now offer the ID field other ways of thinking about learning. Along with advances in technology, they promise design strategies for producing learning environments more complex, more authentic, and more appealing than ever before. The long-term implications of these theories to the ID field are not yet fully known, but they surely offer an invitation to professionals new to the field to help shape that legacy.

Application Questions

1. During the past decade, two authors—Richard Clark and Robert Kozma—have conducted an ongoing debate regarding the role instructional media plays in learning. Their contrasting viewpoints are well described in two articles in the 1994 edition of the journal *Educational Technology Research and Development* (vol. 42, no. 2). Read these two articles. Then review the section of this chapter in which Driscoll describes how proponents of situated learning have used instructional media such as computers and videodiscs to create learning environments such as CSILE and *The Adventures of Jasper Woodbury.* In your opinion, does Drsicoll's description of these learning environments lend support to Kozma's viewpoint or does it support the views of Clark? Explain why you feel this way.
2. Towards the beginning of the chapter, Robert Gagné is quoted as suggesting that most practical and purposeful activities are learned in settings that employ instruction. Take the perspective of a Skinnerian behaviorist, an information processing theorist, and a constructivist. Argue for or against Gagné's contention from each of these perspectives.
3. According to Driscoll, "Changes in ability that are only temporary are not considered learning . . . learning implies a kind of permanence." Do you agree with her statement? What are the implications of her statement? Have you had experiences in your life that could support your viewpoint? In a small-group setting (either in class or in a chat room or threaded discussion environment), list and discuss the implications of this assertion to instructional design.
4. Select a specific learning goal (e.g., add and subtract multidigit numbers). Split the class into learning groups representing the following theories discussed in this chapter: behaviorism, information processing, Gagné's theory, schema theory, cognitive load theory, situated learning, and constructivism. In each group, outline the approach that should be taken to achieve the goal.
5. Events that occur at one point in time are likely to influence theories that are developed some time thereafter. For example, the theory Gagné first put forth in the 1960s was most likely influenced by his work designing military training during the 1940s. Think about current day events and how they may shape future views of learning and instruction. Based on your ideas, describe an instructional theory that may appear in the next 20 years and discuss the events today that are likely to shape that theory.

References

Atkinson, R. C., & Shriffin, R. M. (1968). Human memory: A proposed system and its control processes. In K. Spence & J. Spence (Eds.), *The psychology of learning and motivation* (Vol. 2). New York: Academic Press.

Briggs, L. J. (1980). Thirty years of instructional design: One man's experience. *Educational Technology, 20*(2), 45–50.

Cognition & Technology Group at Vanderbilt. (1990). Anchored instruction and its relationship to situated cognition. *Educational Researcher, 30*(3), 2–10.

Cognition & Technology Group at Vanderbilt. (1991). Technology and the design of generative learning environments. *Educational Technology, 31*, 34–40.

Driscoll, M. P. (2005). *Psychology of learning for instruction* (3rd ed.). Needham Heights, MA: Allyn & Bacon.

Gagné, R. M. (1972). Domains of learning. *Interchange, 3*, 1–8.

Gagné, R. M. (1985). *The conditions of learning* (4th ed.). New York: Holt, Rinehart, & Winston.

Gagné, R. M. (1995/1996). Learning processes and instruction. *Training Research Journal, 1*(1), 17–28.

Gagné, R. M., & Medsker, K. L. (1996). *The conditions of learning: Training applications*. Fort Worth, TX: Harcourt Brace.

Gagné, R. M., & Merrill, M. D. (1990). Integrative goals for instructional design. *Educational Technology Research and Development, 38*, 23–30.

Holland, J., & Skinner, B. F. (1961). *The analysis of behavior*. New York: McGraw-Hill.

Kirshner, D., & Whitson, J. A. (Eds.) (1997). *Situated cognition: Social, semiotic, and psychological perspectives*. Mahwah, NJ: Lawrence Erlbaum Associates.

Kulhavy, R. (1977). Feedback in written instruction. *Review of Educational Research*, *47*(2), 211–232.

Lave, J. (1997). The culture of acquisition and the practice of understanding. In D. Kirshner & J. A. Whitson (Eds.), *Situated cognition: Social, semiotic, and psychological perspectives*. Mahwah, NJ: Lawrence Erlbaum Associates.

Lemke, J. L. (1997). Cognition, context, and learning: A social semiotic process. In D. Kirshner & J. A. Whitson (Eds.), *Situated cognition: Social, semiotic, and psychological perspectives*. Mahwah, NJ: Lawrence Erlbaum Associates.

Mayer, R. E., & Moreno, R. (2003). Nine ways to reduce cognitive load in multimedia learning. *Educational Psychologist*, *38*(1), 43–52.

Saxe, G. B. (1990). *Culture and cognitive development: Studies in mathematical understanding*. Hillsdale, NJ: Lawrence Erlbaum Associates.

Scardamalia, M., & Bereiter, C. (1994). Computer support for knowledge-building communities. *Journal of the Learning Sciences*, *3*(3), 265–283.

Scardamalia, M., & Bereiter, C. (1996a). Adaptation and understanding: A case for new cultures of schooling. In S. Vosniadou, E. deCorte, R. Glaser, & H. Mandl (Eds.), *International perspectives on the design of technology-supported learning environments*. Mahwah, NJ: Lawrence Erlbaum Associates.

Scardamalia, M., & Bereiter, C. (1996b, November). Engaging students in a knowledge society. *Educational Leadership*, 6–10.

Schwartz, D. L., Lin, X., Brophy, S., & Bransford, J. D. (1999). Toward the development of flexibly adaptive instructional designs. In C. M. Reigeluth (Ed.), *Instructional-design theories and models* (Vol. 2). Mahwah, NJ: Lawrence Erlbaum Associates.

Skinner, B. F. (1938). *The behavior of organisms: An experimental analysis*. Englewood Cliffs, NJ: Prentice Hall.

Skinner, B. F. (1969). *Contingencies of reinforcement*. Englewood Cliffs, NJ: Prentice Hall.

Skinner, B. F. (1987). Whatever happened to psychology as the science of behavior? *American Psychologist*, *42*, 780–786.

Sweller, J., van Merriënboer, J. J. G., & Paas, F. G. W. C. (1998). Cognitive architecture and instructional design. *Educational Psychology Review*, *10*(3), 251–296.

Tripp, S. D. (1993). Theories, traditions, and situated learning. *Educational Technology*, *33*(3), 71–77.

van Merriënboer, J. J. G., Kirshener, P. A., & Kester, L. (2003). Taking the load off a learner's mind: Instructional design for complex learning. *Educational Psychologist*, *38*(1), 5–13.

Wenger, E. (1998). *Communities of practice*. New York: Cambridge University Press.

CHAPTER 5

Constructivism and Instructional Design: The Emergence of the Learning Sciences and Design Research

David Jonassen, Dan Cernusca, and Gelu Ionas
University of Missouri

Editors' Introduction

A portion of the previous chapter briefly described how constructivism has influenced the instructional design field. In this chapter, David Jonassen, Dan Cernusca, and Gelu Ionas discuss this issue in more detail, focusing on how constructivism has affected the nature of instructional activities and the instructional design process. Constructivist thought has also served as one of the underpinnings for the emergence of a new academic discipline—the *learning sciences*. The authors describe the scientific perspectives and views of learning, the learner, and learning activities that underlie the learning sciences. They also describe the nature of the learning environments that learning scientists create. The authors discuss how some in the learning sciences community are trying to integrate research and design by engaging in what has been called *design research*. In the second half of this chapter, they describe design research processes and provide examples of how that approach has been implemented.

Knowledge and Comprehension Questions

1. Compare the beliefs of objectivists with those of constructivists.
2. Describe how constructivist beliefs have influenced the nature of instructional activities and the instructional design process.
3. Describe the learning sciences perspective regarding (1) learning, (2) learning activities, (3) the individual learner, (4) groups of learners, and (5) learning outcomes.
4. Describe the characteristics of the types of learning environments designed by learning scientists.
5. Describe the overall goal of design research.
6. Explain why the authors feel that design research is likely to produce contextually bound understandings of learning. Do the authors see this as a benefit or shortcoming of the design research process? Why do they feel this way?

Well over a decade ago, Jonassen (1991) asked whether a paradigm shift was occurring in the field of instructional systems design. At that time, instructional systems design, like most fields associated with learning psychology, was beginning to be substantively influenced by voices espousing constructivist conceptions of learning. Since that time, the question seems ever more rhetorical. A constructivist epistemology has significantly impacted our field. One need only briefly peruse the content lists of any instructional systems technology professional conference proceedings over the past decade to perceive the effects of constructivism on the belief systems of instructional designers. The questions that we are asking and the assumptions that we are making are decidedly different from those of a decade or two ago. However, those belief systems often misconstrue constructivism. Why?

Constructivism is too often characterized as a pedagogy or instructional methodology. It is important to point out, however, that constructivism is a philosophy that underlies theories from which pedagogies and models are derived. *Constructivism* is primarily an epistemological and ontological conception of what reality, knowledge, the mind, thought, and meaning are. Objectivists, who controlled academic beliefs throughout most of the twentieth century, believe that reality is structured by entities and their relationships to each other. The role of the mind is to reflect the inherent structures of reality, so that the meaning that is ascribed to phenomena is independent of the organism attempting to understand those phenomena. Constructivists, on the other hand, believe that reality is constructed by individuals and social groups based on their experiences with and interpretations of the world. The mind constructs its own conceptual ecology for interacting with, interpreting, and making meaning for that world. Rather than being objectively independent from the knower, knowledge, according to constructivists, is embodied in human experience, perceptions, imaginations, and mental and social constructions.

Constructivism is also frequently misconstrued as a theory of learning, rather than an epistemology that underlies a variety of psychologies, sociologies, and anthropologies. Therefore, comparing behaviorism to constructivism represents a category error. Constructivism should be contrasted with objectivist or positivist epistemologies that underlie behaviorism and a fair amount of cognitive psychology. That is, behaviorism and many kinds of cognitive and social psychology make very objectivist assumptions about learning, while other kinds of cognitive and social psychology make more constructivist assumptions. When contrasting theoretical points of view, it is important to compare coordinate belief systems, not superordinate or foundational ones.

Not only have the epistemological and ontological assumptions about the nature of learning changed as a result of constructivist influences, but the nature of instructional activities also have changed dramatically. At the risk of oversimplification, the most obvious change in the instructional systems field has been a shift from emphasis on instructional communication to an emphasis on practice-based learning. Historically, the instructional design field focused on designing instructional communications to support learning about content. Constructivist learning environments engage students in activities applying content.

Instructional systems evolved, in part, from the field of educational communications (ergo, the Association for *Educational Communications* and Technology), which focuses on designing ever-more effective messages to communicate content. Because the explicit goal of instructional systems has been the more efficient transmission of knowledge, a key belief of many professionals in the field has been that the more effectively messages are designed, the more efficiently students can learn about the world. Designers of instructional communications determine an objective reality that they then try to map onto learners' knowledge through the use of instructional strategies that control learning behaviors and processes (e.g., mathemagenic) used to interpret the messages. During the 1970s and 1980s, message design dominated the research literature.

There are epistemological problems with instructional communications. The sense that any student makes of any instructional communication depends mostly on prior knowledge, which depends on previous experience. Beginning with the watershed paper on situated cognition (Brown, Collins, & Duguid, 1989), constructivists have argued that meaning is situated or embedded in authentic contexts, and that when we abstract ideas from their context, the ideas lose their meaning. Constructivists argue that knowledge is both individually constructed and socially co-constructed from interactions and experiences with the world. That is, meaning emerges from practice (or activity) and from discussion and reflection on that practice. That activity may occur in *simulated practice fields* or more *authentic fields of practice* (Barab & Duffy, 2000). Meaningful learning involves willful, intentional, active, conscious, constructive practice that engages reciprocal intention-action-reflection cycles (Jonassen, Hernandez-Serrano, & Choi, 2000).

Constructivism has changed the emphasis of the instructional design process. It has resulted in a shift from attempts to communicate to students about the world in efficient ways to attempts to create learning situations that promote the engagement or immersion of learners in practice fields (simulations and project-, inquiry-, and problem-based activities) and fields of practice (communities of practice, apprenticeships, workplace activities). Concomitant changes include a shift from direct instruction and instructional strategies that support learner acquisition of given facts, concepts, and rules to an approach that focuses on coaching and scaffolding meaningful experiences as well as providing opportunities to reflect on those experiences. Academically, these changes have resulted in the emergence of a new discipline, the learning sciences, which provides a theoretically rich set of assumptions for the design of meaningful learning experiences. The learning sciences begin with different philosophical assumptions and use a different research approach to instruction, learning, and research.

What Are the Learning Sciences?

Over the last decade of the twentieth century, constructivist epistemologies ushered in the learning sciences as an alternative to the instructional sciences. The learning sciences examine learning from a substantively different set of assumptions and scientific perspectives than do instructional sciences, such as instructional design. Learning, from a learning sciences perspective, is activity or practice based, rather than communicative. *Learning sciences* are the convergence of design of activity systems, cognition, and sociocultural context. The learning sciences apply theories to the design of technology-enriched learning environments that engage and support learners in accomplishing more complex, authentic (contextually mediated), and meaningful learning activities with the goal of meaningful learning and conceptual change.

The learning sciences are theory based. Like traditional instructional sciences, the focus is grounded in the cognitive sciences. Unlike them, the learning sciences rely more extensively on more constructivist cognitive disciplines such as cognitive anthropology, situated learning, everyday cognition, ecological psychology, distributed cognition, and Deweyian pragmatism, rather than on information processing theories of learning. From the perspective of learning sciences, the learner is an intentional, active, and reflective agent who is responsible for constructing personal mental models. The learning sciences also rely heavily on social theories of learning and meaning making, such as social cognition, activity theory, motivation, and case-based reasoning that examine the social, organizational, and cultural dynamics of learning processes. The learning sciences also ascribe agency to groups who collaboratively co-construct group mental models. Finally, the learning sciences draw from computer sciences, especially computational modeling and artificial intelligence, as a means for designing technology-enhanced learning environments. Learning scientists view learning through substantively different theoretical lenses than do instructional scientists.

Because of different theoretical emphases, learning outcomes from a learning sciences perspective are often of a different nature than the type of learning outcomes often specified in the instructional sciences. The instructional sciences usually emphasize the acquisition of behaviors and discrete skills. In contrast, learning outcomes in the learning sciences tend to focus on knowledge building, conceptual change, reflection, self-regulation, and socially co-constructed meaning making.

Learning scientists are actively engaged in design. Learning scientists apply theories to the design of technology-enhanced learning environments. Unlike instructional approaches, these learning environments use a learning-by-doing approach that conceives of learning as practice where learners are engaged in some complex, authentic activity that poses some real-world challenge. These environments are inquiry based or project based, typically beginning with a problem to be solved, such as designing something, developing a policy, or making decisions. They engage learners in different forms of model-based reasoning. Learning environments are interactive, not by a prescribed sequence of behaviors, but by a sense of direct engagement. The environments use combinations of multimedia, multiple perspectives, artificial intelligence, and computer support to engage learners.

Learning environments designed by learning scientists also tend to promote collaboration among learners. Learners often work in emergent learning communities, knowledge-building communities, or practice communities to solve vexing problems. Outcomes of collaboration are socially co-constructed knowledge and, again, socially mediated meaning making.

Like many sciences addressing learning, the learning sciences are research based. Rather than exclusively experimental, learning scientists use a variety of research approaches to study learning, including ethnographies, cognitive analyses of problem solving, studies of social policy and organizational change, analyses of social interactions, technology design, and human-computer interaction studies. Learning scientists study learning in authentic contexts as well as in learning environments. Much of the impetus for the learning sciences is qualitative research examining individual cognition and social cognition in everyday settings. Learning scientists focus not only on knowledge in the head, but also on conversation, knowledge, and artifacts in the world, because knowledge is distributed among these.

Another significant change in the focus of learning sciences is the integration of design and research. Historically, instructional science research has used quantitative research methods to establish generalizable theories that could be applied to the design of instructional materials. In the learning sciences, research and design are integrated in a more seamless activity, known as design research. *Design research* integrates the design of learning environments with the development of *prototheories* (emergent, developmental theories) of learning (Design-Based Research Collective, 2003). That is, we develop theories of learning while designing. Design is research, and research is design. Design research uses continuous cycles of design, implementation, analysis, and redesign. Design research not only uses but also produces sharable theories that have implications for practitioners and designers with a focus on design in authentic setting. In the next section, we describe design research in more depth.

Design Research

How does instructional design differ from design research? Nearly every model of instructional design includes formative evaluation of the instructional materials that are produced. Design researchers use formative experiments—that is, iterative processes that combine factors such as arrangements for teacher training, curriculum development, and production of classroom materials—to develop instructional environments that can be used by both teachers and students to carry out various instructional tasks while undertaking research activities. Formative evaluation considers only the materials, while formative experiments consider the process and the context in which learning takes place.

Building on the potential of formative experiments and on the conceptual developments associated with design experiments (e.g., Brown, 1992), Cobb (2001) emphasizes the dynamic reciprocal relationship between instructional design and classroom-based analysis in his representation of the *design research cycle.* The design research cycle can be viewed as a process that has a series of microcycles covering in-class learning tasks, grouped together in macrocycles associated with a given segment of instruction (e.g., unit, quarter, or semester). The overall goal of the entire design research process is to contribute to the development of a "theoretical model of learning and instruction rooted in a firm empirical base" (Brown, 1992, p. 143) by conducting retrospective analyses on the data collected over the course of several macrocycles. The assumption of design research is that instructional design should fundamentally be a research rather than a procedural process. Figure 5.1 conveys the complex, multilayered, and dynamic character of the design research process.

The design process that design researchers use is different from the one that instructional designers use. Rather than beginning with task analysis, design research starts with a "thought experiment" (Cobb, 2001, p. 456), which uses instructional design theory and methods to develop a tentative, provisional, and revisable learning trajectory that describes both the potential learning routes and the means to support and scaffold learning along them. The result is a succession of learning tasks that represents

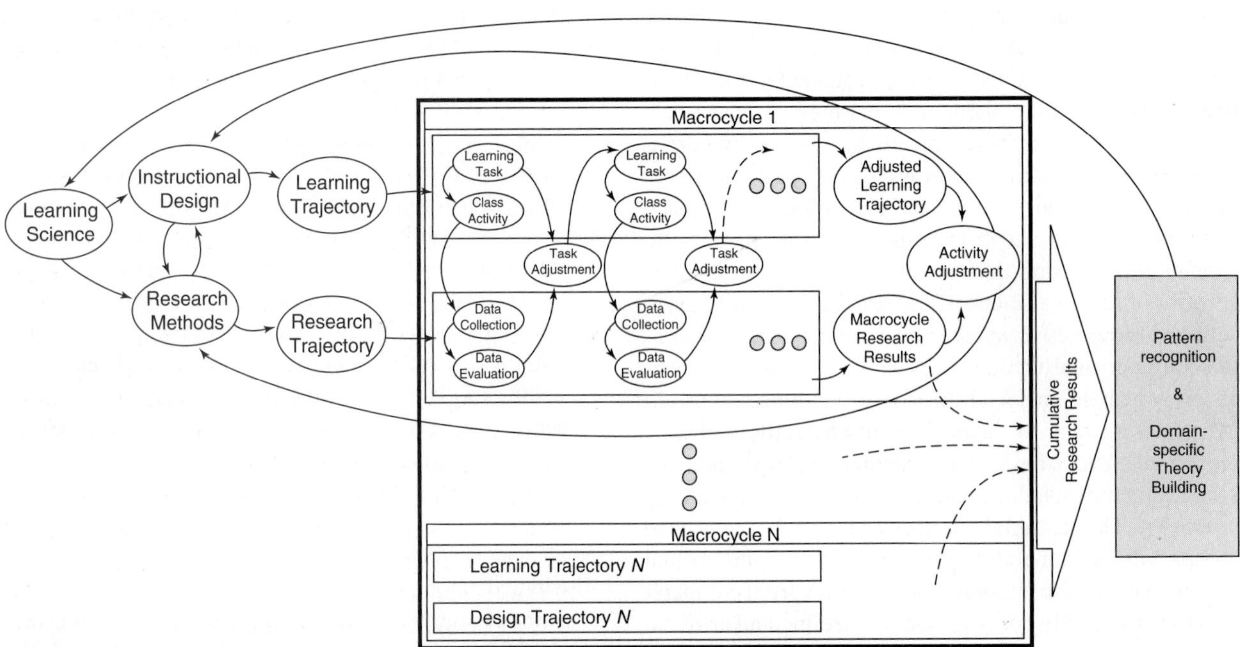

FIGURE 5.1 The design research process.

independent class activities. The development of the learning trajectory is bounded by both the theoretical perspective on learning assumed by the design team and the available empirical research results as reflected in the current learning science body of knowledge. Fundamentally, this is an instructional design process that, when implemented, includes a series of informal feedback-based adjustments that will adapt the learning trajectory to the real class settings.

Design research introduces a higher level of complexity to the entire design process by formalizing feedback and adjustment using appropriate research methods. Therefore, at the beginning of the first macrocycle the research team reconciles the instructional design methodology with the available research methods. The outcome is a hypothetical research trajectory that mirrors the learning trajectory at the microcycle level.

This initial planning stage results in a series of microcycles composed of both learning-related activities and research-related activities. Each microcycle is associated with a learning task of the projected learning trajectory and starts with the implementation of the task. During classroom activities, the research team collects a variety of data, according to the preplanned research methodology. The collected data is analyzed and compared to the forecasted learning task outcomes and used to define potential task adjustments of the next microcycle. Therefore it is important that, at the tactical level, the next microcycle's classroom activities are developed only one or two days prior to the actual implementation (Cobb, 2001). This sequence of events is reiterated until the macrocycle's learning trajectory is completed.

At the conclusion of the current macrocycle the research team defines an adjusted learning trajectory which, reconciled with the cycle's research results, defines the needed changes at the activity level. These changes are used in the next iteration (macrocycle) on one side in the instructional design process to produce an adjusted learning trajectory, and on the other side to select the research methods to be included in the adjusted research trajectory.

Each macrocycle feeds its research results into a cumulative pool of research data. The first cycle's research results are used to identify potential variables and patterns that might form the foundations of a domain-specific theory, the final goal of the entire design research process. To ensure a firm empirical base the process should be run over several successive macrocycles associated with the same learning activity. Each such cycle will follow a path similar to the first one described, building in this way on the previous findings. The number of macrocycles depends on the research team's ability to recognize one or more stable patterns that can be synthesized into a localized theory. Once the theory is clearly defined, it becomes part of the learning science body of knowledge.

So far, we have concentrated on the conceptual aspects of the design research process. At the implementation level, the designer has to deal with specific methodological issues. In the attempt to support the practice of design research, a set of methodological guidelines concerning the identification of specific design and research methods and the way they fit together is emerging in the literature (Cobb, Confrey, diSessa, Lehrer, & Schauble, 2003; Collins, Joseph, & Bielaczyc, 2004).

Based on the conceptual framework presented in Figure 5.1, the existing design and research methodological guidelines might be used as follows:

- *Initial design stage*—Since each design research environment and focus is different, the concern in the initial phase of the process is with identifying the critical variables and their interactions. For example, in a physics environment, the designer would identify the forces and the characteristics of the objects to be simulated in the environment. Recording the outcomes of this initial stage is critical since it provides the basis for future analyses and adjustments.
- *Data collection, measurement, and analysis*—As Figure 5.1 shows, during each microcycle (preceding each "Task Adjustment") a complex set of dependent and independent variables is collected and processed. For example, the literature proposes the settings, the nature of the learners, and the technical or the financial support might serve as independent variables, while cooperation (among members of the learning group), learning (disposition, metacognition, etc.), and system adoption might be included in the dependent variables set. A clear recording of each variable in each microcycle is essential both for efficient data processing and for further retrospective analysis.
- *Macrocycle level analysis*—At the end of each macrocycle the collected data is analyzed from multiple perspectives including individual cognition, interpersonal, group, and classroom relationships, and resources and organizational impact, an approach that has the potential to reflect the complexity of real learning environments. The purpose of this analysis is to develop a set of adjustments that in the following macrocycle will better adapt the learning and research trajectories to the actual characteristics of the researched environment.
- *Design adjustment*—The identified adjustments are used in a subsequent instructional design process and in the selection of the associated research methods. The process follows the steps described in the initial design stage to which is added a clear descriptive documentation of the rationales behind the modifications in design.

- *Research reporting and theory building*—The final stage of design research is the analysis and synthesis of the results collected during the tryouts. The documentation associated with this stage should include a clear and thorough description of at least the following elements: the overall goals of the design and research, the structure of each element of the design, the settings where it was implemented, the structure and outcomes of each macrocycle, and the findings and the lessons learned. This entire stage is designed to support the theory building that is the ultimate goal of the design research method. In the end, the final product is presented to the scientific community for acknowledgment and validation in an attempt to contribute to the learning science body of knowledge.

Examples of Design Research

Interpreting the Gospels

The Learning Sciences Institute at the University of Missouri comprises a group of faculty and graduate students who provide consultation and assistance for higher education faculty across campus. During one of these projects, "Interpreting the Gospels," the long-term relationship between the client and the research team met the basic conditions for the design research approach.

The project was conducted in conjunction with an undergraduate religious studies class on the New Testament. One of the goals of the class was to engage students in the hermeneutic analysis of biblical texts (i.e., using various—in this case, four different—methods to interpret biblical texts). The very sensitive nature of the subject matter, revealed during the research team's interactions with both the client and the students, clearly necessitated an iterative process in which adjustments could be made based on intermediary research findings.

The design process started by conducting an anticipatory thought experiment aimed to develop a learning trajectory and a research trajectory, as shown in Figure 5.1. As a first step, an analysis of the current class conditions was conducted. The research team discovered a large heterogeneous student body of about 150 students, most of them freshmen and sophomores, coming from diverse backgrounds—humanistic, engineering/business, sciences, and social sciences. The development of a Web-based learning environment was considered the most suitable approach for such a heterogeneous class.

The theoretical orientation most closely aligned with hermeneutics is cognitive flexibility theory, a model based on constructivist beliefs (Spiro, Feltovich, Jacobson, & Coulson, 1992). Cognitive flexibility hypertexts are well suited to represent alternative interpretations, including narrative, feminist, redaction, and historical, as main perspectives to guide students' interpretation of the Gospels. The research team selected a summer camp, "Camp Hermeneutica," as the key metaphor of the learning environment.

To operationalize the chosen learning trajectory, the students were required to follow a succession of activities inside this environment for at least two of the four methods of interpretation. First, all students were required to visit a fictive medicine cabinet to choose a metaphorical pair of glasses, each representing one of the perspectives. After choosing one pair of glasses the students were guided to follow a path that led them through an initial sequence of activities that exposed them to Gospel passages interpreted through the different perspectives. The subsequent activity required them to practice on a set of guided interpretations combined with immediate feedback (predefined suggested answers provided by the course instructor) that allowed them to reflect on the specifics of the perspective they were engaged in. The students then tried on two different "pairs of glasses" with which they could examine Gospel passages from different perspectives. At the conclusion of each cycle, they were required to write an essay based on the perspective they practiced in the environment.

The research trajectory associated with the first macrocycle was designed to collect data from discussion boards, student–instructor interactions, two short essays, a final exam, and a questionnaire that measured the student's epistemological beliefs. The short essays measured the near transfer while the final exam measured the far transfer of the target skills. The research had two major objectives. One was to measure the impact of the designed environment on the overall quality of the learning process by comparing current outcomes with those of previous years. The second was to analyze the potential moderating effect of the student's epistemological beliefs on the effectiveness of the environment.

Compared to the general design research cycle, this research focused on a short time span, covering one third of a semester, including the use of the environment outside the formal class periods. These factors imposed certain restrictions on data collection and analysis. Therefore, the collected data was analyzed only at the end of the macrocycle and the conclusions were used to improve the design of the following macrocycle. After analyzing the data collected during the first macrocycle, two issues became evident.

First, the initial design of the learning environment contained several overlapping metaphors (camp, glasses, etc.) which proved to be counterproductive in naturalistic settings. Second, some activities (e.g., those related to historical interpretation) were too time consuming for both the instructor and the students. Based on these findings, the learning environment was redesigned to incorporate only one major metaphor, the film critic (working for a magazine). This new environment, now called "Cinema Hermeneutica" incorporates two distinct areas. One of them engages the students as film critics where they review a real movie as practice for understanding the basics of the method and the environment. The second area is directly related to the class subject matter, the Gospels.

On the research side, the lack of pretreatment data made the environment impact detection difficult, especially for the near transfer of skills. Also, the tool used to measure the epistemological beliefs proved to have a very low internal reliability for this group of students.

In response, for the current macrocycle, more reliable tools are being used: short pretreatment and post-treatment essays along with a new and improved epistemological beliefs questionnaire, administered at the beginning and the end of the class. Currently, this second macrocycle is in its data evaluation stage and based on the results, the researchers anticipate further adjustments of the learning trajectory.

Gene Flow

The Learning Sciences Institute has also been working with a client who teaches an introductory course in biological anthropology. While determining the learning trajectory, the design team found that the most pressing need in this course was student comprehension of the effects of environmental perturbations on gene flow between two populations, resulting in the creation of a new genotype. While determining the learning task, the team determined that the important variables included existing genotype, resulting genotype, and the causal effects of environmental factors such as language, religion, physical similarity, and others on the resulting genotype. Causal reasoning was the learning outcome most in need of support.

Conceptual analysis showed that there are two major conceptual frameworks for studying causal reasoning, covariational and mechanism based. Repeated occurrences of the association and covariation between the cause and effect are a necessary condition for a causal relationship. The covariational approach involves comparing and contrasting an event with others to determine the probability of the event being the cause. Mechanistic explanations link causes to effects by describing the chain of intermediary events. A mechanism-based explanation describes the causal agent and the effect, as well as the underlying mechanism that explains "how" and "why" the cause(s) produces the effect.

During design, the researchers collected numerous instances of gene flow and gradually refined learning activities. It was imperative that students be able to experiment with the effects of environmental factors on gene flow. A thought experiment showed that manipulable simulations would best enable that experimentation. However, students needed to use multiple simulations, so a model-based approach was selected. The model was adjusted several times based on feedback from the faculty member. Environmental factors in the model could be easily changed by renaming the causal agent and including different coefficients to describe the quantitative relationships. These models were converted to Web-ready simulations. Finally, mechanistic models (influence diagrams) were produced to describe the chain of intermediary cause–effect events. These were used to supplement the simulations.

As of this writing, these materials are being tested with students in the class. Data collection includes qualitative assessments of causal reasoning and scaffolded argumentation where students must identify appropriate causal mechanisms in different contexts. Based on student responses to test items and interviews with students following the use of these materials, the design team anticipates further adjustments to the materials. This research not only will validate the effectiveness of the design solution but also will contribute to an emerging prototheory of causal reasoning.

Summary

What has constructivism wrought in the theory and practice of instructional design? The shift in philosophical emphasis from the positivistic and deterministic assumptions made by instructional scientists to the social, historical, and constructivist assumptions made by learning scientists is the most obvious intellectual legacy. The preferred design method of learning scientists is design research, a process that integrates design and research. Rather than applying theories (most of which are inadequately established by empirical research), design researchers integrate theories and design activities in an iterative process. The prototheories that emerge have a much greater potential for affecting the design process than have traditional approaches, which have sought unified principles of instruction rather than contextually bound understanding of learning.

In short, the primary effect of constructivism on instructional design has been the shift from an instructional sciences approach to a learning sciences approach to design. For learning scientists, the design process is based on cognitive and social constructivist assumptions, and it interacts extensively with the context of learning. As noted, we believe this design process is likely to produce more local, and thus more useful, instructional solutions to learning problems.

Application Questions

1. Many of the instructional principles associated with constructivism are clearly described in J. R. Savery and T. M. Duffy, 1995, "Problem-Based Learning: An Instructional Model and Its Constructivist Framework," *Educational Technology*, *35*(5), 31–38. Find the article and read the first four pages. Also reread the section of Chapter 4 in which Marcy Driscoll describes some of the characteristics of constructivist-type learning environments. Based on the information contained in these two readings and your own knowledge of the topic, prepare a list of what you think are four to six of the key instructional principles associated with constructivism.
2. Examine some recent issues of *Journal of the Learning Sciences* and find an article in which a technology-enriched learning environment is described. Read the article, focusing your attention on whether the instructional principles you identified in response to question 1 seem to be incorporated into the learning environment described. Prepare a brief report indicating which of the principles seems to have been built into that environment, and describe the manner in which each principle was incorporated.
3. *Educational Researcher* is a major research journal in the field of education. A large portion of the January/February 2003 issue (vol. 32, no. 1) consisted of articles discussing design research. Read at least three of the articles in that issue and prepare a short report that summarizes the benefits of engaging in design research. Conclude with a section in which you describe the benefits that might be derived if design research methodology was used to help improve a course in which you are, or have been, enrolled.

References

Barab, S. A., & Duffy, T. M. (2000). From practice fields to communities of practice. In D. H. Jonassen & S. L. Land (Eds.), *Theoretical foundations of learning environments* (pp. 25–55). Mahwah, NJ: Lawrence Erlbaum Associates.

Brown, J. S., Collins, A., & Duguid, P. (1989). Situated cognition and the culture of learning. *Educational Researcher, 18,* 32–42.

Brown, L. A. (1992). Design experiments: Theoretical and methodological challenges in creating complex interventions in classroom settings. *Journal of the Learning Sciences,* 2(2), 141–178.

Cobb, P. (2001). Supporting the improvement of learning and teaching in social and institutional context. In S. M. Carver & D. Klahr (Eds.), *Cognition and instruction: Twenty-five years of progress.* Mahwah, NJ: Lawrence Erlbaum Associates.

Cobb, P., Confrey, J., diSessa, A., Lehrer, R., & Schauble, L. (2003). Design experiments in educational research. *Educational Researcher, 32*(1), 9–13.

Collins, A., Joseph, D., & Bielaczyc, K. (2004). Design research: Theoretical and methodological issues. *Journal of the Learning Sciences, 13*(1), 15–42.

Design-Based Research Collective. (2003). Design-based research: An emerging paradigm for educational inquiry. *Educational Researcher, 32*(1), 5–8.

Jonassen, D. H. (1991). Objectivism vs. constructivism: Do we need a new paradigm? *Educational Technology Research and Development, 39*(3), 5–14.

Jonassen, D. H., Hernandez-Serrano, J., & Choi, I. (2000). Integrating constructivism and learning technologies. In J. M. Spector & T. M. Anderson (Eds.), *Integrated and holistic perspectives on learning, instruction, and technology.* Amsterdam, NL: Kluwer Academic.

Spiro, R. J., Feltovich, P. J., Jacobson, M. J., & Coulson, R. L. (1992). Cognitive flexibility, constructivism, and hypertext: Random access instruction for advanced knowledge acquisition in ill-structured domains. In T. M. Duffy & D. H. Jonassen (Eds.), *Constructivism and the technology of instruction: A conversation* (pp. 57–76). Hillsdale, NJ: Lawrence Erlbaum Associates.

CHAPTER 6

Epistemology and the Design of Learning Environments

Michael J. Hannafin and Janette R. Hill
University of Georgia

Editors' Introduction

In the first part of the previous chapter, positivist (also called objectivist) and relativist (also called constructivist) views of learning were briefly compared. In this chapter, Mike Hannafin and Janette Hill discuss this issue in more depth, contrasting the positivist and relativist epistemologies (views regarding the nature of learning and understanding). The authors note that positivists believe that knowledge exists independent of individuals, that there are absolute truths that exist in the world. In contrast, relativists believe there are no absolute truths, that knowledge is relative to and constructed by each individual. As the authors note, these two viewpoints have quite different implications for how instruction is designed, and they describe design practices that reflect each set of beliefs. Finally, in contrast to many individuals who have taken strong positions in support of one or the other of the two sides of this issue, Hannafin and Hill call for an understanding and respect for both sets of beliefs about knowledge and both sets of design practices.

Knowledge and Comprehension Questions

1. Describe the main characteristics of postivist and relativist epistemologies.
2. Describe the differences between *instructional objectives* and what the authors call *integrative learning goals*.
3. Describe what the authors mean by the term *grounded design*. In doing so, try to go beyond simply restating the definition provided by the authors.
4. Compare and contrast instructional and constructional design practices.

Significant shifts have occurred in the instructional design and technology field reflecting alternatives to the traditional foundations and assumptions associated with the field. Professional designers need to become informed consumers as well as producers in a field whose knowledge base continues to shift. Do different epistemological perspectives influence the design of learning environments? How? Are the differences real? Are they important? Where do similarities and differences exist? What, if anything, does it mean for the design of learning systems? In this chapter, we introduce and compare positivist and relativist perspectives and examine design frames linked with each: objectivism and constructivism. We attempt to provide a balanced assessment of both perspectives and design frames, and describe their implications for the design of grounded learning environments. Table 6.1 provides a summary of epistemological perspectives, design frameworks, and design practices.

Epistemology, Psychology, and Design Practices

Epistemology is the branch of philosophy concerned with the nature of knowledge and understanding—their foundations, assumptions, and validity. We all have epistemological beliefs—some formal and others tacit. These beliefs influence how we design, sometimes consciously, sometimes unconsciously (see, e.g., Armstrong, Henson, & Savage, 2005; Segall & Wilson, 1998). Kuhn (1999) identifies a continuum of formal epistemological perspectives, suggesting basic differences in assertions, views of reality, and the role of critical thinking. Inasmuch as positivists believe that knowledge exists independently of the individual, it follows that they generally employ instructional methods designed to transmit knowledge, so as to help individuals "learn" or acquire it. Conversely, inasmuch as relativists believe that knowledge is not absolute

TABLE 6.1 Epistemological perspectives, design frameworks, and design practices

Epistemological Perspectives	Design Frameworks	Design Practices
Positivism	*Objectivism*	*Instructional Design*
• Knowledge exists independent of the learner	• Transfer knowledge from outside to inside the learner	• Classroom
• There is an absolute truth	• Arrange conditions to promote specific goals	• Directed • Teacher directing; learner receiving • Goal predetermined • Objectives defined
	• Knowledge engineered externally	• Activities, materials, assessment teacher driven • Products given to teacher for assessment
Relativism	*Constructivism*	*Constructional Design*
• Knowledge is constructed by the learner	• Guide the learner in constructing knowledge	• Environment • Learner centered
• Truth is contextual	• Provide a rich context for negotiation and meaning construction	• Teacher facilitating; learner controlling • Learning goals negotiated • Learning problems and contexts authentic
	• Knowledge constructed internally	• Activities, materials, assessment context driven and individually constructed • Artifacts shared and reflected on, collectively and individually

but rather what the individual constructs, they typically rely on instructional methods intended to promote judgments and evaluations that facilitate personal interpretations and refine understanding.

Epistemology and psychology have several interesting intersections in the design and development of learning environments. Positivism has been the cornerstone epistemological perspective of the ID field, laying the foundation for many current instructional design practices. Though significant differences exist between behavioral and cognitive perspectives on learning, both reflect positivist epistemology. Behaviorists believe that learning is mediated by relationships among external stimuli, overt responses, and reinforcement principles (see, e.g., Burton, Moore, & Magliaro, 2004; Driscoll, 1999; Hannafin & Rieber, 1989; Silber, 1998). Cognitive psychologists, while emphasizing the thinking processes associated with learning, focus on the relationship between external and internal activities (see Gagné's [1985] events of instruction). Traditional instructional practices have tended to reflect these positivist perspectives, characterized by beliefs that reality exists external to the individual (see, e.g., Hwang, 1996; Jonassen, 1991; Yarusso, 1992). Learning involves the acquisition of these external "truths"; instruction is the principal means to "transmit" or "deliver" them in a consistent manner across learners.

Relativist epistemology reflects fundamentally different views about the nature of knowledge and knowing. Relativists believe that reality is not directly knowable, and can only be inferred or assigned by convention or consensus. They assume that individuals actively assign different meanings to common objects, events, and circumstances that cannot be judged simply as "correct" or "incorrect" by comparing to convention (see, e.g., Driscoll, 1999; Hannafin & Land, 1997; Hwang, 1996; Wilson, 1996; Yarusso, 1992). Knowledge therefore is uniquely constructed rather than uniformly transmitted. *Learning* involves the individual's negotiating meaning in an effort to evolve personal understanding; *design* involves the creation of materials and activities that assist learners in constructing and refining individual representations and personal understandings.

It is apparent, therefore, that different epistemologies have different psychological frameworks, which in turn have different implications for instructional design. In this regard, epistemology, psychology, and design practices should be inextricably linked regardless of the specific beliefs themselves; frequently, however, they are not (Hannafin, Kim, & Kim, 2004; Hannafin & Land, 2000). The extent to which epistemic beliefs and psychological theory and research shape our design practices distinguishes professional designers from others (Armstrong et al., 2005; Segall & Wilson, 1998). By design, instructional materials and methods should reflect beliefs and evidence about the nature of learning and understanding in ways that are consistent with key foundations and assumptions (Hannafin & Hannafin, 2003).

Systems Approaches and Design Practices

The processes used to organize instructional design and development activities are also critical. Instructional design professionals use systematic processes to design, develop, implement, and evaluate methods and materials. Systems approaches enable designers to do more than simply develop individual instructional materials; they provide generalizable processes that aid in focusing, organizing, and managing available resources across diverse learning problems and needs (Dick, Carey, & Carey, 2005).

What "drives" systems design processes, and how do they in turn influence the associated activities? Design practices themselves can either constrain or enable diverse learning environments. Consider a key element in typical instructional systems design (ISD) approaches: the learning objective. Virtually all ISD approaches specify a learning objective as a necessary (usually central) component of the design process (cf. Gustafson & Branch, 1997). The learning objective specifies explicitly what will be learned, and implicitly what will be taught. It also influences how learning will be demonstrated, supported, and evaluated. In ISD approaches, the learning objective specification has tremendous influence on each of the other components. Explicit objectives require methods and materials that are correspondingly precise in their support of the objective in terms of content, conditions of assessment, response, and required performance standard.

Integrative learning goals created in constructivist learning environments, in contrast, are less prescriptive (Hay & Barab, 2001). The goals may be induced externally (e.g., by designers, teachers, parents, school board, management) or generated entirely by learners who seek to clarify, negotiate meaning, generate personal understandings, and otherwise construct knowledge. Varied resources are made available. Tools are provided to assist individuals in their attempts to reason and manipulate, and multiple perspectives are available from which to hone one's own beliefs. Guidance is provided to facilitate the individual's efforts and understandings (Hill & Hannafin, 2001). As we will demonstrate, the processes used to design constructivist learning environments are no less systematic, only less directive in their expectations and learning sequences (cf. Kafai & Resnick, 1996).

The question remains of how different approaches drive design. It is not simply a question of systematic versus nonsystematic design processes; both objectivists and constructivists use systematic design approaches. Vastly different learning environments can result from seemingly minor variations in objectives or learning goals using the same systematic approach. The manner in which epistemological beliefs influence the definition of learning needs has a dramatic impact on the resulting learning environment (Dinter, 1998). Goals are central to both objectivist as well as constructivist design processes, but they have dramatically different impacts on the corresponding learning environment's focus and features. Also, they reflect different perspectives on the nature of learning and understanding—one attempts to convey knowledge and skills to the learner, the other invokes thoughts and actions to help the learner construct knowledge.

In the remainder of this chapter, we introduce the process of grounded design, elaborate on the foundations and assumptions of objectivism and constructivism, and provide examples of grounded design practices associated with each epistemological perspective. The link among epistemological beliefs, psychology, and design practices is important to professionals in the instructional design and technology field. Our intention is to neither minimize nor exaggerate the similarities or differences among approaches, but to underscore the potential of the approaches and clarify their design implications.[1]

Grounded Design

Grounded design is the "systematic implementation of . . . procedures that are rooted in established theory and research in human learning" (Hannafin, Hannafin, Land, & Oliver, 1997, p. 102). By grounding design practices, professionals are better able to make, explain, and defend decisions within a powerful and empirically based theoretical framework. According to Bednar, Cunningham, Duffy, and Perry (1995, pp. 101–102), "effective design is possible only if the developer has reflexive awareness of the theoretical basis underlying the design . . . [it] emerges from the deliberate application of some particular theory of learning." When designers recognize the utility of various approaches and perspectives, and understand key foundations and assumptions, they are able to design learning environments that are aligned philosophically and substantively with such perspectives. Grounded design promotes articulation of and alignment among the underlying principles, not the inherent superiority of one epistemological perspective, theoretical framework, or methodology over another. It supports approaches that enable important epistemological beliefs to be reflected in the materials and activities embodied in learning environments. This is an important contribution: the ability to design qualitatively different, yet equally grounded, learning environments (Hannafin, Hill, & Glazer, in press).

Grounded designs are anchored in a *defensible* theoretical framework, based on relevant research and theory, and validated through successive implementations. The framework must be articulated clearly and differentiated from other perspectives. That is, it must establish connections among key foundations, identify the assumptions consistent with the corresponding foundations, and lead to methods consistent with them. This is true independently of the epistemological perspectives from which they emerge. The approaches must be consistent with the outcomes of research conducted to test, validate, or extend the theories on which they are based; that is, linked to established, proven instructional methods. The methodologies must be applicable to more than a specific setting or problem—they transcend the individual instances in which isolated success may be evident, and can be adapted or adopted by other designers. Finally, designs are validated iteratively through implementation. The design processes and methods continuously inform, test, and validate or contradict the theoretical framework and assumptions on which they are based.

As summarized in Table 6.1, the key for grounded learning systems design is not the specific epistemological perspective or design framework employed, but the correspondence between the perspectives and frameworks and the design practices that link them. Grounded design practices have emerged that are consistent with objectivist epistemology (Dick et al., 2005; Gagné, Wager, Golas, & Keller, 2005); different but grounded design practices have emerged that are consistent with constructivist epistemology (Honebein, 1996; Kafai & Resnick, 1996). Both employ systems approaches for design, development, implementation, and evaluation, but the approaches derived from each tend to reflect basic differences in beliefs and values.

Table 6.2 summarizes fundamental learning systems design concepts: analysis, design, development, implementation, and evaluation. In the following section, the applicability of these concepts for each design framework will be examined.

[1] See Jonassen (1991) for distinctions between objectivism and constructivism; Grabinger (1996) for different assumptions about learning and learning environments; Winn (1997) for distinctions between the assumptions of instructional design and situated cognition; Silber (1998) for contrasts between behavioral and cognitive approaches to instructional design; and Phillips (1995) for distinctions among constructivist theorists.

TABLE 6.2 **ISD phases with objectivist and constructivist design activities**

ISD Phases	Objectivist Design Activities	Constructivist Design Activities
Analysis	• Content • Learner • Instructional need • Instructional goal	• Context • Learner • Problem described • Key concepts identified
Design	• Instructional objectives • Task analysis • Criterion-referenced assessment	• Learning goals • Identify learning sequences (group and/or individual) • Context-driven evaluation
Development	• Develop instructional materials	• Construct learning resources/artifacts
Implementation	• Teacher: conveying, directing • Learner: receiving, acquiring • Focus: objective attainment	• Teacher: consulting, facilitating • Learner: directing, controlling • Focus: problem solving
Evaluation	• What a learner knows • Knowing that, knowing how	• How a learner knows • "Knowing your way around"

Objectivism and Instructional Design Practices

Objectivists believe that knowledge exists independently of the learner; instruction focuses on transferring that knowledge to the learner. To *instruct* is "to provide with knowledge, esp. in a methodical way;" *instruction* is "an imparted or acquired item of knowledge; a lesson" (*American Heritage College Dictionary*, 1993, p. 705). Instructional design—the systematic analysis, design, development, implementation, and evaluation of instruction (e.g., Dick et al., 2005)—reflects fundamental beliefs in the power of *instruction*. Instruction involves the deliberate arrangement of learning conditions to promote the attainment of some intended goal (see Case & Bereiter, 1984, for descriptions and applications of behavioral and cognitive psychology in instructional design). Instructional design methods help to transmit meaning consistently and efficiently across learners. The learner's task, guided by the designer, is to recognize and label relevant objects and events, organize them into coherent chunks, and integrate new with existing knowledge and skills.

Formal education and training have largely reflected objectivist approaches to instruction consistent with behavioral and cognitive psychological foundations and assumptions (Hannafin & Hannafin, 2003; Silber, 1998). Objectivist learning environments are generally structured and prescribed to facilitate the acquisition of knowledge and skills deemed important by teachers and/or subject matter experts. The emphasis is placed on the product (e.g., specific knowledge or skills) resulting from the instruction, and the tasks and activities used to move the learner toward creation of the product. Objectivists focus on design according to discrete stages (Cennamo, Abell, & Chung, 1996).

How are objectivist approaches grounded? Consider how we might develop instruction for a weather unit. Consistent with Table 6.2, the designer *analyzes* the content to be taught, the instructional setting itself, and the learners' prior knowledge. Based on this analysis, an instructional need will be identified and a goal established (e.g., "The learner will develop a better understanding of weather forecasting."). Next, the designer will move into the *design* phase, during which instructional objectives will be defined (e.g., "Given a list of terms related to measuring moisture, the learner will be able to define the terms with 95% accuracy"; or "Given a list of weather forecasting instruments, the learner will be able to identify the purpose of 90% of the tools."). The objectives are then broken down into sequences and hierarchies denoting what needs to occur to obtain the objective. The designer might then use each objective to establish specifications for criterion-referenced assessments of relevant content (e.g., "A barometer is used to measure (a) precipitation, (b) humidity, (c) atmospheric pressure"), materials related to the objectives, or instructional activities (e.g., "Students will read a chapter in text"; "Small groups will complete a worksheet on the procedures for recording temperature and wind").

The materials *developed* for the unit (e.g., worksheets, *PowerPoint®* presentations) will help to facilitate learners' achievement of the objectives and goals. When the unit is *implemented*, the learning environment will convey the information and guide students in accomplishing the prescribed objectives by having them read the instructional materials, engage in instructional activities, produce responses, and receive feedback. Finally, *evaluation* will focus on the learner demonstrating "knowing that" or "knowing how" (Ryle, cited in Perkins, 1996) as specified in the objectives and reinforced in the materials and activities. The objective signifies the knowledge or skill to be learned; the system design methods draw on significant psychological research and theory to prescribe and execute materials and activities designed to ensure that knowledge or skill has been acquired and standards have been met.

Constructivism and Constructional Design Practices

For constructivists, objects and events have no absolute meaning; rather, the individual interprets each and constructs meaning based on individual experience and evolved beliefs (Steffe & Gale, 1995). Individuals construct knowledge as they attempt to make sense of their experiences. They come to an "acceptable" understanding of truth within a particular context. Models of how things work (e.g., gravity, solar system, learning) do not necessarily reflect reality; rather, they represent the best construction of current experience (Driscoll, 1999). Whereas objectivists emphasize decomposing and external control, constructivists tend to eschew the breaking down of content into component parts in favor of environments wherein knowledge and skills are inextricably tied to context and need to know. The individuals assume responsibility for constructing personally relevant understandings and meanings.

To *construct* is "to form by assembling or combining parts; to build"; *construction* is "the act or process of [building]" (*American Heritage College Dictionary*, 1993, p. 299). Constructional design, then, focuses on the creation of learning environments that enable and support individual construction by engaging in design and invention tasks. The design task is to create an environment where knowledge building tools (affordances) and the means to create and manipulate artifacts of understanding are provided, not one in which concepts are explicitly taught. An underlying assumption in constructional design practices is that the learner is an active, changing entity. As such, there is a need for "layers of negotiation" among the teacher, learner, and/or designer of the learning space (Cennamo et al., 1996). According to this model, the varied aspects of the learning environment are defined and redefined continually to accommodate an individual's evolving needs. Neither the meaning of the knowledge and skills embodied in a learning environment nor means through which they are engaged by the individual are fixed. Rather, as beliefs and understandings emerge or questions and uncertainties surface, both the meaning of the learning resources and the environment's support features evolve.

Constructivist learning environments create "a place where learners may work together and support each other as they use a variety of tools and information resources in their pursuit of learning goals and problem-solving activities" (Wilson, 1995, p. 27). Constructivist learning environments are process based (e.g., weather forecasting), question driven ("How does the weatherperson forecast weather for a week?"), and cyclical in nature ("I thought I wanted to know about forecasting, but I really am more interested in calculating humidity levels."). They undergo continual revision and evolve as the learner engages the environment (Jonassen, 1991; Resnick, 1998).

Constructional design is linked closely to constructivist epistemology; there are, of course, many other design methodologies adhering to this framework (see Wilson, 1996, for constructivist learning environment case studies). Constructional design involves four learning-by-design principles (Papert, 1980): (1) individuals are active learners and control their own learning process; (2) individuals create concrete, tangible evidence (artifacts) that reflect their understanding; (3) artifacts are shared collectively as well as reflected on individually to extend one's understanding; and (4) the learning problems and contexts are authentic, that is, they focus on solving a practical problem. The design task for the constructionist, therefore, is one of providing a rich context within which meaning can be individually negotiated and ways of understanding can emerge and evolve.

Systems approaches are also important to the design of grounded constructivist learning environments (Honebein, 1996; Wilson, 1996). Context is the principal organizer, not content. During *analysis*, the designer focuses on a vision of the learning environment and then determines how to create it (Dick, 1997; Wilson, 1996). This involves analyzing how the problem under study might be encountered. To guide the creation of the context, the designer may focus on the description of a problem ("People are interested in weather, but many do not understand the forecasting process."), and/or identification of key concepts related to the problem (e.g., temperature, atmospheric pressure, measuring moisture) (Duffy & Cunningham, 1996). The designer's task, however, is to create a learning environment within which the individual can explore and construct, not to impose a particular "correctness."

According to constructionists, the learner is also a designer, not merely a receiver of designed material and activities. During the *design* phase, the learner establishes individual learning goals (e.g., "Understand how to use a barometer," or "Understand the influence of dew point on relative humidity"), evaluates and decides whether to engage in potential sequences of learning activities (including group interactions and individual work), locates and evaluates potential resources, and chooses methods to assess their solution to the problem posed (e.g., establishing a backyard weather station).

Learning resources are *developed* and/or made available on an as needed basis. Some development will be done by the designer, but development in its purest sense is what individuals do as they construct and create artifacts and refine meaning (e.g., a spreadsheet used to compare hourly temperature and relative humidity readings). During *implementation*, learners will decide what to do, when to do it, and whom to consult (e.g., experts, peers, teachers) as they engage in problem solving and artifact construction. The designer or other facilitators will serve as consultants as learners manage their own learning needs. *Evaluation* will focus on articulation (Collins, Brown, & Newman, 1989) and the learner "knowing her/his way around" (Perkins, 1996) the learning object (e.g., weather forecasting), as exemplified by the assessment method determined by the learner (e.g., the successful creation of a backyard weather station to track weather for a month). The learning goal and problem being studied drive the learning environment as the individual attempts to understand the process, asks questions, and assesses work and progress.

Can Both Perspectives Be "Right"?

The debate over the elusive "best" approach has been lively and occasionally rancorous, if not always productive. Some have questioned the very legitimacy of constructivist approaches for instructional designers (Merrill et al., 1996). Others have suggested that the presumed differences may simply reflect different mindsets rather than fundamentally different approaches (Lebow, 1993). Still others, however, note that the perspectives represent fundamentally different core foundations and assumptions and philosophical differences as to render them potentially incompatible with one another (Hannafin et al., 1997). Finally, some suggest pragmatically that the perspectives are complementary, expanding the designer's "toolkit" (Rieber, 1993; Winn, 1997; Young, 1993).

Is each approach valid, even where vastly different learning environments are developed and implemented? Both perspectives *can be* considered valid provided the tests of groundedness are addressed; that is, *if* they employ methods that are consistent with the underlying epistemological frame. The differences in underlying frames *require* associated differences in approaches and methods. We should not only recognize approaches reflecting different underlying foundations and assumptions—we should *expect* them.

Still, not all supposed instruction adheres to the tenets of objectivism, and not all purportedly student-centered learning reflects the core values of constructivism. Calling an activity instruction because it uses objectives, or an activity constructivist because it claims to be student centered misleads designers and subverts the values of grounded design. We should not tacitly accept a designer's claims as valid simply because it is consistent with our beliefs and values; nor should we categorically reject them based on their differences with our beliefs and values. Learning systems need to manifest the core values on which they are based regardless of those values. We need designs and procedures that optimize and genuinely support important differences, not materials and approaches that diminish or marginalize them (see Dinter, 1998, for a detailed description of the role of epistemology in design).

The Emerging Design Landscape

Instructional designers need to both recognize and support a range of client needs, contextual factors, and perspectives on the nature of learning, knowing, and understanding. It seems both unwise and counterproductive to reject (or remain oblivious to) the design revolution underway in learning environments rooted in nontraditional epistemological perspectives. Significant efforts have been advanced in a variety of fields, some of which have transformed teaching and learning practices in very fundamental ways (see, e.g., the WWild Team (2005) website [**http://it.coe.uga.edu/wwild/**] for a compilation of objectivist and constructivist learning environments in a variety of fields). We need to better understand these approaches—the materials and methods as well as the core foundations and assumptions—if we are to benefit from them. The extent to which we, as a field, learn and expand our role may well determine the extent to which the field survives, grows, and prospers.

Application Questions

1. Collect 10 goals, objectives, or other student expectation statements from 3 or 4 different sources (e.g., textbooks, course syllabi, instructional materials). Using the descriptive information in the chapter, classify each as representative of an integrative learning goal or instructional objective (make whatever revisions are needed so that it best fits as either an integrative learning goal or instructional objective). Then, revise each to create a new version of each that is consistent with the other epistemological perspective. You should have each of the 10 original statements stated in the form of both an instructional objective *and* an integrative learning goal.
2. Select two instructional objectives and two integrative learning goals from item 1. For each, identify two or three grounded teaching–learning activities and describe why you believe that they represent grounded design practices.

References

American heritage college dictionary (3rd ed.). (1993). Boston: Houghton Mifflin.

Armstrong, D. G., Henson, K., & Savage, T. V. (2005). *Teaching today: An introduction to education* (7th ed.). Upper Saddle River, NJ: Merrill/Prentice Hall.

Bednar, A., Cunningham, D., Duffy, T., & Perry, J. (1995). Theory into practice: How do we link it? In G. Anglin (Ed.), *Instructional technology: Past, present, and future* (2nd ed., p. 100–112). Englewood, CO: Libraries Unlimited.

Burton, J., Moore, D. M., & Magliaro, S. (2004). Behaviorism and instructional technology. In D. Jonassen (Ed.), *Handbook of research for educational communications and technology* (2nd ed., pp. 3–36). New York: Macmillan.

Case, R., & Bereiter, C. (1984). From behaviourism to cognitive behaviourism to cognitive development: Steps in the evolution of instructional design. *Instructional Science, 13*, 141–158.

Cennamo, K. S., Abell, S. K., & Chung, M. L. (1996). A "layers of negotiation" model for designing constructivist learning materials. *Educational Technology, 36*(4), 39–48.

Collins, A., Brown, J. S., & Newman, S. E. (1989). Cognitive apprenticeship: Teaching the crafts of reading, writing, and mathematics. In L. B. Resnick (Ed.), *Knowing, learning, and instruction: Essays in honor of Robert Glaser* (pp. 453–494). Hillsdale, NJ: Lawrence Erlbaum Associates.

Dick, W. (1997). Better instructional design theory: Process improvement or reengineering? *Educational Technology, 37*(5), 47–50.

Dick, W., Carey, L., & Carey, J. O. (2005). *The systematic design of instruction* (6th ed.). Boston: Allyn & Bacon.

Dinter, F. R. (1998). Constructivism in instructional design theory. *Journal of Structural Learning & Intelligent Systems, 13*(2), 71–89.

Driscoll, M. (1999). *Psychology of learning for instruction* (2nd ed.). Boston: Allyn & Bacon.

Duffy, T., & Cunningham, D. (1996). Constructivism: Implications for the design and delivery of instruction. In D. Jonassen (Ed.), *Handbook of research for educational communications and technology* (pp. 170–198). New York: Macmillan.

Gagné, R. (1985). The conditions of learning (4th ed.). New York: Holt, Rinehart, & Winston.

Gagne, R. M., Wager, W. W., Golas, K. C., & Keller, J. M. (2005). *Principles of instructional design* (5th ed.). Belmont, CA: Wadsworth.

Grabinger, R. S. (1996). Rich environments for active learning. In D. H. Jonassen (Ed.), *Handbook of research for educational communications and technology* (pp. 665–692). New York: Macmillan.

Gustafson, K. L., & Branch, R. M. (1997). Revisioning models of instructional development. *Educational Technology Research and Development, 45*(3), 73–90.

Hannafin, K. M., & Hannafin, M. J. (2003). Transitioning perspectives to optimize training designs. *Human Systems IAC Gateway, 14*(1), 3–6.

Hannafin, M. J., Hannafin, K. M., Land, S. M., & Oliver, K. (1997). Grounded practice and the design of constructivist learning environments. *Educational Technology Research and Development, 45*(3), 101–117.

Hannafin, M. J., Hill, J., & Glazer, E. (in press). Designing grounded learning environments: Linking epistemology, pedagogy, and design practice. In G. Anglin (Ed.), *Critical issues in instructional technology*. Englewood Cliffs, NJ: Libraries Unlimited.

Hannafin, M. J., Kim, M., & Kim, J. (2004). Reconciling research, theory and practice in Web-based teaching and learning. *Journal of Computing in Higher Education, 15*(2), 3–20.

Hannafin, M. J., & Land, S. (1997). The foundations and assumptions of technology-enhanced, student-centered learning environments. *Instructional Science, 25*, 167–202.

Hannafin, M. J., & Land, S. M. (2000). Technology and student-centered learning in higher education: Issues and practices. *Journal of Computing in Higher Education, 12*(1), 3–30.

Hannafin, M. J., & Rieber, L. P. (1989). Psychological foundations of instructional design for emerging computer-based instructional technologies: Parts I & II. *Educational Technology Research and Development, 37*(2), 91–114.

Hay, K. E., & Barab, S. A. (2001). Constructivism in practice: A comparison and contrast of apprenticeship and constructionist learning environments. *Journal of the Learning Sciences, 10*(3), 281–323.

Hill, J., & Hannafin, M. J. (2001). Teaching and learning in digital environments: The resurgence of resource-based learning. *Educational Technology Research and Development, 49*(3), 37–52.

Honebein, P. (1996). Seven goals for the design of constructivist learning environments. In B. Wilson (Ed.), *Constructivist learning environments: Case studies in instructional design* (pp. 11–24). Englewood Cliffs, NJ: Educational Technology Publications.

Hwang, A. (1996). Positivist and constructivist persuasions in instructional development. *Instructional Science, 24*(5), 343–356.

Jonassen, D. H. (1991). Objectivism versus constructivism: Do we need a new philosophical paradigm? *Educational Technology Research and Development, 39*(3), 5–14.

Kafai, Y., & Resnick, M. (1996). Introduction. In Y. Kafai & M. Resnick (Eds.), *Constructivism in practice: Designing, thinking, and learning in a digital world* (pp. 1–8). Mahwah, NJ; Lawrence Erlbaum Associates.

Kuhn, D. (1999). A developmental model of critical thinking. *Educational Researcher, 28*(2), 16–26, 46.

Lebow, D. (1993). Constructivist values for instructional systems design: Five principles toward a new mindset. *Educational Technology Research and Development, 41*(3), 4–16.

Merrill, M. D., Drake, L., Lacy, Pratt, J., & the ID2 Research Group at Utah State University (1996, September). Reclaiming instructional design. *Educational Technology*, 5–7.

Papert, S. (1980). *Mindstorms: Children, computers, and powerful ideas*. New York: Basic Books.

Perkins, D. N. (1996). Minds in the hood. In B. Wilson (Ed.), *Constructivist learning environments: Case studies in instructional design* (pp. v–viii). Englewood Cliffs, NJ: Educational Technology Publications.

Phillips, D. (1995). The good, the bad, and the ugly: The many faces of constructivism. *Educational Researcher, 24*(7), 5–12.

Resnick, M. (1998). Technologies for lifelong kindergarten. *Educational Technology Research and Development, 46*(4), 43–55.

Rieber, L. P. (1993). A pragmatic view of instructional technology. In K. Tobin (Ed.), *The practice of constructivism in science education* (pp. 193–212). Hillsdale, NJ: Lawrence Erlbaum Associates.

Segall, W. E., & Wilson, A. E. (1998). Putting philosophy to work in culturally diverse classrooms. In W. E. Segall & A.E. Wilson, *Introduction to education: Teaching in a diverse society* (pp. 125–150). Upper Saddle River, NJ: Merrill/Prentice Hall.

Silber, K. (1998). The cognitive approaches to training development: A practitioner's assessment. *Educational Technology Research and Development, 34*(4), 58–72.

Steffe, L. P., & Gale, J. (1995). *Constructivism in education.* Mahwah, NJ: Lawrence Erlbaum Associates.

Wilson, B. (1995). Metaphors for instruction: Why we talk about learning environments. *Educational Technology, 35*(5), 25–30.

Wilson, B. (1996). What is a constructivist learning environment? In B. Wilson (Ed.), *Constructivist learning environments: Case studies in instructional design*. Englewood Cliffs, NJ: Educational Technology Publications.

Winn, W. (1997, January–February). Advantages of a theory-based curriculum in instructional technology. *Educational Technology*, 34–41.

WWILD Team. (2005). Home page. Retrieved from the World Wide Web, http://it.coe.uga.edu/wwild/

Yarusso, L. (1992). Constructivism vs. objectivism. *Performance and Instruction, 31*(4), 7–9.

Young, M. (1993). Instructional design for situated learning. *Educational Technology Research and Development, 41*(1), 43–58.

M. David Merrill
Brigham Young University, Hawaii

CHAPTER 7

First Principles of Instruction: A Synthesis

Knowledge and Comprehension Questions

1. In your own words, briefly describe each of the five first principles of instruction discussed in this chapter.
2. Merrill briefly indicates why each of the first principles is important. Briefly summarize his position regarding the importance of each principle and then indicate, for each principle, whether you agree or disagree with his point of view. Explain why you feel this way.
3. Provide an example of each of the five types of learning tasks discussed in this chapter.
4. Examine the corollary principles in one of the six categories (problem-centered, activation, demonstration, application, integration, and implementation) described in the second half of this chapter. Describe how each corollary principle within that category is related to the category.
5. Briefly describe how learner understanding of the structure of what is to be learned can be supported during each of the four phases of the instructional cycle.

Editors' Introduction

In Section 2 of this book, several of the authors point to differences in design practices between positivists (objectivists) and relativists (constructivists). In this chapter, David Merrill takes a different tack. Having spent several years studying a number of different instructional design theories and models, including a variety of positivist and constructivist approaches, he concludes that these different theories and models do share common instructional principles, which he labels *First Principles of Instruction*.

In the first half of this chapter, Merrill describes and presents a four-phase cycle of instruction that incorporates these principles. In the second half, he presents a series of empirically verified corollary instructional principles derived from published research studies and reviews of research literature. Merrill concludes by indicating that in many of the instructional products he and his colleagues have reviewed, these principles have not been implemented. He expresses the hope that in the future these principles will be more widely applied, thereby resulting in more effective, efficient, and appealing instruction.

Recent years have seen a proliferation of instructional design theories and models. Instructional design theory varies from basic descriptive laws about learning to broad curriculum programs that concentrate on what is taught rather than on how to teach. Are all of these design theories and models merely alternative ways to approach design? Do all of these design theories and models have equal value? Do these theories and models have fundamental underlying principles in common? If so, what are these underlying first principles? Previously (Merrill, 2002a) I outlined a set of First Principles of Instructional Design derived from a study of a number of different instructional design theories and models. It was concluded that these different theories and models do share common principles and that they do not incorporate fundamentally different principles. No theory or model previously reviewed includes principles that are contrary to those identified. Concise versions of those principles I identified are listed here:

1. Learning is promoted when learners are engaged in solving real-world problems.
2. Learning is promoted when existing knowledge is activated as a foundation for new knowledge.
3. Learning is promoted when new knowledge is demonstrated to the learner.
4. Learning is promoted when new knowledge is applied by the learner.
5. Learning is promoted when new knowledge is integrated into the learner's world.

Description of the First Principles

The identification of first principles does more than merely collect a set of prescriptive principles that might be used to select or design effective instruction. These principles are interrelated to one another. A four-phase cycle of instruction related to these principles was identified, consisting of activation, demonstration, application, and integration (Figure 7.1). Effective instruction involves all four of these activities repeated as required for different problems or whole tasks. Each of these activities is described in the following paragraphs.

Learning is facilitated when the first activity in a learning cycle *activates* relevant prior knowledge. Learning is facilitated when the instruction directs learners to recall, relate, describe, or apply knowledge from relevant past experience that can be used as a foundation for the new knowledge. If learners have limited prior experience, learning is facilitated when the instruction provides relevant experiences that can be used as a foundation for the new knowledge.

Learning is facilitated when the next activity in a learning cycle *demonstrates* the new knowledge to be learned, rather than merely telling information about the new learning. Too much instruction merely tells information. Information is usually general and abstract, and refers to many specific situations. Learning is facilitated when instruction also shows portrayals of the information. *Portrayals* are representations of specific cases that are concrete and that illustrate how the information applies to a single situation.

Learning is facilitated when the third activity in a learning cycle provides opportunity for learners to *apply* the new knowledge to new specific situations. Application involves more than merely remembering information; it requires learners to use the information to complete specific concrete tasks or to solve specific problems. Application involves solving whole problems or doing whole tasks and is more than merely answering questions about one step, one action, or one event in the whole.

Finally, a learning cycle is completed when learners have an opportunity to *integrate* the new knowledge and skill into their everyday activities. Learning is facilitated when the instruction provides an opportunity for learners to publicly demonstrate their newly acquired knowledge and skill; when the instruction provides an opportunity to reflect on, discuss, or defend their new knowledge; and when it provides an opportunity for the learners to create, invent, or explore new and personal ways to use their new knowledge and skill.

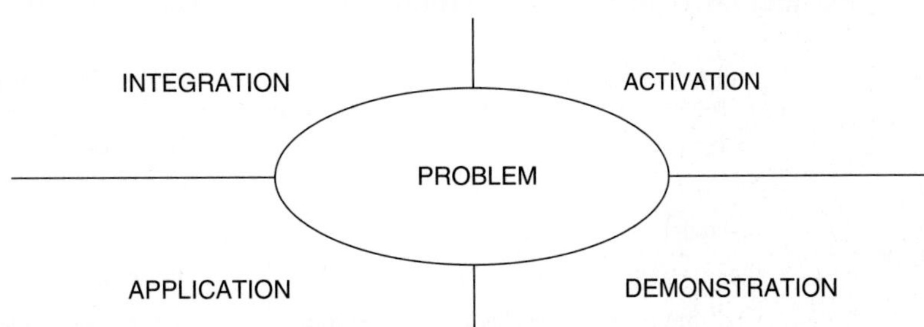

FIGURE 7.1 Phases of effective instruction.

Perhaps as important as the four-phase cycle of instruction is the notion that *effective instruction is problem centered*; that is, individual components are most effectively taught in the context of a progression of real-world problems where the student is shown a problem, taught the components, and then shown how the components are used to solve the problem or do the whole task. This problem-centered approach combines the solving of problems with more direct instruction of problem components, as contrasted with problem-based approaches in which students are placed in collaborative groups, given resources and a problem, and left to construct their own solution for the problem.

Most tasks or problems are complex aggregations of component tasks. Learning is facilitated when these components are directly taught in the context of a progression of whole problems or tasks. Too much instruction focuses on component tasks or individual topics and leaves their integration to the student. Too often after a series of topics or component tasks are taught, the student is given a broader task or problem as a culminating experience and asked to use the skills and/or knowledge related to the component tasks or topics to complete the broader task or problem. These typical topic-centered approaches are far less effective than an integrated approach that combines problem-centered instruction with direct instruction of the individual component tasks. An example of the latter approach is the "pebble-in-the-pond" approach to instructional design (Merrill, 2002b), which prescribes worked problems early in the sequence of instruction and a gradual fading of this guidance or coaching as the instruction proceeds.

Varying Instructional Strategies Based on Types of Learning Tasks

The specific instructional strategy one might use to help learners acquire the skills necessary to perform a particular learning task is dependent in part on the type of task involved. A number of different schemes for identifying types of learning tasks have been proposed. Most include the following categories: information-about, parts-of, kinds-of, how-to, and what-happens. These terms are more easily understood by subject matter experts than some of the more technical terms used by other schemes. Nevertheless, these simplified terms correspond sufficiently with previous knowledge classification schemes to allow specification of different demonstration and application conditions for each type of learning task.

How might instructional strategies differ based on the type of learning task involved? An example can be drawn by looking at how the instructional elements that take place during the demonstration phase should vary depending on the type of learning task. During this phase, instruction for each type of learning task should involve a general information ("tell information") element and one or more specific portrayal ("show portrayal") elements. The information and portrayal elements for each component category are given in Table 7.1.

The demonstration applied to individual learning tasks is not effective unless the information and portrayals involved are consistent with the type of task being taught. *Consistency* means that the information and portrayals used correspond to the type of task being taught. Consistency has been extensively described by Gagné (1985) and Merrill (1994). Similar notions of consistency apply to the application phase of the instructional cycle.

First Principles, Corollary Principles, and Related Instructional Prescriptions

For this chapter I have gathered empirically verified instructional principles from several recent works and related them to my earlier list of first principles (Merrill 2002a). Each of these corollary instructional principles is listed in question form following the first principle that it is related to. In that earlier publication I related these principles to theories or models of instruction; here I have

TABLE 7.1 Types of learning tasks and related demonstration (tell and show) elements

Learning Task	Tell Information	Show Portrayal
Information-about	Facts or associations	Not applicable
Parts-of	Name and description	Location
Kinds-of	Definition	Examples and nonexamples
How-to	Steps and sequence	Illustration of steps for specific cases
What-happens	Describe process, conditions, consequences	Illustration of specific conditions and consequences for specific cases

selected sources that provide research support for a given principle. Moreover, none of these sources contain any contrary principles.

Each of the corollary principles is followed by one or more quotes, taken from published research studys or reviews of the research literature, which describe closely related instructional prescriptions. Some of the prescriptions cited provide more detail than our statement of first principles. The prescriptions were not transformed to correspond to the principles but are quoted as stated by their authors. The reader is encouraged to study the original sources for a clearer picture of the relationship between prescriptions and principles. These sources include a description of the research support, as well as application examples for the prescriptions.

Readers of the previous work (Merrill, 2002a) will note that there have been modifications in some of the corollary principles. I have also added a final section, "Implementation," to include prescriptions that reviewers of our work have often cited as an omission.

First Principle: Problem centered (Let me do the whole task!)

1. Does the instruction involve authentic real-world problems or tasks?
   - "Interactions should mirror the job" (Clark & Mayer, 2003, p. 53).
   - "Use job contexts to teach problem solving processes" (Clark & Mayer, 2003, p. 251).
   - "Focus training on thinking processes versus job knowledge" (Clark & Mayer, 2003, p. 256).
   - "Incorporate job-specific problem-solving processes" (Clark & Mayer, 2003, p. 264).
2. In place of a formal objective, does the instruction show the learners the whole task they will be able to do or the whole problem they will be able to solve as a result of completing the instruction?
   - "When instruction provides clear (to the learner) and complete procedural 'how to' examples of the decisions and actions needed to solve problems and perform necessary tasks to be learned, then learning and transfer will be increased" (Clark, 2003, p. 16).
   - "Instructional goals narrow what students focus on" (Marzano, Pickering, & Pollock, 2001, p. 94). Note that this is probably because most objectives are component or topic oriented rather than whole-task or whole-problem oriented.
   - "Instructional goals should not be too specific" (Marzano et al., 2001, p. 94). Note that when objectives are very specific they are usually topic oriented rather than whole-task oriented. Sometimes objectives are specific to only one instance of a task rather than to a class of tasks.
   - "Begin a lesson with a short statement of goals" (Rosenshine, 1997, n.p.). Note that this is the classic prescription. Rosenshine cites research showing that goals are better than no goals. R. E. Clark's (2003) research shows that illustrating the task is better than providing formal objectives.
3. Does the instruction teach the component tasks of the problem or task and then help the learner use these components in solving the whole problem or doing the whole task? (See Figure 7.1.)
   - "Students should practice the parts of a process in the context of the overall process" (Marzano et al., 2001, p. 142).
   - "Present new material in small steps, providing for student practice after each step" (Rosenshine, 1997, n.p.). Note that Rosenshine stresses that teaching components is better than not teaching components but Marzano's findings indicate that it is better still when this component instruction is related to the whole task.
4. Does the instruction involve a progression of problems, not just a single application?
   - "Use job-realistic or varied worked examples" (Clark & Mayer, 2003, p. 186). Note that the emphasis here is on a varied sequence of job-related tasks rather than on a single task.

First Principle: Activation (Where do I start?)

1. Does the instruction direct learners to recall, relate, describe, or apply prior knowledge from relevant past experience that can be used as a foundation for the new knowledge? If learners have limited prior experience, does the instruction provide relevant experience that can be used as a foundation for the new knowledge?
   - "Cues and questions are ways that a . . . teacher helps students use what they already know about a topic. . . . Cues and questions should focus on what is important as opposed to what is unusual. . . . 'Higher level' questions produce deeper learning than 'lower level' questions. . . . Questions are effective learning tools even when asked before a learning experience" (Marzano et al., 2001, pp. 112–114).
   - "[P]roviding cues to encourage learners to activate relevant preexisting knowledge facilitates learning" (Andre, 1997, p. 246).
   - "Help students develop their background knowledge" (Rosenshine, 1997, n.p.).
   - "Review . . . relevant previous learning [and] prerequisite skills and knowledge" (Rosenshine, 1997, n.p.).
2. Does the instruction help learners see its relevance and to have confidence in their ability to acquire the knowledge and skill to be taught?

- "Designers can help students to become actively engaged in a course or lesson and to persist or stay 'on track' when distracted by helping students connect their personal goals and interests to course goals, by clearly communicating the utility of the course goals (and the risk of not achieving them), and by helping students maintain their confidence in achieving the course goals (by pointing out past successes with similar goals)" (Clark, 2003, p. 20).
- "[S]imply demonstrating that added effort will pay off in terms of enhanced achievement actually increases student achievement" (Marzano et al., 2001, p. 51).
- "Students should be encouraged to personalize the teacher's goals" (Marzano et al., 2001, p. 94).

3. Does the instruction provide or encourage the recall of a structure that can be used to organize the new knowledge?
   - "Representing similarities and differences in graphic or symbolic form enhances students' understanding of and ability to use knowledge" (Marzano et al., 2001, p. 16).
   - "Being aware of the explicit structure of information is an aid to summarizing information" (Marzano et al., 2001, p. 32).
   - "Graphic organizers are perhaps the most common way to help students generate nonlinguistic representations. . . . The more we use both systems of representation—linguistic and nonlinguistic—the better [learners] are able to think about and recall knowledge" (Marzano et al., 2001, p. 73, p. 75).
   - "Advance organizers should focus on what is important as opposed to what is unusual. . . . 'Higher level' advance organizers produce deeper learning than the 'lower level' advance organizers. . . . Advance organizers are most useful with information that is not well organized" (Marzano et al., 2001, p. 118).
   - "[C]oncrete AOs [advance organizers] seem to be more effective than more abstract AOs" (Andre, 1997, p. 248).
   - "Providing learners with a conceptual model can facilitate the acquisition of problem-solving skills" (Andre, 1997, p. 247).
   - "[P]roviding students with appropriate maps and diagrams has been shown to enhance their learning. . . . Concept or semantic mapping has promise of helping students acquire the interrelationships component of a knowledge domain" (Andre, 1997, p. 253).
   - "Provide and teach a checklist" (Rosenshine, 1997, n.p.).

First Principle: Demonstration (Don't just tell me, show me!)

1. Does the instruction demonstrate (show examples of) what is to be learned, rather than merely telling information about what is to be learned?
   - "Replace some practice problems with worked examples" (Clark & Mayer, 2003, p. 177).
   - "[E]xamples in teaching concepts, principles, and problem-solving procedures [result in] substantial benefits . . . presenting learners with worked-out examples . . . led to more effective learning" (Andre, 1997, p. 255).
2. Are the demonstrations (examples) consistent with the content being taught?
   - Are there examples and nonexamples for kinds-of (concepts)?
   - "New concepts should be taught by providing a definition of the concept, examples from the work environment, and practice exercises in which learners are asked to correctly classify many different work-relevant concept examples. If new concepts are presented with these supports, learning of concepts is enhanced. If highly novel applications of the concept are required, then provide practice on many different novel examples of the concept" (Clark, 2003, p. 24).
   - "In teaching concepts or classification skills, it is important to provide students with a range of examples of particular concepts and also to provide contrasts between examples of closely related concepts" (Andre, 1997, p. 256).
   - "[I]nstruction should activate misconceptions and then induce learners to be in a state of disequilibrium or dissatisfaction about the misconception" (Andre, 1997, p. 257). Note that one role of nonexamples is to allow students to see where the information does not apply or where they may have mistakenly thought it applied when it does not. This principle is an elaboration of the examples and nonexamples prescription.
   - Are there demonstrations for how-to (procedures)?
   - "When teaching procedures, the more that instruction is based on expert-based descriptions of the sequence of actions and decisions necessary for goal achievement, and is accompanied by a worked example and the opportunity for part-whole practice that is scaffolded to reflect the learner's prior knowledge and accompanied by a conceptual elaboration of the declarative knowledge base supporting the procedure, the more effective will be the learning and transfer of the procedure back to the job environment" (Clark, 2003, p. 30).

- Are there visualizations for what-happens (processes)?
- "When designing instruction for a process (how something works), give students a clear narrative description integrated with a visual model of the sequence of events that characterize the process, and describe each stage in the process and what key events or actions occur at each stage to produce a change that leads to the next stage" (Clark, 2003, p. 26).
- "When teaching causal principles, the more that the instructional presentation provides a statement about the cause and resulting effects, provides instruction using a worked, prototypical example drawn from the application setting, and helps the learner to first elaborate the elements and sequence of the causal chain and then to apply it to gradually more novel and complex examples, the more effective will be the learning and transfer to the job" (Clark, 2003, p. 28).

3. Are some of the following learner guidance techniques employed?
   - Is the learner's attention directed to relevant information?
   - "People learn better from narrated animations when the narration highlights the key steps and the links between them" (Mayer, 2003, p. 47).
   - "Presenting students with explicit guidance in identifying similarities and differences enhances students' understanding of and ability to use knowledge" (Marzano et al., 2001, p. 15).
   - Asking students to independently identify similarities and differences enhances students' understanding of and ability to use knowledge" (Marzano et al., 2001, p. 15).
   - "[U]se of signaling devices generally has positive effects on memory for the presented information" (Andre, 1997, p. 255).
   - Are multiple representations included and explicitly compared?
   - "Visual representation of text material is helpful in improving comprehension of complex material" (Dembo & Junge, 2003, p. 60).
   - "People learn better from corresponding words and graphics (e.g., animation, video, illustrations, pictures) than from words alone" (Clark & Mayer, 2003, p. 51).
   - "The more we use both systems of representation—linguistic and nonlinguistic [graphic]—the better we are able to think about and recall knowledge" (Marzano et al., 2001, p. 73).
   - "People learn better when corresponding words and graphics are placed near rather than far from each other on the screen" (Mayer, 2003, p. 49).
   - "People learn better when corresponding animation and narration segments are presented simultaneously" (Mayer, 2003, p. 51).
   - Are learners assisted to relate the new information to the structure that was recalled or provided?
   - "Teach learners to self-explain examples" (Clark & Mayer, 2003, p. 190). Note that if this self-explanation assists learners to relate the new information to previously learned information or the structure that was recalled or provided then it will facilitate learning.
   - "Make learners aware of their problem-solving processes" (Clark & Mayer, 2003, p. 260). Note that the processes that facilitate learning are those that help students relate previous knowledge to new knowledge or to the structure that was provided.
   - "[Use] a variety of structured tasks to guide students through generating and testing hypotheses" (Marzano et al., 2001, p. 106). Note that testing hypotheses is another way to relate specific cases to general information.
   - "[R]elating to-be-learned instructional events to preexisting knowledge . . . leads to superior learning and performance" (Andre, 1997, p. 250).
   - "Give clear and detailed instructions and explanations" (Rosenshine, 1997, n.p.).
4. Are the instructional media relevant to the content and used to enhance learning?
   - "Present words as speech rather than onscreen text" (Clark & Mayer, 2003, p. 86).
   - "People learn better from animation and narration than from animation, narration, and on-screen text" (Mayer, 2003, p. 45).
   - "Avoid presenting words as narration and identical text in the presence of graphics" (Clark & Mayer, 2003, p. 99).
   - "People learn better from narrated animations when the narration has a human voice with a standard accent rather than a machine voice or an accented voice" (Mayer, 2003, p. 53).
   - "People learn better from multimedia messages when extraneous words, pictures, and sounds are excluded rather than included" (Mayer, 2003, p. 33).
   - "Avoid e-lessons with extraneous sounds, . . . extraneous pictures, . . . extraneous graphics or . . . extraneous words" (Clark & Mayer, 2003, pp. 111–126).

First Principle: Application (Let me do it!)

1. Do learners have an opportunity to practice and apply their newly acquired knowledge or skill?

- "Critical tasks require more practice" (Clark & Mayer, 2003, p. 159).
- "Provide a high level of active practice for all students" (Rosenshine, 1997, n.p.).
- "Ask a large number of questions, check for student understanding, and obtain responses from all students" (Rosenshine, 1997, n.p.).

2. Are the application (practice) and assessment (tests) *consistent* with the stated or implied objectives?
   - Does "information-about" (factual information) practice require learners to recall or recognize information?
   - Does "parts-of" practice require learners to locate, name, and/or describe each part?
   - Does "kinds-of" (concept) practice require learners to identify new examples of each kind?
   - "Asking students to apply taught concepts to new examples facilitates students' acquisition or construction of the concept" (Andre, 1997, p. 251).
   - Does "how-to" (procedure) practice require learners to do the procedure?
   - Does "what-happens" (process) practice require learners to predict a consequence of a process given conditions, or to find faulted conditions given an unexpected consequence?
3. Is the practice followed by *corrective* feedback and an indication of progress, not just by right-wrong feedback?
   - "Effective feedback about learning progress results in better learning and transfer of such learning to the work environment" (Clark, 2003, p. 18).
   - "Feedback should be 'corrective' in nature. [S]imply telling students that their answer on a test is right or wrong has a negative effect on achievement. . . . The best feedback appears to involve an explanation as to what is accurate and what is inaccurate in terms of student responses" (Marzano et al., 2001, p. 96).
   - "Feedback should be specific to the criterion" (Marzano et al., 2001, p. 98).
   - "Provision of [feedback] typically results in superior performance on later tests than no [feedback] and providing the correct response is usually more effective than simply saying right or wrong" (Andre, 1997, p. 259).
   - "Provide systematic feedback and corrections" (Rosenshine, 1997, n.p.).
4. Does the application or practice enable learners to access context sensitive help or provide *coaching* when they are having difficulty in solving the problem or doing the task? Is coaching gradually diminished with each subsequent task until learners are performing on their own?
   - "Use onscreen coaches to promote learning" (Clark & Mayer, 2003, p. 138).
   - "Guide students during initial practice. . . . Provide procedural prompts or facilitators. . . . Provide models of the appropriate responses. . . . Think aloud as choices are being made. . . . Anticipate and discuss potential difficulties. . . . Regulate the difficulty of the material. . . . Provide a cue card" (Rosenshine, 1997, n.p.).
   - "When teaching higher-level tasks, support students by providing them with cognitive strategies. . . . Help students learn to use the cognitive strategies by providing them with procedural prompts and modeling the use of these procedural prompts" (Rosenshine, 1997, n.p.).
   - "Increase student responsibilities" (Rosenshine, 1997, n.p.).
5. Does the instruction require learners to use their new knowledge or skill to solve a varied sequence of problems or complete a varied sequence of tasks?
   - "Use a variety of structured tasks" (Marzano et al., 2001, p. 106).

First Principle: Integration (Watch me!)

1. Does the instruction provide techniques that encourage learners to integrate (transfer) the new knowledge or skill into their everyday life?
2. Does the instruction provide an opportunity for learners to publicly demonstrate their new knowledge or skill?
3. Does the instruction provide an opportunity for learners to reflect on, discuss, and defend their new knowledge or skill?
   - "The process of explaining their thinking helps students deepen their understanding of the principles they are applying" (Marzano et al., 2001, p. 105).
4. Does the instruction provide an opportunity for learners to create, invent, or explore new and personal ways to use their new knowledge or skill?

Implementation

1. Does the instruction facilitate learner navigation through the learning task?
   - "Use links sparingly to augment the lesson" (Clark & Mayer, 2003, p. 239). Note that too many links may lose the learner in hyperspace and make it difficult to navigate through the primary lesson material.
   - "Allow learners to control pacing" (Clark & Mayer, 2003, p. 240).
   - "Use course maps to provide an overview and orient learners" (Clark & Mayer, 2003, p. 241).
   - "Provide navigation options on all screens" (Clark & Mayer, 2003, p. 241).
   - "Make important instructional events the default navigation option" (Clark & Mayer, 2003, p. 236).

2. Is the degree of learner control appropriate for the learning goals and your learners?
   - "Use learner control for learners with high prior knowledge or high metacognitive skills" (Clark & Mayer, 2003, p. 234).
   - "Add advisement to learner control" (Clark & Mayer, 2003, p. 238).
   - "As the extent of learner control increases, learning decreases except for a very small number of the most advanced expert learners" (Clark, 2003, p. 14).
3. Is collaboration used effectively?
   - "Make assignments that require collaboration among learners" (Clark & Mayer, 2003, p. 207).
   - Assign learners to heterogeneous groups" (Clark & Mayer, 2003, p. 208).
   - "Organizing groups based on ability levels should be done sparingly" (Marzano et al., 2001, p. 87).
   - "Structure group assignments around products or processes" (Clark & Mayer, 2003, p. 208).
   - "Cooperative groups should be kept rather small [3 or 4 members] in size" (Marzano et al., 2001, p. 88).
4. Is the instruction personalized?
   - "People learn better from multimedia lessons when the words are in conversational style rather than formal style" (Mayer, 2003, p. 39).
   - "Use conversational rather than formal style" (Clark & Mayer, 2003, p. 133).

Learner Understanding of the Structure of What Is to Be Learned

As one reviews the four-phase instructional cycle and related principles described in this chapter, it is interesting to note the importance that is placed on learner understanding of the *structure* of what is to be learned. Indeed, several researchers have pointed to the importance of this principle. For example, Marzano et al. (2001) state, "In general, research has demonstrated that making students aware of specific structure in information helps them summarize that information [and subsequently be able to remember and use this information more effectively]" (p. 32).

How is learner understanding of the structure of what is to be learned related to each of the four phases of the instructional cycle? During the activation phase first principles prescribe that students should be encouraged to recall relevant knowledge or skills, or the instruction should provide an organizing structure based on what students already know. This structure should then be used to facilitate the acquisition of the new knowledge. Later, during the demonstration phase, first principles suggest that *guidance* can be used to help students relate the new material to the structure provided during the activation phase.

During the application phase, *coaching* can help students use this structure to facilitate their application activities. Finally, during the integration phase, first principles indicate that students should be guided to summarize what they have learned and *reflect* on how the new knowledge is related to what they previously knew via the structure that was recalled or provided. This focus throughout the four-phase instructional cycle on learner understanding of the structure of what is to be learned deserves more study and research.

Conclusion

It would appear from the limited sources quoted in this chapter that first principles are not only common to and prescribed by many instructional design theories and models, but that they are also consistent with empirical research on instruction. It is hoped that as instructional design matures that this set of first principles can form a foundation on which future instructional design models and prescriptions can build. These principles are deliberately general and their implementation can take many forms. These principles do not require the adoption of any particular philosophical "-ism." First principles can be found in some form in almost all instructional design theories and models. We have not identified any principles that are contrary to these first principles. And yet, with this general agreement on fundamental foundational principles of instruction, many of the instructional products we have reviewed fail to implement even the first level of these principles; i.e., these products often fail to provide sufficient demonstration of worked examples, often fail to provide appropriate practice beyond remember-what-you-were-told questions, and seldom are centered in real-world problems. Few instructional products implement the activation and integration phases. Even fewer instructional products implement the next level of first principles by providing demonstrations and practice that are consistent with a variety of different instructional outcomes. Moreover, almost none of the products we have reviewed involve an emphasis on learner understanding of the structure of what is to be learned. If these *are* the first principles of instruction, let's hope that they will become more widely applied, thereby resulting in instruction that is more effective, efficient, and appealing.

Study Guide for First Principles of Instruction

For an overview of the First Principles of Instruction:

Merrill, M. D. (2002). First principles of instruction. *Educational Technology Research and Development, 50*(3), 43–59.

Merrill, M. D. (2002). A pebble-in-the-pond model for instructional design. *Performance Improvement, 41*(7), 39–44.

McCarthy, B. (1996). *About learning*. Barrrington, IL: Excel.

The following text is perhaps the best advanced presentation of an instructional design model consistent with the First Principles of Instruction:

van Merriënboer, Jeroen J. G. (1997). *Training complex cognitive skills: A four-component instructional design model for technical training*. Englewood Cliffs, NJ: Educational Technology Publications.

Application Questions

1. Assume you are trying to teach sixth-grade students to add fractions (or choose another learning task). Briefly describe how you would apply each of the first principles in this situation.
2. Find and read a reference that describes Gagné's Nine Events of Instruction. Then create a table or chart that compares and contrasts those events with the first principles described in this chapter.
3. Merrill contrasts the problem-centered approach described in this chapter with what he describes as "problem-based approaches in which students are placed in collaborative groups, given resources and a problem, and left to construct their own solution for the problem." Find and read a reference that describes problem-based learning. Then prepare a paper in which you compare and contrast the two approaches (problem centered and problem based). Indicate which approach you feel is more likely to support student learning and provide a rationale for your position.
4. Select a textbook chapter that clearly indicates the skill(s) that the chapter is intended to help students learn. Examine that chapter in light of the first principles, and write a brief report describing the extent to which the various principles are adhered to in the chapter. Provide examples to support the points that you make.

References

Andre, T. (1997). Selected microinstructional methods to facilitate knowledge construction: Implications for instructional design. In R. D. Tennyson, F. Schott, N. Seel, & S. Dijkstra (Eds.), *Instructional design: International perspective* (Vol. 1, pp. 243–267). Mahwah NJ: Lawrence Erlbaum Associates.

Clark, R. C., & Mayer, R. E. (2003). *E-learning and the science of instruction*. San Francisco: Jossey-Bass/Pfeiffer.

Clark, R. E. (2003). What works in distance learning: Instructional strategies. In H. F. O'Neil (Ed.), *What works in distance learning* (pp. 13–31). Los Angeles: Center for the Study of Evaluation.

Dembo, M., & Junge, L. G. (2003). What works in distance learning: Learning strategies. In H. F. O'Neil (Ed.), *What works in distance learning*. Los Angeles: Center for the Study of Evaluation.

Gagné, R. M. (1985). *The conditions of learning and theory of instruction* (4th ed.). New York: Holt, Rinehart & Winston.

Marzano, R. J., Pickering, D. J., & Pollock, J. E. (2001). *Classroom instruction that works: Research-based strategies for increasing student achievement*. Alexandria, VA: Association for Supervision and Curriculum Development.

Mayer, R. E. (2003). What works in distance learning: Multimedia. In H. F. O'Neil (Ed.), *What works in distance learning* (pp. 32–54). Los Angeles: Center for the Study of Evaluation.

Merrill, M. D. (1994). *Instructional design theory.* Englewood Cliffs, NJ: Educational Technology Publications.

Merrill, M. D. (2002a). First principles of instruction. *Educational Technology Research & Development, 50*(3), 43–59.

Merrill, M. D. (2002b). A pebble-in-the-pond model for instructional design. *Performance Improvement, 41*(7), 39–44.

Rosenshine, B. (1997). Advances in research on instruction. In E. J. Lloyd, E. J. Kameanui, & D. Chard (Eds.), *Issues in educating students with disabilities* (pp. 197–221). Mahwah, NJ: Lawrence Erlbaum Associates. Retrieved January 22, 2006, from http://eppa.asu.edu/barak/barak.html

Jeroen J. G. van Merriënboer
Open University of the Netherlands

CHAPTER 8

Alternate Models of Instructional Design: Holistic Design Approaches and Complex Learning

Knowledge and Comprehension Questions

1. Define what is meant by the term *complex learning* and discuss why the interest in promoting this type of learning has increased in recent years.
2. Identify a key goal of holistic design models and briefly describe the three problems these models are designed to overcome.
3. Discuss how each of the following approaches attempt to overcome one of the three problems you identified in response to question 2:
   a. Whole-task approach
   b. Scaffolding
   c. Mathemagenic methods
4. Breifly describe each of the four components of the 4C/ID-model.

Editors' Introduction

At the conclusion of the previous chapter, David Merrill indicated that Jeroen van Merriënboer's four-component instructional design (4C/ID) model is one instructional design model that is consistent with the First Principles of Instruction. In this chapter, van Merriënboer presents this model as an example of what he calls *holistic* instructional design models.

Van Merriënboer argues that traditional instructional design models, in which complex tasks are reduced into simple elements, are not well suited for designing instruction that enables learners to perform complex learning tasks. He indicates that in current-day society it is becoming increasingly important for humans to perform such tasks, and posits that *holistic* instructional design models are much better suited to enable them to do so. According to van Merriënboer, the key features of holistic design models are (1) a focus on *meaningful, whole learning tasks,* (2) the use of *scaffolding* to help learners coordinate different aspects of the whole tasks, and (3) the employment of *mathemagenic methods* to support the transfer of learning. He discusses each of these features in detail, and he concludes the chapter by discussing his own holistic design model, the 4C/ID-model.

Complex learning aims at the integration of knowledge, skills, and attitudes; the coordination of qualitatively different constituent skills; and the transfer of what is learned to daily life or work settings. The current interest in complex learning is manifest in popular educational approaches such as project-based education, the case method, problem-based learning, and competence-based learning; and in theoretical models for instructional design such as 4-Mat by McCarthy (1996), cognitive apprenticeship learning by Collins, Brown, and Newman (1989), collaborative problem solving by Nelson (1999), constructivist learning environments by Jonassen (1999), instructional episodes by Andre (1997), learning by doing by Schank (Schank, Berman, & MacPerson, 1999), multiple approaches to understanding by Gardner (1999), and star legacy by the Vanderbilt Learning Technology Center (Schwartz, Lin, Brophy, & Bransford, 1999). What these approaches have in common is their focus on authentic learning tasks that are based on real-life tasks as the driving force for learning (Merrill, 2002; Reigeluth, 1999; van Merriënboer & Kirschner, 2001).

It would be wrong to view the current interest in complex learning as a whim of fashion. It is an inevitable reaction to societal and technological developments as well as to students' and employers' uncompromising views about the worth of education. Due to new technologies, routine tasks are being taken over by machines, and complex cognitive tasks that must be performed by humans are becoming increasingly important. Moreover, jobs are rapidly changing and information quickly becomes obsolete. This poses higher demands on the workforce—and employers stress the importance of problem solving, reasoning, and creativity. This should allow employees to flexibly adjust to the rapidly changing environment. For instance, many aspects of the job of an air traffic controller have been technically automated over the last decade, but nevertheless the complexity is greater than ever before due to the enormous increase in air traffic, the amount of safety regulations, and the advances in technical aids. The same is true for modern medical doctors, who not only need to care about physical, psychological, and social aspects of their pateients, but who are also confronted with a much more varied list of clients with different cultural backgrounds, a flood of new medicines and treatments, and issues dealing with registration, liability, insurances, and so forth.

The field of education and training is very conscious of the new demands posed by society, business, and industry. There are many attempts to better prepare students for the labor market, which becomes manifest in educational approaches that stress complex learning and the development of professional competences throughout the curriculum. But educational institutions lack proven design approaches, and thus innovations aimed at better preparing students for the labor market have met with varying success. A common complaint of students is that they experience the curriculum as a disconnected set of courses, with implicit relationships between courses and unclear relevance to their future profession. Students have difficulties integrating the things they learn into an integrated knowledge base and employing this after their study to solve new problems in their work and daily life.

Future instructional design theory should support the development of training programs for students who need to learn and transfer professional competences or complex cognitive skills to an increasingly varied set of real-world contexts and settings. The basic claim of this chapter is that a holistic design approach may help to reach this goal. In a traditional *atomistic* approach, complex contents and tasks are reduced into simpler elements. Reduction continues up to a level where the elements can be transferred to the learners through presentation and/or practice. This approach works well if there are few interactions among the elements. But, according to a holistic approach, it does not work well if the elements are interrelated to each other. Then, the whole is *more* than the sum of its parts. *Holistic* design approaches basically try to deal with complexity without losing sight of the relationships among elements.

Holistic approaches should at least offer a solution for three highly persistent problems in the field of education—compartmentalization, fragmentation, and the transfer paradox. This chapter first discusses the undesirable compartmentalization of learning into a cognitive, psychomotor and affective domain. *Whole tasks*, which are based on real-life tasks and aim at the development of professional competences, are presented as a way to reach integration. Second, it discusses the fragmentation of instruction in small elements that correspond with low-level objectives. The *scaffolding* of whole-task performance prevents piecemeal instruction and helps learners to coordinate integrated objectives. Third, the transfer paradox is described, indicating that instructional methods that are most effective to reach specified objectives are often ineffective to reach transfer of learning. Instead, *mathemagenic methods* should help students to mindfully abstract away from their concrete experiences and allow for transfer performances that go beyond a limited list of objectives. The four-component instructional design (4C/ID) model (van Merriënboer, 1997; van Merriënboer, Clark, & de Croock, 2002; van Merriënboer, Jelsma, & Paas, 1992) is briefly described to illustrate the holistic design approach. The chapter ends with some general conclusions.

Whole Tasks: From KS&A to Professional Competences

Traditional instructional design models typically focus on one particular domain of learning, such as the cognitive, psychomotor, or affective domain (Bloom, 1956), which roughly corresponds with the triplet Knowledge, Skills, and Attitudes (KS&A). Another common distinction in the cognitive domain is between models for declarative learning, with an emphasis on instructional methods for the construction of conceptual knowledge, and models for procedural learning, with an emphasis on methods for the acquisition of intellectual skills (Clark, 1989). This compartmentalization has had undesirable effects on, especially, the field of vocational and professional education. Imagine that you have to undergo surgery. Would you prefer a surgeon with great technical skills but with no knowledge of the human body? Or a surgeon with great knowledge of the human body but with 10 thumbs? Or one with great technical skills but a hostile attitude towards her patients? These questions clearly indicate that it makes little sense to distinguish domains of learning when we are primarily interested in real-life performance. Many complex surgical skills simply cannot be performed without an in-depth knowledge of the structure and working of the human body, because such knowledge allows for the necessary flexibility in behavior. And many skills cannot be performed in a socially and professionally acceptable fashion if the performer does not exhibit particular attitudes.

Holistic design models for complex learning therefore aim at the integration of declarative learning, procedural learning (including perceptual and psychomotor skills), and affective learning. Many superordinate terms that encompass KS&A have been proposed in the literature, including *expertise, complex skills*, and (professional) *competences*. With regard to *expertise*, which is probably the oldest of the three terms, most authors (e.g., Chi, Glaser, & Farr, 1988; Sternberg, 1995) agree on three basic characteristics. First, expertise covers declarative, procedural, and conditional knowledge that is related to a specific task domain. Second, it includes the use of automated routines that allow an expert to solve familiar aspects of problems fast and with few errors. And third, it refers to the metacognitive knowledge necessary to monitor and regulate task-related activities in the domain. Furthermore, it should be noted that expertise only seems to exist if colleagues in the professional peer group acknowledge it. While "expertise" may be developed and range from low to high, it is often associated with "expert performance" and reserved for professionals who are at least proficient in their domain.

With regard to *complex skills*, van Merriënboer (1997; see also van Merriënboer et al., 1992) provides an analysis that shares many features with the concept of expertise, but without the connotation of expert performance. In this analysis, complex skills contain both nonrecurrent aspects, which are defined as constituent skills that involve problem solving and reasoning, and recurrent aspects, which are defined as constituent skills that involve the straightforward use of procedures or the application of routines. Nonrecurrent constituent skills can only be performed thanks to the availability of rich, declarative knowledge structures that take the form of conceptual models (how a task domain is organized) and cognitive strategies (how to approach problems in the domain). To perform constituent skills in an acceptable fashion, the task performer must exhibit particular attitudes. Like conceptual models and cognitive strategies, those attitudes are treated as subordinate to, although fully integrated with, the constituent skills that together make up the complex skill. Concluding, the effective coordination of the different constituent skills involved in real-life task performance is of utmost importance and requires "reflective expertise"; that is, the ability to monitor one's own performance and to reflect on the quality of problem-solving processes and reached solutions.

At present, the most popular term to indicate the integration of KS&A is *competence*, including more specific terms such as social competence, learning competence, career or job-market competence, academic competence, professional competence, and so forth. On the basis of a comprehensive, analytical study on the concept of competence, van Merriënboer, van der Klink, and Hendriks (2002) conclude that three dimensions are basic to the use of this term. The first dimension is *integrativity*, and indicates that competence always combines, in a greater or lesser degree, KS&A as well as aptitudes of the task performer. The second dimension, *specificity*, indicates that a competence is always bound to a context that can be highly specific (e.g., a profession) or more general (e.g., a career). The third dimension, *durability*, indicates that a competence is more or less stable in spite of changes in tools, working methods, and technologies. A positioning of various types of competences on the three dimensions shows that professional competences can be seen as largely synonymous with complex skills, because both integrate KS&A; they are specific to the complex tasks that form part of a profession; and their durability is moderate due to continuous changes in technologies and tools.

The shift in focus from KS&A to professional competences or complex skills has important implications for instructional design. First, holistic models of instructional design need to describe final attainment levels in terms that avoid compartmentalization in different domains of learning. Qualitative descriptions of key problems that professionals encounter (Onstenk, 1999), competence maps (Stoof, Martens, van Merriënboer, & Bastiaens, 2002), and intertwined skill hierarchies (van Merriënboer, 1997) are examples of representations that try to reach this goal. Second, and most important, learners must be confronted with learning activities that encourage them to develop an integrated knowledge base—without separating skills, knowledge, and attitudes from each other. Most holistic models of instructional design try to reach this by the use of "whole," meaningful learning tasks that are based on real-life tasks (Merrill, 2002).

Scaffolding Whole-Task Performance: From Single to Integrated Objectives

Traditional design models analyze a learning domain in terms of distinct learning or performance objectives, after which instructional methods are selected for reaching each of the separate objectives. A rather old taxonomy of objectives that is still widely used was introduced by Bloom (1956). While Bloom described three independent taxonomies for the cognitive, psychomotor, and affective domains, the term *Bloom's taxonomy* is typically used to refer to his taxonomy for the cognitive domain, in which six types of performance objectives are distinguished: (1) knowledge; (2) comprehension; (3) application; (4) analysis; (5) synthesis; and (6) evaluation. Gagné (1985) introduced another widely used taxonomy for the cognitive domain. This taxonomy makes distinctions among verbal information, intellectual skills, cognitive strategies, attitudes, and psychomotor skills. The intellectual skills are at the heart of the taxonomy and include five subcategories: (1) discriminations; (2) concrete concepts; (3) defined concepts; (4) rules; and (5) higher-order rules. This taxonomy reflects the fact that some intellectual skills enable the performance of other higher-level skills. For instance, the ability to apply rules or procedures is prerequisite to the use of higher-order rules (i.e., problem solving). If you teach an intellectual skill, it is important to identify, in a "learning hierarchy," the lower-level skills that enable this skill. In teaching, one starts with the objectives for the skills lower in the hierarchy and successively works toward the objectives for the skills higher in the hierarchy.

The taxonomies of Bloom and Gagné inspired many authors to come up with alternative classifications of objectives. But a common premise is that different objectives can best be reached by the application of particular instructional methods (the "conditions of learning," Gagné, 1985). The optimal method is chosen for each objective; the objectives are usually taught one by one; and the general educational goal is believed to be met after all separate objectives have been taught. This often yields instruction that is fragmented and piecemeal. For instance, if complex skills are taught, each objective corresponds with one enabling or constituent skill, and sequencing the objectives naturally results in a part-task sequence. Thus, the learner is taught only one or a very limited number of constituent skills at the same time. New constituent skills are gradually added to practice, and—if at all—it is not until the end of the instruction that the learner has the opportunity to practice the whole complex skill. Obviously, part-task sequencing is a highly effective approach to simplification, because performing only one or a few constituent skills is much easier than performing all constituent skills simultaneously.

In the 1960s, Briggs and Naylor (1962; Naylor & Briggs, 1963) reported that a part-task approach is only suitable if very little coordination of constituent skills is required and if each of the separate constituent skills is difficult for the learners. In the early 1990s, authors in the field of instructional design also started to question the value of a part-task approach to reach "integrative" goals or objectives (e.g., Gagné & Merrill, 1990). For most complex skills or professional competencies, there are many interactions between the different aspects of task performance and their related goals—with extremely high demands on coordination. In a part-task approach, the different aspects are mostly taught in isolation. This makes it impossible to pay sufficient attention to the coordination of all aspects. Performing a particular constituent skill in isolation is simply different from performing it in the context of a whole task. It leads to different mental representations, and a constituent skill that has been learned in isolation can often not be properly performed in the context of the whole task (Elio, 1986). By now, there is overwhelming evidence that breaking a complex domain or task down in distinct elements or objectives and teaching those objectives without taking their interactions and required coordination into account does not often work because learners are not able to integrate and coordinate the elements in transfer situations (e.g., Clark & Estes, 1999; Perkins & Grotzer, 1997; Spector & Anderson, 2000).

Holistic design models replace a part-task with a whole-task paradigm, stressing the importance of integrated sets of objectives. For instance, imagine that a complex skill has some aspects that require problem solving (i.e., higher-order rules) and some aspects that require the application of procedures (i.e., rules). In a part-task approach, you would first teach the application of the rules, then the higher-order rules, and finally the top level-skill—with few opportunities for explicitly teaching the coordination of the problem-solving and procedural aspects of the whole task. In a whole-task approach, it is acknowledged that coordinating the—sometimes many—different constituent skills that make up complex performance is at least equally important as performing each constituent skill separately. In other words, the parts need to be coordinated and controlled by higher-level strategies from the beginning of the training program. Many of the constituent skills will make little sense without taking their context, that is, their related constituent skills and associated knowledge and attitudes, into account. Therefore, constituent skills can better be viewed as aspects of the complex skill than as its parts; this is also the reason that the term *constituent skill* is preferred to the older term *subskill*.

The paradigm shift from a part-task to a whole-task approach has important implications for instructional design. First, descriptions of final attainment levels should not only avoid compartmentalization in different domains of learning, but also should replace distinct objectives with highly integrated sets of objectives. In fact, single objectives should no longer function as a basis for the selection of instructional methods! Instead, instructional design decisions should be directly based on the results of a task analysis, which may take one of a variety of forms, such as a description of key problems that learners must be able to solve after the training, a competence map, or an intertwined skill hierarchy. Second, simplification should no longer be reached by partitioning the learning domain into small elements, but must be reached in another fashion. Scaffolding learners' performance offers an effective alternative. For instance, one might ensure that learners start their training with the simplest version of the whole task by creating all possible conditions that simplify the performance of the task. Or one might provide problem-solving support to help students to coordinate the different aspects of task performance.

Mathemagenic Methods: From Teaching for the Test to Teaching for Transfer

The use of a nonintegrated list of specific learning objectives as the basis for instructional design may lead not only to fragmented instruction, but also to low transfer of learning. This is related to the fact that often one objective corresponds with both one element of instruction and one test item. Logically, the designer will select instructional methods that minimize the "costs" to reach the objectives, that is, to make sure that learners will pass the test items that correspond with the objectives. *Costs* may refer to the necessary number of learning tasks, the time on the learning tasks, learners' investment of effort, and so forth. As an example, suppose that a troubleshooting task is trained where three types of malfunctions (m1, m2, m3) may occur in four different components of a technical system (c1, c2, c3, c4). If there are three objectives referring to the ability to diagnose the malfunctions m1, m2, and m3, the following training schedule fully practices the skills for troubleshooting one particular type of malfunction before the skills for troubleshooting the other types of malfunctions. Thus, it treats the objectives one by one:

m1c1, m1c2, m1c3, m1c4	(practice malfunction 1)
m2c1, m2c2, m2c3, m2c4	(practice malfunction 2)
m3c1, m3c2, m3c3, m3c4	(practice malfunction 3)

After the training, the students will typically be tested on their ability to troubleshoot malfunction 1, malfunction 2, and malfunction 3. Indeed, this practice schedule will be most efficient to reach the three objectives, and minimize the required time on task and the investment of effort from the students. However, it yields *low* transfer of learning! The reason for this is that the chosen instructional method invites students to construct highly specific knowledge for diagnosing each distinct malfunction, which only allows them to perform as specified in the objectives but not to show performances that go beyond the given objectives. If a designer aims at transfer of learning, and the objective is to train the students to diagnose as many malfunctions as possible in the technical system, it is better to practice troubleshooting the malfunctions in a randomized order, such as:

m2c1, m1c4, m3c1, m3c4, m2c4, m3c2, m1c1, m1c3, m1c2, m2c2, m3c3, m2c3

This practice schedule is less efficient than the previous one to reach the three separate objectives, because it increases the necessary time on task and the investment of effort by the learners (you may even need more learning tasks to reach the same level of performance for each objective). But every bit of these higher costs pays itself back in a *higher* transfer of learning! Thus, if a test item asks the learners to diagnose malfunction 1 in component 5 (i.e., a known malfunction in an unfamiliar component), malfunction 4 in component 1 (an unfamiliar malfunction in a known component), or even malfunction 5 in component 6 (an unfamiliar malfunction in an unfamiliar component), students who practiced in a random order do better on this transfer test than students who practice the malfunctions one by one (de Croock, van Merriënboer, & Paas, 1998; van Merriënboer, Schuurman, de Croock, & Paas, 2002). This is due to the fact that randomization sequences the learning tasks in such a way that they each require different solutions, stimulating students to construct general, abstract knowledge that eventually better allows them to diagnose new malfunctions they have not encountered before. The general phenomenon, that the best instructional methods to reach isolated, specific objectives are often different from the best instructional methods to reach integrated learning goals and transfer of learning, has been called the *transfer paradox* (van Merriënboer, de Croock, & Jelsma, 1997).

A holistic design approach takes the transfer paradox into account and always aims at learning goals that go beyond a limited list of highly specific objectives. In order to reach this, it is of utmost importance to identify which aspects of complex performance are identical between learning tasks and transfer tasks and which aspects may differ. The former aspects are called *recurrent constituent skills*; they can be developed into routines during the training that can also be applied when transfer tasks are performed. The latter aspects are called *nonrecurrent constituent skills*; they involve problem solving and reasoning, and these aspects of transfer tasks can only be performed thanks to the availability of general, abstract knowledge (e.g., conceptual models, cognitive strategies) that can be interpreted in an unfamiliar situation to find an acceptable solution. The differentiation between different types of constituent skills should ensure that students who are confronted with transfer tasks have specific knowledge to perform the familiar aspects as well as general, abstract knowledge to perform the unfamiliar aspects of those tasks.

Most importantly, the development of this general, abstract knowledge requires the use of mathemagenic instructional methods that "give birth to learning," as opposed to methods that aim at reaching specific objectives with lowest possible costs. The random sequencing of learning tasks as described is only one example of a mathemagenic method. Another example of a powerful method pertains to variability of practice, indicating that learning tasks must differ from each other on all dimensions that also differ in the real word, such as the conditions under which the tasks are performed, the way they are presented, the saliency of their defining characteristics, and their familiarity (Quilici & Mayer, 1996; Sweller, van Merriënboer, & Paas, 1998). As a final example, leading questions that are sprinkled throughout a learning task may help students to mindfully abstract away from the given information and reach a more general understanding.

The Four-Component Instructional Design Model

An example of a holistic design model that has been developed over the last decade is the 4C/ID-model (van Merriënboer, 1997; van Merriënboer, Clark, & de Croock, 2002; van Merriënboer et al., 1992). This model describes the final attainment level of a training program in an intertwined skill hierarchy. Such a hierarchy interrelates all recurrent and nonrecurrent constituent skills to each other, specifies the knowledge structures (e.g., conceptual models, cognitive strategies) that underlie the performance of those skills, and identifies the attitudes that must be exhibited for acceptable performance. *Learning tasks* are the first of the four components and are at the heart of the model (they are indicated as circles in Figure 8.1). To avoid compartmentalization, each learning task offers whole-task practice, meaning that it confronts the learner with all or most of the constituent skills, together with their associated knowledge and attitudes, that are important for real-life task performance.

It is clearly impossible to use very difficult learning tasks right from the start of a training program. A first solution offered by the 4C/ID-model to deal with complexity, while preventing fragmentation, is to let learners start their work on relatively simple learning tasks and progress towards more difficult tasks. There are categories of learning tasks or "task classes," each representing a version of the whole task with a particular level of difficulty. For instance, a training program for process operators may start with a task class in which they work on troubleshooting tasks in order to diagnose one malfunction, while a later task class may also contain tasks that require the diagnosis of *multiple* malfunctions. Learning tasks within a particular task class are always equivalent to each other in the sense that they can be performed on the basis of the same body of knowledge. The first task class contains learning tasks that are representative of the simplest tasks a professional might encounter in the real world. A more difficult task class requires more knowledge or more embellished knowledge for effective performance than the preceding, simpler task classes. In Figure 8.1, the learning tasks are organized in an ordered sequence of task classes (i.e., the dotted boxes) that represent simple-to-difficult versions of the whole task.

A second solution offered by the 4C/ID-model to deal with complexity is giving learners guidance and support—especially when they start to work on a new, more complex task class. This support diminishes in a process of scaffolding as learners acquire more expertise. There are many types of support and guidance specified by the 4C/ID-model. One highly effective type of scaffolding is known as the "completion strategy" (van Merriënboer, Kirschner, & Kester, 2003) and works from case studies to conventional tasks. Highest support is then provided by a case study; for instance, one can present the learners a real-life problem together with an acceptable solution. They must carefully study and evaluate the given solution on its strong and weak points. Intermediate support might be provided by an incomplete case study or "completion problem," which

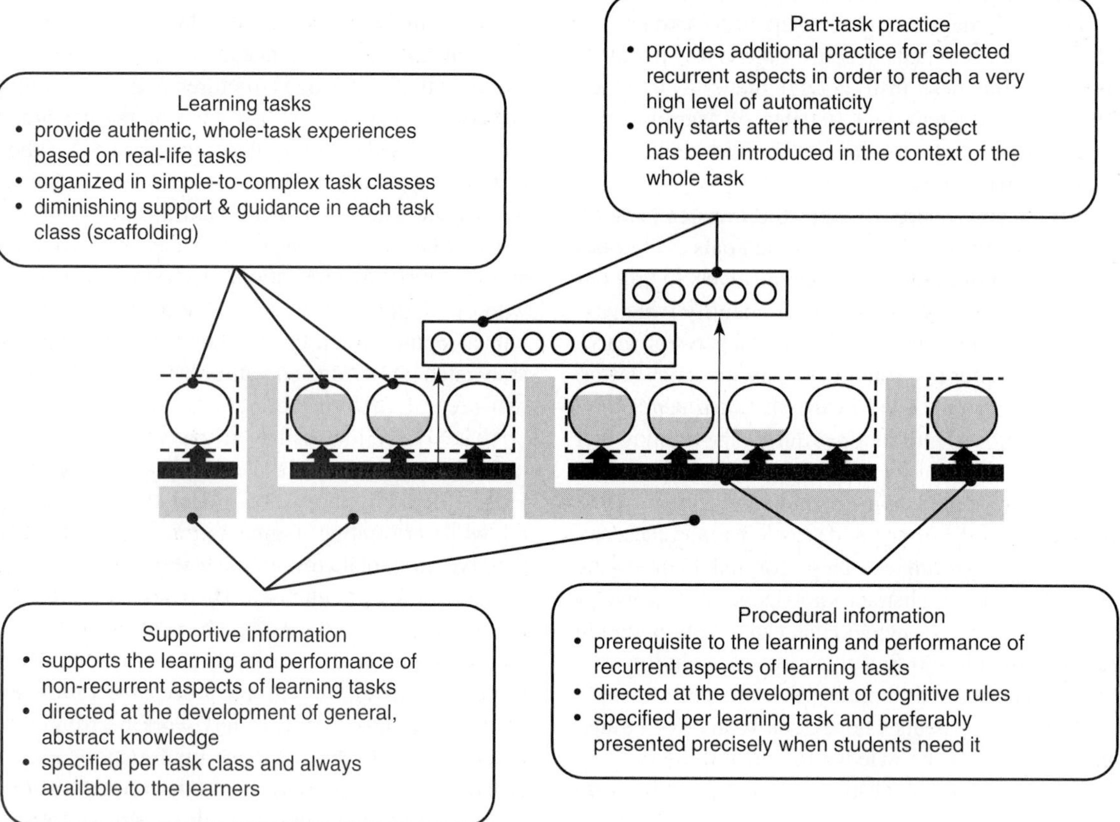

FIGURE 8.1 Schematic representation of a training blueprint showing the four components: (1) learning tasks, (2) supportive information, (3) procedural information, and (4) part-task practice.
Source: From "Blueprints for Complex Learning: The 4C/ID-Model," by J. J. G. van Merriënboer, R. E. Clark, and M. B. M. de Crook, 2002, *Educational Technology, Research & Development, 50*(2), pp. 39–64. Copyright 2002 by ETRD. Reprinted by permission.

presents a problem and a partial solution that learners must complete. Finally, no support is given by a conventional task, for which learners have to perform all actions by themselves. In Figure 8.1, each task class starts with one or more learning tasks with a high level of guidance (indicated by the filling of the circles), continues with learning tasks with a lower level of guidance, and ends with conventional tasks without guidance.

To deal with the transfer paradox, the 4C/ID-model makes a distinction between supportive and procedural information. *Supportive information* is the second design component and is particularly important for learning nonrecurrent constituent skills, that is, those aspects of performance that require problem solving and reasoning. It explains to the learners how a learning domain is organized and how to approach problems in this domain. It provides a bridge between what learners already know and what they need to know to fruitfully work on the learning tasks within the same task class (i.e., equivalent learning tasks that can be performed on the basis of the same body of knowledge). Mathemagenic methods should stimulate learners to develop general, abstract knowledge that allows for transfer of learning. For this reason, learning tasks within the same task class should exhibit a high level of variability and learners are encouraged to deeply process new supportive information, in particular, by connecting it in a process of elaboration to what they already know. Because supportive information is relevant to all learning tasks within the same task class, it is typically presented before learners start to work on a particular task class and kept available for them during their work on this class. For instance, before process operators start to work on troubleshooting tasks that require them to diagnose multiple malfunctions, they may study causal models that describe how particular types of malfunctions mutually influence each other and so affect the behavior of the whole technical system. In Figure 8.1, the L-shaped shaded areas depict the supportive information.

Procedural information is the third design component and is particularly important for learning recurrent constituent skills. It specifies to the learners how to perform the routine aspects of learning tasks. It preferably takes the form of directive, step-by-step instruction that is given by an instructor, a job aid, a quick reference guide, and so forth. Instructional methods for the presentation of procedural information should help learners to develop highly specific knowledge. Because procedural information is relevant to the routine aspects of learning tasks, it is best presented to learners when they first need it to perform a task (i.e., "just in time") and then quickly faded away for subsequent learning tasks. For instance, when process operators work on their first troubleshooting tasks that require them to diagnose malfunctions, it is best to tell them how to operate particular controls precisely when they need it. In Figure 8.1, the dark gray beam with upward pointing arrows linked to the separate learning tasks depicts the procedural information.

Finally, the shift from a part-task to a whole-task paradigm may make it necessary to include additional *part-task practice* in a training program, which is the fourth design component. If a very high level of automaticity is desired for particular recurrent aspects, the series of learning tasks may not provide enough repetition to reach this level. For those aspects, additional part-task practice may be provided—such as children drilling multiplication tables, musicians practicing musical scales, or process operators learning to recognize dangerous situations from the displays in a control room. Part-task practice for a particular recurrent aspect only starts after this aspect has been introduced in a meaningful, whole learning task, so that the learners start their practice in a fruitful cognitive context. In Figure 8.1, part-task practice is indicated by the series of small circles representing practice items for a selected recurrent constituent skill.

Conclusion

In this chapter we have discussed the current shift from atomistic to holistic models of instructional design. Three issues characterize this shift. First, the compartmentalization of learning into cognitive, psychomotor, and affective domains is questioned. The use of whole learning tasks is promoted to stimulate learners to integrate KS&A and to develop professional competences. Second, the fragmentation of educational programs into highly specific objectives and small pieces of instruction is rejected. Instead, learners' whole-task performance is scaffolded so that they can learn to coordinate integrated sets of objectives. Third, the transfer paradox is taken into account by employing mathemagenic instructional methods explicitly aimed at the development of more general, abstract knowledge that should allow learners to perform unfamiliar aspects of transfer tasks.

The main ideas of the 4C/ID-model were briefly presented to illustrate the holistic approach. The most important characteristic of the 4C/ID-model, as well as most other holistic models, is that the reduction of complex learning domains and complex tasks into small elements is rejected as the "regular" approach to deal with complexity. If it is done at all, reduction is only a last resort. "Modeling the model" is a viable alternative to deal with complexity (Achtenhagen, 2001). In this two-step approach, simple-to-complex models of reality or real-life tasks are developed first. Here, it is essential that even the simplest models are yet powerful enough to give learners a truthful impression of the learning domain. In the 4C/ID-model, this is mainly reached by the specification of a sequence of task classes, where—if possible at all—the first task class contains learning tasks that are representative for the simplest tasks that professionals encounter in the real world. As the second step, the models are modeled from a pedagogical perspective. In this step, it is essential to identify sound instructional methods to convey the models to the learners. In the 4C/ID-model, methods for providing support and guidance as well as methods for the presentation of supportive and procedural information help learners to construct their own *mental* models that eventually allow them to perform real-life tasks.

The development of holistic instructional design models such as the 4C/ID-model can be seen as a reaction to societal and technological developments. Their application should better prepare learners for a society in which more and more routine tasks are taken over by machines, in which information quickly becomes obsolete, and in which jobs are quickly changing. These alternate models offer new approaches to deal with complexity in learning, but should at the same time meet good old-fashioned standards of instructional design.[1] For instance, alternate models should still be systematic and help to make design processes more time and cost effective. They should be precise and consistent, offering the possibility to develop computer-based systems and tools that sustain design processes by techically automating the routine aspects of those processes and providing online help for other aspects (e.g., de Croock, Paas, Schlanbusch, & van Merriënboer, 2002). And last but not least, they must be based on sound experimental research. Evidence-based instructional procedures are too often missing in the field of education, but are badly needed to develop instructional design models capable of making a real difference to educational practice.

[1] See http://www.enovateas.com for computer-based ID tools based on the 4C/ID-model.

Application Questions

1. Some of the pioneers in the instructional design field recognized the need for holistic design models. Find and read the article by Gagné and Merrill (1990) that appears in the References for this chapter. Then discuss how the approach described in that article is similar to, and different from, the key features of the holistic design models described in the chapter.
2. Identify a complex learning task. Briefly describe how you might use the whole-task approach, scaffolding, and mathemagenic methods to help students learn to perform that task.

References

Achtenhagen, F. (2001). Criteria for the development of complex teaching–learning environments. *Instructional Science, 29*(4–5), 361–380.

Andre, T. (1997). Selected micro-instructional methods to facilitate knowledge construction: Implications for instructional design. In R. D. Tennyson, F. Schott, N. Seel, & S. Dijkstra (Eds.), *Instructional design—International perspectives: Theory, research, and models* (Vol. 1, pp. 243–267). Mahwah, NJ: Lawrence Erlbaum Associates.

Bloom, B. S. (1956). *Taxonomy of educational objectives: Cognitive domain.* New York: David McKay.

Briggs, G. E., & Naylor, J. C. (1962). The relative efficiency of several training methods as a function of transfer task complexity. *Journal of Experimental Psychology, 64*(5), 505–512.

Chi, M. T. H., Glaser, R., & Farr, M. J. (1988). *The nature of expertise*. Hillsdale, NJ: Lawrence Erlbaum Associates.

Clark, R. E. (1989). Current progress and future directions for research in instructional technology. *Educational Technology, Research & Development, 37*(1), 57–66.

Clark, R. E., & Estes, F. (1999). The development of authentic educational technologies. *Educational Technology, 39*(2), 5–16.

Collins, A., Brown, J. S., & Newman, S. E. (1989). Cognitive apprenticeship: Teaching the craft of reading, writing and mathematics. In L. B. Resnick (Ed.), *Knowing, learning, and instruction: Essays in honor of Robert Glaser* (pp. 453–493). Hillsdale, NJ: Lawrence Erlbaum Associates.

De Croock, M. B. M., Paas, F., Schlanbusch, H., & van Merriënboer, J. J. G. (2002). ADAPTit: Instructional Design (ID) tools for training design and evaluation. *Educational Technology, Research & Development, 50*(4), 47–58.

De Croock, M. B. M., van Merriënboer, J. J. G., & Paas, F. G. W. C. (1998). High vs. low contextual interference in simulation-based training of troubleshooting skills: Effects on transfer performance and invested mental effort. *Computers in Human Behavior, 14*(2), 249–267.

Elio, R. (1986). Representation of similar well-learned cognitive procedures. *Cognitive Science, 10*(1), 41–73.

Gagné, R. M. (1985). *The conditions of learning* (4th ed.). New York: Holt, Rinehart & Winston.

Gagné, R. M., & Merrill, M. D. (1990). Integrative goals for instructional design. *Educational Technology, Research & Development, 38*(1), 23–30.

Gardner, H. (1999). Multiple approaches to understanding. In C. M. Reigeluth (Ed.), *Instructional design theories and models: A new paradigm of instructional theory* (Vol. 2, pp. 69–89). Mahwah, NJ: Lawrence Erlbaum Associates.

Jonassen, D. H. (1999). Designing constructivist learning environments. In C. M. Reigeluth (Ed.), *Instructional design theories and models: A new paradigm of instructional theory* (Vol. 2, pp. 215–239). Mahwah, NJ: Lawrence Erlbaum Associates.

McCarthy, B. (1996). *About learning*. Barrington, IL: Excel.

Merrill, M. D. (2002). First principles of instruction. *Educational Technology, Research & Development, 50*(3), 43–59.

Naylor, J. C., & Briggs, G. E. (1963). Effects of task complexity and task organization on the relative efficiency of part and whole training methods. *Journal of Experimental Psychology, 65*(3), 217–224.

Nelson, L. M. (1999). Collaborative problem solving. In C. M. Reigeluth (Ed.), *Instructional design theories and models: A new paradigm of instructional theory*

(Vol. 2, pp. 241–267). Mahwah, NJ: Lawrence Erlbaum Associates.

Onstenk, J. H. A. M. (1999). Het duale leertraject als krachtige leeromgeving. In K. Schlusmans (Ed.), *Competentiegerichte leeromgevingen* [Competence-based learning environments] (pp. 225–237). Utrecht, The Netherlands: Lemma.

Perkins, D. N., & Grotzer, T. A. (1997). Teaching intelligence. *American Psychologist, 52*(10), 1125–1133.

Quilici, J. L., & Mayer, R. E. (1996). The role of examples in how students learn to categorize statistics word problems. *Journal of Educational Psychology, 88*(1), 144–161.

Reigeluth, C. M. (Ed.) (1999). *Instructional design theories and models: A new paradigm of instructional theory* (Vol. 2). Mahwah, NJ: Lawrence Erlbaum Associates.

Schank, R. C., Berman, T. R., & MacPerson, K. A. (1999). Learning by doing. In C. M. Reigeluth (Ed.), *Instructional design theories and models: A new paradigm of instructional theory* (Vol. 2, pp. 161–181). Mahwah, NJ: Lawrence Erlbaum Associates.

Schwartz, D., Lin, X., Brophy, S., & Bransford, J. D. (1999). Toward the development of flexible adaptive instructional designs. In C. M. Reigeluth (Ed.), *Instructional design theories and models: A new paradigm of instructional theory* (Vol. 2, pp. 183–213). Mahwah, NJ: Lawrence Erlbaum Associates.

Spector, J. M., & Anderson, T. M. (2000). *Holistic and integrated perspectives on learning, technology, and instruction: Understanding complexity.* Mahwah, NJ: Lawrence Erlbaum Associates.

Sternberg, R. J. (1995). Expertise in complex problem solving: A comparison of alternative conceptions. In P. A. Frensch & J. Funnke (Eds.), *Complex problem solving: The European perspective* (pp. 295–321). Hillsdale, NJ: Lawrence Erlbaum Associates.

Stoof, A., Martens, R. L., van Merriënboer, J. J. G., & Bastiaens, T. J. (2002). The boundary approach of competence: A constructivist aid for understanding and using the concept of competence. *Human Resource Development Review, 1*(3), 345–365.

Sweller, J., van Merriënboer, J. J. G., & Paas, F. (1998). Cognitive architecture and instructional design. *Educational Psychology Review, 10*(3), 251–296.

Van Merriënboer, J. J. G. (1997). *Training complex cognitive skills.* Englewood Cliffs, NJ: Educational Technology Publications.

Van Merriënboer, J. J. G., Clark, R. E., & de Croock, M. B. M. (2002). Blueprints for complex learning: The 4C/ID-model. *Educational Technology, Research & Development, 50*(2), 39–64.

Van Merriënboer, J. J. G., de Croock, M. B. M., & Jelsma, O. (1997). The transfer paradox: Effects of contextual interference on retention and transfer performance of a complex cognitive skill. *Perceptual & Motor Skills, 84*(3), 784–786.

Van Merriënboer, J. J. G., Jelsma, O., & Paas, F. (1992). Training for reflective expertise: A four-component instructional design model for training complex cognitive skills. *Educational Technology, Research & Development, 40*(2), 23–43.

Van Merriënboer, J. J. G., & Kirschner, P. A. (2001). Three worlds of instructional design: State of the art and future directions. *Instructional Science, 29,* 429–441.

Van Merriënboer, J. J. G., Kirschner, P. A., & Kester, L. (2003). Taking the load off a learner's mind: Instructional design for complex learning. *Educational Psychologist, 38*(1), 5–13.

Van Merriënboer, J. J. G., Schuurman, J. G., de Croock, M. B. M., & Paas, F. G. W. C. (2002). Redirecting learners' attention during training: Effects on cognitive load, transfer test performance and training efficiency. *Learning and Instruction, 12*(1), 11–37.

Van Merriënboer, J. J. G., van der Klink, M. R., & Hendriks, M. (2002). *Competenties: Van complicaties tot compromis. Een studie in opdracht van de onderwijsraad* [Competences: From complications towards a compromise—A study under the authority of the National Educational Council]. Gravenhage, The Netherlands: Onderwijsraad.

John M. Keller
Florida State University

CHAPTER 9

Motivation and Performance

Knowledge and Comprehension Questions

1. To integrate motivation into instruction, instructional designers should look at three levels of motivation. Briefly explain each one.
2. Describe the three primary categories of influence on performance discussed in this chapter.
3. What is the difference between *intrinsic* and *extrinsic* motivation? Give three examples of each.
4. Why should instructional designers consider state and trait when developing instruction?
5. What is *authenticity* with respect to activity design? Give an example in your area that you would likely see in training or instruction.

Editors' Introduction

As is pointed out in this chapter, *motivation* refers to a person's desire to pursue a goal or perform a task. Because a person's motivation can be influenced by external events, and because motivation does influence learning and performance, instructional designers usually are concerned about how to motivate learners. In this chapter, John Keller answers six fundamental questions about motivation and the design of instruction.

This chapter also describes Keller's ARCS (Attention-Relevance-Confidence-Satisfaction) model of motivational design, which instructional designers frequently use to incorporate motivational tactics into instruction. The four categories of motivation described in the model are presented and the steps in the ARCS design process are displayed.

A concern for motivational design has been a growing trend in instructional design. Keller's 1979 article, "Motivation and Instructional Design: A Theoretical Perspective," described the lack of attention to motivation in the instructional design literature and introduced an approach for integrating motivation into models of learning environment design. At that time, there were only two well-known considerations of motivation in instructional design. The first and major one was application of contingencies of reinforcement to shape and sustain behavior. In this theoretical perspective, motivation was generally established by deprivation; that is, by assuming learners would have some perception of a need or desire that would be fulfilled by the rewards to be gained from learning. The other consideration was a principle embedded in Gagné's (1985) conditions of learning, which stated that it is necessary to gain students' attention before they will learn. Certainly there was a large existing psychological literature on motivation, but neither it nor the previously mentioned areas of research provided an adequate understanding of motivation to learn or how to integrate motivation into instructional design.

Following the publication of Keller's (1979) paper, there was a slow growth in interest in motivation and its integration into instructional and learning environment design, and in recent years it has grown exponentially. This has resulted from the work of people such as Wlodkowsky (1999), Brophy (1983, 1998), and the continued work of Keller (1987a, 1999a). These researchers have built holistic models of motivational influences in instruction and learning, and have developed principles and techniques that can be applied and tested for validity. Interest in motivation and learning has also been stimulated and supported by growing numbers of applied and theoretical studies (Small & Gluck, 1994; Means, Jonassen, & Dwyer, 1997).

Even though there has been this increased activity, it can still be difficult for an instructional design specialist to obtain a quick overview of this literature and its relevance. Consequently, we have formulated six questions that provide a structure for understanding the current situation, the major characteristics of motivation and motivational design, and trends in this area of activity.

Understanding Motivational Design: Six Questions

1. What do I need to know about motivation? Why should I have to know anything about it if my focus is on instructional design and technology?

Effective instructional design does not occur in a vacuum. Employers sometimes complain that instructional design and technology graduates who are well versed in the various authoring and graphics applications for designing computer-based and Web-based instruction often produce instruction that is pedestrian—if not actually boring—and not sufficiently effective. To produce high-quality products, instructional designers must be thoroughly grounded in the processes of both motivational and instructional design. Recognition of this is illustrated by several instructional design texts that now include a section on motivational design (e.g., Dick, Carey, & Carey, 2005; Smith & Ragan, 1999).

Another reason for developing competency in motivational design is the trend in our field to move from the perspective of instructional design to the broader perspective of human performance technology (HPT). From this perspective, instructional designers must understand and be able to identify all of the factors that influence human performance and to use a team approach in designing systems for improving performance. For example, training or education is only one influence on human performance. Also important are motivation, social climate, incentives, resources, leadership methods, and the consistency of all these things with organizational goals.

Within this new frame of reference, motivation is critical at three levels. The first is motivation to learn, second is motivation to work, and third is self-motivation. Motivation to learn, the primary focus of this chapter, refers to learners' internal characteristics combined with external tactics and environmental factors that stimulate and sustain learner motivation. To accomplish this requires knowledge of motivational principles, methods for analyzing learner motivation, and methods for designing relevant motivational tactics. This is critical because of the constantly growing amount of training and education that is occurring throughout an employee's career, even after graduating from a formal educational program. Motivation to work is similar to motivation to learn in that it refers to designing work environments that match external tactics and stimuli to the motivational characteristics of employees. However, there are substantial differences in the motivational dynamics in the two environments.

The remaining concern is with self-motivation, which has been formally studied, (McCombs, 1984), but primarily in school settings. However, this is changing. A current trend in the United States is for employees to take more personal responsibility for learning and development (Cusimano, 1995), which accompanies the development of knowledge management systems in many organizations. With the growing availability of the Internet, intranets, and electronic performance support systems, employees are being expected to build digital literacy (Glister, 1997) in order to use these systems effectively and to contribute to the development of corporate knowledge. Consequently, in addition to the importance of motivation to learn and to work, self-motivation for learning has acquired a new level of importance and instructional designers will benefit from having some knowledge of motivation at all three of these levels.

2. What is motivation (and what isn't it—what is it different from)? Most writers in this field of human performance development (Gilbert, 1978; Porter & Lawler, 1968; Rummler & Brache, 1990) identify three major categories of influence on performance. They can be classified as capability, opportunity, and motivation (Keller, 1999a). *Capability* refers to a person's knowledge, skills, and aptitudes, which determine what a person is able to do. *Opportunity* refers to resources and information that are necessary for a person to perform a task. These can include clear statements of goals, instructional content and tests that are matched to the goals, availability of tools and equipment, sufficient time to perform the task, and guidelines for performing the job. Finally, *motivation* refers to a person's desire to pursue a goal or perform a task, which is manifested by choice of goals and effort (persistence plus vigor) in pursuing the goal.

To design effective learning environments, or to develop holistic programs of human performance development, the instructional designer must understand and integrate all three of these influences in relation to their influences on effort, performance, and satisfaction (Keller, 1983, 1999a). The motivational element is particularly important because it pertains to a person's basic decisions as to whether to accept responsibility for a task and to pursue a given goal. Without this initiation of behavior, none of the other things matter.

3. What are the assumptions and issues in learning and applying motivational design principles and processes? *Assumptions Pertaining to Motivational Design.* Experience has shown it can be difficult to convince educators and instructional designers to accept responsibility for motivational design, and that they sometimes have inappropriate conceptions of their responsibilities for learner motivation. It helps to overcome these obstacles if one understands and accepts three basic assumptions underlying systematic motivational design.

The first assumption is that people's motivation can be influenced by external events. Even though this may appear to be a truism, it runs counter to a frequently held assumption of many teachers and instructional designers, who believe their job is to provide the best-quality instruction they can and that it is the student's responsibility to want to learn the material. Ultimately, students do have control over their motivation, but even motivated students will become disinterested if the instruction is boring and disorganized, just as they may become inspired by an enthusiastic teacher. Teacher behavior, instructional materials, and other elements of a learning environment all will affect motivation.

The second assumption is that motivation is a means, not an end, in relation to learning and performance improvement. Too often, educators equate motivation with entertainment and fun; they believe that if learners are truly motivated they will be smiling and having fun. Certainly, it is enjoyable when learning is fun, but that is not the primary goal of motivational design. The goal is to have learners *engaged* in learning or work activities, not simply entertained by them.

The third assumption is that systematic design can be used to predictably and measurably influence motivation. Instructors sometimes, maybe frequently, believe that to be motivating one must have charisma and wit. On the contrary, there are fundamental characteristics of motivation, and processes for influencing it, that can assist teachers in having motivating instruction regardless of their personal styles. The models to be mentioned in this chapter illustrate this.

The point to remember from these assumptions is that although people are ultimately responsible for their choices and other aspects of personal motivation, the design of learning and performance environments will have positive (or negative!) influences on motivation.

Issues in the Study of Motivation. There are many issues to consider in the study of motivation and development of motivational principles. Among these, three are found frequently in the literature and are particularly relevant to having a solid conceptual foundation for the study of motivation. First is the distinction between intrinsic and extrinsic motivation. Second is the distinction between motivational characteristics as states or traits and how this influences design decisions. Third is the overall conceptual frame of reference for motivation. Some researchers view motivation as being within the affective domain, while others see it as a composite construct having both cognitive and affective elements.

Intrinsic vs. Extrinsic Motivation. In what ways can motivation be considered to have intrinsic or extrinsic elements? Generally, there is a consensus among researchers on the distinction between intrinsic and extrinsic motivation. According to Deci (1975), *intrinsic* motivation occurs when one engages in tasks for which there is no apparent reward except the pleasure of engaging in the activity (also see Stipek, 1998). In contrast, *extrinsically* motivated individuals engage in tasks for rewards associated with successful accomplishment. Naturally, there can be a mixture of the two elements in a given situation, but there can also be conflicts such that extrinsic rewards reduce one's intrinsic motivation for learning, as demonstrated by researchers such as Deci (1972) and Lepper and Green (1978). Other researchers reported that extrinsic motivation, when carefully prescribed, can be used to build learners' intrinsic motivation (Kruglanski et al., 1975). Despite the inconclusiveness of this research, there are specific tactics that promote intrinsic motivation, and others that provide guidance for the effective use of extrinsic rewards (Condry, 1977; Stipek, 1998).

Trait vs. State. Motivational characteristics, like other psychological characteristics, have been conceptualized as both traits and states (Brophy, 1983; Keller, 1983; Rotto, 1994). A *state* is a condition brought on by a situational stimulus or process, whereas a *trait* is a stable psychological need or drive. Berlyne (1965) indicates that curiosity, for example, can be a trait, but it also has state characteristics; that is, people differ in their stable, trait-level degree of curiosity, but some situations will awaken state curiosity more than others. Rotto (1994) makes the same point in regard to intrinsic motivation, and virtually all motivational characteristics have both trait and state features.

This issue has implications for instructional design. Similar to ability, which is considered to be a stable trait and not likely to be changed by specific episodes of instruction, motivational characteristics that are traits will not easily be changed. In these situations, the instructional designer's goal would be to identify the relevant traits and design motivational tactics to accommodate them. But it is reasonable to assume that because many elements of motivation are at the state level, they will be influenced by immediate situational factors and will change from time to time during a period of instruction (Visser & Keller, 1990). Therefore, motivational design models must accommodate both the stable trait and changeable state aspects of motivation, and incorporate means for identifying them during audience motivation analysis to identify and respond to both.

Affective vs. Cognitive Domain. Does motivation belong to only the affective domain, or does it relate to the cognitive domain as well? Some theorists have considered motivation as contained within the affective domain (Martin & Briggs, 1986; Tennyson, 1992). A slightly different position is taken by Briggs (1984) who discusses motivation as an independent area from the affective domain, an area to be intensively studied.

However, if motivation is defined as an internal determinant of the force and direction of effort that drives a student to learn (Keller, 1983), then motivation must be viewed as having both affective and cognitive components. For example, attributional theories of motivation (Rotter, 1966; Weiner, 1974) are primarily cognitive. These theories focus on people's interpretations of the causes of outcomes, combined with the value they attach to the outcomes, as a major influence on whether they will pursue given goals. However, emotions, which are an affective component, must also be considered because of their influence on motivation and behavior (Astleitner, 2000; Ledoux, 1996; Ortony, Clore, & Collins, 1988).

These issues are present in much of the literature of motivation, but simply possessing knowledge of them is not sufficient for motivational design. Motivation is a complex internal construct embedded in experiences, expectations, and perceptions. What is motivating to one person may not be motivating to another. How, then, can instructional designers hope to approach the challenge of motivational design systematically? There are two major requirements of an answer to this question. The first is to understand the major elements of human motivation, and the second is to employ a design process that assists one in diagnosing learner's motivational requirements and prescribing appropriate tactics. The next two sections of this chapter provide a brief introduction to major concepts and theories of motivation and give an overview of design approaches.

4. What are the major characteristics of motivation, in particular the characteristics that will be useful for me to know? There are many characteristics of human beings that must be considered in understanding motivation. For example, people differ in the amount of curiosity they bring to a situation, their desires to be competitive in pursuing challenging goals, and their beliefs as to whether success and failure result from luck, personal effort, or ability. The full array of motivational literature can be daunting to one who wishes to acquire an adequate understanding of how to influence people's choices and efforts. Syntheses such as those provided by Keller (1983), Keller & Burkman (1993), Wlodkowski (1999), and contemporary textbooks (Brophy, 1998; Petri, 1991; Stipek, 1998) are helpful, but one is still faced with a broad spectrum of concepts, theories, and research.

However, based on an analysis of shared attributes among these concepts, there is a somewhat limited list representing the major thrusts in motivational research, and these can be synthesized into higher-level categories making them even easier to remember. In 1983, Keller listed twelve motivational concepts that, combined with principles of behavior analysis and management (Jenson, Sloane, & Young, 1988; Skinner, 1954), continue to represent most of the primary areas of motivational research (Table 9.1).

The theories in each of these subgroups have certain key features in common. Each concept in part A of Table 9.1 is an attempt to explain how certain types of goals become

Representative motivational constructs and categories

A. *Value*-Related Concepts	B. *Expectancy*-Related Concepts
Self-Actualization—Maslow (1954)	Attribution—Weiner (1985)
	Personal Causation—deCharms (1976)
Need for Achievement—McClelland (1976)	Locus of Control—Rotter (1966)
Sensations Seeking—Zuckerman (1978)	Learned Helplessness—Seligman (1975)
Competence—White (1959)	Self-Efficacy—Bandura (1977)
Reinforcement Value—Rotter (1966)	Expectancy for Success—Fibel & Hale (1978)
Curiosity—Berlyne (1965)	

important to people and influence their behavior. Maslow (1954), for example, indicates that there is a hierarchically organized set of needs that explain the basis of human motivation. Other theories focus on specific motivators such as curiosity arousal (Berlyne, 1965), need for achievement (McClelland, 1976), and the need for personal competence (White, 1959). In other words, each of these theories addresses some aspect of the question of what are the important goals, needs, or values motivating a person.

In contrast, all of the theories in part B of Table 9.1 are concerned with the question of expectancy for success. Any time people attempt to accomplish goals, they have personal, subjective opinions about their probability of succeeding. Each of the theories in this group explains causes or effects of various types of success expectancies. For example, attribution theory (e.g., Weiner, 1985) explains how a person's tendency to attribute successes or failures to such causes as luck or task difficulty, as opposed to effort or ability, will affect his motivation to persist in trying to accomplish easy versus challenging goals. Self-efficacy (Bandura, 1977) explains how a person's belief in her capabilities to achieve desired goals affects expectancy for success. Each of these theories has unique aspects, but they can be aggregated into one category because of their shared focus on expectancies.

It is possible to aggregate both of these groups of concepts and theories into a single, macro-level theory that is called *expectancy-value theory*. There are several specific formulations of this theoretical perspective (Petri, 1991), but all of them contain the same basic assumption that motivation, or behavior potential, is a function of expectancies and values. It purports that human beings will be motivated to achieve a goal if (1) they have a positive expectancy for success, and (2) the goal has positive value for them. People have multiple needs and goals, so the goals with the highest resultant motivation are the ones that will receive the most effort.

Even though expectancy-value theory has proven to be satisfactory as a macrotheory to synthesize many of the microtheories that explain the internal, psychological factors of motivation, it does not provide a holistic view of motivation and performance. It is also necessary to consider the influences of behavioral and emotional consequences on motivation and how all of these motivational elements are related to learning, as in Keller's (1983, 1987a, 1999a) systems model of the effects of motivation, learning, and environment on effort, performance, and satisfaction.

Not all concepts listed in Table 9.1 represent currently active areas of research. Without question, the most active are self-efficacy and attribution theory, with a recent elevation of interest in competency motivation. However, some of the other areas, such as curiosity, would benefit from a renewed interest, especially in relation to designing instruction for Web-based instruction and other distance learning and multimedia environments.

With respect to other new developments, there has been a relatively recent growth of interest in the concepts of flow (Csikszentmihalyi, 1990) and learned optimism (Seligman, 1991). In addition, there are studies of motivation embedded in theories, models, or problem areas related to learning and design. These include research on (1) self-regulation, which has become a popular area of research because of its presumed relation to studying successfully in decentralized learning settings (Schunk & Zimmerman, 1994), (2) constructivism (Duffy, Lowyck, & Jonassen, 1993), which attempts to build learning environments fostering the development of self- and group-generated knowledge and concepts, and (3) continuing motivation, which was first introduced by Maher (1976) more than two decades ago.

Given this array of motivational concepts and theories, why is it important for instructional designers or human performance technologists to know something about them? There are several writers offering lists of tactics for designers to choose and apply (for example, Keller, 1987b; Keller & Suzuki, 1988; Stipek, 1998; Wlodkowski, 1999). But without knowledge of the underlying concepts, designers are not likely to choose appropriate tactics for a situation or to adapt them to fit a situation's unique requirements. Judgment is required to know which motivational tactics will be effective and feasible based on learner needs, development costs, and implementation issues. Therefore, to be able to apply a systematic process to motivational analysis and design, as described in the following section, instructional designers must understand the underlying concepts of motivation.

5. How can I apply this knowledge of motivation in the context of instructional design and human performance technology? The effort to build applied models of motivation is not new, but the emphasis has changed. The early models tended to focus on one specific motivational characteristic, as in Alschuler's work on developing the achievement motive in children (Alschuler, 1973; Alschuler, Tabor, & McIntyre, 1971).

The concepts and process in these models can be useful to an instructor who wishes to encourage development of these characteristics, but instructors would not normally attempt to be responsible for formally changing learners' personalities. Instructors will more typically be concerned with how to create learning environments that motivate learning. To do this, one has to estimate learners' motivational characteristics, and then design the learning environment to match their motivational requirements. This implies that one must work holistically with motivation and not be limited to one or two specific motivational characteristics.

There are two well-published models of motivational design that are holistic: the time-continuum model of Wlodkowski (1999) and Keller's ARCS model (1984). Wlodkowski's model contains categories of motivational tactics and prescribes when to use them during an episode of instruction. The question of how many tactics or specifically what kinds of tactics to use in each of the six categories is left to the teacher's judgment.

The ARCS model is similar to Wlodkowski's (1999), but differs in two important ways. Tactic selection in the ARCS model is done systematically from its sets of categories and subcategories. The major categories provide a macro-level frame of reference, while the subcategories (Table 9.2) provide guidance for more specific subsets of motivational tactics. The second difference is that the ARCS model is a problem-solving approach. Selection of tactics is based on a systematic design process, including an analysis of audience motivation, which provides a basis for selecting appropriate tactics, both number and type.

The full application of the ARCS design process has 10 steps (Figure 9.1) and integrates well with lesson planning and instructional design processes. The process begins with information about the lesson or course to be enhanced, the teachers (if it is an instructor-led course), and the students. It then proceeds to analysis of the audience and current materials for the course. Based on this information, the designer or teacher can write motivational objectives, select or create motivational tactics, and then develop and test them.

Both Wlodkowski's (1999) and Keller's (1984) models have elements of prescription, but in different ways. Wlodkowski's approach is prescriptive in that it tells the teacher what types of tactics to use at each stage of an instructional episode. With the ARCS model, prescription does not occur until after an analysis of audience motivation has been conducted, at which time the analysis produces the prescriptions for tactics (Keller, 1987c). In the strictest sense of the word *prescription*, both models are more heuristic than prescriptive. That is, they provide guidance for the selection and application of motivation tactics, but personal judgment is required of the teacher, or instructional designer, with respect to selecting and creating activities that represent the tactics. By having a systematic audience analysis and problem-solving focus, the ARCS model helps provide a rational basis for tactic selection.

6. What are the trends or future directions in motivational research and application to learning environment design? Several currently popular areas of research, such as attribution theory and self-regulation, are mentioned throughout this chapter. In addition to these construct-specific areas of research, in recent years there has been a growth of interest in several other areas of motivational research. First, within the domain of training and human resource development there has been increasing interest in human performance technology (HPT) (see, for example, Section 4 of this book). This is leading instructional designers to be more concerned about motivation in the workplace (Keller, 1999a) and self-motivation (McCombs, 1984). This multilevel set of concerns is likely to grow in importance because of the growing number of organizations adopting HPT.

Second is the role of motivation in the constructivist approach to learning environment design, which promotes learners' self-evelopment of insight and knowledge structures. Within this approach, motivation tends not to be singled out as a specific area of emphasis but is embedded in other concepts. For example, there is a strong emphasis on the principle of *authenticity*, which refers to developing learning activities and tests that are closely related to, or preferably located within, a real-world context. This

TABLE 9.2 ARCS model categories and subcategories

Attention	
Perceptual Arousal:	What can I do to capture their interest?
Inquiry Arousal:	How can I stimulate an attitude of inquiry?
Variability:	How can I use a variety of tactics to maintain their attention?
Relevance	
Goal Orientation:	How can I best meet my learners' needs? (Do I know their needs?)
Motive Matching:	How and when can I provide my learners with appropriate choices, responsibilities, and influences?
Familiarity:	How can I tie the instruction to the learners' experiences?
Confidence	
Learning Requirements:	How can I assist in building a positive expectation for success?
Success Opportunities:	How will the learning experience support or enhance the students' beliefs in their competence?
Personal Control:	How will the learners clearly know their success is based upon their efforts and abilities?
Satisfaction	
Intrinsic Reinforcement:	How can I provide meaningful opportunities for learners to use their newly acquired knowledge/skill?
Extrinsic Rewards:	What will provide reinforcement to the learners' successes?
Equity:	How can I assist the students in anchoring a positive feeling about their accomplishments?

principle would be an element of "relevance" in the ARCS model, and is also related to classical research on transfer of learning, in which transfer is enhanced when the learning environment closely resembles the application environment (Travers, 1977).

Third, within the field of instructional design and human performance technology, there is growing interest and research on motivation in Web-based instruction, computer-based instruction, and distance learning. In most distance learning contexts the noncompletion rate is unacceptably high, and learner motivation problems are generally considered to be a primary cause. However, the number of formal studies is fairly small, although growing (Visser, 1998). With respect to computer-based instruction, Song (1998), building on the work of Astleitner & Keller (1995), demonstrates how one can produce motivationally adaptive computer-based instruction. He embedded motivational self-checks in the lessons. Based on the learner's responses, the computer determined the amount and type of motivational tactics to use in the subsequent segment of the lesson.

Fourth, there is a growing interest in understanding the affective components of motivation in regard to both the internal emotional characteristics of people (Astleitner, 2000) and the affective properties of machine-based learning environments (Baylor, 1999; Picard, 2000). There is no doubt that emotions are highly related to approach and avoidance behaviors, but there is little research on how to understand and systematically influence this aspect of motivation in regard to motivation to learn. Astleitner's (2000) FSEAP model provides a conceptual structure and application guidelines that appear to be a promising development in this area. Picard (2000) is investigating ways to invest computers with emotional properties, while Baylor (1999) and others (Atkinson, 2002) are exploring the effects of various types of animated agents on learning and motivation.

Fifth, a challenge in motivational design, as well as in instructional design, is how to make the design process quick as well as effective. A full-featured process that includes all the relevant levels of analysis, design, development,

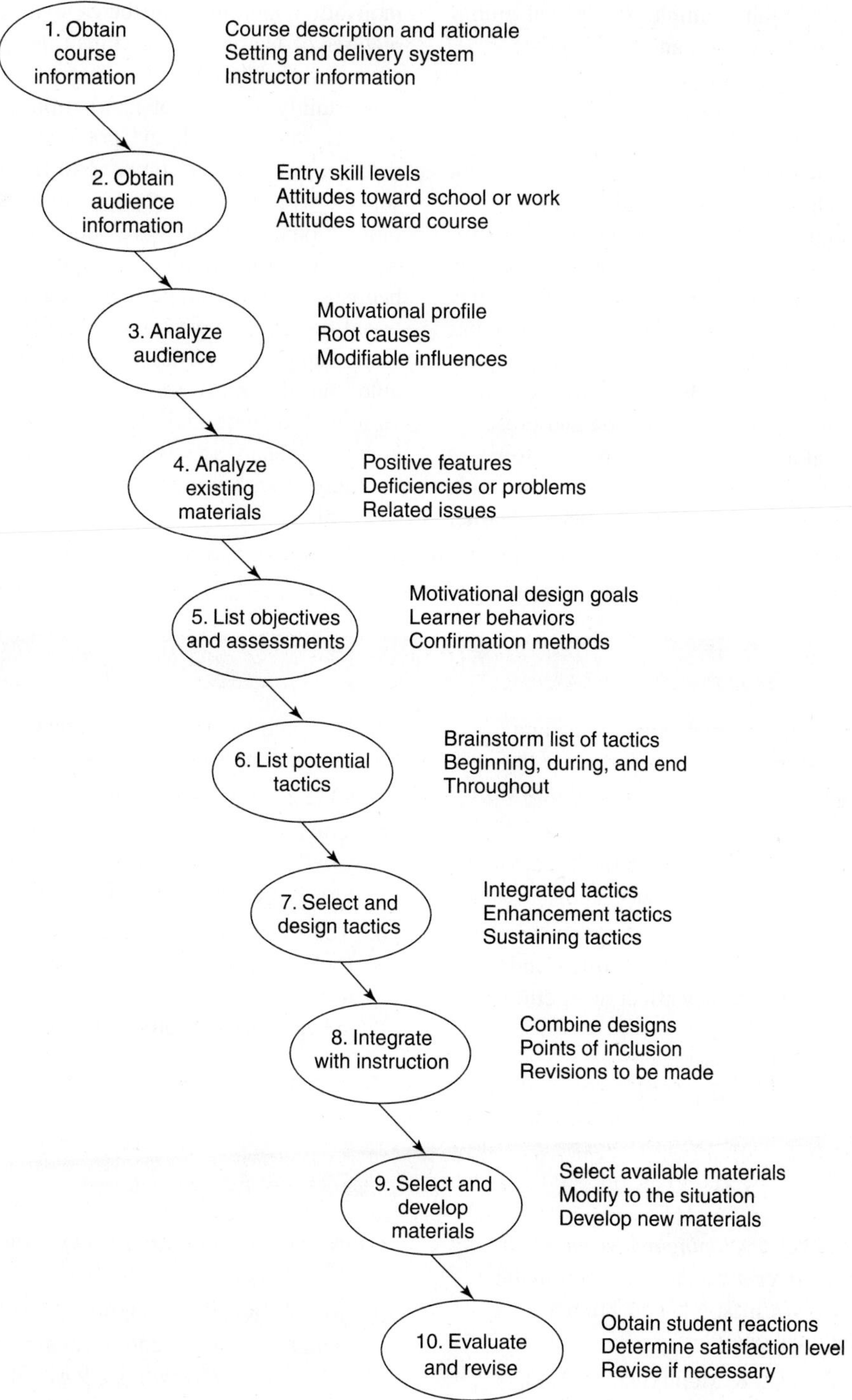

FIGURE 9.1 Steps in motivational design.

formative testing and revision, and validation can be quite time consuming. Within the mainstream of model and tool development in instructional design there is a strong concern about how to reduce the cycle time from project initiation to completion. The same thing is true in motivational design. Recently, Keller and Suzuki (Keller, 1999b; Suzuki & Keller, 1996) introduced a simplified approach to motivational design that has been applied and validated in two additional contexts internationally (Keller, 1999a, Song, 1998; Visser, 1998). In this model, teachers or instructional designers are provided with a simple matrix that guides them through a shortened analysis and design process.

Conclusion

Even a casual comparison of today's instructional design and educational psychology literature with that of 15 years ago illustrates a dramatic growth of attention to motivational factors in learning and performance. As with any field of research on human learning and performance, there is much to be learned, but there is also much that has been learned. In the past, motivation was generally regarded as being too elusive and changeable to encompass in a holistic theory or model of explanation and prescription. However, several areas of research and development have shown that it is possible to build valid, systematic approaches to understanding and influencing learner motivation, and this contributes significantly to the larger pictures of learning environment design and human performance development.

Certainly the field of instructional design can benefit from current research and practices in motivation. Inasmuch as what causes someone to learn is never a precise science with easy-to-follow guidelines, incorporation of motivational techniques is essential to maximize learning. As stated earlier, motivation is an internal construct embedded in personal experience and expectations. Instructional designers must not only be fully cognizant of the entire range of motivational methods and models available, but also must know how to integrate them into a variety of instructional situations. Even the most accurate content, related activities and diligent preparation can be ineffective without the systematic incorporation of motivation.

Application Questions

1. You see a room where learners are smiling and happy and the instructor is entertaining. Are the learners motivated? Why or why not, and how do you know?
2. Do you view motivation as being in the affective or cognitive domain? Support your answer.
3. Compare and contrast value-related and expectancy-related motivational constructs and concepts in terms of how they affect instructional design.
4. Research Wlodkowski's Time Continuum model of motivation. How would you apply each of the six categories to instructional design?
5. Compare and contrast Wlodkowski's Time Continuum model with Keller's ARCS model in terms of approaches to instructional design.
6. You have been hired to design a training course for a topic in your area of specialization. Using Table 9.2 as a template, what would you incorporate into each subcategory to motivate learners?

References

Alschuler, A. S. (1973). *Developing achievement motivation in adolescents: Education for human growth*. Englewood Cliffs, NJ: Educational Technology Publications.

Alschuler, A. S., Tabor, D., & McIntyre, J. (1971). *Teaching achievement motivation: Theory and practice in psychological education*. Middletown, CT: Education Ventures.

Astleitner, H., (2000). Designing emotionally sound instruction: The FEASP approach. *Instructional Science, 28*(3), 169–198.

Astleitner, J., & Keller, J. M. (1995). A model for motivationally adaptive computer-assisted instruction. *Journal of Computing in Education, 27*(30), 270–280.

Atkinson, R. K. (2002). Optimizing learning from examples using pedagogical agents. *Journal of Educational Psychology, 94*(2), 416–427.

Bandura, A. (1977). Self-efficacy: Toward a unifying theory of behavioral change. *Psychological Review, 84*(2), 191–215.

Baylor, A. (1999). Intelligent agents as cognitive tools for education. *Educational Technology, 39*(2), 36–40.

Berlyne, D. E. (1965). Motivational problems raised by exploratory and epistemic behavior. In S. Koch

(Ed.), *Psychology: A study of a science* (Vol. 5, pp. 284–364). New York: McGraw-Hill.

Briggs, L. J. (1984). Whatever happened to motivation and the affective domain? *Educational Technology, 24*(5), 33–44.

Brophy, J. E. (1983). Conceptualizing student motivation. *Educational Psychologist, 18*(3), 200–215.

Brophy, J. E. (1998). *Motivating students to learn*. New York: McGraw-Hill.

Condry, J. (1977). Enemies of exploration: Self-initiated versus other-initiated learning. *Journal of Personality and Social Psychology, 35*(7), 459–477.

Csikszentmihalyi, M. (1990). *Flow: The psychology of optimal experience*. New York: Harper & Row.

Cusimano, J. M. (1995, August). Turning blue-collar workers into knowledge workers. *Training and Development, 49*(8), 47–49.

deCharms, R. (1976). *Enhancing motivation change in the classroom*. New York: Irvington.

Deci, E. L. (1972). Intrinsic motivation, extrinsic reinforcement, and inequity. *Journal of Personality and Social Psychology, 22*(1), 113–120.

Deci, E. L. (1975). *Intrinsic motivation*. New York: Plenum.

Dick, W., Carey, L., & Carey, J. O. (2005). *The systematic design of instruction* (6th ed.). Boston: Allyn & Bacon.

Duffy, T. M., Lowyck, J., & Jonassen, D. H. (Eds.) (1993). *Designing environments for constructive learning*. Berlin: Springer-Verlag.

Fibel, B., & Hale, W. D. (1978). The generalized expectancy for success scale: A new measure. *Journal of Consulting and Clinical Psychology, 46*(5), 924–931.

Gagné, R. M. (1985). *The conditions of learning* (4th Ed.). New York: Holt, Rinehart & Winston.

Gilbert, T. F. (1978). *Human competence: Engineering worthy performance*. New York: McGraw-Hill.

Glister, P. (1997). *Digital literacy.* New York: Wiley.

Jenson, W. R., Sloane, H. N., & Young, K. R. (1988). *Applied behavior analysis in education: A structured teaching approach*. Englewood Cliffs, NJ: Prentice Hall.

Keller, J. M. (1979). Motivation and instructional design: A theoretical perspective. *Journal of Instructional Development, 2*(4), 26–34.

Keller, J. M. (1983). Motivational design of instruction. In C. M. Reigeluth (Ed.), *Instructional-design theories and models: An overview of their current status* (pp. 383–434). Hillsdale, NJ: Lawrence Erlbaum Associates.

Keller, J. M. (1984). The use of the ARCS model of motivation in teacher training. In K. Shaw & A. J. Trott (Eds.), *Aspects of educational technology, Vol.* 17: *Staff development and career updating* (pp. 140–145). London: Kogan Page.

Keller, J. M. (1987a). Development and use of the ARCS model of motivational design. *Journal of Instructional Development, 10*(3), 2–10.

Keller, J. M. (1987b). Strategies for stimulating the motivation to learn. *Performance & Instruction, 26*(8), 1–7.

Keller, J. M. (1987c). The systematic process of motivational design. *Performance & Instruction, 26*(9), 1–8.

Keller, J. M. (1999a). Motivational systems. In H. D. Stolovitch & E. J. Keeps (Eds.), *Handbook of human performance technology* (2nd ed., pp. 373–399). San Francisco: Jossey-Bass.

Keller, J. M. (1999b). Simplified motivational design: Multinational applications of the ARCS model in technology-supported and distance learning environments. In M. Theall (ed.), *Motivation in teaching and learning: New directions for teaching and learning* (pp. 39–47). San Francisco: Jossey-Bass.

Keller, J. M., & Burkman, E. (1993). Motivation principles. In M. Fleming & W. H. Levie (Eds.), *Instructional message design: Principles from the behavioral and cognitive sciences* (pp. 3–54). Englewood Cliffs, NJ: Educational Technology Publications.

Keller, J. M., & Suzuki, K. (1988). Application of the ARCS model to courseware design. In D. H. Jonassen (Ed.), *Instructional designs for microcomputer courseware* (pp. 401–434). New York: Lawrence Erlbaum Associates.

Kruglanski, A. W., Riter, A., Amitai, A., Margolin, B. S., Shabtai, L., & Zaksh, D. (1975). Can money enhance intrinsic motivation: A test of the content-consequence hypothesis. *Journal of Personality and Social Psychology, 31*(4), 744–750.

Ledoux, J. (1996). *The emotional brain: The mysterious underpinnings of emotional life.* New York: Touchstone.

Lepper, M. R., & Green, D. (Eds.) (1978). *The hidden costs of reward: New perspectives on the psychology of human motivation*. Hillsdale, NJ: Lawrence Erlbaum Associates.

Maher, M. L. (1976). Continuing motivation: An analysis of a seldom considered educational outcome. *Review of Educational Research, 46*(3), 443–462.

Martin, B. L., & Briggs, L. J. (1986). *The affective and cognitive domains: Integration for instruction and research.* Englewood Cliffs, NJ: Educational Technology Publications.

Maslow, A. H. (1954). *Motivation and personality.* New York: Harper & Row.

McClelland, D. C. (1976). *The achieving society.* New York: Irvington.

McCombs, B. L. (1984). Processes and skills underlying intrinsic motivation to learn: Toward a definition of motivational skills training intervention. *Educational Psychologist, 19*(4), 199–218.

Means, T. B., Jonassen, D. H., & Dwyer, F. M., (1997). Enhancing relevance: Embedded ARCS strategies vs. purpose. *Educational Technology Research & Development, 45*(1), 5–18.

Ortony, A., Clore, G. L., & Collins, A. (1988). *The cognitive structure of emotions.* Cambridge, UK: Cambridge University Press.

Petri, H. L. (1991). *Motivation: Theory, research, and applications* (3rd ed.). Belmont, CA: Wadsworth.

Picard, R. W. (2000). *Affective computing.* Cambridge, MA: MIT Press.

Porter, L. W., & Lawler, E. E. (1968). *Managerial attitudes and performance.* Homewood, IL: Richard D. Irwin.

Rotter, J. B. (1966). Generalized expectancies for internal versus external control of reinforcement. *Psychological Monographs, 80*(1, Whole No. 609).

Rotto, L. I. (1994). Curiosity, motivation, and "flow" in computer-based instruction. In M. R. Simonson (Ed.), *Proceedings of selected research and development presentations at the 1994 National Convention of the Association for Educational Communication & Technology.* (ERIC Document Reproduction Service No. ED 373 755)

Rummler, G. A., & Brache, A. P. (1990). *Improving performance: How to manage the white space on the organizational chart.* San Francisco: Jossey-Bass.

Schunk, D. H., & Zimmerman, B. J. (Eds.). (1994). *Self-regulation of learning performance: Issues and educational applications.* Hillsdale, NJ: Lawrence Erlbaum Associates.

Seligman, M. E. (1975). *Helplessness.* San Francisco: Freeman.

Seligman, M. E. (1991). *Learned optimism: How to change your mind and yourself.* New York: Knopf.

Skinner, B. F. (1954). The science of learning and the art of teaching. *Harvard Educational Review, 24*(2), 86–97.

Small, R. V., & Gluck, M. (1994). The relationship of motivational conditions to effective instructional attributes: A magnitude scaling approach. *Educational Technology, 34*(8), 33–40.

Smith, P. L., & Ragan, T. J. (1999). *Instructional design* (2nd ed.). Upper Saddle River, NJ: Prentice Hall.

Song, S. H. (1998). *The effects of motivationally adaptive computer-assisted instruction developed through the ARCS model.* Unpublished doctoral dissertation, College of Education, Florida State University, Tallahassee.

Stipek, D. J. (1998). *Motivation to learn* (3rd ed.). Boston: Allyn & Bacon.

Suzuki, K., & Keller, J. M. (1996, August). Creation and cross cultural validation of an ARCS motivational design matrix. Paper presented at the annual meeting of the Japanese Association for Educational Technology, Kanazawa, Japan.

Tennyson, R. D. (1992). An educational learning theory for instructional design. *Educational Technology, 32*(1), 36–41.

Travers, R. M. W. (1977). *Essentials of learning* (4th ed.). New York: Macmillan.

Visser, J. (1998). *The development of motivational communication in distance education support.* Unpublished doctoral dissertation, Educational Technology Department, University of Twente, The Netherlands.

Visser, J., & Keller, J. M. (1990). The clinical use of motivational messages: An inquiry into the validity of the ARCS model of motivational design. *Instructional Science, 19*(6), 467–500.

Weiner, B. (Ed.) (1974). *Achievement motivation and attribution theory.* Morristown, NJ: General Learning Press.

Weiner, B. (1985). *Human motivation.* New York: Springer-Verlag.

White, R. W. (1959). Motivation reconsidered: The concept of competence. *Psychological Review, 66*(5), 297–323.

Wlodkowski, R. J. (1999). *Enhancing adult motivation to learn: A comprehensive approach to support learning among all adults.* San Francisco: Jossey-Bass.

Zuckerman, M. (1978). The search for high sensation. *Psychology Today, 11*(9), 38–46, 96–97.

SECTION 3

Evaluating, Implementing, and Managing Instructional Programs and Projects

Overview

As was pointed out in the first section of this book, the phases of the instructional design process include *analysis, design, development, implementation*, and *evaluation*. Moreover, careful *management* of the entire instructional design process is crucial to the success of most projects. The last few chapters of the previous section offered a variety of suggestions regarding the *design* of instruction. In this section of the book, we focus on trends in three of the other crucial areas—*evaluation*, *implementation*, and *management*.

Chapter 10 focuses on two models of *evaluation*. The first is Stufflebeam's CIPP (Context, Input, Process, and Product) model. This program evaluation model is often used to evaluate large-scale educational projects. The second approach is Kirkpatrick's four-level evaluation model. The third and fourth levels of this model, which focus on the performance of workers and on organizational results, is of particular relevance today.

Chapter 11 focuses on the *implementation* stage of instructional design, which is one of the most important parts of the process. While it was once common to believe that effective, well-designed instructional innovations would be readily adopted, that belief has proven to be a fallacy. A variety of social, personal, organizational, economic, and technical factors combine to influence the rate at which an innovation is adopted and diffused. Chapter 11 describes a variety of strategies for increasing the likelihood that innovations will be properly implemented and adopted.

Many instructional design projects take place over an extended period of time and involve teams of professionals, including instructional designers, computer programmers, artists, subject matter experts, and others. The *management* of such projects is often a complex process. Chapter 12 focuses on some of the skills that are necessary to be a successful manager of such projects.

Those in charge of instructional design projects must be able to manage the people, time, and money resources that are available to them. Given that every training organization has a limited amount of these resources, this is no easy task. Chapter 13 discusses the factors that affect the amount of resources an organization has available and describes strategies a training manager can adopt in order to address the problems presented by resource scarcity.

Walter Dick
Florida State University

R. Burke Johnson
University of South Alabama

CHAPTER 10

Evaluation in Instructional Design: The Impact of Kirkpatrick's Four-Level Model

Knowledge and Comprehension Questions

1. Explain the important concepts in Scriven's definition of *evaluation*.
2. What is the major distinction between *formative* and *summative* evaluation, and how do these two approaches differ?
3. Describe each of the four components of Stufflebeam's CIPP evaluation model.
4. Describe each of the four levels of Kirkpatrick's evaluation model.
5. Explain how Kirkpatrick's model can be used to assess the impact of (1) training, and (2) other types of solutions to performance problems.
6. Provide a case where (1) you would choose to use Kirkpatrick's evaluation model, and (2) where you would choose to use Stufflebeam's evaluation model. What factors should affect the decision to use one evaluation model rather than another?

Editors' Introduction

Evaluation is an essential phase in the instructional design process. In this chapter, Walter Dick and Burke Johnson focus on how the nature of evaluation activities has changed (and, in some ways, remained the same!) over the past half century. In the first half of the chapter they provide a useful definition of evaluation, discuss the purposes and characteristics of formative and summative evaluation, and discuss a popular model of program evaluation, one that is often used to evaluate large-scale educational projects—Stufflebeam's CIPP (Context, Input, Process, and Product) model.

In the second half of this chapter, Dick and Johnson focus on Kirkpatrick's four-level model of evaluation, a model developed over 45 years ago, but which seems to be particularly relevant today. They describe how this model can be used for formative as well as summative purposes, and indicate how its emphasis on the performance of workers and on organizational results is consistent with the human performance technology movement.

Psychologists and training personnel with roots in the empirical sciences were primarily responsible for developing the original instructional design models. One of the fundamental components of these models is evaluation. The collection of data and information on the effectiveness of newly created instruction was critically important in the verification of the design process and in the revision of the instruction. The purpose of this chapter is to describe the original role of evaluation in the design process, how that role has evolved in practice in business and industry, and how Kirkpatrick's model of evaluation has influenced the evaluation process.

Evaluation in Instructional Design

The evaluation of educational innovations in the 1950s and 1960s usually consisted of research designs that involved the use of experimental and control groups. A posttest was used to determine if the experimental group that received the instruction did significantly better than the control group, which had received no instruction. This approach was used to determine the effectiveness of new instructional innovations such as educational television and computer-assisted instruction. In these studies, the effectiveness of instruction delivered via the innovation was compared to the effectiveness of "traditional instruction," which was usually delivered by a teacher in a classroom. The major purpose of the evaluation was to determine the value or worth of the innovation that was being developed.

In the 1960s, the United States undertook a major curriculum reform. Millions of dollars were spent on new textbooks and approaches to instruction. As the new texts were published, the traditional approach to evaluation was invoked; namely, comparing student performance with the new curricula with the performance of students who used the traditional curricula. While some of the results were ambiguous, it was clear that many of the students who used the new curricula learned very little.

Several leaders in the field of educational psychology and evaluation, including Lee Cronbach and Michael Scriven, recognized that the problems with this approach to instruction should have been discovered sooner. The debate that followed resulted in a reconceptualization of educational evaluation, and the coining of the terms *formative* and *summative* evaluation by Michael Scriven in 1967 (Scriven, 1967; also see Scriven, 1991, 1996). Here are Scriven's (1991) definitions of formative and summative evaluation:

> *Formative evaluation* is evaluation designed, done, and intended to support the process of improvement, and normally commissioned or done by, and delivered to, someone who can make improvements. *Summative evaluation* is the rest of evaluation: in terms of intentions, it is evaluation done for, or by, any observers or decision makers (by contrast with developers) who need evaluative conclusions for any reasons besides development. (p. 20)

The result of the discussions about the role of evaluation in education in the late 1960s and early 1970s was an agreement that some form of evaluation needed to be undertaken prior to the distribution of textbooks to users. The purpose of this evaluation was not to determine the value or worth of the texts, but rather to determine how they could be improved prior to being released. During this evaluation phase, there is an interest in how well students are learning and how they like and react to the instruction. But this information is to be used to make the instruction more effective, rather than to make an overall decision about how good it is. Thus, the evaluation is *formative* in that it takes place during the development of the instruction. In contrast, *summative* evaluation takes place after the developers have done all they can to make the instruction as effective as possible. During a summative evaluation it is appropriate to ask such questions as the following: "Is this new instruction as good as our old form of instruction? Is this Web-based version of the course as effective as the CD-ROM version? Which one requires more time to complete? Which one is more expensive? Which one do learners prefer?"

Instructional design models, which were first published in the late 1960s and early 1970s, all had an evaluation component. Most included the formative/summative distinction and suggested that designers engage in some process in which drafts of instructional materials are studied by learners and data are obtained on learners' performance on tests and their reactions to the instruction. This information and data were to be used to inform revisions.

The evaluation processes that were described in the early instructional design models incorporated two important and unique features. The first is that testing should focus on the objectives that have been stated for the instruction. This is referred to as *criterion-referenced* or *objective-referenced* testing. The argument is made that the assessment instruments for systematically designed instruction should focus on the skills that the learners have been told will be taught in the instruction. The purpose of testing is not to sort the learners to assign grades, but rather to determine the extent to which each objective in the instruction has been mastered. Instruction for those objectives for which assessments indicate low performance should be reviewed and revised. Therefore, the assessments, be they multiple-choice items, essays, or products developed by the learners, should require learners to demonstrate the skills as they are described in the objectives in the instruction.

The second feature of evaluation within instructional design is a focus on learners as the source of data to be used for making decisions about the instruction. While subject matter experts are typically members of the instructional design team, they cannot always accurately predict which instructional strategies will be effective and which will not. Formative evaluation in instructional design should include a subject matter specialist's review, and that of an editor, but the major source of input to the process is the learner. Formative evaluation focuses on learners' ability to learn from the instruction, and to enjoy it. The work of Kirkpatrick is important because it has extended the range of variables that should be of interest to the instructional designer.

Defining *Evaluation*

Before we continue with our historical development of evaluation in instructional design, we want to provide you with a formal definition of *evaluation*. Because of the prominence of Scriven in educational evaluation (as stated), we will use his definition, which comes from his Evaluation Thesaurus (Scriven, 1991):

> Evaluation is the process of determining the merit, worth, and value of things, and evaluations are the products of that process. (p. 139)

By *merit* Scriven is referring to the "intrinsic value of the evaluand" (the *evaluand* is what is being evaluated). By *worth*, Scriven is referring to the "market value" of the evaluand or its value to a stakeholder, an organization, or some other collective. By *value*, Scriven has in mind the idea that evaluation specifically involves the making of value judgments.

Scriven's (1980) "logic of evaluation" includes four steps. First, you select the criteria of merit or worth. Second, you set specific performance standards (i.e., the level of performance required) for your criteria. Third, you collect performance data so that you can compare the level of observed performance with the level of required performance dictated by the performance standards. Fourth, in an evaluation, you must make an evaluative (i.e., value) judgment. In short, evaluation is about identifying criteria of merit and worth, setting standards, collecting data, and making value judgments.

Models of Program Evaluation

Many evaluation models were developed in the 1970s.[1] These evaluation models were to have a profound impact on how designers would come to use the evaluation process. The new models were used on projects that included extensive development work, multiple organizations and agencies, and multiple forms of instructional delivery. These projects tended to have large budgets and many staff members, and were often housed in universities. The projects had multiple goals that were to be achieved over time. Examples were teacher corps projects that were aimed at reforming teacher education and modern math projects that attempted to redefine what and how children learned about mathematics.

These projects often employed new models of evaluation. Perhaps the most influential model of that era was that of Stufflebeam (1971). This model is referred to as the CIPP evaluation model. The acronym stands for Context, Input, Process, and Product. These are four distinct types of evaluation, and they all can be done in a single comprehensive evaluation or a single type can be done as a stand-alone type of evaluation.

Context evaluation indicates the requirement to assess the environment in which an innovation would be used, to determine the need and objectives for the innovation, and to identify the factors in the environment that will impact the success of its use. This context analysis is typically called a *needs assessment*, and it helps in making *program planning decisions*. According to Stufflebeam's CIPP model, the evaluator should be present from the beginning of the project, and should assist in the conduct of the needs assessment and in the interpretation of its results.

The second step or component in the CIPP evaluation model is *input evaluation*. Here, evaluation questions are raised about the resources that will be used to develop and conduct the innovation or program. What people, funds, space, and equipment will be available for the project? Will these be sufficient to produce the desired results? Is the conceptualization of the program adequate? Is the program design likely to produce the desired outcomes? Are the benefits of the program expected to outweigh the costs of the prospective innovation or program? In short, this type of evaluation is used to examine what occurs or should occur during program operation, and it is especially helpful in making *program structuring decisions*. Once again, in this model the evaluator plays a key role in assessing the input to the project and analyzing the adequacy of the resources and program conceptualization to meet the identified need.

The third step or component in the CIPP model is called *process evaluation*. This step corresponds more closely to the kinds of evaluation that were being done by designers under the label *formative evaluation*. Process evaluation is used to examine the ways in which an innovation is being developed, the way it is being implemented, and the initial effectiveness and revisions of the innovation. Likewise, is the program following required legal and conceptual

[1] Additional evaluation models are being developed today, and many of the older models continue to be updated. For a partial listing of older and newer models, see Stufflebeam, Madaus, & Kellaghan (2000). Also see Chen (1990), Patton (1997), and Rossi, Lipsey, and Freeman (2004).

guidelines? Data are collected on a regular basis during the project to inform the project leader (and other program personnel) of the current status of the project, how it is being implemented, and how the innovation is being revised to meet the implementation or process objectives. In general, process evaluation helps in making *implementing decisions*.

The fourth step or component in the CIPP model is *product evaluation*, which resembles summative evaluation in that assessments are made of the success of the innovation in producing the desired outcomes in the target environment. Product evaluation includes the specific outcomes of the program, measuring the outcomes specified in the program objectives, attempting to identify unintended outcomes, assessing the merit of the program, and conducting a benefit-cost or ROI (return on investment) assessment.[2] Product evaluation is very helpful in making *summative evaluation decisions* (i.e., "What is the merit and worth of the program? Should it be continued?").

The CIPP model continues to be a popular evaluation model today. If you would like more information about this model (including model updates), go to the Evaluation Center website at Western Michigan University (**http://www.wmich.edu/evalctr/**; see especially **http://www.wmich.edu/evalctr/checklists/cippchecklist.htm**) and read the chapter on the CIPP model in Stufflebeam et al. (2000).

Several things should be noted about the introduction of the CIPP model to the fields of evaluation and instructional design. It changed dramatically the involvement of the evaluator in the development process. The evaluator is now a fulltime member of the project team. Similarly, evaluation is no longer something that just happens at the end of the project, but rather it is a process that continues throughout the life of the project. The purpose of nearly all evaluation is evolving to one of assisting in the improvement of the products being produced by the project team (formative), rather than only determining the absolute usefulness or effectiveness of those products (summative).

While the use of models of evaluation was changing both in instructional design and in large-scale educational projects (which might be using instructional design methods to develop the innovation), evaluation seemed to lag in business and industry. As academics wrote about their new evaluation models, industry tended to continue to rely on learner responses to postinstruction attitude questionnaires as the major or only source of evaluation data about the effectiveness of their training. This was the case in spite of the fact that in 1959, Kirkpatrick published an extensive evaluation model for use in business and industry. The Kirkpatrick model, which became very popular in business and industry during the 1970s up through the present, is described in the next section.

Kirkpatrick's Four-Level Model of Training Evaluation

Kirkpatrick's model was published initially in four articles in 1959 (for a review and references, see Kirkpatrick, 1996). Kirkpatrick's purpose for proposing his new model was to motivate training directors to see the importance of evaluation and to increase their efforts to evaluate their training programs. In other words, Kirkpatrick specifically developed a model for *training* evaluation. What he originally referred to as *steps* later became the *four levels* of evaluation. Evaluators might only conduct evaluations at the early steps or they might evaluate at all four levels. The early levels of evaluation are useful by themselves, but they are also useful in helping one interpret evaluation results from the higher levels. For example, one reason transfer of training (level 3) might not take place is because learning of the skills (level 2) never took place; likewise, satisfaction (level 1) is often required if learning (level 2) and other results (levels 3 and 4) are to occur. (This point will make more sense as you read about the four levels.)

The four levels of the Kirkpartick model of training evaluation are described next. As you read about them, remember that the distinction between formative and summative evaluation would not be made for another decade after the first introduction of the Kirkpatrick model to the literature (1959). The levels as described by Kirkpatrick were often thought to refer to what we would now call summative evaluation; however, it is important to understand that applications of Kirkpatrick's model can be used for summative and formative purposes (i.e., the results can be used to make summative judgments about training programs *and* to provide formative information that can be used to improve training programs).

---

[2] In business, financial results are often measured using the return on investment index (ROI). ROI is calculated by subtracting total dollar costs associated with the program from total dollar benefits (this difference is called *net benefits*); then dividing this difference by total dollar costs, and multiplying the result by 100. A value greater than zero on ROI indicates a positive return on your investment. An index that is commonly used with governmental programs is the *benefit–cost ratio,* which is calculated by dividing total dollar benefits by total dollar costs. A benefit–cost ratio of 1 is the break-even point, and values greater than 1 mean the benefits are greater than the costs. Because it can be difficult to translate many benefits that might result from training and other interventions into dollar units (e.g., attitudes, satisfaction), cost-effectiveness ratios are often used rather than benefit–cost ratios. To calculate a *cost-effectiveness ratio* the evaluator translates training program costs into dollar units but leaves the measured benefits in their original (nondollar) units. A cost-effectiveness ratio tells you how much "bang for the buck" the training provides (e.g., how much improvement in job satisfaction is gained per dollar spent on training).

Level 1: Reaction

The first level of evaluation is the assessment of learners' reactions or attitudes toward their learning experience. Typically, anonymous questionnaires are used to get honest reactions from learners so that information can be provided to management about the instruction. These reactions, along with those of the training director, should be used to evaluate the instruction, but should not serve as the only type of evaluation. It is generally assumed that if learners do not like the instruction, it is unlikely that they will learn from it.

Although level 1 evaluation is used to study the reactions of participants in training programs, it is important to understand that data can be collected on more than just a single overall reaction to the program (e.g., "How satisfied were you with the training event?"). Detailed level 1 information can also be collected about multiple and specific program components (such as the instructor, the topics, the presentation style, the schedule, the facility, the learning activities, and how engaged participants felt during the training event). It also is helpful to include open-ended items (i.e., where respondents respond in their own words rather than only selecting from a set of predetermined responses). Two useful items are (1) "What do you believe are the three most important weaknesses of the program?" and (2) "What do you believe are the three most important strengths of the program?" When conducting a level 1 evaluation, it is usually best to use a mixture of open-ended items (such as the two questions just provided) and closed-ended items (such as providing a statement or item stem such as "The material covered in the program was relevant to my job" and asking respondents to use a 4-point rating scale such as: very satisfied, satisfied, dissatisfied, very dissatisfied). Kirkpatrick (1998) provides several examples of actual questionnaires that you can use or modify for your own evaluations. The formal research design used for level 1 evaluation typically is the one-group posttest-only design (Table 10.1).

Level 2: Learning

In level 2 evaluation, the goal is to determine what the participants in the training program learned. By *learning* Kirkpatrick (1998) has in mind "the extent to which participants change attitudes, improve knowledge, and/or increase skill as a result of attending the program" (p. 20). Learning outcomes can include changes in *knowledge* (e.g., "What are the differences between the CIPP and Kirkpatrick models of evaluation?"), *skills* (e.g., "Can participants use *Dreamweaver* to design a Web page?"), and *attitudes* (e.g., "Have participants' attitudes toward computers improved?"). Some training events will be focused on knowledge, some will be focused on skills, some will be focused on attitudes, and some will be focused on a combination of these three outcomes.

Level 2 evaluation should be focused on measuring what specifically was covered in the training event and on the specific learning objectives. Kirkpatrick emphasizes that the tests should cover the material that was presented to the learners in order to have a valid measure of the amount of learning that has taken place. Knowledge is

TABLE 10.1 Research designs commonly used in training evaluation

Design *Strength*	Design *Depiction*	Design *Name*
1. Very weak	$X \quad O_2$	One-group posttest-only design
2. Moderately weak	$O_1 \quad X \quad O_2$	One-group pretest-posttest design
3. Moderately strong	$O_1 \quad X \quad O_2$	Nonequivalent comparison-group design
	$O_1 \quad\quad O_2$	
4. Very strong	$RA \quad O_1 \quad X \quad O_2$	Pretest-posttest control-group design
	$RA \quad O_1 \quad\quad O_2$	

*X stands for the treatment (i.e., the training event)
O_1 stands for pretest measurement
O_2 stands for posttest measurement
RA stands for random assignment of participants to the groups
Design 3 has a control group but the participants are not randomly assigned to the groups; therefore, the groups are to a greater or lesser degree, "nonequivalent."
Design 4 has random assignment and is the gold standard for providing evidence for cause and effect.
For more information on these and other research designs, see Johnson and Christensen (2004).

typically measured with an *achievement test* (i.e., a test designed to measure the degree of knowledge learning that has taken place after a person has been exposed to a specific learning experience), skills are typically measured with a *performance test* (i.e., a testing situation where test takers demonstrate some real-life behavior such as creating a product or performing a process), and attitudes are typically measured with a *questionnaire* (i.e., a self-report data-collection instrument filled out by research participants designed to measure, in this case, the attitudes targeted for change in the training event). Level 2 evaluation should be done immediately after the training event to determine whether the participants in the event gained the desired knowledge, skills, and attitudes.

The one-group pretest-posttest design is often sufficient for a level 2 evaluation. As you can see in Table 10.1, this design involves a pretest and posttest measurement of the training group participants on the outcome of interest. The estimate of learning improvement is then taken to be the difference between the pretest and posttest measure of leaning. Kirkpatrick recommends that a control group also be used when possible in level 2 evaluation. In training evaluations, this typically means that you will use the nonequivalent comparison-group design shown in Table 10.1 to demonstrate that learning has occurred as a result of the instruction. Learning data are not only helpful for documenting learning; they can also be helpful for training directors as they justify their training function in an organization.

Level 3: Behavior (Transfer of Training)

Here the evaluator's goal is to determine whether the training program participants change their on-the-job behavior (OJB) as a result of having attended and participated in the training program. Kirkpatrick found from his experience that just because learning occurs in the classroom or other training setting, there is no guarantee that a person will demonstrate those same skills in the real-world job setting. Thus, the training director should do a followup evaluation several months after the training to determine whether the skills learned are being used on the job.

To determine whether the knowledge, skills, and attitudes are being used on the job, and how well, it often is necessary to contact the learners and their supervisors, peers, and subordinates. Kirkpatrick oftentimes seems satisfied (e.g., in his 1998 book) with the use of a retrospective survey design (asking questions about the past in relation to the present) to measure transfer of training. A *retrospective survey* involves interviewing or having trainees and their supervisors, peers, and subordinates fill out questionnaires several weeks and months after the training event to measure their perceptions about whether the trainees are applying what they learned. Kirkpatrick (1998) provides several examples of actual questionnaires that can be used in this way. To have a rigorous and more valid indication of transfer of training to the workplace, Kirkpatrick also suggests using designs 2, 3, and 4 shown in Table 10.1. Level 3 evaluation is usually much more difficult to conduct than evaluation done in the classroom, but the resulting information is very important to decision makers; if no transfer takes place then one cannot expect to have level 4 outcomes, which are the original reason for conducting the training.

We developed Table 10.2 to provide you with a fuller understanding of the factors that can facilitate transfer of training. After you examine the table it will be clear that many strategies can be implemented during the training event to increase the likelihood of transfer. Other factors exist in the persons undergoing the training, and additional factors exist in the work environment that trainees return to after undergoing training. Instructional designers and performance technologists must be well versed in how to conduct effective training because without transfer, training investments will fail to produce any meaningful effects.

In discussing transfer, Kirkpatrick (1998) points out that there are five types of environments related to whether transfer of training will take place: (1) preventing environments (e.g., where the trainee's supervisor does not allow the trainee to use the new knowledge, attitudes, or skills), (2) discouraging environments (e.g., where the supervisor discourages use of the new knowledge, attitudes, or skills), (3) neutral environments (e.g., where the supervisor does not even acknowledge that the training ever took place), (4) encouraging environments (e.g., where the supervisor encourages the trainee to use new knowledge, attitudes, and skills on the job), and (5) requiring environments (e.g., where the supervisor formally monitors and requires the use of the new knowledge, attitudes, and skills in the work environment). For more information about transfer of training, we recommend Broad and Newstrom (1992).

Level 4: Results

Here the evaluator's goal is to find out if the training leads to "final results," including but *not* limited to financial results such as a positive return on investment (see note 2). Level 4 outcomes include any outcomes that affect the performance of the organization. Major financial, organizational, and employee results that are often hoped for as a result of training include reduced costs, higher quality of work, increased production, lower rates of employee turnover, lower absenteeism, reduction in scrap rate (i.e., less wasted resources), improved quality of work life, improved human relations, improved organizational communication, increased sales, fewer grievances, higher worker

TABLE 10.2 Factors facilitating transfer of training*

Pre-Training Work Environment Factors
Manager and employee agree on the need and importance of the upcoming training event
Manager and employee agree on appropriate learning goals
Manager and employee agree on appropriate transfer expectations upon employee's return to work posttraining
Training Design Factors (factors occurring during training)
Trainer uses transfer objectives in designing and delivering training program
Trainer provides guidance on transfer goals and strategies
Trainer encourages mastery learning
Training is based on relevant knowledge and skills (based on needs analysis and includes manager and employee input)
Trainer uses situated learning and authentic learning approaches
Trainer provides real-world examples and actual experience, in multiple settings and contexts if possible
Trainer makes sure trainees understand the general principles underlying the learned behaviors (called "transfer through principles")
Trainer makes sure trainees understand the importance and applicability of learning for future on-the-job performance
Trainer has trainees practice what they have learned
Trainer provides training on the use of metacognitive and transfer strategies
Trainer promotes transfer of self-efficacy beliefs
Personal and Motivation Factors
Trainee is satisfied with the training received
Trainee perceives value and importance of new knowledge, skills, and attitudes
Trainee gains intrinsic motivation/satisfaction from using new knowledge, skills, and attitudes
Trainee has high self-expectations, a desire for success, and high self-efficacy
Trainee has shared "ownership" of training content and event
Absence of trainee intrapersonal inhibiting factors (e.g., conflicting knowledge, values, and attitudes)
Trainee has intelligence, ability, aptitude, and prior knowledge
Personality type or individual difference variables (e.g., some people enjoy change; creative personality; mastery orientation; high need for achievement; internal locus of control; learner has learning goals rather than only performance goals)
Posttraining Work Environment and Organizational Factors
Availability of needed resources
Supportive organizational cultural and climate
Opportunities to use what was learned (i.e., new knowledge, skills, and attitudes)
Management and supervisor provide support, guidance, coaching, goal setting, and extrinsic rewards (such as praise, encouragement, help, increased freedom and responsibility, pay increases, formal and informal recognition)
Management works with trainee in posttraining goal setting and provides periodic feedback and reinforcement
Peer support and organizationwide commitment to training program success
Lack of inhibiting factors (e.g., lack of incentives, competing attitudes and competing work behaviors)

*To locate empirical research on these and additional factors, search education, business, and psychology databases starting with these general search terms: "transfer of training" and "transfer of learning."

morale, fewer accidents, greater job satisfaction, and, importantly, increased profits. Level 4 outcomes are often more distal rather than proximal outcomes (i.e., they often take time to appear after the training event). The behaviors acquired by learners during training should result in changes in the organization in the directions noted.

Kirkpatrick acknowledges the difficulty of being able to validate the relationship between the performance of learned skills and changes in the performance of an entire organization. Because there are so many other factors other than the training that also influence level 4 outcomes, stronger designs are often needed (e.g., designs 3 and 4 in Table 10.1). A potential problem is that implementation of these designs can be expensive and difficult. Nonetheless, it was Kirkpatrick's hope that training directors would attempt to conduct sound level 4 evaluations and thus enhance the status of training programs.

Implementation of Kirkpatrick's Model in Business and Industry

Are Kirkpatrick's levels of evaluation currently being implemented in business and industry? The American Society for Training and Development (ASTD) publishes an annual report on training operations in the United States. In ASTD's 2005 report (Sugrue & Rivera, 2005), 18 companies selected as Benchmarking Forum (BMF) organizations—large Fortune 500 companies and public sector organizations that share data and best practices with one another—identified the levels of evaluation they examined to assess the effectiveness of their training programs. Listed following are the percentage of programs offered by these organizations in which a particular level of evaluation was measured:

Reaction (Level 1)	91%
Learning (Level 2)	54%
Transfer of training (Level 3)	23%
Results (Level 4)	8%

These data indicate that in these exemplary organizations, over 90% of all programs offered are accompanied by questionnaires to measure learner attitudes toward the learning experience. However, learning is only measured in about half of the programs, and transfer to the job is only measured in one quarter of them. Moreover, in fewer than 10% of the cases is there any attempt to determine whether a program is having the desired impact on the organization. These data indicate that even though Kirkpatrick's ideas have had wide appeal in the training community, there is little evidence that the total evaluation model is being applied.

Implications of Kirkpatrick's Model for Instructional Design

Kirkpatrick's model can be used as part of both instructional design and human performance technology, and has traditionally been interpreted as a summative evaluation model. It has often been applied after training is completed to measure reactions, learning, and subsequent behaviors and results to validate the work of the training team and to be persuasive with top management about the importance of the training function. However, Kirkpatrick does note that his model can also be used to improve subsequent offerings of the training program (i.e., as formative evaluation).

Dick, Carey, and Carey (2005) have noted that Kirkpatrick's level 1 and 2 assessments are similar to the questionnaire and posttest approaches used for several decades by instructional designers with various drafts of their instruction. The resulting data are used as the fundamental information for a formative evaluation; that is, they indicate what problems learners have with the instruction and suggest what changes might be made to improve the instruction.

It is possible to view level 3 and 4 evaluations from the formative point of view as well as from the more traditional summative point of view. We believe that it is invaluable for designers to determine whether the knowledge, attitudes, and skills learned in training are being used in the performance context, and if not, to determine why not. It also is invaluable to determine the implications for improving training. Interviews with supervisors, peers, and subordinates provide evidence about the extent of use and the effectiveness of new skills employees acquire through training. Likewise, the impact of using the newly trained skills must be determined. Is transfer of training having the desired effect? Is transfer of training impacting sales, reducing costs, and so on? If not, how can the training be modified to provide the knowledge, attitudes, and skills that will have the desired effect? It is clear that Kirkpatrick's four levels of evaluation are just as useful to the instructional designer as they are to the training manager. Information from all four levels can be used to indicate the current effectiveness of the instruction and how it can be improved.

Implications of Kirkpatrick's Model for Performance Technology

More and more designers are becoming human performance technologists. This means that they begin projects with a performance analysis to determine the gap in the organization's goals and its accomplishments. These gaps are examined to determine their causes, and solutions are identified that are responsive to these causes. Performance technologists often find that training, when it is required at all, often is only a part of a total solution to an organizational problem. Thus, a team is required to design, develop, implement, and evaluate the total solution.

Kirkpatrick's model is consistent with the human performance technology approach. Certainly, designers will want to measure attitudes and learning outcomes for participants in any training they develop as part of the solution to a performance problem. It is also necessary to determine whether the newly learned skills are being used on the job, along with the other components of a solution such as improved technology or changes in procedures. Designers will also want to determine whether the implementation of the total solution is having the desired impact on the organization. The long-term solution should solve the underlying problem that led to the development of the solution. Thus there is a direct fit with the four levels of Kirkpatrick's model and the evaluation of the solution to an organization's performance problem.

Conclusion

Evaluation has always been an essential component of the instructional design process. Stufflebeam's CIPP model is an important one for instructional designers and human performance technologists to consider because it expands the role of evaluator to include context evaluation and needs assessment, input evaluation, and implementation or process evaluation, as well as traditional summative or product evaluation. Kirkpatrick's model of evaluation has been helpful because it expands the application of evaluation to performance on the job site. The Kirkpatrick model also is consistent with the major concepts of human performance technology that are used to solve human performance problems within organizations. Data indicate that training departments in the best training organizations still are not consistently conducting the full range of evaluations (neither CIPP nor Kirkpatrick), and thus are losing the benefits of this valuable information. It will be up to the designers of the future to rectify this situation.

Application Questions

1. Recent research indicates that most companies conduct level 1 evaluations, and many conduct level 2 evaluations. However, few organizations conduct evaluations at levels 3 and 4. Describe several possible reasons why companies conduct relatively few evaluations at the higher levels, and discuss the possible consequences of failing to conduct level 3 and level 4 evaluations.
2. Identify a recent instructional design or performance technology project on which you have worked. If you have not worked on any such project, interview someone who has. Describe how you did (or would) evaluate the project by using Kirkpatrick's four-level evaluation model. Discuss any problems you might encounter in attempting to apply the evaluation model, particularly with regard to conducting evaluations at level 3 and level 4.
3. It turns out that there are many evaluation models in addition to CIPP and Kirkpatrick's model. Conduct an Internet search and identify at least three additional evaluation models. Provide brief summaries (in your own words) of the ones that sound most promising to you.

References

Broad, M. L., & Newstrom, J. W. (1992). *Transfer of training: Action-packed strategies to ensure high payoff from training investments*. Cambridge, MA: Da Capo.

Chen, H. T. (1990). *Theory-driven evaluation.* Newbury Park, CA: Sage.

Dick, W., Carey, L., & Carey, J. O. (2005). *The systematic design of instruction*. (6th ed.) Boston: Allyn & Bacon.

Johnson, R. B., & Christensen, L. B. (2004). *Educational research: Quantitative, qualitative, and mixed approaches*. Boston: Allyn & Bacon.

Kirkpatrick, D. L. (1996). Great ideas revisited. *Training and Development, 50*(1), 54–59.

Kirkpatrick, D. L. (1998). *Evaluating training programs: The four levels*. San Francisco: Berrett-Koehler.

Patton, M. Q. (1997). *Utilization-focused evaluation: The new century text*. Thousand Oaks, CA: Sage.

Rossi, P. H., Lipsey, M. W., & Freeman, H. E. M. W. (2004). *Evaluation: A systematic approach.* Thousand Oaks, CA: Sage.

Scriven, M. (1967). The methodology of evaluation. In R. W. Tyler, R. M. Gagné, & M. Scriven (Eds.) *Perspectives of curriculum evaluation* (pp. 39–83). Chicago: Rand McNally.

Scriven, M. (1980). *The logic of Evaluation.* Inverness, CA: Edge press.

Scriven, M. (1991). Beyond formative and summative evaluation. In M. W. McLaughlin & D. D. Phillips (Eds.), *Evaluation and education: At quarter century* (pp. 19–64). Chicago: University of Chicago Press.

Scriven, M. (1996). Types of evaluation and types of evaluator. *Evaluation Practice, 17*(2), 151–161.

Stufflebeam, D. L. (1971). *Educational evaluation and decision making*. Itasca, IL: F. E. Peacock.

Stufflebeam, D. L., Madaus, G. F., & Kellaghan, T. (2000). *Evaluation models: Viewpoints on educational and human services evaluation* (2nd ed.). Boston: Kluwer Academic.

Sugrue, B., & Rivera, R. J. (2005). 2005 state of the industry report: ASTD's annual review of trends in workplace learning and performance. Alexandria, VA: American Society of Training & Development.

Daniel W. Surry
University of South Alabama

Donald P. Ely
Syracuse University

CHAPTER 11

Adoption, Diffusion, Implementation, and Institutionalization of Instructional Innovations

Knowledge and Comprehension Questions

1. Describe each of the following concepts related to Rogers's work on the diffusion of innovations: (1) adopter stages, (2) adopter categories, (3) perceived attributes of innovations, and (4) the S-shaped adoption curve.
2. Describe at least three of the main forms of resistance to innovations.
3. Describe each of the eight conditions that facilitate the implementation of an innovation.
4. Describe what it means for an innovation to have become institutionalized. Be sure to refer to the six commonly accepted indicators of institutionalization (Eiseman, Fleming, & Roody, 1990).

Editors' Introduction

The integration of instructional innovations into both academic and corporate settings is one of the most important parts of the instructional design process. While it was once common to believe that effective, well-designed instructional innovations would be readily adopted, that belief has proven to be a fallacy. Research, much of it based on the work of E. M. Rogers, has shown that a variety of social, personal, organizational, economic, and technical factors combine to influence the rate at which an innovation is adopted and diffused. In this chapter, Dan Surry and Don Ely provide an overview of diffusion theory and describe the key findings of diffusion researchers working within the field of instructional design and technology. The authors also discuss the emerging view that implementation and institutionalization, rather than adoption and diffusion, should be the focus of research in this area.

A large telecommunications company develops an electronic performance support system but, after initial widespread use, workers gradually stop using the system and the project is discontinued. A university starts a completely online M.B.A. program, but the program suffers from low enrollments and poor evaluations and is cancelled before any students ever graduate. A military unit purchases a simulator for training armored vehicle drivers that will be safer and save money in fuel and repair costs; however, trainers continue to use traditional methods whenever possible. A large K–12 school district adopts an innovative reading curriculum, but after two years, evaluators determine that the curriculum was never widely used by classroom teachers. These are but a few examples of how new, innovative, well-designed educational technology products often fail to have a significant impact on the organizations in which they are used. The purpose of this chapter is to provide an overview of research and theory concerning the adoption, diffusion, implementation, and institutionalization of educational innovations.

Educational technology is a field that supports innovation and change. The products and practices developed by educational technologists often require dramatic shifts in the way we think about, deliver, administer, and assess instruction and training. Using our example of a university starting an online M.B.A. program, we can see how the adoption of an innovative delivery approach would require major changes in the way courses are developed and taught, how students are assessed, how faculty performance is evaluated, and the nature of faculty–student interaction. Even though online delivery may have been the "best" technology from the university's perspective, the new degree program failed due to a variety of other factors.

Studying the adoption, diffusion, implementation, and institutionalization of innovations is appropriate for the field of educational technology because many of the innovations designed and developed by those in the field have suffered from a lack of widespread acceptance (Burkman, 1987). While it is possible to point to some notable exceptions, such as the common use of electronic mail or word processors in higher education (Green, 1996) or the growing use of performance technology in industry (Desrosiers & Harmon, 1996), many innovative educational technologies and practices have failed to be fully utilized.

One reason for the lack of intended utilization is that educational technologists have traditionally concentrated their efforts on developing instructionally sound and technologically superior products while giving less consideration to the context of their use. Technological superiority, while important, is not the only factor that determines whether or not an innovation is widely adopted—it might not even be the most important factor (Pool, 1997). A complex web of social, economic, technological, organizational, and individual factors interact to determine which technologies are adopted and the effect of a technology once adopted (Segal, 1994). To fully understand the field of educational technology, practitioners have to understand more than just hardware, software, design models, and learning theory. Understanding why people use educational technology and, perhaps more importantly, why they don't, is at the core of the process. That is where the study of adoption, diffusion, implementation, and institutionalization assists in bringing about change.

In this chapter, we discuss the adoption, diffusion, implementation, and institutionalization of educational technology. We begin by introducing some of the best-known theories of adoption and diffusion. Following this, we discuss examples of adoption and diffusion theory that have been incorporated into the field of educational technology. An important trend we then discuss is the gradual shift of focus from adoption (the initial decision to use an innovation) to the process of implementation and institutionalization. We define *implementation* and *institutionalization* and explore reasons this shift is occurring. We provide a list of conditions that contribute to and facilitate implementation (Ely, 1999) and close with a summary and conclusion.

Overview of Adoption and Diffusion

There has been a long and impressive history of research related to the adoption and diffusion of innovations (Surry & Brennan, 1998). Many of the most important and earliest studies in this area were conducted by researchers working in the field of rural sociology (Rogers, 1995). A study investigating the diffusion of hybrid-seed corn (Ryan & Gross, 1943) is considered to be the first major influential diffusion study of the modern era (Rogers, 1995). Other researchers have investigated the diffusion of innovations in such diverse fields as solar power (Keeler, 1976), farm innovations in India (Sekon, 1968), and weather forecasting (Surry, 1993).

The most widely cited and influential researcher in the area of adoption and diffusion is Everett Rogers. Rogers's *Diffusion of Innovations* is perhaps the single most important book related to this topic and provides a comprehensive overview of adoption and diffusion theory and applications. It is now in its fifth edition (Rogers, 2003).

One of the important theories discussed by Rogers is the Innovation-Decision Process model. This model suggests that the adoption of an innovation is not a single act, but a process that occurs over time. Potential adopters go through five stages when interacting with an innovation (Rogers, 2003). The first stage is "Knowledge," in which potential adopters discover an innovation and gain a basic understanding of what it is and how it works. The second stage is "Persuasion," in which potential adopters form a positive (or negative) impression of the innovation. It is only in the third stage, "Decision," that the innovation is actually adopted or rejected. The fourth stage, "Implementation," occurs when the innovation is actually used. In the fifth stage, "Confirmation," the adopter seeks information about the impact of the innovation and either continues or discontinues its use. The confirmation stage might also describe a later adoption of an innovation that was previously rejected.

Rogers (2003) also discusses the concept of *adopter categories*. This concept states that for any given innovation, a certain percentage of the population will readily adopt the innovation, while others will be less likely to adopt. According to Rogers, there is usually a normal distribution of the various adopter categories that forms the shape of a bell curve. Innovators, those who readily adopt an innovation, make up about 2.5% of any population. Early Adopters make up approximately 13.5% of the population. Most people will fall into either the Early Majority (34%) or the Late Majority (34%) categories. Laggards, those who will resist an innovation until the bitter end, comprise about 16% of the population. The concept of adopter categories is important because it shows that all innovations go through a natural, predictable, and sometimes lengthy process before becoming widely adopted within a population.

The concept of *perceived attributes* (Rogers, 2003) has served as the basis for a number of diffusion studies (e.g., Fliegel & Kivlin, 1966; Wyner, 1974). This concept refers to the opinions of potential adopters who base their feelings about an innovation on how they perceive that innovation in regard to five key attributes—relative advantage, compatibility, complexity, trialability, and observability. In short, this construct states that people are more likely to adopt an innovation if the innovation offers them a better way to do something; is compatible with their values, beliefs and needs; is not too complex; can be tried out before adoption; and has observable benefits. Perceived attributes are important because they show that potential adopters base their opinions of an innovation on a variety of attributes, not just on relative advantage. Educational technologists should think about how potential adopters will perceive an innovation in terms of all of the five attributes, and not exclusively on technological superiority.

The S-shaped adoption curve is another important idea that Rogers (2003) describes. This curve shows that a successful innovation will go through a period of slow adoption before experiencing a sudden period of rapid adoption and then a gradual leveling off. When depicted on a graph, this slow growth, rapid expansion, and leveling off form an S-shaped curve (Figure 11.1). The period of rapid expansion, for most successful innovations, occurs when social and technical factors combine to permit the innovation to experience dramatic growth. For example, one can think of the many factors that combined to lead to the sudden widespread acceptance of the World Wide Web between the years 1993 and 2000.

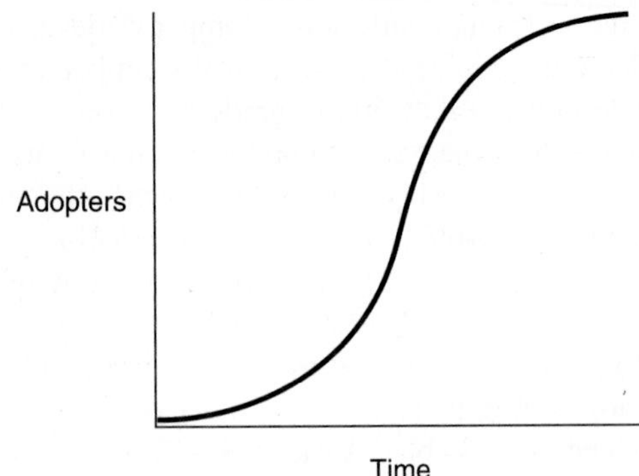

FIGURE 11.1 Example of an S-curve showing initial slow growth, a period of rapid adoption, and a gradual leveling off.

Diffusion Theory Applied to Educational Technology

The theories and concepts discussed by Rogers in *Diffusion of Innovations* (1995, 2003) are applicable to the study of innovation in almost any field. A number of researchers (e.g., Surry, 1993; Litchy, 2000) have used these theories and concepts to study the adoption and diffusion of educational technology innovations. In the field of educational technology, diffusion theory has most often been applied to the study either of artifacts, such as computers, or of knowledge, such as innovative teaching techniques (Holloway, 1996). Put another way, educational technology innovations can be broadly categorized as either "technology" innovations or "process" innovations. Burkman (1987) specifically links diffusion theory with educational technology. Burkman realized that innovations associated with the field of educational technology had been suffering from a lack of utilization and turned to diffusion theory for a possible solution. He used perceived attributes to develop a method for creating instructional products that would be more appealing to potential adopters. Burkman called his new approach "user-oriented instructional development (UOID)." The five steps in Burkman's UOID are:

1. Identify the potential adopter.
2. Measure relevant potential adopter perceptions.
3. Design and develop a user-friendly product.
4. Inform the potential adopter (of the product's user friendliness).
5. Provide postadoption support.

In addition to Burkman, other researchers have incorporated diffusion theory into educational technology applications. For example, Stockdill and Morehouse (1992) use diffusion concepts in a checklist of factors to consider when attempting to increase the adoption of distance learning and other educational technologies. Farquhar and Surry (1994) use diffusion theory to identify and analyze factors that might impede or assist the adoption of instructional innovations within organizations. Sherry, Lawyer-Brook, and Black (1997) use diffusion concepts as the basis for an evaluation of a program intended to introduce teachers to the Internet. A growing amount of dissertation research is being conducted in the area of diffusion theory as it relates to educational technology.

From Adoption and Diffusion to Implementation

As mentioned earlier, there is a trend in innovation research away from focusing on adoption and diffusion towards focusing on implementation and institutionalization. *Implementation* is defined as the actual use of an innovation in a practical setting (Fullan, 1996). Until Fullan and Pomfret (1977) spelled out the process and issues in their review of implementation research, not much was said about the steps after adoption. Now, many researchers are interested in understanding the critical role that implementation plays in the change process. Implementation should be from the beginning an integral part of a comprehensive and systematic change plan.

From Replication to Mutual Adaptation

In the process of implementation, innovations that require replication for successful outcomes have traditionally followed a process by which each product, procedure, and practice had to maintain a high fidelity to the original or else success could not be guaranteed. Fullan and Pomfret (1977, p. 360) introduced the concept of "mutual adaptation," whereby local conditions should be considered and modification of original materials and procedures should be altered accordingly. It was felt that the local professionals could make better assessments of the needs and potential reception of the innovation than the original developer or researcher. Purists, however, felt that if replication was not identical to the original specifications, implementation might fail.

Once professional educators realized that they could modify programs, products and practices, it was a short step to an approach that was less "lockstep." Local participation in the modifications has created a greater sense of ownership.

Other Models

One of the tools often used to guide implementation efforts in schools is Hall's Concerns Based Adoption Model (CBAM) (Hall & Hord, 1987). In the implementation phase of this model, the Levels of Use (LoU) scale is introduced (Hall & Loucks, 1975). The basic levels are Nonuse, Orientation (initial information), Preparation (to use), Mechanical use, Routine, Refinement, Integration, and Renewal. The last four levels actually move into the area of institutionalization discussed later in this chapter. A modification of the LoU, Levels of Technological Implementation (LoTi), based on measurement of classroom use of computers, has been proposed by Moersch (1995). Moersch modifies Hall's levels to provide guidance for determining the extent of implementation using seven levels: Nonuse, Awareness, Exploration, Infusion, Integration, Expansion, and Refinement.

What About Resistance to Innovations?

Over the years there have been studies and explorations of the resistance factors that thwart diffusion and implementation efforts. Prominent among those who have journeyed into this puzzling morass are Zaltman and Duncan (1977). These authors define *resistance* as "any conduct that serves to maintain the status quo in the face of pressure to alter the status quo" (p. 61). The basic argument has been that if we knew what types of resistance exist, perhaps we could design strategies to combat them.

There are many different types of resistance. Pajo and Wallace (2001) categorize barriers to the use of Web-based learning in higher education as "personal barriers," "attitudinal barriers," and "organizational barriers." Berge, Muilenburg, and Van Haneghan (2002), identify 64 barriers to the adoption of distance learning and conduct a factor analysis resulting in 10 factors, including "threatened by technology," "legal issues," and "access." Barriers can also be classified as cultural, social, technological, psychological; other designations also may be used. Using the examples at the beginning of this chapter, we can see how researchers traditionally would have looked at reasons for resistance to each of the failed innovations. Researchers looking at the failed electronic performance support system developed by the telecommunications company might look at the organizational structure, communications channels, and attitudes of the workers towards the company. Those studying the simulation for armored vehicle drivers might identify organizational culture, tradition, attitudes towards technology, and motivation as reasons for lack of full implementation. Studying the barriers to implementation, while important and necessary, is limited in that it is only effective for fostering implementation when strategies for overcoming specific points of resistance have been developed.

Looking for Facilitative Conditions

A less common but emerging approach to understanding the process of implementation has been to tease out reasons for successful implementation rather than to identify the barriers. What are the conditions that appear to facilitate the process where innovations have been adopted and successfully implemented? Are there consistencies among the facilitating conditions from innovation to innovation and from place to place? This logic changes the focus of the research from resistance to a more positive one of facilitating factors, thus providing avenues for further exploration. Rather than come up with ways to get around resistance, a series of studies looked at successful implementation of innovations and asked, "Why were these innovations successful?" The findings of these studies uncovered eight conditions that contribute to implementation (Ely, 1999):

1. *Dissatisfaction with the status quo.* A belief on the part of the end users that things could be better or that others seem to be moving ahead while we are standing still. Dissatisfaction is based on an innate feeling or can be induced by external strategies. Strategies typically used by change agents to induce dissatisfaction with the status quo include product demonstrations, dissemination of "best practices" or research findings, visits to sites using newer/better products or practices, personal testimonials, trips to conferences or trade shows, and use of marketing and other information provided by vendors.
2. *Knowledge and skills exist.* Knowledge and skills are those required by the ultimate user of the innovation. Without them, people become frustrated and immobilized. Training is usually a vital part of most successful innovations.
3. *Availability of resources.* Resources are those things that are required to make implementation work—the hardware, software, audiovisual media, and the like. Without them, implementation is reduced.
4. *Availability of time.* Time is necessary to acquire and practice knowledge and skills. This means good time—"company" time, not just personal time at home.
5. *Rewards and/or incentives exist.* An *incentive* is something that serves as an expectation of a reward—a stimulus to act. A *reward* is something given for meeting an acceptable standard of performance.
6. *Participation.* This is shared decision making; communication among all parties involved in the process or their representatives.
7. *Commitment.* This condition demonstrates firm and visible evidence that there is endorsement and continuing support for the innovation. This factor is seen most frequently in those who advocate the innovation and their supervisors.
8. *Leadership.* This factor includes (1) leadership of the executive officer of the organization and, sometimes, by a board and (2) leadership within the institution or project related to the day-to-day activities of the innovation being implemented.

These eight facilitative conditions identified by Ely (1999) have been the basis for a number of other implementation studies. For example, Jeffrey (1993) used the conditions to study the implementation of a peer coaching program in school districts and found that "dissatisfaction with the status quo" and "knowledge and skills" were necessary conditions. Surry and Ensminger (2002) also found significant differences in the relative importance of the conditions for those working in education and those in business. A number of other studies (e.g., Ravitz, 1999; Bauder, 1993; Varden, 2002) also have been based on the eight facilitative conditions.

Variables in the Setting and the Innovation Itself

It is clear from prior research in this area that the eight conditions are present in varying degrees whenever examples of successful implementation are studied. What is not so clear is the role of the setting in which the innovation is implemented. The setting and the nature of the innovation are major factors influencing the degree to which each condition is present. Some of the variables in the setting include organizational climate, political complexity, and certain demographic factors. Some of the most important variables regarding the innovation are the attributes of the innovation discussed earlier—its relative advantage (when compared with the current status), compatibility with the values of the organization or institution, its complexity (or simplicity), trialability before wholesale adoption, and observability by other professionals or the public. But . . . is implementation the final stage?

Implementation should lead to institutionalization. Institutionalization takes place when an innovation is assimilated into the structure of an organization and changes that organization in a stable way (Miles, Eckholm, & Vandenburghe, 1987). Some writers refer to this process as *routinization* or *continuation*. The ultimate criterion for a successful innovation is that it is routinely used in settings for which it was designed. It has become integral to the organization or the social system and is no longer considered to be an innovation.

Indicators of Institutionalization

According to the Regional Laboratory for Educational Improvement of the Northeast and Islands (Eiseman, Fleming & Roody, 1990), there are six commonly accepted indicators of institutionalization:

1. Acceptance by relevant participants—a perception that the innovation legitimately belongs.
2. The innovation is stable and routinized.
3. Widespread use of the innovation throughout the institution or organization.
4. Firm expectation that use of the practice and/or product will continue within the institution or organization.
5. Continuation does not depend on the actions of specific individuals but on the organizational culture, structure, or procedures.
6. Routine allocations of time and money.

Once implementation has been achieved, one more decision must be made: "Is this innovation something we want to continue for the immediate future?" If it is, the listed criteria could be used to assess the extent to which the innovation is institutionalized. Several other indicators of routine use, called "passages and cycles" are listed by Yin and Quick (1978): support by local funds; new personnel classification; changes in governance; internalization of training; and turnover of key personnel.

Fostering Implementation and Institutionalization

Now that we as a field have a better understanding of some of the issues relating to implementation and institutionalization, the next step is to apply these ideas to actual implementation situations. The goal is to use the ideas to foster the implementation and institutionalization of innovations. The complexity and uniqueness of each change situation means that no single, simplistic, "magic" prescriptive plan for fostering implementation exists. However, the eight facilitative conditions discussed in this chapter can be used as a framework for studying local situations and developing a plan for fostering change.

There are, perhaps, two main ways that change agents can use the eight conditions to foster implementation and institutionalization. The first is to use the conditions as the basis for an "implementation analysis." Such an analysis would involve defining each of the conditions for a specific innovation and determining the level at which each is present within an organization prior to adoption. In the previous example of a K–12 school district adopting a new reading curriculum, an implementation analysis would look at each of the eight conditions from the perspective of all stakeholder groups; for example, defining "dissatisfaction with the status quo" and determining the extent that district and school level administrators, teachers, support staff, parents, and students are dissatisfied with the current way of doing things. Once change agents understand how stakeholders define and value each of the conditions in regard to a specific innovation, it will be possible to develop a plan for maximizing the impact of the more important conditions. If, for example, "rewards and incentives" was identified as the most important condition, it would be possible to build strategies for maximizing that condition into an implementation plan.

The second way that change agents can use the eight conditions to foster implementation and institutionalization is to develop an organizational culture that includes all eight conditions in an ongoing, holistic, systematic way. This is much more difficult than doing an implementation analysis for a specific innovation but is also probably more effective in fostering implementation and institutionalization. Developing an organizational climate for implementation involves two activities. The first is a continuous assessment by change agents and management of the definition of each condition, the level that each condition is present within the organization, and the relative importance of each condition for each stakeholder group within the organization. The second activity is a sincere effort on the part of management to create, update, and maintain the appropriate level of each condition within the organization.

Summary and Conclusion

Case studies of diffusion, adoption, implementation, and institutionalization have been conducted in many organizations and settings. One important conclusion is that there is no formula for this process. There are many elements and principles that should be considered, most of them outlined in this chapter. However, simple transfer of these principles to specific environments would likely be futile. Just as most instructional design projects require a systemic approach, so does the change process. There is no substitute for a "front-end analysis" or needs assessment that yields the goals and objectives to be attained. Communication among all participants throughout the process is essential. A strategy or plan for achieving the goals is the best way to proceed when considering the many variables that are likely to affect the outcomes. Evaluation should be a constant partner during the process.

All of this activity should be coordinated by a change agent—a person who is sensitive to the variables that will impinge on the process. The change agent could be an internal person or an external specialist. Awareness and experience with the change process are essential for a successful outcome.

Application Questions

1. Think of an innovative product or practice that was introduced in the last several years. Individually or as a class, ask a number of people when they first "adopted" or began to use the innovation. Make a graph with the vertical axis representing the number of people who adopted the innovation and the horizontal axis representing time, beginning when the innovation was first introduced. The adoption of electronic mail or the Internet might serve as excellent examples. Does the distribution on the graph resemble an S-shaped curve? If so, is the curve more of a steep or sloping curve? Does your experiment tend to support or contradict the concept of the S-shaped adoption curve discussed in this chapter?
2. The five perceived attributes of an innovation are relative advantage, compatibility, complexity, trialability, and observability. Think of an innovation that you, your organization, or someone you know has recently adopted. Which of the perceptions do you think were most important in the adoption decision? Which perceptions were not important? Do you believe it is possible to measure people's perceptions and design a product that is "perception friendly"? Why or why not?
3. Review Ely's eight conditions that facilitate the implementation of an innovation. Do you believe that each of the conditions is equally important, or are some more important than others? If you believe some are more important, describe which ones you think are more important and discuss why you feel that way. If you believe all of the conditions are equally important, discuss why.

References

Bauder, D. Y. (1993) Computer integration in K–12 schools: Conditions related to adoption and implementation (kindergarten, twelfth-grade). (University Microfilms, DAI-A 54/08, 2991)

Berge, Z. L., Muilenburg, L. Y., and Van Haneghan, J. (2002). Barriers to distance education and training: Survey results. *Quarterly Review of Distance Education, 3*(4), 409–418.

Burkman, E. (1987). Factors affecting utilization. In R. M. Gagné (Ed.) *Instructional Technology: Foundations* (pp. 429–455). Hillsdale, NJ: Lawrence Erlbaum Associates.

Desrosiers, S. M. & Harmon, S. W. (1996). Performance support systems for education and training: Could this be the next generation? In M. L. Bailey & M. J. Jones (Eds.) *Selected Papers from the Fifth Annual LEPS research symposium: Technology, education, and work* (pp. 3:1–3:9). Dekalb, IL: Northern Illinois University.

Eiseman, J. W., Fleming, D. S., & Roody, D. S. (1990). *Making sure it sticks: The school improvement leader's role in institutionalizing change*. Andover, MA: The Regional Laboratory.

Ely, D. P. (1999). Conditions that facilitate the implementation of educational technology innovations. *Educational Technology, 39*(6), 23–27.

Farquhar, J. D., & Surry, D. W. (1994). Adoption analysis: An additional tool for instructional developers. *Education and Training Technology International, 31*(1), 19–25.

Fliegel, F. C., & Kivlin, J. E. (1966). Attributes of innovations as factors in diffusion. *American Journal of Sociology, 72*(3), 235–248.

Fullan, M. (1996). Implementation of innovations. In D. P. Ely & T. Plomp (Eds.), *International encyclopedia of educational technology* (pp. 273–281). Oxford: Elsevier Science.

Fullan, M. (2003). *Change forces with a vengeance.* Toronto: Taylor & Francis.

Fullan, M., & Pomfret, A. (1977). Research on curriculum and instruction implementation. *Review of Educational Research, 47*(1), 335–397.

Green, K. C. (1996, March/April). The coming ubiquity of information technology. *Change,* 259–263.

Hall, G., & Hord, S. (1987). *Change in schools: Facilitating the process.* Albany, NY: SUNY Press.

Hall, G., & Loucks, S. (1975). Levels of use of the innovation: A framework for analyzing innovation adoption. *Journal of Teacher Education, 26*(1), 52–56.

Holloway, R. E. (1996). Diffusion and adoption of educational technology: A critique of research design. In D. H. Jonassen (Ed.), *Handbook of research for educational communications and technology* (pp. 1107–1133). New York: Macmillan.

Keeler, J. D. (1976). Application of innovation attributes dimension to a new solar energy product: Implications for advertising and public relations. *Dissertation Abstracts International, 37,* 7386A. (University Microfilms, 77–11, 540)

Lichty, M. (2000). The innovation-decision process and the factors that influence computer implementation by medical school faculty. (University Microfilms, DAI-A 61/03, 954)

Miles, M. B., Eckholm, M., & Vandenburghe, R. (Eds.). (1987). *School improvement: Exploring the process of institutionalization.* Leuven, Belgium: ACCO.

Moersch, C. (1995). Levels of technology implementation (LoTi): A framework for measuring classroom technology use. *Learning & Leading with Technology, 23*(3), 40–42.

Pajo, K., & Wallace, C. (2001). Barriers to the uptake of web-based technology by university teachers. *Journal of Distance Education 16*(1), 70–84.

Pool, R. (1997). *Beyond engineering: How society shapes technology.* New York: Oxford University Press.

Ravitz, J. L. (1999). *Conditions that facilitate teacher Internet use in schools with high Internet connectivity: A national survey. (*University Microfilms, DAI-A 60/04, 1094)

Rogers, E. M. (1995). *Diffusion of innovations* (4th ed.). New York: Free Press.

Rogers, E. M. (2003). *Diffusion of innovations* (5th ed.). New York: Free Press.

Ryan, B., & Gross, C. (1943). The diffusion of hybrid seed corn in two Iowa communities. *Rural Sociology*, 8, 15–24.

Segal, H. P. (1994*). Future imperfect: the mixed blessings of technology in America.* Amherst: University of Massachusetts Press.

Sekon, G. S. (1968). Differential perceptions of attributes of innovations by professional advocates and their clientele. *Dissertation Abstracts, 30,* 1245A. (University Microfilms, 69–14, 567)

Sherry, L., Lawyer-Brook, D., & Black, L. (1997). Evaluation of the Boulder Valley Internet Project: A theory-based approach to evaluation design. *Journal of Interactive Learning Research, 8*(2), 199–234.

Stockdill, S. H., & Morehouse, D. L. (1992). Critical factors in the successful adoption of technology: A checklist based on TDC findings. *Educational Technology, 32*(1), 57–58.

Surry, D. W. (1993). The role of perceptions in the development and adoption of three computer-based learning modules. (Doctoral Dissertation, University of Georgia, 1993). *Dissertation Abstracts International, 54*(9), 3409A–3410A.

Surry, D. W., & Brennan, J. P. (1998). *Diffusion of instructional innovations: Five important, unexplored questions.* (ERIC Document Reproduction Service No. ED 422 892).

Surry, D. W., & Ensminger, D. (2002, April). *Perceived importance of conditions that facilitate implementation.* Paper presented at the annual meeting of the American Educational Research Association, New Orleans, LA.

Varden, C. H. (2002). Application of Ely's conditions in implementation of a wireless laptop program. (University Microfilms, DAI-A 63/01, 154)

Wyner, N. B. (1974). A study of diffusion of innovation: Measuring perceived attributes of an innovation that determine the rate of adoption. *Dissertation Abstracts International, 35,* 3583A. (University Microfilms, 74-26, 628)

Yin, R. K. & Quick, S. K. (1978). *Changing urban bureaucracies: How new practices become routinized.* Lexington, MA: D. C. Heath.

Zaltman, G., & Duncan, R. (1977). *Strategies for planned change.* New York: John Wiley & Sons.

Brenda C. Litchfield
University of South Alabama

CHAPTER 12

Instructional Project Management: Managing Instructional Design Projects on Site and at a Distance

Knowledge and Comprehension Questions

1. Explain the difference between *leadership* and *management*. Give an example of each one.
2. Describe how personality and behavior affect a person's performance as an instructional project manager. What are some positive attributes and some negative attributes?
3. Using Figure 12.1, describe the type of typical communications an instructional project manager would have with each person or group.
4. In what ways can creative people pose interesting communication challenges for instructional project managers?
5. Consider the attributes of successful project managers. Which are your own three strongest attributes? Give an example of a situation in which you used each one.
6. How would being both the leader and the project manager of an instructional project present unique challenges for an individual? What would be the easiest part and the most difficult part of having both jobs on the same project?
7. What do you consider to be the three most important aspects of managing a project at a distance?

Editors' Introduction

As was pointed out in earlier chapters, instructional design projects usually involve teams of professionals, often including instructional designers, computer programmers, artists, subject matter experts (SMEs), and others. Such projects often take place over an extended period of time, sometimes several months or more. In cases such as these, someone must manage the instructional design project. Often these managers are graduates of instructional design programs who have worked as designers for a few years and have now moved up to a position that requires them to manage instructional design projects.

In this chapter, Brenda Litchfield discusses some of the skills needed to be a successful manager of instructional design projects—effective leadership skills, interpersonal communications skills, and team-building skills. Litchfield provides suggestions related to acquiring and improving your skills in each of these areas. She also describes the trend toward managing instructional design projects at a distance, and discusses the skills necessary to manage projects of this nature.

Consider the following scenarios involving instructional design projects:

> *Scenario 1*—Your supervisor comes to you and says, "Someone from the Department of Corrections called and wants us to do some work. Instead of having the correctional officers sit and listen to long lectures for recertification, the department wants it all on computers. There are 10 separate topics and they are to be interesting and informative. You will be the project manager for this instructional design project and I need a detailed plan by next week." (Final team—15 members.)
>
> *Scenario 2*—A contract is given to an organization to design a comprehensive set of online courses for restaurant managers on topics such as dealing with employees, budgets, and general food service management. Eight online course designers who live in different locations are hired to design and develop courses. They must work with programmers and graphic artists. All courses must be in a similar format with the same look and feel. The project has a seven-month timeline. (Final team—15 members.)
>
> *Scenario 3*—Repeat offenders convicted of driving under the influence of alcohol (DUI) are attending essentially the same program as first-time offenders, and it is not effective. The Office of the State Supreme Court calls and asks you to design a program that is 20 hours in length with interactive activities. The activities do not have to be original, as long as you cite the source. You are given three months to deliver the materials. (Final team—3 members.)
>
> *Scenario 4*—The three-year, $4 million National Science Foundation (NSF) multimedia design project proposal was meticulously written, rewritten, and submitted, and is finally approved. Everything is in there—objectives, timelines, cost breakdowns, design specifications, content, evaluation procedures. You have been chosen to be the project manager. All you have to do is get out the schedules and follow them, and everything will be easy. (Final team—35 members, 5 in another town.)

How would you react to each of these scenarios? What would you do first? As a manager for these instructional design projects, what leadership and management skills will you need? What communication skills will you need? How would you organize things? How would you get these different teams motivated and moving in the same direction to complete each project on time and within budget? How will you manage a virtual team?

Each scenario is an example of an instructional design project requiring instructional project management skills. These projects vary considerably in many aspects. Some will have all the staff under one roof while others will use developers in different locations. Some have a complete design document specifying all procedures and deliverables. For others, it is up to you to do all the planning. One example involves just a few team members. Others require staffs of 15 to 35 talented individuals. The timeline for one is three months, another will take three years.

The common thread running through each project, regardless of scope and complexity, is your ability as project manager to manage and lead your team. It is often thought that a small instructional design project is much easier than a large one. This is not necessarily true. Regardless of size, you should be able to monitor progress, solve problems, motivate (Keller, 1999), and move your team forward by communicating your instructions and desires. Individuals on a team will commit to tasks and projects that pay off for them in a number of ways (Clark, 1999). Your job is to find out what the desired payoffs are and use them to the project's and your advantage.

There are numerous books and articles on project management detailing how to budget, schedule, produce documents, and evaluate projects (e.g., Bennatan, 1992; Fuller, 1997; Gilbreath, 1986; Greer, 2001; Lewis, 1995). This chapter will not focus on areas considered to be *tools* of project management. In this chapter we concentrate on the aspects of project management and leadership related to the basic personal qualities that can help make you an effective project manager and team leader while producing a quality instructional product. The areas we consider especially important for successful project management are development of effective leadership skills, learning to communicate with your team, and developing effective teams.

Management and Leadership

When you read books and articles on management, you will often read different definitions of *management*. The most commonly reoccurring component of management definitions is that a manager is tasked with achieving certain organizational goals with a team or staff of individuals. Specific tasks are to be carried out; it is up to the manager to make sure they are accomplished. Hersey, Blanchard, and Johnson (2001) offer one definition encompassing many aspects of what a manager does: "Management is the process of working with and through individuals and groups and other resources (equipment, capital, technology) to accomplish organizational goals" (p. 8). Strong interpersonal skills are paramount to the success of a manager.

Project management employs many of the components of general management (e.g., program management and administrative management). It does, however, differ because of the nature of projects. What is a project? According to Lewis (1995), a *project* is a one-time job that has definite starting and ending points, clearly defined objectives, a prescribed scope of work, and (usually) a budget. This is an ideal definition because (as you will find out) some projects never seem to end due to unclear objectives and scope, along with an inadequate budget. As illustrated in the introductory scenarios, each project is different and can take on a life of its own. To see an instructional project through to completion, your personal management style will be a critical factor in ensuring the team meets deadlines and produces its deliverables.

Successful project management also requires leadership. *Management* and *leadership* are terms often used synonymously but are operationally two different sets of actions and philosophies. Leadership deals with a broader aspect of achieving goals and objectives. Leaders function more as innovators, visionaries, trust builders, and influencers of people. Leaders influence people through charisma and earned respect. Managers execute the plan, keep the closest goal in sight, and focus on production and deadlines. As Warren Bennis states, "Managers do things right, leaders do the right things" (as quoted in Carter-Scott, 1994, p. 11).

Because management skills (meeting deadlines, supervising staff, staying within budget, and so forth) are usually understood more easily than leadership skills, we will touch briefly on some important aspects of leadership. In the past, it was widely accepted that some people are "born leaders" and others were not. Today, however, it is believed individuals can become successful leaders through work experience, hardship, opportunity, education, role models, and mentors. These situations can further be enhanced through personal characteristics such as intelligence, physical energy, and social potential (Conger, 1992).

According to Hersey et al. (2001), leadership involves three interrelated competencies. These areas represent cognitive, behavioral, and process skills. Being able to diagnose the environment in terms of assessing the current situation and planning what can be done to solve a problem is considered a cognitive skill. Adapting behavior and other resources to match whatever actions are required to solve the problem is a behavioral skill. The process skill is communication. Being able to communicate with staff members and have them understand plans and goals while you listen and respond to their suggestions and concerns is the third essential competency of an effective leader.

Certainly, there are numerous aspects of diagnosing, adapting, and communicating, with each being worthy of further study. The important thing to remember is that as an instructional project manager you must integrate these skills in your daily routine because *you* are responsible for the ultimate success or failure of your project. You must always know the status of the project on which your staff and team members are working. If they are behind schedule or do not understand project objectives, not only must you recognize this, you must be able to design a solution to remedy whatever the problem is.

So, as a person in the position of directing an instructional project, should you be more of a manager or a leader? You must be both. As an instructional project manager, you are in a unique position requiring both management and leadership skills. In instructional projects such as the ones described in the beginning of this chapter, there may be as few as 3 people or as many as 35 on a project. Unless you are working for a large instructional design or training organization where many teams and numerous projects run concurrently, you will probably be working with a relatively small group of individuals. In these cases, as project manager you will be responsible for meeting your goals, timelines, and budget. At the same time you will be the person leading and motivating your team with your energy, insight, and encouragement.

The ability to influence your team depends heavily on your personality and behavior. Maslow (1998) posits that enlightened management can produce more well-rounded employees. If management is fair, rewarding, and understanding, then employees develop more positive actions among each other and with people they know. Lewis (1995) surveyed participants in many of his workshops about what they thought it took to be a successful project manager. Participants mentioned characteristics such as being a good listener, being a team builder, providing feedback, having a sense of humor, showing mutual respect, knowing how to delegate, being a good decision maker, challenging the team to do well, and being flexible as just some of the traits they desired in a manager.

From this list it is evident the skills considered most critical to successful project management were not the abilities to create schedules, define objectives, develop a budget, or conduct formative evaluation. They were interpersonal skills that direct and motivate a team. Certainly, technical skills are important; a project would ultimately fail if the project manager could not handle these aspects of the job. But the personality and behavior you exhibit toward your team is the underlying foundation that builds all relationships and determines whether you are respected or simply tolerated as a leader. You must be flexible and adapt to a variety of situations and people throughout the course of a project.

In the late 1960s, Hersey and Blanchard (Hersey et al., 2001) developed a leadership model labeled Situational Leadership. Since then it has gone through modifications and has evolved into a four-phase comprehensive model for developing leadership skills and influencing individuals. It is based on three factors: (1) the amount of guidance and direction a leader gives; (2) the amount of socio-emotional support a leader provides; and (3) the readiness level followers exhibit in performing a specific task, function, or objective. From your basic personality and behavior you develop a leadership style. Different situations and people require different responses (Bolton & Bolton, 1996). Your leadership style should not remain consistent. This may seem like odd advice, but to treat all situations and all people exactly the same will result in your handling some situations effectively and others ineffectively. By adapting your leadership style (and resources) based on correctly analyzing specific situations you will be more effective.

Using the Situational Leadership approach involves a cycle of phases based on the maturity of your project team. If your team is inexperienced and unsure (often at the beginning of projects) your leadership style (phase 1) would be directive, detailed, and supervisory without being overbearing or appearing to be demanding. As your team gains more confidence but is still learning (phase 2), you can move from a more directive role to one where you explain and clarify decisions and reward improvements in direction and knowledge. At this point you are securing the team's "buy in" of the process and product. The more they learn, the more they can function on their own. Now your leadership role (phase 3) changes to focusing on results and making sure your team is rewarded for effort and production. The last stage (phase 4) involves less of your involvement as a director and more as a monitor. Your team has learned how to work together to produce a product and you can step back and let them work without the close supervision that was necessary in the beginning of the project.

In each of the four phases there are fine lines between being effective or ineffective in your management. For example, while you may see your decrease in direct, observable monitoring as an indication of your trust in your team, the team members may see it as a lack of interest on your part. What is important in each phase is how you communicate what you want to those involved in designing and producing the product.

Communication

Effective communication among all individuals is an essential skill that is becoming more important as we move to a wider base of workers and businesses (Tosca, 1997). Communication with your team members, whether they are housed in the same building or located in different states or countries, can be challenging. Everyone requires concrete instructions as well as enthusiasm, motivation, and acceptance. Your team will want to know exactly what you expect, when you expect it, and what quality you expect. There is no room for errors in communication when *you* are ultimately responsible for deadlines, budgets, and products. Do not assume people know what you are thinking. Make it crystal clear—regardless of how many people you are communicating with. Often serious communication problems can arise when you are working on a small project with just a few people because it is easy to believe you are all thinking the same way.

Discipline problems among some team members are unavoidable in most projects. In numerous situations you will have to recognize inadequate or improper actions and have a serious meeting with some of your team members. How you handle these situations can have a strong bearing on other team members' perception of your leadership. To recognize a discrepant situation and not act quickly can make you appear to be uninterested, uninvolved, or showing favoritism. A classic in the field of management, *The One-Minute Manager* (Blanchard & Johnson, 1982), stresses the importance of "the one-minute reprimand." Reprimand immediately, explain exactly what was done wrong and how you feel about it, focus on the action, not the person, remind that you value them, and end it. No overblown confrontations, just straight-to-the-point communication.

As an instructional project manager, you will have to communicate with a variety of people individually and as groups. Figure 12.1 illustrates the typical communication pattern of a project manager. The arrow width indicates the frequency of communication with each individual or group. You will also have to negotiate and interpret communication between groups and individuals even though you may not attend meetings or interact with some individuals directly. In these cases you may act as a mediator between groups—an important function and one that is necessary to keep the project running smoothly and on time.

Team Communication

A team working on an instructional design project usually consists of instructional designers, assistant project managers (large projects), writers, artists, and (in video/computer projects) videographers, scriptwriters, and other technical people such as programmers. The majority of your communication will be with the team itself. Your primary tasks with the team are to motivate and monitor progress. These are the individuals with whom you will be most involved over the term of the project. Whether you have a team of 3 or 35, accurate, timely, and genuine communication with the team is the most critical element in successfully completing an instructional project. The bulk of your communication with the team will focus on project direction and motivation. You should communicate your enthusiasm and monitor progress regularly. Even

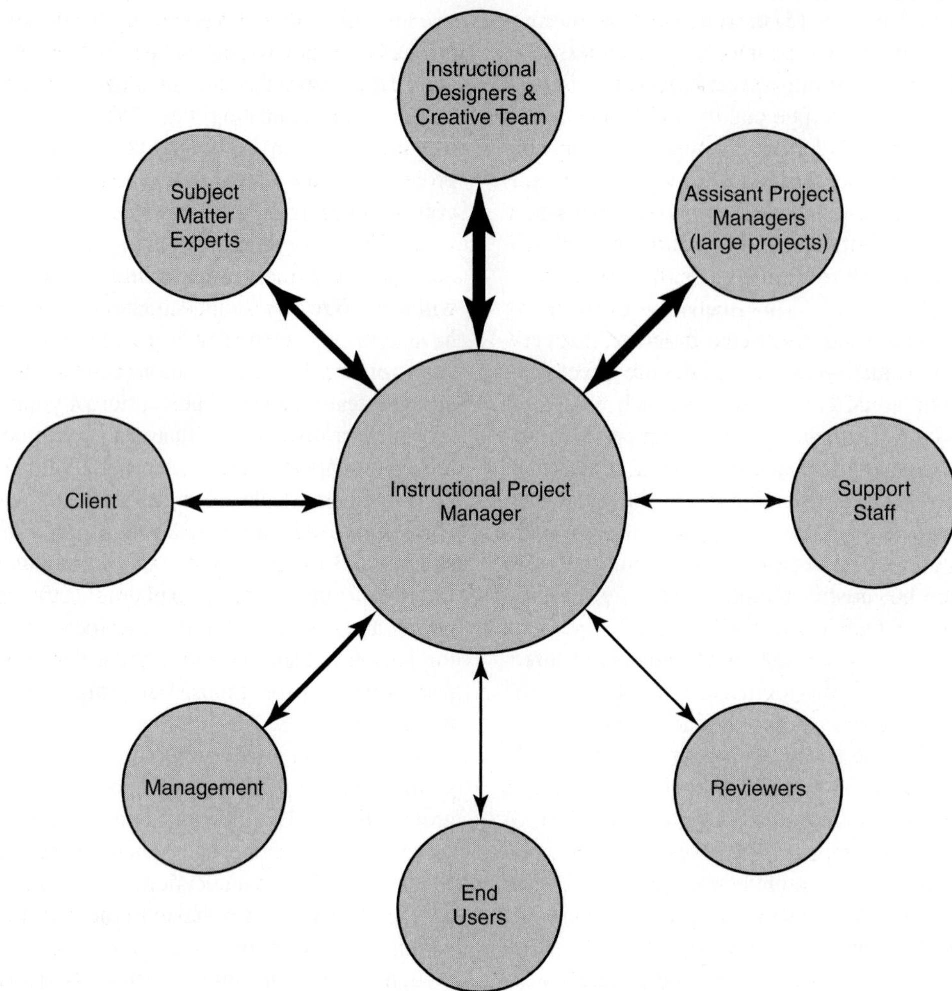

FIGURE 12.1 Communication pattern of a project manager.

though these individuals are competent in their respective fields, the particular combination of personalities in a specific instructional project may present unique problems—all of which you will be expected to handle.

Creative team members. One of the most interesting challenges for an instructional project manager is working with creative people. Creative team members have been described with words such as *weird, disruptive, disorganized,* or *eccentric* (Mattimore, 1993). The majority of instructional projects require writers, editors, graphic designers, artists, Web page designers, and other individuals who may not be in the mainstream in most office environments. If you approach management of creative people the same way you approach traditional management, you may find resistance and misunderstanding. Most views of management are meeting deadlines, budgets, and so forth. Creative people are not often driven by the same goals.

Creativity on demand is difficult, if not impossible, to achieve. Often what is required with creative individuals is flexible work hours and scheduling. Other staff members usually do what they are told (assignments are prescriptive) when working on a project. Creative individuals often take their jobs very seriously because their egos are in each idea and presentation. Critiquing the work of a creative individual takes a bit more sensitivity because of these issues. To most employees, when something is not done to the supervisor's liking, it is easy for them to say, "That's what you told me to do." Not so with creative team members. They put themselves and their creativity on the line each time they explore a way to design a lesson, create a page design, or write a script.

Creative people are not necessarily driven by monetary reward (Stevens, 1992). More important for many is an appreciation of their efforts, along with freedom to be creative without fear of being criticized for trying new ideas. Creative people should be approached with sensitivity and knowledge of the processes they go through to produce their "product," which they may consider to be a reflection of themselves. Sometimes the legendary temperamental and stubborn side of creative people actually comes from misunderstandings or feelings of being limited creatively. They have ideas about a design or an approach and at least want to be heard before you say it will not work or is totally in the wrong direction.

This is not to say that creative people call for special treatment and less responsibility than other team members—just a different approach. Flexible working time (if possible), working in teams, freedom to express ideas without fear, and active listening on your part are simply a few of the techniques that work well with your creative team members. Remember, creative individuals are not necessarily difficult to work with; they just require a bit of special care and understanding if you want your instructional project to succeed.

Instructional designers. Perhaps the most important member of your team is the instructional designer. This is the person (or persons) responsible for researching, designing, and developing the instructional product. It may be that *you* are the instructional designer as well as the manager because the project is small; or, as in the case of a large project, there may be several instructional designers. Your relationship with the instructional designer is probably the closest bond you will have. You are the team members who should be able to communicate best because of your common backgrounds.

Two important variables to be considered in your management of other instructional designers are the levels of experience and skills represented and differentiation of roles. If your level of skill is greater than those of the persons you are managing, you can serve as a coach to assist their development. Regardless of whether your skill level is greater, lesser, or just different from those you manage, it is your responsibility to review their work for quality and to provide feedback. Secondly, you must separate the role of manager from that of "doer." If you are managing other designers, it will be difficult to get used to the fact that their styles and products will be different from what you would have done, and you will be tempted to do it yourself whenever possible. However, it is vital to remember that you are responsible for their development, and you obtain the products you want by means of clear communication of expectations, coaching, and feedback, not by doing it yourself. Even though you are a designer, team members will still look at you as a manager first and expect the guidance and direction that comes with that position.

Assistant project managers. If yours is a large project, multiple teams may be necessary, which will require assistant project managers (APMs). Your main focus with these individuals is to motivate, direct, and inform. They are responsible for communicating with their specific team members. Because directions and procedures are going through APMs, each communication should be especially clear and precise. It may be best to provide APMs with written directives and memos to ensure exact communication. Instructional design is particularly detail oriented and those details must make it to the right person intact.

It is also helpful if you have APMs file a weekly report to you about the progress of their team and fill out a team status report. This consists of each of the development phases (e.g., research, writing, editing, filming) and what stage they are currently in, noting any pending issues, problems, and so on. It is too easy in a large project to lose touch with the specific activities, obstacles, and achievements that are affecting progress.

Subject Matter Experts

Communication between you and the subject matter expert (SME) and between the SME and the team takes on many forms. As the project manager, your main jobs here are to explain the limits and roles, interpret needs and wants, and settle disputes. Subject matter experts rarely know what instructional design (ID) is, much less how it works. Often SMEs are "appointed" to work on a project and sometimes this means extra work for them with no extra time or pay. These situations are sometimes challenging due to inaccurate perceptions and less-than-positive attitudes of some SMEs.

The limits of what you and your team can do and what the finished product will look like is something the SME should know at the outset of the project. You must work with your instructional designers to make sure they understand the techniques of working with SMEs and understand that this is often a trying task because two people are often in effect speaking different languages. SMEs want to be aware of the consequences of changes (more time, money) and develop specific signoff procedures. Identification of problems and quick solutions are the key to careful monitoring of this critical relationship.

Greer (1999) suggests getting SMEs involved very early in the process. This can prevent many problems later. In addition, he recommends asking for overviews of their field or information that will help you understand what they do. Requests for such information also makes it clear you respect the SME's professional judgment. You want to develop a close relationship with SMEs because they are often vital to a project, especially as relates to meeting deadlines.

The Client

The amount of communication you have with the client actually depends on the size of the project. If the project is small, such as the aforementioned DUI scenario (staff of 3), you may have direct contact with the client. In contrast, in the case of the restaurant management scenario (staff of 15) or the $4 million NSF project (staff of 35) there may be a separate project director who oversees the general components of the project while you run the daily operations. Sometimes the project director will have more direct contact with the client.

Assuming you have direct contact with the client, your tasks are to interpret ideas, explain limits, get approvals and signoffs, and most of all, make and keep the client happy. In an ideal project, you will not have much contact with the client if everything is going according to schedule. Your communications will focus mainly on where you are in the schedule and what progress you are making. It is important to communicate to the client (as you do to the SME) that changes to the set plan are serious and can have time and money consequences. A solid, direct understanding about this early on will save many problems later. It is desirable at the beginning of the project to gain firm client commitment to supporting the project by providing *and motivating* SMEs and reviewers, and providing in a timely manner all other input information that will help the project.

You may be required to mediate communication between the client and SME. If the SME gets upset about something the instructional designer cannot do, a meeting with the client often ensues. Then you may have the "them against me" situation that you will have to interpret, analyze, and solve. Keeping a client happy involves good communication so there are no surprises. Nothing is worse than surprising a client with statements such as "We are going to require three extra weeks to finish this part," or "Because you changed this, I forgot to tell you it would cost $5,000 more" (as you hand over the bill). The secret with client communication is keeping it to regular intervals and filling it with pertinent details.

Management

Management in this context refers to your supervisor. Your communication with this person focuses on information about progress and problems with the client. Unless something goes wrong, these communications take the form of regularly scheduled meetings or status reports. Management does not need to know about specific problems with the team—these are yours to solve. The more you can handle yourself, the more capable you appear. Management and the client tend to want the same information: where you are in terms of progress.

Management should be consulted if something gets beyond your control; for example, if the client makes unreasonable requests or wants substantial changes. You may not have total authority to make these decisions depending, again, on the size of your project. If you do, make sure you get things in writing and have everyone sign off on the new schedule and process.

End Users

At first thought, it would seem that as an instructional project manager you would not communicate with the end users. Actually, communicating with them during the initial stages of the project is essential. If possible, at the initial stage conduct a face-to-face meeting. If this is not feasible, send out a questionnaire. The purpose of a meeting or questionnaire is to ascertain if the direction or approach is appropriate and realistic for this particular audience. Although your initial communication with end users is not extensive, it can make a tremendous difference in the acceptance of your instructional product. After this point, the instructional designer carries out the majority of the interaction with the end user.

It is especially helpful for the instructional designer to communicate with the end user when planning and designing instruction for children and young adults. It is easy to get so involved in the design that the overall approach is overlooked and may turn out to not be interesting to the audience. An adult designing for children is tricky in that you may have the skills but lack an understanding of relevant strategies that would capture children's interest and keep them motivated.

Reviewers

The most difficult thing to successfully communicate to reviewers is the importance of timely turnaround. You will often not meet reviewers in person. Your contact with them is usually only through a cover letter explaining the process and what they are expected to do, such as how to fill out an evaluation form and what specific aspects of the program they will be addressing. Because everyone is busy and some reviewers are taking on this task in addition to their other work, you will rarely get all reviews back by the specified date. Others you may never get back at all. It is most helpful to gain support from the managers of the reviewers, especially when your client is their manager. This will help to ensure the reviewers understand that their timely cooperation is expected.

Some reviewers may need another request for completion. As in all other instances of working with your team and staff, you must be assertive but not aggressive in your request. An important gesture with reviewers is to take the time to send a short thank-you note, especially if they are doing the review without payment. They will not forget this and will be more likely to work with you in the future.

Support Staff

The support staff consists of a number of individuals, such as editors, keyboardists, copyright specialists, and researchers, who are essential to the timely function of the project. Although the support staff will mainly be communicating with the design team, you should make it a point to periodically check with the support staff to find out if things are progressing smoothly and on time. You will always be on a tight schedule and these individuals can make or break you in meeting deadlines. Support staff like clear, unambiguous instructions with enough time to do the job well. Do not underestimate the importance of communicating to establish and maintain good rapport with them.

Building Productive Teams

As the problems we are required to solve continue to become more and more complex and interrelated, teamwork becomes more of a necessity (Russell & Evans, 1992). As an instructional project manager you have to be both a manager and a leader, and communicate well enough to get your team moving in the same direction at the same time. An integrated, high-performing team can accomplish a great deal and make a project a success (Robbins, 1998). You have to guide them to want to accomplish the goals and objectives you, the client, and management set forth. This is not an easy task with a diverse group of talented individuals. What motivates teams is a complex issue.

Keeping your team relaxed and happy amid deadlines and pressure is one way to make sure people are motivated to produce a quality product. Most workers are members of one or more work groups with whom they may interact more frequently than with members of their immediate family (Vroom, 1995). In addition to the usual project planning and formal communications, you must develop some interesting ways to boost morale and engagement and keep everyone working well. Garstang (1994) surveyed people who worked in teams about what they enjoyed most when working on projects. Two of the categories he identified, Personal Qualities and Morale, relate directly to making the extra effort to build team cohesion. Under the Personal Qualities category, he suggested that a project manager should be open to questions, provide clear feedback, show appreciation, allow team members space, and encourage them to take care of themselves. Advice from the Morale category was to create traditions as a team, keep a sense of humor, get together outside of work, create a variety of tasks, and provide challenges. This is also illustrated by Wellins, Byham, and Wilson (1991), who indicate that teams are both business entities and social groups and the key factors in team development are the following:

- *Commitment*—committed to group goals above and beyond personal goals.
- *Trust*—faith in each other, behaving in a consistent and predictable fashion.
- *Purpose*—understanding how they fit into the organization, knowing their roles.
- *Communication*—style and extent of interactions with team and others.
- *Involvement*—sense of partnership with each other.
- *Process orientation*—clearly established processes for getting things done.

In addition to developing and nurturing the working relationship of a team, you as project manager must be able to see your team through its growing stages. Your objective should be to get your team to the final stages of the key factors listed. This does not happen quickly. There are distinct but often overlapping stages in team development. Simply put, these stages are beginning, middle, and closure.

In the beginning, your job and how you handle yourself are most critical. You are responsible for setting the initial course and motivating your team. The project manager's ability to immediately take charge is extremely important (Murphy, 1994). This sets the tone for the entire project. Roles must be defined and everyone should be clear about responsibilities. Another important task is to define and clarify the relationships between the team and other members and groups in the organization, funding agency, or business (Moeller, 1994).

Thinking back to our creative team members (who may have freelanced prior to this job, or who may be freelancing with your project) and first-time team members, they may not be cognizant of organizational relationships. This beginning stage can be confusing as personalities, new roles, and responsibilities come together for the first time. Professionals like to know what the ends are and to be given some control over the means. You will need to provide a great deal of guidance and monitor progress in a manner that is supportive without being overbearing—not an easy task.

In the middle of a project, team members are, hopefully, moving along and understanding their roles and the direction of the project and developing their skills in accordance with project specifications. They will still need to be guided and monitored, but not as closely as in the beginning. At this point they should have a clear idea of what they are doing and how to do it. They are becoming more familiar with each other and the design and development task.

In the closure stage, the team is functioning at its upper limit and neither requires or requests very much guidance from you. You must continue to diligently monitor and keep track of team progress and address any problems that arise. In some ways, your job has become easier now that team members know what to do and are producing products and taking pride in their work. But even though things are working well, there can be problems. The addition of new team members, changes in funding or direction, or not enough monitoring often result in new challenges. The most common project management mistake at this stage is to not pay enough attention to the team. It is important to monitor and motivate during both the drudgery and stress periods of a project, especially as you approach the end of the project, which is almost always stressful as everyone is struggling to meet deadlines and coordinate the final production of deliverables. Your interaction must be ever present but with a varying focus throughout the stages of a project.

The Future of Instructional Project Management

One major area for the future of instructional project management is managing at a distance. With phone, FAX, e-mail, and video conferencing you can select, direct, and manage a project and never meet your team members in person. Team members will be chosen for their knowledge and skills along with their computer and electronic access. Managing at a distance can produce a whole new set of challenges for you as a manager, but it basically requires an extrapolation from in-person communication to electronic communications.

Remote management requires that managers be aware of feedback systems and develop methods where they can detect early warning signs of potential problems (Morgan, 1988). Managing at a distance can be a challenge for even an experienced project manager because the procedures are different. Leadership skills become e-mail based, communication can be impersonal, and development of effective teams takes place in cyberspace.

Duarte and Snyder (2001) provide some practical suggestions for successfully managing virtual teams. It is important that you keep in very close contact with all team members even if they are highly competent individuals. Often managers of virtual teams hire competent individuals and think they do not need much guidance. There is a difference between guidance and interaction. You can interact with team members without giving them guidance if they are truly competent and self-directed. Don't make the mistake of just leaving someone alone. You will still need to coach and communicate. Consistent, frequent feedback is critical. Think of it as "walking" around the office and talking to your team. You can drop in on the computer just as you would in an office. Unsolicited feedback is important and can be very motivational.

The compatibility of technology cannot be overemphasized. Just because everyone has a computer and similar software does not mean there is technology compatibility. A simple thing such as different page breaks in documents can cause problems during virtual team meetings. Make sure you match the technology to the tasks.

Building trust and keeping virtual team members informed is even more critical than when working with a site-based team. Communicating with e-mail is efficient and fast but lacks the human interaction of site-based teams. You must be careful not to sound terse in messages. It is easy to send a quick one- or two-sentence response to a question without adding any other feeling or information. Try to avoid this. Always start by using the person's name in a salutation and ending the e-mail with your name. This sounds simple to do, but it's suprising how *many* managers leave off these short courtesies.

Planning every minute detail and controlling all processes can stifle a virtual team. This sounds counterintuitive to the project manager who likes to have everything organized and systematic. Keep in mind that you may have team members from different regions, cultures, and backgrounds. What works in Mobile may not work in New York, Paris, or Tokyo. A virtual team is a fluid, dynamic entity that may have to change in response to customer needs. It is best to have a standard procedure with room for flexibility.

Just as with site-based teams, building group cohesion is an important component. Develop a team homepage with photos and vitas. This will give everyone an idea about who the other members are, and put a face with each name. This does not have to be elaborate, just informal and informational. There are many techniques you can use to develop the sense of community and team spirit of a virtual team.

Regardless of new media and managing virtual teams, instructional project management will always need the perception, sensitivity, and problem-solving skills required of a site-based project manager. If you can do these things effectively in person then you are well on your way to adapting them to managing at a distance.

Conclusion

Instructional project management is a complex human endeavor requiring psychology, management, science, and counseling. It would be impossible to say, "In this situation, do this." Management does not work this way because people are individuals and often unpredictable. This goes for team members as well as clients and management. At times you need to be a leader and at others a manager. You should be able to identify, diagnose, and solve problems with people and production in a manner that is sensitive and fair while being firm and directive.

So, how do you learn project management skills? Read, watch, talk, listen, and practice. Each instructional design project is unique with different objectives, teams, and clients. Regardless of the differences, successful project managers should always lead by example while providing direction and motivation to their teams. It is the mastery of interpersonal skills that enable instructional project managers to understand their teams and guide them to produce the best products.

Application Questions

1. Examine some of the literature that discusses Situational Leadership. Write a paper or present a talk on its main components and how they are applied in work situations.
2. Assume that you have received a two-year grant to develop a 12-unit, multimedia training program. You are the project director and are responsible for timely completion of the product. Using Situational Leadership as a guide, describe how you would lead your team through each of the four phases.
3. BCL Enterprises employs 225 people: 25 management positions and 200 workers divided into 10 teams. Several teams are having problems meeting deadlines and getting along with each other. You have been hired as a team-building expert to evaluate the situation and develop solutions to the problems. Explain what you would do and why.
4. It is 10 years into the future and you are an instructional project manager. Describe how you would assemble a team. How would you convey project objectives and enthusiasm? How will you monitor people and products? How will you give feedback? Finally (and most importantly!), how will you celebrate the end of a successful project?

References

Bennatan, E. M. (1992). *On time, within budget.* New York: John Wiley & Sons.

Blanchard, K., & Johnson, S. (1982). *The one-minute manager.* New York: William Morrow.

Bolton, R., & Bolton, D. G. (1996). *People styles at work.* New York: American Management Association.

Carter-Scott, C. (1994). The differences between leadership and management. *Manage, 46*(2), 10–12.

Clark, R. E. (1999). Motivation systems. In D. G. Langdon, K. S. Whiteside, & M. M. McKenna (Eds.), *Intervention resource guide* (pp. 227–236). San Francisco: Jossey-Bass.

Conger, J. A. (1992). *Learning to lead: The art of transforming managers into leaders.* San Francisco: Jossey-Bass.

Duarte, D. L., & Snyder, N. T. (2001). *Mastering virtual teams.* San Francisco: Jossey-Bass.

Fuller, J. (1997). *Managing performance improvement projects.* San Francisco: Jossey-Bass.

Garstang, M. (1994). Checklist for training project management: The team's perspective. *Journal of Instruction Delivery Systems, 8*(1), 29–33.

Gilbreath, R. D. (1986). *Winning at project management.* New York: John Wiley & Sons.

Greer, M. (1999). *Project management.* Amherst, MA: HRD Press.

Greer, M. (2001). *The project manager's partner.* Amherst, MA: HRD Press.

Hersey, P., Blanchard, K., & Johnson, D., (2001). *Management of organizational behavior.* Upper Saddle River, NJ: Prentice Hall.

Keller, J. M. (1999). Motivational systems. In H. D. Stolovitch & E. J. Keeps (Eds.), *Handbook of human performance technology* 2nd ed. (pp. 277–293). San Francisco: Jossey-Bass.

Lewis, J. P. (1995). *Project planning, scheduling & control.* Chicago: Irwin.

Maslow, A. H. (1998). Maslow on management. New York: Wiley & Sons.

Mattimore, B. W. (1993). *99% inspiration: Tips, tales & techniques for liberating your business creativity*. New York: American Management Association.

Moller, L. (1994). Project management of instructional development: Phase II: Organizing. *Performance and Instruction, 33*(1), 12–14.

Morgan, G. (1988). *Managing the waves of change*. San Francisco: Jossey-Bass.

Murphy, C. (1994). Utilizing project management techniques in the design of instructional materials. *Performance and Instruction, 33*(3), 9–11.

Robbins, S. P. (1998). *Organizational behavior*. Upper Saddle River, NJ: Prentice Hall.

Russell, P., & Evans, R. (1992). *The creative manager*. San Francisco: Jossey-Bass.

Stevens, L. (1992, January–February). Do traditional management techniques work with creative types? *CBT Directions,* 10–14.

Tosca, E. (1997). *Communication skills profile.* San Francisco: Jossey-Bass.

Vroom, V. H. (1995). *Work and motivation*. San Francisco: Jossey-Bass.

Wellins, R. S., Byham, W. C., & Wilson, J. M. (1991). *Empowered teams*. San Francisco: Jossey-Bass.

CHAPTER 13

Managing Scarce Resources in Training Projects

James J. Goldsmith and Richard D. Busby
Accenture

Editors' Introduction

The previous chapter focused on the variety of skills one needs to be a successful manager of instructional design projects. One skill crucial to such success involves being able to successfully manage the people, time, and money resources that are available to you. In this chapter, Jim Goldsmith and Rich Busby focus their attention on this topic.

As Goldsmith and Busby point out, resource scarcity is a reality within every training organization. That is, every training organization has a limited amount of people, time, and/or money available to complete a project, and this limited resource availability undoubtedly will affect the scope and success of the projects the organization undertakes. Goldsmith and Busby discuss the knowledge and skills those in the instructional design field need to successfully address these circumstances.

The authors begin the chapter by defining what they mean by *resources* and *resource scarcity*, and then go on to describe how resource availability and the scope of a project affect one another. They then discuss such basic economic concepts as supply and demand and the economic cycle, factors that have a profound influence on resource availability. Goldsmith and Busby conclude by providing strategies a training manager can adopt to address the problems presented by resource scarcity.

Knowledge and Comprehension Questions

1. Describe the three categories of resources. For each category, discuss how a decrease in that category is likely to affect needs in the other two categories.
2. Define the terms *scarcity, inefficiency*, and *equilibrium*. Describe an example of each of these conditions, other than the examples used in the chapter.
3. Describe the four stages of the economic cycle.
4. Discuss how training departments are affected by the rise and fall of the economic cycle.
5. Based on the descriptions in this chapter, do you think the condition of "scarcity" is good or bad? Explain why you feel this way.

Kirk Scofield, a manager in the training department of a large corporation, is scheduled to meet with his boss, Josephine ("Jo") Bouvier in just a few minutes for their weekly status update. As Kirk walks over to Jo's office, he reflects on the current state of the company and of the training department in particular.

Despite a couple of tough years, the company is now on the rebound and the prospects for the coming year are very promising. And though there was a round of layoffs 18 months earlier that affected about 5% of the training staff, the training department survived the economic downturn relatively unscathed. In fact, right now there is more work than the current staff can handle.

Kirk is hoping that the increase in demand for training products could eventually lead to his promotion to senior manager. With more projects underway, there will be a greater need for experienced people to lead projects and he hopes that he will be among those to fill this gap. He would like to explore this opportunity with Jo during the status meeting.

Kirk knocks on Jo's door and enters.

"Hello, Kirk. Please come in."

"Thanks. I've been looking forward to our meeting today. There are several things that I'd like to discuss with you . . ."

Initially, Kirk and Jo spend time discussing Kirk's current projects. As this discussion winds down, Kirk comments, "From what I hear, our department will be getting quite a bit more work in the near future."

"Yes, that seems to be the case."

"That's great. So, does this mean you'll be filling some more entry-level positions soon, Jo?"

"I'm sorry?"

"You'll be adding positions to the department, right?"

"Interesting that you should say that, Kirk. In fact, I've been spending a lot of my time lately looking for ways to keep us from having to reduce our current staffing level."

Kirk is surprised by this statement. Jo has always impressed him as a capable leader, but this just doesn't make sense. Why would she want to just maintain or even reduce the current training staff when there was clearly a need to staff up?

Obviously, Jo has some practical insights behind her decision to not alter the staffing model in the training department. She made her decision based on a thorough understanding of the concepts associated with scarcity of resources. Resource scarcity is a reality within all training organizations, large and small. The purpose of this chapter is to explain resource scarcity and to offer guidelines to effectively manage this commonplace situation in training organizations. We'll review the key concepts that a training manager needs to understand to operate effectively, starting with a definition of the term *resource*. Other key concepts, such as *supply and demand* and the *economic cycle*, will also be explained and their impact examined in the context of resource scarcity.

Defining *Resources*

From a training development perspective, *resources* are those assets essential to engaging in a training project. Whether in the context of business, academia, or elsewhere, there are three broad categories of resources:

1. *People* (those who plan, develop and/or deliver training)
2. *Time* (the period needed to complete a training project)
3. *Money* (capital available to invest in training)

Obviously, it is not possible to have unlimited people, time, or money resources to complete a training project, so thought needs to be given on how to invest resources effectively. This decision requires consideration of the tradeoffs between project outcomes and limited resources. In fact, the interaction between outcomes and resources has two facets:

1. Outcomes determine the resource requirements.
2. Resource constraints shape the project outcomes.

In the first instance, the length, depth, breadth, complexity, and overall quality requirements of the project (a.k.a., its *scope*) are defined up front. Then, the appropriate number of people and amount of time and money are allocated to meet these requirements. For example, a global workshop with both multiple content areas and a complex learning environment will require many resources to develop. Each unique content area will require significant commitments of instructional designers, content experts, and executive resources.

In this example, the amount of resources allocated depends on the content areas required. In other words, project requirements drive how resources are assigned. All other things being equal, this may seem to be a quite rational way to plan a project. However, projects are often constrained by resources.

This brings us to a second consideration for resource planning; specifically, how scarce resources shape the project scope. Suppose the CEO of the company in our previous example gets a major new client account. Unexpectedly, 50% of the content experts and sponsors are removed from the training project to work on the new account, but the mandate to deliver training remains.

To address this need, one option is to reduce the scope of the course, based on the remaining resources available to the team. In this case, resource scarcity places limits on the scope of the final training outcome.

The interplay among people, time, and money can become quite complex, especially given the possible tradeoffs

TABLE 13.1 Changes driven by decreases in people, time or money

If there is/are *less* . . .

People	Time	Money
Then . . . You need more *Time or* You can decrease the project scope and/or quality	*Then . . .* You need more *People or* You can decrease the project scope and/or quality	*Then . . .* You can decrease the project scope and/or quality by reducing the number of *People or* decreasing the *Time*

among project outcomes and scarce resources. For example, increased money resources enable investment of more people and time to the project. Conversely, a reduction of money implies fewer people and/or less time can be allocated to the project. Table 13.1 illustrates some of the scenarios that can result when there is a reduction in a key resource.

Of course, if there are unlimited resources, these relationships could change significantly. However, in a corporate training environment, the supply of resources is typically limited or "scarce" and must be considered carefully because the supply is likely to behave as illustrated in Table 13.1. Let's examine this concept further.

Defining *Scarcity*

Broadly speaking, *scarcity* occurs when demand exceeds, or has the potential to exceed, supply. This occurs when there is a finite amount of people, time, and/or money available to meet an objective. An argument can be made that scarcity is the normal state of things so, rather than holding an abundance mentality, the experienced manager will assume that resources will be limited, at best.

With this assumption, the goal of the efficient business manager or academic administrator is to occupy the narrow line in which just the right amount of resources is applied to meet a need. That this is a challenge is an understatement. Both the need (demand) and the ability to meet the need (supply) are likely to fluctuate, sometimes wildly, and both can be difficult to anticipate accurately.

Given the challenges that it poses, scarcity is often viewed as a bad thing. But this is not necessarily true. Let's explore supply and demand a little further to understand why.

Supply and Demand

Supply and demand are two broad measures used to describe an economic condition. Simply stated, *supply* refers to available and accessible resources; *demand* refers to the requirements to be met. In a corporate training environment, the supply of resources typically includes the money in the development budget, a team of training developers, time, materials, and tools. Demand is represented by the requirements for the training program. Typically, demand measures include the volume of people to be trained, time available, required performance outcomes, and so on.

The relationship of supply to demand is a convenient reference point to cite when describing conditions both within and across economic contexts.

To this end, let's explore the impact of supply and demand in the context of training. We will examine three conditions, as marked on Figure 13.1:

- Point A: demand exceeds supply (called *scarcity*)
- Point B: supply exceeds demand (called *inefficiency*)
- Point C: supply equals demand (called *equilibrium*)

"Classic" Scarcity

The condition in which demand exceeds supply (point A) is one of "classic" scarcity. In a corporate environment, this would be a situation where training resources are inadequate to meet the task at hand. For example: There is a high level of demand for an end-to-end corporate accounting training program for a new line of business services. However, none of the company offices are willing to release seasoned accountants from daily duties to develop the courseware or deliver the training. In this case, the level of faculty (supply) is lower than training delivery requirements (demand). In the end, if demand exceeds supply, some requirements of demand simply cannot be satisfied. Organizational performance suffers as a result.

Inefficiency

A situation when supply is greater than demand (point B on Figure 13.1) may be appropriately labeled *inefficiency* (sometimes referred to as *overabundance*). How does this condition come about? Inefficiency is typically caused when either of the following occur:

1. Demand drops below existing levels of supply.
2. Supply increases above the level demanded.

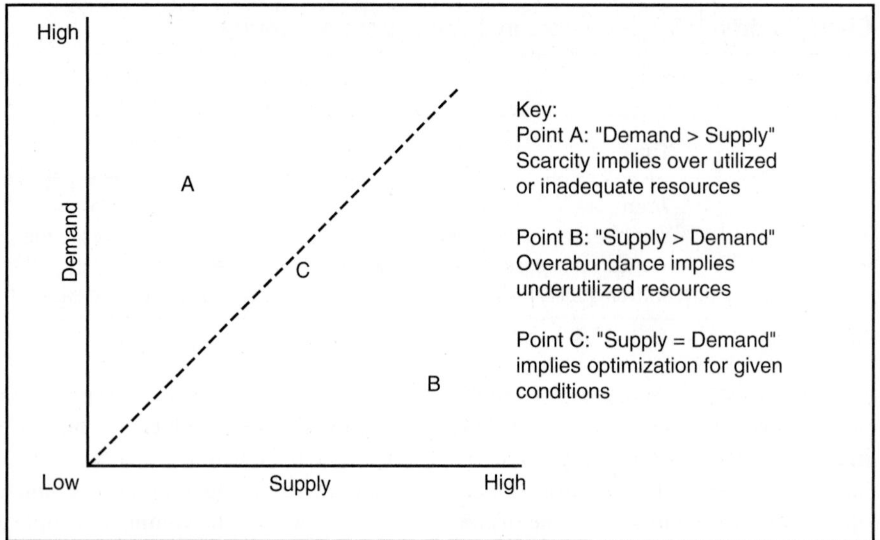

FIGURE 13.1 Supply and demand.

Whatever the cause of inefficiency, businesses cannot afford to sustain this condition because resources are costly.

Here is an example of inefficiency related to training. A technology consulting company agrees to prepay a five-year training contract with network software maker NetSmart. The contract enables the consulting company to quickly hire and train a significant number of technologists to write programs using the unique network software from NetSmart. One year into the contract, the consulting company has a large number of skilled consultants and is selling customized network software based on the programs from NetSmart. The demand for NetSmart programming skills has grown beyond expectations. A year later, now two years into the contract, a new company, Budget Network, Inc., introduces a cheaper, more secure network management program. This causes a dramatic decrease in demand for NetSmart programming skills (condition 1). The consulting company's supply of marketable programming skills is now out of sync with demand for these skills. Furthermore, the training budget is strained, due to the five-year commitment of funds as stated in the contract with NetSmart. The consulting board of directors is quite concerned, since the company finds itself with a large supply of consultants with skills for which there is little demand (condition 2). The CEO calls the training department to ask how much it will cost to retrain the consultants to use Budget Network, Inc. software. The corporate training director, anticipating the question, responds with an estimate that, while shocking, includes a recommendation to use a virtual training approach to lower overall training cost.

The previous example relates to demand as it impacts the supply of a trained workforce; we will now take a look at another example of inefficiency. This time we will examine the impact of inefficiency within the training department itself. A global company with an extensive global training organization enters a prolonged decrease in business. The economic slowdown causes management to cut expenses to maintain profitability. As a result, budgets for new training development are slashed; additionally, the training schedule is reduced dramatically. This leaves the training team underutilized. In this case the level of staffing in the training department (supply) is too high for both the amount of new training to be developed and the number of training sessions to be conducted (demand). The typical business response is to reduce the training budget by a percentage dictated by the senior executive team. This percentage will likely be based on overall profitability targets rather than a thorough analysis of minimal training requirements.

The bottom line is that conditions of inefficiency will not be tolerated in a corporate environment. Thus, as a training manager it is important that you try to avoid inefficiencies in training resources. Your understanding of scarcity will help you avoid such problems.

Equilibrium

The condition in which supply equals demand is called *equilibrium* (point C on Figure 13.1); the condition in which supply levels are not significantly above or below demand is *near equilibrium*. Equilibrium is the ideal for which businesses strive. Near equilibrium is a more realistic goal. In a corporate training environment, equilibrium occurs when the allocated resources enable the development and deployment of required courses.

For example, a training manager is given $500,000 to develop and deploy a corporate accounting curriculum to 400 employees in one year. Based on past experience with the development team and the training content, the manager estimates that $200,000 is required to develop 16 hours of the targeted courseware. This leaves $300,000 to pay for the support and travel required to enable qualified faculty (selected accountants) to deliver the training over a scheduled period of six months. After verifying the estimates, the manager is confident that the resources are sufficient to enable project success.

The bottom line is that management decisions favor the condition in which the allocated supply of resources equals the demand for said resources. Therefore, as a training manager you should try to move your organization toward a state of equilibrium. If a state of resource abundance exists, it is the manager's responsibility to ensure that all excess resources are allocated quickly and efficiently to avoid a state of disequilibrium.

At this point you may be thinking, "So to be successful I just need to make sure I follow the continuum, ensuring resource supply equals demand, and I will be fine, right?" Not really, because you also have to take into account the influence of the broader economic cycle.

Explaining the Economic Cycle

The economic cycle is a conceptual model for assessing the state of the business environment. Understanding the economic cycle will enable a manager to make informed judgments about short- and longer-term consequences of supply and demand decisions. For the purposes of this discussion, the *economic cycle* refers to significant advances and declines in economic activity. Positions on the economic cycle are based on an aggregate measure of many economic indicators. When these broad measures are plotted on a timeline, the resulting graph clearly shows the cyclical nature of the economy. So why is the economic cycle relevant to training professionals? A more detailed analysis of the cycle will reveal the reasons.

Economic Cycle Stages

A training manager needs to observe and react appropriately to the cyclical nature of the economy. This ability requires an understanding of four significant stages of the economic cycle (see Figure 13.2):

- Growth
- Peak
- Decline
- Trough

Definite upward trend lines indicate a "growth" in the economic cycle. This stage is typically characterized by increases in market activity. During this stage, entrepreneurs often react by starting new businesses and companies often invest in greater levels of supply to meet anticipated high levels of demand. Consumers may benefit as well by having more product choices, as new entrants introduce alternative products into the market.

However, growth is not unlimited. As the economic cycle matures, the curve becomes increasingly horizontal until it finally reaches its highest point (the "peak"). At this point, there is still a high level of work. From a training development perspective, there is also increased competition

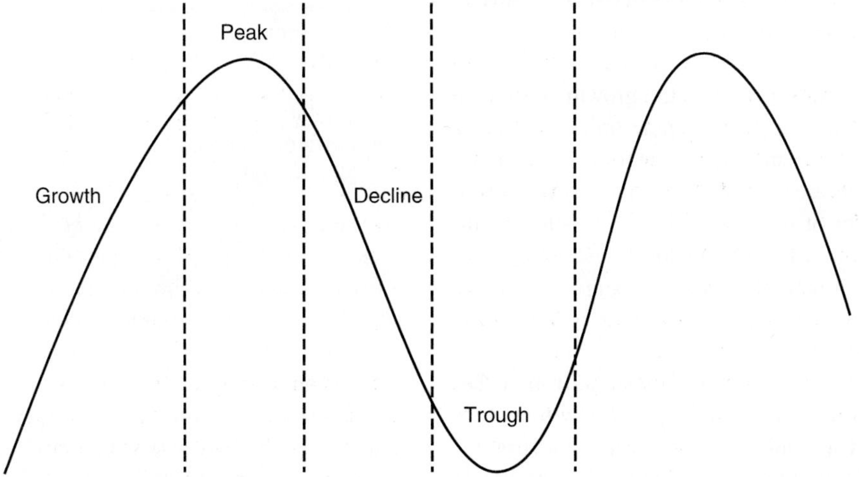

FIGURE 13.2 The economic cycle.

for that work since the economy is no longer expanding. It is also a period of risk, as aggressive business investments made during the heady growth stage may not yield the benefits imagined. For example, in a nontraining business, inventories may start to accumulate on warehouse shelves. In a corporate training environment, the training staff may find a decreasing number of new project opportunities as the level of work flattens.

After the peak stage, the economic cycle begins to "decline" as demand decreases significantly. At this point the impacts to business become obvious. For example, orders for products drop significantly, causing warehouse storage costs to rise; consequently, these costs cut sharply into company profit margins. For training businesses, staffing levels are often dramatically reduced to meet ever-shrinking budget targets issued by the executive team. The decline stage of the cycle causes many businesses to merge or cease to exist. On a positive note, the pressures of a declining market force surviving companies to become extremely efficient, minimizing operating costs.

The "trough" stage occurs after the decline levels off and begins to "hit bottom." This is a stage typified by high levels of unemployment, coupled with lower than average levels of demand. By this stage of the cycle, excess company inventories may have either been sold at a loss or exhausted, with little or no new orders for replenishment. The trough stage may leave some training departments in one of three situations: (1) operating with minimal staff; (2) replaced by outside contractors; or (3) out of business.

Ultimately, the level of impact of any stage depends on both the extent of change and how much time elapses. Two measures are helpful to determine the impact of a given economic cycle:

- Magnitude
- Duration

Magnitude refers to the height and depth of the cycle. The difference between the starting point of the growth stage and its peak is the magnitude of the cycle. For example, a training department starts the growth stage with 10 personnel and an average of 5 new training projects each quarter. Business increases to a peak stage where 40 new training projects are required each quarter. As a result, the training department staffing model changes to accommodate the new demand levels. In some cases additional personnel may be hired. This is one example of how a training manager might make adjustments based on the magnitude of demand.

Duration is the length of time a cycle lasts, from its beginning to its end. Short duration cycles are by their very nature volatile. As a result, when there is a precipitous downswing there is little that the training manager can do to minimize the inherent negative impact of this condition. There is not enough time to make the necessary adjustments to budget, staffing levels, and so on. Conversely, in an equally precipitous upswing it may be difficult to take advantage of the opportunities this condition offers. There is not enough time to quickly increase budget and headcount levels to do whatever is necessary to deliver more training products. So, it is difficult to make effective management decisions when duration is short and significant, regardless of whether there is an upswing or downswing.

Longer cycles, on the other hand, are easier to manage. This is because the manager has more time to understand the impact of the cycle and, subsequently, make prudent management decisions to adjust to the environment. For example, in a gradual upswing, a manager might hire a contractor or even a permanent employee based on a prediction of long-term growth in an expanding market. Managers can make these decisions with greater confidence because the time frames are more generous and the conditions require fewer adjustments.

However, there are exceptions to these assumptions about short- and long-term duration. A savvy manager needs to know about these exceptions. For example, with more monetary resources a manager may choose to endure a difficult short-term trend with no adjustments to resources. But this is not necessarily a good decision, because it requires use of monetary resources that could have been applied to invest in future projects. It may be more prudent to reduce training operations in the current period to preserve scarce training department resources for the future.

At this point we have explored the impact on resource supply and demand of the broad economic cycle in each of its stages. Do these concepts provide enough bases to make training management decisions? Not quite, because there are still some other variables to consider.

Characteristics of the Economic Cycle

The economic cycle is dynamic. In fact, the economic cycle can be:

- Unstable
- Difficult to predict
- Not smooth

The economic cycle is *unstable* in that no stage is fixed. Change may happen at any point or time in the cycle. Unforeseen changes in the broader environment will stimulate fluctuations or dramatic changes in the economic cycle. The impact of the terrorist attacks on September 11, 2001, is an example.

The cycle is *difficult to predict.* If it were easy, more companies (and individuals) would find success and wealth. Given this, successful businesses are those with the capability to adjust and operate flexibly throughout the cycle.

The cycle is *not smooth.* Economic trend lines often appear smooth, as if the rate of growth and decline were constant. This is the effect of charting a moving average. In fact, a more accurate chart would show actual daily fluctuations in leading economic indicators. Though the stock market is only a component of the larger economic cycle, the jagged movement of the Dow Jones Industrial Average provides a useful illustration of variability.

Managers need to have an awareness of each stage as well as the variable nature of the economic cycle. These concepts are relevant to training managers due to their tremendous impact on the people, money, and time resources previously discussed.

So, given this overview of the economic cycle, what are some of the implications for a corporate training department?

Implications of the Economic Cycle

Lag. The business manager or academic administrator who can correctly anticipate and exactly match the economic cycle with what is happening in her own department is either extremely gifted, very lucky, or has signed a pact with the devil. For the rest of us, no matter how hard we try, we always seem to be somewhat behind what is happening in the economy in general. Our goal is to be proactive and to anticipate change, but too often the best we can do is to react. The disconnect between what is happening in the economy in general and our own business and training departments is known as *lag.* Though lag seems inevitable, it can and should be managed. How well it is managed determines whether lag has "good" or "bad" implications. Here are some examples of both.

Good lag. "Good lag" occurs when a training department operational model adjusts appropriately to the economic cycle with minimal delay. Quickly adapting to the cycle will help departments minimize risk. Good lag occurs when a training department's resource level is adjusted to each stage of the economic cycle. So, as the general economy peaks, so do the resource levels of the training department. Conversely, when the economic cycle reaches trough, the training department will reduce resource levels accordingly. Moving in parallel with the economic cycle helps minimize the impact of changes caused by the cycle. For example, if a training department of 30 people is asked to increase production of e-learning assets by 33% over the next six months, they will need to adjust their staffing model. In this situation the training manager must ask several important questions, among them the following:

- Should we hire?
- Should we contract?
- If so, will the resources be part time or full time?
- How many?
- What skills?
- For how long?
- What resources can I afford?

If a company experiences a decline, then its resources should be adjusted to meet the new requirements. However, though it may seem counterintuitive, these changes do not necessarily mean either the hiring or firing of core personnel. In fact, personnel *churn* (characterized by rapid, frequent increases and decreases in the number of people in a department) is a sign that the manager or administrator does not understand the implications of the supply/demand line when placed in the context of the economic cycle.

As an example, a well-run training department will have the capability to monitor and forecast demand levels in order to adjust the supply of resources as appropriate. Additionally, the department's limited resources would be allocated to the highest-value projects.

An awareness of lag may also have positive results. For example, a training manager may intentionally lag behind an emerging market trend. In some cases, the time lag can be an opportunity to see what does and does not work. Early entrants into any new market incur the most risk as novel ideas are tested by consumers. Managers may choose to lag behind the early entrants to reduce risk. In this way, managers may enter the fray better positioned with lessons learned from observing others.

Bad lag. "Bad lag" occurs when there is a disconnect between what is happening in the training department specifically versus what is happening in the economy in general. In an extreme case, the department's resource levels peak just as the general economy moves to trough; conversely, its trough occurs when the economy peaks. This is something like having a clothing store that sells nothing but winter coats in June. There may be a few buyers for these coats but most will be looking for other products. Moving out of step (and, worst case, in the opposite direction) with the economic cycle will increase the impact of changes caused by the cycle. It represents inefficiency and lost opportunity.

The Economic Cycle's Impact on Resources

The periodic and inevitable rising and falling of the economic cycle can have a significant impact on resources. This is because resource requirements are not fixed over time, but are dynamic. For example, when the economic cycle rises, there is typically a greater demand for staff (people), creating an environment of "scare resources" in which the existing staff is overutilized. In this situation, overtime becomes the norm, people are given assignments outside of their area of expertise, and the workforce soon becomes tired, frustrated, and inefficient. Conversely, when the economic cycle falls, there is a reduced demand for staff, creating a situation of underutilized resources. This leads to restructuring, consolidations, and staff reductions, which can have a devastating long-term impact on the corporate culture. In both cases, the end result is something to avoid. Cyclical growth and decline must be monitored carefully and appropriate adjustments should be made to minimize negative impact.

Figure 13.3 illustrates the interplay of the three variables when resources determine project requirements. In particular, notice the inverse relationship of time and money. The impact of these variables as the cycle progresses should be of interest to all conscientious managers and administrators.

Conclusion

We have talked about economic and management concepts related to scarce resources. Before we summarize the concepts introduced in this chapter, let's revisit our opening scenario to understand why Jo made what may initially seem like a counterintuitive decision. When we left the story, Kirk was puzzled about Jo's decision not to hire new staff to meet an increasing workload.

Kirk returns to Jo's office the next day with a question. "Jo, do you have a minute?"

Jo responds, "Sure, I think I can squeeze you in before my next meeting. Come on in."

Kirk says, "I wanted to talk to you about something you said yesterday. I just don't understand why you won't hire more people now when everyone is so busy."

Jo considers this point for a second, then replies, "The reason I don't want to hire anyone now is because I may have to fire them later. And, besides, it's my job as a training executive to run an efficient operation—'lean and mean' if you will. I agree that, right now, we have too few people to manage the current workload but I can deal with that easily by getting help from contractors. What I'm worried about is when the pipeline dries up and we don't have enough to do. If I have people sitting around doing nothing, the executive board is going to be all over me. And I'll be under a lot of pressure to let them go. Of course I don't want to be in that situation, especially when *I* can control it. In fact, my bias is always to have fewer rather than more people. That way, I'm less likely to have to let anyone go. Does any of this make sense to you?"

Kirk responds. "It does. Up to now, I never made a conscious connection between training and supply and demand. But training is just like any other business. A good manager will monitor supply and demand and make adjustments, recognizing the constraints present in the current environment . . ."

Jo and Kirk continued to explore the ramifications of scarce resources in the context of a training environment for several more minutes but, at this point, let's step out of the story to review some of the key ideas expressed or implied in their conversation.

In our story, Jo's decisions are based on two significant concepts:

- *Supply and Demand:* Two broad measures used to describe an economic condition which can be either optimal or suboptimal depending on prevailing economic conditions. These measures can be plotted to reflect current conditions and then extrapolated to predict future conditions, enabling the training manager to make appropriate adjustments.
- *The Economic Cycle:* A conceptual model for assessing the state of the business environment. This model enables training managers to understand the cycle and its many characteristics, including *stages* (growth, peak, decline, trough), *measures* (magnitude, duration) and *attributes* (good and bad lag), as well as its current status. This enables the manager to make the adjustments necessary to run an efficient training department.

	GROWTH	PEAK	FALL	TROUGH
People	Increased need for staffing	Staffing requirements at maximum	Decreased need for staffing	Staffing requirements at minimum
Time	Less time available	Available time at minimum	More time available	Available time at maximum
Money	More money available	Available money at maximum	Less money available	Available money at minimum

FIGURE 13.3 Economic cycle impact on resources.

The implications of the discussion between Jo and Kirk are noteworthy:

- Resource decisions need to take into account both present and future conditions to ensure the training organization runs efficiently. Basing decisions just on what's happening now is risky. As Jo pointed out, additional hiring, though ostensibly warranted by the department's current demand, could be a mistake, resulting in displacing staff and incurring other risks to the training department.
- Managers are required to take calculated risks to invest limited resources. Because the future is unknown, managers apply frameworks and principles to help them mitigate risks and make efficient resource investment decisions. Monitoring and actively managing to the requirements of supply and demand and the economic cycle enable managers to reduce risks and position the training department to operate efficiently.
- All trainers will face constraints and limitations. In fact, some level of resource scarcity is the norm rather than the exception. However, scarce resources are not necessarily a bad thing. The manager needs to embrace the notion that scarcity is reality. Understanding scarcity can even be a competitive advantage when managed well.

Our intent in this chapter has been to help you understand the impact of scarcity to a training department. To this end, we have described several frameworks and concepts that can have an impact on managing scarce resources in a training department.

Scarcity can seem daunting, but as we have tried to illustrate in this chapter, the training manager has many options at his disposal, including the following strategies:

- *Adopt a global to local approach:* Increase awareness of broad economy/business conditions that impact the business of training.
- *Have a bias towards scarcity rather than abundance:* If you can postpone or avoid adding resources in uncertain times, you will be better positioned to avoid staffing entanglements, budget shortfalls, and other problems. However, this has to be weighed carefully against the impact to current resources and/or the ability to meet business obligations.
- *Select resources carefully:* Since training resources are precious, do the research and choose them wisely. Hiring and retaining the right people resources is the most important resource decision a training manager can make. A strong core team will be more capable of adapting to, even flourishing in, the inevitable difficult times.
- *Treat resource scarcity as a strategic issue:* Training resources are often thought of in tactical terms (e.g., books, computers, whiteboard, etc.). Instead, consider resource management as a strategic initiative that can enable you to have an advantage over your competitors. Simply put, your organization will operate more efficiently than a competitor who does not consider scarcity when making training management decisions.
- *Consider interactions among resources:* Managers have many options to adjust the people, time, and money resources to meet the requirements of demand. Explore all options before making a hiring decision.

In conclusion, the effective training manager will view scarcity not with trepidation but with an informed perspective that empowers good decisions. Our hope is that you will consider the concepts discussed herein when you are asked to make your own resource decisions and that application of these concepts will prove useful to you in the demanding arena of training development.

Application Questions

1. Business leadership predicts a significant expansion of the business during a rise in the economic cycle. What actions might a good manager take? What adjustments to resources might be expected?
2. The economic cycle is changing from a rise to a fall condition. What adjustments to resources should be expected if the training department is managed well?
3. A customer wants a training project completed more quickly than originally planned. Based on the relationships among resources described in this chapter, what actions can a training manager take to meet this new requirement?

SECTION 4

Human Performance Technology

Overview

Instructional designers are often called on to design solutions to learning problems (e.g., students are not acquiring desired skills and knowledge) and/or performance problems (e.g., workers are not performing adequately on the job). In the past, when faced with such problems, instructional designers usually focused on designing instructional solutions (e.g., lessons, instructional modules, training programs) intended to improve learning. However, in recent years, professionals in our field, as well as those outside of it, have come to recognize that in many cases the best solution to a learning or performance problem may not involve instruction; that a noninstructional solution may be a better remedy. Moreover, many such individuals have come to recognize that in many cases the best measure of the effectiveness of such solutions is how they influence job performance, as well as the overall success of the organization in which solutions were implemented.

The recent emphasis on noninstructional as well as instructional solutions, and the recent focus on job performance and organizational success are part of a movement or field that has been called *human performance technology* (HPT), or *human performance improvement* (HPI). Chapter 14 defines these terms, discusses the history of this field, and discusses many of the key ideas and practices associated with HPT/HPI.

Chapter 15 focuses on electronic performance support systems (EPSS). The authors describe how systems of this nature provide a variety of tools and resources, some instructional and others noninstructional, to help solve performance problems. These tools and resources are available at the *time of need*, and may be designed to address the performance needs of individual workers, a work group, and/or an entire organization.

Chapter 16 discusses another means of improving the performance of individuals and of organizations—the creation and use of knowledge management (KM) systems. Such systems are designed to help organizations get the right information to the people who need it at the time they need it. The chapter focuses on the key principles associated with the design and use of knowledge management systems and describes a variety of examples of such systems.

Informal learning has been defined as learning other than that which typically takes place in the classroom or in an environment established to deliver formal instruction at a distance (e.g., online instruction, instruction delivered via a video conference). Chapter 17 discusses how informal learning activities have been, and can be, used to help improve the performance of individuals and of the organizations for which they work.

Harold D. Stolovitch

CHAPTER 14

The Development and Evolution of Human Performance Improvement

Editors' Introduction

During the past 15 years, and particularly within the past 10, the field of human performance technology (HPT), also known as human performance improvement (HPI), has had a substantial impact on the instructional design field. In this chapter, Harold Stolovitch describes the HPT/HPI[1] field. He begins by providing a definition of human performance improvement and describing why the field has grown rapidly in recent years. He goes on to describe the roots of the field and, in doing so, discusses many of the key ideas and principles associated with HPT/HPI. He also discusses a current-day model of the HPT/HPI process as put forth by the International Society for Performance Improvement, a leading professional organization in the HPT/HPI field.

Many instructional designers have adopted a number of the practices described in this chapter. For example, when faced with a situation where worker performance is not as good as expected, many instructional designers, rather than assuming that the cause is poor instruction, will carefully analyze the problem and try to identify its actual causes. As a result they may discover that the problem is not due to poor instruction; instead some other problem, such as a poor incentive system or lack of appropriate feedback to workers, may be the actual cause of the poor performance. In such cases, the instructional designer is likely to suggest a noninstructional solution to the performance problem, perhaps recommending the use of a set of worker incentives, or designing a new way for supervisors to provide workers with timely and useful feedback regarding their job performance. This chapter will provide you with a clearer understanding of HPT/HPI practices such as these.

Knowledge and Comprehension Questions

1. In one of the first sections of this chapter, Stolovitch defines the term *human performance improvement* (HPI). Examine this entire section and then answer the following questions:
   a. What are some of the goals of HPI?
   b. What are some of the "systematic means" that are used to accomplish these goals?
   c. What does the term *performance* (within the phrase "human performance improvement") mean?
   d. When a HPI project is undertaken, who are the likely "stakeholders" (those who stand to benefit as a result of the project)?
2. Stolovitch points out that even though instructional designers may produce training programs that result in workers learning more, the instructional designers may not solve the performance problems that an organization is facing. Explain why this may be the case. Use Gilbert's Behavioral Engineering model (Figure 14.1) to support your point of view.
3. In several sections of this chapter, Stolovitch lists a variety of noninstructional solutions to performance problems. List three of these noninstructional solutions and, for each one, describe a specific situation where that solution may be appropriate.
4. Examine the definition of *human performance technology* that is presented in this chapter, as well as the definitions provided in at least two of the other sources listed in the chapter. Identify the definition you prefer, or write your own definition. Describe why you prefer the definition you have specified.

[1] In this chapter, Stolovitch primarily employs the term '*human performance improvement*', but indicates that it and '*human performance technology*' are often considered to be synonymous. We will consider these two terms as interchangeable and, with the exception of this chapter, will use the term *human performance technology* throughout this textbook.

Human Performance Improvement (HPI), what a wonderful sounding term! Is there anyone who does not wish to "improve" in some way? Is this also not the mission of so many personal and organizational development programs? What is special and unique about HPI? Where did it come from? How did it grow into the embodiment of a professional field that is currently making assertive noises throughout the world? How, through its origins and evolution, does it affect individuals and organizations seeking to achieve workplace success in our ever-increasingly complex world? Finally, is HPI just another fad in the long list of miracle cures we have all seen roar into our busy work environments, disrupt our routines, offer incredible promises, only to fade away like broken dreams into the mists of organizational forgetfulness?

These are questions this chapter addresses. It begins by establishing a clear definition and positioning for HPI. It then steps back and reviews the foundations, origins, and evolution of HPI and its parent field, human performance technology (HPT), from which the term *HPI* issued. The chapter then characterizes HPI in terms of where we are today. Along the way, this chapter helps us discover how HPI found its way to its current incarnation, what has been happening with it, and, above all, its growing relevance as an important workplace movement. The chapter concludes with a brief summary of key points and a speculative preview of what we may expect from this evolving field of professional practice in the future.

Defining Human Performance Improvement

There is power in words, but only when their meanings are made manifestly clear. What follows, then, is a definition of the term *human performance improvement* from three perspectives: vision, concept, and desired end. Subsequently, we define the term by examining each of the words that constitute it.

HPI: Vision, Concept, and Desired End

The vision of HPI is relatively simple: achieve, through people, increasingly successful accomplishments that are valued by all organizational stakeholders: those who perform, their managers and customers, their peers and colleagues, shareholders, regulatory agencies, and ultimately, society itself.

Conceptually, HPI is a movement with a straightforward mission—valued accomplishment through people. Via systematic means, from analysis of performance gaps, design and development of appropriate, economical, feasible, and organizationally acceptable interventions through to implementation and long-term monitoring and maintenance of these interventions, HPI concerns itself with achieving organizational goals cost effectively and efficiently. Unlike other movements with similar missions, HPI draws from a unique parent field, HPT, which contains a formidable array of processes, tools and resources, a scientific base, and a history of precedents that document attainment of valued results.

With respect to its "end," valued accomplishment, HPI provides an operational definition. Gilbert (1996) has written extensively about what he has termed "worthy" performance (P_w), the ratio of valued accomplishment (A_v) to costly behavior (B_c):

$$P_w = \frac{A_v}{B_c}$$

In the HPI universe, the desired end is performance whose cost is considerably lower than the value of the result.

HPI: What Does Each Word Mean?

Another way of examining the meaning of the term *human performance improvement* is to define each of three words that constitute the term. Let's do so.

Human. HPI is a professional field of endeavor centered on the efforts and results of people operating in work settings, although there are increasing examples of the principles of HPI being applied to educational and societal situations (e.g., Harless, 1998; Kaufman, 1995; Lande, 2002).

Performance. This word creates difficulties from two perspectives. Some people, when they first encounter it, think of performance in the theatrical sense. It therefore trails connotations of the stage rather than of being substantive (Stolovitch & Keeps, 1999). Nevertheless, *performance* is an appropriate term as it also denotes a quantified result or the accomplishment, execution of something ordered or undertaken, including the accomplishment of work. Nickols (1977) defines performance as "the outcomes of behavior. Behavior is individual activity whereas the outcomes of behavior are the ways in which the behaving individual's environment is somehow different as a result of his or her behavior" (p. 14). Outcomes, accomplishments valued by the system or achievements—these are the focus of HPI (Stolovitch & Keeps, 1999). The second difficulty with performance is that it is an almost uniquely English term. Many languages do not posses an exact, equivalent word for it. In applying various similar words or paraphrases to convey its precise meaning, something often gets lost in the translation. Despite this annoyance, its operational sense, as Gilbert (1996) has suggested, remains clear. *Performance* is the valued accomplishment derived from costly behavior. Lowering the behavioral (activity) cost and markedly increasing the valued result or benefit is what HPI is about.

Improvement. The meaning of this word is almost self-evident. It refers to making things better. In the work environment, *improvement* is operationally defined in many ways: increased revenues and/or market share; greater speed to market; decreased wastage and/or costs; more successful conformance to regulatory requirements; and better safety and health data, to name only some of the more common ones.

Taken together, these three words have created a major business movement—one that endeavors to bring about changes in such a way that organizations are improved in terms of the achievements they and all stakeholders value.

HPI: Why Has Its Time Come Now?

A significant confluence of ideas and events has recently occurred to favor the growth of HPI. Among these are the renewed interest in human capital, the recognition of the importance of systemic thinking, the dramatic surge in organizational complexity, and the focus on performance.

Human Capital

Nobel laureates Theodore Schultz (1981) and Gary Becker (1993) established the importance of human capital at macroeconomic levels. They demonstrated with convincing data that as the knowledge and performance capabilities of populations improve so, too, do the economic successes of countries and their peoples. One need only examine singularly successful smaller nations with limited natural resources and landmasses, such as Japan, Israel, and the Netherlands to confirm the validity of this thesis. Their vast and varied accomplishments attest to the enormous power of leveraging human capital.

The power of human capital has also been demonstrated at the organizational level (Crawford, 1991; Davenport, 1999; Edvinsson & Malone, 1997; Fitz-enz, 2000; Halal, 1998; Pfeffer, 1998; Stewart, 1997). Lickert and Pyle (1971), Stewart (1994), and Bradley (1996) have empirically shown that human capital yields higher rates of return than physical capital in corporate settings. HPI has adopted at its core the maximization of human capital achievements.

Systemic Versus Linear Thinking and Acting

There is a growing demand for systemic as opposed to linear thinking and acting in the workplace (e.g., Senge, 1990). General systems theory (e.g., de Rosnay, 1975) opened the business world to conceiving of organizations as organic entities with interacting subsystems. In the human resource and development arenas, individual types of interventions (e.g., scientific management, management by objectives, management by walking around) have yielded to more systemic and integrated approaches (e.g., quality circles, reengineering, teamwork, six-sigma). This has fostered movements such as HPI, which views performance outcomes as the end result of a number of interacting elements such as clear expectations, timely and specific feedback, access to required information, adequate resources, properly aligned policies, efficient procedures, appropriate incentives and consequences, targeted training, comprehensive selection systems, communication of values, knowledge sharing, and varied management support activities, as well as many others. The demonstrated ineffectiveness of single-solution, miracle interventions to improve performance have bred mistrust for the next "flavor of the month" and a receptiveness to the systemic approach of HPI.

Growth in Organizational Complexity

As instantaneous communication across the world, global markets and 24/7 service availability become our realities, more of the burden of decision making and customer satisfaction falls on the individual worker's shoulders. Companies no longer produce single products. Each product line has a shorter life cycle. Workers and managers must access and share information and knowledge with extreme speed.

In this atmosphere of continuous pressure and upheaval, accompanied by frequent mergers and acquisitions of enterprises, people have to be supported by an environment that facilitates agility, encourages independent activity, and provides easy-to-use links to others for assistance, expertise, and reassurance. Here is where HPI stands out. The professional HPI practitioner—the performance consultant (PC) (Robinson & Robinson, 1995, 1998; Rummler, 2004; Stolovitch & Keeps, 2004b)—is essentially an internal account manager with close links to client groups. As changes are planned or occur, or as problems manifest themselves, the PC is there to identify gaps between desired and actual performance, analyze them, isolate the systemic factors affecting the gaps, and recommend an integrated set of suitable interventions to rapidly and effectively eliminate them. The PC's toolkit is the set of resources, processes, and job aids HPI provides.

Focus on Performance

The impatience with training and other groups of single intervention specialists is that these focus on individual isolated stimulus solutions rather than on the required responses. Gilbert (1978, 1996) lays out a number of principles and theorems that at first sight appear counter-intuitive until examined closely:

- If you pit the individual against the environment, the environment will ultimately win.
- Hard work, great knowledge, and strong motivation without valued accomplishment is unworthy performance.
- A system that rewards people for their behavior (e.g. hard work, knowledge, motivation) without accounting for accomplishment encourages incompetence.
- A system that rewards accomplishments without accounting for behavior invites waste.

These and other principles emphasize the need to account for the many environmental factors that affect how people perform their work, achieve their business-valued results, apply their work processes, and exhibit their behaviors. The growth in availability of alternative means for achieving business-driven success and the demand by management to demonstrate such success concretely (Van Buren & Erskine, 2002) have paved the way for HPI to showcase its relevance.

The Relationship Between HPI and HPT

There are several ways that one might look at the relationship between human performance improvement and human performance technology. In one sense, human performance *improvement* is what we wish to achieve and *human performance technology* is the means we use to achieve it. However, in another sense, the two terms can be viewed as synonymous. The term *human performance improvement* is relatively new. In a strict sense, it is a euphemism (a less direct expression used in place of one considered offensive). It emerged in the 1990s, most likely because of its softer sound than human performance technology (HPT).

Human performance technology is a field of professional practice that began to take form during the 1970s and became recognized in its own right in the 1980s. It is an offspring of general systems theory applied to organizations (Stolovitch & Keeps, 1999). In the mid 1980s, Geis (1986) stated a number of assumptions underlying the HPT that are still true today. Some of the key assumptions are:

1. Human performance follows specific laws and can often be predicted and controlled.
2. Knowledge of human behavior is limited (although growing rapidly), and so HPT must rely on practical experience as well as scientific research.
3. HPT draws from many research bases while generating its own.
4. HPT is the product of a number of knowledge sources: cybernetics, behavioral psychology, communications theory, information theory, systems theory, management science, and, more recently, the cognitive sciences and neuroscience.
5. HPT is neither committed to any particular delivery system nor confined to any specific population and subject matter area. It can address human performance in any context, but it is most commonly applied within organizational, work, and social improvement settings.
6. HPT is empirical. It requires systematic verification of the results of both its analysis and intervention efforts.
7. HPT is evolving. Based on guiding principles, it nevertheless allows enormous scope for innovation and creativity.
8. Although HPT cannot yet pretend to have generated a firm theoretical foundation of its own, the theory- and experience-based principles that guide it are molded by empirical data that have accumulated as a result of documented, systematic practice. In many ways, HPT shares attributes with other applied fields (for example management, organizational development, medicine, and psychiatry).

It may be said that these assumptions hold true regardless of whether you prefer to use the term *HPI* or *HPT* to describe the field.

The notion that these terms can be used interchangeably is further reinforced by examining some of their formal definitions. Harless (1995) defines *HPT* as "an engineering approach to attaining desired accomplishment from human performers by determining gaps in performance and designing cost-effective and efficient interventions" (p. 75). Stolovitch and Keeps (1999) have defined HPI in much the same way.

Human Resources Development, Organizational Effectiveness, and Organizational Development

The preceding paragraphs may lead one to conclude that what has been said of HPI and HPT might just as easily be restated with respect to human resource development (HRD). This is largely true. As Gilley, Maycunich, and Quatro (2002) state, the traditional role of HRD professionals has mainly been a transactional one, mostly focused on training interventions. They emphasize that these roles must change to become more transformational and performance focused. In their assertion that "the challenges facing organizations require HRD professionals to adopt a role that improves firm performance, enhances competitive readiness and drives renewal capacity and capability" (p. 25), they closely approach the goals of HPI.

This convergence is to be expected given the evolving nature of enterprises. One sees a similar viewpoint emerging from the field of organizational effectiveness (OE), with growing emphasis on the ability of the organization to fulfill its mission through a blend of sound management, strong governance, and a persistent rededication to achieving results. This includes meeting organizational and shareholder objectives—immediately and long term—as well as adapting and developing to the constantly changing business environment. OE professionals focus on the overall functioning of an organization. HPI is about engineering effective human performance in specific ways. The link between the two is both evident and natural.

What is true for OE can also be said for organizational development (OD). While generally operating at the macro level of organizations, OD professionals serve a mission of increasing organizational effectiveness and health through planned interventions in the organization's processes or operations. OD adopts less of an engineering emphasis and is characterized more by its communication and facilitation style. Nevertheless, its purpose, just as with HPI, is to deliver valued organizational results, largely through people. Both are concerned with improving human performance.

HPI: How Did We Get Here?

Rosenberg, Coscarelli, and Hutchinson (1999) provide an excellent accounting for the evolution of HPT, which to a large extent, is also that of HPI. Others, such as Dean (1994) and Dean and Ripley (1997) also offer a great deal of detailed information about the significant thinkers and milestones of HPI. This chapter adopts a somewhat different recounting of how HPI came about. It begins with the examination of a basic, successfully growing company.

The Story of a Typical Company

Imagine an enterprise that produces unique, high-quality rocking chairs. The products, of which there are a number of models, are crafted in a very special manner. To achieve the high level of success, the company engages master craftspersons, each with recognized qualifications, experience, and demonstrable skill. As the company gains success through its marketing and sales plus the undoubted quality of its rocking chairs, it foresees that there will soon be an insufficient supply of master craftspersons. It therefore engages apprentices who will be trained by the masters.

Long term, the results will be good. Apprentices over a period of years will acquire the craft. However, in the case of our rapidly evolving company, problems are occurring. First, the time to form a craftsperson from an apprentice is taking longer than the business can tolerate. Secondly, it soon becomes evident that an excellent craftsperson does not always translate into being an excellent trainer of apprentices.

What to do? The ready answer is to hire training professionals who, drawing from the expert rocking chair producers, are able to build successful training programs that take less time than traditional apprenticeships to develop competent rocking chair makers. Soon, a training department is established with its infrastructure, catalogue of courses, and e-learning initiatives. Before long, as with many departments in organizations, a training empire comes into being. Although the training department's explicit mission is to produce excellent rocking chair craftspersons who, in turn, create products that continuously build company success, a more immediate, implicit mission emerges: departmental survival.

The company has grown in size and complexity. There are competing demands for funds. To survive, the training department now turns to greater revenue-generating ventures. While rocking chair craftspersons are the lifeblood of the company, their needs are often very specific, with only a few "trainees" for each specialty. There are much larger gains for the training group to acquire by offering programs on word processing, e-mail, spreadsheet software, and sexual harassment. The populations for these are so much larger than a few craftspersons. As survival of the training department becomes more of an issue, its value to the organization begins to decline. Its initial *raison d'être* fades beneath the day-to-day struggle to maintain its existence.

This is not an uncommon scenario. Somehow, as organizations evolve, the original missions of training departments become buried in the tumult and confusion of internal pressures and events. Training and HRD are particularly vulnerable. As budgets for their activities tighten, they are forced to "sell their wares" for survival. Since their "wares" are training, their recourse is to find large populations as buyers. The small but significant—even crucial—needs of the organization may get ignored.

Early Precursors to Performance Improvement

Let us stop in the midst of the issues related to our rocking chair company and its training department to examine how HPI came to be. In the process, we may discover a way out for both the company and its training group.

In the beginning, there were apprenticeships. The master–apprentice model formed the basis for acquiring workplace performance capability. Whether the learner bore the official title of apprentice or some other nomenclature such as "page," "squire," or even "scullery maid," the idea was that a young person was taken into service and taught a trade. She or he learned through observation, instruction, practice, and feedback, all of which were virtually continuous. It also took a long time.

With the introduction of workplace literacy, those youngsters who could read about their work gained a competitive edge. The Industrial Revolution of the nineteenth century gave rise to the need for literate workers. Public education arose to provide basic reading and calculation skills. Literate, mathematically capable workers tended to be more productive in the increasingly complex, industrial world. With the introduction of printed, illustrated texts, the combination of pictures and words made a great difference in the efficiency and effectiveness of learning.

This fed directly into the audiovisual movement. First photos and then projected images, films, and television brought to life what could not always be experienced directly. Educators were able to bring the world to the classroom. For industrial trainers, these additions made a dramatic difference. They could show objects, products, results, even processes, without the need to "be there" physically. More trainees could be formed and generally in less time than by older methods.

With the arrival of the Second World War and the need to train millions of soldiers rapidly, the audiovisual discoveries were combined with those of the rapidly growing field of behavioral psychology. The result was well-designed audiovisual training materials that structured and presented learning content in ways that facilitated the acquisition of new skills and knowledge. Learners were shown how things worked, were coached and prompted as they learned, and then were released and monitored as they performed.

By the end of World War II, the use of behaviorally designed audiovisual training programs had also found adherents in the war-related industries. Then, as soldiers went back to school and to the general workplace, acceptance extended to schools, universities, and business organizations.

However, something was lacking. Audiovisual training materials were only perceived as training tools and aids. Their use was essentially tactical. When, in the 1950s and 1960s, general systems theory was discovered by the training community, a major shift occurred that gave birth to instructional technology. All of the pieces were now in place. By focusing on the array of elements affecting learning—learner characteristics, learning context, tasks to be mastered, clearly defined learning objectives, criterion measures, media, and delivery systems—a more comprehensive view of learning systems arose. This fit with the surge in knowledge production and the evolution toward a global service- and knowledge-based economy. Learning was no longer narrowly viewed as a prerequisite for obtaining a job position and functioning within it. It now became evident that lifelong, continuous learning was a workplace necessity for both worker and organizational survival.

Instructional technology led to the development of instructional systems design (ISD), which has evolved into the standard for engineering effective learning. The key advantage of this systematic and systemic approach was that it took into account the essential variables for learning. ISD provided a clearly defined and documented pathway for designing, developing, implementing, and evaluating learning—one that was replicable and transferable and that had a demonstrable record of success.

Yet within the very euphoria of having created an effective training–learning technology, one based on the best knowledge acquired from both human and physical sciences, there was disquiet in the professional training community. True, the newly engineered learning systems were demonstrating success. People learned. However, when the instructional systems designers verified whether the learning transferred to the job or the extent to which things changed or improved in terms of business criteria, they were frequently dismayed (Esque & McCausland, 1997).

This brings us back to our rocking chair enterprise. The initial requirement was to increase rocking chair production capability for a growing enterprise. The mission of the training department was to ensure a steady flow of this capability to meet growth demands as well as product change requirements based on market shifts and evolving technologies. The criteria for success defined by the training department were number of training hours delivered, number of persons trained, training revenue dollars generated, number of courses available, and variety of delivery mechanisms available. However, for the company, success criteria were time to market, market share, repeat business, new markets, reduced costs, improved productivity, revenue per employee, and profits. Between the two we observe an obvious misalignment of missions. Is there any way to reconcile the differences? Perhaps through a new direction and a new mission for the training group: HPI.

An Idea Is Born: HPT/HPI

Thomas F. Gilbert is generally considered to be the father of HPT. As a graduate student of B. F. Skinner, Gilbert was steeped in the principles and practices of behaviorism. He became an ardent and able practitioner of programmed instruction, which Skinner had initiated through his research and development of teaching machines.

Taking Skinner's principles and venturing into the workplace arena, Gilbert soon developed a new science of *mathetics* (Gilbert, 1962), derived from the Greek *mathein,* "to learn." His *Journal of Mathetics* attracted the attention of a group of like-minded individuals, including many from learning research laboratories and the American military. They and others, fascinated with the possibilities offered by the science of learning, formed the National Society for Programmed Instruction (NSPI). Together with Geary Rummler, Gilbert soon progressed beyond issues of learning and by the mid 1970s had created his Behavior Engineering model (Gilbert, 1978) that lays out six major categories of variables affecting workplace performance (Figure 14.1). This was a significant milestone and is still used as a fundamental analytic HPI tool.

At approximately the same time, Joe Harless, a former student of Gilbert's, was developing his own performance improvement process (PIP). In 1970, Harless published an interactive volume entitled *An Ounce of Analysis Is Worth a Pound of Objectives*, in which he introduced his now-famous front-end analysis methodology. This had a marked influence on practitioners of training, especially instructional designers. Harless had discovered, through followup evaluation posttraining, that "despite the training having been well-designed in accordance with the standards of the time" (Dean & Ripley, 1997, p. 94), and although students performed well on tests, the skills and knowledge were not being transferred to the workplace. His PIP model, which incorporated front-end analysis, laid the foundation for the numerous performance improvement models that were to follow.

Another slim but immediately popular publication, by Robert F. Mager and Peter Pipe, *Analyzing Performance Problems Or "You Really Oughta Wanna"* (1970), also appeared on the scene at this time. This volume had a tremendous impact on instructional designers, trainers, HRD professionals, and educators. Their very sensible approach to solving workplace performance problems resonated clearly with both practitioners and training managers. It provided ammunition to stimulate significant changes in how human performance at work was viewed.

These models created an enormous stir (and support) among many, who were ill at ease with the impact of their training–learning solutions in the workplace. Even more importantly, they helped effect two fundamental shifts in thinking. The first of these was opening the minds

Stimulus	Response	Consequences
Cell 1: Environment Information	**Cell 2: Environment Resources**	**Cell 3: Environment Incentives**
• Description of what is expected of performance • Clear and relevant guides on how to do the job • Relevant and frequent feedback on adequacy of performance	• Tools, resources, time, and materials designed to achieve performance needs • Access to leaders • Sufficient personnel • Organized work processes	• Adequate financial incentives contingent upon performance • Non-monetary incentives • Career development opportunities • Clear consequences for poor performance
Cell 4: Individual Knowledge	**Cell 5: Individual Capacity**	**Cell 6: Individual Motives**
• Systematically designed training to match requirements of exemplary performers • Opportunity for training	• Match between people and position • Good selection processes • Flexible scheduling to match peak capacity of workers • Prostheses or visual aids to augment capacity	• Recognition of worker's willingness to work for available incentives • Assessment of worker's motivation • Recruitment of workers to match realities of work conditions

FIGURE 14.1 Gilbert's Behavior Engineering model.
Source: Adapted from *Human Competence: Engineering Worthy Performance* (ISPI Tribute Edition), by T. F. Gilbert, 1996, Washington, DC: International Society for Performance Improvement. Copyright 1996 by ISPI. Adapted by permission.

of training and HRD professionals to the fact that many human performance problems could be solved via means other than training; that there are an infinite array of possible interventions to improve human performance. These interventions include new incentive systems, improved and more timely methods for providing feedback to employees, better worker selection procedures, and a host of other performance improvement techniques. Somewhat frightened ("After all, is this our concern?" "Are we the right people to involve ourselves in this?"), yet excited and exhilarated, training and HRD professionals began to see their horizons expanding, their challenges increasing, and at the same time the possibility of having a much greater influence on bottom-line business results.

The second shift in thinking was the growing awareness that the HRD/training community could now offer stronger, more convincing arguments to senior management that what they were engaged in should be viewed as an organizational investment rather than a cost. This naturally led to an emphasis on evaluation, the demonstrable leveraging of organizational human capital and human performance and return on investment calculations (e.g., J. J. Phillips, 1997; P. P. Phillips, 2002; Stolovitch & Keeps, 2004a).

One of the most important milestones in the evolution of HPI was the appearance of another volume, *Improving Performance: How to Manage the White Space on the Organization Chart* (Rummler & Brache, 1995) that presented a comprehensive performance improvement model and set of practices that were more strategic and detailed than earlier approaches. Rummler and Brache examine the organization as a whole and identify key variables affecting performance at the organizational, process, and individual worker level. Their model integrates all of these levels in a tightly integrated manner and with a single purpose: to engineer performance.

Stolovitch and Keeps (1999) have produced an Engineering Effective Performance model that is highly prescriptive and is accompanied by a large number of performance aids (Stolovitch & Keeps, 2004b). What is unique about their contribution is the very practical, procedural guidelines and tools they have produced, which make it relatively easy for training, OD, OE, or HRD professionals to apply. Their work has helped build momentum for the emergence of the PC in organizations.

Finally, to sum up the evolution of HPT/HPI, we present in Figure 14.2 a generalized HPT model (Van Tiem,

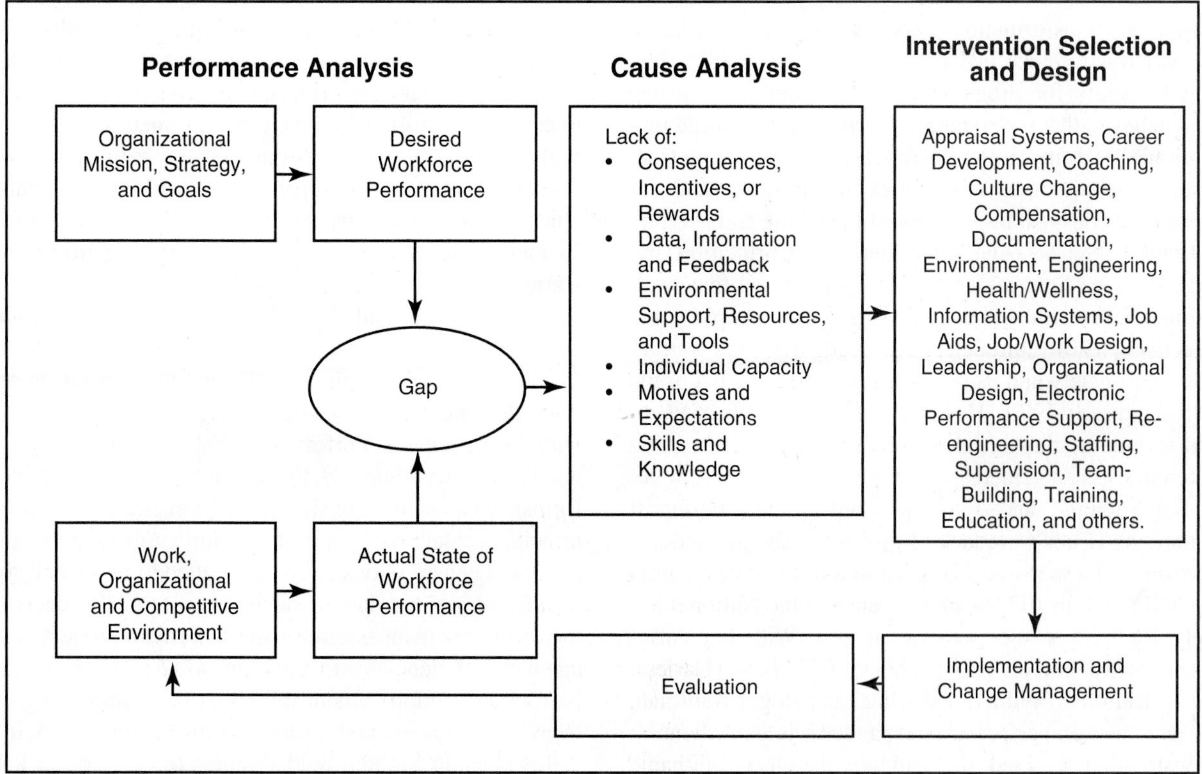

FIGURE 14.2 HPT model of the International Society for Performance Improvement.
Source: From *Fundamentals of Performance Technology* (2nd ed.) (p. 3), by D. M. Van Tiem, J. L. Moseley, and J. C. Dessigner, 2004, Washington, DC: International Society for Performance Improvement. Copyright 2004 by ISPI. Reprinted by permission.

Moseley, & Dessinger, 2004) which has probably had the most global exposure. This is the HPT model adopted by the International Society for Performance Improvement (ISPI), a professional organization that many HPI practitioners worldwide consider to be their professional home.

To conclude our story of the rocking chair company, the training department, perhaps through no fault of its own, became the prisoner of its single-solution mission. Through HPI, as characterized by the preceding models, this department has an opportunity to acquire a new, more relevant and robust mission—that of helping the company achieve business success through its people in systematic, systemic, and scientific ways. By transforming itself into a HPI organization, its focus becomes more aligned with the company's overall business goals. However, is this realistic or achievable? What follows addresses this question.

The Role of Professional Societies in the Evolution of HPI

The short answer to the question, "Can a training department within a company or other workplace organization become a HPI group?" is, "Yes." That is what the International Society for Performance Improvement (ISPI) has been attempting to encourage for many years worldwide. ISPI's own transformation bears witness to the possibility.

ISPI was founded in 1962 under the name NSPI (National Society for Programmed Instruction) by a group who believed that programmed instruction (PI) would revolutionize learning. From the founders' view—many from research laboratories, universities, the military, and defense industries—at last a science of teaching and learning existed! Based on behaviorist theory and principles and drawing from hard research data, they posited that well-defined, behaviorally specified tasks could be rapidly and effectively learned through scientifically designed instruction. The society and its beliefs flourished for most of the 1960s and early 1970s. However, the golden glow of PI began to fade as flaws in the effectiveness of the learning outcomes became increasingly apparent, both from research findings and practical applications. Foremost among the issues were lack of transfer to the job and impact on business results. This led to a broader orientation for NSPI and, in 1973, a name change to the National Society for Performance and Instruction. With key influencers such as Robert Mager, Thomas Gilbert, Joe Harless, Geary Rummler, William Deterline, and Roger Kaufman, the emphasis on performance expanded while its attention to instruction declined. Interestingly, the change in name and focus coincided with an increase in membership from the business sector and, as importantly, greater attention from the international community. In 1995, NSPI became ISPI, the International Society for Performance Improvement, with over 10,000 members globally and 55 chapters representing 40 countries.

ISPI has transformed its mission from learning to performance. Through its publications, conferences, seminars, and other live and online events, it has fostered a major shift in organizational thinking about the roles of training and HPI. Its influence has also spread to other major professional "training" associations. The American Society for Training and Development (ASTD) began offering seminars in HPI starting in the mid 1990s. In 2002, ISPI and ASTD joined forces to offer certification (Certified Performance Technologist) in HPI complete with a rigorous, performance-based program for qualification.

Other organizations, such as Training, long known for its conferences and publications, and the International Federation of Training and Development Organizations (IFTDO), have turned their attention to HPI. In 2003, Training began a PC certificate program at its annual conference. IFTDO held its annual international conference jointly with ISPI in 1999. The emphasis was on HPI internationally.

In addition to the aforementioned professional societies, a variety of workplace organizations have adopted an HPI approach. For example, the famous California-based Wells Fargo Bank has long supported the HPI thrust and since 1983 has had a "performance improvement" organization in place. Prudential Real Estate and Relocation possesses a performance enhancement group. Hewlett-Packard has many performance consultants and a Performance and Learning Lifecycle model, methodology, and tools that it evangelizes throughout the entire company. The oldest retail store company in the world, the venerable Hudson's Bay Company (established in 1670), has turned its attention to transforming its various training groups into learning and performance support teams.

A host of titles and names have arisen to replace "training" or to signal a merged HPI philosophy and orientation that brings together training, OD, and OE specialists and often even includes knowledge management teams. Groups with names such as Performance Enhancement, Learning and Performance Support, Performance Improvement, Performance Consulting, or simply Performance are springing up with accelerating regularity in North American organizations. Their missions range from attending to small, yet significant projects, largely tactical in nature (e.g., decreasing downtime in an assembly line; improving project management efficiencies), to medium sized and meaningful performance improvement initiatives (e.g., improving the overall efficiencies and customer satisfaction ratings in a call center), to big and bold ventures (e.g., working with senior management to improve the quality of human performance in all of its production facilities; participating in corporate strategic planning).

This leads us to two forms of closure. The first is with respect to HPI as a growing field of professional practice. HPI is not simply alive and well, it is thriving. As has been demonstrated to this point, the mission and meaning of HPI is both clear and known. Publications on subjects related to HPI are flourishing. (Go to http://www.ispi.org, http://www.astd.org, or http://www.amazon.com to view the array of recent titles). Increasing numbers of universities offer programs related to HPI (e.g., University of Southern California's doctoral program in Human Performance at Work and Boise State Idaho master's program on Performance and Instructional Technology) or, at the least, courses on the subject (e.g., Indiana University; Florida State University; Concordia University, Canada; San Diego State University). Professional societies with a HPI orientation are in growth phases. Certification is not only under way, but is in great demand. (For example, in 2002, the first year ISPI launched its Certified Performance Technologist progam, 170 candidates enrolled for it. By late 2004, the number had risen to over 1,000.) Finally, numerous large corporations have turned their attention to HPI. These organizations include software producers (e.g., Microsoft; Crystal Decisions), high-technology companies (e.g., Sun Microsystems; Hewlett-Packard), financial institutions (e.g., Wells Fargo; Nationwide Insurance) and a host of other well-established industries in fields as diverse as telecommunications, real estate, transportation, utilities, and manufacturing.

The second form of closure is for our rocking chair company that now has an opportunity to regain, through HPI, coherence between training department survival and the company business needs. By transforming itself from purveyor of courses to that of partner in performance success, the "training department" can enlarge its mission, create new financing models, and help the company attain accomplishments from which everyone benefits.

The Future of HPI

All signs point to a healthy, expanding future for HPI and its professional practitioners who will play increasingly significant organizational roles. The most important indicator of this is the steady evolution and growth of HPI and HPT. It is not a field of practice that has suddenly appeared on the scene. It has emerged slowly but forcefully over the past 40 years to attain a position of prominence among those seeking to effect significant, bottom-line change through people. It is not only very present in North America, but also in Europe (see, for example, the *Performance Improvement Journal* special issue highlighting the application of HPI in Europe and globally [Mueller & Voelkl, 2004]).

As attention focuses more and more on return on investment in learning and performance (e.g., J. J. Phillips, 2003; Stolovitch & Keeps, 2004a), the demand for HPI professionals will increase. Already, as the 2003 American Society for Training & Development *Industry Report* shows, performance consultants are highly visible in organizations and paid significantly more for their contributions than "training practitioners" (Sugrue, 2003, p. 20). All of this augurs well for the future of the field.

Conclusion

HPI is not a flavor of the month, radical departure, or off-the-wall movement. Rather, it is a natural evolution toward systemic alignment of human capital management with organizational requirements to meet tough and competitive demands. Its vision of achieving, through people, increasingly successful accomplishments that are valued by all stakeholders is appropriate to this moment in time.

Although HPI originated and has had its most dramatic developments in North America, it is not unique to this geography. The need for and interest in HPI is a worldwide phenomenon. Groups of training, HRD, OE, and OD professionals have come together in Australia, Europe, Asia, and the developing world to espouse the vision and practices of HPI (Stolovitch & Keeps, 1999).

This chapter has responded to the key questions raised at its outset. It has explained what is special and unique about HPI, recounted where it came from and how it has grown into a professional field that is asserting its message globally. It has also traced its origins and evolution demonstrating how it can assist individuals and organizations to achieve workplace success. Finally, it has demonstrated that HPI is not just another disruptive fad, but a rational and reasonable next step in building valued human performance—one that makes eminent sense in today's exacting world of work.

Application Questions

1. Examine the three major sections of the HPT model presented in Figure 14.2, and answer the following questions:
   a. what seems to be the major purpose of the performance analysis phase of the process?
   b. why is the cause analysis phase of this model crucial? Use some of the terms listed in that section of the model to support your point of view.
   c. select three of the interventions (other than training and education) listed in the intervention selection and design phase. Using other resources, locate definitions of three of these interventions, and write a definition for each. For each of the three, describe whether you feel an instructional designer would need extra training to adequately plan an intervention of that type. Explain why you feel that way.
2. Assume that the chairperson of an academic department is holding a discussion with the person responsible for handling all the paperwork associated with student applications for admission to the department. In explaining the reasons for existing problems, the admissions clerk states, "The office manager never told me exactly what I was expected to do in this job, and she never gives me any help or tells whether I'm doing good work. She also has me answering phone calls that I think should be answered by our office receptionist. On top of that, I often have to walk to the other end of the office to fax copies of admissions forms to the university admissions office, and that takes up a lot of my time. Also, the faculty often ask me to copy textbook materials for them, and whenever they ask me to do so, I put down whatever else I'm working on so that I can get the copying done." Identify the categories of performance problems apparent in the clerk's statement. For each problem you identify, describe an appropriate solution.
3. Some students who are enrolled in instructional design and technology (ID&T) programs, on first learning about human performance technology, feel that their training will not adequately prepare them to perform the many tasks listed in Figure 14.1. However, many graduates of ID&T programs now refer to themselves as performance improvement specialists, and/or engage in many of the activities listed in the figure. With the help of a faculty member, identify two graduates of your program who now consider themselves to have some expertise in human performance technology. Interview these individuals and try to ascertain (1) what HPT skills they employ, and (2) how they acquired those skills. Write a brief report describing your findings. Conclude the report by providing an assessment of how you think you might go about acquiring these skills.

References

Becker, G. S. (1993). *Human capital: A theoretical and empirical analysis with special reference to education* (3rd ed.). Chicago: University of Chicago.

Bradley, K. (1996). Intellectual capital and the new wealth of nations. Lecture delivered to the Royal Society of Arts, London, October.

Crawford, R. (1991). *In the era of human capital: The emergence of talent, intelligence and knowledge as the worldwide economic force and what it means to managers and investors.* New York: HarperBusiness.

Davenport, T. O. (1999). Human *capital: What it is and why people invest in it.* San Francisco: Jossey-Bass.

Dean, P. J. (1994). *Performance engineering at work.* Batavia, IL: International Board of Standards for Training, Performance and Instruction.

Dean, P. J., & Ripley, D. E. (1997). *Performance improvement pathfinders: Models for organizational learning systems, Vol. 2.* Washington, DC: International Society for Performance Improvement.

de Rosnay, J. (1975). Le macroscope, vers une vision globale. Paris: Le Seuil.

Edvinsson, L., & Malone, M. S. (1997). *Intellectual capital: Realizing your company's true value by finding its hidden brainpower.* New York: HarperBusiness.

Esque, T. J., & McCausland, J. (1997). Taking ownership for transfer: A management development case study. *Performance Improvement Quarterly, 10*(2), 116–133.

Fitz-enz, J. (2000). *The ROI of human capital: Measuring the economic value of employee performance.* New York: American Management Association.

Geis, G. L. (1986). Human performance technology: An overview. In M. E. Smith (ed.), *Introduction to performance technology* (Vol. 1, pp. 1–20). Washington, DC: National Society for Performance and Instruction.

Gilbert, T. F. (1962). Mathetics: The technology of education. *Journal of Mathetics, 1*(1), 7–74.

Gilbert, T. F. (1978). *Human Competence: Engineering worthy performance*. New York: Mc Graw-Hill.

Gilbert, T. F. (1996). *Human competence: Engineering worthy performance* (ISPI Tribute Edition). Washington, DC: International Society for Performance Improvement.

Gilley, J. W., Maycunich, A., & Quatro, S. (2002). Comparing the roles, responsibilities, and activities of transactional and transformational HRD professionals. *Performance Improvement Quarterly, 15*(4), 23–44.

Halal, W. E. (1998). *The infinite resource: Creating and leading the knowledge enterprise*. San Francisco: Jossey-Bass.

Harless, J. (1970). *An ounce of analysis is worth a pound of objectives*. Newman, GA: Harless Performance Guild.

Harless, J. (1995). Performance technology skills in business: Implications for preparation. *Performance Improvement Quarterly*, *8*(4), 75–88.

Harless, J. (1998). *The Eden conspiracy: Educating for accomplished citizenship*. Wheaton, IL: Guild V Publications.

Kaufman, R. (1995). *Mapping educational success*. Thousand Oaks, CA: Corwin.

Lande, R. (2002). Performance improvement. *Population Reports*, *30*(2). (Special issue, Family Planning Programs Series J. no. 52, Baltimore MD: Johns Hopkins Bloomberg School of Public Health, Population Information Program.)

Lickert, R., & Pyle, W. C. (1971). Human resource accounting: A human organizational measurement approach. *Financial Analysts Journal*, *27*, 101–102, 75–84.

Mager, R. F., & Pipe, P. (1970). *Analyzing performance problems or "you really oughta wanna."* Belmont, CA: Fearon.

Mueller, M., & Voelkl, C. (Eds.). (2004). Sustaining performance [Special issue]. *Performance Improvement Journal, 43*(6).

Nickols, F. W. (1977). Concerning performance and performance standards: An opinion. *NSPI journal*, *16*(1), 14–17.

Pfeffer, J. (1998). *The human equation: Building profits by putting people first*. Boston, MA: Harvard Business School Press.

Phillips, J. J. (1997). *Return on investment in training and performance improvement programs*. Houston, TX: Gulf.

Phillips, J. J. (2003). *Return on investment in training and performance improvement programs* (2nd ed.). Burlington, MA: Butterworth-Heinemann.

Phillips, P. P. (2002). *The bottom line on ROI: Basics, benefits and barriers to measuring training and performance improvement*. Atlanta, GA: CEP.

Robinson, D. G., & Robinson, J. C. (1995). *Performance consulting: Moving beyond training*. San Francisco, Berrett-Koehler.

Robinson, D. G., & Robinson, J. C. (1998). *Moving from training to performance: A practical guidebook*. San Francisco. Barrett-Koehler/Alexandria, VA: American Society for Training and Development.

Rosenberg, M. J., Coscarelli, W. C., & Hutchinson, C. M. (1999). The origins and evolution of the field. In H. D. Stolovitch & E. J. Keeps (eds.), *Handbook of human performance technology: Improving individual and organizational performance worldwide* (pp.24–26). San Francisco: Jossey-Bass.

Rummler, G. A. (1983). Technology domains and NSPI. *Performance and Instruction*, *22*(9), 32–36.

Rummler, G. A., (2004). *Serious performance consulting—According to Rummler*. Silver Spring, MD: International Society for Performance Improvement.

Rummler, G. A. & Brache, A. P. (1995). *Improving performance: How to manage the white space on the organization chart* (2nd ed.). San Francisco: Jossey-Bass.

Schultz, T. W. (1981). *Investing in people: The economics of population quality*. Berkeley: University of California Press.

Senge, P. M. (1990). *The fifth discipline: The art and practice of the learning organization*. New York: Doubleday.

Stewart, T. A. (1994). Your company's most valuable capital: Intellectual capital. *Fortune* (March 10), 68–74.

Stewart, T. A. (1997). *Intellectual capital: The new wealth of organizations*. New York: Doubleday Dell.

Stolovitch, H. D., & Keeps, E. J. (1999). *Handbook of human performance technology: Improving individual and organizational performance worldwide*. San Francisco: Jossey-Bass.

Stolovitch, H. D., & Keeps, E. J. (2004a). *Front-end analysis and return on investment toolkit.* San Francisco: Jossey-Bass/Pfeiffer/Wiley.

Stolovitch, H. D., & Keeps, E. J. (2004b). *Training ain't performance*. Alexandria, VA: American Society for Training & Development.

Sugrue, B., (2003). *State of the industry:ASTD's annual review of U.S. and international trends in workplace learning and performance.* Alexanderia, VA: American Society for Training and Development.

Van Buren, M. E., & Erskine, W. (2002). *State of the industry: ASTD's annual review of trends in employer-provided training in the United States.* Alexandria, VA: American Society for Training and Development.

Van Tiem, D. M., Moseley, J. L., & Dessinger, J. C. (2004). *Fundamentals of performance technology: A guide to improving people, process, and performance* (2nd ed.). Washington, DC: International Society for Performance Improvement.

CHAPTER 15

Electronic Performance Support Systems: Visions and Viewpoints

Jan McKay
Walter W. Wager
Florida State University

Editors' Introduction

As described in the previous chapter, the field of human performance technology (HPT) places an emphasis on improving human performance in the workplace, as well as improving organizational results. HPT also stresses the value of noninstructional as well as instructional solutions to performance problems. Electronic performance support systems (EPSS) fit right in with these emphases. As Jan McKay and Walter Wager indicate in this chapter, EPSS provide a variety of tools and resources, some instructional and others noninstructional, to help solve performance problems. These tools and resources are available at the *time of need*, and may be designed to address the performance needs of individual workers, a work group, and/or an entire organization.

Knowledge and Comprehension Questions

1. The authors present several definitions of electronic performance support systems (EPSS). Examine these definitions plus at least two more you locate on your own (via the Internet or other sources). Indicate which definition you prefer and describe why you prefer it.
2. Think of an electronic support system you are familiar with (e.g., an electronic tax return preparation program or a word processing program). Identify which of the five components of an EPSS are incorporated into the system, and describe how those components are incorporated.
3. Describe the major factors that have led to increased interest in electronic performance support systems in recent years.
4. Describe how electronic performance support systems can support (1) individuals, (2) work groups, and (3) entire organizations.
5. Describe some of the reasons that electronic performance support systems (1) have not been more widely used and (2) are likely to become much more prevalent in the future.

In recent years the use of electronic performance support systems (EPSS) has emerged as a viable and effective way to support human performance within the work environment. These electronic systems provide workers with the information and tools needed to do their jobs through on-demand access to information, online help, expert systems, and other electronic tools. One of the newest tools in the performance technology toolbox, electronic performance support systems provide yet another option for improving performance in the workplace.

This chapter examines the evolving definition and primary goals of EPSS. It describes factors that have led to the emergence of the EPSS approach and the potential scope of electronic performance support within organizations. In addition, the chapter analyzes the current status of EPSS and possibilities for the future, providing varied examples of electronic performance support systems in use in business and industry.

What Is an Electronic Performance Support System?

Exactly what *is* an electronic performance support system? The concept of EPSS has been gradually evolving since it first emerged in the late 1980s. Pioneers of the EPSS movement include Barry Raybould, who proposed ways computers could be used to solve human performance problems (Raybould, 1990), and Gloria Gery, who coined the phrase "electronic performance support system" (Gery, 1991). These innovators first envisioned a comprehensive electronic system with a suite of electronic tools and resources *integrated to work together* in a single computer application. Using the system, workers could access a variety of tools and resources on demand, just when needed in the context of doing their work. As Raybould (1995) has indicated, early definitions of electronic performance support systems viewed them as electronic systems that provided integrated access to (1) information, (2) advice, (3) learning experiences, and (4) tools to help someone perform a task with minimal support from others.

Components of an Electronic Performance Support System

Ideas vary regarding necessary components of an electronic performance support system. The components described here reflect the early definitions of EPSS, mentioned previously. A scenario then is presented to illustrate how integrated access to these electronic tools and resources might provide performance support in a business setting.

An Information Base. The information base contains the content of the EPSS. It includes the reference information needed by workers in performing their jobs, organized in a way (e.g., hyperlinked, searchable) which makes it easily accessible at the moment needed. Online reference information includes information databases, online documents, and case history databases. Information can be presented in one or more media (text, graphics, video, still images, or audio) to enhance understanding as appropriate to personal learning style and the task at hand.

Learning Experiences. Learning experiences are typically brief segments of interactive computer-based instruction, tutorials, and simulations that address a particular task the user wishes to perform. Workers can access the instruction just at the time it is needed and apply what they learn *as they are performing* the task.

Embedded Coaching and Help Tools. Intelligent coaching and help tools provide assistance in using the system, as well as in performing job tasks. These can be activated either by the user or by the system as it notices a need based on user input.

An Expert Advisor. In its expert advisor role, an EPSS provides decision-making support for difficult or non-routine tasks. Using case-based reasoning the advisor assists the user with on-the-job problem solving. Often the electronic advisor presents a series of questions about the problem. Based on the answers of the user, the system suggests a course of action.

Customized Tools. These electronic tools may include business applications and productivity programs (e.g., word processing, spreadsheet, database, and flowcharting applications) with customized templates and forms specific to the job. Electronic tools are often used to automate work processes and tasks.

Let's consider how this EPSS model might look in action. Imagine you have just been hired as a sales associate in a large company. On your first day of work you enter your office and turn on your computer. A screen appears that asks you to type in your name and job title. When you do, an interface appears that provides instant access to an *integrated* system of electronic tools specifically designed to help you perform your job effectively. With a simple click of the mouse you can have the EPPS provide you with:

- Online reference information including searchable databases that contain your client records, the latest information about the products you will be selling, inventory and shipping schedules, and online reference manuals. (These databases are continuously updated as needed, so you are always provided with the most current information.)

- Wizards that take you step by step through the process of completing and submitting sales forms, generating required reports, and performing other tasks.
- Productivity software such as word processing software with customized form letters to clients, vendors, and so on that are linked to corresponding databases.
- A troubleshooting system that allows you to enter questions about sales strategies and receive advice based on company policies and past experiences of expert employees.
- Short segments of context sensitive computer-based training that you may access just prior to undertaking a new task (e.g., calling a prospective client).
- System-activated help systems that monitor your use of the EPSS and offer guidance as needed (e.g., when you enter information that does not seem appropriate, or when you try unsuccessfully to complete a task).
- Access to current company news of interest to sales associates.

The electronic system is designed so that you can easily access the type of support you need, and use that support when and how you need it to do your job with minimal assistance from your coworkers. With little or no training you are up and running, planning your sales route for the coming week.

Evolving Views of EPSS

The conception of EPSS just described has continued to shape design efforts in recent years. Over time, however, different interpretations and variations of the original definition of EPSS have also evolved. A more pragmatic view of EPSS has gradually emerged as businesses grappled with solving performance problems in the real world (see Mayor, 1996). In a practical sense, an *EPSS* may be considered a computer application that performs any combination of the aforementioned functions (components) as needed to support performance (Stevens & Stevens, 1995). Thus, for some, an EPSS may be as basic as a searchable database containing company policies and procedures, and a context-sensitive help system. This view of electronic performance support acknowledges that performance can often be improved with relatively simple electronic tools. It allows companies to ease into the EPSS arena by successfully addressing a particular performance problem on a small scale, and then expanding the use of EPSS as needed.

At the same time, others involved in the EPSS movement have *broadened* the vision of EPSS by proposing that an EPSS should perform all the functions described—and more. In this view, an EPSS should also function as the "electronic infrastructure that captures, stores, and distributes individual and corporate knowledge assets throughout an organization" (Raybould, 1995, p. 11). The knowledge base grows as workers use the system. In essence, the EPSS is *dynamic*; ongoing synergistic input from the users continuously changes the system (Laffey, 1995). For example, each task completed can provide a case history of a problem solved on the job that is automatically made available to other users of the system. Using this type of EPSS enables organizations to develop expertise that is continually updated and shared.

More recently Gery (2002) has gone on to describe electronic performance support systems as software applications or computer-mediated work environments that provide integrated support for process (i.e., task support), knowledge, tools, data, and communication. The performance support systems may be built from scratch as originally envisioned, or may be constructed using software that integrates a number of different systems workers already use to do their jobs (Warshawsky, 2001).

Goals of EPSS

Though EPSS has come to mean different things to different people, there is general consensus regarding the goals of EPSS and the characteristics of electronic support systems that help to support human performance in the workplace. Advocates agree that *the primary goal of an EPSS is to enable people to perform their work more effectively by providing workers with whatever is needed, at the time it is needed to perform a task.* Using an EPSS a worker should be able to perform a task "in less time, with fewer errors, with better results, or with less training or external support" (Miller, 1996, p. 1). Though workers often learn new skills and knowledge through using an EPSS, the main purpose of an EPSS is to facilitate performance in the workplace (Dickelman, 1999; Hudzina, Rowley, & Wager, 1996, Rosenberg, 1995). This emphasis on performance is in line with the focus of the performance technology movement.

A secondary goal of an EPSS is to provide the support necessary to enable novice workers to perform like more experienced workers, with little or no training, while at the same time accommodating expert workers. Using an EPSS, new workers can access knowledge and tools that enable them to perform their jobs like workers with more expertise. Guidelines and/or prescriptions for "best practices" for on-the-job performance and work strategies are built into the EPSS, and inexperienced workers are led through these "best practices." Gery (1995) maintains that a well-designed EPSS should enable "Day 1" performance by all users. Day 1 performance implies that both novice and expert users are able to use the system to perform their jobs effectively from the very first day. A key element is an intuitive graphical user interface that can be easily understood even by novice users. At the same time, the interface is designed to accommodate expert users. This may be accomplished by providing alternative views of the information or by layering the information and allowing the user to request more detailed information as needed.

Why Electronic Performance Support Systems?

The use of EPSS has emerged as a performance-improvement intervention in response to a variety of factors, including the changing demands of the workplace and the development of new technological capabilities (Laffey, 1995). Today's workplace has become increasingly complex. For most organizations, information overload brought on by computer use and a rapidly changing knowledge base is a major problem. Businesses compete in a rapidly changing global market. They face the continual challenge of increasing productivity while maintaining quality. At the same time, they must accommodate a workforce that is more diverse and transient in nature than ever before (Warshawsky, 2001).

Computer technology has enabled the development and implementation of electronic performance support systems in the workplace. Computers currently in widespread use in business and industry provide a readily available infrastructure for *implementation* of electronic support. Access to wireless, mobile technology makes it possible for workers to receive electronic support almost anywhere it is needed while performing their jobs. In addition, new software applications have emerged over the past decade that make the *development* of electronic performance support systems quicker and more cost effective. Other advances in technology have enabled the *integration* of electronic tools in ways that were previously not possible (Warshawsky, 2001).

A basic premise of the EPSS approach is the notion that training is ineffective and inefficient for many performance problems facing companies today. With the rapid pace of change in the business world, training is often too slow and too expensive to meet constantly changing performance needs. For example, the rollout of a new product in a large company may require retraining thousands of sales associates. Time devoted to training becomes extremely costly both in terms of salaries being paid to trainees and the decrease in sales while workers are away from their jobs. In addition, training is often less effective than desired because it takes place out of the job context and is too far removed in time from actual job performance. Workers often forget what they have learned before they can apply it on the job. In contrast, with an EPSS training is done precisely when it is needed in the context of the job. This "just-in-time" training means the worker is performing effectively on the job in a much shorter period of time.

Potential Scope of Performance Support

Obviously, the EPSS approach can be implemented in a variety of ways. EPSS may range in complexity from relatively simple standalone systems to large-scale, highly integrated systems. An EPSS may be designed to support the performance of an individual worker, a work group, or an entire organization. The scope of performance supported is contingent on the scale of the EPSS and the degree to which it is integrated into organizational work processes.

Performance Support for Individuals

Many EPSS provide support to individual workers performing a specific task. These EPSS are often standalone applications, running on a personal PC. For example, at Honda Corporation, a troubleshooting EPSS running on a laptop may be used by a technician in the field to diagnose problems with a motorcycle's electrical system and to help make repairs to the unit (Plus Delta Performance, Inc. & American Honda Motor Co., Inc., 1999). A system that supports customer service associates at a telephone-banking center in daily interactions with customers is another example of a tool that supports individual performance. These systems are sometimes referred to as electronic performance support *tools* (EPST).

Performance Support for Work Groups

EPSS designed to support the job performance of work groups generally run on local or wide area networks and the application is shared by the workers. All individuals in the group use the EPSS to perform an *interdependent* task. They may work collaboratively to plan a project or produce a report. The EPSS may facilitate synchronous or asynchronous, person-to-person or group conferencing. It may also help guide the group through key processes involved in completing the collaborative task (Malcolm, 1998). *Lotus Notes* is an example of a commercial software application that supports work group projects by enabling group conferencing and shared access to written documents and online references. In addition, communications tools such as e-mail, fax, chat rooms, and other methods of computer-mediated interactions now play an important role in electronic support for collaborative work (Gery, 2002).

Performance Support for the Organization

Large-scale, highly integrated EPSS include applications that integrate a number of different aspects of an organization and support the performance of many people. These EPSS are integrated into the company's computer networks, requiring centralized security control and maintenance. The point-of-sale system used by most large department stores is an example of an EPSS that provides organizational-level support. The point-of-sale system integrates the inventory, distribution, floor planning, buying, and sales systems. When a product is scanned at the register, a program notes the sale, adjusts the corresponding inventory records, and checks to see if more of the product is on hand. If so, it alerts the floor manager; if not, it checks to see if more should be ordered (possibly based on an expert system that computes whether the floor space might be more effectively used for a different product). The system even compiles and transmits the order to the distribution center. An EPSS such as this facilitates the performance of many different employees. It also changes (automates) many of the jobs that workers previously did manually.

Designing Electronic Performance Support Systems

EPSS design benefits from the use of a systems model that analyzes the nature of the job tasks and work processes, establishes performance objectives, and uses feedback from potential users to improve the product. Large-scale, highly integrated EPSS are generally designed and developed by a multidisciplinary team that brings together expertise from a variety of fields, such as human performance technology, knowledge management, systems engineering, and others (Huber, Lippincott, McMachon, & Witt, 1999). The process for the design and development of large-scale, highly integrated EPSS is typically complex and time intensive. In contrast, standalone electronic support tools and less complex networked EPSS are often developed over a relatively short period of time by a small group of innovative individuals with skills in multiple areas.

One model of instructional design, developed by Digital Research in the 1980s, was the D4M2 model of EPSS Design and Development (Brown, 1996). *D4M2* stands for Define, Design, Develop, Deliver, Manage-Measure. Brown redefined and expanded this process into a book on EPSS design, and called the new model the ED4: EPSS Define, Design, Develop and Deliver. Each of the four phases is described briefly.

1. *Define Phase*—Analysis of the performer and the performance environment. The purpose is to assess the performer's needs, define the EPSS goals and requirements, define the technical functionality, and plan the development process.
2. *Design Phase*—Create flowchart or storyboards of the detailed design. The purpose is to create the blueprint that the software engineers and instructional designers will use to create the EPSS—the design is formatively evaluated by the potential users using rapid prototypes or storyboard reviews. Important parts of this step are to make the EPSS "user friendly," including attention to suggestions made by the potential users. The design team often includes a project manager, a potential user, an instructional designer, and an information systems person.
3. *Develop Phase*—This phase includes the development and testing of a functional prototype. The prototype might be built in stages, testing each one before moving on to the next. When the prototype is satisfactory, it can be turned over to the systems developers, who will put the product into a distributable form. Most EPSS include or are built around a database system, and the expertise of a software engineer is important to the success of the system. Any help system or instructional materials (user's manual) needed for the EPSS is also developed during this phase.
4. *Deliver Phase*—After development, the EPSS has to be "rolled out" so that the performers can use it. This might necessitate installation procedures, training, notification of procedure changes, media or company announcements, equipment upgrades, and other things that were planned for back in the design phase.

Last, but not least, the design team should develop a maintenance plan. Technology and hardware, as well as business practices, change over relatively short periods of time. Brown (1996) suggests that questions as to whether to maintain, redesign, or reuse the EPSS should be asked on a periodic basis.

Effective EPSS designers are problem solvers. They must determine the nature of performance problems within an organization and/or identify possible opportunities for enhancement of work processes and decide if an EPSS is indeed a viable solution. They must then match the performance problems to appropriate types of electronic support (Stevens & Stevens, 1995). For example, if performance is compromised because the users lack sufficient knowledge, computer-based learning experiences may be needed. If quality control is a problem, embedding coaching and help tools may be used to improve performance.

EPSS designers must be able to establish a business case for the electronic system that will be endorsed by critical sponsors. They will then work with end users to produce a *prototype* of the EPSS that represents the design for the solution. The prototype has the look and feel of the real system, but it may or may not be the actual working model. The prototype is used to demonstrate to sponsors and potential users how the EPSS will function.

The focus of EPSS design is on the end user. Throughout the design and development phase, the EPSS is continually refined based on feedback from novice and expert workers. Utilizing a "performance-centered design" process (Gery, 1995, 1997) helps to create an EPSS that may be effectively integrated into the work context and used intuitively by workers to improve performance. This is such an integral aspect of EPSS, that the term *performance-centered systems* (PCS) is now often used interchangeably with EPSS (Gery, 2002).

It is also important to address other factors that will influence successful implementation of an EPSS in the organizational context. No matter how well designed, an EPSS must be considered and implemented in conjunction with other critical interventions that affect performance (Stevens & Stevens, 1996). Such things as laying the proper groundwork to minimize employee resistance to change, making sure that workers are provided with incentives for using the EPSS on an ongoing basis, and providing supplementary training as needed to ensure workers are comfortable using the EPSS are all critical to successful implementation and sustained performance improvement.

Current Use of EPSS

What is the current status of electronic performance support in the workplace? Despite the obvious potential of electronic performance support systems and growing interest in their use by many companies, "training, backed up by peer and advisory support and further supported by reference materials, is still the predominant model for improving performance" (Gery, 2002, p. 465).

The EPSS approach has not been widely accepted for a variety of reasons. There is a lack of awareness of the EPSS concept and the potential of EPSS on the part of many organizations (Kemske, 1997). Even for organizations that understand the benefits of EPSS, a fear of upfront cost and time required for EPSS development and implementation may be deterrents (Driscoll & Hynes, 2002). Uncertainty surrounding the potential costs and benefits of implementing and maintaining an EPSS may make it difficult to assess the future return on investment and present a level of risk that management is unwilling to accept (Desmarais, Leclair, Fiset, & Talbi, 1997). Depending on the complexity of the EPSS, this concern may or may not be justified. For example, Stevens and Stevens (1996) describe a relatively inexpensive yet highly effective EPSS developed to help managers in a medical industry at 170 locations throughout the country access critical information needed to make decisions. Using *RoboHelp* and *Toolbook* software, the total development cost was only $11,700, or about $70 per facility. On the other hand, large-scale, highly integrated EPSS may cost hundreds of thousands of dollars to design, develop, and implement. Depending of the size of the company, the number of employees whose performance will be enhanced, and the resulting rate of return on the initial investment, an EPSS may or may not be a cost-effective option.

For some, a reluctance to implement EPSS may be due to a commitment to the status quo (Gery, 2002) and resistance to change. Indeed, those who have implemented an EPSS have found themselves facing the challenge of change management that is inevitable with infusion of innovations that alter the corporate culture. While an EPSS may be effective in increasing overall worker performance, it represents a new way of doing things that some employees may find threatening, particularly if it involves redesign of the work process. Betty Mackay at American Express describes the painful development and implementation process of a title transfer EPSS designed to improve customer service by streamlining the title transfer process for death settlements (Paul, 1999). The EPSS was very effective, and was ultimately adopted. However, many of the workers in the department were unhappy with how the EPSS redefined their jobs, and they eventually left the company. This scenario illustrates the need to address change management issues prior to developing an EPSS.

In terms of EPSS that are currently in use, we know the following things:

- **Most EPSS in use today in the corporate sector contain only a subset of the tools and resources proposed by Gery and others.** In most cases, the particular components and resources built into an EPSS depend on the performance problems to be addressed, available funds for EPSS development, and the expertise of the design team. The design of EPSS has not kept pace with the myriad support options possible through existing technology. For example, text and graphics remain the most commonly used media types in EPSS, though varied forms of media might more effectively support cognitive processing (i.e., through visual and auditory channels) and increase accessibility for workers with special needs (Schubert, 2002).
- **Implementing EPSS has reduced, but not totally eliminated, the need for training.** Businesses are finding that even with the best EPSS, Day 1 performance

is more a dream than a reality. However, training time is greatly reduced, sometimes resulting in significant savings to the company. Using an EPSS for new customer service employees enabled American Express to reduce initial training time by 83% while at the same time improving entry-level productivity and accuracy on the job (*Selling the Concept*, 1999). Other companies are finding it beneficial to implement an EPSS as part of the training (Sherry & Wilson, 1996). The benefit of this approach is that upfront training time is greatly reduced, and workers are subsequently better able to use the EPSS to perform their work effectively.

- **In cases where costs have been examined, EPSS have often proven to be cost-effective solutions to performance problems.** In some cases, major financial benefits have been reported. For example, using a Web-based EPSS for customer care agents called *Web Source,* Hewlett-Packard saved millions of dollars in reduced call time and elimination of traditional training for new products (*Hewlett-Packard Call Agent Performance-Centered Design,* 2001). Payless ShoeSource implemented a retail performance support system (RPSS), used by employees in over 4,500 stores in the United States and Canada, which led to an average sales increase of 4.5% for each store and greatly reduced employee training time (Chiem, 2001; Dickelman, 2001; Gery, 2002). However, it is difficult to make general conclusions about cost effectiveness of EPSS. This is partly because even though there are numerous success stories, "use of EPSS is a relatively new concept, and not much is known about their critical success factors" (Altallib, 2003, p. 13). In addition, many companies fail to conduct an evaluation of the use and outcomes of implementing an EPSS (Kemske, 1997). Even when cost effectiveness is considered, financial information about company management is generally proprietary, and not published. Consequently, there are still significant gaps in the EPSS literature regarding proven cost effectiveness.

The Future of EPSS

Obviously, the potential of EPSS has yet to be fully realized. It seems logical that electronic performance support systems will become more widely used as electronic technology becomes an increasingly integral part of the way we work and live.

There will be growing acceptance of EPSS in the workplace. As more EPSS are successfully implemented in business and industry, managers will become more willing to turn to EPSS to address performance problems or opportunities. Employees, the majority of whom now use computers in their workplace, will become more comfortable using electronic performance support systems as they perform their jobs. They will come to *expect* more electronic performance support as they gain experience with EPSS methodologies currently being incorporated into commercial consumer products such as Intuit's *TurboTax* and e-commerce websites such as eBay or Expedia.com (Gery, 2003). Employers will also find EPSS to be an effective support strategy for younger employees who grew up with computers and video games and are often more comfortable accessing information through visual sources than print materials (see Chiem, 2001).

In the future it is likely that EPSS will more effectively support the performance of *groups* as they do their work, while also enabling continuous growth of the EPSS content as workers use the system. There will be increased exploration into effective ways to support *interdependent group work* in the context of ongoing work flow, while at the same time enabling *dynamic* updating of the information in EPSS (Malcolm, 1998). The use of electronic sensors that work behind the scenes to analyze data and provide workers with information regarding trends that impact business will be further explored. For example, electronic sensors may analyze data stored in an EPSS, such as patterns in customer service calls, or changes occurring in the environment, such as trends in consumer spending. In addition, building environmental *predictors* into EPSS will enable workers to anticipate new knowledge (Malcolm, 2003).

As new technologies continue to evolve, so will the nature of electronic performance support systems. Already on the horizon are voice-recognition wearable EPSS for equipment repair technicians (Kiser, 2000). These EPSS will provide needed support in a manner that frees up the hands of the technicians so that they can perform repair procedures while using the EPSS. Voice-recognition technology enables workers to give verbal, rather than keyboard-entered, commands. Information and instructions are displayed on a tiny LCD panel attached to the worker's headgear, in a multimedia format including video, audio, graphics, and text. This type of EPSS has been tested by U.S. Postal Service machine technicians, airline mechanics, and other repairmen who require hands-free electronic support. It is also
ality technology may be used
enhance electronic support cap

Regardless of the directions
ture, the approach is sure to pl
workplace performance. It seer
for electronic performance sup
in the years to come. Indeed, w
of new technologies, the futur
only limited by our imaginatic

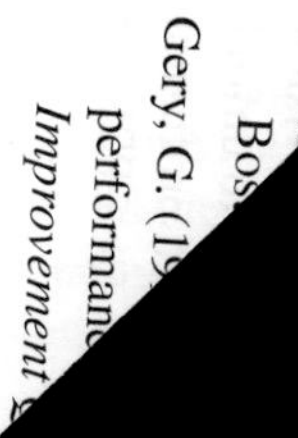

Application Questions

1. Suppose that you work as a training performance manager for a midsized manufacturing concern. You recommend to your boss that your company needs an EPSS to facilitate performance. Your boss wants to you to present some examples of ways that an EPSS would be beneficial to the company's bottom line. What types of examples would you present? Why?
2. Imagine that you are designing an EPSS for new sales employees of a large insurance company. What components would you include? Why?
3. Describe how performance objectives and feedback can be used in the design of an effective EPSS.
4. Outline the design of a prototype EPSS that would aid in accomplishing a simple task such as purchasing car tires or optimizing storage in a closet.

References

Altallib, H. (2002). ROI calculations for electronic performance support systems. *Performance Improvement Journal, 41*(10), 12–22.

Brown, L. A. (1996). *Designing and developing electronic performance support systems.* Newton, MA: Digital Press.

Chiem, P. X. (2001, August). A better fit: Payless Shoesource provides just-in-time support for in-store processes. *Knowledge Management.* Retrieved July 15, 2005, from http://www.destinationkm.com/articles/default.asp?ArticleID5311&KeyWords5 payless11AND1shoesource

Desmarais, M. C., Leclair, R., Fiset, J., & Talbi, H. (1997). Cost-justifying electronic performance support systems. *Communications of the ACM, 40*(7), 39–48.

Dickelman, G. (1999). Performance support in Internet time: The state of the practice. *Performance Improvement Quarterly, 39*(6), 7–17.

Dickelman, G. (2001). Award-winning performance & consulting: An interview with Burt Huber. *Performance Improvement Quarterly, 40*(7), 9–15.

Driscoll, M., & Hynes, C. (2002). Back to fundamentals: The business realities of funding for performance-support projects. *Technical Communications on Line, 49*(4), 453–466.

Gery, G. J. (1991). *Electronic performance support systems: How and why to remake the workplace hrough the strategic application of technology.* ton: Weingarten.

95). Attributes and behaviors of e-centered systems. *Performance Quarterly, 8*(1), 47–93.

Gery, G. (1997). Granting three wishes through performance-centered design. *Communications of the ACM, 40*(7), 54–59.

Gery, G. (2002). Achieving performance and learning through performance-centered systems. *Advances in Developing Human Resources, 4*(4), 464–478.

Gery, G. (2003). Ten years later: A new introduction to attributes & behaviors and the state of performance-centered systems. In G. Dickelman (Ed.), *EPSS revisited: A lifecycle for developing performance-centered systems* (pp. 1–3). Silver Spring, MD: International Society for Performance Improvement.

Hewlett-Packard call agent performance-centered design: Closing the gap between training and working. (2001). Retrieved on July 15, 2005 from http://www.pcd-innovations.com/infosite/pcd2001/hp/index.htm

Huber, B., Lippincott, J., McMahon, C., & Witt, C. (1999). Teaming up for performance support. *Performance Improvement Journal, 38*(7), 10–14.

Hudzina, M., Rowley, K., & Wager, W. (1996). Electronic performance support technology: Defining the domain. *Performance Improvement Quarterly*, *9*(1), 36–48.

Kemske, F. (1997). Midmorning after the dawn of EPSS: Summary and highlights of the 1997 EPSS report. Retrieved from http://www.totallearning.com/Report/Study5.htm

Kiser, K. (2000). Wearable training. Retrieved on July 15, 2005, from http://www.jamesroach.com/Cover%20Story%20Wearable%20Training.htm

Laffey, J. (1995). Dynamism electronic performance support systems. *Performance Improvement Quarterly, 8*(1), 31–46.

Malcolm, S. E. (1998). Where EPSS will go from here. *Training*, *35*(3), 64–69.

Mayor, T. (1996, January 15). Doing equals learning. *CIO Magazine, 1999*, 52–59.

Miller, B. (1996). EPSS: Expanding the perspective. Retrieved July 15, 2005, from http://www.pcd-innovations.com/infosite/define.htm

Paul, L. G. (1999, January). American Express: Performance under pressure. *Inside Technology Training*, 1–6.

Plus Delta Performance, Inc. & American Honda Motor Co., Inc. (1999). GoldWing 1500 Electrical Troubleshooting EPSS. Retrieved July 15, 2005, from http://files.epsscentral.info/samples/contest98/deltaplus.htm

Raybould, B. (1990). Solving human performance problems with computers. *Performance & Instruction*, *29*(10), 4–14.

Raybould, B. (1995). Performance support engineering: An emerging development methodology for enabling organizational learning. *Performance Improvement Quarterly*, *8*(1), 7–22.

Rosenberg, M. J. (1995). Performance technology, performance support, and the future of training: A commentary. *Performance Improvement Quarterly, 8*(1), 94–99.

Schubert, D. (2002). Use and rationale of media types in performance-centered design. *Performance Improvement Quarterly, 41*(10), 34–38.

Selling the concepts to management: Case studies. (1999). Retrieved from http://www.epss.com/1b/how/sell.htm#cs

Sherry, L., & Wilson, B. (1996). Supporting human performance across disciplines: A converging of roles and tools. *Performance Improvement Quarterly, 9*(4), 19–36.

Stevens, G., & Stevens, E. (1995). *Designing electronic performance support tools*. Englewood Cliffs, NJ: Educational Technology Publications.

Stevens, G., & Stevens, E. (1996). The truth about EPSS. *Training & Development, 50*(6), 59–61.

Warshawsky, J. (2001). One on one: Gloria Gery—Performance support, ten years later. Retrieved July 15, 2005 from http://files.epsscentral.info/gery/pdfarticles/one_on_one.pdf

Marc J. Rosenberg
Marc Rosenberg and Associates

CHAPTER 16

Knowledge Management and Learning: Perfect Together[1]

Knowledge and Comprehension Questions

1. Think about the many pieces of knowledge that exist within an organization with which you are familiar (e.g., the academic department in which you are a student). Drawing on that knowledge base, identify examples of each of the four kinds of knowledge described by Rosenberg.
2. Some have said that knowledge management is nothing more than the electronic storage and retrieval of knowledge. Indicate whether you agree or disagree, and explain why.
3. Explain what is meant by the following statement: Collaboration can make tacit knowledge explicit and will enable it to be codified.
4. Select 3 of the 10 types of organizations identified in the section, "Knowledge Management Applications." For each, describe one example of explicit knowledge and one example of tacit knowledge that is likely to exist within that type of organization.
5. Describe what is meant by the term *blended learning*. Also describe how the use of a knowledge management system as part of a blended learning approach can overcome some of the problems inherent in this approach.

Editors' Introduction

As was pointed out in the first chapter in this section, instruction is not always the best or only solution to a human performance problem. In this chapter, Marc Rosenberg discusses another means of improving the performance of individuals and of organizations—the creation and use of knowledge management (KM) systems. Rosenberg describes *knowledge management* as the creation, archiving, and sharing of valued information, expertise, and insight within and across communities of people and/or organizations with similar interests and needs, in order to improve competitive advantage. In other words, a knowledge management system helps organizations get the right information to the people who need it at the time they need it.

Rosenberg states that knowledge management systems are built on three main interrelated components—codification, collaboration, and access—and he describes all three. In doing so, he also points to the role technology plays in knowledge management systems. He also describes a variety of examples of knowledge management systems.

As noted, in this section of the book we are emphasizing the notion that instruction is not the only solution to performance problems. Rosenberg emphasizes this point when he discusses the complementary roles that can be played by training and knowledge management. He does so when he discusses blended learning (a combination of classroom learning and online learning), describing why knowledge management systems should be a integral part of a blended learning approach to improving performance.

[1] Portions of this chapter are based on content from Marc Rosenberg, *Beyond E-Learning: Approaches and Technologies to Enhance Organizational Knowledge, Learning, and Performance*, Pfeiffer, 2006.

Knowledge management (KM) is a revolution in the way we manage information, and the way we share and use it. More practically, for training/learning professionals, it changes the way we see the boundaries of our practice—from the tools and processes we use, to our sphere of influence and the impact we make in organizations.

In this chapter, we will explore three sides of knowledge management, its potential, pitfalls to watch out for, and what this all means for organizational learning.

What Is Knowledge Management?

Organizations are awash with data—customer data, financial data, employee data, product data, market data, and so on. To make sense of it all, we organize data in ways that are meaningful for us. We create tables and relationships, documents and presentations, databases and websites where data are transformed into information. When people use that information to make a decision, change a viewpoint, or take an action, that information becomes internalized as knowledge.

Types of Knowledge

In most organizations, knowledge is of four kinds: explicit, tacit, common, and undiscovered (Figure 16.1).

Explicit knowledge is knowledge that can be codified or documented in textbooks, magazines and newspapers, websites, procedural manuals, user guides, audio and video programs, and training courses and other media.

Tacit knowledge is the knowledge of experience and insight. There is usually much more tacit knowledge within an organization than there is explicit knowledge, and it is often more valuable. But, it is more difficult to identify, articulate, and manage. When you look at your best performers, and ask yourself, "What makes them more productive, more insightful, or just plain smarter than the others?" you are often asking questions about their tacit knowledge. It's not just a process, because you know that simply looking up steps to that process will not get you all the way to equaling that superior performer. There must be something more. So you extract it the only way you know how, by asking and watching over time, hoping you get the "nuggets" of insight and expertise you are looking for. This is the challenge of tacit knowledge.

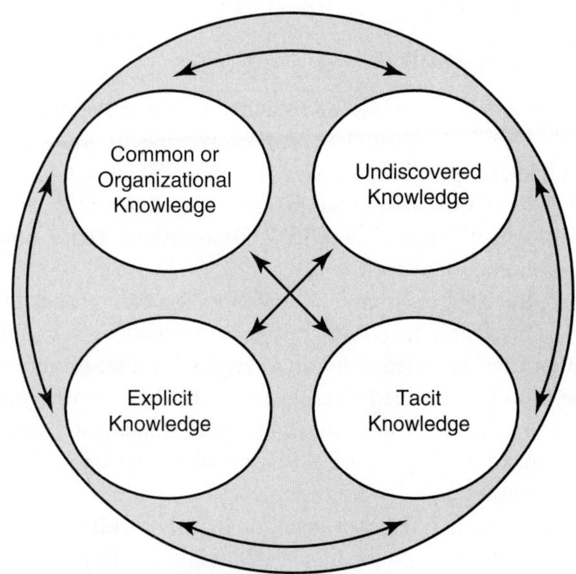

FIGURE 16.1 The four types of knowledge.

Explicit and tacit are the most common ways of classifying knowledge. In most cases, the goal is to turn as much tacit knowledge into explicit knowledge as possible, despite the inherent difficulties in capturing, describing and codifying it. But in determining the value of knowledge management in an organization, two other views about knowledge may be more useful. These perspectives—common and undiscovered knowledge—go to the heart of what KM is supposed to do: make information known and available to all who need it.

In any work setting, there are countless volumes of standard operating procedures, rules and regulations, training courses, and manuals. But if you need specific information and you don't know where that information is, you're as much in the dark as if that information was never published. Thus the third type of knowledge is *common* (or *organizational*) *knowledge*, explicit knowledge that everyone who needs to know (or know about), actually does.

Finally, the fourth type of knowledge is *undiscovered knowledge*. Undiscovered knowledge represents the greatest challenge to any business. The product improvement no one sees, the innovation that goes unnoticed, or the new idea that's buried in thousands of e-mails all represent knowledge that might greatly benefit the organization, if anyone was aware of its existence. Sometimes undiscovered knowledge stares you in the face but you don't see it. Other times it's buried in complex patterns of work activities and communications, requiring a detective to ferret it out.

Defining *Knowledge Management*

KM strives to enable the easy and systematic creation of explicit knowledge and facilitate its dissemination so that it is commonly known. It seeks to create opportunities for collaboration that brings tacit and undiscovered ideas to the surface, where they have value.

Knowledge management is the creation, archiving, and sharing of *valued information*, expertise, and insight within and across *communities* of people and organizations with similar interests and needs, the goal of which is to build *competitive advantage*. Essentially, it is getting information from people who have it to people who need it.

KM requires a sound process, meaningful management and organizational leadership, and unique software tools; but like a three-legged stool, if you remove one of the legs, the stool (KM) can't stand. KM should not be confused with *training*, which focuses on instruction rather than information. It is not simply a website or a search engine, although those are critical components. And it is not just technology, which should be viewed more properly as a critical *enabler* of KM.

Knowledge Management Myths

Knowledge management solutions fail most often when those responsible for its design and implementation often fall victim to one or more KM myths (Rosenberg, 2002):

- *Myth: KM is all about knowledge storage.* Archiving information is good, but not nearly enough. We create KM systems to harness knowledge for valued purposes, such as profit, customer satisfaction, improved product reliability, and enhancing human performance. To view KM as just about information storage and retrieval is to restrict thinking about how knowledge can be used to add value.
- *Myth: KM is all about technology.* The rush to first buy KM-related technology and *then* figure out what to do with it confuses means with ends. This approach has sent many KM initiatives towards failure, jading lots of sponsors along the way. Understanding the business and performance issues for which KM might be a solution, and *then* carefully selecting the technology and tools that will help get there, is a far superior approach to successful KM implementation.
- *Myth: KM solutions must be huge.* Many KM projects overreach in terms of what can be accomplished with the resources (financial and personal) on hand. A better way to look at KM projects is to think big, but start small (with a supportive sponsor) and then be ready to scale up when the project is successful.
- *Myth: KM is about knowledge control.* Some organizations institute a KM system to control or restrict access to information. A better alternative is to do the opposite—to democratize access to critical business and technical content. Of course, there is always some information that must be restricted, but in successful KM systems, locking up information is done only when deemed absolutely necessary.
- *Myth: If you build it, they will use it.* If e-learning represents a major change in the way people are trained, requiring special care in bringing them aboard, knowledge management will require even more work in this area. A comprehensive change management effort is essential to any KM deployment.

Knowledge Management Components

Comprehensive KM systems are built on three main interrelated components: codification, collaboration, and access (Figure 16.2).

Codification

Codification is focused primarily on documenting, and storing for easy retrieval, explicit knowledge. Perhaps the best known codified KM system is the public library. Almost anyone can quickly find the resource(s) they are looking for in any library, including ones they've never been to before. Why is this so? First, all libraries have a common organizing scheme, in this case the Dewey Decimal System (or in university libraries, the Library of Congress System). These classification approaches are based on *metadata*, "information about the information," to ensure that similar content is stored and found in similar ways, regardless of who is looking for the information or who is providing it. *Metatags*, systematically assigned to all content "objects" (document, website, media, etc.), enable proper management of the expanding knowledge base, while at the same time facilitating the searching, linking, and browsing that's so essential in finding high-quality information in a reasonable amount of time.

Training materials are codified, explicit content. So are books, maps, user guides, troubleshooting tips, frequently asked questions, product specifications, and so on.

Collaboration

The other side of knowledge management is collaboration. *Collaboration* focuses on tacit knowledge by providing vehicles for people to surface and share what they know. Over time, this sharing validates the tacit knowledge to a point where it can be codified and published. That's how best practices are born.

In the right environment, collaboration can be as natural as breathing. Incentives that reward knowledge sharing rather than knowledge hording, leadership that promotes the time people need to collaborate, facilitators who encourage, manage, and motivate collaborators, and tools that make it all easy are all essential for success. Even more important, collaboration thrives when it reflects topics of genuine interest or need, or when the collaboration facilitates the accomplishment of a work task in ways that are easier and more reliable than previous approaches.

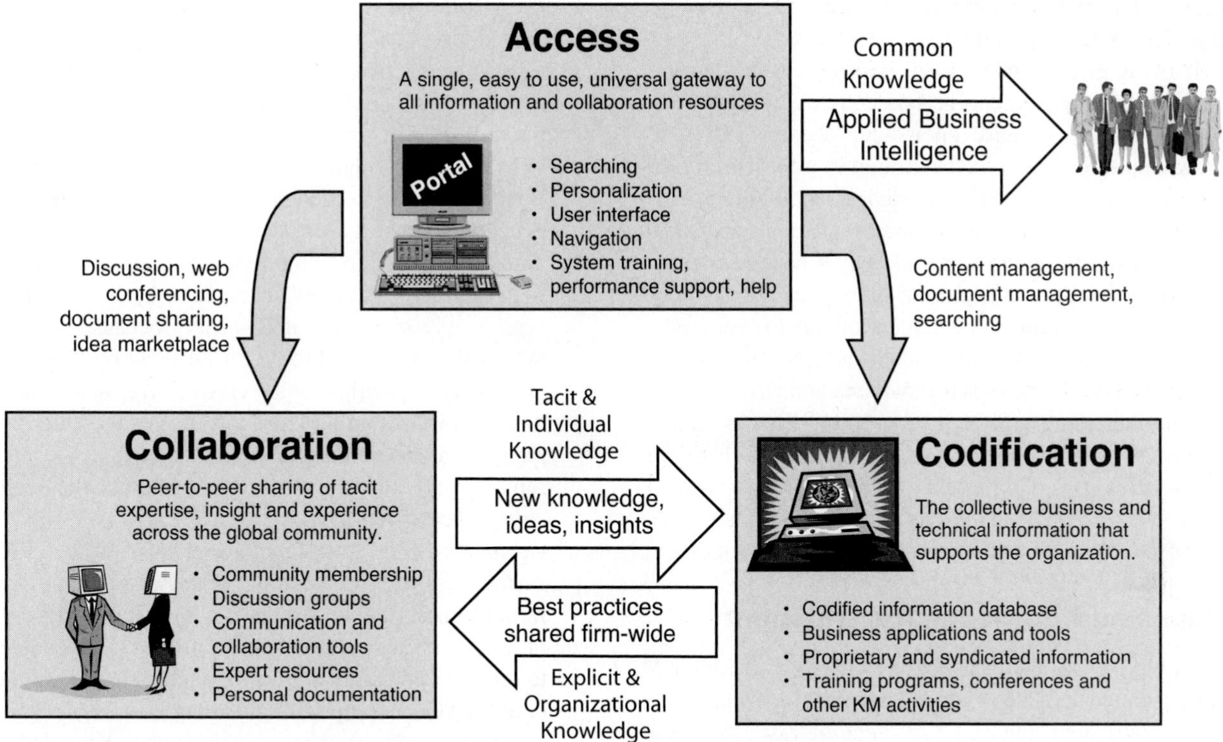

FIGURE 16.2 Knowledge management components: codification, collaboration, and access.

This is why the creation of *communities,* or *communities of practice,* is so important. Efforts to foster collaboration simply by setting up discussion threads or chat rooms have largely been unsuccessful, primarily because people have difficulty figuring out how to use these tools to solve meaningful problems, or how to locate other people for assistance. In these situations, they merely fall back on their more comfortable methods of calling on colleagues who may or may not have a correct answer, sending out e-mail blasts asking anyone for help, or resorting to trial and error until they figure out what they needed to know. Naturally, this can be extraordinarily wasteful and costly, not to mention frustrating.

Communities of practice facilitate collaboration by enabling people with similar interests, needs, and responsibilities to work together across time and distance. Project groups, trainers and their students, sales teams, committees and task forces, researchers, executives, user groups, and customers are natural candidates to benefit from communities of practice.

It would be nice if everyone could collaborate in person, at meetings, over lunch, or just in casual conversation inside and outside the workplace. But the sheer volume of knowledge and the increasing number of people who need it, coupled with the decentralization of those resources, requires technological solutions to make collaboration work. The emergence of online communities and networks has helped define a new category of collaborative tools called *social software* that moves significantly beyond the classroom to embrace e-mail, threaded discussions, chat rooms, instant messaging, synchronous conference tools, and other technologies. These new technologies put people in touch with each other, often in real time. They also help identify who is available and when, use filters to zero in on the right expertise, and ultimately document the interaction for possible codification as explicit knowledge.

Access

The interplay between codification and collaboration is what drives value in knowledge management. But any KM system is quickly overwhelmed if *access* to knowledge—documents, websites, experts, communities, and so on—is haphazard, difficult, or time consuming. The key is to *synchronize* all the knowledge into a well-defined common access strategy, where all knowledge seekers can quickly find what they are looking for, and all knowledge providers can contribute information and expertise in a similar way that makes it easy to find.

On the Web, *portals* are one way to synchronize knowledge for a user. "My Yahoo" and other websites that allow users to customize what content they see, and how they see it, are examples of portals.

It is not enough to package information in websites, online training, documents in shared drives, or in countless e-mail inboxes, because knowledge seekers still don't know where content is or how to find it. New search technologies enable the user's knowledge requirements to be matched with knowledge resources (through metatags) and displayed through the portal, which becomes a gateway to the intellectual capital of the organization. This is the process of making knowledge available to everyone.

As jobs become more distributed and less office centric, the ability to access knowledge anytime and anywhere will become increasing critical (Gotta, 2004). This is what is driving the move to e-learning as a supplement to classroom training. But just having access to online instruction will not be enough; access to online information will also be required to support the performance of the mobile work force.

Managing Knowledge Management

Behind the scenes there is a lot of technology making KM work. Content and document management tools enable the categorizing, archiving, and versioning of vast amounts of information in a variety of formats. Sophisticated search engines find specific information, and then can adapt it to the user's preferences for level of detail, content recency, or selected sources, for example. Knowledge management systems usually include an organizationwide database of eligible users that allows the KM system to identify each user and associated *entitlements*, such as allowing only people at a certain level or working in a certain department to see specific content, or restricting the ability to change a document, while allowing everyone to read it. Links into the organizational e-mail system allow users to be notified when new content that meets their predefined interests is published. Finally, community tools create member-based groups of employees, customers, or partners that enable secure interactions around a common interest, project, or goal.

When done well, all of this technology—from the word processor that a contributor uses to create content to the document manager that classifies and stores it and the search engine that finds and distributes it—creates a seamless process that significantly enhances the value of what the organization, and the individuals who comprise it, knows.

Knowledge Management Applications

Opportunities for knowledge management abound in all types of organizations and in all types of functions. Whenever people need to share information, work in teams or improve the efficiency of projects, KM can be a valuable tool. Here are 10 representative examples.

1. *Call centers.* KM is at work when hotel rooms are reserved, users get support for their computers, or customers seek product information for a possible purchase. Call center representatives certainly should be well trained, but training can't possibly keep up with the almost daily changes in product specifications, prices, and schedules. Today, the accepted expectation is that a representative provides customers with information from multiple databases of information, and certainly does not recite it by heart. When service levels decline, it is usually because the rep takes too long to find the right information, supplies incorrect information, or says those dreaded words, "I don't know." Good KM systems fix this by better organization and delivery of information to call center reps in ways that make customer interactions seem easy and responsive.
2. *Customer relationship management (CRM).* CRM systems collect a vast amount of customer data, from initial transactions to overall buying habits (past and predicted). But this knowledge is useless unless it gets to the right person in a timely manner. Training alone could never keep up with changing customer demographics, buying patterns, and interests. Knowledge management takes a more real-time approach, asking such questions as "Who should get this information? When should they get it? How is it different from 'yesterday's' information? How should it be structured?" KM systems collect CRM information, structure and parse it into appropriate "buckets" of knowledge, and distribute it to those who need it, when they need it, in a format they can use. For example, being able to get customer buying behavior to the *right* marketing managers at the *right* time creates tremendous competitive advantage for inventory management, product design and placement, and sales.
3. *E-commerce.* With the Web firmly established as a critical piece of almost every company's market strategy, knowledge management is playing a more important role beyond the sale. Customer satisfaction with after-purchase support is consistently cited as a major factor when deciding if they will purchase additional products from a company. As customers become increasingly comfortable with e-commerce, businesses are responding with online access to user manuals, product demonstrations, troubleshooting and support resources, user communities, online training, and other knowledge-rich environments that help build customer loyalty. The application of knowledge management principles of content organization, searching, and personalization creates a high-quality user experience (as opposed to a chaotic one) that strengthens this bond.

4. *Government.* Serving a diverse citizenry is as important to governments as serving diverse customers is to corporations. The challenge is to provide access to mountains of public information without overwhelming the user. Good KM practices help meet this obligation, thus helping government agencies better serve their constituencies. Today, most state and local governments provide an extraordinary amount of information on the Web. The federal government is moving quickly to do even more, especially at the agency level (e.g., the Internal Revenue Service, the Food and Drug Administration, etc.). But the biggest user of KM is undoubtedly the military. The U.S. Army's information needs are so voracious that its KM system, *Army Knowledge Online*, has over 6 trillion documents, making it one of the largest online repositories in the world. Imagine managing all that information without a disciplined KM approach!
5. *Human resources.* Human resource (HR) departments were early users of online information. As the Web emerged in the 1990s, HR was quick to see the potential of putting benefit information online, allowing employees to manage their pay and medical claims over the Web, in a self-service mode. Now, internal (and external) job markets and performance management systems are moving to the Web; and it's not just the forms and the process, but associated tools and training as well. Because employees naturally value this type of information, they quickly became comfortable in the online world, making it easier for the business to Web-enable information of other business functions.
6. *Information technology (IT).* Perhaps nowhere else in an organization is there more complexity and more risk than IT. Today, no organization can succeed without significant support technology; when it fails, the business falters. Keeping track of a company's substantial IT investment, from facility, hardware, and software assets to the process documentation, user manuals, and training that keeps it all running, is vital. When technology does fail, quick and reliable access to accurate information for disaster recovery, system restoration, troubleshooting, and so on can mean the difference between a short service interruption and closing down the business.
7. *Partner–supplier relationships.* As companies create longer and stronger ties with partners and suppliers, a symbiotic relationship develops and the need to share information becomes essential. Through knowledge management, businesses can share certain knowledge with partners and suppliers, while restricting information that should not be shared. For example, the company can share its procurement processes with suppliers to improve the supply chain. It can share marketing materials with retailers to enhance sales. And these partners and suppliers can feed product/service performance, cost, and customer data back to the business. In these ways and others knowledge sharing improves productivity as all parties learn how best to use mutually created and shared information to its greatest advantage.
8. *Professional services.* Consulting and other professional services firms rely on the expertise of their people as their primary and sometimes only asset. With consultants spending most of their time at client sites, their ability to access information, collaborate, and learn would be severely restricted without KM. Tapping into information databases and using technology to support collaboration at a distance overcomes the physical separation—from knowledge and from each other—that consultants often feel. When executed well, knowledge management enables individual contributors to call on the collective "smarts" of the organization as if they were just down the hall, rather than across the country or around the world. And they can represent those collective smarts to a client, which significantly increases their value.
9. *Sales.* Salespeople spend most of their time with customers, and often see office work and classroom training as unproductive. Many sales organizations are discovering that knowledge management can keep distributed sales teams up to speed on customer characteristics, product specifications, competitive intelligence, and other key topics without reducing customer "face time." Furthermore, as salespeople learn more about a customer or industry, they can feed that information back to a small KM core team that republishes the information to everyone else. This turns the tacit knowledge of a single salesperson into explicit knowledge, and ultimately into common knowledge as the information spreads throughout the sales force.
10. *Training.* What should be apparent from these business functions is that each incorporates knowledge management to support learning—customer learning, employee learning, and partner and supplier learning—in a variety of unique ways. Likewise, training programs can incorporate knowledge management principles. There also may be times when training is a less appropriate solution to a learning or performance problem than is KM. How to recognize and capitalize on knowledge management opportunities in this context is the subject of the next section.

Knowledge Management and Training

When training is used to address performance problems, the assumption is that an *instructional* solution is what's needed; i.e., learners *must* be *taught* what they need to know. This is often appropriate. There are countless people who must be able to perform their skills automatically—often perfectly—without the aid of references or other supports. Surgeons, pilots, soldiers, and quarterbacks clearly fall into this group. There are also many roles that require training as a prerequisite to performance, but after that, much of the learning may be more informational than instructional. Salespeople must be trained to make a good product presentation before they can win a sale. But once in the field, knowledge about changing product specifications or customer preferences can be accessed more efficiently than it can be taught. Call center representatives need initial systems training as well as training on customer relationship skills, but on the job, they rely on knowledge databases to keep up to date on product promotions and customer buying habits. Training will help new managers develop coaching skills, but in the field, they can also access online expertise if they face unique supervisory situations.

Seeing everything as just instructional in nature will result in missed opportunities that limit the potential for knowledge management and that reduce overall learning effectiveness. On the other hand, blending KM into a learning strategy significantly enhances the options available to improve performance.

The Blended Learning Dilemma

Although computer-based training (CBT) has been around for decades, until recently classroom training dominated the learning landscape. CBT made little headway until the Internet and Web virtually eliminated most of the access and interoperability issues that plagued technology-based learning. Because of the Web, online training was able to put forth a compelling economic argument that propelled it to the forefront of training innovation. The mistaken assumption that Web-based learning would some day eliminate the classroom has been replaced by a recognition that *balance* between the value still offered by classroom learning and the promise offered by online training is what's needed. The result is *blended learning*, an approach to instruction that seeks to combine the best of both worlds.

But this view of blending is woefully inadequate for four main reasons:

1. It assumes that all learning solutions require an instructional approach, when informational approaches may be more appropriate and more cost effective.
2. It focuses exclusively on what happens in formal, instructional environments (classroom or online). In reality, most learning—about 90%—takes place informally, on the job and in the context of everyday work. Opportunities to impact informal, workplace learning are often missed.
3. It drives all actions to what can be the most expensive solution—training—without first considering less costly alternatives.
4. Finally, by focusing on training solutions to the exclusion of other, noninstructional alternatives, there is an increased likelihood that the developed training may be inappropriate and may not yield the results expected; i.e., it may not work.

From Blended Learning to a Learning and Performance Architecture

True blended learning crosses the line between formal and informal learning. It must recognize that the learning needs of people only increase as they apply to their jobs what they've been taught in a formal training setting. Thus, it is important for training professionals to look beyond just the blending of instructional solutions.

E-learning is a lot more than e-training. By embracing knowledge management, as well as performance support, the entire definition of e-learning changes to include a much wider array—or blend—of tools and approaches.

Why Training Professionals Should Care About KM

Knowledge management is not just an interesting tool that sits on the periphery of learning and performance, it is in its dead center. Besides greatly expanding the notion of blended learning, KM fundamentally adds new dimensions to traditional training programs:

1. It makes interactions with original company resources easier and more powerful. Because critical business and technical information can be much more reliable and accessible online, learners have opportunities to use these materials to a far greater extent than before. This reduces reliance on student guides and compels the training organization to incorporate workplace tools and documentation as primary learning materials. Doing so adds tremendous authenticity to the course by getting learners to interact with the same knowledge resources they will use on the job.
2. Learner communities will become much more important. Formal training is episodic. People come for a week of training then go back to work for some time before they get back in the classroom. Online training is the same way. Learners log on, take a course (or part of a course) and then log off. If the program is good enough, they may repeat this process many times. But what happens *between* these events? A well-managed community of students (and instructors) can be a powerful way to continue learning even when they are not in a formal class.

3. It should be much easier for workers to access learning content (perhaps in a format different than for the original course) on the job. It will become extremely important for training organizations to put training content online and keep it continuously updated and available to everyone in the organization, not just to current learners.

On the job, knowledge management has even more impact. With the bulk of learning taking place in workplace settings and in the context of job performance, knowledge management can be an indispensable resource in a number of key ways:

1. Using powerful search, content management, and publishing technologies, access to critical business and technical information becomes not just an easier but a *preferred* way of getting information in a timely fashion—anytime and anywhere. Learning and performance is enhanced because just the right knowledge is delivered to the right people at the right time. This makes the business more agile and responsive in the marketplace.
2. Access to expertise augments codified knowledge. Workers can reach out across distance to communities of practice and subject matter experts to get the insights and perspective that come from experience. New collaboration technologies enable this learning to be captured and disseminated across the organization.
3. KM can streamline work by eliminating downtime devoted to training. While training will not be eliminated completely, more content can be built directly into work processes, in the form of help systems, decision tools, FAQs, performance support, and so on. Work processes become more streamlined, efficient, and easier to use.

While the convergence of KM and learning, especially e-learning, may seem extremely advantageous, there are barriers to overcome. Brandon Hall Research (n.d.) suggests four key obstacles:

1. *Organizational and functional barriers.* KM and learning professionals are very much separated in most organizations. They rarely talk or work on the same projects, even though their goals are quite similar.
2. *Divergent communities of practice.* Professional activities (journals, conferences, education) for these two groups rarely cross paths.
3. *Complex and ambiguous concepts.* KM concepts still need much more clarity and focus before they are truly accepted.
4. *Divergent technologies.* KM tools and technologies (and their vendors) are hardly known to the learning/e-learning community, and vice versa. There is little effort to link the two technology sets—yet.

For the integration of KM and learning/e-learning to really take place, these barriers must be overcome; there must be much more collaboration of the two practice areas.

Knowledge Management in Action

Knowledge management enables organizations to improve human performance through easier, more direct access to reliable information and expertise, often bypassing interim steps such as training. Sometimes, KM reduces the need for training; other times it augments it. The key, of course, is considering KM when making design and implementation decisions and when developing broad-based blended solutions. Table 16.1 illustrates how this worked in four industry examples: telecommunications, services, finance, and petroleum.

Learning to Learn—in Real Time

By immersing people in a knowledge culture, not just a training culture, they learn to be better knowledge seekers and better researchers. They learn to discern important and valid content from drivel. In doing so, they develop a critical skill: the ability to identify, access, evaluate, and effectively use information. Once this skill is mastered and supported by a sound knowledge management strategy, KM will no longer be seen as playing a secondary, supporting role to training. Rather, the reverse may be true. Knowledge management could become the primary tool for disseminating knowledge in the organization, with training playing a supporting, albeit continuingly important, skill-development role.

Furthermore, waiting for a training course—in the classroom or online—is no longer acceptable. Training professionals are well advised to expand their thinking about what both learning and e-learning are, and to include KM in their repertoire of solutions. When information is needed to win a sale, solve a technical problem, design a product, or manage any other process, speed is the premier asset of the competitive business. Learning through knowledge management—in the workplace and in real time—is essential for a smarter, more productive enterprise.

TABLE 16.1 Knowledge management in action

Performance Challenge	KM Approach	Why Training Wasn't the Complete Solution
A major telecom company wants to land a global contract with a bank to handle electronic funds transfers worldwide.	*Networking and collaboration.* Several times a day, the sales team sent competitive intelligence and customer information to a core KM group at company headquarters, which in turn republished this critical information to everyone. On awarding the contract to this company, the bank commented on how well the entire team always "knew" the customer.	The team was already highly trained; any additional training would have been redundant. Thus no training resources needed to be diverted from the company's core sales and technical training programs.
Field technicians are having trouble fixing machines at client locations, resulting in increased costs and lower customer satisfaction.	*Collaboration.* Frustrated with new technical issues that were not covered in training and not addressed in the field manual, technicians began e-mailing each other for advice and help. Responses were often immediate and very useful. In addition, the collaboration enabled the company to identify new problems much earlier than before, enabling it to solve them before any major negative customer impact.	Training and technical manuals, even online, were valuable, but only to a point. Additional training for each unique problem would have been costly, but more importantly, would have taken a long time to reach all technicians. Even a help desk had trouble responding quickly enough to some unique, previously undiscovered technical issues.
The IT department of a major New York financial services company wanted to be sure everyone had consistent and reliable access to key methods and procedures.	*Knowledge repository.* During a knowledge audit in connection with Y2K, the firm discovered that most technical knowledge was embedded in the "heads" of employees and that the ability of the firm to respond was dependent not only on finding the right person with the right knowledge, but also on making that knowledge available to all in a reasonable time. The firm built a secure knowledge repository around critical IT procedures, including disaster recovery. After September 11, 2001, the firm was able to recover its operations much faster because this KM system was in place.	To ensure the right response (i.e., the right performance) training had to be blended with access to critical business and technical knowledge. Besides ensuring the people were knowledgeable, training focused on how to use, and rely on, the KM system, which contained key information that no single person or group of individuals could master.
A global petroleum company must keep highly sophisticated production equipment operating at peak efficiency. When problems occur, it takes a great deal of time to get experts to the sites to diagnose and fix the problem.	*Collaboration and solution archiving.* The option of flying key experts halfway around the world was no longer viable due to cost and the scarcity of true expertise. The company built a collaborative network of knowledge sharing resources, including videoconferencing tools that enabled experts to consult from a distance in a much timelier manner. In addition, consultation can be captured and kept in a knowledge repository for future reference, again improving response time and lowering costs.	While intensive training coupled with significant on-the-job experience could increase the number of experts available, there were significant time and cost barriers that limited this approach. Making the existing expertise more responsive and available through KM technologies increased real-time access to knowledge more substantially than could have been accomplished through any long-term training program.

Application Questions

1. Describe a hypothetical (or real) example of how a knowledge management system might be (or is) used to support operations within one of the types of organizations listed. Your example should be one other than those used in the chapter. Types of organizations: (1) call center, (2) customer relations department, (3) government agency, (4) military organization, (5) human resources department, (6) consulting agency, (7) sales department.
2. Identify a real (or hypothetical) performance problem that does (or might) exist in one of the types of organizations listed in question 1. Describe how a blended learning approach, including the use of a knowledge management system, might be used to solve that problem.
3. Assume that you are working for one of the types of organizations mentioned in question 1. Further assume that your supervisor is reluctant to approve the development of a knowledge management system for the organization. The supervisor has asked you to write a one-page memo describing three reasons why a knowledge management system will be useful to the company. Write the memo!

References

Brandon Hall Research. (n.d.). Learning management and knowledge management: Is the Holy Grail of integration close at hand? Retrieved July 15, 2005, from **http://www.brandon-hall.com/public/whitepapers/lmkm/whitepaper_lmkm260101.PDF**

Gotta, M. (2004). *On the road to knowledge management* (Delta Report 2726). Stamford, CT: META Group.

Rosenberg, M. (2002, August/September). The seven myths of knowledge management. *Context Magazine,* 12–13.

Allison Rossett
Bob Hoffman
San Diego State University

CHAPTER 17

Informal Learning

Knowledge and Comprehension Questions

1. Using the section of this chapter, "What Is Informal Learning?" as a guide, describe the general characteristics of informal learning.
2. Think of an example of an informal learning situation that you are familiar with (e.g., a group of students who form a study group to prepare for their masters or doctoral comprehensive examination). Describe this situation in terms of the six factors the authors identify in the section, "How Informal Learning Works."
3. The authors describe how inexperienced sales representatives at Xerox acquired some of their skills. Discuss how this situation serves as an example of each of the following: (1) informal learning, (2) the distinction between *explicit* and *tacit* knowledge, and (3) a community of practice.
4. Describe how people's interest in authentic objects parallels their interest in informal learning. Discuss how instructional designers can use this interest to their advantage when they design learning experiences for workers.
5. What do the authors mean when they state that an informal learning experience is a product of careful design processes?
6. Describe what is meant by the term *action learning*. What seems to be the key factor that makes this type of experience successful?
7. The authors describe several ways that instructional designers can promote and enhance informal learning. Identify three of the techniques that seem particularly useful to you and explain why you think these techniques are likely to be effective.

Editors' Introduction

The previous two chapters have described several means (focusing on electronic performance support systems and knowledge management systems) other than *formal* instruction that instructional designers might employ to help solve human performance problems. In this chapter, Allison Rossett and Bob Hoffman describe how *informal* learning activities have been and can be used to help improve the performance of individuals and of the organizations for which they work.

Rossett and Hoffman begin by describing informal learning as learning beyond the control of people who mange training programs; learning other than that which typically takes place in the classroom or in an environment established to deliver formal instruction at a distance (e.g., online instruction, instruction delivered via a video conference). They go on to describe how informal learning works by describing six factors related to it, and by providing examples of informal learning in corporations and other settings. They conclude the chapter by indicating that in the future they expect that informal and formal learning opportunities will be blended together more closely than is currently the case. With this occurrence, they anticipate improvements in individual learning and performance, as well as organizational results.

Winston Churchill said, "Personally, I'm always ready to learn, but I do not always like being taught."

Bob: *There. That's it. Many are like Winston Churchill. They want experiences, immersion. They need learning to be more like their lives and less like a lesson.*

Allison: *Sure. But not all students or employees, for that matter, put themselves in the way of natural learning opportunities. Some do. Many don't. Would we wait for them to decide when and what to learn if they were our nine-year-old or our customer service reps? What if they'd rather not learn to read or get fluent on a new software package? What if they'd just as soon pass on a trip to the Air and Space Museum?*

Bob: *Well, that would be an issue, admittedly.*

Allison: *We are instructional designers. Our task, and it's a noble one, is to create opportunities to help people and organizations achieve learning and performance goals. I don't think that's arguable.*

Bob: *Still, I think that too much of instructional design is overly planned and thus too distinct from life and work.*

Allison: *Then maybe the work of the instructional designer is to integrate aspects of informal learning into our plans, to endeavor to enhance authenticity, experience, conviviality, and even spontaneity in learning experiences. Informal learning is one way.*

That is our purpose. We'll look at informal learning in several settings, from museums to corporations, to seek implications for learning and performance.

What Is Informal Learning?

Informal learning tends to be authentic, typically happening beyond the control of the people who manage training programs, outside the limits of classrooms and environments established to deliver formal instruction at a distance (e.g., online instruction, instruction delivered via a video conference). Informal learning gives learners more control of what, where, and how they learn and usually involves intrinsic motivation.

Informal learning can take many forms, such as when individuals chat with one another about business strategy, search in a knowledge base for information about anthrax, share opinions with a coach about the Electoral College, compare approaches to an ethical dilemma, plunge a hand into a pool with dolphins, and give and receive feedback about a proposal submitted to a client. It happens over coffee, online, at lunch, in the lounge, at the museum, on the way to the parking lot, and through e-mail.

Some organizations, such as Hewlett-Packard, favor the term *work-based learning* over *informal learning* because it highlights personalization, authenticity, activity, and integration into the work. While we are interested in informal learning that occurs at work, we are also intrigued with other environments, such as museums and online experiences.

Informal learning is a growing force. A 1998 study by the Center for Workforce Development at the Education Development Center (*The Teaching Firm,* 1998) confirmed an earlier finding by the U.S. Bureau of Labor Statistics: the preponderance of what is learned at work happens through informal means.

How Informal Learning Works

How does informal learning work? Let's think about it in light of six factors: nature of the outcomes; nature of the experience; origin; role of the student; role of the instructor; and role of the instructional designer. Note that no setting is specified because the possibilities exist just about everywhere.

Nature of the outcomes. While most informal learning has a reason for being, such as staying up to date on equipment repair or fondness for astronomy or checking out the work of a new artist, it is rare to find specific objectives and matched tests. That is one reason why constructivists are particularly keen on informal learning, while objectivists acknowledge the benefits, but worry about outcomes and measurement.

Nature of the experience. Informal learning tends to be vivid, emotional, unexpected, and idiosyncratic. Individuals willingly immerse themselves in experiences that are real, often social, and essentially engaging. Informal learning must attract its participants; if they don't find the moments at the museum or the online chat with other reps compelling, they will not elect to participate.

Origin. Where does informal learning come from? More often than in conventional training, it happens because students or employees make it happen themselves. Gay and lesbian employees form an affinity group at their company to support and coach each other as they attempt to traverse the organizational ladder. Another group decides to invite auditors online once each month to chat about the challenges they are facing. Individuals keen on art and surfing queue up to see a surfboard art exhibit. While some examples of informal learning are initiated by organizations, a frequent, but not necessary, attribute of informal learning is that it is more often born of the efforts and interests of the people themselves.

Role of the student. Informal learning depends on a willing, active individual. The father willingly logs on to that website to talk with other parents about alternative treatments. The middle schooler chooses to take yet another look at the Civil War museum exhibit. The new sales associate fixes her schedule so that she can be where many other sales people lunch.

Role of the instructor. Informal learning typically does not involve an instructor, although people with more and less expertise often find themselves together at a gathering online or face to face. As an organization takes advantage of more informal approaches, instructors might do more motivating, anticipating, and connecting people to ideas and resources.

Role of the instructional designer. Informal learning is the way it sounds—informal, offhand, and natural. However, the way it seems from the outside does not mean that it is unplanned on the inside. There are distinct roles to be played by training professionals in nurturing informal learning in corporations, agencies, and museums. We'll focus on this at the conclusion of the chapter.

Why Informal Learning Has Value

Microsoft's learning evangelist, Bob Mosher, touts informal learning in the July 2004 issue of *Chief Learning Officer* magazine. Mosher describes the popularity of informal learning with these words: "The first two [reasons for popularity] have to do with immediacy and relevancy. Informal methods of learning are often found right in the work environment. They are seen as techniques that a learner can take advantage of right away and with work-related resources. Another reason these methods are so popular is because they are often very short. Advanced learners tell us that they don't have the time or budget to attend more formal learning. Even the immediacy of e-learning is seen as something that will take too much valuable time" (n. p.).

Mosher is acknowledging the shift in schools, government, and businesses in two key directions: (1) towards convergence of learning and work; and (2) to more authentic approaches. In San Diego, schoolchildren spend a week living in the country and learning about each other and the natural environment. The goals are numerous, and it is certainly not unplanned, but it is also experienced by the students as educational, informal, convivial, personal, and realistic.

Corporations are intrigued by this movement. Communities of practice, e-coaching, threaded message boards, and FAQs are examples of a more informal tilt. Mosher (2004), in touting their emergence, remarks, "They have existed under the radar screen of most training programs for years" (n. p.).

Informal learning isn't expensive, at least not in the usual ways. There is no need to hire instructors, provide lunches, separate people from their work, purchase a learning management system, or develop an online learning module. Because informal learning bubbles up naturally, often fueled by individuals themselves, as likely in a coffee shop as a convention center, there is no need to hire a hall or a band. This is particularly appealing to organizations attempting to shave costs.

In an article in the *Harvard Business Review,* Brown and Duguid (2000) describe the value that comes from learning in social groups. Their example comes from Julian Orr's work at Xerox. Orr noted the divergence between the formal descriptions of employees' work processes and the tacit improvisations involved in handling unforeseen problems with equipment.

How did inexperienced reps learn, if the formal processes enshrined in policies and training were not accurate? Orr pointed to the informal aspects of their lives, elements that contribute to getting the job done. For example, the reps ate breakfast together. During the meal, they collaborated on problems and shared war stories, which probably led to enhancements in old documentation and training materials.

Another appealing aspect of informal learning is that it moves individuals towards autonomy. As many organizations shift to policies associated with career self-reliance for employees, informal learning is of special interest as a means for developing independent habits.

The Museum Experience

What do museum experiences have to do with informal learning? Quite a bit, we think.

Although informal learning moves us away from the four walls of classrooms, museums take us somewhere else. That place is of central importance.

Those places come in many shapes and sizes. There are art museums, science museums, and natural history museums. Aquariums, botanical gardens, and zoos all qualify as museums, too. There are also park museums (such as our national parks), social history museums (for example, historic or ethnic costume or toy museums), place museums (Colonial Williamsburg) and even entertainment museums (Sea World and Disneyland qualify here).

As we've seen, informal learning in the workplace can take place anywhere from the lunchroom to the cubicle or the production floor. The museum experience, on the other hand, requires . . . a museum!

Why then talk about the museum experience in the same breath with the informal learning that takes place in organizations? We think there are some important parallels between the two experiences. One involves the attraction we feel for authentic objects.

Art provides an example. Suppose you found yourself thinking, "What's the big deal with Leonardo Da Vinci's *Mona Lisa*?" Online, via a Web browser, you could find a variety (more than 26,000 at this writing) of images of *Mona Lisa*—big ones, little ones, details, parodies, you name it. You could spend as much time as you liked, read a lot about it, and examine the picture itself in minute detail.

Now suppose you heard that your local art museum was bringing *Mona Lisa* to town? Would you say, "Naw, I know what she looks like," or "Hey, I can see her for free right here on my computer?" It's a good bet that you—and many other people in your town—would pay handsomely to get tickets to see the real thing.

The same holds true for other kinds of objects as well. Students, faculty, and visitors stood in line recently at San Diego State University for the privilege of a few minutes viewing—through glass—a rare copy of the first printed edition of the American Declaration of Independence. Certainly it wasn't because they wanted to read it. More legible copies are available online or in books. And it wasn't because they hoped to gain new insights about the content. Yet many felt drawn to just stand in its presence.

There is discussion about the phenomenon of the attraction of authentic objects in the literature on informal learning (Paris, 2002), but few claim to entirely understand it. Perhaps the closest anyone has come to explaining the lure of objects is Nemeroff and Rozin (2000, cited in Evans, Mull, & Poling, 2002) who describe it as "magical." Not magical in the supernatural sense, but rather as a prevalent mode of human thinking that ascribes a transfer of power or energy through proximity with celebrated people or objects—hence the phenomenon of celebrity. Some of the good (or bad) qualities of the original "rub off" on those fortunate enough to approach or establish a physical relationship, however tentative. In some Eastern cultures this manifests as the idea of *darshan*, by which the disciple gains enlightenment merely by being in the presence of the master. In some Western religions, the same occurs when healing or other benefits occur in the presence of saintly relics.

Whether magical or not, experiences with authentic or celebrated objects draw people to Greenfield Village in Michigan to file inside the Wright Cycle Shop instead of being content to watch a film reenactment of the first powered flight. It attracts visitors to the Museum of Costume in Bath, England, to inspect the coat of a young Scottish gentleman from 1720, instead of looking it up in a coffee table book. And it is the power of objects that brings adults and children to the Birch Aquarium in La Jolla, California, to touch and hold the creatures in a simulated tide pool instead of gazing at pictures on the Web in the comfort of their homes.

Objects are often necessary—but not sufficient in themselves—for a substantive experience. Museums also rely on explanation and interpretation. Consider the labels on the pictures in the Metropolitan Museum of Art in New York City, the signage at the National Museum of Natural History in Washington, DC, the audio tour in Mystic Seaport in Connecticut, or the docent guide at the Japanese American National Museum in Los Angeles. Each of these helps visitors understand and appreciate the objects themselves. A rock is just an ordinary chunk of minerals without the label, "moon rock." With the label, it is exotic, special, and worthy of attention.

How does this affinity for objects resemble the kind of informal learning that takes place in organizations? We sometimes refer to informal learning in the workplace as "on-the-job training." Learning is driven by the real-life situations that arise. It happens in response to actual requests from supervisors, authentic opportunities in the marketplace, genuine problems with work flow, and so on. These are not cases we're reading about as part of a workshop exercise, or principles we study as an example of human performance technology. They are the real things, the genuine articles. They resemble life and work in a way that only the real bicycle shop, authentic copy of the Declaration of Independence, and the living creatures of the tide pool can. These objects, environments, and situations are more gripping than "mere" media representations.

There is another important similarity between museums and informal learning in the workplace. When viewed from the visitors' perspective, of course, time in a museum is unstructured. But that informal environment is the product of careful design processes by museum administrators, exhibit designers, and educators. As with informal learning in the workplace, someone in the museum is trying to put magic in a bottle, and at the same time assessing audience needs, specifying purposes, devising strategies, evaluating results, and continuously improving efforts.

Can museums take their place alongside other informal learning strategies in organizations? Why not? The Motorola Museum of Electronics in Schaumburg, Illinois, targets employees of Motorola along with their families and the community. The goal of the museum seems not to be to help workers improve their performance, but rather to foster appreciation of the importance of communications technology, the role of the company in the development of technology, and even the wonder of semiconductors and radio waves.

Informal Corporate Experiences

When San Diego State University alumnus Ari Galper took a delivery job at United Parcel Service in Atlanta, he was expected to put on the brown uniform and work in the field before creating a moment of training. When queried about his experience on the trucks, he was very positive. He noted that it was a great way to get a real feel for the business and to see the work from the perspective of employees and customers.

Marguerite Foxon (in Rossett & Sheldon, 2001) describes the GOLD process, Motorola's program to prepare high-potential managers for success in the diverse, global organization. They use action learning, which is a bridge between formal training and daily life at work. *Action learning*, according to Marquardt (1999), engages small groups in using what they are learning to solve real-world problems while simultaneously reflecting on the learning process itself.

Foxon said about the project, "In designing GOLD, we recognized that no matter how mind stretching and job relevant the content is, training alone cannot accelerate the development of a new generation of leaders. Tying the course content to the business challenges provided our managers with the perfect opportunity to put the new learning into action, real time" (Rossett & Sheldon, 2001, p. 216). Two alumni from Motorola's GOLD process had this to say about their experience: "When we were working hard on our business challenge, we all felt like we might actually be able to make a difference in the organization. This was different from attending other management/leadership courses where you get all pumped up during the class about the 'right' way to do things, then go back to your job but nothing changes" (pp. 216–217).

Reality. Connection. Effort. Action. Serendipity. All were critical to GOLD.

They are also central to how Whirlpool Corporation prepares managers. At a big house in Benton Harbor, Michigan, new employees learn about company products by living with them. When residing in the house, employees are expected to wash and dry clothes, cook in microwaves, and unload and load dishwashers. As Steelcase Inc. writes about the Whirlpool program on its Web page (Milshtein, 2003), "Rather than studying from a book and being tested in a standard format, these trainees really see how their products work—from the end-user perspective. Not only does this support an enhanced method of training it also provides a level of product confidence one could never get from simply reading a stack of product operation manuals or attending a two-day training seminar" (n. p.).

Technology and Informal Learning

Online Communities of Practice

Online communities of practice are electronic gatherings that develop, evolve, and disperse according to the energy of participants. Typically, membership is open, structure is loose, and rules are scarce. Most communities of practice lack beginning and ending dates. According to Wenger (1998), a community of practice is a different kind of entity than a task force or a team, which is established by the organization to do something in particular. Technology enables gatherings at the water cooler to transcend physical locations as gays and lesbians, parents of newborns, petrochemical engineers out on oil rigs, and aspiring actors get together.

Interestingly, an online community of practice is becoming a staple in blended learning programs. Early blending efforts were characterized by adding online conversations to face-to-face classes in universities, agencies, and companies (Bersin, 2004; Rossett, Douglis, & Frazee, 2003). While less motivated by the participants themselves, this online connection adds a social and informal dimension via threaded discussions, listservs, and chats. What better way to transcend the walls of the classroom and continue conversation and relationships?

E-Coaching

Not all informal learning is collective, of course. Some is more individual and personal, but nonetheless augmented by technology. An example is e-coaching.

Goldsmith (2001) posits e-coaching as the future of learning. "This is going to be a huge breakthrough in the way people learn, a huge breakthrough for coaching, a huge breakthrough in the way people get developed" (n. p.). Complaining that traditional learning methods give everybody the same thing even if they do not need it, he writes, "With E-coaching, you're going to get the opportunity to learn what you need, when you need it, from whom you need it, from the best sources" (n. p.).

Elliot Masie, a major figure in the learning and technology world (see, for example, **http://www.masie.com**), described enormous benefits from frequent, personal, and tailored interactions with his e-coach. After as many as three contacts per day with his online health coach, Masie reported the loss of 22 pounds and improved blood pressure and cholesterol (Dwyer, 2004).

Informal Learning and Training

In our view, formal training is one way to develop employees, and informal learning is another. Although informal learning is not produced in the same ways that classes or online modules are, it can be promoted and enhanced, and it should be. The challenge for the professional is unique—how to encourage informal learning without taking away its grassroots, idiosyncratic aspects. Rossett & Sheldon (2001) highlight several ways that learning and performance professionals can leverage informal learning.

Find It

How much informal learning is going on in your organization? Note examples and anecdotes. Find the people and groups who do it and profit from it. Collect favorite homegrown job aids and knowledge bases. Where is it happening? When? How did it start? Why does it endure? To what challenges does it contribute? In what ways is technology involved?

Learn from It

How are mentors making a difference? What materials are being created by tutors, high performers, and coaches and handed off from employee to employee? How can you leverage the impact of these informal artifacts? Where do people gather? What rivets their attention? What topics provide focus for online communities? What wisdom, errors, and misconceptions are being conveyed? How can you second key messages and correct flawed information?

If employees are chatting online about a customer problem or how to fix a software bug, perhaps this topic should be introduced into formal classes or the knowledge management system. Lunch conversations about new global efforts could become the basis for an international mentoring program, war stories about customer complaints could be repurposed into elements in classes or online modules.

If employees are coming together online to chat informally, are there ways to seed their efforts and direct that energy to strategic goals? Can you sponsor action learning groups that devote attention to substantive priorities, as Motorola did?

Honor It

There is a fine line between recognizing and valuing informal learning and changing its nature with structure, attention, and kudos. Provide examples of coaches at all levels in the organization, from the CEO mentor to the truck driver peer tutor. Consider involving informal learning leaders in formal training events. Do they want to teach? Produce videos with their ideas and stream them around everywhere. Schedule synchronous presentations and archive them for continuous availability. Give credit where it is due, but ask first. Some informal learning participants prefer the ad hoc and sub rosa nature of their contributions and relationships. Others will enjoy the advocacy of the organization.

Support It

Look for small ways to be a friend to informal learning. How can you plant the seed during orientation and training? Can you ensure space in a building? Provide a pizza? Connect the group to a person familiar with the technology that interests them? Is it time to create a website and knowledge base to support their efforts? Does the informal group want more people to know about their existence? Can you help a group in a distant land to upgrade its technology platform? Can you provide an informal guide to informal groups as part of orientation? Do instructors know about the ways that their messages are represented in the underground, informal network?

Redefine Roles

If employees are thriving when coached on the job, it's time to consider ways to encourage it more broadly. Can such coaching be modeled and defined in classes? Might the role of instructors be changed to involve more coaching and followup in the field and less presentation in classes? The Defense Acquisition University (DAU) has moved in this direction (personal communication, n. d.). Are managers recognized for the ways that they nudge professional development? Is it part of their performance appraisal process?

What about individual employees? Perhaps the most important role for museums and other informal learning environments is that of promoting the love of learning itself. If we are born to learn, and some are put off to some extent by formal schooling, informal learning in any of its incarnations has the potential to revive an innate urge to understand and communicate.

Into the Future

As we move to the future, we hope that the distinction between formal and informal learning will diminish. Now, still, when customers ask for training, they envision a room with an instructor and students. The unusual client might incline towards an online module.

What we see for the future is a richer palate from which professionals can paint. It would include dynamic displays and experiences provided by museums as well as relationships, online and in space, cultivated by peer teachers and coaching colleagues. And it would have classroom experiences side by side with phone coaches, online communities, and knowledge bases. Which is formal? Which informal? Why would we care?

We don't. What we do care about is the ability of professionals and employees to make learning happen, continuously, and not just within four walls. Informal learning presents more and varied ways of creating options for individuals and results for the organization. Isn't it time to integrate the approaches and roles and forget about the tag?

Application Questions

1. Assume you are working for the training department for a large automobile manufacturer, and that your particular training group focuses on improving the sales skills and product knowledge of all of the car salespeople working for the company. Each year new courses are created for all of the sales personnel. You have now worked for the company for several years and have found that much of what the salespeople learn is done through informal means, such as discussing sales techniques with other salespeople at their car dealership and from other dealerships when they attend the annual convention of sales personnel. You would like to start a project designed to promote and enhance these and other informal learning experiences, but your supervisor is reluctant to have you devote any time to this effort. Write a one- or two-page memo to the supervisor explaining why you think it will be worthwhile for the company to support the type of project you are proposing.
2. Assume you are a professor in the Department of Instructional Design and Technology at Solid State University, and your chairperson has asked you to propose a series of strategies to promote informal learning among graduate students in the department. Describe the following:
   a. *How* you will identify the types of informal learning activities you will focus on.
   b. The specific activities you think you might identify.
   c. How you will promote and enhance each of those activities.

References

Bersin, J. (2004, January). Blended learning: Finding what works. *Chief Learning Officer.* Retrieved July 15, 2005, from **http://www.clomedia.com/content/templates/clo_feature.asp?articleid=357&zoneid=30**

Brown, J. S., & Duguid, P. (2000). Balancing act: How to capture knowledge without killing it. *Harvard Business Review*, *75*(3), 73–80.

Dwyer, J. (2004). E-coaching. Retrieved July 15, 2005, from **http://edweb.sdsu.edu/people/ARossett/pie/Interventions/ecoaching_1.htm**

Evans, E. M., Mull, M. S., & Poling, D. A. (2002). The authentic object? A child's-eye view. In S. Paris (Ed.), *Perspectives on object-centered learning in museums.* Mahwah, NJ: Lawrence Erlbaum Associates.

Goldsmith, M. (2001). E-coaching: The future of learning. Retrieved July 15, 2005, from **http://www.athenaonline.com/knowledge/tview/t_view_goldsmith.asp#**

Marquardt, M. J. (1999). *Action learning in action.* Palo Alto, CA: Davies Black.

Milshtein, I. A. (2003). Livin' it: Whirlpool's "The Real Whirled" program brings a touch of reality television to management training. *Steelcase 360.* Retrieved 03 February 2006 from **http://www.steelcase.com/na/files/daa09281243b42808a3d83edd7d2bc85/LivinItWhirlpool.pdf**

Mosher, B. (2004, July). The power of informal learning. Chief Learning Offices. Retrieved July, 18, 2005, from **http://www.clomedia.com/content/templates/clo_col_selling.asp?articleid=557&zoneid=5/**

Paris, S. G. (Ed.). (2002). *Perspectives on object-centered learning in museums.* Mahwah, NJ: Lawrence Erlbaum Associates.

Rossett, A., Douglis, F., & Frazee, R. V. (2003, July). Strategies for building blended learning. *Learning Circuits*. Retrieved July, 18, 2005, from **http://www.learningcircuits.org/2003/jul2003/rossett.htm**

Rossett, A., & Sheldon, K. (2001). *Beyond the podium: Delivering training and performance to a digital world.* San Francisco: Jossey-Bass.

The teaching firm. (1998). Newton, MA: Center for Workforce Development, Education Development Center.

Wenger, E. (1998). *Communities of practice: Learning, meaning, and identity*. New York: Cambridge University Press.

SECTION 5

Trends and Issues in Various Settings

Overview

Over the years, professionals in the IDT field have worked in a variety of settings, ranging from public schools (where the visual and audiovisual instruction movements had their birth) to the military (where the pioneers of the instructional design field began applying their skills) to business and industry (where the performance technology movement has really taken hold). In the chapters in this section of the book, recent IDT activities in six different settings—the aforementioned three plus the health care field, higher education, and the international arena—are discussed.

Business and industry is the setting where it is commonly held that most instructional designers in the IDT field are employed. Chapter 18 focuses on the expanding set of roles being played by instructional designers in business and industry, as well as on the challenges professionals in this setting are likely to face now and in the future.

The IDT field has also had a significant impact in the military, with several of the branches of the United States military officially adopting a systematic approach to the design of training. Moreover, in recent years, interest in the use of instructional media and instructional design practices has remained strong. Chapter 19 reviews the reasons for this continued interest and describes current trends in IDT in the military.

The IDT field also plays an important role in the health care field, particularly with regard to professional education in this area. Chapter 20 reviews the history of medical education and the role the IDT field has played in that history. The current status of education and training in the health care field is also discussed and implications for IDT professionals are described.

The influence of the IDT field in P–12 education in the United States has been rather limited. Chapter 21 examines some of the reasons why the IDT field has not had a greater impact in schools and offers some suggestions as to how that impact might be increased.

As has been the case in schools, IDT has had minimal impact on instructional practices in higher education. However, the challenges currently being faced by institutions of higher education worldwide are presenting IDT professionals with an excellent opportunity to have a far greater impact in this arena. In Chapter 22, the authors describe higher education in both an Australian and a U.S. context.

On the international scene, over the years the field of IDT has had a significant impact on the educational systems of several nations. Today, the issues of cost, access, and quality of instruction are prompting many educational leaders in many nations to turn to distance learning and instructional design and technology for solutions. Chapter 23 focuses on the issues both developing and developed nations are facing, the IDT solutions that are being proposed, and the skills professionals in our field will need to implement those solutions.

Rita C. Richey
Wayne State University

Gary R. Morrison
Old Dominion University

Marguerite Foxon
Motorola Corporation

CHAPTER 18

Instructional Design in Business and Industry

Knowledge and Comprehension Questions

1. Describe the three ways in which designers work. What are the implications of these roles for daily work?
2. List and describe three new paradigms that influence the instructional design process.
3. Identify at least three individuals (other than the designer) who work on design teams. What are their roles? What are the ideal characteristics and qualifications of each?
4. How does the client influence the instructional design process? How can the client facilitate and/or constrain the process? How can a change in the client's representative impact the design process?
5. What are the various assessment and evaluation tasks undertaken by instructional designers? What conditions facilitate and/or constrain the completion of these tasks?
6. Outline the specific challenges facing instructional designers leading virtual design teams. In what skill or knowledge areas do you personally need to improve in order to lead a virtual design team?

Editors' Introduction

Business and industry settings are where much of the instructional design practice has occurred in the last quarter century. According to Rita Richey, Gary Morrison, and Marguerite Foxon, the growth is likely to continue.

In this chapter, the authors discuss the expanding set of roles played by instructional designers in business and industry today. They also describe several factors that designers should consider to ensure the success of their efforts in this arena. The authors then turn their attention to two issues that are currently influencing the nature of instructional design in business and industry: reducing design cycle time and enhancing training effectiveness and efficiency. They describe several approaches instructional designers are using to address these concerns. The authors close with a discussion of the implications of the globalization of training.

Since the 1980s, the preponderance of instructional design (ID) practice has occurred within the private sector, primarily in business and industrial settings. This coincides with the steady growth of employee training[1] as an integral part of most organizations. In the United States alone, the training industry was a $62.5 billion endeavor in 1999, up from the 1990 estimate of $45.5 billion as reported by the American Society of Training and Development (Industry Report, 1999). Remarkably, these data are only partially descriptive, since they reflect only the direct cost of formal training in organizations with 100 or more employees. Informal, on-the-job training is not included. Training in smaller firms throughout the United States is not included. Moreover, such growth is not unique to this country, but is duplicated to a great extent worldwide. More recently, most of the largest organizations have continued to increase their training expenditures per employee, and all have increased the number of training hours per employee (Sugrue, 2003).

This growth reflects an emphasis not simply on producing a more knowledgeable workforce, but increasingly on improving employee on-the-job performance and on solving organizational problems. Correspondingly in today's market, instructional design to many is not merely an organized approach to product or course development, but is instead a generic process for analyzing human performance problems and determining appropriate solutions to such problems (Rothwell & Kazanas, 2004). In addition, designers and training managers must often predict future problems and likely organizational changes and project ways to prepare employees for these new situations (Pieters, 1997).

The expansion of instructional design practice in the corporate sector over the past 30 years, not surprisingly, has been complemented by the development of new approaches to instructional design and a concomitant augmentation of designer competencies. Nonetheless, the majority of ID practice is still dominated by instructional systems design (ISD) models (e.g. Dick, Carey, & Carey, 2005; Morrison, Ross, & Kemp, 2004; Seels & Glasgow, 1998; Smith & Ragan, 1999) or by similar models adapted specifically to the business environment (e.g. Rothwell & Kazanas, 2004). In most cases, the performance improvement orientation is also rooted in instructional systems design (ISD) with an emphasis on analysis, specifically problem analysis (Rummler, 1999).

New paradigms have evolved. Visscher-Voerman and Gustafson (2004) describe three additional paradigms—communicative, pragmatic, and artistic. The first two directly reflect typical corporate training characteristics in which the perceptions and needs of stakeholders are sought and emphasized. The communicative paradigm emphasizes reaching consensus among these parties throughout the design process. The pragmatic approach is distinguished by repeated tryout and revision based on stakeholders' perceptions. The artistic approach (typical of many technology-based design and development projects) relies on the developer's own subjective criteria as well as those of clients. Often corporate training blends these approaches with traditional ISD procedures.

With the expansion and increased sophistication of ID practice, designer skills have expanded as well. New competencies are required, specifically pertaining to technology applications, project management and collaboration, advanced analysis techniques, noninstructional strategy design, and business skills (Atchison, 1996; Harless, 1995; Richey, Fields, & Foxon, 2001). Designers were previously well served with basic training in the ISD process supported by subsequent work experience. Today, corporate designers are expected not only to demonstrate basic skills, but also to have design specialization and fundamental business acumen. In addition, the best designers also have an insider's understanding of the industry of their parent organization, often referred to as "the business of the business." ID competency identification, demonstration, and certification are increasingly important to the business community (Mulder, Nijhof, & Brinkerhoff, 1995; Richey et al., 2001). Moreover, in keeping with the advancements in the field, designer competencies are now viewed in terms of both novice and expert skill sets (LeMaistre, 1998; Perez & Emery, 1995; Richey et al., 2001; Rowland, 1992).

On the other hand, the business training industry includes a large sector of external suppliers of training products, programs, and, in many cases, the delivery of instruction itself. Of the $62.5 billion spent on corporate training in 1999, nearly one quarter of those dollars went to outside providers of training products and services (Industry Report, 1999). This outsourcing trend has grown even more in recent years, with the number of internal instructional designers in large organizations decreasing and the number of external performance consultants increasing (Sugrue, 2003).

In this chapter we will expand on the nature of instructional design practice in the business environment today. We will discuss:

- The work environment, including work patterns and conditions and potential legal issues.
- Trends in corporate instructional design and development, including the demands for cycle time reduction and increased effectiveness and efficiency.
- The impact of globalization, a key emerging issue confronting designers in the first decade of this century.

[1] We are not distinguishing here between the concepts of "education" and "training." Consequently, under the umbrella of the term training we are including all types of professional development activities, from technical training to executive development.

The Nature of Instructional Design in Corporate Settings

The growth of instructional design in the corporate sector has resulted in different approaches to instructional design. In this section, we will examine these approaches and the factors that can constrain or facilitate the design process.

Roles of Instructional Designers

There are three very broad categories of roles that instructional designers may take in a corporate setting—as sole designer, as a consultant, or as a member or leader of a team. Particular approaches can vary by organization and by project. The following is an examination of each approach.

Sole designer. In some smaller companies and on small-scale projects, the instructional designer may serve as the only "permanent" team member. The subject matter expert (SME) typically serves as a consultant and is involved on an as-needed basis. Design, development, assessment, formative evaluation, revision, and implementation are typically the responsibilities of the designer rather than the SME. A subject matter expert, however, who is also the instructor may take a greater interest and responsibility in the design and implementation of the intervention. During the production phase, the designer might hire a photographer, video crew, or graphic artist to assist with the technical aspects of the production process, but maintain overall control and responsibility. The designer's span of control is quite large, and responsibility for the success of the project is the designer's sole burden.

Designer as consultant. Instructional designers can also serve as consultants to instructional design/training projects. Internal instructional design consultants often serve as consultant to a development team that may be led by an instructor or SME. The designer's role is often one of advising rather than taking a proactive role for instructional design. In this environment the designer may provide only feedback or a "blessing" of the materials, or may work on an equal partner level with the SME or other team members. The designer's role is often negotiated early in the project, but may change as problems arise (i.e., instructional, timeline, technical, or budgetary). A variation of this approach is used at the British Open University, where the designer is considered a *transformer* (Hawkridge, 1994). The subject matter expert prepares a draft of the materials and then the instructional designer "transforms" the draft into an effective set of instructional materials.

A second type of consultant is the external instructional designer. In this approach, the client company will hire an instructional design company to produce a product. Typically, the instructional design team consists of all external members except for the subject matter expert, who is provided by the client's company. The SME might also be an external consultant.

Team member/leader. Larger-scale projects typically require a team approach. The number of instructional designers can vary from one to several, and the responsibility level can vary from that of the senior or lead designer to the instructional designer or technologist. Other members of the team will vary depending on the type of technology used for delivery and the scope of the project. Table 18.1 provides a list of team members.

TABLE 18.1 Instructional design team member

Team Member	Assignment
Instructional designer(s)	Duration of project or design phase
Subject matter expert	Begins with analysis stage and stays through production
Evaluator	Duration or starts prior to conducting formative evaluation
Project manager	Duration, often starts prior to design planning phase
prior to design Text editor	Begins during production
Multimedia/computer programmer	Begins after strategy design or start of production
Video/audio production	Begins at production phase
Scriptwriter	Begins after strategies are designed or at production phase
Graphic artist	Begins with production phase
Learners	Begins with learner analysis and continues through formative evaluation

However, teams themselves vary depending on the type of organization and the complexity of the project. Three of the more common types of work teams are virtual teams, cross-functional teams, and contractor-led teams.

With increased globalization and decentralization of organizations, instructional designers participating in or leading project teams in large and medium-sized organizations are more likely to find themselves part of a virtual team, rather than a colocated team. (A *colocated* team works in the same building and can physically meet together; members of a *virtual* team are located in different places). In some cases the team members may be in the same general geographical area, but unable to physically meet. More common, however, are virtual teams with members in different time zones within one country, or in different countries around the globe. Virtual design teams must use forms of electronic communication for needs assessments, design reviews, and meetings. While conference calling is the most common method for conducting meetings, a more costly medium such as videoconferencing allows for much more effective team interaction.

Over the past 10 years the boundaries between many workplace disciplines have blurred, and design and performance improvement project teams are often staffed by a variety of specialists working together (Foxon, Richey, Roberts, & Spannaus, 2003). A typical work team might draw members from human resources, organizational development, and communications as well as from training. As the roles and tasks of these functions become less clearly delineated, designers may find themselves partnering with human resource staff on a needs assessment or contributing to a human performance intervention led by organizational development or communications professionals.

During the recent economic downturn, management in major U.S. companies recognized the financial advantages of replacing internal instructional designers with external contract designers. Today much of the design work in major companies is outsourced to organizations or individuals offering design expertise. As a result, many instructional designers working in major companies have experienced a subtle shift in their role. Much of their time is now spent as project managers, supervising contractors with varying degrees of instructional design expertise. In turn, they are now doing relatively little design work themselves.

Constraints

Identifying the client. One problem designers face when starting a new project is identifying the client (Foshay, 1988; Morrison, 1988, Tessmer, 1988). Often there is more than one client for an instructional design project. In the simplest environment the client "owns" the problem usually by virtue of being the supervisor or manager of the target audience that has a performance problem. When the design team grows in size, when the designer is a consultant, or when the funding of the project is at issue, it is often more difficult to identify the client. For example, if the designer is working as an outside consultant there may be two clients. First is the individual who is funding the project and second is the owner of the problem (e.g., manager of the target audience). An additional level of complication is added when one manager funds the project and another individual serves as project manager. When we add the individual who owns the problem and is usually identified as the client, the client list grows! Some projects are even more complicated when one considers the training manager or others who can influence design reviews or decisions.

Each instructional design project will have at least one client. The task, however, is to identify all the clients who can influence the instructional design process. Identifying the various clients and their responsibilities will help the designer both to solve and to prevent problems.

Client's knowledge of ID process. A study by Loughner and Moller (1998) revealed differences between the client's and training personnel's (e.g., training mangers, instructional designers, and consultants) perceptions of the instructional design process. For example, almost 80% of the respondents surveyed agreed that task analysis is the most important part of the instructional design process. Only 21% indicated that their organization felt this to be true. Almost 41% of the respondents surveyed reported that their clients did not understand the importance of conducting a task analysis, while 24% did not express an opinion.

Instructional designers of all levels of expertise may experience frustration when designing instruction due to the lack of understanding of the basic steps (e.g., task analysis) and the organization's failure to realize the importance or need for such steps. This lack of understanding of importance might lead to shortened timelines, making it more difficult for the designer to adequately design a project. Other factors that affect the design process include the type of training (e.g., sales, technical, or management), time frame, and budget (Loughner & Moller, 1998). A more encouraging finding was that two thirds of the respondents indicated their organization supported their development of instructional design–related skills.

Project management v. Instructional design. Projects with a significant budget, milestones, and personnel typically require someone to serve as project manager. Often this responsibility is either delegated or assumed by the instructional designer, since this individual is often the de facto leader/manager of the project. The larger the project in terms of budget, timeline, or products, the greater is the project management responsibility. As this responsibility grows, the instructional designer is often faced with the dilemma of choosing between completing instructional design tasks or project management tasks. Neglecting the instructional design process will affect the quality of the product. Neglecting the project management process will affect the schedule, personnel, production, and budget. To avoid this dilemma, very large projects often employ either a project manager specialist or delegate the full responsibility to one of the senior instructional designers, who then concentrates on the management tasks.

Many organizations have chosen to downsize their instructional design group, often in response to budget pressures, and outsource work to design consultants on an as-needed basis. The remaining instructional designers then function as project managers rather than designers. They monitor and track projects, ensuring that organizational design standards are met.

Legal issues and training. Most of us have probably seldom, if ever, heard of a lawsuit resulting from training. Eyres (1998) identifies several common legal problems related to training, which are summarized in the following sentences. First is the failure to perform government-mandated training for employees. For example, airline companies are required to train their agents in the proper handling of hazardous goods. Failure to develop and offer training and to certify employees can result in legal action by the federal government. Second are legal cases resulting from injury while participating in training. A popular training exercise in recent years has combined physical activities such as tug-of-wars and mountain climbing with team building. Employees injured during such exercises have filed suit for injuries received during the training. Disabled employees have also filed discrimination suits when acceptable alternatives were not provided. A third legal problem is the result of infringement on intellectual property rights. The Internet makes it very easy to find information, ideas, and graphics; however, using this material in your training may be an infringement on the intellectual property rights of others. For example, copying a picture of a new car from **http://www.ford.com** could violate their copyright agreement as posted on their website. Lawsuits filed because of discriminatory content in training are the fourth problem. Eyres describes lawsuits resulting from diversity training classes where evidence of discrimination was produced as a result of an informal survey. Other lawsuits are the result of sexually, racially, or ethnically based comments made during a training session. A fifth category of problems are those involving injuries as a result of human error. An employee injured during required training may sue the company if it can be proven that the training personnel were negligent in their actions. The implication is that the instructional environment must be carefully designed and monitored to ensure the safety of all. The last category of legal problems concerns tests that prevent access to training. Employees who are kept from receiving training that will promote them to a different job may have a basis for litigation. Testing procedures that discriminate against employees both in hiring and promotion can cause legal problems (see Shrock & Coscarelli, 1996).

As a result of our litigious society, instructional designers need to be aware of the laws governing training, develop instructional materials and testing procedures that do not discriminate, design an instructional environment that provides qualified trainers and a safe environment for the trainer and trainee, and respect the intellectual property rights of others. Instructional designers need to be aware of general laws (e.g., sexual harassment) and the laws governing specific industries (e.g., discharge of pollutants).

Facilitators

In the following paragraphs we will examine factors that contribute to the success of a project and contributions from information technology that can facilitate a project.

Success factors. Klimczak and Wedman (1997) attempted to identify the factors that contribute to the success of an instructional design project. They had instructional designers, trainers, sponsors, and learners rate 23 project success factors. As a group, they felt the two most important factors for a successful training project were training strategies and tangible resources. Trainers rated implementation support as relatively important, while instructional designers rated it as least important for success of a project. Klimczak and Wedman suggest that this difference is due to the orientation of the two groups. The trainers are often directly responsible for implementation, while the designer might consider the task mostly completed by the time it is implemented. An alternative explanation is that designers may ignore the implementation of a project while focusing on other elements of the instructional design process. Regardless of the explanation, instructional designers and instructional design models should focus on planning the implementation of a project.

Information technology. Information technology has had and will continue to have a significant impact on the instructional design process. To realize the full impact of information technology, let's consider an instructional designer working in the mid 1970s. The designer's key tool was a pencil (or a pen if one had a lot of confidence) or a simple typewriter and paper. A draft of the instruction was written by hand or typed and then given to a secretary for final typing. Depending on the secretary's workload, turnaround time might be 24 hours or a week. Major revisions to the draft could take just as long, as typewriters have no memory and you can only put a few additional lines onto an existing page. The introduction and wide use of word processors (i.e., dumb terminals connected to a minicomputer) in the early 1980s significantly increased the designer's productivity. It was now possible to create several drafts of the *same* document in a *single* day! Editing was very easy compared to completing the task on a typewriter. The introduction of personal computers, sophisticated word processing, page layout applications, and laser printers provided another platform for increasing the instructional designer's productivity. A designer could now compose, edit, and format the final materials while embedding pictures into the electronic document rather than taping or gluing pictures to the printed pages.

Similarly, the introductions of spreadsheets, databases, and project management software have made the project management task much simpler for the designer. One can now use "boilerplate" information for a proposal, add the project-specific information, create a budget with a spreadsheet, and produce a timeline for a proposal in a relatively short time. Once the proposal is funded, the same tools are used to produce the instructional products and manage the project.

Trends in Corporate Design and Development

Today, there are many changes in the training industry. None are more firmly established than the demands for design cycle time reduction, and at the same time, for increased effectiveness and efficiency of the training itself. In other words, training design and development must be completed in less time, the training must be delivered quickly with minimal loss of employee work time, and the training should result in improved job performance and a positive impact on the mission and profits of the corporation. ID theorists and practitioners alike are in the process of responding to such challenges.

Reducing Design Cycle Time

Many instructional designers are tackling the problems associated with reducing design cycle time. Some seek ways to modify the design process itself (e.g., Tessmer & Wedman, 1990, 1995). Others are exploring ways of reducing cycle time while still adhering to the same ISD approach they feel has been validated by repeated successful use. A description of two such tactics follows.

Rapid prototyping. Rapid prototyping methodologies are commonly used in software engineering and those principles have been adapted to instructional design projects. Here rapid prototyping involves the development of a working model of an instructional product that is used early in a project to assist in the analysis, design, development, and evaluation of an instructional innovation. Many view prototyping methods essentially as a type of formative evaluation that can be effectively used early and repeatedly throughout a project (Tessmer, 1994); for others, rapid prototyping involves more profound changes in traditional ID.

Basically, *prototypes* are either workable models of the final product or simply shells that demonstrate the projected appearance of the product. Formats vary depending on the medium and use of the final product. In some instances the prototype is discarded after use, while in others it evolves into additional prototypes and ultimately into the final product (Hix & Hartson, 1993; Reilly, 1996). All prototypes enable designers to determine the best product format and the most effective instructional strategies while acknowledging, rather than minimizing, the complexity of actual instructional situations (Tripp & Bichelmeyer, 1990).

Rapid prototyping is thought to decrease design cycle time for two reasons. First, these methodologies reduce production time because (1) using working models of the final product early in a project tends to eliminate time-consuming revisions later on, and (2) design tasks are completed concurrently rather than sequentially throughout the project. Second, rapid prototyping methodologies will ensure, if not a quality product, at least satisfied customers, because they have been involved in an extensive formative evaluation of the actual product throughout its design and development. This logic has been supported by research in natural work settings (Jones & Richey, 2000).

In the Jones and Richey (2000) research, rapid prototyping ID is an iterative undertaking, due to a great extent to the concurrent analysis phase permeating much of the project. Consequently, overall cycle time (and especially development time) is shortened, even as analysis time is extended. The endeavor is totally collaborative and highly dependent on technology support and a high level of designer expertise.

While such an approach to ID is not commonplace throughout the field, tactics such as these are likely to be increasingly popular as ways to reduce cycle time without sacrificing product quality. Moreover, it is possible to be flexible and responsive to client needs, even while adhering to fundamental ISD tenets.

Enhancing Training Effectiveness and Efficiency

The need to save time in training design is matched by the need to save time in training delivery. To a great extent this is being done in two ways: (1) using technology to reduce training time and costs; and (2) using more sophisticated evaluation techniques to ensure training effectiveness, thereby avoiding the need for followup instruction.

Technology-based training delivery. Technology not only provides a solution to the cycle time problem, but most designers also expect it to facilitate more efficient training delivery. Over 70% of training in the United States is still delivered classroom style, with nearly 20% of the training in large corporations is delivered via the computer (Industry Report, 1999). In the 2003 ASTD benchmarking study, up to 29% of training in Fortune 500 organizations involved technology-based delivery. Service organizations tended to rely on CD-ROM training, but 74% of the technology-based training offered by the Benchmarking Forum organizations[2] was delivered via the Internet (Pfefer, 2003). This not only enabled them to decrease travel costs, but online training is increasingly seen as a way to negate the need for classroom training altogether, thus avoiding much lost work time.

This delivery system is likely to mushroom. Internet-based training can be either synchronous (with two-way real time communication) or asynchronous (with two-way delayed communication). It can involve online interaction in terms of practice, feedback, discussion, and assessment. Alternately, training can be relatively passive, more like online reading. Web-based training can be a collaborative activity or it can be self-study. The Web-based materials may even serve more as job aids than instruction.

To a great extent, designers are in the process of determining the guidelines for effective Web-based instruction. Hannafin and Hannafin (1995/1996) have suggested such guidelines, including the need to:

- Optimize the technological capabilities.
- Promote active, engaging learning.
- Establish meaningful contexts for learning.
- Establish open communication among learners and facilitators.
- Build effective management systems.

It is likely that corporate training will take full advantage of the benefits of Web-based instruction only to the extent to which designers master these new techniques.

[2] The Benchmarking Forum of ASTD consists of Fortune 500 and other large-sector organizations. Each year they share detailed data on their spending and other practices.

Advanced evaluation techniques. Effective training is often viewed as that which results in performance improvement in the workplace, as well as improvement in organizational outcomes. Consequently, productive evaluation must measure not simply learning, but also transfer of knowledge gains to the workplace and impact on the organization.

Trainers commonly interpret such evaluation in terms of the higher levels of the Kirkpatrick Model (Kirkpatrick, 1994). Here, initial evaluation, level 1, is of trainee reactions. Level 2 evaluates learning. Level 3 measures on-the-job behavior, and level 4 measures organizational or business impact (see Chapter 10 for a more detailed discussion).

High-level evaluation is not simply an end-of-course activity, it is a traditional summative evaluation endeavor. To adequately measure transfer and organizational impact one must engage in what has been called *confirmative evaluation* (Dessinger & Moseley, 2004). There is a lapse of time between training and confirmative evaluation to allow for transfer and impact to occur. This delay coincides with Foxon's (1993) view of transfer as a five-stage process (not an event) that occurs over time after training. Her concept of transfer moves from intent to initiation to partial transfer to conscious maintenance of skills/knowledge, and finally to unconscious maintenance.

Organizational impact evaluation is also complex. It relates to organizational change (McArdle, 1990), and fundamentally to what an organization sees as valuable (Kaufman, Keller, & Watkins, 1996). In most settings this value is intimately tied to "the monetary worth of the effects of changed performance" (Fitz-enz, 1994, p. 58). Many designers find impact evaluation a formidable task, but Brinkerhoff's (2003) success case method provides a rigorous yet relatively simple approach to evaluating the qualitative and quantitative impact of training on an organization.

Phillips (1998) proposes a level 5 evaluation that measures return on investment (ROI). ROI is usually expressed as a percentage and is arrived at by comparing the costs of designing, developing, and delivering the training with the measurable outcomes. Because relatively few such evaluations have been done, instructional designers have little guidance for conducting them (Russ-Eft & Preskill, 2001). In particular it is difficult to take into account the many organizational factors that, in addition to training, are likely to affect organizational outcomes. In asking for ROI evaluation, many organizational decision makers are actually seeking the kind of data that comes from an impact evaluation. The challenge for the instructional designer is to evaluate training interventions at the higher levels and to provide organizations with meaningful and valid evidence that the training has made a measurable difference.

Globalization of Training

As corporations grow and expand beyond individual country boundaries, the internal operations of companies from information systems to sales to training must also cross these boundaries. These boundaries represent not only geopolitical divisions but cultural and language differences. Instructional designers must address the issue of how to prepare and/or adapt instructional materials for different cultures.

Designing instruction for different cultures is not a new issue for the instructional technology field (Stevens, 1969, 1970a, 1970b). Problems and solutions resulting from the use of software in different cultures provide contexts and strategies for designing instruction for different cultures. Software and information system specialists describe two concepts for developing software for use in a global market. First, any cultural context is extracted from the product, including from the software, packaging, hardware, switches or buttons, and other labeling. This process is referred to as *internationalization* (Taylor, 1992) and results in a generic package that is shipped to each country or culture. Specialists with a knowledge and understanding of the local culture and language then add various features and elements to adapt the generic or internationalized software to the local culture. This process is referred to as *localization*. Internationalization produces a culturally free product, while localization produces a culturally dependent product. Software programmers and instructional designers cannot expect to localize a product by simply translating the words to the language of a target audience (Hars, 1996).

What are some of the issues localization must address to adapt the product? Hars (1996) suggests colors be changed to avoid cultural problems. For example, Hars notes it is best to avoid yellow in Russian materials, blue in Egyptian materials, and red and white for materials destined for Quebec. Similarly, cursors that use a pointing finger are associated with thieves in some cultures. Video and audio can create problems as some cultures will not accept female presenters or female voice-overs. Instructional designers must also be aware of text conventions used on computer screens and in print. The expression of a date can vary from culture to culture so that 1/6/00 can be interpreted as either January 6 or June 1. Similarly, different cultures express time in a 24-hour format rather than the American 12-hour format and it may be written with a colon (e.g., 8:30) or with a decimal (e.g., 8.30).

Localization of text goes beyond simply formatting a date or time. Nakakoji (1994) discusses how text and instructional strategies must be modified for different cultures. For example, people in Western cultures tend to prefer text written in a declarative manner. People in Oriental and Russian cultures prefer to have material written in a procedural format with a summary at the end. Instructional strategies may also need to be adapted. Some cultures place a high value on teamwork while others value individual achievement. Thus, a training program that stresses teamwork would not be well received in a culture that values individual contributions over team contributions. Western cultures want to control their own environment and want to take active control over a computer. Oriental cultures are more oriented towards external control where they try to harmonize with the environment and may prefer a passive control approach to using a computer.

Recent advances in machine translation systems can translate instructional materials from one language to another quickly and fairly accurately. This wholesale approach to localization of materials, however, ignores the nuances of the culture and may produce offensive and/or seldom-used materials. To develop effective instructional materials for the global marketplace, the instructional designer must first internationalize the instruction by removing the cultural elements, and then localize the instruction by adapting it to each culture.

Conclusion

The most prevalent applications of instructional design now occur in corporate settings. The complexities and pressures of these work settings shape not only the roles of designers, but also in many cases the design processes themselves. Demands for increased efficiency, lower training budgets, and globalized products, for example, are stimulating the evolution of instructional design. As such, current ID is more reliant on technology, is more interdisciplinary, and produces more data to support its impact on performance and organizational improvement.

Application Questions

1. Using the library, the Internet, and other resources, what is the level of training activity in the United States in dollars today? To what extent does this figure reflect internal training and outsourcing? What types of training delivery systems are now most common? How might these expenditures impact today's design practice?
2. Define and give an example of *rapid prototyping*. Given a specific project, how could you use this tool? What are the factors that facilitate or constrain its use?
3. You are designing a job aid for how to wash your hands before working. This tool is to be used by restaurant employees. How would you localize the job aid for a particular geographical region? How would you internationalize it to facilitate its use worldwide?
4. Consider the scenario in question 3. How would you use your knowledge of evaluation to assess the effectiveness of this job aid?
5. In recent years, we have seen an increasing emphasis on the Internet as a delivery tool and have seen the evolution of e-learning. What are the implications of these trends for the role of the designer? What are their implications for the design process?
6. Locate at least three laws, regulations, or judicial decisions that could influence a designer's job. Do these laws, etc., vary for designers working in different industries? How?
7. Think about a global organization you would like to work with. What issues would affect your role as the designer of new employee orientation training for that organization?

References

Atchison, B. J. (1996). Roles and competencies of instructional design as identified by expert instructional designers. Unpublished doctoral dissertation. Detroit, MI: Wayne State University.

Brinkerhoff, R. O. (2003). *The success case method: Find out quickly what's working and what's not.* San Francisco: Berrett-Koehler.

Dessinger, J. C., & Moseley, J. L. (2004). *Confirmative evaluation: Practical strategies for valuing continuous improvement*. San Francisco: Pfeiffer.

Dick, W., Carey, L., & Carey, J. O. (2005). *The systematic design of instruction* (6th ed.). Boston: Allyn & Bacon.

Eyres, P. (1998). *The legal handbook for trainers, speakers, and consultants*. New York: McGraw-Hill.

Fitz-enz, J. (1994). Yes . . . you can weigh training's value. *Training, 31*(7), 54–58.

Foshay, W. R. (1988). I don't know is on third. *Performance & Instruction, 27*(3), 8–9.

Foxon, M. (1993). A process approach to the transfer of training. Part 1: The impact of motivation and supervisor support on transfer maintenance. *Australian Journal of Educational Technology, 9*(2), 1–12.

Foxon, M., Richey, R. C., Roberts, R., & Spannaus, T. (2003). *Training manager competencies: The standards* (3rd ed.). Syracuse, NY: ERIC Clearinghouse on Information and Technology.

Gagné, R. M. (1993). Computer-based instructional guidance. In J. M. Spector, M. C. Polson, & D. J. Muraida (Eds.), *Automating instructional design: Concepts and issues* (pp. 133–146). Englewood Cliffs, NJ: Educational Technology Publications.

Hannafin, K. M., & Hannafin, M. J. (1995/1996). The ecology of distance learning environments. *Training Research Journal, 1*, 49–69.

Harless, J. (1995). Performance technology skills in business: Implications for preparation. *Performance Improvement Quarterly, 8*(4), 75–88.

Hars, A. (1996). Localization is not just a multilingual issue; it's also multicultural. Retrieved from **http://www.byte.com/art/9603/sec18/art1.htm**

Hawkridge, D. (1994). Which team for open and distance learning materials production? In F. Lockwood (Ed.), *Materials production in open and distance education* (pp. 97–102). London: Paul Chapman.

Hix, D., & Hartson, H. R. (1993). *Developing user interfaces: Ensuring usability through product & process*. New York: John Wiley & Sons.

Industry Report, 1999. *Training, 36*(10), 37–80.

Jones, T. S., & Richey, R. C. (2000). Rapid prototyping in action: A developmental study. *Educational Technology, Research & Development, 48*(2), 63–80.

Jury, T., & Reeves, T. (1999). An EPSS for instructional design: NCR's quality information products process. In J. van den Akker, R. M. Branch, K. Gustafson, N. Nieveen, & T. Plomp. (Eds.), *Design approaches and tools in education and training* (pp. 183–194). Dordrecht, the Netherlands: Kluwer Academic.

Kaufman, R., Keller, J., & Watkins, R. (1996). What works and what doesn't work: Evaluation beyond Kirkpatrick. *Performance & Instruction, 35*(2), 8–12.

Kirkpatrick, D. L. (1994). *Evaluating training programs—The four levels*. San Francisco: Barrett-Koehler.

Klimczak, A. K., & Wedman, J. F. (1997). Instructional design success factors: An empirical basis. *Educational Technology, Research & Development, 45*(2), 75–83.

LeMaistre, C. (1998). What is an expert instructional designer? Evidence of expert performance during formative evaluation. *Educational Technology, Research & Development, 46*(3), 21–36.

Loughner, P., & Moller, L. (1998). The use of task analysis procedures by instructional designers. *Performance Improvement Quarterly, 11*(3), 79–101.

McArdle, G. E. H. (1990). What is evaluation? *Performance & Instruction, 29*(7), 43–44.

Merrill, M. D. (1999). Instructional transaction theory (ITT): Instructional design based on knowledge objects. In C. M. Reigeluth (Ed.), *Instructional-design theories and models. Volume 2: A new paradigm of instructional theory* (pp. 397–424). Mahwah, NJ: Lawrence Erlbaum Associates.

Morrison, G. R. (1988). Who's on first. *Performance & Instruction, 27*(3), 5–6.

Morrison, G. R., Ross, S. M., & Kemp, J. E. (2004). *Designing effective instruction* (4th ed.). Hoboken, NJ: John Wiley & Sons.

Mulder, M., Nijhof, W. J., & Brinkerhoff, R. O. (Eds.). (1995). *Corporate training for effective performance*. Boston: Kluwer Academic.

Nakakoji, K. (1994). Designing software for a different culture calls for an awareness of its subtleties and unwritten assumptions: Japan is a case in point. Retrieved from **http://www.byte.com/art/9406/sec7/art5.htm**

Perez, R. S., & Emery, C. D. (1995). Designer thinking: How novices and experts think about instructional design. *Performance Improvement Quarterly, 8*(3), 80–95.

Pfefer, J. (2003). Deep in benchmarking: Using industry standards to access training programs. *SIGUCCS 2003*, 33–37.

Phillips, J. J. (Ed.). (1998). *Implementing evaluation systems and processes*. Alexandria, VA: American Society for Training & Development.

Pieters, J. M. (1997). Training for human resources development in industrial and professional organizations. In S. Dijkstra, N. M. Seel, F. Schott, & R. D. Tennyson. (Eds.), *Instructional design: International perspectives. Volume 2: Solving instructional design problems* (pp. 315–340). Mahwah, NJ: Lawrence Erlbaum Assoiciates.

Raybould, B. (1995). Performance support engineering: An emerging development methodology for enabling organizational learning. *Performance Improvement Quarterly, 8*(1), 7–22.

Reilly, J. P. (1996). *Rapid prototyping: Moving to business-centric development*. Boston: International Thompson Computer Press.

Richey, R. C., Fields, D. F., & Foxon, M. (with Roberts, R. C., Spannaus, T., & Spector, J. M.). (2001). *Instructional design competencies: The standards* (3rd ed.) Syracuse, NY: ERIC Clearinghouse on Information and Technology & The International Board of Standards for Training, Performance & Instruction.

Rothwell, W. J., & Kazanas, H. C. (2004). *Mastering the instructional design process: A systematic approach* (3rd ed.). San Francisco: Jossey-Bass.

Rowland, G. (1992). What do instructional designers actually do? An initial investigation of expert practice. *Performance Improvement Quarterly, 5*(2), 65–86.

Rummler, G. A. (1999). Transforming organizations through human performance technology. In H. D. Stolovitch & E. J. Keeps (Eds.), *Handbook of human performance technology* (2nd ed.) (pp. 47–66). San Francisco: Jossey-Bass/Pfeiffer.

Russ-Eft, D., & Preskill, H. (2001). *Evaluation in organizations: A systematic approach to enhancing learning, performance, and change*. Cambridge, MA: Perseus.

Seels, B., & Glasgow, Z. (1998). *Making instructional design decisions* (2nd ed.). Upper Saddle River, NJ: Merrill/Prentice Hall.

Shrock, S. A., & Coscarelli, W. C. C. (1996). *Criterion-referenced test development: Technical and legal guidelines for corporate training and certification*. Washington, DC: International Society for Performance and Improvement.

Smith, P. L., & Ragan, T. J. (1999). *Instructional design* (2nd ed.). New York: Macmillan.

Spector, J. M. (1990). *Designing and developing an advanced instructional design advisor* (AFHRL-TP-90-52). Brooks AFB, TX: Human Resources Laboratory, Training Systems Division.

Stevens, W. D. (1969). Sign, transaction, and symbolic interaction in culture mediation. *AV Communication Review, 17*(1), 150–158.

Stevens, W. D. (1970a). Affection and cognition in transaction and mapping in cultural space. *AV Communication Review, 18*(2), 440–445.

Stevens, W. D. (1970b). Formation, information, and instruction in culture mediation. *AV Communication Review, 18*(4), 180–185.

Sugrue, B. (2003). *State of the industry: ASTD's annual review of U.S. and international trends in workplace learning and performance*. Alexandria, VA: American Society of Training & Development.

Taylor, D. (1992). *Global software: Developing applications for the international market*. New York: Springer-Verlag.

Tessmer, M. (1988). What's on second. *Performance & Instruction, 2*(1), 6–8.

Tessmer, M. (1994). Formative evaluation alternatives. *Performance Improvement Quarterly, 7*(1), 3–18.

Tessmer, M., & Wedman, J. F. (1990). A layers of necessity instructional development model. *Educational Technology, Research & Development, 38*(2), 77–85.

Tessmer, M., & Wedman, J. F. (1995). Context-sensitive instructional design models: A response to design theory, practice, and criticism. *Performance Improvement Quarterly, 8*(3), 38–55.

Tripp, S., & Bichelmeyer, B. (1990). Rapid prototyping: An alternative instructional design strategy. *Educational Technology, Research & Development, 38*(1), 31–44.

Visscher-Voerman, I., & Gustafson, K. (2004). Paradigms in the theory and practice of educational and training design. *Educational Technology, Research & Development, 52*(2), 69–89.

CHAPTER 19

Instructional Design Opportunities in Military Education and Training Environments

Mary F. Bratton-Jeffery[1]
U.S. Naval Education and Training Command

Suzanne Q. Hoffman
Independent Consultant

Arthur B. Jeffery
University of South Alabama

Editors' Introduction

Over the past 60 or 70 years, the field of instructional design and technology has had a significant impact on training in the military. Many of the founding figures in the field began their professional careers designing training for the military during World War II. Moreover, during the 1970s, several military organizations officially adopted a systematic approach to the design of training.

Today, the IDT field continues to play an important role in the design and presentation of military training. In this chapter, Mary Bratton-Jeffery, Suzanne Hoffman, and Arthur Jeffery provide an overview of the military culture, the changing roles and responsibilities of the military, and the role of instructional design and development within that culture. The authors examine military visions for the future from an international perspective and how they will affect the role of instructional designers working with the military.

Knowledge and Comprehension Questions

1. Describe the characteristics an instructional designer should have to be successful when working with large-system clients.
2. What are some of the constraints that a designer might face when working with a federal client?
3. If you want to know more about a country's Department or Ministry of Defense, what are some strategies you might use to find planning documents, organizational structures, or mission and objective statements?
4. The primary mission of most countries' militaries is that of national defense. What are some of the additional roles or responsibilities that are accomplished by military organizations?
5. How does the Advanced Distributed Learning Initiative impact large-scale, technology-based education and training systems in the United States and internationally?
6. Why should an instructional designer working in a diverse military training environment be well versed in learning theory and instructional strategies?

[1] The views presented by Dr. Bratton-Jeffery are those of the author and do not necessarily represent the views of the U.S. Department of Defense or its components.

The military forces of any nation, whether it be the United States Army, the British Royal Marines, the Royal Dutch Air Force, the German Bundeswehr, the Singapore Armed Forces, or the Australian Defence Force, are an integrated, dedicated, and astute group of individuals who share a camaraderie unmatched in the corporate world. Their culture is one born of the ever-present threat of war and the necessity to trust one another with their lives. Despite a common mission to protect the lives and fortunes of those at home and abroad and a responsibility to respond to that mission, those who comprise today's international military units are individuals with diverse interests and personal goals. An enhanced appreciation for the individual's needs has spurred a dynamic change in the military training of today. Those involved in that training—possibly you as an instructional designer—must produce training that meets the requirements of the military as well as the needs of the individual. Today's servicemen and women volunteer to serve their country, but they expect something in return.

Among the challenges to instructional designers working within a military environment are (1) recognizing that ineffective instruction can have catastrophic consequences, (2) creating training that addresses the needs of the military while considering the interests of the individual, (3) designing for an environment that is constantly changing, (4) using technology wisely when technology is evolving more rapidly than the ability to accommodate change, (5) assuming the responsibilities dictated by one's role and relationship to the military (federal worker or contractor), and (6) designing for individual projects, which may be repurposed into other training products or delivery environments.

Instructional designers play a significant role in the transformation to accommodate the needs of today's servicemembers and move the military of today to the military of tomorrow. This role requires the following: knowledge of learning theories and instructional strategies and how to use them effectively; understanding how to apply technology at the optimal level to meet the needs of the user in a variety of learning environments; ability to create a blend of learning solutions; ability to work within budget; understanding and appreciation of the military culture both at home and abroad as well as the culture of international forces; and the ability to communicate with clients.

This chapter provides an overview of the major issues and challenges for instructional designers and developers in international military communities, from classroom to combat environments. Reading this chapter will help you gain insight into the roles and responsibilities of the instructional designers and developers who create training products for the military.

The chapter begins with an overview of the military culture and the role of instructional design and development within that culture. The following section addresses the changing roles and responsibilities of the military. Next, we investigate the international military visions for the future. Finally, we describe the role of instructional designers working with the military. A glossary appears at the end of the chapter to assist with terminology unique to the military environment.

Military Culture and the Role of Instructional Design and Development within that Culture

Since the end of World War II, America's national protective force has evolved from national to global defense. In 1948, the United Nations Security Council established the United Nations Peacekeepers to oversee the fragile truce between the Arabs and Israelis ("Peacekeepers," 2004). Ten years following the end of World War II, Germany became a member of the North Atlantic Treaty Organization (NATO). Since that time the Bundeswehr has grown to the largest European conventional armed forces contingent within NATO (Germany Info, 2004). In 2001, the United Nations Security Council authorized the establishment of an International Security Assistance Force (ISAF) comprised of military personnel representing 19 countries. This joint force was tasked to assist the new Afghan Interim Authority with the provision of security and stability in Kabul (Joint Operations Command, Press & Information Centre, 2004). This global military evolution demonstrates the increased logistical demand for training across cultures and around the world.

But winning wars and providing security is only part of the military mission. All of the NATO allies are committed to peacekeeping efforts as well as providing humanitarian relief assistance. These commitments require well-trained men and women, and it is within the realm of training that instructional designers will have an opportunity to apply their knowledge and skills.

To work effectively in the military environment, instructional designers must understand and appreciate the transitions the military will make in the years ahead. Military training will evolve alongside this transition, and the use of and emphasis on technology will have a significant impact on that training.

The military clients that instructional designers work with are subject matter experts (SMEs) in their occupational fields. They are not usually familiar with educational principles, learning theories, or instructional technology applications. Their knowledge of the classroom and learning is based on their personal experiences as students. Their knowledge of technology is through experience in the workplace. They place a great deal of trust in the instructional design team to provide them with the best recommendations for how and when to apply a theory or a technology to achieve optimal learning solutions and to help them stay within the financial and environmental constraints. Instructional designers must "know their stuff," and they are expected to keep abreast of the instructional technology field. Anything less is not in the best interests of the client or the design firm the team represents. Flawed designs or inefficient use of technology can result in hundreds of thousands of dollars wasted. Mistakes such as these will not enhance your company's reputation or lead to follow-on contracts.

Changing Roles and Responsibilities of the Military

Over the years, military forces in the United States and other developed nations have evolved into huge, technologically sophisticated, multifaceted, integrated organizations with an overwhelming number of responsibilities (Figure 19.1). Allied military have also assumed responsibility for protecting and defending the freedom of other nations. For example, the British Royal Navy has an ongoing commitment to support four standing NATO forces—Standing Naval Force Atlantic, Standing Naval Force Mediterranean, and Mine Countermeasure Forces North and South (Royal Navy, 2004). Similarly, the Australian Defense Force is deployed in more than 10 operations including border protection, UN and coalition operations, and third-country deployments (Australian Department of Defense, 2002). The Singapore Armed Forces, as well, have supported 13 operations in 11 different countries since its first involvement in 1989 ("Peacekeepers," 2004).

These added responsibilities have altered the lives of each nation's military personnel. These long-term global assignments impact personal lives and professional goals as never before. Instructional designers may be asked to provide learning solutions that will support training and learning opportunities both at home and abroad. Some of the major issues associated with the changing roles and responsibilities of the military and the role of the instructional designer with regard to those changes are discussed in the following sections.

The military of all nations will face a number of common challenges. Two of these challenges that may impact the role of a designer are:

- International responsibilities of a national military force
- New technologies

The global corporate world thrives on international partnerships. Designers must recognize the cultural diversity of the clients and select training or learning solutions that can accommodate dissimilar audiences. Further complexities may be encountered when designing products that may be purchased by international forces. Many U.S. allies purchase American instructional products and access to the training as well as the weaponry. The German air force and navy combat jet crews and all surface-to-air missile operators are trained entirely in the United States and Canada (Germany Info, 2004). Other countries offer exchange-training programs and support joint exercises at U.S. military training sites.

New technologies exist on every front, in every business, and in every home. Students share classroom experiences with children around the world via the Internet. Low-cost, digital communications have placed international friends and relatives within a finger's reach. These new technologies are also available to adversaries. Using

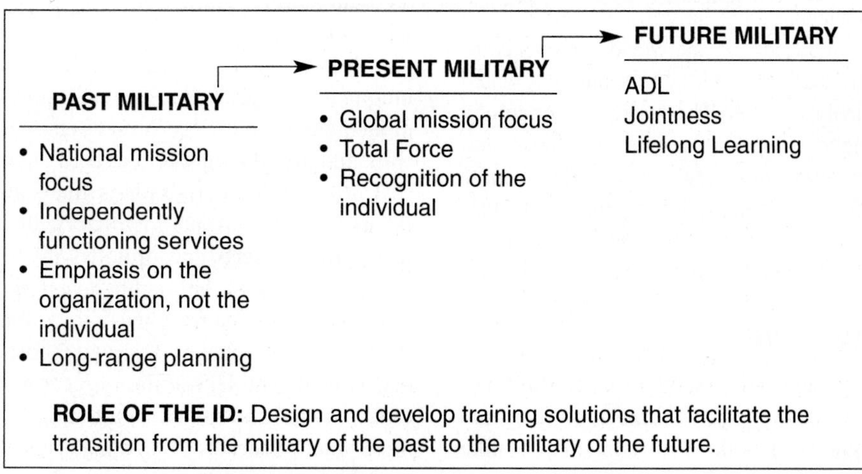

FIGURE 19.1 The evolving military culture: Current status.

secure networks and limiting the number of applications are just two ways in which the military tries to prevent illegal access. But these security solutions may cause instructional designers to adjust the design and delivery of training products. Designers must learn to work within the system.

Military Issues

Funding

The challenge for each service in any country is how to best utilize the money it has available for training. In most instances, tradeoff decisions must be made to stay within budget. A low-tech training solution, such as a paper-based job aid, may not be the most desirable approach, but may well be the option selected to accomplish the training task and stay within budget. The desire to utilize all the capabilities of technology is a temptation that may be hard to resist, but using dollars injudiciously can quickly be the undoing of a design firm. For the instructional designer, suggesting new approaches to training using low- and high-tech methods incorporated with the mission equipment is an option that should be considered.

An instructional designer must be able to articulate carefully and accurately the cost of the training solution and provide alternative choices while keeping the project within budget. Whatever funds are applied to one project may be taken from another, and the designer must be able to help the client weigh the costs or tradeoffs.

Technological Range

Instructional designers working with the military find themselves supporting the development of instructional products that range from the simplest paper-based, pocket-sized job aids to advanced computer-based simulations. At the higher end of technology, the military employs the most sophisticated simulations in the world, such as combat fighter pilot simulations and large-scale automated command and control exercises. The range of technology available to training developers presents ever-increasing opportunities to improve training realism and effectiveness while also presenting an ever-expanding range of challenges for instructional designers as they work to adapt to the variety of instructional and performance requirements.

Delivery Environment

Like their civilian counterparts, members of the military must constantly learn new things to achieve professional success and survive in hostile environments. Unlike the civilian operational environment, training is always center stage. Except for new employee or new equipment training, training in the civilian environment is generally separated from the workplace or jobsite. In the military, training is part of the job and is integrated into the workplace, which means it represents a larger proportion of day-to-day activities than in the civilian environment. Because of this, training in the military is pervasive, and the quantity and diversity of training products tend to be much higher. Instructional designers recognize that training takes place in the classroom, in garrison, in base and shipboard environments, and wherever personnel are deployed—even in combat (Figure 19.2). This variable training delivery environment means training products must be adaptable to all environments.

Design Constraints

Large-systems design is an area that presents unique challenges to instructional designers. The larger and more widely dispersed the system, the greater the challenge. Designing for the military differs from designing for large corporations on a number of fronts: management, configurations, implementation, and expertise of training instructors.

The management philosophy within a large corporation generally follows a single directive from the board of directors. The military prides itself on the diversity and the mission scope of each of the independent services. Especially when working within the joint arena, the instructional design team may find itself trying to please a number of clients with strong, service-specific opinions.

The configuration component of any technology-based solution is probably the most difficult aspect of a project. Each service has its own network infrastructure(s) and equipment purchased over a number of years. In the majority of cases, designers will work with legacy (existing) systems and with integrating new hardware and software.

Once the project has been completed and beta tested in an ideal setting, the instructional design team may assist with implementation or provide instructions to the government's implementation team(s). Implementation presents unique challenges because it will more than likely be implemented in a variety of settings—in the field, aboard ship, and around the world as well as in the classroom.

Unlike major corporations that have training departments and professional instructors, the military uses subject matter experts and provides them with instructional materials to assist them with "teaching." Instructional designers must create train-the-trainer materials that explain the lesson plans step by step and incorporate learning theory as well. The U.S. military recognizes Master Instructors, and while assignments are short lived (no longer than three years) instructors need materials that clearly explain all components of the learning package, including the theories underlying the design.

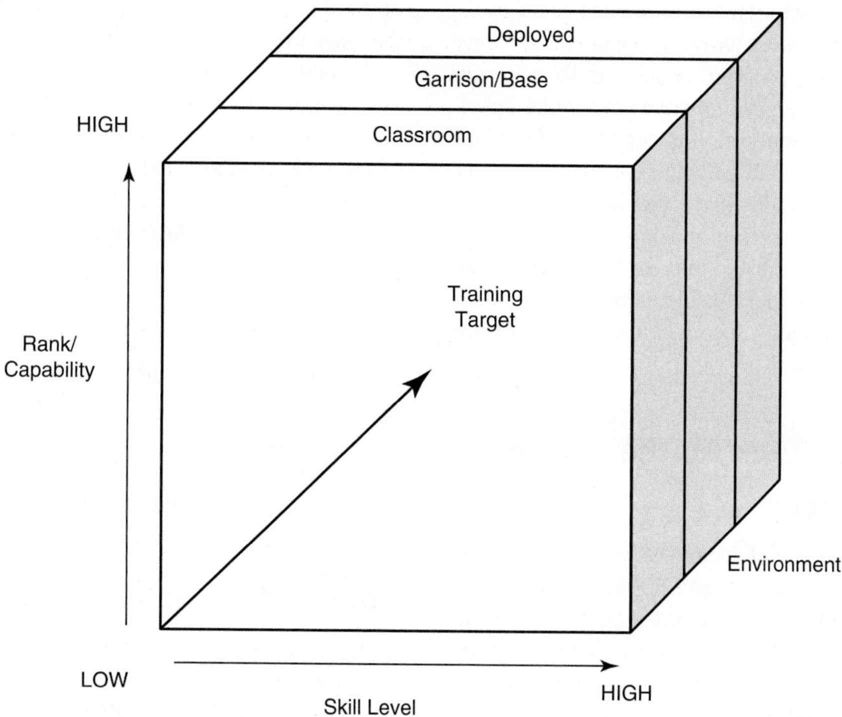

FIGURE 19.2 Full-spectrum use of training products.

People

The most critical challenge to all of the services is recruiting good people and retaining highly trained and skilled servicemembers. The national defense planning documents of many of the allied nations address the need to recruit and retain highly qualified people (Australian Department of Defense, 2002; Director for Strategic Plans & Policy, 2000; U.K. Ministry of Defence, 2001). These plans also recognize the need to provide for quality of life, especially in the areas personal and professional growth.

Alternative Training Solutions

Instructional designers are accustomed to examining the skill and knowledge levels of the target audience to determine how to design the instruction and what level of language to use. Particularly important is the ID's knowledge of learning theories and instructional strategies. Historically, training has been designed for and delivered to the "group." Servicemembers who did not achieve the desired performance during the first iteration of training were remediated until mastery was achieved. This remediation was often done in the same manner in which the original instruction was presented.

In the case of remediation activities, rather than presenting the same information in the same format or the same information in a slightly different format, the instructional designer might recommend completely different instructional approaches. Allowing individual learners to select learning options allows for the learner control that is a basic tenet of adult learning.

The technological options now available to instructional designers afford them an opportunity to recommend varied training solutions that address a variety of instructional challenges at the individual level. Take, for instance, a scenario in which a computer-based training product has been ordered to replace the resident classroom instruction for cooks in the Army. An examination of the ethnic composition of the client's cooks reveals that a large number of Hispanic/Latino soldiers are in that occupational specialty. Technology access studies indicate that members of that community come to the workplace with less computer experience than any other ethnic group (McGee, 2002). Hofstede's 1997 work (cited in McGee, 2002) in cross-cultural theory is the basis of Web-based design identified by Marcus and Gould (cited in McGee, 2002) that specifically addresses culturally based instructional considerations for this community. These include minimal emphasis on individual achievement; active learning; simple, straightforward design; consistent and repetitive visual cues, and an intimation of consequences before taking action or making decisions. The instructional designer might suggest to the client a blended solution that provides team-based review sessions or laboratory assignments or experiments. The computer software program or adjunctive materials would use minimal graphics and increased white space. Visual cues would orient the learner throughout the program and assist with intuitive navigation features. And finally, the program would allow the learner to select and access alternatives before making final decisions. Designing instruction such as this that adheres to the culturally based instructional considerations specific to the Hispanic/Latino community increases the likelihood that these learners will succeed.

The Military's Vision for the Future

Guiding Documents

Each country has a number of documents written by the military that describe its vision and goals for the future, and that are submitted to its governing body (Figure 19.3). In the case of the United States, the *Quadrennial Defense Review Report (QDR)* (required by Congress) articulates the military's posture for capabilities that will be needed in the future to promote peace, sustain freedom, and encourage prosperity (U.S. Department of Defense, 2001). This document establishes the vision for all efforts by each of the individual services, including "exploitation of new approaches to operational concepts and capabilities, [and] the use of old and new technologies" (p. 29). Each service must examine its current means of doing business and transform itself against the measures provided in the *QDR*. The vision statements written by each of the services in alignment with the *QDR* are excellent starting places when working as an instructional designer creating training for the military. A familiarity with the visions and plans of the particular branch of the military with which you are working will aid you in the quest to provide the best training solution possible.

Should you work with an international military service, you will be able to locate many of these planning documents via the Internet by visiting the country's Department of Defense (or equivalent) website.

Long-Range Planning

By the time a plane or ship is designed, prototyped, and ordered, technology has surpassed the original plans for the aircraft or ship. An instructional designer must be able to "look into the future" and provide input as to how technology and learning research may evolve and the impact this evolution will have on future training needs.

The key to the future of military training lies in three major areas: advanced distributed learning; jointness, within a nation and internationally; and lifelong learning.

Advanced Distributed Learning (ADL)

"The Advanced Distributed Learning (ADL) Initiative, sponsored by the U.S. Office of the Secretary of Defense (OSD), is a collaborative effort between government, industry and academia to establish a new distributed learning environment that permits the interoperability of learning tools and course content on a global scale. ADL's vision is to provide access to the highest quality education and training, tailored to individual needs, delivered cost-effectively anywhere and anytime" (Advanced Distributed Learning, 2004a, n.p.).

Initially a U.S. endeavor, ADL hosted the first International Plugfest in 2004 attended by European and Asian e-learning standardization and specification bodies. The United Kingdom and Canada have signed partnership agreements with the U.S. ADL Initiative and it is

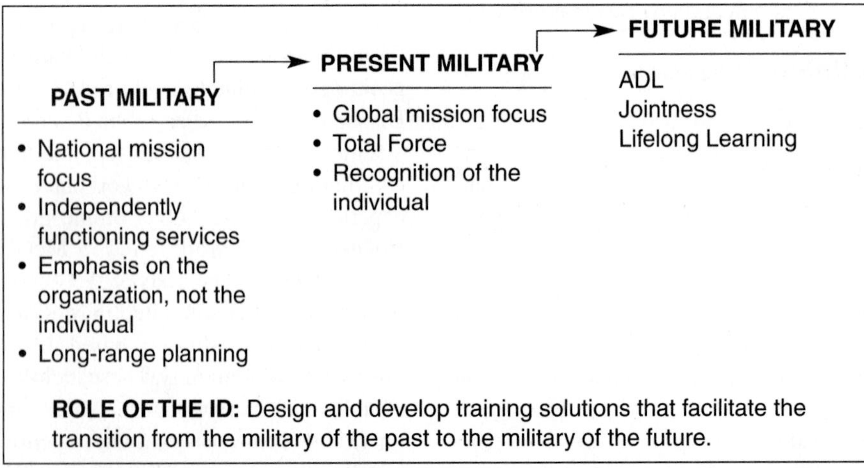

FIGURE 19.3 The evolving military culture: Future status.

anticipated that many of the 37 countries represented at the Plugfest will follow suit (Advanced Distributed Learning, 2004b).

Technology-based efforts such as ADL address the requirement of systems and software communicating on a global scale. The ADL effort will eventually reduce costs, increase the capacity to write joint programs, and support the building of an expert knowledge base.

Jointness

Maximum advantage of funding, acquisition, technology, and people can be attained through collaboration. The U.S. military and its allies fight as a combined force—an integrated whole of the service branches and ally counterparts. This dictates that training be joint as well, necessitating training products that are developed to enhance the joint war-fighting skills of disparate forces. Inherent in this instructional design mission is recognition of the diversity of the force in terms of service perspective (i.e., Army, Air Force, Navy, and Marines), doctrine of allied forces (such as the case in NATO or UN coalitions with many different national armed forces and their associated war-fighting strategies and tactics), and even cultural diversity such as differences in language and religion.

Lifelong Learning

Military leadership supports and encourages learning beyond the military requirements for a number of reasons. Continued learning opportunities within the service improve servicemembers within their occupational specialty and open the doors to many opportunities for those who leave service. The United Kingdom, for example, offers advanced learning opportunities through its resident universities and the Open University. The U.K. government has an established Lifelong Learning Policy; its military component is the Learning Forces Initiative, which is open to all ranks (British Army, 2004).

The European Union (EU) has instituted Europewide educational reforms to allow students to "study without borders." The European Credit Transfer System (ECTS) simplifies accreditation between institutions. This open system allows military students to continue their personal learning goals while serving their countries abroad (Germany Info, 2004).

The words of the U.S. Chief of Naval Operations, Admiral Vern Clark, evidence a respect for and recognition of the individual's learning goals:

> The people that make up our military decide that they are going to give of themselves. Every human being who puts on the uniform . . . makes tremendous sacrifices. . . . There should be a commitment from the leadership for the promise sailors make to us. I believe that promise has to be kept by people like me—to make sure people have the tools that they need to succeed. We've got to offer to them a chance to make a difference. They want us to give them a chance to show what they can contribute. They want a chance to grow and develop. (Kennedy, 2000, n.p.)

The Role of Instructional Designers Working with the Military

The instructional design profession prides itself on creativity, ingenuity, and research. That means the instructional designer can and should suggest a number of innovative solutions. A novice instructional designer working with a military client might assume that the "bank" would have open doors for funding spectacular projects. That is not the case. Limited funding will require tradeoffs for every project. Using a technique similar to that of the Quality Function Deployment model for instructional design (Bratton-Jeffery & Jeffery, 2003), the Scenarios Solution Discussion Matrix (Figure 19.4) suggests a systematic methodology for working through the tradeoffs that can serve as the basis for discussion between the instructional designer and the client.

In this section we present four scenarios dramatizing different types of challenges designers who work with the military may face. In each, you are the designer. As you examine the scenarios, identify what you know; make a list of questions to ask your client; and list possible solutions based on instructional technology practices and theories. Use the Scenarios Solution Discussion Matrix to guide your thinking. Be sure to consider areas in which the instructional designer will be involved when reviewing the solutions.

Scenario 1: Degree Completion vs. Deployment

Army Reserve Sgt. John King faces a 12-month rotation in Iraq as a member of his Reserve unit. His unit along with a signal battalion from the state's National Guard will support coalition forces in promoting stability and safety in the war-torn country. Sgt. King's company will be part of a larger force designed to patrol and collect information.

Sgt. King currently works for a large corporation that has been paying for his college work in business management. To advance in the company, he must complete his degree. Unfortunately, the deployment will now interrupt his efforts and jeopardize his place in the company. The big question in Sgt. King's mind is what will happen to his personal goals as he takes time from his career to serve his country overseas.

REMEMBER: When designing and developing training solutions for the military, the instructional designer must take into account design considerations as well as specific human- and technology-related issues unique to the military environment.

	DESIGN CONSIDERATIONS					
DESIGN ISSUES	**Learning Theories**	**Technology Applications**	**Blended Solutions**	**Budget**	**Military Culture**	**Communication**
Funding						
Long-range Planning						
Joint Training						
Low-tech vs. High-tech						
Delivery Environment						
Alternative Training Solutions						
Design Constraints						
Motivation						
Cultural Diversity						
Knowledge Levels						
Skill Levels						
Learner Past Experiences						

FIGURE 19.4 Scenarios Solution Discussion Matrix.

Problem. You are a member of an instructional design team that has been formed to address deployment and distance learning options. Identify strategies that will meet the needs of the individual servicemember while serving the requirements of the organization.

The Army's solution. Sgt. King is representative of the new Army in which soldiers are expected to be educated and technology-savvy enough to succeed in the missions and on the battlefields. The Army, in support of the Joint Vision, provides an organizational structure that rewards professional expertise and encourages personal growth (Office of Secretary of the Army, 1999). Recognizing the increased demand of the global mission, the Army worked with instructional technology firms to launch eArmyU in January 2001. eArmyU adds a Web-based component to its education system for resident and nonresident instruction to support servicemembers actively pursuing college degrees.

Currently, eArmyU offers approximately 150 certificate and degree programs from 27 member colleges, and the opportunities for individual professional growth are increasing rapidly (eArmyU.com, 2004). More than 3,000 courses have been delivered online to more than 250,000 students. Soldiers receive 100 percent funding for tuition, books, fees, a personal laptop, an e-mail account, and an Internet Service Provider (ISP). A 24-hour help desk for technical support is provided as well.

Funding for eArmyU lies primarily with the Army; however, the Army has arranged collaborative partnerships with IBM, the Council on Academic Management, and several distance learning solution providers, as well as with the academic institutions (eArmyU.com, 2004).

Scenario 2: Contextual Learning to Improve Motivation and Retention

Ensign Martha Gilmore has just completed her four-year degree at George Washington University in political science. To cover her college expenses, she joined the Navy Reserve Officer Training Corps (ROTC). Now, to fulfill her military obligation, she reports for active duty. Traditionally, the Navy officer training schools are several months long. Students receive a thorough indoctrination into the Navy culture as well as the intricacies of a particular war-fighting speciality. The thought of another six months of classwork after completing a four-year program is not what Ensign Gilmore had in mind. Whatever happened to the recruiters' pictures of exotic ports and world travel? From the Navy's perspective, here's a novice sailor who has no concept of what it means to serve watch, supervise a work team, or participate in a drill.

Problem. Your firm has been called in to examine the issue of motivation and retention. Students indicate that lengthy classroom engagements are not what they had in mind when they joined the Navy; many junior officers leave once their initial obligation has been met. Those responsible for sending trained and prepared officers to the Fleet believe that students must understand their jobs thoroughly before going aboard ship. What instructional strategies can your firm recommend that address both the expectations of the individual and the needs of the training organization?

The Navy's solution. Training a young ensign to assume the responsibilities of a division officer aboard ship is a complex and lengthy task. In years past, a young ensign would, in many cases, complete four years of college and then attend a six-month resident course at the Surface Warfare Officers School (SWOS) in Newport, Rhode Island. While the experience was valuable, the lengthy classroom training drained the motivation of the young junior officers.

To remedy the motivation issue, to contextualize the technical training, and to indoctrinate the young officers more quickly into shipboard life, the Navy has implemented a blended learning solution, Division Officer at Sea (Leppo, 2004). Ensigns are assigned to ships directly after graduating from college. While aboard, they complete a regimen of self-paced, computer-based training, seminars, and practical, hands-on exercises. Many senior officers have used the seminars to elaborate on specific topics contained in the computer modules, have organized tours of the various types of ships, and have arranged, when possible, for ensigns to discuss the training process with visiting admirals.

While completing the blended training, the ensigns fulfill division officer responsibilities to gain management and leadership experience. Once they have completed the "At Sea" component and earned their Officer of the Deck Underway, they return to SWOS in Newport for a three-week simulation-based course to fully qualify as Surface Warfare Officers.

According to Ensign Adam Terral, "the new program allows Junior Officers the benefit of reinforcing the information they learn on the computer with experiences that can only be found aboard their ship" (Leppo, 2004, p. 5).

Scenario 3: Full-Spectrum Training

Staff Sergeant Rios is exhausted. His recon team consisting of three Bradley fighting vehicles and two M1 Abrams tanks has just come off the "point" on the Third Division's march to Baghdad. They are still in a hostile and deadly environment, but it is a welcome relief from the gut-wrenching mission of being the lead element of the entire American force. His CO has told him the company will be in reserve for at least the next 24 hours.

Sergeant Rios has his team set up a security perimeter before they go about the business of getting ready for combat. The team is resupplied with ammo, fuel, water, and rations. They carefully check and service their weapons and vehicles. They rest and then wait. To Sergeant Rios, time is a precious commodity. He needs to get some of the new Bradley crewmen cross-trained on a different weapon and his RTO (radio telephone operator) seems shaky when using the latest upgrade of the secure radio system. He is glad he remembered to bring a handful of job aids on the weapons systems from Fort Benning—that will help with the cross-training. However, the job aids aren't current enough to include the new system "mods." They have the current technical documentation, but he isn't sure of the best way of going about integrating the new procedures into the training. He also doesn't have the changes to the manuals for the secure radio upgrades, so he will need to get that information in order to train the RTO.

Finally, he reminds himself to take time to "train the trainers" so the crew chiefs will automatically conduct needed "hip-pocket" training during lulls in the fighting without his supervision. He tries to recall the "train-the-trainer" techniques and other training "tricks" he learned during his last professional development course, but with all the confusion of the past few days, he can't remember them. If he could just call that instructor . . .

Problem. Your client wants to provide training anywhere and anytime; yet, when you ask for minimum configuration setups, you are unable to get a consistent answer. How will you design a training solution that provides continuous training in an unstable or unidentifiable environment like that of Sergeant Rios?

The Marine Corps' solution. Design teams working with the Air Force, the Navy, or the Army are able in most cases to identify the technology requirements for implementation at a garrison location or aboard ship. However, the Marines present a unique challenge in that they are completely mobile. A Marine unit may be assigned to the U.S.S. *Eisenhower* for one deployment and to the U.S.S. *Ronald Reagan* for another. Once reaching the area of operations, the unit will leave the ship and move to a shore facility.

By 2006, the Marine Corps will have in place 54 Deployable Learning Resource Centers (DLRC). Each mobile unit consists of a server, network switch, printer, and 20 rugged laptop stations. The unit stores and distributes training courseware and hosts the management tools to monitor, test, and record learner progress. When available, the system can connect to external networks including a shipboard local area network (LAN), shore-based metropolitan area networks (MAN) and wide area networks (WAN). This networking capability can even be sent to field locations via wireless systems. The system uses a reach-back mode to connect to the USMC Institute Automated Information System to receive information updates and send scores back. This solution on wheels provides continuous support to the Marines Professional Military Education program, the military skills training and cross-functional training applicable to all Marines ("Deployed Education Pilot Program," 2004).

Scenario 4: Joint Training U.S. Forces

A joint task force has been formed with the mission to support port security activities at ports on the Gulf Coast. The task force comprises elements from the Air Force, Navy, and Coast Guard. The Coast Guard will have operational control and will coordinate with the Department of Homeland Security.

Proficiency in communications with civil agencies and aviation and marine assets has been identified as a training issue. Although the Coast Guard members are well trained and experienced in the communications procedures of civil agencies such as the police and emergency services as well as commercial aviation and marine resources, the military services are not as familiar with these communications networks. Task force members from the armed services will receive training on these nonmilitary communications procedures in order to coordinate security activities.

Problem. You are a member of an "assembled team" of representatives from each of the services as well as a number of design firms. The team has been charged with finding a means of training all of the forces as a single ready-response unit. What various methodologies present the most realistic training scenario possible and would utilize technology advances both in weaponry and in evaluation of the training?

The Department of Defense's solution. Joint operations have been an integral part of America's ability to engage in and win battles. In the not-so-distant past, the effort was expended by four distinct services assembled for a common effort. Now, joint training is truly integrated.

The Department of Defense requires that every service be prepared to fight in an urban setting and to be able to conduct humanitarian and peacekeeping efforts. Recently, Eglin Air Force Base, in the panhandle of Florida, was selected as the site of a $20 million urban combat and antiterrorism training center for Military Operations on Urbanized Terrain (MOUT). This facility will replicate a city in which America's military and its allies will train in all facets of this new type of warfare—switching from humanitarian to combat at a moment's notice (Blair, 2004).

Conclusion

Although working as an instructional designer in a military environment is challenging, it provides an exceptionally rich opportunity for growth as a professional. The knowledge of learning theories and instructional strategies that will be needed can be employed in virtually any manner: instructor-led or instructor-facilitated classroom, informal self-study, formal online learning courses with synchronous and/or asynchronous options, or a blend of any or all of these.

Many of the challenges the instructional designer faces in a military environment, however, require skill sets that go beyond the basic information learned in either a formal or an informal study program. Perhaps most daunting of these is acquiring an understanding and appreciation for military culture. There is a steep learning curve that encompasses everything from familiarity with ranks to military protocols—things not directly related to instructional design. Also, it is virtually impossible to "bend the rules" when working with the military, and designers face scheduling deadlines and budgeting constraints that require tremendous productivity in record time at a minimal cost to the taxpayer. This can make the ID's job particularly stressful.

A greater emphasis on the professional needs of the individual in tandem with the needs of the organization, budget limitations, and quickly evolving technologies are all challenges that make a career as an instructional designer in the military education and training environment difficult but rewarding. Instructional designers who work in the military environment are never bored and, given enough time, will have the opportunity to work in every aspect of instructional design from analysis to evaluation.

Application Questions

1. You've been asked to assist an organization that is establishing computer-based training opportunities for the military system in a third-world nation. Prepare a short (1–2 page) briefing paper of the considerations and constraints for program implementation. Use the Scenarios Solution Discussion Matrix (see Figure 19.4) to assist you with framing your answer.
2. Your client wants to utilize technology in its training program; however, the field of operation does not always provide electronic access. What alternatives might you suggest for a successful program? Use the Full Spectrum diagram (see Figure 19.2) to guide your thoughts. Prepare a table that provides the learning outcome and a comparison of the technology-based strategy with one or more complementary alternatives including capability, skill level, the delivery environment, and development issues or constraints.
3. Humanitarian efforts are a major role for the military of many countries. Prepare a list of Web-based training materials to assist servicemembers charged with learning how to conduct relief efforts. Consider checking websites for first aid, disaster or famine relief, wildfires, and so on.

References

Advanced Distributed Learning. (2004a). About ADL. Retrieved February 8, 2004, from **http://www.adlnet.org/Index.cfm?fuseaction=abtadl**

Advanced Distributed Learning. (2004b). ADL's first International Plugfest showcases global e-learning progress. Retrieved March 31, 2004, from **http://adlnet.org/index.cfm?fuseaction=newsstory&newsid=163**

Australian Department of Defense. (2002). *Force 2020.* Canberra, Australia: Office of Public Affairs & Corporate Communication.

Blair, K. (2004, January 13). Eglin plans for street fight: Proposed training facility would replicate city for urban warfare. *Pensacola New Journal*, p. 1A.

Bratton-Jeffery, M. F., & Jeffery, A. (2003). Integrated training requires integrated design and business models. In A. M. Armstrong (Ed.), *Instructional design for the real world: A view from the* trenches (pp. 218–244). Hershey, PA: Idea Group.

British Army. (2004). Education for personal development. *Serving Soldier*. Retrieved March 15, 2004, from **http://www.army.mod.uk/servingsoldier/career/usefulinfo/epd/ss_cmd_epd_w.html**

Deployed education pilot program. (2004, January 16). U.S. Marine Corps Press Release #0121-04-0746. Retrieved January 29, 2004, from **http://www.usmc.mil/marinelink/mcn2000.nsf/releaseview/B6028E5FBD62821585256E22**

Director for Strategic Plans & Policy. (2000). *Joint vision 2020.* Washington, DC: U.S. Government Printing Office. Retrieved February 8, 2004, from **http://www.dtic.mil/jointvision/jvpub2.htm**

eArmyU.com. (2004). Homepage. Retrieved from **http://www.earmyu.com**

Germany Info. (2004). Background papers: German Armed Forces. Retrieved March 15, 2004, from

http://www.germany-info.org/relaunch/info/archives/Background/armedforces.html

Joint Operations Command, Press & Information Centre. (2004). German contribution to the ISAF. Retrieved March 3, 2004, from **http://www.operations.mod.uk/fingal/germany/isaf_english.htm**

Kennedy, D. (2000, June 22). Clark will leave legacy of progress. Retrieved February 8, 2004, from **http://www.chinfo.navy.mil/navpalib/cno/covenant.html**

Leppo, D. (2004, January 21). Divo-At-Sea training rises to new level [Electronic version]. *Mayport Mirror*. Retrieved February 4, 2004, from **http://pub.mayportmirror.com/Sections.aspx?sec=6101&art=35148&tb=88605**

McGee, P. (2002). Web-based learning design: Planning for diversity. *USDLA Journal, 16*(3). Retrieved June 27, 2004, from **http://www.usdla.org/html/journal/MAR02_Issue/article03.html**

Office of Secretary of the Army. (1999). *The Army vision: Soldier on point for the nation.* Retrieved December 27, 2003, from **http://matthew7hayes.tripod.com/army.htm**

Peacekeepers in the service of peace. (2004). Retrieved March 1, 2004, from **http://www.mindef.gov/sg/peacekeepers/peacekeepers.htm**

Royal Navy. (2004). Joint Operations, North Atlantic Treaty Organisation (NATO). Retrieved March 3, 2004, from **http://www.royal-navy.mod.uk/static/pages/content.php3?page=164**

U.K. Ministry of Defence. (2001). *The future strategic context for defence*. London: Author.

U.S. Department of Defense. (2001). *Quadrennial defense review report.* Retrieved February 8, 2004, from **http://www.defenselink.mil/pubs/qdr2001.pdf**

Glossary

Active duty Servicemember is assigned to an active unit and serves full time as a member of the regular force.

Advanced Distributed Learning Federal initiative that supports a collaboration of government, academia, and industry to provide a philosophy of accessibility, durability, interoperability, and reusability in network and software solutions.

Deployment The active force moves from its standing residence within the United States to an overseas location for a designated period of operation.

Jointness The term exemplifies the independent U.S. Services (Air Force, Army, Marine Corps, Navy) operating as an integrated force sharing resources, personnel, and operational missions.

Joint Vision 2020 The military document that defines the vision and requirements of the Armed Forces in the future. The Joint Vision is published in 10-year increments (e.g., 2010, 2020, 2030).

Total Force All those who work with the U.S. military including active duty, reserves, National Guard, and federal employees.

CHAPTER 20 Performance, Instruction, and Technology in Health Care Education

Craig Locatis
National Institutes of Health

Editors' Introduction

In this chapter, Craig Locatis discusses the role of instructional design and technology in health care settings, especially as related to educating and training physicians and other health professionals. Although professional education is stressed, he also addresses related areas, such as patient and consumer health education. The chapter begins with an overview of education in different areas of health and a brief history of medical education. The latter is used to frame a discussion of education and training in the health care field and the factors currently driving the application of technology and the design of instruction. Educational issues important to the health science community are identified, and an attempt is made to portray the overriding concerns of those working with education and training in health care.

Knowledge and Comprehension Questions

1. Name five settings for performance technology and education and training in health care, and two areas where performance technology is applied and education is developed that cut across the other five settings.
2. Name three reports that affected health professions education and discuss the impact of each.
3. What is content specificity in clinical problem solving and what are its implications for health professions education?
4. What is problem-based learning and what salient research findings of clinical reasoning support it?
5. What is evidence-based medicine and what is the relationship between evidence-based medicine and problem-based learning?
6. What characteristics and features of health professions education besides problem-based learning and evidence-based medicine are important to consider when designing performance and education interventions involving technology?
7. Name four factors affecting the development of technology-based performance and instruction applications in the health care field.

Education and performance technology are employed in different settings. General societal forces affect each context, and those working in a given setting have their own priorities, values, and culture. All of these factors affect the education and training agenda and, consequently, the way technology is used and instruction is created. In this chapter, I review the role of technology in supporting performance and instruction in health care settings, especially as it relates to educating and training physicians and other health professionals. I emphasize medical education particularly, since many trends in medicine carry over to other health science disciplines. Although professional education is stressed, related areas, such as patient and consumer health education, also are addressed.

The chapter begins with an overview of education activities in different health contexts and a brief history of medical education. The latter is used to frame discussion of education and training in health care and the factors currently driving technology application. Clinical reasoning, problem-based learning, and evidence-based medicine are discussed and educational issues important to the health science community are identified.

At the end of this chapter appears a list of annotated URLs to online applications that are either examples of education and performance technology in varied health settings or illustrations of how a theoretical approach has been instantiated in practice. Readers are encouraged to consult the URLs, which are organized to coincide with certain sections of the chapter. They will add meaning and definition to the concepts presented, and some are useful in their own right as health information sources.

The Health Care Education Context

One of the first things that you learn working in the health care field is that it is very broad. Most of us associate health care with hospitals and doctors' offices. The health care field not only involves the delivery of health services, but also biomedical research. It includes the medical profession and its varied subspecialties plus the professions of veterinary medicine, dentistry, nursing, allied health, and public health. Biotechnology (the use of DNA and protein sequences to engineer biological substances) and medical informatics (the application of information and communication technology to support medical research, practice, and education) are emerging as new subspecialties due to advances in genetics and computer science. The health field not only includes varied professions and specialty groups, it also embraces such related sciences and disciplines as anatomy, biochemistry, molecular biology, physiology, and psychology. In addition to academic institutions, hospitals, clinics, and research centers, the health care field also can include certain regulatory agencies and industries involved in drug manufacturing, genetic engineering, and medical instrumentation. When you take a pet to the vet, visit a pharmacy, eat in a restaurant, or buy food at the grocery store, someone in the health sciences, either directly or indirectly, has affected your life.

Health care is comprised of varied subsettings that include (1) academic medical centers and health professions schools, (2) government agencies, (3) pharmaceutical and biotechnology companies and private foundations, (4) professional societies and health associations, and (5) hospitals, clinics, and other caregiving institutions. Two other "settings" are consumer health and continuing education.

The most obvious subsettings for education and training in health care are the professional schools. Medical schools have departments of medical education that evaluate students and courses and develop curricula; departments of biomedical communication that do medical illustration, photography, and video; and academic departments in medical informatics doing teaching and research related to the application of computer and information technologies. They may have telemedicine offices for distant consultation and learning. Medical libraries provide computing and information resources supporting research, practice, and education and, typically, have learning resource centers. Other health professional schools may have one or more similar departments depending on size, and large university medical centers may have several professional schools sharing a single medical library. Health professions schools not only offer courses, but also develop interactive multimedia education programs on CD-ROM or for the Internet.

Government health agencies, pharmaceutical companies, hospitals, and clinics train staff internally and often provide training to others. Some of the external training is geared to keeping public health and other professionals up to date, but much of it is focused on educating the general public and providing consumer health information.

Private foundations focusing on health underwrite the development of health education programs and publish their own materials of interest to professionals and consumers. Professional associations are most actively involved in continuing education. In addition to holding conferences and publishing journals, they produce tutorials and case studies online, on CD-ROM, or in other media formats. Some offer virtual journal clubs online, electronic bulletin boards where health professionals can discuss information appearing in publications. They also offer information in their medical specialty areas for the general public.

Consumer health and continuing education cut across the other health education and training settings. Consumer health includes general education about wellness, health issues, and specific diseases as well as skills training (e.g., first aid) and patient education. Most health professionals are required to complete a certain number of hours of continuing education each year and almost every medical school and professional society has a continuing medical education (CME) program. Sometimes CME credit is provided for attending workshops and conferences, but it also can be obtained by documenting use of educational materials, many of which are online.

Medical Education: a Brief History

Another of the first things that you learn in the health field is the key roles physicians play in providing health care and in leading teams of other health professionals. This leadership extends to management and other areas outside the direct delivery of care (e.g., hospital administration and drug development). Trends and standards in medical education often spill over into other domains as a consequence. But there are additional reasons why medical education affects other health professions. There tends to be more research and evaluation of medical education programs, so much of the empirical evidence guiding education and training in health care emanates from medicine. Other health professions often mimic medicine's teaching methods. Nursing and public health schools, for example, have adopted many of the case-based teaching methods that are currently popular in medicine. Knowing the evolution of medical education is very helpful in understanding the culture of health care and the role of technology.

In the United States, medical education does not commence until one has obtained a baccalaureate degree, and the education process itself can be divided into three phases—undergraduate education comprising the years in medical school, graduate education comprising time in residency, and postgraduate and continuing education to obtain knowledge and certification in additional areas or keep current in one's field. The history of medical education also can be divided into three phases: a prescientific phase, a scientific or "Flexner" phase emphasizing selected disciplines and specialties, and a post-Flexner phase focusing on problem solving and cognition in addition to science.

Prescientific Phase

It can be argued that educational technology has had a place in medicine from the time of Andreas Vesalius and Leonardo da Vinci. Their drawings, based on dissection of anatomical structures, were some of the first attempts to codify medical knowledge based on direct observation rather than speculation, superstition, or religious beliefs, and can be viewed as "research works" as well as teaching aids. Although "science" in medicine dates back to the Renaissance, it was not until the early 1900s that there was a concerted movement to develop a scientific foundation for the medical curriculum, at least in the United States.

Scientific Phase

In 1910, a report by Abraham Flexner to the Carnegie Foundation for the Advancement of Teaching documented the evolution of medical teaching from apprenticeship to more formal education. The "Flexner Report" noted that the first medical schools in the United States in the late 1700s were university affiliated and devised to more efficiently teach basic information that would better prepare students for apprenticeship. At the time of the report, most schools were independent, commercial enterprises that emphasized didactic instruction, and had minimal facilities and no hospital affiliation. Doctors could graduate by memorizing symptoms and doses (e.g., if fever, give quinine). Laboratories, except those used for dissection, were usually absent and there was very little emphasis on the biological sciences and new medical technologies (e.g., stethoscopes, thermometers, x-rays, and laboratory tests) that were revolutionizing medicine at the time.

The Flexner Report called for the reaffiliation of academic programs with colleges, universities, and hospitals, and the introduction of scientific rigor. The following key observation was elaborated in later sections of the report:

> For purposes of convenience, the medical curriculum may be divided into two parts, according as to the work is carried on mainly in laboratories or mainly in the hospital; but the distinction is only superficial, for the hospital is itself in the fullest sense a laboratory. In general, the four year curriculum falls into fairly equal sections: the first two years are devoted mainly to laboratory sciences—anatomy, physiology, pharmacology, pathology; the last two to clinical work in medicine, surgery, and obstetrics. (p. 57)

Scientific rigor and empiricism were the primary concerns, and the scientific method was the glue holding the two parts of the curriculum together. It was assumed that the scientific method could be employed for diagnosing and treating individuals as well as for biomedical research.

The Flexner Report was very influential, revolutionizing teaching and practice by introducing the concept of "scientific medicine" (Bonner, 1998). While medical education improved as a result, the form of medical education the Flexner Report established remained essentially unchanged for 70 years (Association of American Medical Colleges, 1984). Whether intentional or not, its categorization of laboratory and clinical science led to bifurcation of the medical curriculum.

Post-Flexner Phase

In the 1960s and 1970s a movement for problem-based learning (PBL) began that was a reaction to what many perceived as the uncoupling of scientific and clinical content (Albanese & Mitchell, 1993). Its proponents differentiated between learning content within a problem-solving context and applying knowledge to solve problems after it is acquired, arguing that the former approach lets students determine what they need to know and enables them to synthesize information from multiple disciplines, develop transferable problem-solving competence, and acquire effective self-study skills for lifelong learning (Barrows & Tamblyn, 1979). The methodology proposed for attaining these goals was exposing students to a rich array of real and simulated patient cases. Cases are presented and students, usually working in groups, have to distill the patient's problems, generate hypotheses, gather data, and, if their background knowledge is lacking, independently research and discuss information bearing on the case (Barrows & Tamblyn).

Interest in PBL increased when the Association of American Medical Colleges's Panel on the General Professional Education of the Physician and College Preparation in Medicine issued *Physicians for the Twenty-First Century* in 1984 (Albanese & Mitchell, 1993). The *GPEP Report*, as it is often called, recommended (1) reducing lectures and providing more time for independent study, (2) integrating basic science and clinical education, (3) requiring more active problem solving, (4) promoting application of information science and computer technology, (5) considering social science and humanities undergraduate coursework in addition to science when admitting students to medical school, and (6) providing clinical learning experiences in settings other than hospitals. There was concern that students entering medicine were too narrowly focused, that memorizing facts took precedent over acquiring skills, values, and attitudes, that too much emphasis was placed on curing disease at the expense of promoting health, and that the population of patients in hospitals did not reflect the patient population most physicians encounter in practice.

The Association of American Medical Colleges (AAMC) issued another report, *Medical Education in the Information Age*, in 1986 that also impacted medical curricula (Salas & Brownell, 1997). It defined *medical informatics* as a developing body of knowledge and set of techniques concerning the organization and management of information in support of medical research, education, and patient care and called for including informatics in the medical curriculum through the use of databases, decision support systems, and computer-based education. The knowledge explosion in medicine mandated the use of these information systems to teach problem solving, to keep physicians current, and to facilitate lifelong learning.

Factors other than reports from the AAMC have influenced change. Indeed, the reports themselves are to some extent an outgrowth of some of the research and development on clinical problem solving, medical education, and computer-based instruction that was going on at the time, that continues to be conducted, and that still drives reform.

Problem-Based Learning and Evidence-Based Medicine

Allowing students to learn basic and clinical science in the context of cases is supported by research on clinical reasoning indicating that expertise is largely a function of previous problem-solving experience. Problem-solving expertise is dependent on the type of patient cases encountered, rather than involving application of general scientific methods and hypothetico-deductive reasoning as Flexner suggested (Norman, 1985; Patel, Evans, & Groen, 1989). Instead, it depends on acquiring rich, elaborated conceptual information about particular diseases and illnesses (content-specific knowledge) that can be associated with problems patients present (Schmidt, Norman, & Boshuizen, 1990). As expertise develops, problem solving becomes automatic and more a matter of pattern recognition than of formal deduction (Norman, 1985; Patel et al., 1989). Pattern recognition is important in clinical reasoning on several levels. On the one hand, it is recognizing constellations of symptoms patients present as manifestations of different diseases and conditions, but it also involves interpreting images and visual information, such as abnormalities in x-rays or features of skin rashes (Norman et al., 1996).

Other research has documented the benefits of problem-based learning. Meta-analyses and literature reviews indicate that students in PBL curricula perform as well or better than those in traditional programs on clinical reasoning tests, but somewhat less well on basic science exams. PBL students also have much more favorable attitudes about how they are taught (Albanese & Mitchell, 1993; Vernon & Blake 1993). There is also evidence that PBL students tend to integrate, retain, and transfer information better and that they have superior self-directed learning skills (Norman & Schmidt, 1992). Given that the costs and outcomes of traditional and PBL programs are about the same, but PBL is far more enjoyable, some have gone so far as to conclude that the choice between the two approaches is analogous to deciding whether to reproduce by sexual intercourse or by artificial insemination (Norman, 1988).

Since clinical problem solving research strongly supports exposing students to a range of cases representative of what they may encounter in practice and the patients that students are likely to encounter in hospital wards in their clinical clerkships may be unrepresentative and insufficient, computer-based patient management simulations have been identified as one means of providing problem-solving experiences and measuring performance (Barnett, 1989; Norman, Muzzin, Williams, & Swanson, 1985; Piemme, 1988). Computer simulation is an active area of research (Dev et al., 2002; Eva, Neville, & Norman, 1998; Luecht, Hadadi, Swanson, & Case, 1998; Sandrick, 2001).

The movement for evidence-based medicine (EBM) is partially an outgrowth of problem-based learning. EBM involves formulating clinical questions, finding evidence in the medical literature that addresses the questions, critically appraising the evidence, and applying the evidence to specific patients (Craig, Irwig, & Stockler, 2001; Evidence-Based Medicine Working Group, 1992; White, 2004).

One aspect of the EBM movement is to develop meta-analyses and systemic reviews of the literature to produce reliable summaries of the research related to varied medical problems. Another aspect is to apply the methodology in the medical curriculum so that students become so accustomed to consulting information sources while learning that they will continue to do so in practice (cf. Burrows, Moore, Arriaga, Paulaitis, & Lemkau, 2003; Finkel, Brown, Gerber, & Supino, 2003; Wadland, Barry, Farquhar, & White, 1999; White, 2004). There are problems implementing evidenced-based medicine in graduate education and practice where there are time constraints in providing real-time patient care (Green, 2000), and there are many clinical problems where evidence for conclusive solutions is lacking (Myrmel, Lai, & Miller, 2004). Although some have argued that there needs to be more evidence about the effectiveness of evidence-based medicine (Green, 1999), the approach complements problem-based learning.

Other Observations about Health Science Education

Although the current thrust is toward case-based, problem-solving approaches to teaching and the use of evidence in the process of learning and providing care, there are other points that need to be made about health care education. They relate to the roles of risk, altruism and professionalism, sensory perception, science, and educational innovation in health professions curricula. Some of these factors may seem obvious, but they are worthy of discussion nonetheless.

Risk

There is much at stake in health professions education. The subject matter taught, the skills learned, and the techniques and technologies employed can have life-threatening consequences. The health field is one area where errors in learning literally can be a matter of life or death. Moreover, the risks in health education and practice are not only for patients, but also for health practitioners and students. Health professionals do not wear rubber gloves because they are trying to make fashion statements. They are exposed to contagious diseases and work with hazardous substances routinely. The education of health professionals is serious business, which is one reason clinical problem solving and medical education programs are subject to ongoing evaluation and research.

Altruism and Professionalism

The health professions are helping professions. The idea of healing and helping people is more than just rhetoric to those electing careers in health care. The Hippocratic Oath and guidelines published by professional associations and government agencies set standards for conduct. Since the health professions are some of the few where work involves literally laying hands on others, interpersonal skills and open communication are needed to build trust and address the psychosocial aspects of disease (Stewart, 1995; Stewart, Brown, Boon, Galajda, & Sangster, 1999). This dimension of caregiving is so important that medical schools routinely hire actors and laypersons especially trained to mimic varied diseases and conditions that students have to interview and examine. The use of these "standardized" patients and other methods for teaching and assessing professionalism are being actively researched (American Association of Medical Colleges & National Board of Medical Examiners, 2002).

Sensory Perception

It goes almost without saying that most of the work of biomedical practitioners and researchers depends on making observations and reasoning about them. Some of the observations involve numerical data, such as when doctors and nurses take blood pressure or when epidemiologists plot the occurrence and spread of disease. Others involve sounds, such as when doctors and nurses listen to breathing and heartbeat. Most involve images that can be visual representations of numerical values, such as EKGs, or "raw data," such as skin lesions that physicians see during physical examinations, cellular alterations and adaptations that pathologists identify with microscopes, and x-rays and other images that radiologists interpret. The sensory nature of the raw data dealt with by most health professions makes it hard to imagine how biomedical researchers and practitioners could learn without exposure to audiovisual and multimedia information. A diagnosis literally can be seen in a biopsy specimen or a radiograph and there is probably no tougher or sensitive jury when it comes to judging image quality than health professionals.

Science

The role of sensory data in providing health care further underscores the scientific nature of the health professions. Those working with technology addressing performance and instruction in health care collaborate with subject matter experts who are either scientists or practitioners having backgrounds in science, who see teaching as an outgrowth of their efforts to provide care or conduct research, and who are probably less likely than other academics to have their ego involved in their teaching. They are, however, unlikely to accept changes in education without evidence.

Innovation

The penchant for science in health care does not necessarily stifle creativity or engender conservatism, and in fact may foster willingness to experiment with new technologies and teaching methods. Some of the more innovative educational technology applications have been in health care and many of these have been created by health science faculty and practitioners working intuitively on their own. Several of the earliest computer applications in the 1960s involving the development of databases, expert systems, and educational simulations were in the medical field (Blois & Shortliffe, 1990; Hoffer & Barnett, 1990), as were some of the earliest applications of interactive television and satellites for telemedicine (cf. Foote, Parker, & Hudson, 1976; Park, 1974).

Use of advanced computing and network technologies for consultation and education currently are active areas of health science research (Lindberg, 1995). Current work includes representing the entire adult human male and female anatomy digitally (Ackerman, 1998), establishing a collaboratory where scientists and teachers in embryology can work together and provide distance learning online (Cohen, 2002), and developing immersive, virtual reality environments using 3-D images and haptic feedback for surgical planning and training (Dev et al., 2002; Sandrick, 2001). Some innovations are only feasible for use at large medical centers and many may not be widely adopted. Still, on the whole, there is a general inclination in health care to at least experiment with new methods.

Factors and Issues Affecting Performance and Education

Some of the most significant factors affecting performance, the development of instruction, and the application of educational technology in health care are knowledge and research, costs and managed care, regulations and standards, and convergence.

Knowledge and Research

Knowledge advances rapidly in health care, and its currency and integrity are overriding concerns. The volume and timeliness of knowledge has made information technology an important ingredient in education and practice (Salas & Brownell, 1997). As the cost of information technology continues to decline, its use becomes more feasible. When the National Library of Medicine's Medline database of the published medical literature was first ported to CD-ROM, medical libraries could treat searching it as a fixed cost because the database was available by annual subscription instead of on a charge per search basis. This enabled greater student access to current medical research (Rapp, Siegel, & Woodsmall, 1989) and put pressure on faculty to keep themselves more up to date. Now that the Internet has eliminated the National Library of Medicine's need to support a separate telecommunications system for database access, online searching is free to everyone and this may put more pressure on practitioners to keep more current as well. The ubiquity of health information on the Internet from varied sources has expanded the knowledge integrity and timeliness problem, however. It has exacerbated the need to develop standards for health information and guidelines for helping nonprofessionals judge its quality and appropriateness (Robinson, Patrick, Eng, & Gustafson, 1998). One solution is for doctors to prescribe information sources as well as medicine (Bader & Braude, 1998).

Costs and Managed Care

Although tuition for some health professions (e.g., medicine or dentistry) can be high, education is a cost center, not a profit center, for health care institutions. These costs often are underwritten from income generated by hospitals and clinics. Attempts to curtail rising health care costs, especially with the introduction of managed care, not only affect the delivery of health services, but of professional education and training as well. There is more pressure on faculty to spend less time teaching and more time seeing patients and to limit the duration of individual patient encounters, further eroding the time faculty can coach students at the bedside or examination room (American Association of Medical Colleges & National Board of Medical Examiners, 2002).

Managed care has sparked faculty interest in information technology as a way to lighten the burden of teaching, while others have become interested in its use for patient and consumer health education. Ironically, while many health insurers see information and education as a means to control costs (people knowledgeable about health tend to need fewer services), many patients and lay people view it as a way to ensure they are receiving appropriate care (Bottles, 1999).

Regulations, Standards, and Licensure

Regulations and standards affect education and training because they dictate what has to be learned. The recently enacted Health Insurance Portability and Accountability Act (HIPAA) establishes rights of access to medical information and sets standards for privacy that impacts how educators and researchers can use medical records (DiBenedetto, 2003). In addition, many of the substances and devices employed in health care and the procedures for their use are regulated. There also are requirements concerning the certification of health personnel and mandated continuing education that impact curricula. When educational reforms such as problem-based learning are proposed, differences between what the curriculum teaches and what the exams measure have to be addressed (cf. Albanese & Mitchell, 1993; Vernon & Blake, 1993). The PBL movement has spawned research efforts to devise better ways to assess clinical problem-solving on licensure exams (Clyman, Melnick, & Clauser, 1995).

Convergence

Converging technologies are affecting education and training in all fields, including health care. As television, telephony, and computing come together, applications are emerging incorporating these varied modalities. It is possible to stream a video presentation and to simultaneously have a videoconference discussing the presentation's contents. The same conferencing hardware and software may allow physicians to consult each other at a distance and to share whiteboard and application software to discuss information about a case and to find information related to it. Students used to have to use standalone computer-based instruction packages to learn content initially and then needed to access databases separately on CD-ROM or online to search for additional information. As instruction has become more Web-centric and more databases have become Web accessible, educational and information resources can be unified by simply establishing links. The boundaries between educational and informational applications are becoming increasingly murky, especially in problem-based learning and evidence-based medicine, where the use of information resources is part of the learning methodology.

Summary

ID professionals seeking education and performance technology positions in the health care field need to understand the philosophical and empirical foundations of learning and the tensions that exist as teaching institutions move away from the more compartmentalized traditional approaches to teaching that resulted from the Flexner Report. They need to be aware of the roles that risk, professionalism, sensory perception, and science have in developing solutions to performance and instruction problems. They need to understand how knowledge and research, regulations, standards and licensure requirements, managed care, and convergence affect the application of technology in health care and their role in the health care enterprise.

Application Questions

1. *Problem-based learning* and *content specificity* are terms unique to medical education. Identify constructs and concepts in general learning psychology and instructional theory that are related. What findings in general learning research also support the approach?
2. When experienced physicians encounter very unusual cases, their reasoning strategies often regress and become more like those of novice medical students. Why does this happen? How do pattern recognition and content specificity help to explain the phenomenon?
3. When experienced physicians make misdiagnoses, it is often because a less familiar disease or condition mimics many of the symptoms of a more familiar one. How do the reasoning strategies that work well for physicians most of the time create complications some of the time?
4. How can information and performance systems reduce the information practitioners need to memorize? In what ways might they help prevent misdiagnoses?
5. Write a summary describing what, to you, would be the ideal medical (or other health professions) curriculum. Indicate how you would teach and assess needed reasoning and interpersonal skills. Provide a rationale for each key feature of the curriculum,

drawing on problem solving, learning, and educational research.

6. Write a summary of what you believe would be the ideal performance support system for medical practice and provide a rationale for each feature. How would the system relate to existing or proposed systems for computerized medical records and current databases of medical knowledge? Would the system have features for synchronous or asynchronous collaboration among practitioners or patients?

7. Inspect the websites of several schools in the health professions and examine course descriptions and syllabi. Decide whether each school follows a predominately traditional or problem-based learning approach. Identify objectives and resources at each site supporting your judgment.

8. Examine several popular health care sites for the general public. Identify those that appear to provide better or more scientifically sound information. Generate criteria for evaluating the quality of online health information.

Annotated URLs

Academic Educational Resource and Innovation Examples

Loyola University Medical School/LUMEN—The LUMEN project is an effort to make major portions of medical education publicly accessible online. **http://www.meddean.luc.edu/lumen/**

Stanford University Medical School—The websites describe Stanford resources on CD or available online. Advanced educational research projects in surgical simulation are also discussed at the SUMMIT sites.

Educational Learning Technology Services homepage: **http://ane.stanford.edu/Edtech/index.html**

SUMMIT homepage: **http://summit.stanford.edu**

Current projects page: **http://summit.stanford.edu/research/current.html**

University of Iowa Virtual Hospital—The Virtual Hospital was an effort to make major portions of medical education publicly accessible online and to provide other medical information resources to practitioners. Although the site ceased operations in January 2006, much of its content remains available. Homepage: **http://www.vh.org**

University of Utah Medical Library/Knowledge Weavers—The Knowledge Weavers are a group that consults with faculty on the development of course materials. The program at the University of Utah also is part of a consortium supporting the HEAL project, a repository of sharable educational objects for health education.

Homepage: **http://medlib.med.utah.edu/kw/**

Health Assets Education Library (HEAL): **http://www.healcentral.org/index.jsp**

University of Washington/Department of Medical Education and Biomedical Informatics—The sites describe an academic program in medical education and informatics, offer a link to an online patient education program indicative of those used in problem-based learning, and provide examples of online continuing education courses typically offered by medical schools.

Homepage: **https://www.dme.washington.edu/**

Patient simulation page: **https://www.dme.washington.edu/patientsimulation/overview.html**

Continuing education online courses: **http://uwcme.org/site/courses/online.php**

Visible Embryo Project—A project to develop a repository of resources in embryology that can be shared among institutions.

Homepage: **http://netlab.gmu.edu/visembryo/index.html**

Products and animations: **http://www.uic.edu/com/surgery/embryo/index.htm**

Government Educational Resource Examples

Centers for Disease Control and Prevention (CDC)—The sites are to online and other resources that keep public health professionals up to date in epidemiology, biochemistry, and related fields and provide timely training in response to emergencies arising from epidemics or bioterror. The National Training Laboratory Network at CDC uses satellites and the Internet to link state health departments with videoconferences and webcasts.

Homepage: **http://www.cdc.gov**

National Training Laboratory Network: **http://www.phppo.cdc.gov/nltn/**

National Institutes of Health—The various institutes of the National Institutes of Health fund development of educational materials. Its videocast department regularly broadcasts seminars and meetings via the Internet on a range of health topics.

Homepage: **http://www.nih.gov**

Videocast page: **http://videocast.nih.gov**

Visible Human Project—A project to develop an image database of the entire male and female adult anatomy as both gross anatomy and magnetic resonance images (MRIs) and computer tomography (CT) scans that can be used by others to create diagnostic tools and educational programs.

Homepage: **http://www.nlm.nih.gov/research/visible/visible_human.html**

Additional websites—Check out the National Institute of Health and National Library of Medicine websites listed under Consumer Education, following.

Company/Foundation Educational Resource Examples

Pfizer—The site has links to information concerning use of company products and to health resources geared to different populations.

Homepage: **http://www.pfizer.com**

Merck Pharmaceuticals—The company maintains the Merck Medicus website for health professionals and the Merck Source site with resources for the general public.

Merck Medicus: **http://www.merckmedicus.com**

Merck Source: **http://www.mercksource.com**

Foundations—The Kellogg, Nemours, and Robert Wood Johnson foundations are three of the more active in funding health research and education programs. Nemours has funded the DuPont Children's Hospital PedsEducation and KidsHealth websites for health professionals and consumers (see Clinic and Hospital URLs, following).

Kellogg Foundation homepage: **http://www.WKKF.org**

Nemours Foundation homepage: **http://nemours.org**

Robert Wood Johnson Foundation homepage: **http://www.rwjf.org**

Professional Society and Health Association Educational Resource Examples

American Academy of Pediatrics—Its site typifies consumer health information offered by many health professional societies.

Homepage: **http://www.aap.org/**

American College of Cardiology—The ACC has an online catalog to education resources for cardiologists as well as online information and media resources, some of which cardiologists can use with their patients.

Homepage: **http://www.acc.org**

American Heart Association—The AHA website is consumer oriented, with cooking tips and other information for maintaining a healthy heart.

Homepage: **http://www.americanheart.org**

iPeds Interactive Journal of Pediatrics—This electronic journal in pediatrics consists mainly of interactive case presentations. Questions regarding diagnosis and treatment are interspersed throughout the case presentations.

http://www.medconnect.com/ipeds/ipedsmain.asp

Radiological Society of North America Education Portal—The RSNA website provides case studies, tutorials, and a virtual journal club for students and health professionals. It offers information about different imaging techniques for the general public.

http://www.rsna.org/education/

Hospital/Clinic Websites and Educational Resource Examples

Brigham and Women's Hospital—This Harvard-affiliated institution is typical of the kind of information provided by hospitals.

Homepage: **http://www.brighamandwomens.org**

DuPont Children's Hospital—This hospital provides education for health professionals at its PedsEducation website and information on health topics geared especially for children at its KidsHealth website.

DuPont Children's Hospital PedsEducation: **http://www.pedseducation.org**

DuPont Children's Hospital KidsHealth: **http://www.kidshealth.org**

Mayo Clinic—The three websites listed mirror the three activities of the clinic. One provides information about the clinic itself, another provides information for patients and consumers about their health, and the third provides information about its academic programs as a teaching institution.

Patient information: **http://www.mayoclinic.com**

Clinic information: **http://www.mayoclinic.org**

Academic information: **http://www.mayo.edu**

Consumer Educational Resource Examples

National Library of Medicine—The NLM maintains databases to the medical literature that are of primary interest to health professionals, but its MedlinePlus site is for the general public. It has links to online health resources that have been independently vetted to insure content integrity and has medical dictionaries and tutorials to help consumers understand health concepts. The ClinicalTrails website is of interest to persons wanting to participate in clinical trials of new drugs and therapies, usually persons for whom conventional care has been unsuccessful.

Homepage: **http://www.nlm.nih.gov**

MedlinePlus: **http://medlineplus.gov**

ClinicalTrials: **http://clinicaltrials.gov**

National Institutes of Health—All the institutes comprising the NIH offer some form of consumer health information related to the health problems that each addresses. The various institute homepages can be accessed from the NIH institutes page.

Homepage: **http://www.nih.gov/icd/**

Additional websites—Check out virtually all the Clinic and Hospital sites, the Professional Society and Health Association sites, and the Pfizer and Merck sites in the Company/Foundation sites listed previously.

Continuing Medical Education Educational Resource Examples

Cyberounds—This commercial website offers engaging CME involving online discussions about cases in specialties posted by experts.

Homepage: **http://www.cyberounds.com**

University of Florida—This medical school CME website streams presentations made at the school as a way to extend access to practitioners in the field.

Grand Rounds: **http://medinfo.ufl.edu/cme/grounds/index.shtml**

University of Washington—The University of Washington Continuing Medical Education site is typical of the CME offering of many medical schools.

Continuing education online courses: **http://uwcme.org/site/courses/online.php**

Additional websites—See all the professional Society and Health Association websites listed previously.

Websites of Organizations Concerned with Problem-Based Learning

American Association of Medical Colleges—The AAMC has been instrumental in providing information about problem-based learning. It establishes curriculum and evaluation guidelines for medical schools.

http://www.aamc.org

National Board of Medical Examiners—Most states have their own tests for licensure and certification, but the NBME is the primary national licensure and certification agency that is honored by most states. It is developing tests to measure problem solving and has sponsored research about the approach.

http://www.nbme.org

The University of Washington Patient Simulation Page—This is an example of a highly interactive online case that illustrates the approach.

Patient simulation page: **https://www.dme.washington.edu/patientsimulation/overview.html**

Additional websites—Check out most of Professional Society and Health Association websites listed previously.

Websites of Organizations Concerned with Evidence-Based Medicine

Agency for Healthcare Research and Quality—This government agency does technology assessments summarizing the research on different medical practices and therapies. It provides evidence based guidelines for providing clinical care and supports the National Guideline Clearinghouse.

Homepage: **http://www.ahrq.gov/**

National Guideline Clearinghouse: **http://www.guideline.gov**

Bandolier—An independent journal summarizing research evidence related to health. It has been supported by the United Kingdom's National Health Service and is currently supported by Oxford University Medical School and by subscription.

http://www.jr2.ox.ac.uk/bandolier/

Cochrane Collaboration—An independent organization of volunteers contributing summaries of medical research in varied specialty areas.

http://www.cochrane.org

Healthgate—A private company providing evidence-based medicine services. Online tutorials on different evidence-based approaches to care are provided.

http://www.healthgate.com

References

Ackerman, M. (1998). The visible human project. *Proceedings of the IEEE, 86*(3), 504–511.

Albanese, M., & Mitchell, S. (1993). Problem-based learning: A review of the literature on its outcomes and implementation issues. *Academic Medicine, 68*(1), 52–81.

Association of American Medical Colleges. (1984). *Physicians for the twenty-first century.* Washington, DC: Association of American Medical Colleges.

Association of American Medical Colleges. (1986). *Medical education in the information age.* Washington, DC: Association of American Medical Colleges.

Association of American Medical Colleges & the National Board of Medical Examiners. (2002). *Embedding professionalism in medical education: Assessment as a tool for implementation.* Philadelphia, PA: National Board of Medical Examiners.

Bader, S., & Braude, R. (1998). "Patient informatics": Creating new partnerships in medical decision making. *Academic Medicine 73*(4), 408–411.

Barnett, O. (1989). Information technology in undergraduate medical education. *Academic Medicine, 64*(4), 187–190.

Barrows, H. S., & Tamblyn, R. M. (1979). Problem-based learning in health sciences education. (National Library of Medicine Monograph, Contract No. 1 LM-6-4721). Bethesda, MD: National Institutes of Health.

Blois, M., & Shortliffe, E. (1990). The computer meets medicine: Emergence of a discipline. In E. Shortliffe & L. Perreault (Eds.), *Medical informatics: Computer applications in health care* (pp. 3–36). Reading, MA: Addison-Wesley.

Bonner, T. (1998). Searching for Abraham Flexner. *Academic Medicine, 73*(2), 160–166.

Bottles, K. (1999). The effect of the information revolution on American medical schools. *Medscape General Medicine, 1*(7), n.p.

Burrows, S., Moore, K., Arriaga, J., Paulaitis, G., & Lemkau, H. (2003). Developing an "evidence-based medicine and use of the biomedical literature" component as a longitudinal theme of an outcomes based medical school curriculum: Year 1. *Journal of the Medical Library Association, 91*(1), 34–41.

Cohen, J. (2002). Embryo development at a click of a mouse. *Science, 297*(5587), 1629.

Clyman, S., Melnick, D., & Clauser, B. (1995). Computer-based simulations. In E. L. Mancall & P.G. Bashook (Eds.), *Assessing clinical reasoning: The oral examination and alternative methods* (pp. 139–149). Evanston, IL: American Board of Medical Specialties.

Craig, J., Irwig, L., & Stockler, M. (2001). Evidence-based medicine: Useful tools for decision making. *Medical Journal of Australia, 174*(5), 248–253.

Dev, P., Montgomery, K., Senger, S., Heinrichs, W. L., Srivastava, S., & Waldron, K. (2002). Simulated medical learning environments on the Internet. *Journal of the American Medical Informatics Association,* 9(5), 554–556.

DiBenedetto, D. (2003). HIPAA Privacy 101: Essentials for case management practice. *Lippencott's Case Management, 8*(1), 14–23.

Eva, K., Neville, A., & Norman, G. (1998). Exploring the etiology of content specificity: Factors influencing analogic transfer and problem solving. *Academic Medicine, 73*(10), S1–S5.

Evidence-Based Medicine Working Group. (1992). Evidence-based medicine: A new approach to teaching the practice of medicine. *Journal of the American Medical Association, 268*(17), 2420–2425.

Finkel, M., Brown, H., Gerber, L., & Supino, P. (2003). Teaching evidence-based medicine to medical students. *Medical Teacher, 25*(2), 202–204.

Flexner, A. (1910). *Medical education in the United States and Canada: A report to the Carnegie Foundation for the Advancement of Teaching,* Boston: Updyke. Reprinted in 1973 by Science and Health Publications, Bethesda, MD.

Foote, D., Parker, E., & Hudson, H. (1976). *Telemedicine in Alaska: the ATS-6 satellite biomedical demonstration. Final report of the evaluation of the ATS-6 biomedical demonstration in Alaska.* Palo Alto, CA: Institute for Communications Research, Stanford University.

Green, M. (1999). Graduate medical education training in clinical epidemiology, critical appraisal, and evidence-based medicine: A critical review of curricula. *Academic Medicine, 74*(12), 1184–1185.

Green, M. (2000). Evidence-based medicine training in graduate medical education: Past, present and future.

Journal of Evaluation in Clinical Practice, 6(2), 121–138.

Hoffer, E., & Barnett, G. O. (1990). Computer in medical education. In E. Shortliffe & L. Perreault (Eds.), *Medical informatics: Computer applications in health care* (pp.535–561). Reading, MA: Addison-Wesley.

Lindberg, D. (1995). HPCC and the national information infrastructure: An overview. *Bulletin of the Medical Library Association, 83*(1), 29–31.

Luecht, R., Hadadi, A., Swanson, D., & Case, S. (1998). A comparative study of a comprehensive basic sciences test using paper-and-pencil and computerized formats. *Academic Medicine, 73*(10), S51–S53.

Myrmel, T., Lai, D., & Miller, D. (2004). Can the principles of evidence-based medicine be applied to the treatment of aortic dissections? *European Journal of Cardio-Thoracic Surgery, 25*(2), 236–242.

Norman, G. (1985). The role of knowledge in the teaching and assessment of problem solving. *Journal of Instructional Development, 8*(1), 7–10.

Norman, G. (1988). Problem-solving skills, solving problems, and problem-based learning. *Medical Education 22*(4), 279–286.

Norman, G., Brooks, L., Cunnington, J., Shali, V., Marriott, M., & Regehr, G. (1996). Expert-novice differences in the use of history and visual information from patients. *Academic Medicine 71*(Suppl.), S62–S64.

Norman, G., Muzzin, L., Williams, R., & Swanson, D. (1985). Simulation in health science education. *Journal of Instructional Development, 8*(1), 11–17.

Norman, G., & Schmidt, H. (1992). The psychological basis for problem-based learning. *Academic Medicine, 67*(9), 557–286.

Park, B. (1974). *An introduction to telemedicine: Interactive television for delivery of health services*, New York: Alternate Media Center, New York University School of the Arts.

Patel, V., Evans, D., & Groen, G. (1989). Biomedical knowledge and clinical reasoning. In D. Evans & V. Patel (Eds.), *Cognitive science in medicine* (pp. 895–935). Cambridge, MA: MIT Press.

Piemme, T. (1988). Computer-assisted learning and evaluation in medicine. *Journal of the American Medical Association, 260*(3), 367–372.

Rapp, B., Siegel, E., & Woodsmall, R. (1989). Medline on CD-ROM: Summary of a report of a nationwide evaluation. In R. Woodsmall, B. Lyon-Hartmann, & E. Siegel (Eds.), *Medline on CD-ROM* (pp. 172–186). Medford, NJ: Learned Information.

Robinson, T., Patrick, K., Eng, T., & Gustafson, D. (1998). An evidence-based approach to interactive health communication: A challenge for medicine in the information age. *Journal of the American Medical Association, 280*(14), 1264–1269.

Salas, A., & Brownell, A. (1997). Introducing information technologies into the medical curriculum: Activities of the AAMC. *Academic Medicine, 72*(3), 191–193.

Sandrick, K. (2001). Virtual reality surgery: Has the future arrived? *Bulletin of the American College of Surgeons, 86*(3), 42–43, 63.

Schmidt, H., Norman, G., & Boshuizen, H. (1990). A cognitive perspective of medical expertise: Theory and implications. *Academic Medicine, 65*(10), 611–621.

Stewart, M. (1995). Effective physician-patient communication and health outcomes: A review. *Canadian Medical Association Journal, 152*(9), 1423–1433.

Stewart, M., Brown, J., Boon, H., Galajda, J., & Sangster, M. (1999). Evidence on patient-doctor communication. *Cancer Prevention and Control, 3*(1), 25–30.

Vernon, D., & Blake, R. (1993). Does problem-based learning work? A meta-analysis of evaluative research. *Academic Medicine, 68*(7), 550–563.

Wadland, W., Barry, H., Farquhar, L., & White, A. (1999). Training medical students in evidence-based medicine: A community campus approach. *Family Medicine, 31*(10), 703–708.

White, B. (2004). Making evidence-based medicine doable in everyday practice. *Family Practice Management, 11*(2), 51–58.

CHAPTER 21

Trends and Issues in P–12 Educational Change

Charles M. Reigeluth
Indiana University

Francis M. Duffy
Gallaudet University

Editors' Introduction

In this chapter Charles Reigeluth and Frank Duffy argue that piecemeal change is inadequate in P–12 education today and that systemic change is crucial to meeting our students' and communities' needs in the information age. They review some of the different meanings for the term *systemic change* and describe ecological systemic change as addressing three key areas of a school system. They also argue that a "process approach" to ecological systemic change is more important than a "product approach." The role of instructional design and technology specialists in the change process is described as well as two projects that have been conducted for districtwide ecological systemic transformation. Finally, the authors discuss needs and future directions for ecological systemic change in P–12 education.

Knowledge and Comprehension Questions

1. What are the triple societal forces creating pressure for education reform in American school districts?
2. Describe the difference between *piecemeal* change and *systemic* change.
3. Explain why systemic change is needed in P–12 education today.
4. Describe the four different definitions of *systemic change* found in the literature.
5. What is the dominant paradigm for improving P–12 education in America today?
6. What are the three change paths that must be followed simultaneously to create and sustain ecological systemic change?
7. What are the key differences between product and process approaches to change?
8. What are the three major components of the GSTE?
9. What are the five phases of the GSTE's discrete events? Describe the focus of each phase.
10. What conditions need to be in place before launching an ecological systemic change effort?
11. What are the steps in the Step-Up-To-Excellence methodology? Describe the focus of each step.
12. What are the special teams and roles that provide change leadership for the Step-Up-To-Excellence methodology?
13. Describe the role of instructional design and technology specialists in the systemic change process.
14. Describe the ecological systemic change efforts that have occurred in two school districts in the United States.
15. Describe five of the biggest needs for educational reform in P–12 education.

The field of instructional design and technology (IDT) is focused on improving learning and performance (Reiser & Dempsey, 2002). Learning and performance typically occur within organizations (systems), including school districts, universities, businesses, government institutions, and others. IDT professionals design instructional systems to improve learning and performance, but over the past 20 years there has been increasing recognition that organizational characteristics can severely constrain learning and performance within those organizations (Burke, 2002; Cummings & Worley, 2001). Consequently, it is often necessary for IDT professionals to work for significant changes on an organizational level.

Systems thinkers in corporate and educational contexts have made much progress over the past 20 years in developing knowledge about systemic organizational change (see e.g., Ackoff, 1981; Banathy, 1991, 1996; Checkland, 1984; Duffy, 2002, 2003; Duffy, Rogerson, & Blick, 2000; Hammer & Champy, 2001; Jenlink, Reigeluth, Carr, & Nelson, 1996, 1998; Pasmore, 1988). This chapter focuses on issues and trends in systemic organizational change in the P–12 education sector (preschool through 12th grade), but most of these issues and trends are relevant to such change in other sectors and countries.

In the P–12 education sector in the United States, there has periodically been pressure for change, from Sputnik in the early 1960s to the *Nation at Risk* report (National Commission on Excellence in Education, 1983), and most recently the accountability movement as represented by the No Child Left Behind (NCLB) Act. Each of these pressures has been a response to perceived shortcomings of our public education systems in meeting the rapidly changing educational needs and realities of our society.

Although not much has changed in the design and functioning of school systems, what has changed is the amount of political and social pressure being applied by NCLB to school districts to improve the quality of education. The pressure comes in the form of standards, assessments, and accountability and these dynamics can be characterized as the triple engines driving school improvement into the twenty-first century. These dynamics are not going away anytime soon, and school districts desperately need knowledge that will help them respond effectively to these pressures.

In this chapter we begin with a discussion of types of change in education. Then we briefly review current knowledge for systemic redesign, including a discussion of the role of instructional design and technology specialists in the systemic change process, followed by a description of several recent projects for systemic redesign of a school district. We conclude with a discussion of needs and future directions for knowledge in this important area.

Types of Change in Education

Two distinctions may be helpful here: one is between piecemeal and systemic change, and the other is between product and process approaches to change.

Piecemeal vs. Systemic Change

Perhaps the most important distinction among types of change is that between *piecemeal* change, which entails tinkering or adjusting one or two parts of a system but leaving the basic structure of the system intact, and *systemic* change, which entails redesigning or transforming the whole system. When a system's environment is relatively stable, piecemeal change is typically the more appropriate type of change, whereas when a system's environment is undergoing massive changes, systemic change is typically more appropriate. In either event, if a significant change is made in one part of a system, that part will usually become incompatible with other parts of the system, and the system will work to change that part back to what it was before. This pattern of change and reversion has occurred frequently in P–12 educational systems.

The term *systemic change* is used in several different ways, which often results in miscommunication. Squire and Reigeluth (2000) identify four distinct meanings of the term:

1. *Statewide policy systemic change.* Systemic change is statewide changes in tests, curricular guidelines, teacher certification requirements, textbook adoptions, funding policies, and so forth that are coordinated to support one another (Smith & O'Day, 1990). This meaning is how policymakers typically think of systemic change.
2. *Districtwide systemic change.* Systemic change is any changes or programs instituted throughout a school district. This meaning is how P–12 educators typically think of systemic change.
3. *Schoolwide systemic change.* Systemic change is any change or program instituted throughout a school, and it typically involves "a deeper (re)thinking of the purposes of schooling and the goals of education" (Squire & Reigeluth, 2000, p. 144). This meaning is how educators participating in the Coalition of Essential Schools typically think of systemic change.
4. *Ecological systemic change.* Systemic change is based on a clear understanding of interrelationships and interdependencies within the system of interest and between the system of interest and its "systemic environment" (the larger system of which it is a part, its peer systems

within that larger system, and other systems with which it interacts outside of its larger system). It recognizes that a significant change in one part of a system requires changes in other parts of the system. It also recognizes the need for changes in three spheres: the system's core work processes, its social architecture, and relationships with its environment (Duffy et al., 2000). Of necessity, this meaning of systemic change subsumes all the other three meanings, and it is how "systems thinkers" view systemic change (see e.g., Ackoff, 1981; Banathy, 1996; Checkland, 1984; Emery & Purser, 1996; Senge, 1990).

Ever since John Goodlad (1984) wrote *A Place Called School* and argued for school-based management, schoolwide systemic change (see list item 3) has been the dominant paradigm for improving schooling in America's school districts. Yet, after 30 years of using this process, very little has changed in the design and functioning of school systems. We believe that ecological systemic change (see list item 4) is the only kind of change that has the potential to create and sustain systemwide improvement in school districts. This is because the ecological systemic change process requires simultaneous improvements in three key areas of a school system: (1) the core and supporting work; (2) the internal "social architecture" (which includes organization culture, communication, the reward system, and power and political dynamics); and (3) the district's relationship with its external environment. The literature and research on ecological (or whole-system) improvement is clear that organizationwide improvement can only be accomplished by following those three paths (e.g., Duffy, 2002, 2003, 2004; Emery, 1977; Pasmore, 1988; Trist, Higgin, Murray, & Pollack, 1963).

Product vs. Process Approaches to Change

It is helpful to distinguish between the product and process of change. The *product* of the change process is the redesigned or transformed educational system. School change models that are product oriented focus on what the new educational system should look like by describing and prescribing what the schools should be like. For example, the 10 principles of the Coalition of Essential Schools (CES) describe what schools should be like (Sizer, 2002). They offer no guidance, however, to help educators engage in a process that will result in the successful implementation of the principles. The "comprehensive school reform" designs, such as Success for All, CoNECT, and Modern Red Schoolhouse (see e.g., Stringfield, Ross, & Smith, 1996), are similarly product focused. At the 2002 conference of the American Educational Research Association (AERA), researchers presented findings on the NAS models that revealed significant implementation problems and failures. These findings provide growing evidence that we need a better understanding of the *process* of transforming schools and districts, and that no matter how good a design is, it will not succeed in its implementation if a sound transformation process is not used (Joseph & Reigeluth, in press).

Given these considerations, the remainder of this chapter focuses on the process orientation to ecological systemic change. We begin with an overview of the current knowledge for this kind of systemic change. We next describe a few projects that have used this approach. We conclude with a discussion of needs and future directions.

Current Knowledge about the Ecological Systemic Change Process

In this section, we describe two major lines of work regarding the ecological systemic change process: the Guidance System for Transforming Education by Jenlink et al. (1996, 1998), and Step-Up-To-Excellence by Frank Duffy (2002, 2003, 2004). Following this description, we discuss the role of instructional design and technology specialists in the systemic change process.

Guidance System for Transforming Education

The Guidance System for Transforming Education (GSTE) (Jenlink et al., 1996, 1998) is a process model for facilitating systemic change. The GSTE was designed to provide process guidelines to a facilitator engaging in a districtwide systemic change effort. The GSTE does not provide any indication of what changes should be made in the district (the "product" issue). Rather, it provides the facilitator with guidance about the process in which the school district and its community should engage for systemic change to occur successfully.

The GSTE is comprised of:

- A set of core values about the change process (Table 21.1).
- Some "discrete events" (Table 21.2), a chronological series of activities for engaging in systemic change.
- Some "continuous events" (Figure 21.1), activities that must be addressed continuously throughout much or all of the change process (Jenlink et al., 1998).

The discrete events listed in Table 21.2 reflect some tentative revisions based on Reigeluth's experience using the GSTE with a small school district in Indianapolis (described later in this chapter). Furthermore, there are many principles and suggested activities that help one to understand and engage in those events.

TABLE 21.1 Core values underlying the GSTE

Caring for children and their future	Respect
Systemic thinking	Responsibility
Evolution of mindsets about education	Readiness
Inclusiveness	Collaboration
Stakeholder empowerment and ownership	Community
Participant commitment	Ideal vision
Co-evolution	Wholeness
Facilitator	Common language
Process orientation	Conversation
Context	Democracy
Time	Culture
Space	

TABLE 21.2 Revised discrete events in the GSTE

Phase I. Initiate Systemic Change Effort	1. Facilitators assess and enhance their own readiness for the process and form a Support Team. 2. Facilitators establish or redefine a relationship with a school district and discuss per diem payment for Event 3. 3. Facilitators assess and enhance district readiness for change. 4. Negotiate and sign a contract/agreement with the superintendent and board for Phase II.
Phase II. Develop Starter Team	5. Facilitators and superintendent form the Starter Team. 6. Hold a retreat to develop the Starter Team dynamic. 7. Develop Starter Team understanding of systems, design, mental models, the systemic change process, dialogue, and small-group facilitation. 8. Assess and enhance district and community capacity for change. (Identify assets and barriers, and use community forums if needed.) 9. Develop an agreement/contract with the Starter Team and School Board for Phase III, determine resource needs, and plan a budget for internal funding and a proposal for external funding.
Phase III. Develop District-Wide Framework and Capacity for Change	10. Starter Team expands into the Leadership Team, Starter Team becomes facilitators, facilitator becomes an advisor and "critical friend." 11. Hold a one-day retreat to develop the Leadership Team dynamic. 12. Facilitators develop Leadership Team understanding of systems, design, mental models, the systemic change process, dialogue, and small-group facilitation. (Address throughout Events 13–17.) 13. Leadership Team develops a districtwide framework with broad stakeholder participation (community forums). This includes identifying changes in the community's educational needs, and using them to develop a mission, vision, and core values for an ideal school system. It takes this opportunity to assess and enhance district and community interest in, and culture for, systemic change. It develops pyramid groups for broad stakeholder involvement. 14. Leadership Team identifies current and recent change efforts and decides what relation those should have with this effort. 15. Leadership Team develops a change process strategy, including capacity building and funding. Advisor's role is defined and funded for Phase IV.
Phase IV. Create Ideal Designs for a New Educational System	16. Leadership Team forms and capacitates building-level Design Teams and conducts a workshop on the framework. 17. Design Teams create building-level designs and systems for evaluating those designs with broad stakeholder involvement. Leadership Team supports and monitors the Design Teams. 18. Leadership Team forms and capacitates a district-level Design Team. 19. Design Team creates a design for ideal district administrative and governance systems, and systems for evaluating that design, with broad stakeholder involvement. Leadership Team supports and monitors this Design Team.

TABLE 21.2 Continued

Phase IV. Create Ideal Designs for a New Educational System	20. Design Teams create building-level processes for evolving as close as possible to their ideal designs. Leadership Team supports and monitors the Design Teams. 21. Carry out implementation plans, formative evaluations, and revisions of the evolving designs and the implementation processes. 22. Periodically evolve the ideal designs (building level and district level).

Evaluate and improve the change process.
Build and maintain political support.
Sustain motivation.
Develop and sustain appropriate leadership.
Build and maintain trust.
Evolve mindset and culture.
Periodically secure necessary resources.
Develop skills in systems thinking.
Periodically and appropriately allocate necessary resources.
Develop group-process and team-building skills.
Build team spirit.
Engage in self-disclosure.
Engage in reflection.
Develop design skills.
Communicate with stakeholders (two-way).
Build and evolve community.
Foster organizational learning.
Build an organizational memory.

FIGURE 21.1 Continuous events in the GSTE.

Step-Up-To-Excellence

Step-Up-To-Excellence (SUTE) (Duffy, 2002, 2003, 2004) is a process methodology designed to help change leaders in school districts create and sustain whole-district improvement. This methodology combines proven and effective tools for school system improvement. Although these tools have been used singly for more than 40 years in different kinds of organizations, they never have been combined to provide educators with a comprehensive, unified, systematic, and systemic methodology for redesigning their entire school system.

Step-Up-To-Excellence is designed for successful or average-performing school systems that want to step up to the next higher performance level. It can also be used with failing or low-performing districts if these districts develop the necessary conditions for successful whole-district change. These conditions include:

- Senior leaders who act on the basis of personal courage, passion, and vision; not on the basis of fear or self-survival.
- Senior leaders who conceive of their districts as whole systems; not as a collection of individual schools and programs.
- Leaders and followers who have a clear view of the opportunities that systemic redesign offers them; not a view of "We can't do this because . . . "
- Leaders and followers who possess the professional intellect, change-minded attitudes, and change-management skills to move their districts toward higher levels of performance; not people without an inkling about the requirements of systemic change management.
- Sufficient human, financial, and technical resources to launch systemic change with the knowledge that more resources will be required to sustain the effort; not resources solely acquired through a within-district reallocation of funds that undermines the overall operations of the district.

If these conditions are not in place before educators begin a whole-district improvement process, then they need to be developed during the Pre-Launch Preparation phase of SUTE.

Step-Up-To-Excellence is an innovative approach to create and sustain whole-system change in school systems. It is a five-step process preceded by a Pre-Launch Preparation phase as illustrated in Figure 21.2.

One of the most common reasons for organization transformation to fail is lack of good preparation and planning (Kotter, 1995). Therefore, change leaders must take the time to engage their school system in the Pre-Launch Preparation activities. What happens during this phase will significantly influence the success (or failure) of their district's transformation. Remember, quick fixes almost always fail.

The early Pre-Launch Preparation activities are conducted by the superintendent of schools and several hand-picked subordinates. The superintendent also may wish to include one or two trusted school board members in this small planning team. It is important to know that this small team is temporary and that it will not lead the transformation. It has one purpose and one purpose only—to prepare the system to engage in systemic change.

At some point in the Pre-Launch Preparation phase a decision will be made to launch the transformation effort or not to launch it. If a launch decision is made, then the remaining activities are transferred to a Strategic Leadership Team composed of the superintendent and several others, including teachers and building administrators appointed to the team by their peers (not by the superintendent). This team also appoints and trains a Transformation Coordinator who will provide tactical leadership for the transformation.

After the Strategic Leadership Team assumes leadership of the transformation, other educators become involved. One of the key events for involving other educators in a school district is the District Engagement Conference. The results of this conference create a new strategic framework for the district that includes a new mission, vision, and strategic plan.

There are many more Pre-Launch Preparation activities that need to be completed. A full description is found in Duffy (2004).

During Step 1, educators working on small teams within clusters of schools redesign their entire school district by making three simultaneous improvements. They improve their district's core and supporting work processes, the district's internal social architecture, and the district's relationship with its environment. This is a core principle from the field of organization improvement (e.g., see the writings of Fred Emery, 1977; William Pasmore, 1988; and Eric Trist [Trist et al., 1963]).

Following the redesign of a district, change leaders then make a transition to Steps 2–4 of the methodology. Activities during these steps invite educators to align the work of individuals with the goals of their teams, the work of teams with the goals of their schools, the work of schools with the goals of their clusters, and the work of clusters with the goals of the district. This is also called "creating strategic alignment" (Duffy, 2004).

Creating strategic alignment accomplishes three things (Duffy, 2004): First, it ensures that everyone is working toward the same broad strategic goals and vision for the

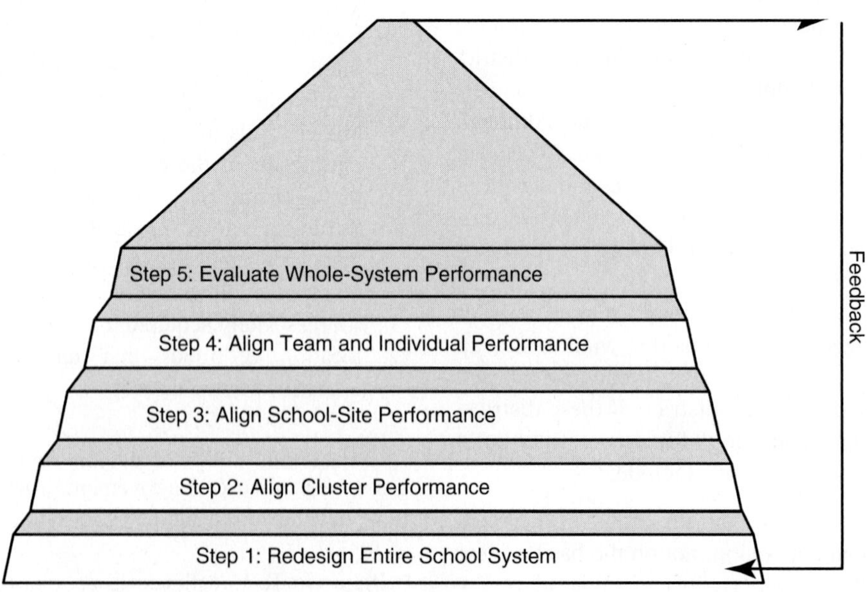

FIGURE 21.2 Step-Up-To-Excellence—Five steps to whole-district improvement.
Source: Copyright © 2002 by Francis M. Duffy. All rights reserved. Reprinted by permission.

district. Second, it weaves a web of accountabilities that makes everyone who touches the educational experience of a child accountable for their own part in shaping that experience. And third, it forms a social architecture that is free of bureaucratic hassles, dysfunctional policies, and obstructionist procedures that limit individual and team effectiveness. You will recall that W. Edwards Deming (1982), among others, says that it is these hassles, policies, and procedures that cause at least 80% of the performance problems that we usually blame on individuals and teams.

After strategic alignment is achieved and the rate of change is slowed down so people can learn the knowledge and skills required by the newly redesigned school system, then change leaders move their district to Step 5. During Step 5, change leaders evaluate the performance of the entire district, including the performance of its clusters, schools, and teams. The purpose of this level of evaluation is to measure the success of everyone's efforts to educate children. Evaluation data are also reported to stakeholders in the environment to demonstrate the district's effectiveness.

The evaluation data from Step 5 are also used to sustain school district improvement by managing the performance of the district, clusters, schools, teams, and individuals. Then, after a predetermined period, the district "steps up" again by cycling back to Step 1: Redesign the Entire District. Achieving high performance is a lifelong journey for a school district.

SUTE is powered by the collective efforts of several teams, informal learning networks, and a special leadership role. Each one is briefly described in the following paragraphs.

Strategic Leadership Team (SLT). The SLT provides strategic leadership for whole-district improvement. It does not get involved with the daily work of improvement. Those tasks go to a special role described later in this section.

The SLT is responsible for initiating SUTE. At a minimum, it is composed of the superintendent, one or two administrative subordinates, and one principal and one teacher from each level of schooling in the district. The principals and teachers are appointed to the SLT by their peers, not by the superintendent. Some districts may decide to include other members such as a teachers' union leader, a school board member, a parent, or a student. Team size should be no larger than 15 people. Teams larger than 15 are notoriously ineffective.

Cluster Improvement Teams. In SUTE, clusters of feeder schools and clusters of supporting workers are the units of change. For example, one cluster would be the central administration staff; a second would be supporting workers such as cafeteria, transportation, and building maintenance staff. Each of these clusters is led by a Cluster Improvement Team.

Site Improvement Teams. Within each cluster there are individual schools or supporting departments. Each school and department must have a Site Improvement Team that focuses on improving what happens inside their building or department and that ensures that what they are doing is aligned with their cluster's goals.

Organization Learning Networks. School districts are knowledge-creating organizations, and teachers are knowledge workers (Duffy et al., 2000). This characteristic requires school systems to create and support opportunities for personal, team, and organizational learning. Organization Learning Networks (OLNs) are informal learning communities that respond to this need.

On-Track Seminars. This mechanism is a variation of the OLN, described previously. While OLNs focus on developing professional knowledge and then distributing that knowledge throughout a school system, On-Track Seminars focus on what Argyris and Schön (1978) call "double-loop" learning.

With single-loop learning, people learn about what happened and may make changes in response to what happened, but they do not uncover and examine "why" things happened the way they did. By adding learning about why something happened, and by surfacing and examining underlying mental models that influenced outcomes, people add a second loop to their learning process, thereby creating double-loop learning. Double-loop learning activities are particularly useful for solving problems that are complex and ill structured and that change over time.

The On-Track Seminars use formative and summative evaluation data to help educators learn what happened in their change process and why it happened.

The Transformation Coordinator Role. Someone has to manage the daily, tactical work of school district improvement. This "someone" is a Transformation Coordinator. This person can be hired from within a district or can be a "new hire." The Frederick County Public School System in Maryland, for example, created a new position called Executive Director of District and Community Relations to coordinate that district's improvement effort. The superintendent, Dr. Jack Dale, hired an outside person to fill this role. Whether from within a district or from outside, the person filling this role must have superior knowledge of organization development and ecological systemic change processes.

Role of instructional design and technology specialists. Many IDT specialists know and understand systems and how they function. Many also understand effective processes for implementation of innovations. This knowledge can be particularly helpful to school districts involved in creating and sustaining ecological systemic change.

Another role that IDT specialists can play is in working to create improvements in the core and supporting work, the first of the three key areas for ecological systemic change listed. The core work of a school district is classroom teaching and learning. IDT specialists have focused on making improvements in this core work, and their expertise can be magnified if it is applied within the context of a whole-system process that creates and sustains improvements in the three key areas listed earlier.

Projects For Systemic Redesign

We are aware of several projects that have been conducted for districtwide ecological systemic transformation and will describe two in some detail in the following subsections. The first project is being facilitated by Charles Reigeluth, who is using the GSTE for guidance. The second was not conducted according to either the GSTE or the SUTE, but nevertheless exhibits most features of a sound transformation process. Several additional districtwide ecological systemic transformation efforts will also be briefly mentioned.

Decatur Township School District

The Metropolitan School District of Decatur Township initiated a systemic change effort in January 2001, a few months after a new superintendent, Donald Stinson, began working there. Charles Reigeluth, a professor at Indiana University, agreed to serve as facilitator for the change effort, along with a graduate student in Instructional Systems Technology, Roberto Joseph, only after being expressly invited by leaders of all the major stakeholder groups in the school district. The facilitators used the Guidance System for Transforming Education (GSTE) described previously to guide their facilitation efforts.

The major objective of the transformation process was to help stakeholders evolve their thinking (mental models or mindsets) about education, to reach consensus on a set of ideal beliefs or core values about education, and to design an ideal system in accordance with those beliefs. To succeed with such a fundamental transformation of their school system, the facilitators believed it was important for as many stakeholders as possible to participate in the change process and feel a sense of ownership of both the process and whatever design resulted. Two strategies were used to accomplish this: (1) forming a Leadership Team comprised of 20–25 key opinion leaders from all of the stakeholder groups in the school system and community; and (2) conducting numerous community forums in which as many stakeholders as possible could participate in shaping and conducting the transformation process. Crucial to the success of both strategies was establishing an appropriate culture for change, central to which was building greater trust and communication among all stakeholder groups.

Forming the leadership team. Because it is difficult to shape the culture and dynamic of a group that size, the GSTE calls for forming a Core Team or "Starter Team" of about five to seven key opinion leaders from all the major stakeholder groups, establishing a culture and understanding of systemic change, and expanding into the Leadership Team. The Starter Team was formed in February 2001 by the superintendent and facilitator. Team members included:

- A school board member
- A principal
- A PTA leader
- The president of the Decatur Education Association
- The superintendent.

From March to May 2001, the Starter Team met weekly with the facilitators to establish a culture for systemic change and develop an understanding of systemic thinking and the systemic change process. The team identified core ideas and values that should guide the process of improving the Decatur Township Schools' ability to meet all children's needs. Those ideas and values placed heavy emphasis on all stakeholders (parents, teachers, students, staff, administrators, employers, and other community members) reaching consensus on the changes that would benefit their children.

Conducting community forums. As its first step to getting many stakeholders involved in the journey toward excellence, the Starter Team held six widely publicized meetings to which all community members were invited. The purpose of those meetings, which took place between January 22 and February 7, 2002, was to start to identify the educational needs of the students and community and how those needs had changed over the past generation or two. Results were reported in the local newspaper with an invitation for more input from community members.

In January 2003, the Starter Team expanded to include about 25 key leaders of all stakeholder groups in the community, and that expanded team's first task was to develop a framework of ideal beliefs or core values about education, along with a strategic plan for helping building-level "design teams" to create ideal designs for their respective schools within the districtwide framework. The development of the framework and strategic plan occurred simultaneously with activities that helped Leadership Team members to function effectively as a team and to evolve their mindsets about education.

When this stage of the process is complete, building-level teams will be charged with creating ideal designs within the boundaries of the districtwide framework. Then it is likely that a district-level design team will be formed, including one person from each building-level design team, to design ideal district-level administration and governance systems to support the building-level designs. Finally, they will develop a strategic plan for evolving their current system as close as possible to their ideal designs as time and resources allow.

Chugach School District

The Chugach School District in Anchorage, Alaska, won one of the first two Malcolm Baldrige Excellence Awards in education. (The other district was the Pearl River District in Pearl River, New York.)

The Chugach School District is small. Its 214 students are scattered throughout 22,000 square miles of remote South Central Alaska. With 30 faculty and staff, CSD is the smallest organization to ever win a Baldrige Award. The district provides instruction from preschool up to age 21 in a comprehensive, standards-based system. Education occurs 24 hours a day, 7 days a week. Instruction is delivered in the workplace, in the community, in the home, and in school. Fifty percent of the students in the Chugach School District are minorities (Native Alaskans).

The process that the Chugach superintendent of schools, Richard De Lorenzo, and his colleagues used was highly influenced by the requirements of the Baldrige National Quality Program (2003). The process is documented in *A Guide to Reinventing Schools* (Chugach School District, 2002) and summarized here.

The Chugach transformation process started in 1994 and culminated when the school district received one of the first two Baldrige Awards in Education in 2001. Their process had four phases—design, delivery, refinement, and continuous improvement.

The design phase. The design phase of the Chugach whole-district improvement process included activities aimed at developing a shared vision among stakeholders for the district, creating a balanced instructional model that was tailored to the needs of their students, writing districtwide standards of performance, developing districtwide assessments to evaluate performance against their standards, and creating aligned tools for reporting the results of their assessments.

The delivery phase. Once the design phase was completed and all the pieces in place, district leaders and teachers implemented their improvement plans.

The refinement phase. During implementation, change leaders and educators in the district focused on phasing in the district's new standards, assessments, and reporting tools. As they phased these elements into their district, they identified and corrected glitches in the process. They also screened their students to identify their individual learning needs and made necessary changes in instruction and teaching schedules to respond to the needs. One of the important tactics they used to respond better to students' learning needs was to petition their State Department of Education for a waiver of the Carnegie Unit formula. They received the waiver.

The continuous improvement phase. At the time of this writing the district was in the continuous improvement phase, which brought members back to where they started, thereby creating a closed loop. They are once again focusing on developing a shared vision for the future of their district, which will lead to them revisiting all of the other phases as summarized.

Other Redesign Efforts

Five other districts that engaged in whole-system change participated in a research study conducted by the Learning First Alliance (Togneri & Anderson, 2003):

- Aldine Independent School District, Texas
- Chula Vista Elementary School District, California
- Kent County Public Schools, Maryland
- Minneapolis Public Schools, Minnesota
- Providence Public Schools, Rhode Island

Although the systemic redesign process these districts used is not clear in the research report, it is clear what they aimed to do through the process they used.

First, change leaders in each district worked to develop their district's readiness and willingness to engage in districtwide reform. This was followed by the development of a vision of where they wanted to take their district. Next, they scouted for new approaches to professional development focusing on improving instructional strategies. They also refined their leadership roles and engaged multiple stakeholders in their improvement process. Details about the outcomes of their efforts are found in a summary report available online at **http://www.learningfirst.org/publications/districts/.**

Needs and Future Directions

The school-based improvement process still dominates the literature and practice of school improvement. One of the biggest needs, therefore, for education reform is for educators and policymakers to recognize the power of using an ecological systems approach to improvement. This recognition, we think, will be facilitated by providing case study examples of successful whole-system improvement efforts such as the ones identified in this chapter.

Another important need is to help educators realize that districtwide ecological systemic improvement is not only needed, but doable. The thought of improving an entire district is a scary one for many people. There is so much that needs doing, so little time to do it, and, on top of all that, educators cannot stop teaching children while they try to redesign their school systems. But, the redesign process *is* learnable and doable, and educators need to learn about this.

A third important need is for policymakers on state and national levels to realize the need for and nature of ecological systemic transformation of school districts. They must recognize that, even though the new systems that districts design will likely not be more expensive to operate, there is considerable expense to redesign and transform the current system into the new one. Without outside financial support, it is unlikely that districts that are ready for systemic change will be able to successfully navigate the treacherous waters of such change. Systemic transformation is far more complex, difficult, and expensive than piecemeal change. Given the scope of this need, charitable foundations and state governments must recognize the importance of this kind of change and help support the transformation process.

A fourth need is related to the third one. Although "extra" money is needed to kick start a districtwide improvement process, a district must find permanent money in its budget to sustain improvements. Unless a district takes steps to create a permanent budget line for continuous ecological improvement and fund that line with permanent dollars, continuous ecological improvement will be unsustainable.

Unlike traditional reform efforts, continuous ecological improvement cannot be sustained solely through small increases in operating budgets. Because ecological improvement touches all aspects of a school district's core operations, it imposes significant resource requirements and demands a rethinking of the way current resources are allocated, as well as some creative thinking about how to use "extra" money that will be needed to jump start ecological improvement (Duffy, 2003).

Financing continuous ecological improvement also requires school-based budgeting that is coordinated and aligned with centralized budgeting processes. Financing ecological improvement is not an "either centralized or school-based" endeavor. It requires both a centralized *and* school-based budgeting approach.

What we are arguing for is the principle that money is an indicator of priorities and commitment. A significant line item in the budget sends a clear message to administrators, teachers, and other stakeholders about the importance of continuous ecological improvement. We are arguing in support of the position that educators should think more creatively and comprehensively about how to fund continuous ecological improvement in the short term to jumpstart the process and for the long term by making these improvement funds a permanent part of a district's core operations. We believe that finding the extra money "out there somewhere" will surely help get a whole-district improvement process moving, but it will not be able to sustain it over time or fund the effort completely. Continuous ecological improvement ought to be a core function of a school system, funded by core resources that can be spent more wisely to transform entire school systems into high-performing organizations of learners (Duffy, Cascarino, & Henson, 2005).

Finally, there is a knowledge need. We need to know more about the ecological systemic transformation process. The GSTE and the SUTE models offer some important, well-validated principles and activities, but the complexity of the process requires additional knowledge about how to manage and lead it. It is also likely that the process should change in important ways from one kind of school district to another. There is, therefore, a strong need for government agencies and foundations to support research on the ecological systemic transformation process.

Summary

In this chapter we discussed why piecemeal change is inadequate in P–12 education today and why systemic change is crucial to meeting our students' and communities' needs in the information age. We discussed different meanings for the term *systemic change*; we described ecological systemic change as addressing three key areas of a school system—(1) the core and supporting work, (2) the internal "social architecture"; and (3) the district's relationship with its external environment; and we discussed why ecological systemic change is so desperately needed today. We discussed why a "process approach" to ecological systemic change is more important than a "product approach."

Next, we described two major lines of work regarding the ecological systemic change process, the GSTE and SUTE. We discussed the role of instructional design and technology specialists in the change process. We described two projects that have been conducted for districtwide ecological systemic transformation. Finally, we discussed needs and future directions for ecological systemic change in P–12 education. Only with a much wider recognition of the need for ecological systemic change among policymakers, school district leaders, funders, and researchers will it be possible for communities to succeed in transforming their school systems to meet their needs in the information age.

Application Questions

1. Review the prerequisite conditions that need to be in place in a school system before it can successfully engage in whole-district change. Determine if these conditions exist in your district and assess their relative strength.
2. Given your assessment of the degree to which the prerequisite conditions exist in your school system, develop an action plan to (1) reinforce those conditions already in place and (2) develop those conditions not yet in place.
3. Interview several key leaders in your school system to diagnose which definition of *systemic change* they hold. Their definition(s) are a reflection of their mental models for change. Make a judgment about whether their mental models will help or hinder whole-district change in your system.
4. Review the Step-Up-To-Excellence methodology and the GSTE. Develop a staff development activity that will introduce both methodologies to your colleagues.
5. Contact change leaders in several of the school districts identified in the chapter that engaged in whole-district change. Interview them about the change process they used, how effective it was, and what they would do differently the next time they engage their districts in whole-system change.

References

Ackoff, R. L. (1981). *Creating the corporate future*. New York: John Wiley & Sons.

Argyris, C., & Schön, D. A. (1978). *Organizational learning: A theory of action perspective*. Reading, MA: Addison-Wesley.

Baldrige National Quality Program. (2003). *Education criteria for performance excellence*. Retrieved September 4, 2003, from **http://www.quality.nist.gov/PDF_files/2003_Education_Criteria.pdf**

Banathy, B. H. (1991). *Systems design of education: A journey to create the future*. Englewood Cliffs, NJ: Educational Technology Publications.

Banathy, B. H. (1996). *Designing social systems in a changing world*. New York: Plenum.

Burke, W. W. (2002). *Organization change: Theory and practice*. Thousand Oaks, CA: Sage.

Checkland, P. (1984). *Systems thinking, systems practice* (Rev ed.). New York: John Wiley & Sons.

Chugach School District. (2002). *A guide to reinventing schools*. Anchorage, AK: Chugach School District.

Cummings, T. G., & Worley, C. (2001). *Organization development & change* (7th ed.). Cincinnati, OH South-Western College Publishers.

Deming, W. E. (1982). *Out of crisis*. Cambridge, MA: MIT Press.

Duffy, F. M. (2002). *Step-Up-To-Excellence: An innovative approach to managing and rewarding performance in school systems*. Lanham, MD: Scarecrow Education.

Duffy, F. M. (2003). *Courage, passion and vision: A guide to leading systemic school improvement*. Lanham, MD: Scarecrow Education & American Association of School Administrators.

Duffy, F. M. (2004). *Moving upward together: Creating strategic alignment to sustain systemic school* (Leading Systemic School Improvement Series, Vol. 1). Lanham, MD: Scarecrow Education.

Duffy, F. M., Cascarino, J., & Henson, C. M. (2005). *Financing whole-district change: Where can we find the money?* Manuscript submitted for Publication.

Duffy, F. M., Rogerson, L. G., & Blick, C. (2000). *Redesigning America's schools: A systems approach to improvement.* Norwood, MA: Christopher-Gordon.

Emery, F. E. (1977). *Two basic organization designs in futures we are in.* Leiden: Martius Nijhoff.

Emery, M., & Purser, R. E. (1996). *The search conference: A powerful method for planning organizational change and community action.* San Francisco: Jossey-Bass.

Goodlad, J. I. (1984). *A place called school: Prospects for the future.* New York: McGraw-Hill.

Hammer, M., & Champy, J. (2001). *Reengineering the corporation: A manifesto for business revolution.* New York: HarperBusiness.

Jenlink, P. M., Reigeluth, C. M., Carr, A. A., & Nelson, L. M. (1996). An expedition for change. *Tech Trends, 15*(3) 21–30.

Jenlink, P. M., Reigeluth, C. M., Carr, A. A., & Nelson, L. M. (1998). Guidelines for facilitating systemic change in school districts. *Systems Research and Behavioral Science, 15*(3), 217–233.

Joseph, R., & Reigeluth, C. M. (in press). Formative research on the initial stage of the systemic change process in a small urban school system. *Journal of Educational Change.*

Kotter, J. P. (1995). Leading change: Why transformation efforts fail. *Harvard Business Review, 73*(2), 59–67.

National Commission on Excellence in Education. (1983). *A nation at risk: The imperative for educational reform.* Washington, DC: U.S. Government Printing Office.

Pasmore, W. A. (1988). *Designing effective organizations: The sociotechnical systems perspective.* New York: John Wiley & Sons.

Reiser, R. A., & Dempsey, J. V. (Eds.). (2002). *Trends and issues in instructional design and technology.* Upper Saddle River, NJ: Merrill/Prentice Hall.

Senge, P. M. (1990). *The fifth discipline: The art and practice of the learning organization* (1st ed.). New York: Doubleday.

Sizer, T. R. (2002). *The common principles.* Retrieved February 11, 2004, from **http://www.essentialschools.org/pub/ces_docs/about/phil/10cps/10cps.html**

Smith, M. S., & O'Day, J. (1990). Systemic school reform. In S. Fuhrman & B. Malen (Eds.), *The politics of curriculum and testing* (pp. 233–267). Philadelphia: Falmer.

Squire, K. D., & Reigeluth, C. M. (2000). The many faces of systemic change. *Educational Horizons, 78*(3), 145–154.

Stringfield, S., Ross, S. M., & Smith, L. (1996). *Bold plans for school restructuring: The New American schools designs.* Mahwah, NJ: Lawrence Erlbaum Associates.

Togneri, W., & Anderson, S. E. (2003). *Beyond islands of excellence: What districts can do to improve instruction and achievement in all schools.* Washington, DC: Learning First Alliance.

Trist, E. L., Higgin, G. W., Murray, H., & Pollack, A. B. (1963). *Organizational choice.* London: Tavistock.

CHAPTER 22

What Do Instructional Designers Do in Higher Education? A Written Symposium

John V. Dempsey
University of South Alabama

Peter Albion
University of Southern Queensland

Brenda C. Litchfield
University of South Alabama

Byron Havard
Mississippi State University

Jacquie McDonald
University of Southern Queensland

Editors' Introduction

What the five authors of this "written symposium" have tried to do is to give you a small window on their world in higher education. The vignettes are written by Australians and Americans discussing different job responsibilities instructional designers have in higher education. By organizing the roles of instructional designers into five common positions at the university level, the authors hope to give a glimpse of some of the day-to-day opportunities and some of the demands of their careers in higher education. The chapter highlights the similarities and differences among these job positions in higher education from the perspective of two countries with diverse traditions.

Knowledge and Comprehension Questions

1. With reference to the higher education systems of Australia and the United States, briefly describe two similarities and two differences.
2. Suggest ways in which expert knowledge of, and experience in, instructional design might allow an academic to make an effective service contribution in a university.
3. What is meant in higher education by the term *faculty development*?
4. Why are many colleges and universities focusing on improving faculty teaching skills?
5. Outline the key competencies that you think are required to be an effective instructional designer.
6. Compare your key competency list from question 5 with the selection criteria of a recently advertised instructional designer position.
7. What courses would you consider necessary for the required core in an instructional design degree program? Does your list reflect what your current program offers? How does your list compare to other programs?
8. Faculty duties at most universities are comprised of teaching, research, and service. What percentage of time should be spent on each? Ask three faculty members in your program of study and compare their percentages to yours.

What do instructional designers do in higher education? What roles do they take? How do these roles change as we progress through our careers? How are those roles dissimilar in different geographical areas? Those are some of the questions we will explore in this chapter.

Our approach is a little different than most other chapters in this book. You may think of this chapter as a type of written symposium. As individuals working in the field, our notion is to discuss—through short, personal vignettes by Australians and Americans—five different job responsibilities instructional designers have in higher education. Although there are certainly differences between the Australian and the U.S. higher education systems, there are also many commonalities. Likewise, although Australia and the United States both have many people practicing in the area of instructional design and technology, Australia thus far has no formal graduate programs such as those that exist in the United States.

As readers you will see that instructional designers' lives are quite similar to other faculty and professional staff members in higher education. Particularly in the traditional assistant/associate/full professor faculty succession, the day-to-day activities of our lives are not greatly distinct from academics in the business, music, or the history departments. What is different is our training and areas of professional concentration. Instructional designers working in support areas such as distance education or faculty development are practitioners. As the use of educational technologies increases in higher education, these individuals are becoming more critical to the success of organizations where faculty members are trained in content but not in pedagogy.

The Australian and U.S. Higher Education Systems

The structure and operations of universities in Australia and the United States are similar in many respects. Universities are divided into separate colleges where semesters are approximately 15 weeks long and the teaching loads average about three courses per semester. Administratively, both systems have deans, associate deans, and department chairs. The distribution of teaching, research, and service is similar, as are the expectations for each component. The number of students per course in the Australian system is a bit higher. There are 38 universities in Australia, which has a population of around 20 million. By contrast, the United States has around 2,500 public and private four-year institutions for a population of 295 million.

The major difference in the two systems is the progression of ranks for faculty. In Australia there are usually five levels of progression in a faculty member's career, each with a specific number of steps. Faculty members move up one step each year to the top of that level. To move to the next level they must apply for and gain promotion. A typical progression is as follows:

- Associate lecturer—Honours or good pass degree (8 steps)
- Lecturer—Master's degree, common beginning level (6 steps)
- Senior lecturer—Doctorate plus publications (6 steps)
- Associate professor—Doctorate plus 1–2 publications per year (4 steps)
- Professor—Doctorate plus significant research reputation

For tenure-track faculty in the United States there are three ranks, assistant (usually 6–7 years), associate (3–4 years minimum), and full professor. Promotion and tenure are two separate things in U.S. universities. A tenure-track faculty member at any rank who comes into a U.S. university must be granted tenure within a specified time period in order to continue working at that university. Although less common, there are two steps for nontenured faculty, instructor[1] and lecturer.

Another important distinction is that in the Australian system very few make it to the title of professor, and there may be only one in each department. In the United States, most faculty members become associate professors and many of these, in time, become full professors. In certain U.S. departments, a majority of tenured faculty members may be full professors.

Byron Havard, Assistant Professor (United States)

My role as an assistant professor is challenging, rewarding, and unfortunately, continuously under the pressure of a timeline with milestones and commitments that must be met for tenure. I'm starting my third year as an assistant professor of Instructional Systems; one of 10 assistant professors in our department composed of 21 full-time faculty members. The department I entered had undergone four years of faculty and departmental changes. Blood and tears were shed but our current department head has created a vibrant and motivated faculty body.

My background may color my perspective on the assistant professor role so I'll share it briefly. On completion of a master's degree in Instructional Design and Development I was accepted into a doctoral program in Instructional Technology. While pursuing my doctorate I worked

[1] Some U.S. universities have a senior instructor level to recognize nontenure-track faculty who are both experienced and skillful.

full time as an instructional designer and training manager for several large corporations. The experiences and activities in which I was engaged and led were priceless and in the beginning the work was invigorating. Eventually I came to the realization that I was not pursuing my true dream that originated during the pursuit of my master's degree. I wanted to teach graduate courses in the field of instructional design and technology.

While it is not my intention to describe the tenure process, the role of assistant professor and tenure are inexorably linked. Fortunately, the university where I'm employed has set minimum guidelines for tenure. This at least provides some direction and permits me to focus my time and effort accordingly. However, there are still many unknowns within the tenure process at my university. My peers at other universities describe a more nebulous tenure process. Happily, 6 of the 10 assistant professors in my department will go up for tenure before me. I'll have the opportunity to learn from their experiences. In the paragraphs that follow I briefly describe a few of the many responsibilities of my role.

Many of my peers pursued a career in academia to pursue their passion of teaching. I share that passion and teach three courses fall semester, two spring semester, and three or four summer semester. My course load is generally divided between undergraduate and graduate courses. My role as assistant professor includes a variety of other responsibilities that are equally if not more important to the university than teaching. I'm interested in research but often it seems that the satisfaction I derive from conducting research falls short compared to the fulfillment I feel from teaching. In the corporate world the phrase "publish or perish" meant little, but now as an assistant professor I know what it truly means and I'm reminded of it almost daily.

As if original research was not demanding enough, the waiting process may be even more arduous. Based on my experience, waiting for periods of several months for a journal article to be accepted or rejected can be excruciating. As a faculty member I wouldn't dare send the same paper for publication acceptance to two different journals at one time, so I wait. If an article is rejected then that time is lost, but the tenure clock keeps on ticking.

In my opinion, the single point of focus for anyone preparing for a tenure-track role in academia is a research agenda. With regard to publishing, as an assistant professor, I'm expected to publish a number of papers in referred journals in a specific amount of time. Having a research agenda sets one up for success in this role. It provides a starting point from which to base an initial thrust into presentations and publications.

At my university, undergraduate academic advisement is another important responsibility of my role. I understand that this is not the norm in many universities across the United States. Advising undergrads is a taxing and tedious process, and is one of my least favorite responsibilities. I'm the coordinator for an undergraduate program in Information Technology Services (ITS). The program continues to grow each semester; we currently have approximately 110 students in the ITS program. While this is an overwhelming drain on my time for writing and fulfilling the research commitment previously described, it has offered me academic leadership responsibilities. A senior faculty member has coached me in the program management and maintenance process and I am grateful to her. Several faculty members and I fulfill the advising tasks for several undergraduate programs. I'm exaggerating, but it seems every moment of available time spent in my office is spent with undergrad students. This was never my intention.

Graduate student advising, especially doctoral student mentoring, is much more gratifying. I'm currently mentoring 3 doctoral students. One is in the dissertation process; she will be my first student to receive a Ph.D. Another advisee has almost completed his coursework, and a third has just started the program. I find mentoring to be almost as rewarding as teaching. It's my opinion that it requires a special bond built on trust and respect. I also advise about 20 master's degree students and I've chosen 4 of these students to work with on a closer basis than required for standard advising. These students show great promise and intend to pursue doctoral degrees at this or another institution. They are involved in presentations and papers, and I generally offer them more of my time and push them a little harder than I do others.

As I continue to learn the ropes I often find myself taking on too much. Again, wondering if this project or that committee will assist in edging me closer to tenure. Our department is currently in the process of program revisions that will take several years to complete. I'm actively involved in several of these programs. Other responsibilities include course development, committee participation and the many ensuing meetings, reviewing papers, and grant writing.

At this point I'm fully engaged in my pursuit of tenure, promotion, and the eventual title of full professor. I have no plans on leaving academia, as the intrinsic rewards are too great. My students and colleagues appreciate me on a personal level, something I never really experienced in the corporate setting.

Jacquie McDonald, Instructional Designer (Australia)

Like many fledgling instructional designers (IDs) my first appointment (1990) was a short-term contract funded by an external grant to design and develop commercial training materials. It took several years of part-time work, a career side step and years of study before I gained promotion and tenure. My educational career began as a primary teacher and after a childrearing break I moved into tertiary education. I will briefly share the variety of roles I have experienced as an Australian instructional designer (ID)—including ID in an academic distance education context, a government health training sector, and a community-based training environment.

Instructional Design Role at University

My initial and current position is instructional designer in the Distance and e-Learning Centre (DeC) at a university (University of Southern Queensland) that has offered distance education for more than 25 years and has approximately 25,000 enrollments, including over 7,400 international students.

In the 1990s, IDs at my university focused only on off-campus learning, working closely with faculty content experts (course/unit leaders) and members of the DeC team to design and deliver distance learning materials based on ID and distance learning theory. These materials have traditionally been designed for independent learning, using a student/content interactive approach (Anderson, 2003). Figure 22.1 shows our organizational structure and the interface between the faculties and DeC in the development of distance learning materials. IDs work with across a range of faculty course leaders on new, online, or blended/hybrid courses, or on courses undergoing major revision.

Many academics employed by the university have little or no experience in distance learning, and some employed for their content expertise have no educational background. As an ID, part of my role is to facilitate the development of learning and teaching strategies and introduce faculty to the distance learning production processes. This role demands a sound knowledge of ID theory and sensitivity to the concerns of academics moving into a new, distance teaching role. This role can lead to tension as timelines for developing distance learning materials is much longer than preparing materials to present in an on-campus lecture. In this context, the ability to interact effectively with faculty staff and "sell" ID theory, which often means more work to time-stressed staff, is a key ID skill. Elsewhere in this chapter, Jack Dempsey talks about the need for junior colleagues to be attuned to "departmentese." I agree that the ability to listen and *hear the real message* is essential, not just to succeed in your own department but also to work effectively as an ID across a number of faculties. The need for ID sensitivity to the beliefs and practices of faculty staff is also articulated by Crawford (2004), who highlights that negotiation is an essential part of the design process.

Going into a design meeting with ID "tunnel vision" (i.e., your knowledge of ID theory will be applied, whatever the context) can be counterproductive. Of course, solid knowledge of ID theory is a given tool of our trade, but sensitivity to the knowledge of other team members is essential. Seely Brown & Duguid (2002) articulate this approach, and although their context is the application of technology it also rings true for ID contexts: "Too often, we conclude, the light at the end of an information tunnel is merely the gleam in a visionary's eye. The way forward is paradoxically to look not ahead, but to look around" (p. 8).

Project management and facilitating smooth integration of timelines for multiple team members are also required ID skills. When you apply for a job, these skills are covered in the *interpersonal* and *teamwork* selection criteria. From my experience of applying for ID positions and being on selection panels, you need to have some prepared examples of how you have successfully demonstrated these skills.

Instructional Design Generator Model

The approach I endeavour to take as I work with faculty is the Instructional Design Generator Model (Figure 22.2). I work closely with unit leaders (subject matter experts) in the initial stages to design a blueprint outlining the key learning and implementation strategies appropriate for the context. In close collaboration with the ID, the course leader develops a sample or module of the course and the ID provides feedback. Once agreed on, this provides a model for the writing of subsequent modules and detailed ID feedback is usually not required. This approach has proven more effective than the *transformer* approach. No doubt we have all experienced the difficulties of redesigning (transforming) materials that are near completion before ID input is sought. Of course the generator is an *ideal* model. In reality the success of this approach depends on context and personalities, not just on the application of a model of practice.

Extending the Possibilities

After five years at my university on rolling contracts I applied for promotion and a permanent position in a major regional hospital that offered professional development and training to rural and remote health professionals. This context called for a range of ID competencies, as the ID was involved at each stage of the instructional systems design, and the development team consisted of two programmers and myself as ID. The required range of ID skills included most of the competencies discussed by Drs. Davidson-Shivers and Rasmussen in Chapter 27. This can

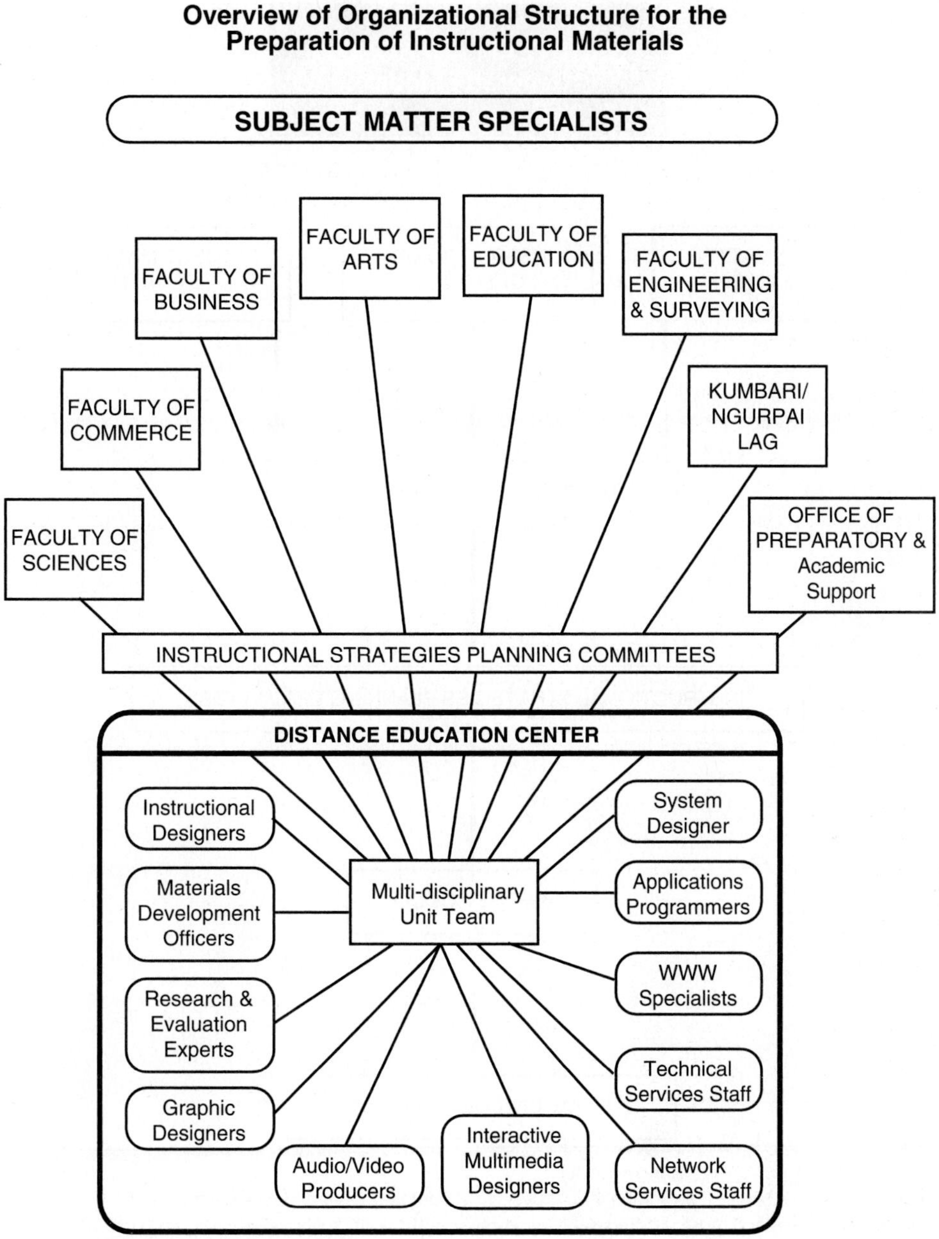

FIGURE 22.1 Organizational structure overview.
Source: From *DeC Visitors Guide* (n.p.), n.d., Toowoomba, AU: University of Southern Queensland. Copyright by the University of Southern Queensland, Australia. Reprinted by permission.

be compared to an academic environment where often the program is accredited and the target audience (students) is a given before the ID becomes involved in the program design. In the government, health service teams were smaller and with shorter development timeframes, and I was often involved in the presentation of face-to-face training. Government health budget cuts eventually meant a reduction in the training budget, and I returned to the university.

Community Role and Application of ID Competencies

Community service is an expected role for an Australian academic and is one of the three promotion criteria. In response to a government initiative to provide access to education and technology facilities for people in rural and remote areas I spent three years as president of a

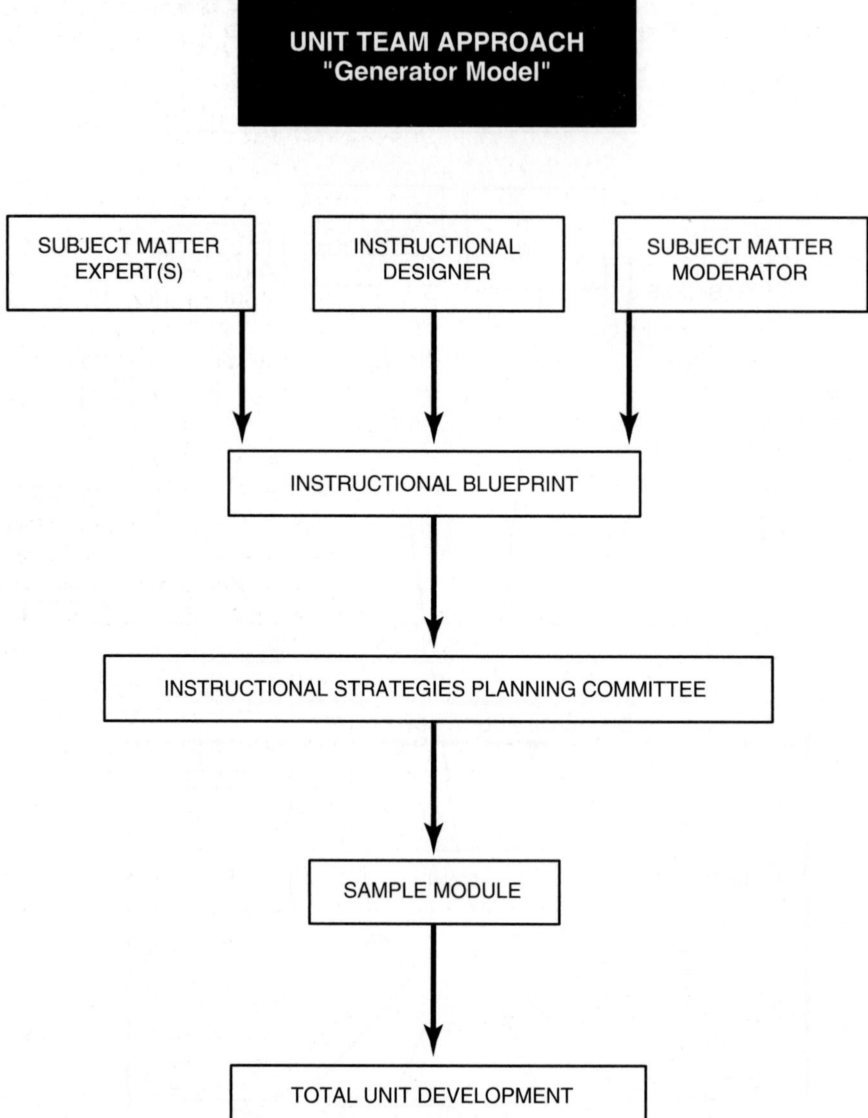

FIGURE 22.2 Instructional design generator model.
Source: From *DeC Visitors Guide* (n.p.), n.d., Toowoomba, AU: University of Southern Queensland. Copyright by the University of Southern Queensland, Australia. Reprinted by permission.

community-based nonprofit organization. As president, I used many of my ID skills to work with a small committee in preparing a funding submission to train long-term unemployed in the use of multimedia. Given the complex nature of the training program, I had to employ a variety of project management skills including budgeting, time management, and the interpersonal skills necessary to maintain project flow. I had to negotiate with a variety of stakeholders including the trainer, clients, commercial training organizations, and other community groups.

Changing Instructional Design Role

The ID role has changed from working with individual course leaders to a group approach (which often filters down to individual interaction) to meet the needs of changing educational initiatives at my university. As online learning became prevalent at my university, IDs participated in the design and development of online courses and training of faculty in application of online pedagogy and technology. The later implementation of a "hybrid" (or blended learning) initiative and new production software by management, plus a reduced ID team, has lead to alternative approaches to the past practice of IDs mainly working with individual course teams.

One faculty (akin to a school or college at a U.S. university) has initiated a collaborative team approach for implementing the hybrid plan, and I'm currently involved in a community of practice (Wenger, 1999) project to facilitate the design, development, and evaluation of hybrid courses. This involves sharing hybrid theory and practice with the group to facilitate the professional development of the participating course leaders. As a result of that project I have recently been seconded to the faculty to work with a range of teams to develop models of good practice for blended learning, and to facilitate a community of practice for research into learning and teaching.

This facilitation, or *change agent* role (Schwier, Campbell, & Kenny, 2004) is an emerging trend in the roles of instructional designers. It is one in which we have an increasing responsibility in facilitating the application of technology to enhance learning. An essential component of this ID role is keeping up to date with ID literature and educational theory and practice (e.g., constructivism, online pedagogy, blended learning, and so forth). As Jack Dempsey mentions later in the chapter, faculty members are trained in content, not pedagogy, so sharing this knowledge with the team and negotiating appropriate application to a course context in a team environment builds the knowledge base of all team members.

My academic role now includes a range of professional development workshops, research, and evaluation of online and hybrid initiatives. I have also team-taught for several semesters in an online instructional design course that is part of a Master's of Education program offered internationally. The hands-on teaching gives me valuable experience in the application of ID theory and credibility when working with faculty members designing online courses. You may find having a direct teaching role will have the same benefits in your work context. When seeking promotion and tenure, hands-on teaching can be an advantage. In the Australia academic context, gaining promotion requires meeting (or exceeding) guidelines for three criteria—teaching and scholarship, research, and community service. IDs can have difficulty addressing the *teaching* criteria, as the ID role is different from the traditional faculty teaching role. ID contribution and output is difficult to measure in a team environment.

Now What?

Where to from here? First, I plan to complete my doctoral studies; then, to further explore the application of learning communities to both my professional and teaching roles. You will read later in the chapter that a professor's role involves committee meetings that can be "enormously time consuming and uninteresting." My current plan is not to seek promotion from senior lecturer position, as this level allows me to work at the coalface, and maintain close working relationships with faculty applying ID theory in practice.

Brenda Litchfield, Faculty Development (United States)

So, you want to get into faculty development in higher education? Are you sure you know what that means? One thing for certain is that as an instructional designer you will be well prepared. Sure, there are non-ID people working as faculty developers in U.S. institutions who are doing a good job. But you, with your training in ID, will be further ahead in your understanding of what faculty members in higher education need to be successful designers, developers, and implementers of instruction.

Although there are several definitions of *faculty development*, the one I will focus on here is the type that assists faculty members in several important areas—the analysis of students and learning contexts, design and development of instruction, innovative methods of implementation, and evaluation of teaching and learning. By using the basic components of systems design, I am able to work with any faculty member and assist in the development of courses that meet student learning needs and improve a faculty member's teaching skills at the same time. Without using instructional designers' terms (*context, implementation, formative, entry behaviors*, and so forth), I can go through each step of the design process in a way that is easily understood by faculty members.

Why do so many institutions spend time and money on faculty development? There are several reasons. Accrediting agencies are requiring more schools to provide training for faculty because they recognize it is a vital part of an institution's mission. In addition, it has long been the case that the majority of faculty members in higher education have not had opportunities to participate in formal training in teaching methods. They teach the way they were taught: they lecture. This is not the most exciting way to keep students' attention (yawn). Finally, students are becoming real consumers these days and often have several choices of junior colleges, four-year colleges, and universities both in town and online. Why would they choose a school where the instructors are boring? An institution with a reputation of excellent instructors can ultimately mean higher student enrollment.

What do faculty development offices look like? That depends on the university. Some U.S. schools have funding to support teaching centers with a director and staff. Some have one person who plans all activities and conducts many of the workshops, and who often has additional responsibilities such as teaching. Other schools have a volunteer committee of individuals from around campus who are interested in improving teaching skills. At my university, a volunteer committee coordinated all non-online faculty development activities. This group worked together for several years but it became evident that the continued success of the program would require one person dedicated to this task. That person became me. I took on this responsibility in addition to my teaching responsibilities. There are also some other individuals and groups involved in my university for more specific faculty development tasks (e.g., online learning).

Just what does a faculty developer do day in and day out? My major function at the beginning of the year is to plan and deliver the orientation for new faculty. This is a full-day event covering a variety of topics such as motivation, presentation skills, syllabus construction, learning styles, and collaborative learning. I provide new faculty members with special attention throughout their first year through workshops and individual meetings.

During orientation, I survey new faculty about which workshops (I give them a list) they want during the year. Based on their choices, I plan the year's workshops. These workshops are also open to all other faculty members. Typical workshops include technology skills, alternative assessment techniques, instructional delivery strategies, course development, problem solving, and critical thinking. In addition to specific teaching skills, faculty members request topics such as grant writing, advising students, tenure and promotion procedures and preparation, and research skills. I have found that an important aspect of faculty development is to include the faculty in the selection of topics. This way, you are meeting their perceived needs and they have a vested interest in attending the workshops.

In addition to workshops, I meet with faculty individually, which gives me an opportunity to analyze what they know about teaching and what they need to know. Even though I work with a diverse group of faculty with expertise in many areas, I look at them as the subject matter experts and go from there. I find out what they consider to be the most important goals and objectives for their courses and then help them design, develop, and implement strategies and activities that will keep their students' attention and increase learning. We also develop evaluation instruments to measure their teaching skills and their students' learning. After this process, faculty members have a greater appreciation for the design process and all its components.

Other aspects of my job as a faculty developer include sending out regular e-mails of what I call "Teaching Tips." Having survived 12 years teaching in the U.S. K–12 public school system, I have many teaching tips that can be applied successfully to teaching in higher education. These tips are mainly things I have experienced and implemented over time, although some are from other sources and books. Faculty respond very favorably to these and say they work well in their classrooms.

I also meet with department chairs and deans to design specific workshops for their faculty. Each department has different needs, so I often design workshops to address certain topics using the department's terminology and concrete examples as a basis for instruction. In these workshops, I match my instruction more directly to one group's needs.

The hardest part of being a faculty developer is getting faculty to come to workshops. Many are reluctant to admit they want or need help with their teaching. They think nothing of going over to the math department for statistical help with a research study but would not dream of calling me to ask about how to create more effective instruction. I spend a lot of time just making faculty aware that there are other ways to teach besides lecturing. When, and if, they agree with this they then are ready to learn more about teaching.

The easiest part of being a faculty developer is being an instructional designer, although no one seems to know what that is. Based on my training, I know methods to identify what should be taught and how to teach it. Through a series of questions, I can guide a faculty member through the steps of the instructional systems design without ever saying it out loud. They end up with a new appreciation for how instruction is designed, developed, and implemented and, hopefully, in some cases, may even continue to practice what they have learned.

If you aspire to work in faculty development in higher education you are already ahead of most individuals in this position because of your training in instructional design and development. This program provides you with a solid foundation of how to design all aspects of instruction. But that's not all there is to faculty development. Working with a diverse group of faculty can be a challenge. I would suggest you take courses, attend workshops, and seek out people who can help you improve in areas such as negotiation skills, presentation skills, dealing with difficult participants, and integrating technology into the curriculum. The more skills you have as a faculty developer, the easier your job will be.

Your efforts will mean a great deal to everyone you work with. It's a rewarding feeling to be able to assist others to create interesting instruction and to improve their teaching skills. For individuals not trained in instructional design, teaching and designing effective and efficient instruction can often be a mystery. You can be the person who helps them solve the mystery.

Peter Albion, Associate Professor (Australia)

As an associate professor in the Faculty of Education at a regional university in Australia, I may well have hit the peak of my academic career. As we mentioned in the introduction to this chapter, our system of academic ranks differs from that in the United States. Full professors are not quite so rare as hen's teeth but we do have just one among about 50 academics in our faculty and I am one of 4 associate professors. In that context, making associate professor is a significant achievement and because, like most of my colleagues, I became tenured while still at lecturer level it can be something of a comfortable plateau in a career. Since relatively few make it to full professor there is hope but no strong expectation or pressure associated with the prospect of further promotion. At the same time, because associate professors are senior in rank and usually in years, they are expected to contribute to leadership in the faculty.

Each academic in our faculty is expected to contribute across the three broad areas of teaching, research/consultancy, and service/administration. The balance among these areas and the specific tasks that make up any one area vary according to the needs of the faculty and the interests, skills, and rank of the individual faculty member. Associate professors have been part of the system at this or another university for long enough that they can negotiate work assignments that are mostly a good fit for their own interests. However, there are some less popular tasks that require a certain level of experience or the responsibility that comes with elevated rank. Most associate professors find themselves taking on one or more of those tasks that they might prefer to leave to others but which they recognize as being important for the benefit of the faculty in which they work.

The teaching assignment of an associate professor may include large courses that are central to a program and require experienced leadership as well as smaller courses that align closely with his or her research interests. For an associate professor working in the area of instructional technology there is an expectation that both the content and presentation of courses will reflect recent and current developments in the field. Over the past several years, obvious developments have included increased focus on the use of presentation tools in regular classrooms and on the use of computer-mediated communications and course management systems for distance, online, and face-to-face classes. In addition to learning the new tools, assessing their potential, and integrating their use into courses, an associate professor working in instructional technology is likely to be called on to offer advice and assistance to other members of the faculty who are considering the application of new approaches in their own teaching. This work can sometimes place significant demands on available time, but it is interesting to see how new techniques work out in different contexts. I have found that assisting colleagues to learn and implement new technologies for teaching and learning is similar to other teaching roles and can generate the same feelings of satisfaction.

As experienced academics, associate professors are expected to have an established profile in consultancy and research, to be able to identify new lines of inquiry together with sources of support, to be productive in research publication, and to provide research leadership for more junior colleagues and research students. The capacity to work with and lead teams is an important quality in this area. An associate professor who pursues idiosyncratic research interests that offer few opportunities for participation by other faculty members is liable to be seen as putting her or his personal satisfaction ahead of the common good of the faculty. Allowing such a perception to develop among those who make decisions about allocation of resources and work assignments within the faculty can have negative consequences. Associate professors working in our field of instructional design and technology are fortunate that there are clear connections between research into effective instruction and both the content and presentation of courses. Colleagues working in other areas are often interested in research into new approaches to teaching because it has potential both to improve the effectiveness of their teaching and to allow them to demonstrate the application of new technologies in ways that may enhance their own opportunities for advancement. Being open to working with colleagues in this way can create opportunities to conduct worthwhile research while simultaneously being seen to contribute to the wider work of the faculty.

In addition to providing leadership in their teaching and research, associate professors are expected to contribute through administration and service to the faculty, university, and professional community. As members of the professional community they can be expected to review papers for scholarly publications and conferences. They may also accept leadership roles as members of committees of professional organizations. Within the faculty, associate professors will be expected to contribute to organizational development. They may find themselves leading degree programs, serving as department head, or taking on more major administrative roles such as associate dean. These are important roles that must be filled if the faculty is to function effectively, and they require knowledge of academic functions and capacity to work with people. Sustaining a research profile while fulfilling a significant administrative role requires careful personal management. Some associate professors are able to manage the balancing act and, after serving their time in an administrative role, are able to return focus to their research programs. Others find that the administrative roles offer real satisfaction through what they can achieve in developing faculty programs and supporting the development of other academics. Associate professors also find themselves representing the faculty on a variety of university committees dealing with matters such as program accreditation and other elements of the academic program. In recent years the enthusiasm for online teaching and learning has created interesting opportunities for those of us working in instructional design and technology to share our knowledge and experience with colleagues in other parts of the university. I have enjoyed the opportunity to work with colleagues from other faculties on the introduction of new instructional technologies.

My work as an associate professor in the area of instructional technology is varied but can mostly be easily connected to my central interest in the application of technologies to improvement of learning. It requires me to keep up to date with developments in both technology and education and especially their intersection. It is at once challenging and fulfilling.

Jack Dempsey, Full Professor (United States)

One of the shocks of middle age is being there. If you live long enough, you may become one of the inmates running the asylum—or at least a trustee. That happened to me. I've been at my university for over 15 years and about 6 years ago I was promoted to full professor. Compared to many of my colleagues, that's not a long time to be one, so I'm speaking from limited time on the job. Plus, shortly after I was promoted to professor, I became a department chair. Now that's a job that takes much from what any academic loathes to give: time and energy—both precious. Also, I know it must make my views of the professor role different than some folks'.

First, I should state what I have heard from a number of senior faculty members—becoming a full professor was kind of anticlimactic. When I became tenured and an associate professor, a couple of colleagues and I went out to dinner and celebrated. When I received notice of my promotion to full, I was happy for the raise, but otherwise it was just another day. In academia, tenure holds the keys to the safe door. Promotion is far from the military or government civil servant models where there are oodles of differentiations among practitioners. The full professor rank is a plateau, not a summit. There are prestige and power levels associated, but at least in the United States these are less overt than one would think. The Australian system that Peter articulated earlier in this chapter seems exceedingly more reflective of the requirements of society in general than does the U.S. system.

It takes a great deal of patience to succeed in your professional life in higher education. I don't mean from anyone else's perspective—I mean from your own. By the time you're a full professor you probably feel more comfortable in your own professional skin. You probably don't even consider many of the things that most worried you as an assistant. You may, but if you do, you've lost the real pleasure of your promotion. Perhaps that's one thing reaching a senior faculty position gives you—reassurance.

Like many a determined faculty-naturalist, I have enjoyed watching the metamorphoses that happen as academics becomes senior faculty. Freed from the pressures of tenure and promotion, they are able to steer their own courses more than almost any other professionals. Almost all change because of their promotion and the occupational stability it brings. Some full professors' careers become superb; some become reasonably solid; others become downright ugly. The superb full professors are at the top of their game, work as hard or harder than they ever have, and are often the most valuable individuals to their academic programs. The downright ugly full professors muddle safely in their tenured mediocrity, become out of touch with their fields, avoid university-related responsibilities, and regularly vote against productive junior colleagues when they come up for promotion in the department.

The notion of full professor varies at different institutions, but all are expected to provide leadership at the academic program, department, college, and university levels. Professors' leadership in academic programs comes, first of all, from maintaining their productivity in their areas of academic interest. Unproductive full professors can only drag a program down. Does this mean research only? Probably not. It's no secret that many of the senior faculty members in some our most celebrated academic programs are not active researchers. Research expectations vary by institution, but in general our system allows some flexibility. At the program level, productivity for full professors is often more related to their personal strengths. Some individuals may concentrate on getting grants or on developing educational projects. Some work on writing articles, chapters, and books in their field. In some institutions, some will focus much more on the technology of teaching. Many full professors regularly go "on the road" with workshops or have consulting businesses related to instructional design that help their academic programs' visibility. Still others look for leadership roles in professional organizations.

Full professors usually provide program leadership on levels other than personal productivity. They have experience and a memory of what has worked and what hasn't in the past. They often have a more complete view of the entire curriculum than do their junior colleagues. If they are active in the field, they have a pretty good instinct about where a program should be headed. Many full professors participate in formal mentoring activities with junior colleagues. Others team with them on writing or teaching endeavors. Being more experienced and frequently older than their counterparts, they often act as sounding boards for research ideas, suggest teaching techniques, and in some cases offer personal guidance.

Many academic departments, especially in colleges of education, are composed of a number of programs. Some full professors serve as department chairs or academic program coordinators. Almost all full professors have increased departmental committee participation. One of the most critical of these at the department level is the tenure and promotion committee. In most institutions, only full professors vote to promote associate professors to full. Although in some institutions, including my own, the recommendation to promote or not is made by the department chair with the promotion committee's input, no chair wants to disregard senior faculty members' input.

At many higher education institutions, full professors are expected to participate more actively on important college and university committees. Some of these, such as accreditation committees, can be enormously time consuming and uninteresting. Others, such as the curriculum review or distance education committee, can at times be very interesting for an individual with a background in instructional design.

Because many readers of this chapter will be considering an entry-level position in higher education, it is probably worthwhile to close this section with a caveat about departmental politics. Academic departments often adopt a certain language that Hume (2003) refers to as "departmentese." This can appear to be a foreign language to a new assistant professor. As chair of a large department, I frequently listen to senior faculty complain about junior faculty for things that have to do with the juniors' inability to "hear the real message." Quite recently, I heard a full professor state how angry he was with a junior colleague who he said refused to be flexible in the course scheduling process. The senior faculty member's expectation was that since he had served his time with less favorable assignments, he didn't understand why the junior professor should complain. He told me because of this person's "inflexibility and abrupt manner during faculty meetings," he would likely not vote for tenure and promotion. The implication of this common scenario in higher education is that senior faculty will sometimes make judgments affecting junior members based on their own self-interests or prejudices. In this case, I doubt that the junior faculty member was insightful enough to observe the damage done. On a number of occasions as an assistant professor, I know I wasn't as perceptive and circumspect as I should have been.

Assistant professors do have the ability to change the status quo without risking a vendetta by senior colleagues, but they should also realize that changes in higher education take time—sometimes years—and compromises. Full professors are the journeymen and journeywomen of academia. Nothing is easily changed in a department without their support.

In most other ways, active senior faculty members spend their time like junior faculty. We observe the dictates of the higher education holy trinity (teaching, academic productivity, and service) and make an effort to improve. We have spouses and kids that are starting to get a little older. We wish we had saved more for our retirement when we were assistants. We live in nicer domiciles. Our insurance costs more. And we often have well-developed biases that junior faculty members abhor.

As I mentioned, I have been a full professor for a limited time. I have friends who have been full professors for 30 years. I am humbled by what a really good full professor who uses those years well can accomplish over time. Another thing these women and men have shown me—much of their good work will go unnoticed. It's expected. A full professor should be able to carry the load.

Conclusion

What we five have tried to do in this chapter is to give you a small window on our world in higher education in two hemispheres. Organizing the roles of instructional designers into five common roles may give a glimpse of some of the day-to-day opportunities and some of the demands of our careers in higher education. For all the tiresome rituals, politics, and inertia in our colleges and universities there are also the professional freedoms, intellectual discoveries, and delightful interactions with learners that are rarely matched outside of higher education.

Here's the kind of thing that sometimes happens. As a university person, you'll find yourself at a social gathering of people who don't work in higher education. You'll hear the well-substantiated complaints about your friends' jobs. You'll think of your own complaints at first. You'll want to contribute your sad stories to the conversation. As the testimonials continue, you'll feel that life is not so bad. You'll hesitate, knowing your work-a-day problems don't compare. As the conversation swirls around you, you'll say nothing. You'll empathize, but you'll smile to yourself, thinking about what a good professional life you have.

Application Questions

1. As a faculty member working in the area of instructional design, you have been approached by a member of another department seeking advice about how to implement new instructional technologies in a course. It is evident that your colleague has limited knowledge of instructional design and that you will need to commit significant unpaid time and effort if the innovation is to be successful. How might you respond in a way that would result in benefits for both parties?
2. One expectation of more senior faculty members is the provision of leadership within the department and university. Junior faculty members seeking promotion are expected to demonstrate capacity for leadership. As a junior faculty member in a department where more senior colleagues fill all formal leadership positions, how might you find or create opportunities to demonstrate your leadership potential?
3. A department chair has asked you to meet with a faculty member who has received poor evaluations for the past two years. The faculty member is receptive to the meeting. What will you do to prepare for this meeting? What will you do during the meeting? What will you do to follow up?
4. Using the situation described in question 3, how would you handle it differently if the faculty member is opposed to the meeting and thinks his or her current methods of instruction and assessment are just fine?
5. Using the Internet, research at least four different colleges or university offices of faculty development. Answer the following questions for each office:
   a. What are the different names used for faculty development offices?
   b. Where is the office housed? What division is it under?
   c. What services does it offer?
   d. How often are programs given? What specifically are they?
   e. What is the range of experience of the staff?
   f. Provide other relevant information you find that further illuminates each office's unique attributes.
6. You are an instructional designer working in a discrete education unit and you have been invited to present a one-hour session on blended learning and its possible application by faculty members. What information would you prepare, and how would you design the session to help the faculty turn that information into practical knowledge?
7. Using the described situation in question 6 and given the range of experience that will exist in your target audience, outline the strategies you would use to balance the presentation of theory and practical application.
8. Possibly as a graduate student and most certainly as a faculty member in an instructional design program, you will be expected to conduct research related to the discipline. Identify three current trends in the field of instructional design that could provide a focus for three separate research studies. Describe the purpose, design, and potential outcomes of each study.
9. Choose three universities with instructional design or educational technology–related programs (not including your current institution), and determine what is required for an assistant professor at each university to receive tenure. In what ways are the tenure requirements similar? How do they differ?
10. This chapter has given a glimpse of what it is like to work in differing professional positions at universities in two different countries. Create a chart by which you could systematically compare the attributes, advantages, and disadvantages of working at higher education organizations among a variety of different countries in relatively similar positions.

References

Anderson, T. (2003, October). Getting the mix right again: An updated and theoretical rationale for interaction, *International Review of Research in Open and Distance Learning, 4,* 2. Retrieved January 21, 2004, from **http://www.irrodl.org/contnet/v4.2/anderson.html**

Crawford, C. (2004). Non-linear instructional design model: Eternal, synergistic design and development, *British Journal of Educational Technology, 35*(4), 413–420.

Hume, K. (2003, January 31). Department politics as a foreign language. *Chronicle of Higher Education*, p. B5.

Schwier, R., Campbell, K., & Kenny, R. (2004). Instructional designers' observations about identity, communities of practice and change agency, *Australasian Journal of Educational Technology, 20*(1), 69–100.

Seely, Brown, J. & Duguid, P. (2000). *The social life of information.* Boston: Harvard Business School Press.

Wenger, E. (1999). *Communities of practice: Learning, meaning, and identity.* Cambridge, UK: Cambridge University Press.

Jan Visser
Learning Development Institute

Katsuaki Suzuki
Iwate Prefectural University

CHAPTER 23

Designing for the World at Large: A Tale of Two Settings

Knowledge and Comprehension Questions

1. Compare the two settings described in this chapter. Identify and discuss differences and commonalities.
2. In this chapter, the authors identify a variety of elements that are particularly characteristic of each of the international settings they describe. What are those elements for each of the settings? Which of them applies also, but perhaps to a lesser extent, to the mainstream setting for instructional design and technology?
3. Based on your reading of this chapter, what are the most crucial problems developing nations are facing? What are some of the implications these problems have for the practice of instructional design and technology in the developing world?
4. This chapter argues that IDT was brought to Japan with the recent e-learning movement. According to the author, what aspects of IDT were brought to Japan with e-learning movement and what had been present in Japan before then? How has the Japanese situation been different from and similar to that of the Western world?

Editors' Introduction

There is tremendous diversity in the world, and being more aware of this will increasingly be important to instructional designers. The authors of this chapter, Jan Visser and Katsuaki Suzuki, take on the challenge of portraying instructional design and technology in the world at large using two alternative settings, each of them clearly distinct from the U.S. context. The authors contrast the developed and less developed areas of the world. The two pieces are purposely quite different, both in style and in what they try to reflect. The authors have made an effort to provide examples of how the developed and the developing sections of the world are set apart and how the instructional design discipline can be viewed across settings. For readers, it should be an interesting exercise to compare the two settings and draw conclusions from such a comparison.

In this chapter we present two almost diametrically opposed settings for instructional design and technology. Both settings also are different from the context of the United States. Working in these settings poses particularly interesting challenges. As authors we take turns, describing each of the settings in detail to give insight into the nature of the challenges faced. We precede our descriptions with a brief exploration of the issue of diversity, arguing that the world as a whole should be considered diverse as well as integral, calling for a vision of instructional design practice that takes context seriously into account.

The Challenge of Diversity

The professional literature of the instructional design field draws heavily on the experience of its application and development in one country, the United States of America. Clearly, the felt needs in the United States during and after the Second World War to intervene in a rational and controllable manner in the restructuring of human performance capability has had a profound influence on the founding and subsequent shaping of the field (e.g., Dick, 1987). Consequently, many researchers and practitioners who contributed to the development of the field either reside in the United States or, if they are active in other parts of the world, choose to discuss their ideas in journals whose readership is largely U.S. based or whose thinking is referenced to the U.S. experience and context. This chapter aims at calling attention to the broader context to which instructional design is relevant, to the diversity that characterizes that context, and to the challenges it poses to the discipline.

For this chapter we have thus chosen to focus on two different settings at opposite ends of the diversity spectrum: (1) the complex agglomeration of countries commonly designated by the somewhat misty concept of "developing nations" and (2) Japan, which, though distinct from the United States in a variety of respects such as culture, is also an industrialized economy. Conditions at these two extremes of the diversity spectrum vary widely, particularly as regards to access to and control over the earth's resources. Even so, we should recognize that those seemingly separate worlds become increasingly intertwined in a global context in which both the powerful and powerless must be concerned with what happens in the rest of the world. Therefore, highlighting in this chapter the particularities of instructional design and technology in two radically distinct non–United States settings may contribute to developing a vision of the profession attuned to the demands of a world that is in acute need of discovering how a small planet with limited resources can accommodate, in a sustainable manner, the developing needs and desires of an ever-growing population.

The reader will appreciate that the two parts of this chapter paint pictures that have not been conceived according to the same rationale nor painted with the same brush. The two authors were deliberately left to explore, separately and individually, the role instructional design and technology has played in their respective, starkly different environments. It is left to the reader to discover and appreciate both the differences and the commonalities that the two pictures reveal.

The Case of the Developing World[1]

Industrialized vs. Developing World

There once was a time when the world was simply the world according to those who defined it. Those people were able, through their supremacy in navigating the seas and their control over means to propagate and consolidate their ideas—particularly through the printed word—to impose their definitions on all others. That time is over. Before the fundamental shift in our perception of the world started to materialize, a process that may not even have entirely completed its course today, it was still perfectly possible and ethically acceptable—rare exceptions apart—for one part of the human population to think of the remaining proportion of the species as not fully human, or at least so far removed from the state of full humanness that it could be considered to be available for the free exploitation by those in power. This was the Colonial era.

This era started to break down following the Second World War. That war was fought with the involvement not only of soldiers of the principal warring nations, but also with those who could be recruited in their dependent colonies. Fighting someone else's war, however, may easily lead to the idea that one can also fight one's own war. This is exactly what happened. As World War II came to an end, territories that had thitherto remained under the control of various colonizing powers engaged in a struggle for, and eventually obtained, their formal independence.

The world changed rapidly in two to three decades. Changing as it did, it had to come to grips with a new reality. If everyone had the same fundamental rights, then the world as a whole must take responsibility for ensuring that everyone on the planet could indeed enjoy those rights. The world was—and, despite progress, continues to be—far removed from that state of affairs. Thus, development was called for.

Initial ideas about what this concept actually meant divided the world into countries that saw themselves as already developed and those that were seen to be in need of

[1] This case was authored by Jan Visser.

development. The latter were initially designated "undeveloped," a term that was later replaced by "underdeveloped" and then "developing" in successive attempts to defray negative connotations. At the same time the designation "developed" for those countries that started to see their responsibility to contribute to the development of others, changed into "industrialized." None of the terms is satisfying as all of them have connotations that are in various respects debatable. Using these terms "you cannot avoid the value judgments that the words contain" (Hancock, 1989, p. 41). What matters is that the role of instructional design in this context cannot be considered in separation from the meaning one is willing to attribute to the term *development*.

A particularly interesting question that students of this text may want to ask themselves is whether so-called developing nations should strive to emulate the achievements of industrialized nations and model the futures they desire for themselves on the ways of life prevalent in the industrialized world. Should the answer to that question be "No," then the next question will be, What kind of situation should all countries strive towards that would represent an acceptable first approximation of the direction in which *all* countries ought to be moving? How one answers these questions has implications for how one sees one's role as instructional designer and how one conceives of instructional design as a practice and a discipline in an international development context.

Situation Sketch

Among the questions that drive the different chapters in this book is this: What can or should instructional designers do in particular settings? To answer that question in my case I must first give a rough sketch of the world I have been working in for the past several decades.

To start with, in accordance with recent statistics of the United Nations Educational, Scientific and Cultural Organization (UNESCO), "nearly one in seven of the world's six billion people cannot read or write" (Sharma, 2003, n. p.). While illiteracy occurs in even the most highly developed nations, the majority of illiterate people can be found in developing countries. In fact, roughly half of them live in the nine so-called high-population countries: Bangladesh, Brazil, China, Egypt, India, Indonesia, Mexico, Nigeria, and Pakistan. If the one-in-seven statistic sounds staggering, then consider that this statistic represents, according to the same source, "a considerable advance on the first survey of world illiteracy published in the 1950s when 44 per cent of the world's population was found to be illiterate" (n. p.).

Considering the crucial importance of being literate as a prior condition to most traditional instructional interventions, it should be no surprise that great emphasis is being placed in the developing world on creating infrastructure and mechanisms through which young people can become literate and retain their literacy. Consider in that context that currently more than 100 million children of school age don't go to school and that those who do go often find themselves exposed to conditions that in other parts of the world would be perceived as wholly inadequate. This means that merely building more schools and filling them with kids and teachers may improve the statistics but does not necessarily contribute to solving the problem. Important questions must be raised regarding what happens inside schools, particularly as regards quality and relevance of learning.

In spite of all the imperfections, the benefits of "as little as three or four years of basic education have been demonstrated on outcomes as diverse as enhanced agricultural productivity, reduced infant mortality, longer lifespan, and increased family income" (Morgan, 1989, p. 48). From that perspective, investing in the development of education is not only a simple matter of doing what is right from a political humanitarian point of view; it is equally sound, as Morgan argues, to do so on the grounds of investing in a developing nation's socioeconomic development. A decision maker must question not only what is sound from a pedagogical or andragogical point of view, but also the effectiveness and efficiency of systems through which people learn designed in response to basic learning needs, including school systems as well as alternative and supplementary frameworks for learning. Considering the extremely scarce financial resources available, instructional designers working in developing countries should be able to think economically and have a good sense of macroeconomic issues. They should also have the capability to judge the concrete societal impact of interventions they plan or evaluate (Kaufman, 1999; Kaufman & English, 1979) and do so from a variety of different perspectives and within the context of multiple possibilities (Hallak, 1990).

The primary concerns of decision makers in developing countries will likely go to creating relevant, effective, and efficient learning opportunities for the young. This should by no means, however, exclude from their attention, the learning needs of the adult population. As a consequence of the lack of educational opportunities at the time the current adult population was young, learning needs of today's adults are both acute and diverse. Attending to all these needs may range from finding innovative solutions for issues as critical as impeding the spread of infectious disease via skills development among illiterate rural dwellers who have no access to electricity or even basic hand tools to developing sophisticated distance education systems to serve learning needs at the graduate level.

One World or Many Worlds?

I alluded earlier to a discernible trend in how developing countries have responded to the learning needs of their populations during the postcolonial era, namely by emulating the models and means known to them from their former colonizers. This tendency is "understandable," as Morgan (1989, p. 49) points out, from the perspective of those who ended up being in charge of their national destinies when former colonies attained political independence. Nevertheless, the tendency to emulate often stifled the development of more creative solutions to problems that were almost invariably more complex than those of industrialized nations. The approach "worked fairly well" (p. 49) as long as the scale of interventions remained restricted to catering to the few, located mainly in urban areas, rather than to the masses. This may explain why it has taken decades for the trend to be challenged.

The political pressure, both from within and without, to cater to the masses in a substantial and serious manner is relatively recent. At the international level it received a particular impetus thanks to the World Conference on Education for All held in Jomtien, Thailand, in March 1990 (Inter-Agency Commission World Conference on Education for All, 1990) and the World Education Forum, held in Dakar, Senegal, in April 2000 (UNESCO, n.d.). Such pressure redefined the felt problems developing nations are facing. It is noted, moreover, that, while educational thinking and patterns of educational practice changed in the industrialized world, developing countries often continued to be influenced by obsolete models from their colonial past, rather than by innovations that were adopted by their respective former colonizers during the postcolonial era. It is thus not uncommon for travelers from industrialized countries who visit developing nations to come across school scenes that can only remind them of the past of their own native countries.

There is both good and bad in the identified trend. Intuitively, it makes sense to try and replicate something that has worked elsewhere in a different context. However, such replication efforts, when undertaken, should go hand in hand with careful scrutiny of what works and what does not in the new context. Such efforts should equally be guided by a clear vision of what is to be achieved; i.e., a perspective and criteria by which to ascertain that something worked or didn't work. Typically, such criteria should not be limited to measures such as a headcount of increased school participation but be an expression of social impact goals to be attained. Moreover, the context within which the viability of a particular approach is being examined should be considered an integral part of the problem under consideration (Arias & Clark, 2004; Tessmer & Richey, 1997). Contextual factors vary widely across developing nations and they are usually starkly different from those in the industrialized world.

From a practical point of view, which recognizes that people learn for diverse purposes in diverse contexts, it makes little sense to strive for solutions that assume the whole world is the same. In fact, even if it were possible to strive for the reduction of diversity so as to allow greater efficiency in the grand-scale application of solutions across local settings, it would be shortsighted to follow such a course of action. Diversity is a great good and should not be sacrificed. Without diversity the conditions for evolutionary growth disappear. This is as true for biological systems (see e.g., Levin, 1999) as it is for the world of knowledge, learning, and the development of thought and creativity. Axelrod and Cohen (1999) argue that diversity is essential to allow variation, interaction, and selection to effectively do their job and contribute to growth. If we are to advance as a species we must thus allow ourselves to learn in diverse ways.

This concern may sound overly sophisticated to instructional designers whose work focuses on a particular sector within a specific country in the industrialized world, where the range of diversity is usually limited. However, as soon as one broadens one's perspective to the world at large, the diversity issue can be ignored only to the peril of the planet and those who inhabit it. The answer to the question in the heading of this section is therefore Yes, the world is one, but it's one in diversity, it's many worlds in one. Consequently, designing for the world at large means designing the conditions of learning with diversity in mind.

Reinvention Rather Than Transfer

Most of the practical wisdom of the instructional design and technology field is conceptualized in terms of the resources and conditions prevalent in the industrialized world. We know, for instance, that science education can't really be successful if students don't get a chance to acquire hands-on experience actually *doing science*. Thus, the all-too-familiar school science lab comes immediately to mind to the instructional designer charged with the task to improve the quality of science education in a particular developing country. Similarly, teacher classroom performance can greatly improve if already practicing or would-be teachers could get a chance to observe their own teaching behavior and if they could carefully practice component skills in ways controlled by effective video feedback before putting those skills together in more complex teaching behaviors. Allen and Ryan (1969) invented microteaching as a technology to facilitate such learning by teachers. No doubt, if anywhere in the world there is an urgent and great need to improve teachers' classroom behavior, it is in the countries of the developing world. Microteaching must thus be assumed to offer potential also in this context. Likewise, everyone knows that language laboratories are proven tools for the pursuit of excellence in the learning of foreign and second languages. Many of the more highly achieving students in developing countries are greatly dependent for their advanced studies on enrolling in institutions of higher learning abroad where teaching occurs in languages different from their own. As professionals, too, they will continue to be dependent on adequate mastery of major languages, particularly English, for their interaction with peers internationally. They would be greatly helped by access to language labs. There is no doubt either that there is enormous potential in giving people in, say, rural areas of Africa access to computers and the Internet so as to open new opportunities for learning to them.

Indeed, science labs, microteaching facilities, language laboratories, and computer-based rural community resource centers have found their way to developing countries thanks to the good, but often somewhat naïve, intentions of experts from more privileged parts of the world as well as following the equally good intentions of developing world decision makers who may have seen those tools performing effectively in the industrialized world. Unfortunately, the mere importation of a technological facility is insufficient to make it work. It is not uncommon for an evaluation team asked to assess a project undertaken by a development agency in a developing country to come across a well-equipped media production studio or language lab merely gathering dust or to find procured equipment still sitting in crates in the port, sometimes years after it had been shipped. One needs competent human beings to install and handle the technology as well as to take care of regular maintenance and upgrading as required. Moreover, none of those facilities lasts forever. Economic conditions must be in place—and if they don't yet exist they will have to be created—to allow for pieces of equipment to be replaced when their limited lifecycle comes to an end. The lesson is simple: Technology must be reinvented in the context in which it will be used.

Indeed, solutions that work are those that, though originally invented for use in entirely different circumstances, were not simply transferred but rather allowed to be invented anew, in a participatory fashion, within the new setting of a developing country. Reinvention, in addition to leading to adaptation to local conditions, also provides an excellent opportunity to create local involvement and thus ownership of the technology in question; i.e., it allows "going beyond appropriate technologies towards the appropriation of technologies" (Faccini & Jain, 1997, n. p.). It may result in the use of hardware components that are more resistant to heat and humidity, less expensive, and more durable. It may equally lead to more basic configurations, such as when a fully equipped microteaching lab is replaced by a single video camera and portable monitor that can be used in any makeshift classroom or even in the open air. Likewise, it could result in choices that are more energy efficient and thus allow alternative energy sources, such as solar energy, to be used. More importantly, it is essential to move beyond the simple concept of appropriate technology to that of *appropriated* technology, including the invention of not just equipment but also ways of usage that are appropriate to given circumstances and purposes.

Appropriating Technologies for Appropriate Uses

The search for appropriate technologies has often been interpreted negatively. Why? Because in the common perception technology as developed for the industrialized world is taken as the standard. By comparison, any technology that is developed or reinvented for less sophisticated environments seems to be a downgraded edition of the original version. Pertinent questions must be asked, however, regarding the value judgments, often propagated by profit-driven marketing, attached to the faster, bigger, and more powerful options that consumers in affluent societies are being told they should acquire lest they lose. I like to contend that there is great beauty and superior intelligence in the invention of things that meet their purpose and are able to do so over a sustainable period of time for people who can adapt the uses of tools to their particular desires and cultural circumstances and that, in addition, produce the minimum of waste. Also consider that solutions that are stripped of their unnecessary oversophistication are more transparent and less mystifying to their users and therefore more effective and thus desirable from a pedagogical or andragogical perspective. This notion applies, for instance, to the development by teachers and students of equipment for the study of science from locally available materials of which excellent examples can be found in the *New UNESCO Source Book for Science Teaching* (UNESCO, 1973), a real classic that can now also be found on the Web (Elfick, 2004). The fact that I am able to quote a source that is more than three decades old, whose history goes back to the close of World War II, and that still is as relevant today as it was then (see e.g., Elfick, 2004), is testimony to the sustainability of the technology in question.

Conclusion

The reality of working as an instructional designer in the developing world varies largely from individual to individual. It depends on persons, their personalities, life choices, worldviews, and the myriad circumstances in which each may end up working. It would also depend on the particular area of instruction one may be concerned with. It is also perfectly possible to end up, as I did, working in almost all possible areas at different points in time and sometimes simultaneously. Such areas may range from basic education and literacy via skills training for rural dwellers to training of secondary school teachers to university education. It may mean that one stays within formal structures, but it could also imply working through informal mechanisms. Besides, it may include dealing with schoolage children alongside adults whose learning may have to be considered in the perspective of curricula covering multiple years or much shorter training interventions. In addition, one's actions may impact groups of people as small as a single community or a school. They may equally target an entire country, a geographical region comprising a variety of countries, half the world (as is the case of the earlier mentioned nine high-population countries), or the entire planet.

Whatever the case, instructional designers dedicated to the cause of international development will live an interesting life, full of challenges their colleagues may not even dream of. No doubt, there is also a downside. Challenges as big as those one gets confronted with within this context can never be fully met and one may have to fight near-impossible battles (e.g. Visser, 2002), such as those against the shortsightedness of the development establishment and bureaucracy. Consequently, in addition to having all the standard skills that define the qualified instructional designer, those seeking employment in an international development context should have a well-developed capacity to think autonomously, creatively, and, at times, unconventionally, as well as a high tolerance of frustration.

The Case of Japan[2]

If You Were Working in Japan in the IDT Field

If you were working in a Japanese firm, you might find yourself suddenly assigned to the training division to become an instructor. Based on your knowledge and skills that you acquired in your job, you would have to start from scratch to teach for two or three years before you might go back to your original job assignment. I am not talking here about the case of a person who has been hired as an instructor or IDT specialist. Rather, I'm talking about what could happen to any of the white-collar workers in a firm. With no training as an instructor, you would be asked to become an instructor. The reason you would be asked to take up such a role is that you have a certain number of years of experience in your particular field of competence. So, you have become a subject matter expert (SME). In Japan it is natural to assume that, if you have subject matter expertise, you can also teach—and teach well—the skills and knowledge that pertain to that particular field. It is not normally considered important that a SME should work with an instructional design and technology (IDT) specialist for effective training.

On the other hand, if you were hired in a company that sells training or educational products, you would receive intensive training in becoming an instructor before doing any job at all. In fact, you may be in training sessions for six to nine months with a fully paid salary, just being trained to be a trainer. After your training, you would be teaching classes of 20 to 30 trainees. The trainees can be from inside the company or they can be fee-paying customers from outside. You would be using a textbook specified by the company. First, you would rehearse yourself in a seminar room after regular classes were over, trying to memorize what you would say in your class. Your group leader would then test you, so that you can modify your teaching following his or her advice. After a final check by the division leader, you would deliver your training. When the class ends, you would be evaluated by the trainees. Using a questionnaire, they would rate your tone of voice, the clarity of your explanation, and your attitude toward your "customers"—mainly at level 1 of Kirkpatrick's four levels of training evaluation (see Chapter 10). The results, in turn, would be used by your boss to judge the quality of your work. After some years you may be assigned to coach younger instructors in your group or to write the textbooks that they use. You may also be assigned to mentoring e-learning courses that the company started to deliver recently, answering trainees' questions by e-mail.

If you were a consultant specializing in human resource development (HRD), you could be asked to propose an intensive plan of change management for training. The majority of the workforce is accustomed to getting the training the firm would offer, and their bosses would put little value in training because training results in absence of the trainee during the period of off-the-job training sessions. The firm would want to reduce training costs. Nevertheless, it would be necessary for both bosses and their subordinates to be aware of all opportunities, including training, that improve their knowledge and skills for the rapidly changing task demands in a knowledge society. As a consultant, you are likely to find it a most urgent and difficult task to change Japanese attitudes towards self-directed job-related competency improvement. So, you would create a management plan to foster these initiatives and focus trainees on setting personal goals attainable as a result of their own efforts and responsibilities.

[2] This case was authored by Katsuaki Suzuki.

The situations discussed here, quite common in Japan, may or may not seem familiar from the perspective of your non-Japanese experience. As an industrialized country that shares a similar technological environment for teaching and learning with the rest of the industrialized world, Japan has long had a prominent position among the leaders in the world economy. However, the field of IDT is different in Japan from the rest of the world because of Japan's unique way of combining rapid westernization with a long history of Asian culture. It may well depend on people, rather than on technology. It may also well depend on how organization has been maintained. How is it different? How is it similar?

Japan has been a country of mystery to Western eyes: It is known as the country of Geisha girls and Shogun, Harakiri and Sukiyaki song. It is also known as a country that once, before and during World War II, had a fascist regime and then became a democracy. The miracle comeback from postwar state to becoming a leading industrial country has attracted many researchers to find out how it happened and to learn from it.

Total Quality Management, a technique invented in Japan, but now exported from the United States back to Japan, is one of the results of such investigations. Group emphasis, called "we-ism" as opposed to personal emphasis, "me-ism"; the bestseller book *Japan as Number One* (Vogel, 1980); or more recently, Prof. Nonaka, guru of Knowledge Management, with his theory of Implicit vs. Explicit Knowledge (Nonaka, 1994) have caught much attention and are seen as clues to uncover the Japanese miracle.

Japan has thus been full of mystery and stereotypes. Speaking of IDT, however, it is yet to be discovered how the field of IDT is different from that of the Western world. In this section, you will find out how the IDT situation in Japan may be different from or similar to the world you are acquainted with. We will look at the business and industry sector first and then proceed to the schools.

IDT Brought to Japan with the e-Learning Movement

Professionals called instructional designers or educational technologists have not been known in Japan until very recently. IDT captured the interests of the HRD sector of the Japanese business and industry sector only with the emergence of e-learning.

The year 2000 is considered to have marked the beginning of e-learning in Japan. An important event in that context was the compilation and publication of the *E-learning White Book* by the Advanced Learning Infrastructures Consortium (ALIC), an affiliated organization of the Japanese Ministry of Economy, Trade and Industry. Such training technologies as computer-based and Web-based instruction, multimedia use, and Internet-based learning merged under the name of *e-learning*, a term that has since become firmly established. IDT was seen as a "new technique" and a key tool to improve and ensure the quality and effectiveness of e-learning.

IDT, as it was brought to the Japanese e-learning industry, meant at first no more than designing appealing and usable screens and providing structure to learning materials. The focus was on better screen layout, adequate use of fonts and colors, and easier navigation techniques. The purpose was to give the materials a professional look. The word *design* played a certain role in leading people to think of the "new technique" as having something to do with visual and artistic design of e-learning. However, they did not understand in what way IDT was different from usability design and visual design.

It thus took time before the focus shifted to the systematic process for bringing about effective results in training. Only after that happened, analyses of training needs, participants, contexts, and available resources were taught as essential steps of IDT. In 2003, several training programs were offered in Japan concerning the basics of IDT in business and industry. This included, for instance, a two-day seminar to introduce the ADDIE model (Analysis–Design–Development–Implementation–Evaluation) to the development of instruction, a one-day workshop on how to use the "Instructional Designer's Tool Kit," and a five-day workshop to become familiar with the basics of the design and development of e-learning material. Lee and Owens's (2000) *Multimedia-Based Instructional Design* was translated into Japanese in 2003 as the first major introductory text on IDT. However, it was still difficult for the Japanese readers to understand in what way IDT was different from project management.

The availability of Japanese texts on IDT grows steadily. The author of this section, for instance, wrote an introductory book in 2002, *Instructional Material Design Manual*, based on the Dick & Carey model. The Japanese translation of the Dick, Carey, & Carey (2001) book itself became available in 2004. In 2003, an experimental five-day intensive course was designed and delivered by the author of this section to introduce the basics of IDT, including research-based principles and models of ID, in the context of e-learning. The course attracted more than 100 individuals who themselves produce and deliver training in business and college settings. The textbook and videotaped sessions were combined into packaged learning material that was made available through the Japan e-Learning Consortium in January 2004.

IDT that combines usability design, project management, and research-based instructional design principles is gradually becoming a recognizable concern in business and industry. Even so, another big step forward has yet to be made. The idea that IDT, in the sense of the design and development of instructional material, should be combined with notions of performance technology that connect training and a company's business strategies must gain greater popularity before a really big impact on the practice of HRD can be expected. This process may, paradoxically, be helped along by the current decline in economic growth in Japan, which has attracted more professionals than ever to become interested in better quality of HRD, higher effectiveness of training, and the design of change processes to better prepare companies to play their part in the unclear and ever-changing world of the knowledge society.

IDT Before the Advent of e-Learning

My earlier assertion that IDT only came to Japan with the advent of e-learning should not be interpreted to mean that media and technology were not used in training prior to that. Although it has been and still is common for many training sessions to be conducted by live instructors in face-to-face group settings, media and technology have been used in many training scenarios. Especially after the CD-ROM drive became a standard part of all personal computers, ample learning materials for this medium entered the consumer market. With the advance of the Internet, many online learning materials also appeared on the market. This trend formed a strong basis for the development of an e-learning infrastructure.

On the other hand, the majority of media-based training materials have not yet fully utilized IDT research-based principles. Many of the available materials are no more than books or instructor talks transformed into electronic media. The lack of analysis and design and an almost total dependence on experience-based rules of thumb can likely be identified as a major reason why IDT has so far not been fully utilized. There are a few exceptions, though. A major Japanese electronics company introduced Robert Mager's work earlier by offering a 20-day course on criterion-referenced instruction. The early mainframe computer system, PLATO, was earlier introduced in order to train pilots for a major Japanese airline company. TUTOR, the authoring language for PLATO, was used to develop a computer-assisted instruction (CAI) courseware package for English instruction. These experiences, however, may have been too few to have strong impact on the mainstream of IDT practices.

The reason why IDT only appeared with the emergence of the e-learning movement is simple: There were no IDT specialists in Japan. We still do not have a graduate program that can produce IDT specialists. The need for establishing the profession of instructional design and technology emerged only recently. Moreover, unlike the United States, there are almost no graduate programs in Colleges of Education geared towards training in business and industry. The focus in such schools has been on teacher education to prepare educational personnel for the school system. Yet another reason why IDT has not been fully employed in Japan can be gleaned from a more detailed look at the tradition of HRD in Japanese business and industry.

Non-IDT Characteristics of HRD in Japan

While there has been a long history of the existence of education and training sections in larger business firms in Japan, there has been little concern for the quality of the training or for adequate return on investment (ROI). Until the collapse of the economy in the late 1980s, the high-growth economy helped companies make profits without seriously training their employees. The major concern of companies was to produce as much as possible. The more they could produce, the more they could sell. Thus, HRD was solely concerned with productivity, not with the personal growth of the employees.

The training function, consequently, has long been regarded as a way to reward employees for their daily good work. The thought behind it was that it is "nice to have a retreat from time to time from the daily chores." In fact, the expectation behind offering training was that it would refresh employees by taking them to a remote training facility, letting them escape from the noise and hassle of their daily routine so that they would come back to work with a revitalized state of mind. Major companies even tried to attract their recruits by making them aware of their excellent training facilities in famous resort areas, rather than by reference to the content and effectiveness of their training programs for personal growth. The content of the training did not need to be readily applicable to the next day's duties, nor to building the employees' job-related competency. Training was merely expected to provide a mindset for the future, in rather indirect ways.

Hannum and Briggs (1982), comparing the systems approach and the traditional approach, point out that in traditional training content comes solely from instructors' experience; instructional strategies are experience based; tests are full of surprise; expected test results are normally distributed; and, should instruction fail, it is considered that the trainees need more time and effort. It is fair to say that the traditional approach as described by Hannum and Briggs still characterizes most of the training conducted in Japan today.

Traditionally the employment practice in Japanese firms has been to hire employees as generalists. Their specific academic background, except for possessing a college diploma, would be of little importance, as in any case new employees would be fully trained by the company after their recruitment. Newly employed personnel would first receive general training to familiarize themselves with how the business works and to acquire information technology (IT)–related skills. After that, and based on the company's judgment, they would be assigned to a section in the company. As employees go through their career, they would experience various types of job assignments. This would allow the best career path to be found for each individual. In this way, all new recruits experienced training that would in the first place serve them to become "family members" of the company. Lifelong employment was the basis for such a tradition.

Typically, newly recruited employees go through a rather intensive training period after entering a company. Such initial training may last three to six months, with full salary paid, before any job assignment is taken up. That is to say, it is as if the company is running its own business school for all the newly employed, with the exception that all the costs are paid by the company itself. It is also like going to school in that all the newly recruited typically spend their entire training at one place all together. This is done for a purpose. The company expects that all the new members will start forming a strong bond among themselves by knowing each other, spending their first time together, and, as we say, by eating rice from the same rice cooker.

Traditionally, Japanese companies do not consider their training divisions—even though they are responsible for the success of the training of new employees as well as for the followup training of employees who are in their second or higher year with the company—to be organizational entities that are made up of specialized professionals. Rather, they consider positions in a training division to be temporary for those who occupy them. People come and go as they advance along their career paths. So, it is very rare for a person to stay more than, say, two or three years in a training division before moving on to another job assignment. It is thus equally rare for accumulated IDT-related knowledge and skills to remain within the training division. As a consequence, the provision of training remains largely intuitive and based on the commonsense principle that past experience can best be repeated. Trainers also take strong cues from how they were taught in school during their childhood: the chalk-and-talk approach.

IDT in Japanese Schools

Until very recently, positions such as those of instructional designer or information technologist were unknown to the 40,000 public schools in Japan. Generally, those expected to play the role of instructional designer/technologist are teachers selected from among those who happen to form the team of teachers in each school. In other words, there are no technicians working at public schools in Japan. Schools are staffed with a principal, one or two vice principals, and teachers. It is a Japanese tradition that no principals are hired from outside the school practice, which means that principals are ex-teachers over 55 years of age. Thus, the entire personnel in Japan's public schools consists of individuals with a teacher background with specialization in one or another subject area. With the exception of technical high schools, they usually teach their subjects without any help from others, such as technicians or librarians. Larger schools, though, may have one full-time licensed librarian, whereas a teacher may take on a part-time role as a librarian in smaller schools.

Even if you were specialized in instructional design and technology, you would still need to have a Japanese teacher's license in a particular subject area, assuming full-time responsibility for teaching that area, before you would be allowed, as a part of your duty, to take care of computer labs, networks, and educational media such as projectors and broadcast equipment, while other teachers are taking care of other school duties. Should you be assigned to another school, which occurs every three to six years, then the new school may assign you to a different role. Special skills and knowledge of IDT and past experience may be taken into account in deciding your role in the new environment, but there is no guarantee that you would be considered as an IDT specialist.

There has been a Ministry of Education initiative to make all teachers conversant with the use of information technology in their own subject matter. Within this "e-Japan II" initiative, not only the goals for hardware and infrastructure were set, the government also set the goal that teachers should be trained in information technology and that by 2005 all teachers should be capable of using IT in their day-to-day classroom practice (e-Japan Strategy II, 2003).

I should note in this context that the emergence of a new technology has always been an opportunity for the IDT field to guide its introduction in the school context. This has been the case when audiovisual aids and personal computers first appeared. It holds equally true for the educational opportunities that result from the introduction of the Internet and the World Wide Web. Such challenges require teachers to think about how they can best integrate the new technology in their existing teaching repertoire and what implications this has for the redesign of their instruction. The recent emphasis in Japan on the use of IT in the classroom may thus become an opportunity for IDT-related concepts and techniques to be disseminated among school teachers.

Government has thus been offering teacher training in basic IT-related skills and IT-enhanced instruction as well as conducting training seminars for school-based IT leaders (Akahori, Horiguchi, Suzuki, & Nambu, 2001). In addition, during preservice teacher training in teacher certificate programs at the college level, a two-credit "IT basics" course is now required for all teacher licenses. Because no periodic renewal is required for teacher licenses, however, reluctant or technophobic teachers may receive no further training once they have their licenses. There are no strong demands or regulations specifying how much IT should be incorporated in the teaching of a particular subject area. So, those teachers who like to use IT will try and will become capable of effective IT utilization, whereas those who do not use IT now may remain nonusers for the rest of their career. Thus the digital divide may well grow among teachers (and those students who are in their classrooms), rather than be diminished.

Good Practices Continue: Where the Japanese Mindset Is Fostered

Although IDT has a weak tradition as a specialization, many Japanese schoolteachers have been creative enough to develop their own teaching styles. There are many methodologies that groups of teachers of a particular subject area have created and that they share as their traditions. Through this process, the teaching tradition of Japan has thus formulated subject matter–specific principles for the design of instruction. In other words, teachers can be regarded as instructional designers in the area of their own subjects.

Because the tradition in each subject area plays such an influential role among Japanese schoolteachers, teaching methods tend to be transmitted from the older to the younger generation. Until the late 1970s, the so-called "overnight alert," in which a small group of teachers stayed awake and engaged in informal communication late into the night, was a part of teachers' duties. It is said that these late-night talks created good opportunities for sharing the wisdom of older teachers with younger ones. The Ministry of Education has since established a mentorship program for first-year teachers to make such an informal sharing of traditions official, but it is difficult to say how much of the school traditions are simply transmitted and to what extent new ones are being created.

Becoming a schoolteacher is still a very competitive matter in Japan and the teaching profession still commands great respect. Local organizations of teachers in all subjects play an important role in nurturing the development of high-quality activities, even without the help of colleges of education. With proper guidelines from the Ministry of Education to lead schools to become better at integrating information technology in their programs, the concepts and techniques of IDT should be expected to start playing a more vital role in the ever-more complex classroom environment. Thus, Japan will continue to foster the younger generations' ability to learn effectively using various media and technologies, as schoolteachers maintain their creative and high-quality practices of teaching.

Multiple Settings, One Tale

In this chapter about instructional design and technology in the world at large we presented two alternative settings, each of them clearly distinct from the U.S. context. Despite the already great differences between these two examples, the available variety in the world is obviously much greater than our two cases are able to reveal. While circumstances may greatly vary from place to place—as they do between the settings discussed in this chapter—the instructional designer who works in an international context is likely to find comfort in the robustness of the instructional design discipline across settings.

Application Questions

1. In this chapter the question is raised whether developing nations should strive to emulate the achievements of the industrialized nations and model the futures they desire for themselves on the ways of life prevalent in the industrialized world or rather choose their own ways and models. How will the fact that countries may visualize their course of development from radically different perspectives affect your work as an instructional designer in an international development context? If you were to recruit an instructional designer to work in an international development context across the globe, what would you put in the person's job description?

2. Consider an instructional technology you are familiar with in the part of the world where you live. Now imagine you are being asked to introduce that technology in a part of the world that is starkly different. Specify major areas of difference between your part of the world and the location where your imaginary journey is going to lead you. Explain for yourself—or if studying this text with other students, discuss with your colleagues—what you would do to ensure appropriation of the technology in the new context and how the ways in which it will be used might change.

References

Akahori, K., Horiguchi, H., Suzuki, K., & Nambu, M. (2001). Development and evaluation of Web-based in-service training systems for improving ICT leadership of schoolteachers. *Journal of Universal Computer Science, 7*(3), 211–225.

Allan, D., & Ryan, K. (1969). *Microteaching*. Reading, MA: Addison-Wesley.

Arias, S., & Clark, K. A. (2004). Instructional technologies in developing countries: A contextual analysis approach. *TechTrends, 48*(4), 52–55, 70.

Axelrod, R, & Cohen, M. D. (1999). *Harnessing complexity: Organizational implications of a scientific frontier*. New York Free Press.

Dick, W. (1987). A history of instructional design and its impact on educational psychology. In J. Glover & R. Roning (Eds.), *Historical foundations of educational psychology* (pp. 183–200). New York: Plenum.

Dick, W., Carey, L., & Carey, J. O. (2001). *The systematic design of instruction* (5th ed.). New York: Longman.

E-Japan Strategy II. (2003). Tokyo: IT Strategic Headquarters.

Elfick, J. (2004). *School science lessons*. Web-based database maintained by J. Elfick, including a revised 2004 version of the *New UNESCO source book for science teaching* (UNESCO, 1973) Retrieved September 5, 2004, from **http://www.uq.edu.au/_School_Science_Lessons/**

Faccini, B., & Jain, M. (1997). Towards open learning communities. In B. Faccini & M. Jain (Eds.), *Technology and learning portfolio: Rethinking today's realities*. Paris: UNESCO. Available from **http://www.unesco.org/education/educprog/lwf/doc/portfolio/portindex.htm**

Hallak, J. (1990). *Investing in the future: Setting educational priorities in the developing world*. Paris: UNESCO; Oxford, UK: Pergamon.

Hancock, G. (1989). *The lords of poverty: The power, prestige, and corruption of the international aid business*. New York: Atlantic Monthly Press.

Hannum, W. H., & Briggs, L. J. (1982). How does instructional systems design differ from traditional instruction? *Educational Technology, 22*(1), 9–14.

Inter-Agency Commission World Conference on Education for All (1990). *World declaration on education for all and framework for action to meet basic learning needs*. Paris: UNESCO.

Kaufman, R. (1999). *Mega planning: Practical tools for organizational success*. Thousand Oaks, CA: Sage.

Kaufman, R., & English, F. W. (1979). *Needs assessment: Concept and application*. Englewood Cliffs, NJ: Educational Technology Publications.

Lee, W. W., & Owens, D. L. (2000). *Multimedia-based instructional design: Computer-based training, Web-based training, and distance learning*. San Francisco: Jossey-Bass/Pfeiffer.

Levin, S. A. (1999). *Fragile dominion: Complexity and the commons*. Reading, MA: Perseus.

Morgan, R. M. (1989). Instructional systems development in third world countries. *Educational Technology, Research & Development, 37*(1), 47–56.

Nonaka, I. (1994). A dynamic theory of organizational knowledge creation. *Organization Science*, *5*(1), 14–37.

Sharma, Y. (2003). Literacy: A global problem—Written out of the script. *The New Courier, No. 2* [Online version]. Retrieved February 22, 2005, from **http://portal.unesco.org/en/ev.php@URL_ID=10513&URL_DO=DO_TOPIC&URL_SECTION=201.html**

Tessmer, M., & Richey, R. C. (1997). The role of context in learning and instructional design. *Educational Technology, Research & Development, (45)*2, 85–115.

UNESCO. (1973). *New UNESCO source book for science teaching*. Paris: UNESCO. Available from **http://unesdoc.unesco.org/images/0000/000056/005641e.pdf**

UNESCO. (n.d.). World Education Forum homepage. Retrieved August 13, 2004, from **http://www.unesco.org/education/efa/wef_2000/index.shtml**

Visser, J. (2002). Technology, learning and corruption: Opportunities and hurdles in the search for the development of mind in an international development context. *Educational Technology, Research & Development, 50*(2), 85–94.

Vogel, E. F. (1980). *Japan as number one.* Tokyo: Tuttle.

SECTION 6

Getting an IDT Position and Succeeding at It

Overview

If you were a student in the field of instructional design and technology (IDT), or someone who is interested in entering it, you most likely would like to know what you should do in order to get a good job in this profession. Similarly, if you already hold a position in the field, you are most likely interested in examining what it takes to get further ahead in the profession. If either of these statements applies to you, this section of the book should be quite useful. (If neither statement applies, read the section anyhow; you paid good money for this book [we hope!] and you might as well try to get as much out of it as possible.) The section focuses on what it takes to get a good job in the IDT field and on some of the actions and skills that will help you succeed at it.

As good instructional designers, we have conducted a careful analysis of what it takes to become successful in the IDT field and have come to the amazing conclusion that one of the prerequisites to success is getting an IDT position, preferably a good one. Chapters 24 and 25 are intended to help you get such a position. In Chapter 24, the author describes his experiences in trying to obtain a position in the higher education field and offers a series of lessons he learned in doing so. These lessons are intended to serve as suggestions to help those seeking positions in the IDT field. Chapter 25 presents a matrix to help you identify your occupational preferences within the IDT field. It also describes many tips (on such topics as preparing a résumé, obtaining letters of reference, and getting ready for a job interview) that should help you obtain a good professional position.

Two of the keys to success in any profession are being active in a professional organization and keeping up with the professional literature. Chapter 26 identifies and describes the major professional organizations in the IDT field, as well as the major professional journals. Suggestions for how to decide which organizations to join and which journals to read are also provided.

What competencies must you possess to be successful in the IDT field? Over the years, many individuals and organizations have put together lists of desired competencies for various positions in the field. Chapter 27 reviews some of these competency lists, including two that recently have been developed by major professional groups. The chapter also presents a discussion of some of the issues related to competency identification, such as the certification of professionals in the IDT field.

Robert A. Reiser[1]
Florida State University

CHAPTER 24

Getting an Instructional Design Position: Lessons from a Personal History

Knowledge and Comprehension Questions

1. Describe how the conditions under which the author of this chapter was seeking a instructional design position are similar to and/or different from your own. Also indicate whether you think these similarities and/or differences affect the usefulness of the author's suggestions (lessons). Explain why.
2. The author states that most of the lessons he describes are applicable regardless of the type of position you are seeking. Describe the type of position you are interested in and identify three or four of the lessons presented by the author that you think will be most useful to you. Explain why you think each of these lessons will be useful.

Editors' Introduction

In this chapter, Bob Reiser presents a series of suggestions intended to help those individuals seeking an instructional design position. However, as the author indicates, individuals who are seeking other types of positions within the field of instructional design and technology are also likely to find many of the suggestions to be useful. The suggestions are in the form of lessons the author learned when he was looking for a job in instructional design.

By the way, the author of this chapter has guaranteed that those who follow his suggestions will be at least as successful in the field of instructional design as he has been. But be forewarned! Some would argue that attaining the author's level of success is not much of an accomplishment!

[1] Portions of this chapter were reprinted with permission of the publisher from Reiser (1987).

The purpose of this chapter is to describe some lessons that I learned when I was looking for my first position in the field of instructional design. By describing these lessons, I hope to provide some useful information to those of you interested in obtaining an instructional design position. As a matter of fact, even if you are interested in obtaining a position in our field that is outside of the area of instructional design, I think many of these lessons will be useful. Nonetheless, since I learned these lessons when I sought an *instructional design* position, I will use that term, rather than the broader term *instructional design and technology,* throughout this chapter. I will leave it up to you whether you want to substitute one term for the other.

Because I am in an instructional design frame of mind, I will now restate the purpose of my chapter in terms that should please those of you who are firm believers in "traditional" instructional design practices (Friendly note to constructivists—please do not read the remainder of this paragraph; you may find it offensive). The objectives of this chapter are as follows: Given a copy of this chapter, the reader will:

1. Choose to apply the lessons described herein.
2. Obtain a desirable position in the field of instructional design.

Before I begin to describe the lessons I learned, I would like to briefly describe some of the conditions under which I learned them. First, I learned the lessons back in prehistoric days, in 1975, to be exact. As many people are fond of saying, "times were different then," but the times weren't all that different! Second, at the time I learned these lessons, I was looking for a *faculty position in academia*. Although a few of the lessons may apply primarily to those individuals looking for a similar position, I believe most of the lessons apply regardless of the type of instructional design position you are seeking. Third, I learned many of these lessons when I was a *doctoral student*. Some of the lessons I will describe may be geared toward doctoral students, but I think most of them should be of value to anyone interested in obtaining a position in our field.

Now that I have masterfully handled any concerns you may have had about the external validity of my findings, let me take you back to those thrilling days of yesteryear . . . the lowly graduate student (me) plods along again!

The Journey Begins

In the first half of the 1970s, a frequently used expression was "the light at the end of the tunnel," and in January 1975, I finally began to see that light. I realized that within a few months I would most likely graduate from Arizona State University's doctoral program in instructional design. At that point, I decided I should start looking for a position I could move into on my graduation. Thus began my job search.

The first source I turned to during my search was the job book that was maintained and updated by the faculty members in my doctoral program. As I looked through that job book, I was reminded of a song that was popular back then: "Is That All There Is?" Needless to say, the number of faculty positions in academia listed was considerably less than I had expected. Thus, I decided to turn to other sources to find out about position openings. This leads me to the first lesson.

Lesson 1. Not every job is listed in a job book. There are many sources that list instructional design job openings. The websites of most of the professional organizations in the field of instructional design and technology include information about current job openings in the profession. The sites I recommend to students who are job seeking include those hosted by the Association for Educational Communications and Technology (**http://www.jobtarget.com/c/search_results.cfm?site_id=136**), the American Society for Training and Development (**http://www.astd.org/astd/Careers/job_bank.htm**), and the International Society for Performance Improvement (**http://www.ispi.org/**). Each of these professional organizations, and many others in our field, also provide some type of job placement assistance at the annual meeting of the organization. At a minimum, such assistance entails posting job openings and résumés at the annual meeting and providing a means for potential employers to contact and interview job seekers either during the meeting or at a later date.

There are numerous other websites you can visit that list current job openings in the field of instructional design and technology. These include careerbuilder.com (**http://www.careerbuilder.com**), and Monster.com (**http://www.monster.com**). Use terms such as *instructional design*, *instructional technology*, or *performance improvement* as keywords when you enter these sites. Moreover, a number of academic programs in our field have websites that list recent job openings. For example, see the site maintained by Indiana University (**http://www.indiana.edu/~ist/students/jobs/joblink.html**). In addition to the sources listed here, the weekly journal *Chronicle of Higher Education*, available in print and online, is an excellent source of information about job openings in higher education.

Unfortunately, many of the sources listed were not available when I was seeking a position. Back in those days, there was no Internet. However, contrary to some of the rumors you may have heard, at the time I was looking for a job the printing press had indeed been invented! Thus I was able to review the openings listed in various professional journals and posted at professional meetings. As I looked through these job listings, I learned several lessons.

Lesson 2. Most instructional design positions are in business and industry. Although this lesson was a bit surprising to me back in 1975, it shouldn't be surprising to anyone today. Indeed, the *vast* majority of positions in the field of instructional design are in business and industry.

Inasmuch as I was looking for a position in academia, I found Lesson 2 to be a bit disheartening. It was not as disheartening, however, as the next lesson I learned.

Lesson 3 (Also known as "the faculty members' lament"). Most high-paying instructional design positions are in business and industry. This lesson still holds true today. Many of the masters-level graduates of the Instructional Design program where I teach (Florida State University) begin their careers in business and industry at higher salaries than those of faculty members with doctoral degrees who have been professors for 7 to 10 years! The average annual salary for instructional designers working in business and industry can be found each year in the October issue of Training magazine.

Lesson 4. Learn how businesses operate. In light of lessons 2 and 3, you may decide that a job in business and industry is in your best interest. If that is the case, it is important that you acquire a clear understanding of how businesses operate. At Florida State, many students have acquired this knowledge by taking a graduate-level business and management course (such as Organizational Development) offered by the College of Business. A similar course at your university should prepare you to better understand the business environment in which you may be working.

Lesson 5. Acquire a strong set of skills in the production of instructional media. As I proceeded through the listings of job openings, I also noticed that many prospective employers were looking for instructional designers with some media production skills. Today, in spite of the fact that approximately 70% of the training in business and industry is presented via a live instructor (Dolezalek, 2004), job announcements often call for skills in the production of instructional media, especially the production of computer-based and Web-based training.

Most programs in our field offer a variety of courses that focus on the production of instructional media, including the development of Web-based courses, computer-based instruction, multimedia programs, and electronic performance support systems. My advice is to take several such courses.

Unfortunately, when I was a graduate student, I did not take many media production courses, and I believe that my lack of skills in that area worked against me when I was being considered for several of the positions I applied for. However, I feel that the instructional design skills and experience I acquired while I was a student and graduate assistant at Arizona State helped me get several job interviews. This leads me to the next lesson.

Lesson 6. Acquire a strong set of design (and analysis!) skills. I believe Lessons 5 and 6 go hand in hand. Although media production skills are likely to help you acquire a job, I believe it is essential to have a strong set of design skills, ranging from being able to describe goals and objectives all the way through to being able to conduct formative evaluations and revise instruction based on the data collected. Moreover, with the recent emphasis on performance technology, and particularly on front-end analysis, I believe it is also important to have a strong set of analysis skills, including skills in the areas of needs assessment, job task analysis, and instructional analysis.

Speaking of analysis, if your analysis of the skills you have (or don't have!) has led you to be concerned about the type of position you will be qualified for, let me assuage your fears—don't worry, you'll manage. And you can take the last part of the preceding statement quite literally. As was the case when I was looking for a position, many current job announcements call for skills in the management of instructional design projects. So, we come to the next lesson.

Lesson 7. Acquire some management skills. Many graduates of instructional design programs have indicated that shortly after they obtain a position, they are thrust into some type of management role. Many graduate programs in our field offer courses and/or experiences in this area, and I believe it is to your definite advantage to gain some skills and experience in the management of instructional projects and personnel.

How was I managing my own job search? After mulling (and occasionally weeping) over the lessons I was learning, I began to apply for some of the positions I read about. Working away at the old typewriter (this was during the pre–word processing age), I sent off many letters of inquiry. And before I knew it, I received my first reply, which leads me to the next lesson.

Lesson 8. Don't be discouraged if you don't get the first job you apply for. As you can tell from this lesson, I did not get the first job I applied for. Unfortunately, the same thing is likely to happen to you, so be prepared for it! With this piece of advice in mind, instead of dwelling on the rejection letter I had received, I waited eagerly for a response from the second potential employer I wrote to. And before I knew it, it came. And with that response, came the next lesson.

Lesson 9. Don't be discouraged if you don't get the second job you apply for. I could go on listing many similar lessons, but rather than dwelling on misfortune, let's just say I had a *long* string of bad luck. But my luck finally changed, and it did so when I attended the annual conference of the Association for Educational Communications and Technology (AECT), which was held in Dallas that year.

At the AECT conference, I registered with the job placement service, I gave several paper presentations, and I spoke with faculty from several universities (in spite of the fact that my professors kept trying to keep me hidden). In other words, in today's parlance, I kept a high profile. And for once in my life, my profile paid off. As a result of my activities at the conference, I was invited to two universities for job interviews, which leads me to the next lesson.

Lesson 10: Become active in professional organizations.[2] There are many ways in which you can become an active member of a professional organization. Two of the most important types of activities you can become involved in are delivering papers at the annual conference and helping various groups within the organization perform their work. To do the former, you need to submit a proposal to the organization (calls for such proposals are sent out to members many months before the conference). To do the latter, all you have to do is contact the head of some group within the organization and volunteer to help! It is rare that such an offer is turned down.

By getting actively involved in a professional organization, you will acquire new skills and knowledge, demonstrate your skills and knowledge to others, and develop a network of colleagues who can be of assistance to you throughout your career. As far as I am concerned, these statements are not trite phrases. As stated, my initial involvement in AECT led to two job interviews, and my continued involvement in the organization throughout my professional life has furthered my career in ways too numerous to mention.

Although my activities at the AECT conference led to my being invited to two universities for job interviews, I believe there was another contributing factor as well. At the time I attended the convention, several manuscripts I had written for class assignments or coauthored for research projects had been published. Since I was seeking a position in the world of "publish or perish," I assume my publication record did not go unnoticed. Thus, my next lesson.

Lesson 11. Publish, don't cherish. Random House Webster's Dictionary (1993, p.112) states that *cherish* means "to cling fondly to something." Instead of clinging to (or flinging out) the papers and reports you have written for classes or projects, my suggestion is to submit them to a journal for publication. Where should you submit your papers? The Klein and Rushby Chapter 26 provides a list of periodicals in our profession that are publication possibilities. Review the types of articles found in those publications and submit your manuscripts to the journals for which they seem best suited. Because I am a strong believer in practicing what I preach, I would like to point out that I have submitted manuscripts to many of the journals listed there. Notice, however, that I used the words *submitted to,* not *published in.* On rare (well, maybe not so rare!) occasions, my manuscripts have been rejected. Which leads me to the next lesson.

Lesson 12. Don't be dejected if your manuscript is rejected. Even if your manuscript is rejected, you are likely to get some valuable feedback from those who reviewed it. If the feedback indicates that the manuscript has some redeeming qualities, I suggest that you use the feedback to revise your manuscript. After you do so, submit the revised manuscript to another journal, or perhaps resubmit it to the same journal. If you follow this strategy, it is likely that your manuscript eventually will be published, but don't be surprised if you receive some more rejection notices first!

Speaking of rejection, let me get back to my story. When we last left me, I was about to go off to job interviews at two universities. The first was at the University of Toledo. (I mention the name of the university only to point out that when I told my wife that I was to be interviewed there, her only reply was "Holy Toledo!")

I remember my interview at Toledo quite clearly. Everyone I met there was very nice and many of them were very interested in me and my work. One faculty member, let's call him Professor X, was particularly interested in one area in which I had professed some expertise (although I don't recall the area, let's say it was mastery learning). Indeed, Professor X himself had done some research in that area. "Have you read my recent study on mastery learning?" Professor X asked. I responded by indicating that I had not read his paper. "Well, have you read Jones's outstanding literature review on mastery learning?" he inquired. Again, I had to respond that I had not read the paper he was referring to. The conversation

[2] See Chapter 26 for a listing of some of the organizations in which you may want to become active.

continued to proceed in this fashion and, as it did, I became more and more certain that I would not get the job. For once, I was right—I didn't get the job, but I did learn two other important lessons, which I discuss next.

Lesson 13. When preparing for a job interview, find out as much as you can about your potential employers. If I had taken the time to find out more about the interests and expertise of the faculty members at the University of Toledo, I most likely would have discovered that Professor X was interested in an area I was interested in. Then, by taking a little bit of time before the interview to look at his work in that area, I would have been well prepared to mention and discuss his work *before* he questioned me. I'm sure that would have created a much better impression of me than the one I left him with.

You can learn from my mistake by taking some time to find out about your potential employers. Then, during the interview, you will be able to demonstrate that you know a good bit about them and their organization. These actions will not only increase the chances that you will get the job you are interviewing for, but will also increase your knowledge about the organization so that you can decide whether you want to work there or at one of the many other places craving to hire you!

Lesson 14. Keep up with the literature in your areas of interest. As revealed by my first job interview anecdote, I had not kept up with the literature in at least one of the areas in which I thought I had some expertise. How do you keep up with the literature in the areas of our field that are of particular interest to you? A good way to start is by examining two or three issues of several of the journals in your area of interest. Ask your professors which ones they think are the most important for you to skim through.

After you have identified the journals you are most interested in, try to skim through them on a regular basis (preferably every few months, but even once a year is okay, at least by my standards!). This suggestion does not mean you have to subscribe to *all* of the journals (let your university do that), nor does it mean you have to read each journal cover to cover. Look at the titles of the articles in each issue, and read the abstracts of the articles whose titles interest you. If you are still interested in an article after having read its title and abstract, I suggest that you make a copy of the article and file it away for future reference (if you are really ambitious, you may even choose to read the article before you file it!).

Filing away articles is easy, retrieving articles when you need them is difficult. Therefore, the next lesson is important.

Lesson 15. Develop a good filing (and retrieval) system for important literature. My filing system usually works for me. I file important articles in folders that are designated by topic headings such as "distance learning" and "constructivism," (No, constructivist articles do not go into my circular file!). My folders are arranged alphabetically in several file cabinets in my office. I used to place the folders in piles all around my office, and this system seemed to work just as well. Testimonial to this fact was given by a student who once asked me for some articles on a particular topic. I immediately went to the right pile and pulled out the appropriate folder. The student, who was obviously impressed, complimented me by stating, "I really like your piling system."

I may possess good filing (and piling) skills, but in 1975 I did not seem to possess good interviewing skills. I didn't get the job at either of the universities at which I interviewed. Shortly thereafter I had a job interview at a research and development center, but again I failed to get the job. This failure was particularly disappointing—I was the only person who was interviewed! I did feel better, however, when I was told that the only reason I was not hired was because there had been an unexpected budget cutback. (At least that's what they told me!)

At this point, I decided to talk to my professors at Arizona State to see if they could give me some advice. This decision turned out to be a wise one because instead of advice, my professors gave me a job; they hired me as a faculty member in their department! This occurrence leads me to two further lessons.

Lesson 16. Let your professors know you are looking for a job.

Lesson 17. (Prerequisite to Lesson 16). Demonstrate to your professors that you do good work. Lesson 16 is important because your professors may be aware of job opportunities that you are not aware of. But Lesson 17 is even more important because it is unlikely that your professors will recommend you for a position, or even inform you of some possibilities, if you have failed to demonstrate to them that you do good work. If, on the other hand, your work is good, your professors are likely to go out of their way to help you attain a good position. Because recommendations from professors often are a critical factor in determining whether a recent graduate obtains a particular job, I suggest that if you are still a student, you should pay careful attention to Lesson 17. (Would you expect a professor to say otherwise?)

When my professors hired me as one of their colleagues, it was with the understanding that if another good job opportunity arose, I would pursue it. Thus, I would be able to broaden my horizons and share the wisdom

I had acquired at Arizona State with faculty members and students at other institutions. Besides, the contract money with which I had been hired wasn't expected to last forever!

Fortunately, well before Arizona State ran out of the contract money that was being used to pay me, I came across an announcement regarding an instructional design position that was available at Florida State University. Unfortunately, although the position sounded very interesting, the position announcement indicated that applicants were expected to have skills in a number of areas in which I had no experience or training. Nonetheless, I decided to apply for the position. And, sure enough, I got the job! Which brings me to the final lesson.

Lesson 18 (Also known as "the formative evaluator's advice"). If the job doesn't fit, revise it. Apply for jobs that interest you, even if you don't have the exact qualifications advertised. Why would an employer hire someone who does not have several of the skills the employer is looking for? I was told that in my case the fact that I was strong in some skill areas more than outweighed the fact that I lacked other skills. Fortunately, as those who hired me at Florida State had hoped, I was able to acquire some of those other skills once I obtained the job.

Now, about 30 years after I first learned the lessons described in this chapter, I'm still at Florida State and I'm still learning. I hope that by following the lessons I have described, you will be able to obtain a position that has been as enjoyable as mine has been. Good luck!

Application Questions

1. Examine several of the sources of job openings identified in this chapter and identify the two that seem to list the largest number of positions that are of interest to you. Examine at least six announcements for positions of this type. Describe the general nature of these positions and list the specific skills most frequently mentioned as being required for this type of job.
2. Identify two journals in our field that are of interest to you. (If you are unaware of two such journals, either ask your professors to identify some for you or examine the list of journals that appears in Chapter 26.) Examine three or four issues of each journal. Briefly review the titles, abstracts (if any), and content of the articles contained in the issues you examined. Also examine any notes or columns written by the editors. Afterwards, describe each journal in terms of the range of topics it addresses and the audience it seems geared towards (e.g., instructional designers, media specialists, researchers, performance technologists, etc.). Then indicate whether it is likely that you will eventually read and/or subscribe to each journal. Explain why.

References

Dolezalek, H. (2004). *Training* magazine's 23rd annual comprehensive analysis of employer-sponsored training in the United States. *Training, 41*(10), 20–36.

Random House Webster's dictionary. (1993). New York: Ballantine Books.

Reiser, R. A. (1987). Getting an instructional design position: Lessons from a personal history. *Journal of Instructional Development, 10*(1), 3–6.

Donna M. Gabrielle
Redding College

Robert K. Branson
Florida State University

CHAPTER 25

Getting a Job in Business and Industry

Knowledge and Comprehension Questions

1. As the authors suggest, describe the positive and negative features of any job you have had.
2. Complete the WorkMatrix™ as indicated in the chapter. Describe what the results of this exercise mean to you regarding:
   a. The kind of work you want to do.
   b. The kind of organization in which you want to work.
3. The authors contend that graduates of instructional systems programs will become supervisors and managers early in their careers. What implications does this contention hold regarding your academic preparedness?

Editors' Introduction

Donna Gabrielle and Bob Branson provide in this chapter useful advice for getting a job in business and industry. Indeed, many of the suggestions are likely to be useful regardless of the setting in which you may want to work. A key feature of the chapter is the WorkMatrix™, a tool for helping you clarify your occupational preferences. This tool is likely to help you come to some important decisions about the types of professional positions you are (and are not!) interested in pursuing. The authors also provide a variety of useful tips designed to help you obtain a good professional position. Some of the many topics covered are preparing your résumé, making and using contacts within an organization, obtaining letters of reference, learning about an organization, preparing for an interview, dressing for success, and using a systems approach to identify and attain professional goals.

A wise man asks, "Do you live to work or do you work to live?" Regardless of your perspective of balance in work and in life, it is important that you enjoy what you do for a living, especially when such a large proportion of your waking hours are spent working. This chapter is intended to help you consider job opportunities in business and industry, to focus on what is important to you as you begin job hunting, and to think about what work environments appeal to your personality and your interests.

First Things First

If you are still in school and are undecided about what you want to do for a living, use the opportunity to explore. For example, search for a part-time job or an assistantship that will give you experience in a work environment that you are interested in pursuing. If you don't like what you are doing, chances are that when you graduate, you won't like it any better.

If you are already working, use this chapter to help you focus on where your career path should go next. As is often said, the best time to find a job is while you have a job.

Also, in today's uncertain times, there is good news and bad news about getting a job in business and industry. The good news is that careers are no longer permanent. It is not uncommon for people to change jobs or careers several times in their lives. The bad news is that careers are no longer permanent. While your parents or grandparents may have worked for the same company their entire careers, today's workforce requires that people be trained and retrained frequently, and that people be prepared to lose their jobs and begin the hunt all over again. Consequently, it is essential to be a self-directed, lifelong learner in order to thrive in your career.

Psychological and Economic Income

There are two important kinds of income in any job. Economic income provides the *money* to exist in society. Psychological income provides the *inspiration* to thrive in society. To determine the importance of both kinds of income requires that you clarify your feelings and goals. What kinds of work do you enjoy? Think about the various classes and assignments you have had and what the really good ones had in common. To find out what kinds of work you dislike, go through the same process. Identify the good and bad features of any job you have had. Talk to people who do what you want to do. Ask them about what they like and dislike about their jobs.

Do you prefer working face to face with people? Would you rather sit at your computer and create products? Is happiness in your job more important than your income level? Do you require support and external approval? Do you aspire to work in occupations that help people? All of these factors and others are important in helping you make good career decisions.

Table 25.1 presents a condensed version of the Work-Matrix™ (Branson, 1999), which provides a decision-making tool for clarifying your occupational preferences. It is intended to help you describe the kind of work you want to do and the kind of organization in which you want to do it. We will assume that your chosen career is performance technology or instructional systems. Column 1 describes attributes of work, location, and organizations. Column 2 asks you to rate each attribute's relative importance on a 10-point scale. Thus, if "High starting income" were very important to you, then you would rate it a 10. If you really don't care where you work and would be equally happy staying where you are or going somewhere else, it would be rated a 1. Multiply each entry in column 1 by the entry beside it in column 2, and put that number in column 3. The result shows how likely it is that you can satisfy that attribute. This is not a psychological test; there is no right or wrong answer to any given question.

It is best to use this table with your spreadsheet program so that you can sort the data after you have entered it. A hyperlink is provided in the Appendix at the end of this chapter to an online version of the spreadsheet. The matrix shows what features of work are most important to you, how likely you are to achieve those features, and the combination of the two as an overall score. You may enter any other feature or attribute that you consider important. When you have the worksheet completed, sort the columns to get a rank ordering of your preferences and your best estimate of the chances of making your preferences become reality.

By using your preferences and research on the Web and at your career center, you should be able to get a better idea of what your prospects might be. For example, suppose that you really want to be a trainer delivering instruction, have no travel, and receive a high starting income. You then look up jobs in which these characteristics might be found and discover that being a trainer in industry might satisfy your requirements. However, many trainers have to travel a lot. So you must now begin the process of trading off your desires with the chances of actually finding your chosen situation.

Ultimately, you will have to decide whether you want to remain a professional performance technologist/IDT specialist or join the company or organization as a supervisor or manager. Remaining a professional provides you the flexibility to move from one organization to another while doing similar work. Becoming a supervisor and manager provides you the opportunity to get a higher salary and more responsibility within an organization. Recent experience for

The WorkMatrix™ is intended to help you describe the kind of work you want to do and the type of organization in which you want to work. Rate each descriptor in the first column on Importance and Likelihood on a 10-point scale. Multiply the rows to arrive at a Score in the final column

Type of Work	Importance	Likelihood	Score
First-level service (Teaching, delivering training)			
Second-level service (Training trainers)			
Third-level service (Designing instructional models)			
Fourth-level service (Creating basic knowledge to inform third-level service)			
Designing instruction			
Developing instruction			
Other			
Features of Work			
Geographic location			
High travel requirement			
High starting income			
High income growth			
High promotion opportunity			
Other			
Economic Sector			
Education			
Public service; Foundation, NGO			
Service industry			
Manufacturing			
Knowledge industry			
Government			
Other			

Source: From Using the WorkMatrix™ to Make Career Choices, by R. K. Branson, 1999, Tallahassee, FL: Branson Professional Associates. Copyright 1999 by Branson Professional Associates. Reprinted by permission.

IDT graduates in industry suggests that they will do technical work for a year or two and then will become supervisors and ultimately managers. It is up to you to manage your own career and to continue your personal preparation. For one glimpse of the future of the profession, see Bowsher's (1998) *Revolutionizing Workforce Development: A Systems Approach to Mastery.*

Searching for the Right Job

A recent poll by CareerBuilder.com (2004) showed that 40% of workers in the United States plan to change jobs this year and that 24% are generally dissatisfied with their jobs. Don't be part of these statistics. If you are not happy in your job, find another job you enjoy. There is nothing worse than waking up in the morning and dreading going to work. For more information about how to find the right job that makes you happy, read Jansen's (2003) *I Don't Know What I Want, But I Know It's Not This: A Step-By-Step Guide to Finding Gratifying Work.*

Most companies post their employment opportunities on their website. Many organizations use a keyword search strategy to help them handle the volume of résumés they receive. Be sure that you have included all the professional keywords and current buzzwords (e.g., *adding value, saving costs, improving job performance*, or *working alone* or *in teams*) in your résumé. Avoid going overboard with extensive formatting and creating large files. Your university placement center has useful information about job searching and presenting yourself and your résumé. Be prudent and consider their advice.

If your academic department permits you to receive mail and telephone calls, use the official address on the résumé. "The Department of Educational Psychology and Learning Systems, Florida State University," sounds better than "123 First Street, Apartment 342A." Even though many employer contacts will be via e-mail or the Internet, the address and telephone number will still look more professional.

Landing the Job Interview and Networking

Having an insider recommend you or send in your résumé will often give you an advantage over people who are simply distributing their résumés to large numbers of organizations. If you know people in the organization, ask them to refer you. If you have no contacts, you might cross-reference people through directories such as those maintained by the International Society for Performance Improvement (ISPI) or the Association for Educational Communications and Technology (AECT). If you can find an inside contact, send that person an e-mail saying who you are and how you found them and ask for advice on getting a job with their organization. Also be certain to attach a cover letter to show the company that you made an extra effort and have the skills it requires.

Business and professional relationships thrive on personal contact and interaction. Begin early to develop relationships with others in the field through memberships in societies, attending professional conferences and meetings, and organizing student groups to build networks. Volunteer on committees to be sure that the relationships are mutually satisfactory. Good relationships are mutually beneficial and thrive on give-and-take opportunities over time. Recent research suggests that providing such support to others may lead to a longer, happier life (Brown, Nesse, Vinokur, & Smith, 2003). Also, take advantage of opportunities to learn more about your personality and what work environment best suits you.

Preparing for the Job Interview

Preparation is the key to success. Before you go on a job interview, research the company's mission and its key people. Company websites are a useful place to begin your research, but you might also consider searching library databases.

You may be interviewed by one person or a team of people. Find out who will be conducting the interview and familiarize yourself with their work and their roles in the company. This research is beneficial during the entire interview, but especially when you will be asked if you have any questions for the interviewer(s). Always have at least one or two thoughtful questions ready for your interviewer.

The Interview Process

All the skills in the world will not land you a job if you don't have good interview skills. The interview process is an opportunity to let your personality shine through. You should demonstrate that you are confident, well spoken, polite, friendly, and capable.

Take advantage of your university career center. Not only will you learn about job opportunities, but you will also learn about how to present your résumé and how to polish your interview skills. There may also be occasions to have mock interviews and receive feedback on your performance.

The more interviews that you have, the more you will see common questions and will be better prepared to answer them. A standard first question might be, "Tell me about yourself." Practice your response to this and other questions, focusing on what your strengths are and how your skills would benefit the organization. More importantly, consider the role of your interviewer and relate your strengths to their job function. For example, if your interviewer is the head of training and development, discuss your use of IDT to benefit instruction. Also, you should have clear, well-rehearsed answers that cover the following topics:

- Why you selected the field of performance technology or IDT.
- A portfolio, if possible, including products that you produced in classes or in past jobs.
- Examples of how your skills have benefited organizations.
- Why you should be chosen over other qualified candidates. (What makes you unique?)
- Examples of how you have handled difficult situations.
- Where you see yourself in your career 5 or 10 years from now.
- Why you think you would like to work for the organization. (Demonstrate your knowledge of the company and relate your skills directly to its needs.)

Adopt the standards for the organization you seek. Dress in professional business attire. When in doubt, dress to a level higher than the job you seek. Develop a firm, but not too powerful, handshake. Be sure that you make eye contact with the person when you are shaking hands and that your hand is warm but not sweaty.

Wear no perfume, aromatic aftershave, or other heavily scented cosmetics. Use moderate amounts of makeup. You are seeking a job in a professional organization, not a role in a play.

Regardless of the culture from which you come, learn to look the other person in the eye when you are interviewed. Popular guides on meeting people suggest that others will get their first impression of you within the first 30 seconds. One never gets a second chance to make a good first impression. If you are uncertain in any of these areas, seek advice and practice.

The students who study the most get the best grades. The expert musician practices more than twice as many hours as the would-be expert does. There is a message here. Rehearsal and practice make an important difference in results. Engage in mock interviews with your colleagues and make sure that they ask difficult or trick questions. For the more specific questions, rehearse specific answers.

Say what you have to say in no more than three minutes, and then wait for questions. Even if you are nervous, avoid babbling and other nervous habits. Remember that you should come away from the interview with knowledge of the interviewer, too.

Avoid undergraduate slang such as "She goes," "He goes," when you mean that she or he *said* something. Avoid using arcane and local acronyms.

Tough interview questions. A question you may encounter at the end of the interview is, "Why should we hire you?" Because you are a hard worker who likes to get things done you have the qualifications and perhaps experience that they are seeking. You work well alone or are a great team player. Think up other reasons.

"What is your greatest strength?" Is it your work ethic? You are really good at learning and updating software. You work well with subject matter experts. You are good at explaining technical information in common language without intimidating people.

"Where do you see the greatest need for improvement in yourself?" There is so much to know and so little time to learn. You have to work on personal priorities to avoid being overwhelmed. You are a perfectionist.

Salary questions. Some employers will probe your minimum salary requirements. We firmly believe that you should avoid this question if at all possible until it is clear that they want to hire you. When discussion begins on the job offer, then you can say that you would expect to be paid comparably to others with your qualifications. However, you need to know what those numbers are. If an organization hires a number of IDT graduates, you will find it more difficult to negotiate salary and terms of employment than if you are the only one being hired (see Branson, 1987). The advantage of working for an organization that hires numerous IDT graduates is that you can develop collegial relationships with others and likely find a good mentor.

The best source of recent salary information is from your colleagues that were last hired. Listservs can provide a source of employed IDT people who might be willing to give you this information. Your college placement service keeps records of positions and salaries by major. The federal government has a job classification for IDT and you can check out the most recent pay schedule on agency websites. Finally, this chapter's Appendix lists resources to help you learn about salary trends in the field.

Environment issues. Some consulting companies do not really have offices. You will be working in the client's locations and will be traveling quite a lot. Be sure that you understand what "80%" travel means. That is four days out of five. That will be hard on your family and social life, if you have either. Travel often sounds exciting, but remember that you are traveling to work and often will not have the time to see the sights.

How important is location? Some people cannot stand long periods of hot or cold weather. If you don't like heat, stay out of the south and the desert. Avoid the northern tier of states if you dislike cold weather. Some people crave cities. Others prefer suburbs or smaller towns. Clarify your feelings on the kind of place that you want to live, or decide if location really matters to you.

Career Enhancements

Three career-enhancing skills are analysis, synthesis, and presentation. Learn to analyze a problem or situation to identify the issues, the basic numbers used to describe it, and the potential cause-and-effect relationships. Generally, you will benefit from understanding the business that your organization pursues. What factors contribute to success and where are the problems? Ordinarily, analyses of this type will be done using spreadsheet programs that display the critical variables. When you learn the business problems, you will be in a better position to see how your efforts can add value to the organization.

Suppose, for example, that you work in the financial services industry. In a conversation with the customer service manager, you learn that one of their largest cost factors is handling customer inquiries. You observe the job and conclude that if they could reduce the length of transactions with clients by 10 or 12 seconds, it would reduce costs significantly. So, you compare the costs of developing and delivering a brief training program to capture those 12 seconds to the costs of maintaining the status quo. The issue is to start with the business problem and work backward into alternative solutions.

Based on your analysis, can you synthesize the findings into a coherent presentation of the issues and explain your conclusions? The synthesis usually occurs first in concept, and then moves toward outlining your presentation. Can you present the results to a group using standard presentation software? Learn to conduct good briefings. Use *PowerPoint* or other presentation software effectively and without the use of too much pizzazz (keep it simple). Use sans serif fonts such as Arial, and be sure to have the font large enough to read from the back of the room. Also, to add realism to your presentation, use photos whenever possible instead of canned clip art. It will give your presentation a more professional and polished look. A hyperlink is provided in this chapter's Appendix to specific information on other tips to improve your presentations.

Preparing effective presentations is an important skill to develop. Practice and rehearsal of oral presentations will improve the impression you make on your listeners. You may be asked to present briefings to senior managers. Those who do this well will find their careers moving at a faster pace than those who stumble through awkwardly.

When writing the results of your efforts, seek editorial assistance and peer feedback to ensure that the story is clearly told and interesting to read. The report or document must not contain poorly written sentences, or grammar or word usage errors. Remember that your word processor's spelling checker will consider "there," their," and "they're" all as correct when only one of them is the right word.

Potential Threats to Success

Potential threats include talking too much and listening too little. This unfortunate behavior often occurs when recent graduates, bursting with a better way to do things, urge changes before fully understanding why the status quo is in place. So, you should learn to do it their way before you try to get them to do it your way. One can learn much more by active listening than from talking.

Gossiping and joining office cliques can lead to dire consequences. Because we are people, there will always be struggles for power, competition for promotions and resources, and social systems operating. Often, disgruntled staff members who believe the organization has done them wrong will lead these cliques. Perhaps they are right, but the issue is not likely to be your battle. Thus, never badmouth your company or your boss. The only exception is to avoid a conviction of perjury in court.

Use a Systems Approach

In career preparation, using a systems approach can greatly enhance your potential. Use the available information sources to decide what your goals are. People who have written goals are more likely to achieve them than those who do not.

Make a careful inventory of your assets and liabilities. What are your personal strengths and gaps? Benefit from your strengths and try to close your performance gaps. This will require study and work. Also, maintain your physical appearance and condition as best you can. People who are in better physical condition find more opportunities than those who are not.

Search deliberately for those opportunities that meet your personal goals. Only you can know all the things that are important to you and how important they are. Use these preferences to help you make career choices.

Beware of the size of your personal debt. If you abuse your credit cards and overextend yourself, you may well make career choices that you don't want simply because you need more money to pay off the debt. Remember, too, that unforeseen but almost certain events will occur in your life that will cause immediate financial problems. Unless you have developed the skill of managing your personal finances, you can well be at risk when you needn't be.

Plan Your Career

Planning your career will probably take as much time as fulfilling the requirements for a difficult graduate course.

Think about that. First, you will need to learn about yourself. Ask yourself the following questions:

- What are your strongest skills?
- What skills must you polish?
- What job-related tasks make you happy?
- What do you dislike doing most?

Then, you should figure out where you fit into the world. Next, research the options available to you. When you have finished this analysis, you will have the information to plan. Think of *planning* as developing a script that lays out what you will do and when. Begin executing your plan and revise as required when you have new information.

To survive and thrive in the future will require a constant and aggressive search for new ideas and new information. Rely on yourself, not just on your employer, to discover new information that you can convert to knowledge that will add value to your job and to yourself.

Staying in the Game

No matter how happy you are in your job, you must be prepared in case you lose it or want to change jobs. This includes staying updated on developments in the field, making connections through professional organizations, and ensuring your résumé or curriculum vita is current.

Read journals and publications to keep updated on developments in the field. Know what publications are most pertinent to your area of interest. Also, identify and take advantage of networking opportunities. For example, if training is your field, join your local chapter of the American Society for Training and Development (ASTD). Most professional organizations, including International Society for Performance Improvement (ISPI) and American Educational Research Association (AERA), have student rates to join. Also, submit academic papers for conferences. Even if your paper is not accepted, attend conferences to learn about research in the field. Volunteer your time at these conferences, not only to offset the registration fees, but also to make valuable contacts and learn from them.

Application Questions

1. Prepare a résumé that emphasizes your capabilities based on your professional experience and academic training. Incorporate keywords that are used in the industry.
2. Select a self-assessment opportunity from the list in this chapter's Appendix. Complete the self-assessment. What did you learn about yourself? What surprised you about the results?
3. Go to your university's career center. If offered, participate in a mock interview. If not offered, work with a group of your classmates to conduct a mock interview for a job in business or industry. Videotape the interview. Take the roles of interviewer and interviewee. When you have finished, critique both each other's and your own performance. What would you have done differently? What were your strengths in the interview?

Appendix Online Resources

The following resources may be of use to you in your job hunt:

- **http://gabrielleconsulting.com/workmatrix.htm**—Online spreadsheet version of the WorkMatrix™ that will automatically calculate the cells for your work preferences.
- **http://www.careeronestop.org**—Online career coach, self-assessment opportunities, job bank, and other free resources for job seekers.
- **http://www.doleta.gov/jobseekers/services.cfm**—U.S. Department of Labor's training and employment services for job seekers.
- **http://www.astd.org/astd/careers**—American Society for Training & Development career center including job bank, self-assessments, résumé writing, and salaries.
- **http://www.jobtarget.com/home/index.cfm?site_id=136**—Association for Educational Communications & Technology career center.
- **http://gabrielleconsulting.com/TipstoImprovePresentations.htm**—Tips on how to improve your presentations including details on font sizes, shortcuts, and organization.

References

Bowsher, J. E. (1998). *Revolutionizing workforce development: A systems approach to mastery.* San Francisco: Jossey-Bass.

Branson, R. K. (1987). Finding a good instructional systems position in business and industry. *Journal of Instructional Development, 10*(1), 7–12.

Branson, R. K. (1999). *Using the WorkMatrix™ to make career choices.* Tallahassee, FL: Branson Professional Associates.

Brown, S. L., Nesse, R. M., Vinokur, A. D., & Smith, D. M. (2003). Providing social support may be more beneficial than receiving it: Results from a prospective study on mortality. *Psychological Science, 14*(4), 320–327.

CareerBuilder.com. (2004). A survey of U.S. worker attitudes toward jobs. Available from **http://www.careerbuilder.com**

Jansen, J. (2003). I don't know what I want, but I know it's not this: A step-by-step guide to finding gratifying work. New York: Penguin.

James D. Klein
Arizona State University

Nick Rushby
British Journal of Educational Technology

Knowledge and Comprehension Questions

1. Make a list of your professional interests and identify which of the organizations described in this chapter you would be inclined to join. Explain why.
2. Scan the table of contents for several of the publications described in this chapter and make a list of the topics included in each one.
3. Select a topic of interest and conduct a search of the publications listed in this chapter to identify those that have published articles on the topic. Read a few articles from different publications related to the topic and explain which journals you believe provided the best source of information.
4. Describe how a conference can be approached as a learning event.

CHAPTER 26

Professional Organizations and Publications in Instructional Design and Technology

Editors' Introduction

Earlier in this book it was noted that by becoming active in a professional organization in our field and by keeping up with the professional literature in your areas of interest, your chances for success in our profession would be greatly increased. In this chapter, Jim Klein and Nick Rushby describe factors to consider when deciding which professional organization(s) to join and which professional publications/journals to read. They also provide brief descriptions of most of the major professional organizations and journals in our field. (Please note that all URLs in this chapter were correct as of time of publication. However, due to the rapidity with which such things can change on the Internet, some addresses may be outdated by the time you read this.)

With this information in hand, you should be ready to make some informed decisions about the professional organizations and publications that are of greatest interest to you.

The field of instructional design and technology (IDT) includes a number of professional organizations and publications.[1] Membership in professional organizations, attendance at conferences, and focused reading of journals are an essential part of your continuing professional development and crucial for developing a network of contacts. Every instructional designer is expected to update and improve their knowledge and skills in IDT and related fields (see, for example, **http://www.ibstpi.org**). Furthermore, many instructional technologists work in small teams, while others work alone. In these circumstances, formal and informal networks help to develop and maintain your professional competence.

But as a new member of the field, how do you know which organizations to join, which conferences to attend, and which publications to read? This chapter provides information about organizations and publications in IDT to help you make informed decisions as a consumer and hopefully, an active member of the field. The chapter opens with an overview of the factors to consider when deciding about an organization, conference, or publication, followed by specific details about 31 professional organizations and 75 publications of interest to members of the IDT field.

Deciding Which Organizations to Join

Most professional organizations have a clearly stated mission or focus and are geared toward meeting the needs of a particular segment of the professional community. Professional organizations in IDT are focused on a variety of areas such as educational technology, human performance improvement, information technology and computers, scholarly inquiry, and training. Further, they are aimed at a range of audiences from academics and graduate students in higher education to practitioners in business and industry.

The decision to join a professional organization should be based in part on whether its mission or focus matches your career goals and interests. For example, if your goal is to work as an instructional designer in a business setting, then you should consider joining a professional organization that focuses on performance improvement or training. If you plan to become a faculty member in higher education, you should think about joining an organization that has a mission related to scholarship and research.

The decision to join a professional organization should also be based on the benefits provided to members. Each organization provides specific benefits to its members; these include annual meetings and conferences, employment assistance, journal subscriptions, professional development opportunities, and access to websites and listservs. These benefits are important because they help you become an active and informed member of the field. For example, conferences provide you with the opportunity to keep up with the latest trends, share ideas and problems, and network with others by forming professional relationships and contacts. In addition, a subscription to a journal or magazine published by an organization can help keep you informed of the latest theories, research, or techniques being employed by other professionals in the field.

The benefits of joining any professional organization should be weighed against the cost of membership. Annual dues can range from a small, nominal fee to several hundred dollars. Conference fees and journal subscriptions can also be expensive. Since most professional organizations have special rates for graduate student members, you should consider joining a few groups while in school to see which are most appropriate for you.

Joining a Web-Based Forum

A relatively new phenomenon is the Web-based association or forum, which may be no more than a loose grouping of people sharing some common interests and posting and discussing their ideas on the Internet. These tend to be ephemeral groups, forming, storming, and falling into neglect over a relatively short time frame. However, some are more robust. A good place to look for fora on the Web is your professional organization's website; you also may learn of sites by talking to like-minded IDT colleagues at the conferences and exhibitions that you attend.

Deciding What Conferences and Exhibitions to Attend

In the days before safety matches and lighters, instructional technologists (and most of the rest of the population) used tinderboxes as a portable source of fire. These contained a flint and steel for striking sparks and some tinder to catch the spark and start a flame. If any of these three were missing, you couldn't make fire. Professional organizations and conferences that focus totally on your specific field are good places for meeting up with old friends, confirming existing ideas, and hearing colleagues preaching to the choir. But progress usually happens because people make connections between apparently unrelated ideas. Sometimes you need to be jolted out of established paths through contact with new ideas from another branch of

[1] We would like to thank Jason Chan, Laura Czerniewicz, Nancy George, John Hedberg, Carol Koroghlanian, Myint Swe Khine, Heng-yu Ku, Kar Tim Lee, Ron Oliver, Gregory Thomas, Philip Towndrow, Martyn Wild, Michael Yip, and Amy MacPherson-Coy for their help with gathering the information presented in this chapter.

IDT—or even from another discipline. Conferences and organizations are like tinderboxes; it is sometimes very enlightening to attend a conference that is not directly focused on your field.

Conferences and exhibitions are learning events. As an informed learner (You are, after all, an instructional technologist!) you should go with clear learning objectives and plan in advance how you intend to achieve them. Most conferences have a website that you can use to help plan your visit. Identify the sessions and the booths that you want to visit. Papers by recognized authorities are usually worth attending but don't ignore the less well-known presenters who may have something important to say about your interests.

Many companies demonstrate learning materials at their booths and this provides an opportunity to critique them and to learn from others' mistakes. Would you have designed them like that? Do the materials work for you? Do you think they would work for the intended audience? How could they be improved? Don't be hesitant about spending time talking to people and working through the learning materials. Exhibitors like their booths to look busy and your presence will help with the impression that they have something worthwhile to display.

Deciding What Publications to Read

The decision to spend time reading a specific professional publication should also be based on whether its focus matches your interests. Like professional organizations, publications have a specific purpose aimed at a particular audience. Some are scholarly academic journals that publish articles on research and theory; others are magazines that publish about current practices. Publications of interest to the IDT community are focused on a variety of topics, including cognition and instruction, distance education, instructional development, multimedia, performance improvement, and visual literacy.

The value or quality of a journal often depends on the interests of readers. A journal that practitioners in business and industry might find very useful may be considered of little value to researchers in the field or to IDT professionals working in school settings. Some factors that you can consider when deciding on the quality of a particular journal are whether submissions are reviewed "blindly" by peer reviewers, the rate of acceptance versus rejection of submissions, and the reputation of the editorial board.

Electronic Journals

In recent years, there has been an increase in the number of electronic journals (e-journals) found on the Web. e-journals can be a good source for you to find information on the latest trends and issues in IDT. However, although a few e-journals apply the same rigorous standards used by peer-referred print journals, others are less careful about the accuracy of information published on the Web. As an educated consumer of information, you should critically analyze the content of what you read regardless of where it has been published.

Professional Organizations in IDT

The following pages provide specific details about 31 professional organizations of interest to members of the IDT field. Much of the information has been taken directly from materials published by these organizations.

Academy of Human Resource Development (AHRD) encourages the systematic study of human resource development theories, processes, and practices. The academy provides opportunities for interaction among individuals with a scholarly and professional interest in HRD from multiple disciplines and from across the globe. It sponsors an annual international conference and several other meetings held in different regions of the world. AHRD publishes several journals, including *Human Resource Development Quarterly.* **[http://www.ahrd.org]**

American Educational Research Association (AERA) is concerned with improving education by encouraging scholarly inquiry and by promoting the dissemination and application of research results. Members include educational researchers, administrators, evaluators, professors, and graduate students from a variety of disciplines. AERA consists of 12 divisions and approximately 150 special interest groups that enable members with a common interest in a specialized topic or issue to exchange information and ideas. Individuals with an interest in IDT often belong to Division C: Learning and Instruction and to the Instructional Technology Special Interest Group. AERA sponsors an annual meeting with several thousand presentations on a range of topics. Individuals seeking employment in academia will find the job placement center at the annual meeting and an online listing of job openings particularly helpful. AERA publishes several journals, including *American Educational Research Journal (AERJ), Educational Researcher (ER),* and *Review of Educational Research (RER).* **[http://www.aera.net]**

American Society for Training & Development (ASTD) provides leadership to individuals and organizations that are committed to workplace learning and performance. Members are from organizations such as multinational corporations, medium-sized and small businesses, government, academia, and consulting firms. ASTD has local chapters in several regions of the world that provide an opportunity to network with training professionals at the local level. The organization sponsors various professional conferences each year and an online job bank to assist individuals seeking employment in the training and performance field. The association also has a global network that is active in Europe and growing in influence. ASTD publishes *T+D Magazine* and *Learning Circuits*, an online source to promote and aid the use of e-learning. [**http://astd.org**]

Asia Pacific Society for Computers in Education (APSCE) was established in 2003 and organizes the International Conference on Computers in Education. [**http://www.apsce.net/**]

Association for the Advancement of Computing in Education (AACE) is an international organization dedicated to the improvement of knowledge, theory, and quality of learning and teaching with information technology. AACE encourages scholarly inquiry related to information technology in education and the dissemination and application of research results. Members include researchers, developers, practitioners, administrators, policy decision makers, trainers, adult educators, and others with an interest in information technology in education. AACE sponsors international conferences each year including ED-MEDIA—World Conference on Educational Multimedia, Hypermedia and Telecommunications; and E-Learn—World Conference on e-Learning in Corporate, Government, Healthcare, and Higher Education. AACE publishes the *Journal of Interactive Learning Research (JILR)*, *Journal of Educational Multimedia and Hypermedia (JEMH)*, and *International Journal on e-Learning (IJEL)*. The organization also hosts an online career center and a digital library with access to thousands of journal articles and conference proceedings. [**http://www.aace.org**]

Association for Applied Interactive Multimedia (AAIM) supports professionals who use and develop interactive multimedia for education and training. The association sponsors conferences and workshops for practicing multimedia professionals, educators, trainers, and those considering using multimedia and related applications. [**http://www.aaim.org**]

Association for Educational Communications and Technology (AECT) links professionals holding a common interest in the use of educational technology and its application to learning. Members include professors and graduate students, school library media specialists, researchers, and instructional developers from business and industry. The association has several divisions and councils to address the specific interests of its members. Individuals with an interest in IDT often join divisions focused on instructional design and development, research and theory, and training and performance. AECT sponsors an annual international convention with several hundred presentations and a job placement center, a summer conference focused on specialized topics, and an online list of employment opportunities in educational technology. AECT publishes *Educational Technology, Research & Development (ETR&D)*, *Quarterly Review of Distance Education (QRDE)*, and *TechTrends*. [**http://www.aect.org**]

Association for Media and Technology in Education in Canada (AMTEC) is a pan-Canadian community of educators, media producers, researchers, librarians, and other professionals who work to facilitate and improve learning through the appropriate application and integration of educational technology. AMTEC holds an annual conference and publishes the *Canadian Journal of Learning and Technology*. [**http://www.amtec.ca**]

Australasian Society for Computers in Learning in Tertiary Education (ASCILITE) is a society for those involved in tertiary computer-based education and training, including educational interactive multimedia. It provides a forum to stimulate discussion of relevant issues in the educational use of technology, as well as promoting research and evaluation. ASCILITE holds an annual conference and promotes cooperation and liaison with other groups and organizations that have complementary aims. [**http://www.ascilite.org.au**]

Australian Council for Computers in Education (ACCE) is a national professional body for those involved in the use of learning technology in education. It strives to encourage and maintain a level of excellence in this field of endeavor throughout Australia. Each state and territory has an independent association that advances the professional development of its members in the use of learning technologies in education. [**http://www.acce.edu.au**]

Australian Society for Educational Technology (ASET) is the Australian national organization for people with professional interests in educational technology. It organizes a biennial conference and publishes the *Australian Journal of Educational Technology*. [**http://www.aset.org.au**]

British Learning Association (BLA) was formed when the British Association for Open Learning merged with the Forum for Technology in Training. It provides impartial information and advice on best practice, techniques, and technologies in learning. It aims to generate opportunities for networking and access to the collective expertise of the membership, supports the use of quality models and promoting continuous improvements, and maintains strategic links with key organizations both in the United Kingdom and worldwide. [**http://www.british-learning.com**]

Chartered Institute of Personnel and Development (CIPD) is a professional body for those involved in the management and development of people. Primarily a U.K. institute, it has an international membership. Much of its activities focus on human resources but there are also some significant initiatives in training. [**http://www.cipd.co.uk**]

Distance Education Association of New Zealand (DEANZ) is a national association committed to fostering growth, development, research, and good practice in distance education, open learning, and flexible delivery systems for education. The association is made up of individual and institutional members mainly from within New Zealand but also from the Pacific Rim. Its aim is to foster high standards in the practice of distance education in New Zealand. Membership is open to anyone or any institution with an interest in distance education or open learning. [**http://www.deanz.org.nz**]

Educational Research Association of Singapore promotes the practice and use of educational research with the view to enhancing the quality of education; encourages schools to carry out action research; stimulates and facilitates collaborative research efforts; seeks to improve the training and facilities for educational research personnel; promotes critical discussion into problems, methods, presentation, and use of educational research; seeks the dissemination of educational research findings; and facilitates closer ties with the international research community. [**http://www.eras.org**]

e-Learning Network is a U.K. organization that is run for users of technology in training by users of technology in training. The objective is to be the source of information and best practice on design, implementation, and evaluation of electronic learning. [**http://www.elearningnetwork.org**]

European Association for Research on Learning and Instruction (EARLI) provides a platform to engage in critical dialogue and systematically exchange and discuss ideas on instructional and educational research, as well as research on industrial training. Members include scholars from all parts of Europe. EARLI sponsors a biennial conference and publishes *Learning and Instruction*. [**http://www.earli.org**]

Institute of IT Training is concerned with developing and promoting high standards of excellence within the training of IT and in the use of technology in training. To this end it has developed and published a set of competences for those involved in training design and development. It publishes a monthly magazine, *IT Training*. [**http://www.iitt.org.uk**]

International Board of Standards for Training, Performance and Instruction (IBSTPI) develops the capability of individuals in the training, education, learning, and performance improvement professions through the development and dissemination of competency-based standards. Members include professionals selected to represent academia, government, businesses, and consultancies from around the world. [**http://www.ibstpi.org**]

International Forum of Educational Technology and Society encourages discussions on the issues affecting the educational system developer and education communities. The forum conducts multiple online discussion threads on specific topics concerning the design and implementation of integrated learning environments. The discussions are aimed to be definitive and helpful in reaching conclusions that are then disseminated to the public. [**http://ifets.ieee.org**]

International Society for Performance Improvement (ISPI) is dedicated to improving productivity and performance in the workplace through the application of human performance technology (HPT). Members include performance technologists, training directors, human resource managers, instructional technologists, and organizational consultants. ISPI has an international network of local and regional chapters across the United States as well as in Canada, South America, Europe, the Middle East, Australia, and New Zealand. The organization sponsors an annual international conference and exposition and several institutes each year that provide information about HPT. ISPI provides information on employment opportunities through an online job bank, at a job fair, and through advertisements in a monthly newsletter. ISPI publishes *Performance Improvement Journal* and *Performance Improvement Quarterly (PIQ)*. [**http://ispi.org**]

International Society for Technology in Education (ISTE) provides leadership and service to improve teaching and learning by advancing the effective use of technology in K–12 education and teacher education. Members include K–12 teachers, administrators, technology coordinators, media specialists, and teacher educators. ISTE supports seven special interest groups—for administrators, computer science teachers, multimedia-focused educators, special education professionals, teacher educators, technology coordinators, and educators focused on telelearning. The organization is responsible for recommending guidelines for the accreditation of programs in educational computing and technology teacher preparation. ISTE sponsors the National Educational Computing Conference (NECC) and publishes *Learning and Leading with Technology, Journal of Computing in Teacher Education (JCTE)*, and *Journal of Research on Technology in Education (JRTE)*. [**http://iste.org**]

International Technology Education Association (ITEA) is devoted to enhancing technology education through experiences in K–12 schools. Members include individuals and institutions throughout the world, with primary membership in North America. ITEA conducts various professional development programs, sponsors an annual conference, and publishes the *Journal of Technology Education*. [**http://www.iteaconnect.org**]

International Visual Literacy Association (IVLA) is concerned with issues dealing with education, instruction, and training in modes of visual communication and their application through the concept of visual literacy. Members are researchers, educators, and artists from a range of disciplines including instructional technology, computer applications, communication, and business. IVLA provides a forum for the exchange of information related to visual literacy, hosts an annual conference, and publishes the *Journal of Visual Literacy*. [**http://ivla.org**]

Korean Society for Educational Technology (KSET) is the main Korean professional association concerned with improving learning environments and solving real-life learning problems with educational technology. Its mission is to provide professionals in educational technology with opportunities for sharing ideas, experiences, knowledge, and skills. KSET sponsors a conference and publishes *Educational Technology International*. [**http://www.kset.or.kr**]

National Association of Distance Education Organizations in South Africa was formed when 58 organizations involved in distance education committed to promoting access to lifelong learning of high quality. Participating institutions include public, private for-profit, and non governmental organizations. All are united in their belief that distance education methods could play a major role in facing South Africa's enormous educational challenges. [**http://www.nadeosa.org.za**]

Open and Distance Learning Association of Australia (ODLAA) is a professional association of members interested in the practice and administration of distance education and open learning. Its aims and objectives are to advance the practice and study of distance education in Australia, foster communication between distance educators, and maintain links with other national and international associations with related aims and objectives. [**http://www.odlaa.org**]

SANTEC—Educational Technology and e-Learning for Development aims to be an enabling network of educational technology practitioners with an interest in educational technology and electronic learning in developing environments, with an initial focus on Southern Africa. It facilitates the conceptualization and execution of sustainable programs in project format. Any individual or organization anywhere in the world with an interest in educational technology and e-learning in developing environments is welcome to join. [**http://www.santecnetwork.org**]

Society for Applied Learning Technology (SALT) is an organization for professionals whose work requires knowledge in the field of instructional technology. It sponsors an annual convention that covers a range of topics such as distance learning, interactive multimedia, development of interactive instruction materials, performance support systems, interactive instruction delivery, and information literacy. SALT publishes the *Journal of Educational Technology Systems, Journal of Interactive Instruction Development* (JIID), and *Journal of Instruction Delivery Systems (JIDS)*. [**http://www.salt.org**]

Society for Information Technology and Teacher Education (SITE) is focused on the integration of instructional technologies into teacher education. The organization promotes research, scholarship, collaboration, exchange, and support among those interested in the use of information technology in teacher education. Members are individual teacher educators and affiliated organizations in all disciplines. SITE sponsors an annual international conference and publishes the *Journal of Technology and Teacher Education (JTATE)*. [**http://site.aace.org**]

South African Institute of Distance Education (SAIDE) was formed as an educational trust to assist in the reconstruction of education and training in South Africa. It promotes open learning principles, the use of quality distance education methods, and the appropriate use of technology. SAIDE works closely with policy makers and providers of educational programs to translate these approaches into practice. [**http://www.saide.org.za**]

Professional Publications In IDT

The following pages provide specific details about 75 professional publications in IDT and related fields. Information about each journal was obtained from either the journal itself or from one of Cabell's directories of publishing opportunities in education (Cabell & English, 2002a, 2002b).

American Educational Research Journal (AERJ) publishes peer-reviewed articles that report on original empirical and theoretical studies and analyses in education. The journal has a section on Teaching, Learning, and Human Development, which contains articles that examine teaching and learning at all educational levels in formal and informal settings. [**http://www.aera.net/publications/?id=315**]

American Journal of Distance Education (AJDE) is a peer-reviewed journal that publishes articles on research, theory, and practice of distance education. The journal is aimed at educators who develop and deliver training and educational programs at a distance and for administrators setting up systems for this kind of education. [**http://www.ajde.com**]

Asia Pacific Journal of Education is a refereed publication of original research from around the world, with special attention to research from the Asia-Pacific region (including Australia, New Zealand, and the Pacific Island territories). Its objective is to provide a forum for the dissemination of well-conceived educational research and for the open discussion of ideas concerning developments in education. [**http://www.nie.edu.sg/nieweb/research/loading.do?id=Research%20Publications&cid= 13664257**]

Australasian Journal of Educational Technology (AJET) is a refereed journal that publishes research and review articles in educational technology, instructional design, educational applications of computer technologies, educational telecommunications and related areas. [**http://www.ascilite.org.au/ajet/ajet.html**]

Australian Educational Computing publishes refereed and non-refereed articles, reports, and reviews related to the use of computers in education. [**http://www.acce.edu.au/journal**]

Australian Educational Researcher (AER) is a peer-reviewed journal that publishes original research and scholarly essays from a variety of disciplinary perspectives on any level of education. The focus of the journal is on issues related to research. [**http://www.aare.edu.au/aer/aer.htm**]

British Journal of Educational Psychology is a peer-reviewed journal that publishes empirical and theoretical studies, case studies, and action research, surveys, experimental studies, and psychometric and methodological research. The focus of the journal is on psychological research that makes a significant contribution to the understanding and practice of education. [**http://www.bps.org.uk/publications/bjep/**]

British Journal of Educational Technology (BJET) publishes peer-reviewed articles on the theory, application, and development of learning technology and communications. The journal is targeted to an international audience of academics and professionals in learning technology. [**http://www.blackwellpublishing.com/journals/bjet**]

Canadian Journal of Learning and Technology (CJLT) is a peer-reviewed journal that focuses on the use of technology in learning. The journal publishes research and evaluation studies, literature reviews, position papers, and reports of instructional development projects. [**http://www.cjlt.ca**]

Cognition and Instruction publishes peer-reviewed articles on cognitive-instructional research and analysis. The focus of the journal is on cognitive investigations of instruction and learning. [**http://www.leaonline.com/loi/ci**]

Computers in Human Behavior is a scholarly journal that publishes theoretical articles, research reports, and literature reviews that examine the use of computers from a psychological perspective. The journal addresses human interactions with computers and the psychological impact of computer use on individuals, groups, and society. [**http://www.elsevier.com/wps/find/journaldescription.cws_home/759/description#description**]

Contemporary Educational Psychology publishes peer-reviewed articles that involve the application of psychological theory to education. Articles include original research reports, literature reviews, theoretical papers, and reports on instructional techniques when the use of adequate controls demonstrates their validity. [**http://www.elsevier.com/wps/find/journaldescription.ews_home/622811/description#description**]

Contemporary Issues in Technology and Teacher Education (CITE) is an online, peer-reviewed journal, established and jointly sponsored by five professional associations (AMTE, AETS, NCSS-CUFA, CEE, and SITE). This is the only joint venture of this kind in the field of teacher education. Each professional association has sole responsibility for editorial review of articles in its discipline. [**http://www.citejournal.org**]

Distance Education disseminates research and scholarship in distance education, open learning and flexible learning systems. [**http://www.odlaa.org/publications/publications.html**]

Educational Researcher (ER) contains scholarly articles of general interest to educational researchers from a range of disciplines. The journal has a features section that publishes peer-reviewed articles that report, synthesize, or analyze scholarly inquiry in education. [**http://www.aera.net/publications/?id=317**]

Educational Technology is a professional magazine that publishes non-refereed articles interpreting research and practical applications of scientific knowledge in education and training environments. The magazine covers a variety of topics related to the educational technology field. [**http://www.bookstoread.com/etp**]

Educational Technology, Research and Development (ETR&D) is a refereed journal that publishes research reports, literature reviews, theoretical and conceptual articles, and descriptions of programs, methods, and models. The journal has two sections. The Research section features well-documented articles on the practical aspects of research as well as applied theory in educational technology, and the Development section focuses on the design and development of learning environments and educational technology applications. [**http://www.aect.org/Intranet/ Publications/index.asp#etrd**]

Educational Technology and Society publishes peer-reviewed articles on the issues affecting the developers of educational systems and educators who implement and manage such systems. The articles discuss the perspectives of both communities and their relation to each other. [**http://ifets.info/others/**]

Educational Technology Review (ETR) provides a multidisciplinary Web-based forum for the exchange of information between disciplines, educational levels, and information technologies. Originally a print journal, *ETR* has been transformed into an online publication to increase timeliness of content and provide readers with current and future electronic resources and Web-based tools. [**http://www.aace.org/pubs/etr**]

e-Journal of Instructional Science and Technology (e-JIST) is an international peer-reviewed electronic journal that publishes articles from practitioners and researchers with a specific focus on or implications for the design of instructional materials. The journal is aimed at policy makers, managers, investors, professional staff, technical staff, and academics within education and training. [**http://www.usq.edu.au/electpub/e-jist/**]

eLearn Magazine is a Web-based source for news, information, and opinions on the field of online education and training. It also offers e-learning professionals a public forum for the exchange of ideas. This publication is a magazine, not a scholarly research journal. [**http://www.elearnmag.org**]

Electronic Journal for the Integration of Technology in Education (EJITE) is an online, refereed journal that features research findings and practical articles on technology integration. [**http://ejite.isu.edu**]

Electronic Journal of Research in Educational Psychology (EJREP) is an online, refereed publication that aims to promote interaction and joint research among academic and professional researchers. It is a bilingual publication, with articles published in both Spanish and English. [**http://www.investigacion-psicopedagogica.org/revista/english**]

European Educational Research Journal is an online journal devoted to European educational research. Although its dominant content is conventional peer-reviewed academic articles, an important area of the journal is devoted to "research intelligence," general announcements, conference news, a discussion area, points of contact and general "notice board" information. [**http://www.wwwords.co.uk/eerj/**]

Higher Education Research and Development is a refereed journal that includes articles covering all aspects of higher education, which seek to improve practice through research, evaluation or scholarly reflection. The Higher Education Research and Development Society of Australasia publishes it. [**http://www.herdsa.org.au/journal.php**]

Instructional Science publishes refereed scholarly articles that focus on the nature, theory, and practice of instructional processes and learning. The journal is targeted to an international audience of academics and professionals interested in learning and cognition. [**http://www.springerlink.com/(d3mn4rvzriiw5d45wyj4kc45)/app/home/journal.asp?referrer=Parent&backto=linkingpublicationresults.1:102905,1**]

Interactive Educational Multimedia (IEM) is an online journal that publishes peer-reviewed and invited articles related to research, implementation, and design of multimedia. The journal covers subjects related to educational multimedia, hypermedia, learning, design, teaching, and evaluation of new technologies when applied in education. [**http://www.ub.es/multimedia/iem/**]

Interactive Multimedia Electronic Journal of Computer-Enhanced Learning is peer-reviewed online journal focusing on innovations in computer-enhanced learning. The journal aims to serve as a model for electronic journals with a high level of multimedia and interactivity and to advance the acceptance of electronic publication as a legitimate form of academic discourse. [**http://imej.wfu.edu/**]

International Journal of Educational Technology (IJET) is a refereed online journal that publishes research articles in the area of educational technology. It is published online twice each year and is available without an access charge. [**http://www.ao.uiuc.edu/ijet/**]

International Journal on e-Learning (IJEL) publishes peer-reviewed articles on research, development, and practice of e-learning. The journal is targeted to an international audience of educators and trainers in corporate, government, health care, and higher education settings. [**http://www.aace.org/pubs/ijel/default.htm**]

International Journal of Instructional Media (IJIM) is a refereed journal that publishes articles focused on all forms of media used in instruction and training. The journal examines topics such as computer technology, computer-mediated communications, distance learning, and media research. [**http://www.adprima.com/ijim.htm**]

International Journal of Training and Development is a refereed journal that publishes theoretical, conceptual, and methodological research articles focused on training. The journal is aimed at an international audience from the academic and corporate communities, as well as those engaged in public policy formulation and implementation. [**http://www.blackwellpublishing.com/journal.asp?ref=1360-3736&site=1**]

International Journal of Training Research publishes peer-reviewed articles that focus on research studies and reviews of research related to vocational education and training in Australia and internationally. [**http://www.avetra.org.au/publications/journal.shtml**]

International Review of Research in Open and Distance Learning (IRRODL) is a refereed e-journal that carries articles about projects and programs in the area of flexible learning. It provides documented research into the ways in which learning occurs via flexible delivery modes. [**http://www.irrodl.org/**]

Journal of Asynchronous Learning Networks (JALN) publishes peer-reviewed articles that describe data-based research on asynchronous learning networks. The mission of the journal is to provide practitioners in online education with knowledge about research in online learning. [**http://www.sloan-c.org/publications/jaln/index.asp**]

Journal of Computer Assisted Learning (JCAL) is a peer-reviewed journal that focuses on the use of information and communication technology to support learning and knowledge exchange. The journal is aimed at an international audience of researchers and practitioners and addresses topics such as collaborative learning, knowledge engineering, and open, distance, and networked learning. [**http://www.blackwellpublishing.com/journal.asp?ref=0266-4909&site=1**]

Journal of Computer-Mediated Communication is a refereed e-journal that disseminates information about computer-mediated communication. The journal publishes theoretical analyses and original empirical research, as well as reviews, synthesis, and meta-analyses of prior research. [**http://www.ascusc.org/jcmc/**]

Journal of Computing in Teacher Education (JCTE) is a refereed journal that publishes practical applications, research reports, and theoretical articles of interest to teacher educators involved with computer and technology education for preservice and inservice teachers. [**http://www.iste.org/jcte/**]

Journal of Distance Education (JDE) publishes scholarly articles and research papers that focus on issues related to distance education. Its aims are to promote and encourage Canadian research and scholarly work in distance education and provide a forum for the dissemination of international scholarship. [**http://www.lib.unb.ca/Texts/JDE/**]

Journal of Educational Computing Research publishes peer-reviewed articles including research reports, critical analyses, design and development studies, and reviews related to educational computing and computer-based education. [**http://www.baywood.com/journals/PreviewJournals.asp?Id=0735=6331**]

Journal of Educational Multimedia and Hypermedia (JEMH) publishes peer-reviewed articles that discuss research, development, and applications of multimedia and hypermedia in education. The journal focuses on the theory and practice of learning and teaching using technological tools that allow the integration of images, sound, text, and data. [**http://www.aace.org/pubs/jemh/default.htm**]

Journal of Educational Psychology is a peer-reviewed journal that publishes original psychological research pertaining to education at all levels. The journal occasionally publishes theoretical and review articles related to educational psychology. [**http://www.apa.org/journals/edu/**]

Journal of Educational Research (JER) publishes peer-reviewed articles that describe or synthesize research on educational practice in elementary and secondary schools and in higher education. The journal gives special consideration to variables that can be manipulated in educational settings. [**http://www.heldref.org/jer.php**]

Journal of Educational Technology Systems publishes articles on the use of computer technologies as an integral component of an educational system. The journal examines the design and development of interactive computer-based systems, techniques for using technology in educational systems, and classroom practices and experimentation with technology. [**http://www.salt.org/salt.asp?ss=1&pn=jets**]

Journal of Experimental Education is a peer-reviewed journal that publishes basic and applied research studies that use a range of quantitative and qualitative methodologies. The journal is divided into three sections: Learning and Instruction; Motivation and Social Processes; and Measurement, Statistics, and Research Design. [**http://www.heldref.org/jexpemanu.php**]

Journal of Instruction Delivery Systems (JIDS) publishes peer-reviewed articles that focus on issues, problems, and applications of instructional delivery systems in education, training, and job performance. The journal is application oriented and is aimed at educators, trainers, and professionals in academia, business, industry, and the military. [**http://www.salt.org/salt.asp?ss=l&pn=jids**]

Journal of Interactive Instruction Development (JIID) is a practical publication that focuses on enhancing the quality, effectiveness, and productivity of interactive systems design. The journal provides how-to information aimed primarily at managers and senior level professionals in training, education, and government. [**http://www.salt.org/salt.asp?=l&pn=jiid**]

Journal of Interactive Learning Research (JILR) is a refereed journal that publishes articles related to the theory, design, implementation, effectiveness, and impact of interactive learning environments in education and training. Types of articles include theoretical perspectives, research reports, literature reviews, and descriptions of learning environments. [**http://www.aace.org/pubs/jilr/default.htm**]

Journal of Interactive Media in Education (JIME) publishes articles on theory, research, and practice of interactive media in education. The journal uses an open peer-review approach where reviewers are named and accountable for their comments, authors have the right of reply, and readers have the chance to shape a submission before it is published. [**http://www.jime.open.ac.uk/**]

Journal of Interactive Online Learning (JIOL) publishes manuscripts, critical essays, and reviews that encompass disciplinary and interdisciplinary perspectives in regards to issues related to higher-level learning outcomes. It is a peer-reviewed e-journal that publishes articles on theory, research, and practice related to interactive online learning. [**http://www.ncolr.org/**]

Journal of Online Behavior (JOB) is a peer-reviewed journal concerned with the empirical study of human behavior in the online environment, and with the impact of evolving communication and information technology on individuals, groups, organizations, and society. The journal is published electronically and in printed form. [**http://www.behavior.net/Job/**]

Journal of Research on Technology in Education (JRTE) publishes refereed articles that report on research studies, system or project descriptions and evaluations, syntheses of the literature, and theoretical or conceptual positions that relate to educational computing. The journal is aimed at an international audience of teachers, teacher educators, technology coordinators, educational policy makers, and industry leaders. [**http://www.iste.org/jrte/**]

Journal of Technology and Teacher Education (JTATE) is a peer-reviewed journal that publishes articles about the use of information technology in teacher education. The journal covers preservice and inservice teacher education, as well as graduate programs in areas such as curriculum and instruction, educational administration, staff development, instructional technology, and educational computing. [**http://www.aace.org/pubs/jtate/default.htm**]

Journal of Technology Education (JTE) publishes peer-reviewed articles that focus on technology education research, philosophy, and theory. [**http://scholar.lib.vt.edu/ejournals/JTE/**]

Journal of Technology, Learning, and Assessment (JTLA) is a peer-reviewed, scholarly online journal that provides an interdisciplinary forum where initiatives that combine technology, learning theory, and assessment are shared. [**http://www.bc.edu/research/intasc/jtla.html**]

Journal of Technology Studies is a refereed journal that provides an open forum for the exchange of relevant ideas in the field of technology studies. [**http://scholar.lib.vt.edu/ejournals/JOTS/**]

Journal of Visual Literacy (JVL) is a refereed journal that publishes articles exploring the empirical, theoretical, practical, or applied aspects of visual literacy and communication. The journal focuses on the effective use of visuals in a variety of fields. [**http://www.cameron.edu/jvl**]

Learners Together is an online magazine developed to contribute to the teaching and learning environment of NgeeAnn Polytechnic and Singapore. Its aims are to showcase best teaching practices, inform readers about teaching and learning, and provide a forum for readers to collaborate, discuss, and ask questions about current teaching and learning issues. [**http://tlcweb.np.edu.sg/lt/**]

Learning and Instruction is a peer-reviewed journal that publishes empirical research studies, theoretical and methodological articles, and literature reviews on learning, development, instruction, and teaching. The focus of the journal is on European work in the field. [**http://www.earli.org/earli_journals/Learning And Instruction**]

Learning and Leading with Technology (L&L) is a non-refereed magazine that emphasizes practical ideas about technology and how to use it in the K–12 curriculum. Articles that appear in *L&L* are written by educators for educators such as classroom teachers, lab teachers, technology coordinators, and teacher educators. [**http://www.iste.org/ll**]

Open Praxis publishes scholarly papers and provides information on worldwide developments in the field of open learning and distance education. It is the journal of the International Council for Open and Distance Education (ICDE) and is distributed free of charge to all members. [**http://www.icde.org/**]

Paradigm carries articles, notes, and reviews promoting the interdisciplinary study of textbooks of all kinds. [**http://faculty.ed.uiuc.edu/westbury/paradigm/**]

Performance Improvement Journal is a non-refereed professional magazine aimed at practitioners of human performance technology in the workplace. The journal deals with all types of interventions and all phases of the HPT process and publishes hands-on experiences with models, interventions, how-to-guides, and ready-to-use job aids, as well as research articles. [**http://www.ispi.org**]

Performance Improvement Quarterly (PIQ) is a peer-reviewed journal that publishes literature reviews, research studies, and other scholarly articles about human performance technology. The journal emphasizes human performance technologies such as front-end analysis and evaluation. [**http://www.ispi.org**]

Practical Assessment, Research and Evaluation is a peer-reviewed e-journal that publishes scholarly syntheses of research and ideas about issues and practices in education. Its purpose is to provide education professionals access to refereed articles that can have a positive impact on assessment, research, evaluation, and teaching practice, especially at the local education agency level. [**http://pareonline.net/**]

Quarterly Review of Distance Education (QRDE) is a peer-reviewed journal that publishes articles related to theory, research, and practice of distance learning. The journal frequently examines issues related to the design of online instruction. [**http://infoagepub.com/products/journals/qrde/index.htm**]

Review of Educational Research (RER) is a peer-reviewed journal that publishes critical, integrative reviews of research literature related to education. The journal contains reviews that interpret and synthesize educational research from a range of disciplines. [**http://www.aera.net/publications/?id=319**]

TechKnowLogia is an international online magazine that deals with issues related to technologies for knowledge and learning. It is aimed at policy makers, strategists, practitioners, and technologists at the local, national, and global levels. [**http://www.techknowlogia.org**]

TechTrends publishes peer-reviewed articles that focus on the practical applications of technology in education and training. It is aimed at professionals in the educational communications and technology field. [**http://www.aect.org/Intranet/Publications/index.asp#tt**]

T.H.E. Journal publishes non-refereed articles that report on the actual experiences of educators integrating technology in both instruction and administration. [**http://www.thejournal.com**]

T & D Magazine publishes non–peer-reviewed articles on current practices, new theories and their applications, and emerging trends in the field of workplace learning and performance. The magazine is aimed at practitioners in business, government, academia, and consulting. [**http://astd.org/astd/publications/td_magazine**]

Training Magazine publishes non–peer-reviewed features such as interviews and profiles of industry leaders, special reports, original research, opinions, and the latest trends in training and workforce development. [**http://www.trainingmag.com/training/index.jsp**]

Turkish Online Journal of Distance Education (TOJDE) is a peer-reviewed e-journal that publishes articles on theory and research related to students enrolled in any level of distance education or open learning applications. [**http://tojde.anadolu.edu.tr/**]

Turkish Online Journal of Educational Technology (TOJET) is a peer-reviewed e-journal that publishes articles on theoretical discussions of technology and teacher preparation, current practices on the use of technology, and previously published "classic" articles that have advanced the discussion of educational technology. [**http://tojet.net**]

UltiBASE is a peer-reviewed e-journal and resource for university and tertiary teachers in Australia. Its aim is to foster understanding of the conditions that enhance effective learning and it regularly publishes material relating to effective online teaching practices. [**http://ultibase.rmit.edu.au**]

Summary

Instructional design and technology is a rapidly evolving field. Although on the surface it may appear to be driven by advances in technology, important advances in learning and performance improvement underpin the design and delivery of instruction and other interventions.

The changing nature of our field requires conscious effort to keep abreast of advances in theory, research, and practice of IDT and related fields. Competent professionals invest significant amounts of time on their own continuing professional development; they become actively involved in professional organizations, they read relevant publications in their field, they participate in Web-based forums, and they contribute to conferences.

In this chapter, we have provided a comprehensive list of professional organizations and publications in IDT. Each has a specific focus aimed at individuals with a particular area of interest. Furthermore, many are international in scope. We are hopeful that the information provided in this chapter assists your continuing professional development as an active member of the IDT field.

Application Questions

1. Write an action plan for your next conference listing your learning objectives, how you expect to meet those objectives, the preparation you will need, and other resources you may need to achieve your objectives (it is easiest if you select a specific conference rather than taking some abstract event!).
2. Visit the websites of two or more professional organizations identified in this chapter and compare them using the following list:
   - Mission
   - Cost of membership
   - Publications
   - Conferences and meetings
   - Opportunities for professional development and networking
   - Employment services
   - Other benefits to members

References

Cabell, D. W. E., & English, D. L. (2002a). *Cabell's directory of publishing opportunities in educational curriculum and methods* (6th ed.). Beaumont, TX: Cabell.

Cabell, D. W. E., & English, D. L. (2002b). *Cabell's directory of publishing opportunities in educational psychology and administration* (6th ed.). Beaumont, TX: Cabell.

CHAPTER 27

Competencies for Instructional Design and Technology Professionals

Gayle V. Davidson-Shivers
University of South Alabama

Karen L. Rasmussen
University of West Florida

Editors' Introduction

What skills are necessary be considered competent in the field of instructional design and technology (IDT)? Over the years, various individuals and groups have tried to answer this question by developing lists of desired competencies for one or more types of positions within the IDT field. In this chapter, Gayle Davidson-Shivers and Karen Rasmussen review some early competency lists and present two lists that have recently been developed. Based on these lists and the definition of instructional design and technology put forth in this book, the authors identify several competency areas (domains) within the field of instructional design and technology. They also describe trends related to the use of competencies and issues that continue to concern the IDT field.

Knowledge and Comprehension Questions

1. What is the difference between *certification* and *licensure*? How does this difference affect an IDT professional?
2. Evaluate the different competencies from the perspective of an IDT professional. How have the competencies changed over time? What competences have remained the same over time? Why? Which set of competencies would you subscribe to? Why?
3. The great debate: Which came first—HPT or IDT? or, Which overarches the other? How do these two fit together? or, Do they fit together? Explain your response.
4. ibstpi took great lengths to define *performance technologist* (PT) in 1998 and began to describe the role of the PT. However, ibstpi has not yet developed PT competencies. Why not? Explain your reasoning.

Competencies for occupations in the instructional design and technology (IDT) field were first proposed over 25 years ago and have continued to evolve. The main focus of this chapter is to explain what is meant by "The Competencies" and discuss their purposes for the field today. the chapter begins with defining the term *competencies*, followed by a historical perspective. Included in this history are the types of competencies found in the IDT field and the purposes of those competencies. The chapter ends with a discussion of trends related to the use of competencies and issues that continue to concern the IDT field.

What is Meant by "The Competencies"?

Competencies are defined as the quality of being competent; as having suitable or sufficient skill, knowledge, experience, or being qualified to perform a task (Harris, Guthrie, Hobart, & Lundberg, 1995; Spector & de la Teja, 2001). To relate directly to an occupation or profession, this definition may be refined to the requirement, or the quality level, which is authoritatively deemed as an acceptable basis for judging performance (Larson, 1977, 1990; Metzger, 1976). Most professions use competencies to facilitate autonomy and self-regulation of its members once a common set of standards is established for the group. Although using different terminology (i.e., *key competencies* in Australia, *core skills* in the United Kingdom, and *essential skills* in New Zealand), such competencies cross international boundaries (Harris et al.). In Australia, competencies are framed from a perspective that employees are expected to apply knowledge and skills to situations as well as to transfer those skills to new circumstances (Harris et al.).

More specific to the IDT field is the definition offered by the International Board of Standards for Training, Performance and Instruction (ibstpi, 2003) which defines *competency* as "knowledge, skills, or attitudes that enables one to effectively perform the activities of a given occupation or function to the standards expected in employment" (n.p.). ibstpi proposes that although competencies may reflect attitudes, they are stated as behaviors, not as personality traits or beliefs, and that those specific behaviors are correlated with job performance.

The ibstpi definition organizes knowledge, skills, and abilities for three practitioners of the IDT field: instructional designers, training managers, and instructors. The growth of ibstpi and the development of competencies have their roots in the early beginnings of the IDT field. The following historical perspective highlights the evolution of the competencies over the past 25 years and lays a foundation for our use of them.

Historical Perspective on Establishing Competencies

The formation of the Association for Educational Communications Technology (AECT) in 1977 helped establish the field of instructional design and technology (Saettler, 1990). Through the auspices of AECT, a group of scholars and practitioners began defining instructional design practices as being distinct from other fields (e.g., human resource development) and from education in general (Richey, Fields, & Foxon, 2000). This initial process immediately focused attention on knowledge, skills, and abilities required of an instructional designer.

Early Efforts of DID/AECT Members

The Division of Instructional Development (DID) of AECT began identifying competencies for the instructional development practitioner in the 1970s. An ad hoc task force, led by Bratton, produced a list of 23 functional competencies for instructional development specialists after three years of work (Division of Instructional Development/AECT Ad Hoc Task Force, 1980; *Instructional Innovator*, 1980). For each competency, knowledge, performance, and evaluation standards were identified.

This set of competencies contained multiple knowledge standards but contained only one performance and one evaluation standard for each. The primary, or essential, competencies were related to instructional design (ID) procedures, training and project management, and practitioner professional development (Table 27.1). With initial competencies identified, the DID/AECT Task Force continued to work with others to streamline the competencies.

Task Forces and the Joint Committee

In 1981, the official DID Task Force on ID Certification was formed and sanctioned by AECT with the charge of determining the viability of certification and developing assessment procedures for evaluating professional performance. However, the task force concluded that decisions on certification were premature until a core list of competencies for professionals could be identified and approved. Members from the organizations of DID/AECT, National Society for Performance and Instruction (NSPI), and American Society for Training and Development (ASTD) provided extensive feedback on these proposed competencies (Task Force on ID Certification, 1981) and the competencies were approved.

This 1981 version streamlined the original set to a total of 16 competencies, and with continued emphasis on procedures associated with the generic ADDIE (analysis–design–development–implementation–evaluation) model.

TABLE 27.1 The original ID competencies by DID/AECT task force

1. Select appropriate projects for instructional development
2. Conduct needs assessment
3. Assess learner/trainee characteristics
4. Analyze structural characteristics of a job, task, and/or content
5. Write statements of learner outcomes
6. Analyze the setting characteristics
7. Sequence learner outcomes
8. Specify instructional strategies
9. Sequence instructional activities
10. Select learning resources
11. Create the specifications for instructional activities
12. Seek extant instructional materials
13. Prepare specifications for to-be-produced materials
14. Evaluate instruction/training
15. Establish a course/training package/workshop management system
16. Develop an instructional development project plan
17. Monitor instructional development projects
18. Communicate orally and in writing according to accepted societal and professional standards
19. Discuss research and theory
20. Use appropriate consulting skills
21. Use appropriate group process skills
22. Encourage the diffusion and adoption of instructional development
23. Engage in professional activities

TABLE 27.2 1981 ID Competencies by the Task Force on ID Certification

	Competencies
A competent instructional/ training development specialist is able to:	1. Determine project appropriate for instructional development. 2. Conduct needs assessment. 3. Assess learner/trainee characteristics. 4. Analyze the structural characteristics of jobs, tasks, and content. 5. Write statements of learner outcomes. 6. Analyze the characteristics of a setting [learning environment]. 7. Sequence learner outcomes. 8. Specify instructional strategies. 9. Sequence learner activities. 10. Determine instructional resources (media) appropriate instructional activities. 11. Evaluate instruction/training. 12. Create course, training package, and workshop systems. 13. Plan and monitor instructional development projects. 14. Communicate effectively in visual, oral, and written forms. 15. Demonstrate appropriate interpersonal, group process, and consulting behaviors. 16. Promote the diffusion and adoption of the instructional development process.

Correspondingly, knowledge, performance, and evaluation standards for each competency were reduced in scope. In addition, the focus was modified to describe the performances of entry-level practitioners. The 1981 version of the competencies is presented in Table 27.2.

The 1981 competencies, not listed in any particular order, were considered as an integral element of core requirements. Recognizing the future evolution of the competencies, "the list was 'final' only to the degree that it [would] not be modified further until the Task Force [explored] ways by which the competencies might be evaluated" (Task Force on ID Certification, 1981, p. 14). When arriving at a "final" list, the Task Force members kept to the following ideas (Bratton, 1983):

- The competencies should reflect the skills of professional instructional/training designers regardless of their current jobs, positions, titles, academic degrees.
- The competencies should be performance-oriented rather than academic-oriented.
- While some employment situations may prevent designers from exercising every competency, professionally

competent designers should be able to perform most (if not all) of the competencies, given the opportunity to do so.

- The competencies should reflect the skills of experienced, professional designers—as opposed to students, trainees, or entry-level designers.

The DID/AECT Task Force was then joined by the NSPI Standards Committee to form the DID/AECT and NSPI Joint Certification Task Force (Bratton, 1995), which became known as simply the Joint Committee. The Joint Committee focused on assessment of the competencies.

The Formation of ibstpi in 1986

In 1984, the Joint Committee formed a new entity, the International Board of Standards for Training Performance and Instruction (ibstpi) (Bratton, 1983, 1995; Richey et al., 2000). ibstpi was founded as an international, not-for-profit service organization with a mission of improving individual and organizational performance. In 1986, this group generated the next version of ID competencies (ibstpi, 1988).

ibstpi changed the focus of the competencies back to entry-level practitioner performances, contrary to the direction of the AECT/DID Task Force. *Entry-level practitioners* were defined as individuals who had academic and informal (e.g., through on-the-job experiences) preparation for instructional design positions (Foshay, 2000). The 1986 version set a proficiency level of at least three years of field experience beyond entry-level training. The competencies continued to be closely associated with common procedures found in traditional ID models and were sequenced in the order that they were typically performed (Rasmussen, 2002).

ibstpi ultimately divided the competencies into three main roles: instructional designers, training managers, and instructors (Bratton, 1995; Foshay, 2000; Foxon, Richey, Roberts, & Spannaus, 2003; ibstpi, 1989, 2003; Richey et al., 2000). A fourth role, performance technologist, was added in 1989. ibstpi has continued to publish modified versions of competencies for the first three IDT roles, but not for the performance technologist.

Current Competencies and Ethical Standards for IDT Practitioners

Instructional Designer

The term *instructional design* is used by ibstpi (1989) rather than *instructional* or *training development* because of its usage in the private sector. Although there are many job titles and specialized ID roles, Richey et al. (2000) point out "while it is not unusual for a designer to perform development tasks as well [as design], those who concentrate totally on development or production tasks are *not* considered designers. For example, graphic artists and programmers may be critical members of a design team, but they are not instructional designers" (p. 36).

The most current list of ID competencies increases them from 16 to 23, with a total of 122 performance standards. These 23 competencies are organized into a conceptual framework based on the four domains of professional foundations, planning and analysis, design and development, and implementation (Richey et al., 2000); evaluation was not included as one of the domains.

Within each domain, the competencies are identified as either *essential*, which must be mastered for an ID professional to be considered competent, or *advanced*, which an experienced, expert ID professional would master (Richey et al., 2000). Table 27.3 identifies the competencies according to domain. In this list, remnants of the original list can still be observed.

Training Manager

As with the ID competencies, training and training management competencies have been explored by individuals and organizations other than ibstpi. ASTD, for example, sponsored early endeavors in validating training (Foxon et al., 2003) as did Deden-Parker (1981). Ibstpi published their first set of competencies for the training manager in 1989.

A training manager "manages the development and delivery of training and all that is associated with those activities" (Foxon et al., 2003, p. 3). Although general principles of management apply across functional areas, Foxon et al. suggest that training managers must possess skills unique to the human resource development function, including new skills related to market globalization, information technology, e-learning, e-business, and knowledge management. These realities of twenty-first century business require role shifts of successful training managers from those traditionally held (Daft, 2003; Foxon et al.; Mosley, Pietri, & Megginson, 1996; Schermerhorn, 1999).

The 2003 version contains 14 training manager competencies with 88 associated performance standards, organized into four general domains: professional foundations. performance analysis and planning; design and development; and administration (Foxon et al., 2003). Unlike the ID competencies, levels of mastery (i.e., essential and advanced) were not identified. See Table 27.3 for training manager competencies.

Instructor

The original set of instructor competencies were developed in 1988 by Hutchison, Shepherd, and Stein (ibstpi, 1989) and updated in 1993 and 2000. The 2000 set

TABLE 27.3 ID, training manager, and instructor competencies

Instructional Designer (2001)	Training Manager (2003)	Instructor (2003)
Professional Foundations	**Professional Foundations**	**Professional Foundations**
1. Communicate in visual, oral and written forms. *(Essential)*	1. Communicate in written, oral, and visual forms.	1. Communicate effectively.
2. Apply current research and theory to practice. *(Advanced)*	2. Comply with established ethical and legal standards knowledge and skills.	2. Update and improve one's professional
3. Update and improve one's skills and knowledge in instructional design and related fields.*(Essential)*	3. Maintain networks to advocate for and support the training and performance function.	3. Comply with established ethical and legal standards.
4. Apply basic research skills to design projects. *(Advanced)*	4. Update and improve professional and business knowledge, skills, and attitudes.	4. Establish and maintain professional credibility.
5. Identify and resolve ethical and legal implications of design and workplace environments. *(Advanced)*		
Planning & Analysis	**Planning & Analysis**	**Planning & Preparation**
6. Conduct a needs assessment. *(Essential)*	5. Develop and monitor a strategic plan.	5. Plan instructional methods and materials.
7. Design a curriculum or instructional	6. Use performance analysis to program. *(Essential)*	6. Prepare for instruction. improve the organization.
8. Select and use a variety of techniques for determining instructional content. *(Essential)*	7. Plan and promote organizational change.	
9. Identify and describe the target population characteristics. *(Essential)*		
10. Analyze the characteristics of the environment.*(Essential)*		
11. Analyze the characteristics of existing and emerging technologies and their use in an instructional environment. *(Essential)*		
12. Reflect on and study the elements of a situation before finalizing design solutions and strategies. *(Essential)*		
Design & Development	**Design & Development**	**Instructional Methods & Strategies**
13. Select, modify, or create a design and development model appropriate for a given project. *(Advanced)*	8. Insure the application of instructional design principles. engagement.	7. Stimulate and sustain learner motivation and
14. Select & use variety of techniques to define and sequence the instructional content & strategies. *(Essential)*	9. Use technology to enhance the training function.	8. Demonstrate effective presentation skills.
15. Select or modify existing instructional materials. *(Essential)*	10. Evaluate training and performance interventions.	9. Demonstrate effective facilitation skills.
16. Develop instructional materials. *(Essential)*		10. Demonstrate effective questioning skills.
17. Design instruction that reflects an understanding of the diversity of learners and groups of learners. *(Essential)*		11. Provide clarification and feedback.
18. Evaluate and assess instruction and its impact. *(Essential)*		12. Promote retention of knowledge and skills.
		13. Promote transfer of knowledge and skills.
		14. Use media and technology to enhance learning and performance.

TABLE 27.3 Continued

Instructional Designer (2001)	Training Manager (2003)	Instructor (2003)
Implementation & Management	**Administration**	**Assessment & Evaluation**
19. Plan and monitor multiple instructional design projects. *(Advanced)*	11. Apply leadership skills to the training function.	15. Assess learning and performance.
20. Promote collaboration and partnership among the key participants in a design project. *(Advanced)*	12. Apply management skills to the training function.	16. Evaluate instructional effectiveness.
21. Apply business skills to managing ID. *(Advanced)*	13. Apply business skills to the training function.	***Management***
22. Design instructional management systems. *(Advanced)*	14. Implement knowledge management solutions.	17. Manage an environment that fosters learning and performance.
23. Maintain the effective implementation of instructional products and programs. *(Essential)*		18. Manage the instructional process through the appropriate use of technology.

Source: Data are from Foxon, Richey, Roberts, & Spannaus (2003); International Board of Standards for Training, Performance and Instruction (ibstpi) (1989, 2003); Klein, Spector, Grabowski, & de la Teja (2004); Richey, Fields, & Foxon (2000). Reprinted by permission of ibstpi as required.

TABLE 27.4 Skills/competencies associated with online instruction

Asynchronous Discussions	Synchronous Discussions
Allow learners time for reflection.	Establish ground rules for discussion.
Keep discussions alive and on a productive path.	Animate interactions with minimal instructor inventions.
Archive and organize discussions to be used in subsequent lessons.	Sense how the online text messages may appear to distance learners.
	Be aware of cultural differences.

included 14 competencies with 83 performance statements. The competencies increased to 18 (ibstpi, 2003) and are organized under the five domains of professional foundations, planning and preparation, instructional methods and strategies, assessment and evaluation, and management (ibstpis 2003; Klein, Spector, Grabowski, & de la Teja, 2004).

Online instructor: Spector and de la Teja (2001) maintain that online teaching requires additional competencies to those skills required of the classroom instructor due, in part, to technology demands and requirements placed on them as they moderate online discussions. To meet such challenges, the authors created a list of online instruction skills (Table 27.4). Even though some of these skills may apply to all teaching situations, the authors argue that the manner in which an online instructor demonstrates the skills are unique and must be identified separately.

Ethical Standards

One of the hallmarks of any field is the adherence to ethical standards that it endorses, and this is no less true for the IDT field. A code of ethics for each IDT practitioner role has been established and is typically found as an appendix to each competency set. For the ID code of ethics, Spector (2000) identifies the four guiding standards as responsibilities to others, social mandates, respecting the rights of others, and professional practice. Specific skills are associated with these ethical standards (Table 27.5).

The four guiding standards for ibstpi training managers are responsibilities to the organization, responsibilities to others, responsibilities to the profession, and responsibilities to society (Foxon et al., 2003). Again, associated with each ethical standard are specific skills that a training manager should be able to perform (see Table 27.5).

As members of ibstpi, Klein et al. (2004) identified five ethical standards for the instructor—responsibilities to learners, responsibilities to other individuals, responsibilities to organizations, responsibilities to society, and responsibility to the profession. Skills associated with these guiding ethics are included (see Table 27.5).

Performance Technologist

The fourth role in the IDT field, performance technologist, had a different beginning as compared to other three

TABLE 27.5 **Code of Ethics for Instructional Designer, Training Manager, and Instructor**

Instructional Designer (2001)	Training Manager (2003)	Instructor (2003)
Responsibility to Others	**Responsibility to Others**	**Responsibility to Other Individuals**
Provide efficient, effective, workable, and cost-effective solutions to client problems.	Be honest and fair in interactions with others.	To assistants, be obligated to treat them with the rights and responsibilities associated with an employer/employee relationship.
Systematically improve human performance to accomplish valid and appropriate individual and organizational goals.	Treat others with dignity and respect.	To employers, be responsible for the accurate reporting of progress and problems to supervisors and managers.
Facilitate individual accomplishments.	Facilitate individual accomplishment.	Do not violate a personal sense of right and wrong.
Help clients make informed decisions.	Facilitate individual accomplishments.	If personal ethics are compromised, make this known to others involved and do everything possible to avoid the conflict, including removing him- or herself from the situation.
Inform others of potential ethical violations and conflicts of interest.	Do not engage in exploitative relationships.	
Educate clients in matters of instructional design and performance improvement.	Do not discriminate unfairly in actions related to hiring, retention, salary adjustments, and promotion.	
	Do not represent the ideas or work of others as one's own.	
Social Mandates	**Responsibilities to Society**	**Responsibilities to Society**
Support humane, socially responsible goals and activities for individuals and organizations.	Support humane, socially responsible goals and projects for the organization.	Recognize oneself, the learners, and employers as citizens and members of society.
Make professional decisions based upon moral and ethical positions regarding societal issues.	Ensure that training products and procedures reflect moral and ethical positions on societal issues.	Recognize that when encountering a wide diversity of learners, some of may come from different cultures and be accustomed to different societies.
Consider the impact of planned interventions upon individuals, organizations, and the society as a whole.	Consider the consequences of proposed solutions upon individuals, organizations, and the society as a whole.	Make explicit the roles and social responsibilities of others whenever possible.
Respecting the Rights of Others	**Responsibilities to the Organization**	**Responsibilities to the Organization**
Protect the privacy, candor, and confidentiality of client and colleague information and communications.	Provide efficient, effective, workable, and cost-effective solutions that advance organizational performance goals.	Represent that organization fairly to learners and others.
Show respect for copyright and intellectual property.	Initiate and collaborate in organizational decision-making.	Accurately report outcomes to the organization and maintaining the confidentiality of organizational records.
Do not misuse client or colleague information for	Educate the organization in matters of instructional design	Treat the organization in much the same way that one would treat an individual.

TABLE 27.5 Continued

Instructional Designer (2001)	Training Manager (2003)	Instructor (2003)
personal gain.	and performance improvement.	
Do not represent the ideas or work of others as one's own.	Inform the organization of potential conflicts of interest, and ethical, legal, and due process violations.	
Do not make false claims about others.	Protect the privacy, candor, and confidentiality of information and communication of the organization and its members.	
Do not discriminate unfairly in actions related to hiring, retention, and advancement.	Do not misuse organizational information for personal gain.	
Professional Practice	**Responsibilities to the Profession**	**Responsibility to the Profession**
Be honest and fair in all facets of one's work.	Seek and acknowledge the contributions of others.	Respect the ethical codes of the professional community or communities.
Share skills and knowledge with other professionals.	Aid and be supportive of colleagues.	Represent the education and training community in a positive way.
Acknowledge the contributions of others.	Commit time and effort to the development of the profession.	
Aid and be supportive of colleagues. Commit time and effort to the development of the profession.	Promote the enforcement of ethical standards.	
Withdraw from clients who do not act ethically or when there is a conflict of interest.		
		Responsibility to the Learners
		Provide learners with guidance and support in achieving instructional goals.
		Respect the rights of learners and being fair in all aspects of instruction to all learners.
		Be familiar with these rights and ensure that learners know their rights.
		Be sensitive to their multiple roles and to the expectations of learners that derive from these multiple roles.
		Make the responsibilities associated with learner's roles explicit.
		When a learner raises an ethical issue, listen first, then gather any additional evidence that may be required, and then consult with others if necessary before reaching a decision.
		When an instructor's decision is challenged or changed, continue to treat all those involved fairly and without bias.

Source: Data are from Foxon, Richey, Roberts, & Spannaus (2003, pp. 157–158); Klein, Spector, Grabowski, & de la Teja (2004, pp. 2747–2748); Spector, in Richey, Fields, & Foxon (2000, pp. 201–203). Reprinted by permission.

professions. In 1988, ibstpi declared it as a profession and defined it as being able to:

> systematically analyze and utilize a variety of technologies [to] improve human performance by providing . . . solutions [that] relate [to] specific, valid, and appropriate tasks or aspects of individual or organizational performance. In doing so, performance technologists assure a link between human performance improvement efforts, results, and consequences. (ibstpi, 1989, p. 8)

At the same time, ibstpi stated the purposes of performance technology and listed tasks associated with its practice and identified special values of the profession. These tasks and mandates are shown in Table 27.6. ibstpi encouraged the development of a code of ethics by listing a set of "don'ts" for this type of IDT practitioner (see Table 27.6). However, for some unknown reason, ibstpi did not revise its original publication into a set of competencies. Instead, two other organizations, ASTD and the International Society for Performance Improvement (ISPI) [formerly NSPI], took on the task of creating performance technology competencies.

According to Chevalier (2004), the current 10 standards (or competencies) provide a set of principles and steps for the professional who desires to pursue a career in human performance technology. These standards focus on outcomes, take a systems view, add value, and facilitate partnership perspectives (ISPI, 2002). Table 27.6 shows the ASTD/ISPI competencies for performance technology. There is an associated code of ethics.

Why the Emphasis on Identifying Competencies?

From the very start, the various task forces, committees, and boards considered competencies as useful tools (AECT Program Standards, 2000; Bratton, 1983, 1995; ibstpi, 1988, 2003). Even though each practitioner set continues to evolve, their utility to the IDT field, organizations, practitioners, and academic programs has not changed. Competencies for IDT can be used as follows (Bratton, 1983, 1995; Deden-Parker, 1981; Foxon et al., 2003; ibstpi, 1988, 2003; Richey et al., 2000):

1. As a source of information for individuals wanting to know more about the IDT field.
2. As a self-assessment tool for experienced practitioners to assess their own knowledge and skills.
3. To provide a common set of concepts and vocabulary to improve the communication among the members of the IDT field.
4. To provide academic programs with information to develop and evaluate curriculum, courses, internships, and program requirements.
5. To provide academic programs with a basis for program evaluation and planning.
6. As a vehicle for communicating with clients, employers, and other professions.
7. As a vehicle for communicating to other fields the applications of IDT.
8. To serve as a model for identifying the competencies in other specialties in the IDT field.
9. To provide IDT academicians with a direction for forming a research agenda.
10. As an aid to employers and organizations in making decisions about the types of training functions that should be established.
11. As an aid to employers in recruitment activities and identifying qualified applicants and consultants.
12. As an aid to employers and managers in evaluating their IDT personnel.
13. To provide a basis for a certification program.
14. To provide a basis for defining the parameters of the IDT field.

Current Paths Toward Certification and Accreditation

As stated, one of the utilities of competencies is that of serving as a basis for certification. Even though certification of the profession was the original focus of the DID/AECT task forces, it has not occurred as anticipated. Only the role of performance technology has a venue for certifying practitioners.

Certified Performance Technology Designation

ASTD and ISPI joined forces specifically to provide certification and accompanying credentials for individuals who work in the performance technology (PT) area. The impetus for the "credentialing" was to provide employers and clients with the ability to identify practitioners who possess appropriate skills in performance improvement and training. In addition, certification offers the PT practitioner a credential that provides credibility and attention to continued professional development (ISPI, 2004).

The Certified Performance Technologist (CPT) is a designation that is based on the individual's performance in relation to the 10 standards (see Table 27.6) and carried out in concert with its accompanying code of ethics. Such performance is shown through description and documentation of professional activities, which includes confirmation letters from clients or supervisors. The CPT designation requires recertification every three years (ISPI, 2004). This recertification requires that the performance technologist

TABLE 27.6 Performance technologist competencies and code of ethics

1988 ibstpi Associated Tasks	2004 ISPI/ASTD PT Competencies
1. Improve the effectiveness and efficiency of organizations and the resources within them.	1. Focus on results and help clients focus on results.
2. Aid the client in solving performance problems by demonstrating systematic approaches to problem identification and problem solving.	2. Look at situations systemically, taking into consideration the larger context including competing pressures, resource constraints, and anticipated change.
3. Facilitate individual accomplishment and remove obstacles to achievement of organizational mission outcomes.	3. Add value in how you do the work and through the work itself.
4. Establish, support, and demonstrate results of performance that effect organizational outcomes.	4. Use partnerships or collaborate with clients and other experts as required.
1988 ibstpi Social mandates & values of PT	5. Be systematic in all aspects of the process including: The assessment of the need or opportunity.
1. Use PT only in support of humane, socially responsible, and life-fulfilling ends for both the individual and organization.	6. Be systematic in all aspects of the process including: The analysis of the work and workplace to identify the cause or factors that limit performance.
2. Serve individuals and organizations in the context of work.	7. Be systematic in all aspects of the process including: The design of the solution or specification of the requirements of the solution.
3. Maintain the widest view of the usefulness for, and impact of, their interventions.	8. Be systematic in all aspects of the process including: The development of all or some of the solution and its elements.
4. Support organizational goals aware of impacts to society as a whole.	9. Be systematic in all aspects of the process including: The implementation of the solution.
5. Take moral/ethical positions on societal issues and make professional decisions according to those positions.	10. Be systematic in all aspects of the process including: The evaluation of the process and the results.
6. Help clients make informed decisions by providing supportable intervention options with objective data, consequences, and recommendations.	
7. Use the highest professional standards of ethics, honesty, and integrity in all facets of their work. They withdraw from clients who cannot act ethically.	
8. Protect the privacy, candidness, and confidentiality of client information and communications.	
9. Have a peer relationship with anyone engaged in the improvement of worthy performance.	
10. Deal with fellow practitioners ethically, honestly, and with integrity.	
11. Share skills and knowledge with other professionals.	
12. Do not represent the ideas of others as their own.	
13. By definition, the intelligent practice of PT includes the education and transfer of the technology to clients.	
14. Commit time and effort to the development of the profession.	
15. Make skills and knowledge of professional available for examination by colleagues and clients.	
16. Give and get support and professional aid from colleagues.	
Responsibility for ethical conduct	
It is unethical to:	
1. Violate professional, academic, or business ethics.	
2. Promise that solutions will work when the opposite may be true.	
3. Make false claims on return on investment (ROI) or any professional behaviors or potential accomplishments.	
4. Falsify data.	
5. Take credit for the work of another.	
6. Use client information for personal or political gain.	

participate in professional development, continues a commitment to the code of ethics, and continues to practice and have proficiency in performance technology.

Additional Certification and Accreditation Efforts

In the 1990s, another arena for certification occurred with the accreditation of teacher education and teacher certification. AECT, in conjunction with the National Council for Accreditation for Teacher Education (NCATE), developed guidelines for basic and advanced programs in educational communications and instructional technologies (ECIT). The guidelines were based on the five domains developed by the AECT Committee on Definitions and Terminology (ACET Program Standards, 2000). The five IDT domains are design, development, utilization, management, and evaluation (Seels & Richey, 1994).

Once approved by the administrative boards of AECT and NCATE, the guidelines were for evaluating academic programs and guiding program development with the focus on NCATE accreditation of teacher education and school library media specialist programs. NCATE required all teacher education/school library media programs seeking NCATE accreditation for initial teacher certification to describe their technology integration and use as part of their NCATE institutional report. These guidelines further stipulated that, although not required, other academic programs could apply for specialty area accreditation (AECT Program Standards, 2000).

In the late 1990s, NCATE began a performance-based accreditation process, resulting in the formation of another AECT task force. This task force revised the guidelines (retermed *standards*) using, again, the five domains of the IDT field. The AECT and NCATE boards approved these new standards in 2000 (AECT Program Standards, 2000).

With the 2000 program standards in place, NCATE now mandates that the curriculum and candidate performances for the preparation of ECIT personnel should be grounded in the knowledge base of the IDT field. Furthermore, program candidates must demonstrate the knowledge, skills, and dispositions, or competencies, that are directly related to the field of instructional design and technology. The standards for the Initial and Advanced ECIT programs include the same 5 domains and 20 subdomains identified previously, but differ by the performance level of the individual candidate, as indicated for each subdomain. Table 27.7 provides a listing of the domains and subdomains.

The 2000 program standards are intended to accompany the NCATE accreditation of professional education units; however, they greatly broaden the scope of the NCATE accreditation from its traditional areas of teacher education and school library media specialist programs to include other advanced programs in higher education such as educational communications and instructional technology (ECIT) programs. According to the AECT Program Standards (2000), advanced ECIT programs are considered to be those graduate programs that provide additional study in the field beyond the entry level and have limited application to IDT in the areas of business and industry and the military; the standards also note that ECIT programs will vary in their concentration on each of the five domains.

Trends and Issues Related to IDT Competencies and Certification

The continued evolution of the competencies naturally, leads to a consideration of how they may evolve and their current and future functions. The two main trends surrounding the competencies are the direct linkage to and integration of competencies with current ID models and continued specialization within the IDT field. The two main issues are the lack of common job or program titles and professional certification of the IDT field.

Trend 1: Integration of the Competencies Within ID Models

From their very inception, the competencies have been directly related to the practices of the IDT field and sequenced according to how they are typically performed by a practitioner. The majority of them are based on the domains of the IDT field as defined by the AECT Task Force on Definitions and Terminology or as seen in the five stages of ADDIE, noting that the current ID competencies do not include evaluation as a major domain. Being directly linked to the practice is one trend that we see continuing.

Furthermore, we see a direct integration of IDT competencies within ID models. For instance, Rothwell and Kazanas (2003) were among the first to infuse the competencies in their model and in their book, *Mastering the Instructional Design Process,* now in its third edition (ibstpi, 2003). The authors state that "The Standards provides a solid foundation for describing the instructional design field. . . . While the *Standards* focuses on *what instructional designers do,* this book focuses on *how to demonstrate competencies of instructional design work.* Its purpose is thus to point the way toward building instructional design competencies" (Rothwell & Kazanas, 2003, p. Emphasis ours). ibtspi (2003) notes that as the chapters present the stages of the design process, the authors relate them back to the competencies and performance statements.

TABLE 27.7 **AECT/NCATE accreditation standards for professional education units for ECIT program curriculum and candidates**

Domains	Subdomains
Standard 1: Design	Instructional systems design Message design Instructional strategies Learner characteristics
Standard 2: Development	Print technologies Audiovisual technologies Computer-based technologies Integrated technologies
Standard 3: Utilization	Media utilization Diffusion of innovations Implementation and institutionalization Policies and regulations
Standard 4: Management	Project management Resource management Delivery systems Management Information management
Standard 5: Evaluation	Problem analysis Criterion-referenced measurement Formative evaluation Summative evaluation

The 2001 edition of Morrison, Ross, and Kemp's textbook also contains the ibstpi code of ethics for instructional designers. In defining the roles of the instructional designer, the authors present a series of scenarios and examples that incorporate the competencies and accompanying knowledge, skills, and attitudes that are required to fulfill those roles (ibstpi, 2003). Similarly, Davidson-Shivers and Rasmussen's text (in press) presents a discussion of their Web-Based Instructional Design model that incorporates skills framed from the ID competencies.

As the discussion of competencies continues, it is expected that they will receive additional exposure in future writings of the IDT field. Such exposure provides a broad cross-section of IDT professionals with the opportunity to review the competencies in their current state, even though we are quite certain that not everyone will agree with what the current competencies entail and how they are used.

Trend 2: Specialization Within the IDT Field

As can be seen, the competencies have evolved from a single set to four main sets, which indicates that the IDT field is becoming (or has become) a field of specializations. Theories that discuss the formation of professions, such as those by Collins (1990), Freidson (1994), Larson (1977, 1990), and Metzger (1976), have a common factor: the increased specialization within an occupation facilitates its status as a profession. Surveying traditionally recognized professions, such as law or medicine, reveal that the differentiation (or specialization) of skills often happens as a field's body of knowledge increases and it moves towards a higher professional level, as compared to other occupations or professions (Davidson, 1985, 1987; Davidson-Shivers & Barrington, 2004). With the division of the original set of competencies, it is clear that IDT is no less complex professional field.

The growth of the IDT knowledge base is comprehensive as well as extensive (Connop-Scollard, 1990; Davidson, 1987; Davidson-Shivers & Barrington, 2004; Richey et al., 2000). Richey et al. discuss the nature of IDT and propose three general specializations—analysis and evaluation, e-learning, and project management. Other areas, including those of designing and developing, might also be included. For instance, Davidson (1987) suggests that designers may focus not only on different aspects of the design process, but may specialize by a particular technology or delivery system (e.g., videography, platform training, computers) or be oriented toward a particular setting (e.g., business and industry, military, health care, education). We anticipate that the trend for specialties within the field will continue, due in part to the broad applications and technological advances that facilitate multifaceted work environments.

Issue 1: Lack of Common Job and Program Titles

With the trend toward specialization comes the issue of name recognition that has plagued the IDT field since its official inception in 1977. Richey et al. (2000) suggest that name recognition for the IDT field exists; although the name of the field is recognized, its practitioners are still known by many names. The 2004–2005 edition of the *Occupational Outlook Handbook* (U.S. Bureau of Labor Statistics, 2004–2005) still does not include the job title of instructional designer, instructional technologist, or other common names associated with the field (Davidson-Shivers & Barrington, 2004; Henderson, 2004).

A lack of easily identified, common titles makes the field difficult to distinguish from other professions in educational and training (Davidson-Shivers & Barrington, 2004; Richey et al., 2000). The lack of common titles for IDT programs at colleges and universities makes it difficult for prospective students to match professional goals to programs. A lack of common job titles makes it difficult, if not impossible, for IDT practitioners to compare job tasks, duties, and compensation packages and to locate new positions. Managers may find it difficult to identify career paths for staff to promote professional development and incentives.

Although the 1994 AECT committee on domains and terminology established a beginning of defining the field, the work must be continued. Perhaps it is time to establish a joint committee among the various IDT organizations to arrive at common titles to encourage growth of IDT as a profession.

Issue 2: Professional Certification

The second issue that surrounds the competencies is that of professional certification. Members of the field have discussed this issue for the last 25 years. Although there are a few organizations that credential certain areas and others that accredit academic programs, there is no overall certification of IDT practitioners. (Remember that the original purpose of the ad hoc and official ACET task forces was ID certification and that identifying competencies was an offshoot of this purpose.) Part of the problem may lay with how certification is being defined.

Certification defined. *Professional certification* has been defined as "the formal recognition individuals received from an independent body of peers who have examined their work and evaluated it against some published external standards" (Bratton, 1995, p. 393). ISPI (2004) defines certification as a credential "that is given to people who satisfy a set of requirements" (n.p.). Bratton (1995) stresses that professional certification and teacher certification are not the same things and that the latter "is a misnomer because it is a form of licensure" (p. 393). Certification can be viewed as recognition by a professional organization that an individual has met an agreed set of requirements.

Stumbling blocks to certification. IDT practitioners must evaluate the value of certification to the profession and practitioners and whether it should even occur. This discussion has not been resolved for the last two decades and still continues today. Some IDT practitioners do not want, nor see a need for, certification while others are and remain advocates for this process. The debate continues.

In addition, certification requires that organizations and the individuals in the profession agree to a set of standards. The IDT field has several sets of competencies, which share commonalities. Yet, there is no single, overarching set of competencies that have been agreed on by the entire field. A common, agreed set of competencies is required to advance the profession and permits professionals to share a common view and framework of their field (Davidson, 1985, Metzger 1976). At present, certification for IDT professionals is not a requirement, but rather a designation of proficiency, specifically in the area of performance technology.

Certification processes imply that assessment procedures are in place and that a designated external agency conducts the process (Bratton, 1995; Davidson, 1985, 1987; Davidson-Shivers & Barrington, 2004). Although several national organizations are identifying procedures for accreditation processes, IDT practitioners have not designated a single entity as "the" external agency responsible for certification. Likewise, no articulated assessment procedures for evaluating practitioners and programs have been identified and approved by IDT practitioners. Selection or determination of the designated external agency will have a vital part in how the field will be shaped and defined in the future.

Finally, professional certification remains of great concern for individual practitioners. National organizations, including AECT, ASTD, ISPI, and NCATE, are vying for control over the certification and accreditation process of IDT field and its practitioners, but it is unclear how this control issue will be settled. How the certification and accreditation process plays out in the future has direct bearing on *who are* and *will become* IDT practitioners and *what are* and *will be* "approved" IDT programs. Discussion on this issue continues with no timetable set for resolution.

Summary

DID/AECT was a forerunner in identifying competencies for IDT professionals (Bratton, 1983); the concern for identifying competencies for instructional design and training professionals was so important that three international organizations worked to define and refine a common set of standards that describe and outline the knowledge, skills, and abilities needed to perform in an IDT environment. Early efforts showed a concern for the diffusion and adoption of the instructional design process and creating a niche in the marketplace for the instructional and training design specialist (Deden-Parker, 1981; Richey et al., 2000). The early works of ibstpi also showed a concern for developing and defining the fourth IDT profession, performance technology. These original competencies for all four types of practitioners served as cornerstones of the current sets of competencies.

As the field developed over these past decades, the competencies were divided by a separation of roles within the field—instructional designer, training manager, instructor, and performance technologist. A code of ethics is included with each set of competencies. These competencies and ethical standards will continue to evolve as the field continues to change.

Two primary trends can be discerned when examining the concept of IDT competencies. Incorporating competencies into ID models has been observed, as each competency/standard mirrors a skill required to implement the model. Another trend has been the development of specialties within the IDT field. We foresee that these trends will continue for sometime in the future.

Two issues surrounding competencies were also identified. One relates to the lack of common job and program titles for the IDT field. The second issue is related to professional certification of the field. Of the two, the issue of IDT certification has major consequences for practitioners, academic programs, and the field itself. For the IDT field to progress and develop further, it is time that its practitioners come to terms with the issue of professional certification.

Application Questions

1. If you were responsible for identifying the domains, competencies, and performance statements for a performance technologist, what would they include? Why?
2. Are the competencies too complex to have utility? Review the conceptual map presented by Connop-Scollard (1990) for a view of the tasks completed by the IDT professional.
3. Should IDT practitioners be certified? What is your position on this issue? Why? Forecast the direction of the debate over the next 25 years.

References

AECT Program Standards. (2000). *NCATE program standards: Initial and advanced programs for educational communications and technology.* Bloomington, IN: Association for Educational Communications and Technology. Retrieved March 16, 2004, from **http://www.aect.org/Affiliates/National/Standards.pdf**

Bratton, B. (1983, November). *Instructional/training design competencies and sources of information about them.* A DID/AECT Occasional Paper. (n.p.).

Bratton, B. (1995). Professional competencies and certification in the instructional technology field. In G. J. Anglin (ed.), *Instructional technology: Past, present, and future* (2nd ed.) (pp. 393–397). Englewood, CO: Libraries Unlimited.

Chevalier, R. (2004). Using the standards of performance technology. *ISPI Vancouver Orientation to Performance Improvement*. Retrieved May 28, 2004 from **http://www.ispi_van.org/htm/articles/chevalier_standards.pdf**

Collins, R. (1990). Changing conceptions in the sociology of the professions. In R. Torstendahl & M. Burrage (Eds.), *The formation of professions* (pp. 11–23). London: Sage.

Connop-Scollard, C. (1990). The ID/D chart: A representation of instructional design and development. *Educational Technology, 31*(12), 47–50.

Daft, R. L. (2003). *Management* (6th ed.). Mason, OH: South-Western/Thomson.

Davidson, G. V. (1985, February). *Specialization within the instructional design profession*. Paper presented at the annual meeting of the Association for Educational Communications and Technology, Anaheim, CA.

Davidson, G. V. (1987, February). *Seven requirements to be a legitimate profession: What happens if the instructional design field doesn't make it?* Paper presented at the annual meeting of the Association for Educational Communications and Technology, Atlanta, GA.

Davidson-Shivers, G. V., & Barrington, M. (2004, October). *Revisiting the professional status of instructional design and technology and the specialization within*. Paper presented at the annual meeting of the Association for Educational Communications and Technology, Chicago, IL.

Davidson-Shivers, G. V., & Rasmussen, K. L. (in press). *Web-based learning: Design, implementation, & evaluation*. Upper Saddle River, NJ: Merrill/Prentice Hall.

Deden-Parker, A. (1981, February). Instructional technology skills sought by industry. *NSPI Journal,* 24–25, 30.

Division of Instructional Development/AECT Ad Hoc Task Force. (1980, Fall). Competencies for the instructional development practitioner. *DID Newsletter,* 1–10.

Foshay, W. R. (2000). Preface. In R. C. Richey, D. C. Fields, & M. Foxon, *Instructional design competencies: The standards* (3rd ed.) (pp. 16–20). Syracuse, NY: ERIC Clearinghouse on Information & Technology.

Foxon, M., Richey, R. C., Roberts, R. C., & Spannaus, T. W. (2003). *Training manager competencies: The standards* (3rd ed.). Syracuse, NY: ERIC Clearinghouse on Information and Technology.

Friedson, E. (1994). *Professionalism reborn: Theory, prophecy, and policy.* Chicago: University of Chicago Press.

Guerra, I. J. (2003). Key competencies required of performance improvement professionals. *Performance Improvement Quarterly, 16*(1), 55–72.

Harris, R., Guthrie, H., Hobart, B., & Lundberg, D. (1995). *Competency-based education and training: Between a rock and a whirlpool*. Hong Kong: Macmillan Education Australia.

Henderson, K. (2004, September 8). What's an instructional designer? Getting businesses to recognize the value of your ID skills. Invited address to the Instructional Design and Development Student Group General Meeting, University of South Alabama, Mobile, AL. Available from **http://www.southalabama.edu/coe/bset/iddsg/idd_brief_files/frame.htm**

Instructional Innovator. (1980, December). Competencies for instructional development specialist. *Instructional Innovator,* 27–30.

International Board of Standards for Training, Performance, and Instruction (ibstpi). (1988). *The professional reference guide to the competencies: The standards for instructors, instructional designers, and training managers.* Chicago: ibstpi, Altshchuler, Melvoin, & Glasser.

International Board of Standards for Training, Performance, and Instruction (ibstpi). (1989). *What competencies must an individual demonstrate to meet minimum standards in each of the three roles*? Chicago: ibstpi, Altshchuler, Melvoin, & Glasser.

International Board of Standards for Training, Performance and Instruction (ibstpi). (2003). Homepage. Retrieved March 18, 2004 from **http://www.ibstpi.org**

ISPI. (2002). *ispi's performance technology standards*. Silver Spring, MD: *ISPI.*

ISPI. (2004). *CPT-certified performance technologist*. Retrieved May 28, 2004 from **http://www.certifiedpt.org/**

Klein, J. D., Spector, J. M., Grabowski, B., & de la Teja, I. (2004). *Instructor competencies: Standards for face-to-face, online, and blended settings* (3rd ed., rev.). Greenwich, CT: Information Age.

Larson, M. S. (1977). *The rise of professionalism: A sociological analysis*. Berkley, CA: University of California Press.

Larson, M. S. (1990). In the matter of experts and professionals, or how impossible it is to leave nothing unsaid. In R. Torstendahl & M. Burrage (Eds.), *The formation of professions* (pp. 24–50). London: Sage.

Metzger, W. P. (1976, Fall). What is a profession? *College and University,* 42–55.

Morrison, G. R., Ross, S. M., & Kemp, J. E. (2001). *Designing effective instruction* (3rd ed.). New York: John Wiley & Sons.

Mosley, D. C., Pietri, P. H., & Megginson, L. C. (1996). *Management: Leadership in action* (5th ed.). New York: HarperCollins.

Rasmussen, K. L. (2002). Competence at a glance: Professional knowledge, skills, and abilities in the field of instructional design and technology. In R. A. Reiser & J. V. Dempsey (Eds.), *Trends and issues in instructional design and technology* (pgs. 375–386). Upper Saddle River, NJ: Merrill/Prentice Hall.

Richey, R. C., Fields, D. C., & Foxon, M. (2000). *Instructional design competencies: The standards* (3rd ed.). Syracuse, NY: ERIC Clearinghouse on Information and Technology;

Rothwell, W. J., & Kazanas, H. C. (2003). *Mastering the instructional design process: A systematic approach* (3rd ed.). San Francisco: Jossey-Bass/Pfeiffer.

Saettler, P. (1990). *The evolution of American educational technology.* Englewood, CO: Libraries Unlimited.

Schermerhorn, J. R. (1999). *Management* (6th ed.). New York: John Wiley & Sons.

Seels, B. B., & Richey, R. C. (1994). *Instructional technology: The definitions and domains of the field.* Washington, DC: Association for Educational and Communications Technology.

Spector, J. M. (2000). The ibstpi code of ethical standards for instructional designers. In R. C. Richey, D. C. Fields, & M. Foxon (Eds.), *Instructional design competencies: The standards* (3rd ed.) (Appendix D.) Syracuse, NY: ERIC Clearinghouse on Information and Technology.

Spector, J. M., & de la Teja, I. (2001, December). *Competencies for online teaching.* Syracuse, NY: ERIC Clearinghouse on Information & Technology. Retrieved March 18, 2004, from **http://www.ibstpi.org** (ERIC Digest, ED-99-CO-0005.)

Task Force on ID Certification. (1981). Competencies for the instructional/training development professional. *Journal of Instructional Development, 5*(1), 14–15.

U.S. Bureau of Labor Statistics. (2004–2005). *Occupational outlook handbook.* Retrieved June 22, 2004 from **http://www.bls.gov/oco/home.htm**

SECTION 7

New Directions in Instructional Design and Technology

Overview

Like many fields, instructional design and technology is hugely affected by the enormous changes brought about largely through the pervasiveness of networked computers. Most of the chapters in this section consider the effect of these phenomena on our present and future learning systems.

The first two chapters of this section both look at distributed learning, but do so in different ways. Chapter 28 considers what effective online learning is and how that possibility causes radical changes to our more traditional views of instructional design. The authors contend that designers should be more aware than ever of interactivity, interactions, and learning communities as well as other factors. In addition, they contend that the emergence of online learning has created great opportunity while increasing expectations, including more clearly establishing our identity as a field to nonpractitioners.

Chapter 29 reviews critical issues of reusability and instructional systems. The meaning and requirements for reusable learning objects, metadata, granularity, copyright issues, and the role of instructional designers in reuse are discussed.

Chapter 30 considers rich media and learning. The authors examine research-based principles to prescribe guidelines for instructional designers to use in enabling effective instructional methods that promote learning.

The final two chapters in this section look to the future in very different ways. The authors of Chapter 31 review a broad spectrum of emerging instructional technologies and select a few that they predict will have a growing impact on the field over the near (or foreseeable) future. In addition, as is the theme of at least three chapters in this section, they argue that a technology-induced and far-reaching paradigm shift is underway in our field.

Chapter 32, the closing chapter of this section and of the book, is a point/counterpoint interaction concerning the future of instructional design and technology. This "conversation" between two well-known theorists in the field samples the diversity of perspectives and philosophical approaches that exist in our field.

John V. Dempsey
University of South Alabama

Richard N. Van Eck
University of North Dakota

CHAPTER 28

Distributed Learning and the Field of Instructional Design

Knowledge and Comprehension Questions

1. Distributed learning can take many forms, varying both by environment and level of implementation. Give a brief description of five different examples of distributed learning, varying your examples by environment and level of implementation.
2. Why do the authors say that instructional designers have a "window of opportunity" in distributed learning? What role does instructional design play in distributed learning? What risk do we run, as instructional designers, by not quickly embracing distributed learning? What are the risks involved with taking a leading role in distributed learning design and development?
3. What kinds of learning outcomes may distributed learning be particularly suited to? Why? What kinds may not be well suited for distributed learning environments? Why?
4. The authors contend that interactions are becoming more important. Answer the following questions about interactions and interactivity:
   - What is the difference between *interactions* and *interactivity*?
   - How will interactivity change with technological improvements?
   - What are the two typologies of interactions? Give an example of each.

Editors' Introduction

In this chapter, Jack Dempsey and Rick Van Eck contend that the explosive growth in distributed learning presents both a challenge and an opportunity for the field of instructional design. The ability of instructional designers to embrace this challenge and opportunity depends greatly on the comprehension of learning outcomes, interactions and interactivity, learning communities, and the constraints imposed by administrative restrictions or mandates in online learning. This chapter presents an overview of some of the most salient processes and issues in the development of distributed learning today.

Our Tools Shape Us

When we wrote our chapter in 2001 for the first edition of this text, we argued that instructional designers could play a critical role in guiding the development of quality online programs. Given the furious pace of innovation in all technology-driven enterprises, it is not surprising that much has changed since then. Our conception of online learning has expanded to address new technologies such as intelligent tutoring systems, learning object repositories, and virtual communities of practice. Once the exclusive purview of researchers in laboratory settings, many of these new technologies are now or will soon be mainstream. The Internet 2 initiative has become a 200 institution network with capabilities of 6.5 gigabits per second (Gbps); bandwidth more than 10,000 times faster than typical broadband access (*Interactions News Wire*, 2004). The Next Generation Internet (NGI) initiative has completed testing and development of the next version of the Internet, called the National LambdaRail. Based on a giant ring of fiber optic cables comprised of 40 channels, each with a throughput of 10 Gbps, the combined potential of this is a network for simultaneous transmission of data at 400 Gbps. But this is only half the story. Internet 2 will be coupled with grid computing, which is a new protocol that allows us to distribute not just information, as the current Internet does, but to distribute tasks, processes, and applications as well. This is the same concept that has allowed people to create supercomputers by hooking multiple computers together to act as one, with processing power distributed among all the computers in the grid. The potential for collaboration over the Internet will increase dramatically overnight with these applications. Moore's law (computer processing power, or the number of transistors on a CPU, doubles every 18 months) is expected to hold true for the next few years, and network capacity has been double that rate for the last few years (Villazon, 2005).

Concurrently, we can expect continual movement toward ubiquitous computing, in which technology and access are everywhere, invisible, and taken for granted. The true promise of Internet 2 is that it will allow grid computing so processing tasks will be automatically distributed among available computers anywhere on the network, or grid (Villazon, 2005). We are looking at a world of information, power, and access that is highly accelerated and exciting—a world where video conferencing will be supplemented by virtual reality and primitive forms of artificial intelligence. Although the Internet remains the prime mover, for this edition we have changed the title and, somewhat the focus, of this chapter from *online learning* to *distributed learning*, a less restrictive concept.

Have instructional designers managed to embrace the opportunities we've had, or are we falling behind? What changes will be required by these advances in technology and delivery? In this chapter we'll address and update things that have changed and attempt to outline some of the new challenges that exist. The essence of learning with instructional design has not changed. We use instructional design to create learning environments and products. The processes or *functional architectures*[1] involved in our work, however, are changing quickly. We will argue that it is necessary to understand and embrace changes in the functional architectures of instructional design to continue to play a meaningful role in the future of distributed learning.

Distributed learning requires a radical change in the professional practices of educators and trainers. Clearly, the prevalence of online learning and information access is growing exponentially (Nielson, 1999) in many areas of our society and to view it as a passing fashion is myopic. Sixty-seven percent of all adults in the United States have access to the Internet, with the largest increase from 2000 occurring in home Internet access and use (*Business Courier*, 2003). And the future is clear; according to Susan Patrick (2005), one of the authors of the National Education Technology Plan, 94% of all teens, 80% of all middle school children, 76% of elementary students, and 50% of all preschool children make daily use of the Internet, and children and young adults spend more time online now than they do watching television.

As Marshall McLuhan (1989) pointed out, we shape our tools, but then our tools shape us. The nexus between computer-managed instruction, common since at least the 1960s with the PLATO system (Bitzer & Boudreaux, 1969), and the Internet, a practical tool since around 1993 with the *Mosaic* browser (Tauber & Kienan, 1995), fits well into the needs of those Rogers would classify as early adopters of innovations (Jacobsen, 2000; Rogers, 1995). The capabilities we have gleaned as instructional designers from years of systematic approaches toward learning and from our early adoption of the computer as a delightful learning tool is coming to fruition. Organizations that a couple of years ago had never contemplated instructional design are now anxious for trained designers to take a major role in renovating their instructional systems. Effective

---

[1] By *functional architecture*, we mean the various functional entities and components involved in an instructional system and the collaborations and interactions among them. Many of these are most obviously influenced by new technologies, but changes in preferences toward social communications certainly affect the functional communications of instructional systems as frequently as do, say, advances in cellular phone technologies.

distributed learning thrives on the systematic organization of instructional materials and effective instructional strategies and technics[2]—two principal strengths of instructional design.

We have observed for some time now that in implementing distributed learning systems we have been experiencing the equivalent of the silent movie era of technological change. Just as sound was inevitable in motion pictures, richer media and more smoothly running delivery systems with few bandwidth limitations are becoming a staple of future online delivery systems. So, to continue with the analogy, we may now be moving from silent movies to talkies. The technology for video and audio conferencing has been used as a matter of course by early adopters and now by innovators and opinion leaders. But like the corresponding move to audio from silent films, it is not yet ubiquitous or effective, particularly in higher education. Nonetheless, we will undoubtedly see highly increased use of video and audio in distributed learning in the next 3–5 years. The challenges that rural states face with rapid consolidation of school districts and the No Child Left Behind Act's teacher quality standards also guarantee that such technologies will not just be limited to higher education and the corporate world. In terms of production, what we call distributed learning today will seem quite primitive in 10 years. Likewise, instructional technology is in a nascent stage. Despite its dramatic growth in the last 3 years, the majority of instructors, trainers, and designers have had little or no experience participating in online learning environments, much less developing learning activities for them. Although we may be comparatively impressed with the available technology, this available technology is rudimentary and underdeveloped. At this point in the development of distributed learning, instructional designers have enormous opportunities and often more responsibility than we bargained for.

What Is Distributed Learning?

Distributed learning is any educational or training experience that uses a variety of means, including technology, to enable learning. It can provide for intentional and incidental learning outcomes and may be separated by time, distance, or both. Distributed learning includes, but is not limited to, distance learning and online learning. Often, regardless of the location of the learning environment, distributed learning eliminates time as a barrier to learning (Oblinger, Barone, & Hawkins, 2001). In *distance learning* the learner is typically separated in space and time with the instructor and peers. In *online learning* the learner is limited to Internet-based learning technologies. Another commonly mentioned subset of distributed learning is *e-learning*, which Clark and Mayer (2003) refer to as, "a combination of content and instructional methods delivered by media elements such as words and graphics on a computer" (p. 311). With the changes in the Internet and in computing technology, the lines between these areas are rapidly becoming blurred, and may cease to exist in the near future.

Distributed learning may occur among people scattered across the globe or among coworkers at a single facility. What characterizes distributed learning is the use of a very flexible functional architecture that takes a variety of manifestations. These could include any combination of on-campus lectures, CBT training modules, online seminars, reference websites, books, DVDs, threaded discussions, videoconferences, weblogs, simulations, performance support systems, and numerous other elements by which learning is accomplished. Another attribute of distributed learning is that it may be *synchronous* (takes place in real time), *asynchronous*, (does *not* take place in real time), or a mixture of both.

Distributed Learning in Academic and Corporate Settings

Distributed learning in academic environments includes established brick-and-mortar institutions that have begun to branch out into online learning and virtual institutions that have never provided onsite classes. Universities now offering online learning opportunities range from those offering a few individual classes to those that have moved entire programs and degrees online. In the former case, some existing classes are often chosen and converted to an online format, often by professors who had formerly taught the class in a classroom. In the case of degree programs, universities may elect to begin by putting a few courses at a time online as described, gradually building to a fully implemented online degree. This latter case requires a great deal more planning, organization, and resources than does the former. Online degree programs usually require "virtual campuses" with a completely online registration system and a full complement of student support services such as library, bookstore, advising, and financial aid. In 2004, there were at least 263 accredited online graduate degrees in five disciplines available in the United States (USNews.com, 2004).

Recently, there has been a marked increase in virtual universities without a traditional brick-and-mortar complement. Such institutions have a physical address but may have little more in terms of buildings, relying instead on

[2] *Instructional technics* are activities or tactics that use technology designed or selected to reach learning outcomes. They are influenced or driven by instructional strategies.

online resources. There are hybrids, of course, offering a limited menu of onsite courses as a supplement to their online presence. Although some academicians consider commercial virtual universities substandard, they are now gaining acceptance, with newer for-profit virtual universities getting accreditation as institutes of higher learning (e.g., Jones International University, accredited by NCATE; and Walden University and Cappella University, accredited by Higher Learning Commission and North Central Association of College and Schools).

Corporate online learning environments often include an intranet (a network similar to the public Internet but secure from outside access) for employees of a corporation. A great deal of training is taking place over corporate intranets. Corporate training budgets are investing billions of dollars in Web-based training alone, and investments are expected to increase for the foreseeable future (Abernathy, 2001). The rationale is that it costs the company money not only to transport and house employees for out-of-town training but also to replace that employee during the training. Moreover, employees are able to get training when and where they need it instead of waiting for the next scheduled training session. Employees can log on to a company intranet and take the classes they need when they need them. Such training is managed by learning management systems (LMSs), which track who has taken what course, at what time, and which individual objectives have or have not been met. LMSs thus allow institutions to track what their employees know or can do. This saves money and simplifies compliance issues.

Online classes may be developed in house by corporate training departments or by outside providers who reduce course costs by leasing the same or slightly modified courses to a number of companies. From 1999 to 2003, companies who spent the most on training in general increased their budget for outside training services from 22 percent of expenditure in 2001 to 28 percent in 2002 (ASTD, 2003). This increased reliance on outside training products may partly account for the significant decrease in the number of instructional designers in these organizations, which fell from 52 in 2001 to 14 in 2002 (ASTD). At the same time, spending on distance learning technologies increased in these same organizations by 29%, indicating that more corporate training departments are looking for distance learning technologies and off-the-shelf learning (ASTD). Our opportunities as instructional designers for distance learning may lie in the development of instructional materials for distance learning vendors, rather than in the corporate market itself. Already in academia, textbook companies are beginning to market online learning development services, including hosting, development, and support. A number of publishers offer development tools for creating websites to accompany textbooks, and offer online courses tied to existing textbooks. Many states are demanding electronic versions of textbooks themselves from the publishers, perhaps signaling a shift toward licensing rather than purchasing.

There are a host of online tools and resources that do not easily fall into the academic or corporate distributed learning categories but which nevertheless constitute distributed learning. Examples include personal websites with detailed information on different topics, research and reference tools, virtual reality sites with avatars and chat rooms where people interact in a cyber-social setting, and virtual communities of practice (VCOP). Examples of a variety of online environments are given in Table 28.1.

The Role of Instructional Design in Online Learning Development

One of the greatest challenges facing those charged with creating distributed learning is the tremendous pressure to generate that learning quickly. Given the increased expenditure on learning technologies in corporate training (ASTD, 2003), the exponential trend toward distributed learning, particularly online, in the corporate world seems to be continuing. Many in higher education are also feeling the pressure to produce better and more distributed learning, sometimes in less time than might be allowed for a comparable traditional classroom course. More than one million students have enrolled in virtual schools, and 90 percent of all four-year public schools offer online education, as do half their counterparts in private schools (Botelho, 2004). And with the $5.1 billion online learning industry growing at a 38% rate, this pressure is not likely to diminish anytime soon (Botelho). This pressure to produce distributed courseware quickly may lead some to think that there is simply no time for instructional design processes. Because there are so many people without instructional design training who are able to create stylish websites in a relatively short time, some managers and administrators may come to expect the same with high-quality distributed learning materials and activities. In fact, many view the creation of online courses and websites as the same activity! This represents both our greatest challenge and greatest opportunity—to convey to others not only what we do but why what we do is valuable. It is the nature of good design to produce effective products that do what they are intended to do. This is accomplished through a tremendous amount of upfront work that is often invisible to outsiders except as extra development time. One can imagine an administrator looking at a finished product and saying, "There's nothing fancy about that site; my high school kid could put that together in half the time it took you." This could be true, of course, but only if that kid

TABLE 28.1 Examples and resources for online learning

Resource Type	URL
Web-based (virtual) campuses	http://www.jonesinternational.edu/ http://www.open.ac.uk/
Learning object repositories	http://www.merlot.org
University clearinghouses & free courses	http://www.gnacademy.org/ http://www.electroniccampus.org/ http://ocw.mit.edu/index.html
Web-enhanced Campuses	http://usaonline.southalabama.edu http://sln.suny.edu/sln/public/cshome.nsf/docs/2
"Full-service" Web-based courses & course systems	http://www.lsal.cmu.edu/lsal/expertise/technologies/online/index.html http://cecal.humberc.on.ca/distance.html
Standalone online activities	http://www.southalabama.edu/coe/idbook/ http://www.oar.noaa.gov/k12/
Course tools and services	http://www.ecollege.com http://www.webct.com
Electronic books	http://www.gutenberg.org/ http://www.exemplary.net/omnimedia/bookstore.html
Reference sources	http://www.eduref.org/ http://www.psycinfo.com
Smart tools	http://www.aproposinc.com http://www.wernerschaudin.de
EPSSs or wizards	http://www.epsscentral.info/ http://openacademy.mindef.gov.sg/OpenAcademy/Learning%20Resources/EPSS/artonlin.htm
Corporate training sites	http://www.getsmartonline.com/ http://www.syberworks.com/
Intelligent tutoring systems	http://www.autotutor.org http://www.pitt.edu/~circle/Projects/Atlas.html
Repurposed instruction	http://builtinvacuum.com/installguides/supervalve/

knew exactly what to do from the beginning and had all the content outlined and organized for him.

Crafting an instructional message that is customized to the environment, learners, domain, and mode requires the complex application of scientific and artistic principles. When we have done our job, the end result is a product that is effective and easy to use, but which consequently shows no outward sign of the effort that went into it. It is our responsibility to educate clients and school administrators about the value of good design. This may be difficult since the advantages (e.g., better student learning, accountability, or the reputation of the school or business) may be invisible in the short term. Nonetheless, if we do not embrace this challenge, we run the risk of abdicating the design of online learning to those who master the tools of creation and ignore the science of learning. It can be argued that artful instructional designs in online learning depend greatly on the designer's comprehension of learning outcomes, interactions and interactivity, learning communities, and constraints imposed by administrative restrictions or mandates. To varying degrees, being able to apply or evaluate "artistic" skills (e.g., graphic design principles) can be a critical part of the development process.

Given the established trend in corporate and educational venues of adopting outside training, and the increasing interest in customized learning and learning objects, one way we may be able to address the "need for speed" without sacrificing quality is through the development of learning objects and reusable content. *Learning objects* are individual components of learning material that can be aggregated or disaggregated to form instructional units of varying size. Objects in theory can be any size, but are most commonly at the objective, module, or unit levels as the larger the object the less reusable it is.

The impetus for learning objects arises from the recognition that instructional designers often duplicate each other's work when developing new training. For example, training on soft skills such as sales is done thousands of times a year in as many different environments. While philosophy and approach to these skills certainly varies with the organization, product, and time in which it is being developed, there are also a striking number of similarities in sales techniques overall. It would be great if we could reuse content we or others created earlier. The problem is that while some of the training could be repurposed, it is aggregated at the course unit, meaning that the prerequisite skills are enmeshed in the overall training unit, with no easy way to extract them for use elsewhere. Learning objects solve this problem by providing a means of not only creating separate objects, but also of identifying what those objects are and how they relate to the content and to the larger domain. The means of creating this identification, or *metadata*, can theoretically take any form, and prior to 1999 organizations were developing their own ways of doing this. But to truly harness the power of learning objects, it quickly became clear that these competing models and standards would result in intraorganizational reusability but no interorganizational reusability. In other words, what was developed in one organization could never be used elsewhere. The call went out for one model and set of standards that could be adopted by all.

The most widely known and accepted model for this process in distributed and computer-based learning is called the Shareable Content Object Reference Model, or SCORM (**http://www.adlnet.org**). SCORM is an emerging set of standards for creating and identifying learning objects for use in distributed and computer-based learning. SCORM arose from the Department of Defense's Advanced Distributed Learning (ADL) initiative. The DoD was charged with working with other federal agencies and the private sector to establish a set of standards. SCORM 1.0 was released in 2000, and SCORM 2004 was released in 2004 as the final working version of the standards and model. All government contractors who develop training must adhere to this model, and most learning management systems implement it now. Understanding how to develop content to this standard thus is a necessity for doing business as well as a good way for instructional designers to shorten development time of new learning without sacrificing quality.

Learning Outcomes

Rich online environments require a wealth of interaction. Human interaction, skillfully designed into almost any learning environment, provides for the richest learning experiences—ones that go beyond simple acquisition of knowledge. As Merrill (1997) and others have suggested, information is not instruction. Two of the most useful conceptual frameworks in instructional design, the nine Events of Instruction (Gagné, 1985) and the ARCS model (Keller, 1983) are as appropriate for online learning as they are for other media. The Events of Instruction and the ARCS model focus on instructional strategies and motivational strategies respectively. In addition, Sweller's Cognitive Load Theory as it relates to the design of electronic learning systems is particularly useful for designing media-rich computer-mediated learning (Kalyuga, Chandler, & Sweller, 1998; Sweller, 1989; Sweller, van Merriënboer, & Paas, 1998).

Probably because of Gagné's neobehaviorist approach to classifying learning outcomes, some educators (e.g., Gillespie, 1999) dismiss systematic design of instruction out of hand. In our view, this may be due to a lack of understanding of the origins and possible uses of these models. Neither Gagné's Events of Instruction nor Keller's ARCS model specifies the nature of the instructional strategies or how the theory used influences those strategies. Rather, these models provide a framework by which instructional designers can examine course topics in intentional learning environments. Kruse and Keil (2000) provide a worthwhile discussion of this area and examples of the use of these instructional and motivational frameworks in online environments. More recently, a delightful book by Iverson (2005) gives a number of creative and practical examples of techniques which may be strategically grounded in Gagné's and Keller's frameworks.

The Internet and its environs are saturated with opportunities for incidental learning outcomes. More than any other medium, the Internet allows for serendipity in acquiring or expanding knowledge. This may be online learning's most powerful and unexplored feature. Without question, incidental learning on the Internet is a rich area for systematic exploration and research by university faculty, corporate R&D groups, and graduate students. What we learn parenthetically is often the spark that fires a burning interest in more sustained learning activities. Conceptual approaches such as constructivism and situated learning address incidental learning more steadfastly than what some individuals refer to as "objectivist" learning approaches, such as the Dick, Carey, and Carey (2005) model.

Often, however, the instructional designer's job is to arrange for intentional learning outcomes. Basic instructional design skills expected in the marketplace are the ability to use taxonomies of learning outcomes such as Bloom's (Bloom, Engelhart, Furst, Hill, & Krathwohl 1956) or Gagné's (1985) and to conduct an analysis to achieve intentional learning outcomes. The methodology required for classifying learning outcomes and conducting learning or instructional analysis is well established and taught in a number of the leading instructional design texts in our field, as are other basic skills such as learner analysis, criterion-referenced assessment, and formative evaluation of instructional materials. In general, it should be noted that the Internet in its current incarnation is more useful for teaching cognitive outcomes. Given the existing technology, it is generally less useful for direct instruction of psychomotor skill development or attitudinal change (with the possible exception of the blogging phenomenon). Designers may expect these limitations to become less restrictive in the next decade as technology and bandwidth continue to evolve.

Interactions and Interactivity

Interactions are often confused with interactivity on the Internet, but it is useful to consider them separately. According to Wagner (1994), *interactions* involve behaviors where individuals and groups directly influence each other. Conversely, *interactivity* tends to focus on the attributes of the technology system. For example, threaded discussion in an online course would mandate interactions among learners. Similarly, effective standalone computer-based training generally features a highly interactive learning environment. What interactions and interactivity have in common in a learning environment are that both contribute to active learning, both tend to be oriented toward expressed or implied goals, and neither was commonly used in the same instructional piece before the Internet.

As a result of our familiarity with computer-based training in its many guises (CAI, CAL, CMI, etc.) and our psychological foundations in programmed instruction (Kulhavy & Wager, 1993), instructional designers have been leading proponents of interactivity. For somewhat the same reasons, courseware developers in our field have been less concerned with interactions, particularly interactions among learners. As the Internet has emerged as the leading tool of distributed learning, this has changed. Some authors even contend that "focusing on real-time, technologically enabled interactivity as a defining attribute of distance learning is an artifact of the past" (Wagner, 1997; p. 21). Although we do not agree with the absoluteness of this statement, interactions clearly have found a safe haven in online learning. Even so, the increasing availability of broadband access to the Internet—60% of all online users have it (Villazon, 2005)—is allowing for interactivity to return as a practical option for online learning. As both interactivity and interaction can promote active learning processes, it seems foolish to dismiss the power of interactivity out of hand. Consider the current limitations in lab courses or ID courses that rely on CBT development tools such as *Authorware, Director,* or *Toolbook;* with the advent of distributed computing and screen-sharing collaboration software over IP, it will soon be possible to teach synchronous courses that require intensive one-to-one mentoring and support during application.

Nevertheless, as many creative instructional designs give emphasis to socially active learning, interactions will become an even more central force in courseware development. Because interactions are so central a part of many online learning environments, it is useful to understand typologies of interactions. Two functional typologies consist of interactions as agents and interactions as outcomes. Three types of interactions are suggested by Moore (1989): interactions that occur (1) between the learner and the instructor, (2) among learners, or (3) between learners and the content they are trying to master. This schema does not consider the intended outcomes of these interaction categories and therefore provides only general information to an instructional designer about the learning environment. Wagner (1997) approaches interaction types in a more serviceable fashion by considering the outcomes of interactions. Wagner's interactions refer to outcomes that emphasize the communicability of educational experiences. These include interactions that increase participation and communication, refer to events of instruction (e.g., interactions to receive feedback or enhance retention and transfer), support metacognition, encourage team development, emphasize discovery and exploration, and provide for clarification and closure. Wagner's effort to emphasize outcomes that include, but are not limited to, specific learning outcomes reflects the increasing importance of social interaction in instructional courseware development as it has been accelerated by the phenomenon of online learning.

The Online Environment as a Learning Community

Although often viewed as an isolating experience, the paradox in online learning is that learners sitting alone in front of a computer monitor may actually be satisfying their human need for community (di Petta, 1999). In addition to the expansion of technological capabilities, the phenomenal rise in virtual or online communities has been attributed to the disintegration of traditional communities around the world (Rheingold, 1993). Online or virtual communities may also be effective vehicles to improve learning overall. According to the American Society of Trainers and Developers (ASTD), 70% of what an employee needs to know to do their job is learned outside of formal training, and virtual communities of practice (VCOPs) are a good way to capture tacit knowledge (Kaplan, 2002). These VCOPs play a critical role in higher education as well as institutions move toward completely online degrees (Haythornthwaite, Kazmer, & Robins, 2000).

If constructivism has one true champion in circumstance, it is the shared construction of learning assignments—an inherently social activity. Many online course developers are coming to see the information they incorporate as less of a product (permanent in the sense of a textbook) and more of a process of a learning group in action among an increasing array of learning options and shared experiences. Research on the benefits of learners as designers, peer tutoring, and collaborative design indicates that this emphasis on process versus. product in online learning design may be one of the unanticipated strengths of developing online instruction and training (Dede, 1995). Participation and creativity not available in conventional classes are becoming commonplace in well-designed online environments (Abrami & Bures, 1996). Properly structured group guidelines, such as those suggested by Palloff and Pratt (1999), describe how teams are structured and led, what authority the team leader has, what responsibilities other members of the team assume, how team projects are graded, and the role of the instructor in arbitration. These are the rules of the social game. These make learning communities eminently viable.

The Instructional Designer's Role on the Development Team

Although some distributed learning environments are designed and implemented by individuals (particularly at universities) most require teams of individuals to accomplish online learning development activities. In addition to an instructional designer, the cast of characters typically includes a project manager, subject matter experts (SMEs), editors, graphic designers, a system manager, legal counsel, programmers, instructors, technical writers, client representatives, evaluators, and marketing specialists. The roles and responsibilities of these team members are well detailed in a number of books and periodicals (Driscoll, 1998; Hall, 1997; Kruse & Keil, 2000; Thach & Murphy, 1995; see also Chapter 12 of this text). An instructional designer has the primary responsibility of making sure the online program accomplishes the learning goals—in essence, that it teaches what it's supposed to teach.

The production of distributed courseware is similar to other educational media efforts. In the best situations, needs assessment and task analysis establish the need for and the goals of the distributed courseware. Once the goals are established, the instructional designer addresses assessment issues and creates the overall design, which includes the processes of instructional, learner, and environmental analyses. Usually, a *treatment* (a detailed narrative description of the project to be used for planning, development, production, and evaluation) is developed and discussed with the client and production specialists. Along with other team members, the designer brainstorms and develops instructional and motivational strategies, contributes to the design of the graphical interface, and prepares a general lesson diagram. Often, the instructional designer will prepare a complete storyboard for the program. Thorough storyboards include sequencing, branching, and general flow of progress of the program. The storyboard also describes the types of media, specifies texts, and illustrates graphics and photos using rough drawings or screenshots, videos, narration, and other audio. From the point that the storyboard enters production, the instructional designer begins the process of quality control (review and revision) and may pilot test the courseware on the target group (formative evaluation). In addition, instructional designers frequently work on online courseware development in many of the other team roles, from project manager to programmer. For obvious reasons, instructional designers with collateral skills, such as graphic design or subject matter expertise, are more valuable to the development group.

Administrative Issues

When we talk about the learning environment we tend to focus on the instructional environment alone, forgetting that the learning environment includes noninstructional elements as well. When learners are onsite, they not only have immediate access to the instructor and their peers for course-related questions, they also have access to other organizational resources. In the corporate setting, such resources might include supporting materials that cannot be supplied electronically and mentors and coworkers outside the class. Employees who do not have prerequisite information in an onsite course may easily get (or be provided) a book or manual for reference, or they may ask a coworker they know outside of class to help explain a concept.

Those who participate in online (i.e., offsite) training may not have as easy access in some regards. So, it is worthwhile for any organization to ask what the primary cost-benefit factors of online learning environments are. A study funded by the Canadian government's National Centre of Excellence in Telelearning in 1999 attempted to respond to this by focusing on six case studies of online courseware (Greengard, 1999). Using several kinds of cost data, these researchers identified three main areas of benefits. These were performance-driven benefits (learning outcomes, student satisfaction, instructor satisfaction, and return on investment), value-driven benefits (access, flexibility, and ease of use), and value-added benefits (reduced traffic and parking needs, spinoffs of new products and services, and increased revenue generation). Clearly, these benefits could be negatively as well as positively assessed (Bates, 2000; Bates & Bartolic, 1999).

Noninstructional concerns may be even more significant in an academic environment where online coursework aimed at a degree or advanced certification tends to occur for greater periods of time and with somewhat less structure. Online students do not have ready access to the entire host of student support services that students who attend classes on campus do. This is especially apparent when we consider that one of the main benefits of asynchronous learning is the ability to "attend" class at odd hours—hours that the school is not open. Services such as financial aid, registration, bursar's office, career counseling, academic advising, and others often cannot be fully utilized by distance education students. For example, how do students clear a financial hold on their records on short notice, handle any paperwork that requires signatures, receive (nonelectronic deposit) financial aid, peruse a thousand company profiles contained at career services, or receive in-depth career exploration and planning from 200 miles away? These are just a few of the issues in student services; dilemmas with student development (e.g., social interaction of living in a dormitory, stopping into the counseling center, career exploration, etc.) present even more challenges for online learning. What is important is that organizational policies address these infrastructure issues in a systematic fashion and either construct a "grow-your-own" virtual campus or contract the construction of these services to one of the increasing number of companies who specialize in this area (e.g., eCollege™ and BlackBoard™). The two most critical components of the educational infrastructure are the merging of the virtual campus environment with existing systems and high-quality, 24/7 student "help desk" availability. Because myriad add-on software products can be accessed within most online course tool environments, the quality of the educational infrastructure and help desk are more critical to the success of an online learning system than are specific pedagogical features available within those systems. In other words, a robust virtual campus with a really useful help desk is more critical to the long-term success of online components of distributed learning than are the particulars of the course tools themselves.

Our Window of Opportunity: The Emerging Role of Instructional Designers

As has been suggested by many authors for a number of years (e.g., Baldwin, 1999; Young, 1997), supplementing or replacing lectures with an online interactive learning experience requires more skill than most educators possess at present. A number of authors, including Turoff (1997), suggest that institutions should be accrediting educators as well as programs. His point is well taken. Candidly, veteran instructional developers working with competent SMEs would likely develop a more effective distributed course than would most university professors or experienced trainers. Professors and content specialist trainers with little or no formal training in delivering instruction are especially mystified at the prospect of organizing an online course.

Of course, this returns us to the familiar question of how we can support the voracious demand for distributed learning without sacrificing quality (i.e., instructional design). We discussed how learning objects can help speed the development process, and how we have to educate others about the vital role that ID can play in quality distributed learning.

One solution may lie in the oft-overlooked field of human performance technology. As instructional designers, we recognize that not all problems we encounter will be solved by training or instruction. Among the tools at our disposal when training is not deemed necessary are electronic performance support systems (EPSS). This term was first coined by Gloria Gery (1991) in her book by the same name. She defined an *EPSS* as

> an integrated electronic environment that is available to and easily accessible by each employee and is structured to provide immediate, individualized on-line access to the full range of information, software, guidance, advice and assistance, data, images, tools, and assessment and monitoring systems to permit job performance with minimal support and intervention by others. (p. 21)

EPSSs are usually knowledge management or decision-making support systems, but their definition and purpose has grown over time. Miller (1996) broadens the definition:

> An electronic performance support system is any computer software program or component that improves employee performance by either reducing the complexity or number of steps required to perform a task (process simplification), providing the performance information an employee needs to perform a task, or providing a decision support system that enables an employee to identify the action that is appropriate for a particular set of conditions. (p. 1)

Electronic performance support systems, specifically, one type of EPSS called an authoring tool, present one solution to this problem. Authoring tools help bridge the gap between experts and learning technology. Most coach an SME through a question-and-answer process and translate her knowledge into a pedagogically effective form that the target learning technology can use.

Authoring tools for intelligent tutoring systems have been in existence for some time (e.g., Macias & Castells, 2001; Murray, 1998; Toole & Heift, 2002). These tools commonly take advantage of a fully developed expert module and provide maximum flexibility and choice for the script designer (Murray, 1999).

The key to these systems is the manner in which they support and encourage the development of content by SMEs according the needs of the tools and pedagogy. These tools use a series of questions and examples to help learners map what they know as SMEs to what is needed by the technology or, in this case, the instructional designer. We can design authoring tools that help guide and coach the SME through the process of developing content for online learning environments. The tool itself becomes a manifestation of a design approach, with the pedagogy embedded in the tool and process. By asking a series of questions about the content, the desired outcomes, and the strategies used in traditional instruction, we can help map what the SME has traditionally done onto the processes, procedures, and tools that can best support them in a distributed learning environment. We must first, of course, have an idea of what kinds of structures and pedagogy we can support in the given online environments, but by focusing our (IDers) attention on these issues rather than on the one-by-one design *and* development of distributed learning, we are able to embed some of our expertise in tools that allow others to at least begin to develop online courses that will be effective. Authoring tools may not be able to entirely replace instructional designers, but they can begin to address the bottleneck of expertise we now face in developing distributed learning, and there is evidence that these tools not only reduce development time, but do so while ensuring a higher level of quality than would be possible if the SMEs were to develop their own, as is often the case in distributed learning (e.g., Van Eck, Adcock, Sussarla, & Tutoring Research Group, 2005).

Brick-and-mortar institutions such as universities and resident training centers in particular are feeling the heat. Universities, perhaps for the first time, are finding themselves vulnerable to direct competition from private industry. At the same time the demand and reward structures for instructional designers are increasing. In the big picture, organizing information and procedures has become more associated with production and less with service. Thus, designers are seen as more critical to the needs of organization than in earlier years.

What do we have to do to take advantage of our opportunities in distributed learning? First, we make sure that those whose job roles and responsibilities are identified as instructional designers are actually competent. Not all instructional designers need master's degrees to develop courseware or programs. After all, neither Steve Jobs nor Bill Gates needed an MBA to be successful corporate executives. Yet, just as many ill-prepared businesses fail through ignorance of effective business practices, many individuals without formal training in instructional design will fail through ignorance of effective instructional practices. University instructional design programs often do a creditable job preparing professional instructional designers. Even so, both new instructional design students and working professionals should demand that ID programs frequently update courses and content to reflect the changes in technology and instructional theory.

Secondly, we should certify instructional designers much as interior designers or architectural designers are certified. This is an idea that has been considered for some time (Bratton, 1991; Dempsey & Rasmussen, 1995). Certification in certain minimum instructional design skills would at least suggest that an individual instructional designer has a basic level of competence in the field. As certification requirements tend to drive professional schools, it would also ensure that university programs do not neglect basic instructional design skills in the pursuit of the latest fashions in educational psychology. Although there is little widespread consensus in the field about standards for certification, there are proposed standards (e.g., the ibstpi and the National Council for Accreditation of Teacher Education [NCATE], and the Association for Educational Communications and Technology, [AECT] standards) that could form the base for such certification efforts (see Chapter 27). Standards and certification are one of the hallmarks of a profession rather than of a trade, and we should get serious about these discussions.

Just as it is important for instructional designers to receive a good basic education in the field, it is critical for them to continue that education. Those of us who have been in the field for some time realize the limitations of the education we received. Developments in technology are constantly upping the ante. How do we expect our skills to stay current without continuous retraining? University instructional design and continuing education programs should take on the task of preparing CEU programs for designers, just as they now do for nurses, lawyers, classroom teachers, and other professionals. Ideally, a certification process and recognition of continuing education would be best, but if a certification movement fails to roll out (as is likely), a consortium of schools in the field or a national association could take on the task of requiring, or at least recognizing, continuing education coursework.

Lamentably, instructional designers have an identity crisis. For various reasons our graduate programs, which tend to teach similar content, are referred to by myriad names: instructional design and development, instructional systems, instructional technology, instructional psychology, educational technology, and so forth. It is no wonder that nonpractitioners do not know what we do! A common terminology is *instructional design technology* (connoting both the system of knowledge and educational software/

hardware of popular parlance). Outside of our immediate field, however, both industry and academia seem to have accepted the term *instructional designer* when referring to what most of us do on the job. Recognition is no small thing. On an acronymic level common to online learning organizations, IDers (instructional designers) are sufficiently different from ITers (information technologists) to avoid confusion. ITers (instructional technologists) are not.

Learning environments are more complex and more demanding of skilled individuals than ever before. Times are good in this field because the field in which we labor is increasingly difficult to plow. More complex instructional technologies, such as direct instruction via the Internet, are relatively new and mystifying. The newness will pass, however. If instructional designers are not seen as highly useful to the course development process, we will see decreases in demand and remuneration just as sharp as the increases in the first few years of this decade.

What makes instructional designers more valuable than before? Like designers in other fields, our job is simply to create order in the environment in which we labor. Just as an architectural designer's job is to work with clients to create order out of disparate elements of a building, an instructional designer's job is to work with clients to create order in a learning environment. Metaphorically, at least, it's that simple. Pelton (1996) theorized that newer fields of study go through a ritualistic process whereby the new discipline is viewed with contempt, then skepticism, then grudging acceptance, and finally anointment. Partially as a result of online learning, instructional design is entering the grudging acceptance stage. Whether we reach the stage of anointment that fields such as computer science have attained depends not only on our ability to more firmly establish our professional identity and competence, but also on how we adapt to change.

Application Questions

1. Given that distributed learning in an academic environment can range from distributed resources used to support a "face-to-face" class to a completely asynchronous distributed course taught in a virtual university, what do you think academic learning will look like 15 years from now? Will all learning be distributed learning? Why or why not?
2. Assume you have been hired as a consulting instructional designer to help an international corporation set up a virtual training network. Describe what steps you would take and what questions you would ask in evaluating the feasibility of this and in developing your proposed system.
3. Using the internet, find 10 examples of distributed learning. Try to find examples of each of the following (one example may fit within several of the categories):
   - Corporate distributed learning
   - Academic distributed learning
   - Distributed resource support
   - Hybrid classes
   - Virtual classes
   - Distributed learning based at physical locations
   - Distributed learning via virtual institutions
   - For-profit distributed learning
   - Free distributed learning
   - Skills-based training (e.g., computer skills training)
   - Knowledge-based learning (e.g., WWII history, introduction to psychology, etc.)

References

Abernathy, D. J. (2001, March). Stats appeal. *Training & Development, 55*(3), 18–19.

Abrami, P., & Bures, E. M. (1996). Computer supported collaborative learning and distance education. *The American Journal of Distance Education, 10* (2), 37–42.

ASTD. (2003). *State of the industry report: Executive summary*. American Society of Training and Development.

Baldwin, R. G. (1999). Technology's impact on faculty life and work. In K. H. Gillespie (Ed.), *The impact of technology on faculty development, life, and work* (pp. 7–22). San Francisco: Jossey-Bass.

Bates, A. W. (2000). *Managing technological change: Strategies for college and university leaders*. San Francisco: Jossey-Bass.

Bates. A. W, & Bartolic, S. (1999). *Assessing the costs and benefits of telelearning: Six case studies.*

Vancouver: University of British Columbia/National Centre for Excellence in Telelearning.

Bitzer, M. D. , & Boudreaux, M. C. (1969). Using a computer to teach nursing. *Nursing Forum, 8* (3), 1–19.

Bloom, B. S., Engelhart, M. D., Furst F. J., Hill W. H., & Krathwohl D. R (ed.)(1956). *Taxonomy of educational objectives*. New York: David- McKay.

Botelho, G. (2004). Online schools clicking with students. Retrieved April 26, 2005 from **http://www.cnn.com/2004/EDUCATION/08/13/b2s.elearning/**

Bratton, B. (1991). Professional competencies and certification in the instructional technology field. In G. J. Anglin (Ed.), *Instructional technology: Past, present, and future* (pp. 227–235). Englewood, CO: Libraries Unlimited.

Business Courier. (2003, February 5). *Latest news*. Retrieved April 26, 2005 from **http://cincinnati.biz journals.com/cincinnati/stories/2003/02/03/daily 33.html**

Clark, R. C., & Mayer, R. E. (2003). *E-learning and the science of instruction.* San Francisco: Jossey Bass/Pfeiffer.

Dede, C. (1995). The evolution of constructivist learning environments: Immersion in distributed, virtual worlds. *Educational Technology, 35*(5), 46–52.

Dempsey, J. V., & Rasmussen, K. L. (1995). Competencies and a new instructional design program. *College Student Journal, 29*(1), 2–7.

Dick, W., Carey, L. & Carey, J. (2005). *The systematic design of instruction* (6th ed.). Boston: Allyn & Bacon.

Di Petta, T. (1999). Community on-line: New professiónal environments for higher education. In K. H. Gillespie (Ed.), *The impact of technology on faculty development, life, and work.* (pp. 34–36). San Francisco: Jossey-Bass.

Driscoll, M. (1998). *Web-based training: Using technology to design adult learning experiences*. San Francisco: Jossey-Bass.

Gagné, R. M. (1985). *The conditions of learning and theory of instruction* (4th ed.). Fort Worth: Holt, Rinehart & Winston.

Gery, G. (1991). *Electronic performance support systems:* How and why to remake the workplace through the strategic application of technology. Boston: Weingarten.

Gillespie, F. (1999). Instructional design for the new technologies. In K. H. Gillespie (Ed.), *The impact of technology on faculty development, life, and work.* (pp. 39–52). San Francisco: Jossey-Bass.

Greengard, S. (1999). Web-based training yields maximum returns. *Workforce, 78*(2), 95–96.

Hall, B. (1997). *Web-based training cookbook*. New York: John Wiley & Sons.

Haythornthwaite, C., Kazmer, M. M., & Robins, R. (2000). Community development among distance learners: Temporal and technological dimensions. *Journal of Computer Mediated Communication, 6*(1), 192–210.

Interactions News Wire. (2004, April 20). New world record announced for Internet performance. *Interactions News Wire*, (24-04). Retrieved April 26, 2005 from **http://www.interactions.org/cms/?pid=1011527**

Iverson, K. M. (2005). *E-learning games: Interactive learning strategies for digital delivery*. Upper Saddle River, NJ: Pearson/Prentice Hall.

Jacobsen, M. (2000, January). *Excellent teaching and early adopters of instructional technology*. Paper presented at ED-MEDIA 2000: World Conference on Educational Multimedia/Hypermedia & Educational Telecommunication, Montreal, Quebec. Retrieved April 19, 2005 from **http://www.acs.ucalgary.ca/~dmjacobs/edmedia/edmedia_2000.html**

Kalyuga, S., Chandler, P., & Sweller, J. (1998). Levels of expertise and instructional design. *Human Factors, 40*(1), 1–17.

Kaplan, S. (2002, August). Building communities: Strategies for collaborative learning. *Learning Circuits*. Retrieved April 26, 2005 from **http://www.learningcircuits.org/2002/aug2002/kaplan.html**

Keller, J. M. (1983). Motivational design of instruction. In C. M. Reigeluth (Ed.), *Instructional design theories and models: An overview of their current status*. (pp. 386–434). Hillsdale, NJ: Lawrence Erlbaum Associates.

Kruse, K., & Keil, K. (2000). *Technology-based training: The art and science of design, development, and delivery*. San Francisco: Jossey-Bass.

Kulhavy, R. W,, & Wager, W. (1993). Feedback in programmed instruction: Historical context and implications for practice. In J. V. Dempsey & G. Sales (Eds.), *interactive instruction and feedback*, (pp. 3–20), New York: Educational Technology Publications.

Macias, J. A., & Castells, P. (2001). *An authoring tool for building adaptive learning guidance systems on the Web*. Unpublished manuscript.

McLuhan, M. (1989). *The global village: Transformations in world life and media in the 21st century*. Oxford, UK: Oxford University Press.

Merrill, M. D. (1997, November–December). Instructional strategies that teach. *CBT Solutions,* 1–11.

Miller, B. (1996). *EPSS: Expanding the perspective*. Retrieved April 26, 2005 from **http://www.pcd-innovations.com/infosite/define.htm**

Moore, M. G. (1989, April). *Three modes of interaction*. Presentation of the NUCEA Forum, "Issues in Instructional Interactivity." Presented at the annual meeting of National University Continuing Education Association, Salt Lake City, UT.

Murray, T. (1998). Authoring knowledge based tutors: Tools for content, instructional strategy, student model, and interface design. *Journal of the Learning Sciences, 7*(1), 5–64.

Murray, T. (1999). Authoring intelligent tutoring systems: An analysis of the state of the art. *International Journal of Artificial Intelligence in Education, 10*, 98–129.

Nielson, J. (1999). User interface directions for the Web. *Communications of the ACM, 42*(1), 65–72.

Oblinger, D. G., Barone, C. A., & Hawkins B. L. (2001). *Distributed education and its challenges: An overview*. Washington, DC: American Council on Education.

Palloff, R. M., & Pratt, K. (1999). *Building learning communities in cyberspace: Effective strategies for the online classroom*. San Francisco: Jossey-Bass.

Patrick, S (2005, February). National Education technology plan. Presentation given at U.S. Department of Education/Public Broadcasting Service "Ready to Learn" summit, Baltimore, MD.

Pelton, J. N. (1996, November-December). Cyberlearning vs. the university: An irresistible force meets an immovable object. *The Futurist*, 17–20.

Rheingold, H. (1993). *The virtual community: Homesteading on the electronic frontier*. Reading, MA: Addison-Wesley.

Rogers, E. M. (1995). *Diffusion of innovations* (4th ed.). New York: Free Press.

Sweller, J. (1989). Cognitive technology: Some procedures for facilitating learning and problem solving in mathematics and science. *Journal of Educational Psychology, 81*, (4), 457–466.

Sweller, J., van Merriënboer, J. J. G, & Paas, F. G. W. C. (1998). Cognitive architecture and instructional design. *Educational Psychology Review, 10*(3), 251–296.

Tauber, D. A., & Kienan, B. (1995). *Mosaic access to the Internet*. San Francisco: Sybex.

Thach, E. C., & Murphy, K. L. (1995). Competencies for distance learning professional. *Educational Technology Research and Development, 43*(1), 57–79.

Toole, J., & Heift, T. (2002). The tutor assistant: An authoring system for a web-based intelligent language tutor. *Computer Assisted Language Learning, 15*(4), 373–386.

Turoff, M. (1997). *Alternative futures for distance learning: The force and the darkside*. Invited keynote presentation at the UNESCO / Open University International Colloquium, April 27–29: Virtual Learning Environments and the Role of the Teacher, Open University, Milton Keynes. Retrieved April 26, 2005 from **http://eies.njit.edu/turoff/ Papers/darkaln.html**

USNews.com. (2004). *E-Learning: Online graduate degrees*. Retrieved April 26, 2005 from **http://www.usnews.com/usnews/edu/elearning/directory/gradonline.htm**

Van Eck, R., Adcock, A., Sussarla, S., & Tutoring Research Group. (2005 March). Embedded design: How authoring tools can ensure that instructional design is present when we can't be there. *Proceedings of the 1st Southeastern Conference in Instructional Design & Technology*, Mobile Alabama March 11–13.

Villazon, L. (2005). Internet 2: Son of Internet. *Maximum PC*, 10(3).

Wagner, E. D. (1994). In support of a functional definition of interaction. *American Journal of Distance Education, 8*(20), 6–29.

Wagner, E. D. (1997). Interactivity: From agents to outcomes. In T. E. Cyrs (Ed.), *Teaching and learning at a distance: What it takes to effectively design, deliver, and evaluate programs*. (pp. 19–26). San Francisco: Jossey-Bass.

Young, J. R. (1997, Oct. 3) Rethinking the role of the professor in an age of high-tech tools. *Chronicle of Higher Education*, p. A26.

CHAPTER 29

Reusability and Reusable Design

Robby Robson
Eduworks Corporation

Editors' Introduction

One of the primary challenges for many organizations in which instructional designers work or with which they consult is reusability. Often characterized in our field simply as designing learning objects, reusability involves a good deal more, including use of metadata, management of rights, technical interoperability, and an understanding of reusable design.

In this chapter, Robbie Robson explains the meaning of and the requirements for reusability. Sections of the chapter discuss generating and using metadata, granting and managing permissions of reusable content, and interoperability. The author explains reusable design in terms of content, context, pedagogy, structure, and presentation. A final section considers the important issue of granularity and the role of instructional designers within reusability environments.

Knowledge and Comprehension Questions

1. List four distinct barriers to reuse.
2. What are the layers of a digital learning resource? Give an example of how each affects reusability.
3. List at least three techniques that a content developer might employ to make it easier for others to reuse the content being developed.
4. List at least three techniques that a learning object repository might use to make it easier for its clientele to reuse the resources found in the repository.
5. What metadata is important for reuse? Why?
6. How does copyright affect reuse? What can be done about it?
7. Give an example where context and pedagogy are not separated from structure and presentation.

What Is Reusability?

This chapter is about reusability for digital learning resources, primarily those that are accessible through a Web browser. *Reusability* is defined as the ability to use the same resource multiple times in multiple ways and in multiple contexts. Reusability also encompasses the ability of developers to use a resource as a building block in their own work.

Some authors distinguish between *reuse* and *repurposing* but no such distinction will be made here. Reuse can take place when content is being designed and developed or when it is being used by instructors and learners. It could involve making changes to a resource (sometimes called *adapting* a resource) or using a resource "as is" (sometimes called *adopting* a resource). Examples of reuse include:

- A development team creating a library of templates and objects that are used multiple times when authoring and developing content.
- An instructor including an applet written by someone else in an online course.
- A learner searching for and finding a module on a topic she is studying and using the exercises from that module to check her understanding of the topic.

Reusers in these scenarios benefit in different ways. Designers and developers save time and money by reusing or repurposing existing content rather than redeveloping it. Instructors have more and better choices and don't have to develop content themselves. Learners benefit by having more learning resources at their disposal, thus increasing the chance that they can find one that is right for them. Reuse is certainly attractive, but it is not necessarily easy to achieve.

Reusability Requirements

What is needed for reusability? From the perspective of an author, instructor, or learner, the ability to reuse a resource boils down to answering four questions in the affirmative:

1. Can I find it?
2. May I use it?
3. Will it work?
4. Can I use it in a way that works for me?

If the answer to any of the first three of these questions is "no" or "not easily," then reuse is a nonstarter. You can't use a resource if you don't know it's there, you can't use a resource for which you do not have appropriate rights and permissions, and you can't use a resource if it won't work. The fourth issue is largely a matter of how a resource is designed.

The design of content for reuse is an important subject, but it should not be forgotten that a lot can be done to enhance reusability by simply ensuring that a resource can be easily found, that proper permissions are granted, and that appropriate standards are followed so that the resource can be used without difficulty. These reusability factors will be addressed first, with design issues coming later.

Metadata

The process of finding appropriate learning resources is often called *search and discovery*, and a fundamental tool for search and discovery is metadata. *Metadata* is information about a resource. It comes in several different flavors:

- *Basic descriptive metadata* (also called *bibliographic metadata*): Title, author, description, identifier, subject, keywords, etc.
- *Contextual metadata*: Information about learning objectives, intended audience, level of difficulty, and other instructionally oriented information. Relationships to other resources can also be considered to be contextual metadata.
- *Rights metadata*: Copyright information, terms of use, and contact information for obtaining permissions.
- *Technical metadata*: Format, platform requirements, software requirements, and structural information.

Taking a broad view of the notion of metadata, it also makes sense to include

- *Usage information*: Documentation and guides.

Full text search engines such as Google™ have largely replaced keyword searches, but full text searches don't work for nontextual content and are of limited value when searching for content that fits into a particular instructional context, that has specific associated rights, that satisfies a given set of technical requirements, or that has adequate associated documentation and usage information. If the promise of e-learning is, as put by Hodgins (2002a, p. 64), the ability to get "just the right stuff to just the right person at just the right time and place in just the right way and with just the right context on just the right device and through just the right medium," then these are all important things to know. It follows that authors and developers should try to provide as much metadata as possible and that learning object repositories should include options to search for resources according to many fields other than title, author, and description.

While on the subject of metadata, it should be noted that search and discovery are not the only uses for metadata. In particular, bibliographic metadata is important for cataloging and preservation, which are increasingly critical issues in the digital world (Library of Congress, 2002; Online Computer Library Center, 2001, 2002). Also, modern search techniques depend on page ranks derived from data such as frequency, clustering, and linking degrees—all of which are arguably forms of contextual metadata.

Generating and Using Metadata

Given the importance of metadata, what techniques are available to authors for generating it and to repositories for using it? In the case of authors, the buzzword is "automated metadata generation" (Cardinaels, Meire, & Duval, 2005; Greenberg, Spurgin, & Crystal, 2005). Few of us are enthusiastic about filling in screen after screen of metadata every time we are involved in developing a new resource, and theoretically this is not necessary. Technical information such as the format or size of a resource can be derived directly from the resource, software used to support the development workflow should be clever enough to know and record information such as the author's name and what learning objectives are being addressed. Such tools do not exist in abundance today, but at the very least tools should be chosen that give designers and developers the opportunity to include rich metadata. Tools that create SCORM content generally do this (Nantel, 2004), and many of them capture at least some technical metadata in the files that are automatically generated as part of the "package" that SCORM, (Advanced Distributed Learning, 2004) uses to transport content from one system to another (Dodds & Thropp, 2004).

Another longtime trend in metadata is standards. By using variations on metadata standards such as IEEE learning object metadata (Institute of Electrical & Electronics Engineers, 2002) or qualified versions of Dublin Core metadata (Dublin Core Metadata Initiative, 2005), educational digital libraries are able to keep track of contextual and technical metadata. Their search interfaces permit users to not only look for resources by keywords but to also search by a combination of criteria such as format, educational level, and copyright restrictions (see Robson, Collier & Muramatsu, 2005, for examples) Beyond that, many of these repositories are using standards such as the Open Archives Initiative Protocol for Metadata Harvesting (Lagoze, Van de Sompel, Nelson, & Warner, 2002) and various standardized query languages (Library of Congress, 2004; Simon et al., 2005) to enable federated searches. Users can find resources (or metadata records) in multiple repositories by searching any single repository in a federation.

Rights

The use and reuse of digital resources is increasingly subject to *intellectual property rights*, including patents, trade or service marks, and copyright. Of these, the one of most concern for reusability is *copyright*. There are several excellent resources on copyright, fair use, the TEACH Act, and related issues in U.S. copyright law (Stanford University Libraries, 2005; University of Texas System, 2005) and in other jurisdictions (e.g., Green & Baulch, 2005; JISC Legal Information Service, 2005; Stanford University, 2005). The high-level summary for instructional designers is as follows:

- Most resources are copyrighted and fair use generally does not cover the types of reuse of existing resources when creating or distributing new ones.
- Copyright can be used to protect the interests of authors, publishers, and distributors who receive money from the sale of content, but copyright can also prevent intended uses. For example, suppose that a university professor writes and posts an applet to a website. Copyright law restricts others from downloading and using the applet without permission, so potential users must go to the trouble of obtaining permission if it is not explicitly granted on the Website. This takes time and effort and may be difficult or impossible if the author is not the copyright holder.

Granting Permissions

Because obtaining permission takes time and effort, people involved in creating or disseminating learning resources should do their best to grant appropriate permissions in advance. An increasingly common approach to doing this is that taken by the Creative Commons (2005). The Creative Commons has developed licenses that express a small set of standard terms and conditions. The licenses have legal forms, plain English forms, and forms for inclusion in a Web page or other resource. Creative Commons licenses can be used to grant the right to copy and modify a resource, require proper attribution, or restrict the licensed use of a resource to noncommercial applications. A simple but effective step that authors can take to increase the reusability of their work is to disseminate it under a license of this type. Conversely, repositories that collect freely available learning resources can help their contributors by making a standard set of licenses available. This helps people who are contributing content that does not already have a license.

Managing Rights

Granting rights is all well and good, but learning resources often already come with their own copyright restrictions and licenses. In that case, it is important that potential users be able to see those restrictions and licenses and be given the information they need to request or purchase further rights. This information can be embedded in standard metadata, including Dublin Core metadata (DCMI, 2005) and the IEEE learning object metadata (IEEE, 2002) used by SCORM. Rights metadata can be as basic as a link to a copyright statement or as sophisticated as a standardized XML rights expression (Coyle, 2004; International Organization for Standardization & International Electrotechnical Commission, 2005; Open Digital Rights Language Initiative, 2005). In either case it is important not only to express rights but also to identify the rights holder so that potential users know where to ask for further permissions if needed.

Rudimentary but successful experiments have shown how rights management can be integrated into content management systems, course management systems, and e-reserves in academic environments (Colin & Simon, 2004; Dalziel, 2002). In these experiments, the systems not only display rights but also enforce them by denying unauthorized access to resources. In thinking about rights, it is important to separate the notions of expressing and displaying rights, which are necessary for reuse, from those of enforcing rights, which requires different technologies (Collier, Piccariello, & Robson, 2004a, 2004b; Duncan, Barker, Douglas, Morrey, & Waelde, 2004). Rights enforcement will not be covered in this chapter.

Interoperability

The basic technical question faced by a potential user is "Will it work in my environment?" This is often a question of *interoperability*; i.e., the ability of two software components to exchange and correctly interpret each other's data. Many of the standards in e-learning, such as the Aviation Industry CBT Committee (AICC) (2005), SCORM, IEEE (2005) standards, and IMS Global Learning Consortium (2005) specifications, address interoperability issues. The point of these standards is to allow content to be developed for use by multiple delivery platforms. Content that conforms to these standards has wider applicability and is not locked into a single learning management system (LMS).

Interoperability does not just apply to content for LMSs. There are even more basic considerations. One is *cross-platform compatibility*, the ability for a resource to be used on different operating systems, with different browsers, and with different software configurations. A resource that requires a specific version of the Windows operating system has a more limited audience than one that can run on any version of a Windows, MACOS, or Unix-based system. Another related consideration is that of requiring specialized plugins, software, or tools. Dependencies of this nature can have a severely limiting effect on reuse. Finally, from the perspective of a developer, a major issue is the availability of source code or editable versions of resources. For example, Flash™ content and Java™ applets cannot be edited unless the source code is made available.

The Role of Standards

Interoperability and platform independence can be greatly enhanced by adhering to *industry standards*. These can either be formal standards—such as those mentioned previously for learning content interoperability—or simply formats that have ubiquitous availability and acceptance. PDF, Flash™, Microsoft Word, and Microsoft *PowerPoint* are example of such formats. It is a safe bet that content written in any one of these formats can be read by the majority of potential users.

The converse is that is a good idea to avoid reliance on specialized plugins and on features that are present in only one version of an operating system or in only one browser, such as active-X controls or the special capabilities of *Internet Explorer*. It is interesting to note that less than a year before this chapter was written in May 2005 one might have argued that *Internet Explorer* was so dominant that content did not really need to be tested in other browsers, at least in the noneducational market. At the moment, however, it appears that Firefox® is making phenomenal gains[1] and that even in corporate circles a second browser may end up with significant market share (Ranger, 2005). Whether or not this happens, it illustrates the advantage of not being unnecessarily tied to a specific product or vendor.

Catering to Content Developers

If a learning resource is to be reused by developers, then a primary consideration is their ability to modify the resource. As indicated, this requires making source code available. Repositories can aid in this respect by including links to source code. Rights also play a role because creating and distributing a modified version requires permission, which should either be granted in advance or should be made as easy as possible to obtain by providing appropriate

[1] According to ClickZ stats (**http://www.clickz.com/stats/sectors/traffic_patterns/article.php/3500691**) Firefox market share jumped from 4.23 in January 2005 to 10.28% in April 2005.

contact information. Finally, developers will need to have appropriate tools to modify and existing resource. Even if a proprietary tool is used to develop a resource, publishing the resource in a standard format will increase the probability that another developer will have the tools needed to reuse the resource.

Reusable Design

Once one gets beyond metadata, rights, and interoperability, there is the more complex issue of *reusable design*, how to intrinsically design content for reuse. Its primary goal is to create content that can be used in as many ways and in as many contexts as possible without sacrificing the quality and effectiveness of the content. Another goal of reusable design is to create content that can be reused in content development and creation processes.

A good way to understand reusable design is to deconstruct learning resources into *layers*. The ones chosen for discussion here are content, context, pedagogy, structure, and presentation. Each layer affects reusability in a different way, and associated with each layer are design principles and techniques that can help ameliorate any negative effects. In addition, it is important not to conflate different layers. For example, presentation styles and sequencing should not impose a particular instructional design or be dependent on a specialized context.

Content

At the heart of any learning resource is content. This the information contained in a resource that is intended to affect a change in cognitive state. It's what the resource is about, but it is important to understand that the same content can be presented in different ways. Whenever a resource is designed, choices are made concerning how the content is structured; what words, images and sounds are used; what learning modes are supported; and so on. All of these choices are separate from the content itself.

The content of a learning resource has an effect on its potential audience. A learning resource that tests a learner's understanding of advanced principles in quantum mechanics has an intrinsically smaller audience than a resource designed to give learners practice in basic presentation skills or that teaches how to add fractions. A resource has to be designed within the constraints imposed by its content, but within those constraints choices can be made that maximize reusability.

Context

Content is interpreted with the aid of language, culture, subject knowledge, and other resources; in other words, within a *context*. Context is what is needed to properly use, understand, and learn from a resource.

There is a natural tension between context and reuse. The more that can be assumed about the context of a learner, the easier it is to design an effective learning resource. For example, suppose that a designer has been asked to create training for a new billing system for Company X. The training will likely be more effective if it uses examples, terminology, and procedures that are in fact used by Company X. At the same time, this makes it far less reusable by someone in a different company. Assumptions about shared vocabulary, prerequisites, notation, linguistic abilities, knowledge of procedures, cultural icons—all of these things help people learn but impact the potential for reuse. (See Chapter 23 for a related discussion, concerning designing instruction for global markets.)

There are several ways in which content can be designed so that contextual dependencies become less of an issue:

- The use of language, images, and scenarios should be inspected to make sure that any cultural assumptions are appropriate and contribute to the effectiveness of the resource. If cultural dependencies are unproductive, they should be removed.
- References to external resources should be examined. If they are not generally available online, then it is worthwhile looking for substitutes.
- Implicit assumptions about notation, terminology, and background should be teased out. To the extent reasonable for the subject at hand, it is good practice to create separate sections for background material or to provide links to existing resources that provide it.
- Content should follow Web accessibility guidelines (World Wide Web Consortium, [W3C] 2005.
- Multilingual versions of the same resources should be considered. Translation is aided by not embedding words into graphics and by using tools that support authoring in multiple languages if they are available.

Pedagogy

Learning takes place in many settings, including classroom settings, blended learning, online classes, self-study, and mentored learning. Learning resources also embody learning strategies and instructional designs, as is discussed at length throughout in this book.

Designing a resource for a single setting or instructional strategy limits its reusability. For example, a resource that requires an instructor to do a physical demonstration will be hard to use in online settings. Similarly, a resource that is built as a drill-and-practice module may be difficult to repurpose for discovery learning.

As with context, the key to reusable design is to isolate components that require specific pedagogical settings or approaches. If a lab experiment is required, it should be discussed in a separate section rather than sprinkled throughout the entire content. Teacher and student guides should also be kept separate, as should assessments. Assessments can be used in different ways (formative, normative, or as learning material) and can frequently be taken from one resource and used in another. Assessments embedded in the midst of other content are much harder to reuse than those that are self-contained.

Structure

Digital resources are often structured into smaller conceptual and physical units. Conceptual units include "information objects" (Horn, 1993) such as introductions, facts, principles, explanations, examples, assessments, and so on. Physical units are such things as Web pages, *PowerPoint* slides, and paragraphs.

Many types of reuse involve parts of larger learning resources. A learner may want to use only one module in a course, and instructor may want to use only an assessment, and a developer might want to reuses only an image or an applet. The physical and conceptual structure of a resource can either help or hinder this.

As an example, consider a resource used for teaching musical notation and suppose it consists of 30 pages that are linked via "forward" and "back" buttons and can only be navigated in order. A developer wishing to use just a few pages would have to remove or edit these buttons, and if an instructor assigned just a portion to a class, the learners would have to somehow get to the right pages and stay there. On the other hand, suppose that the same resource had clearly delineated sections on time signatures, clefs, the values of notes, and soon, and had midi examples that could be played independently. A teacher, student, or developer would then be better equipped to use just what they needed and to do so with a lot less effort.

Learning objects and content models. Examples such as the ones given lead to the principle that reusability is enhanced if digital learning resources are structured into self-contained sections that address single learning objectives.[2] These are often called learning objects (Barritt & Lewis, 2000), although the term is also used more broadly (Wiley, 2000). The notion of a learning object is tied to the more general concept of a *content model* that can be used to identify the components of a learning resource according to their granularity and pedagogical characteristics. The most common content model in use these days is that promoted by the Learnativity Group (Hodgins, 2002b; Wagner, 2002). Table 29.1 is a variant of this content model. It shows how different levels of granularity are inherently more or less reusable by different reusers (authors, instructors, and learners) and helps explain why learning objects fall in the "sweet spot."

The idea of using learning objects is implicit in IMS specifications, AICC guidelines, and SCORM. All of these have notions of self-contained units that can be delivered and sequenced by an LMS (or equivalent delivery platform) according to instructions that are encoded with but separate from the content. In this paradigm, the LMS can be given instructions that determine how learners go from learning object to learning object. Whether using standards or not, it is important to avoid hard-coded navigation among different learning objects. Doing so destroys their self-contained nature and makes it harder to use them individually. Instead, inter–learning object navigation should be put into a frame or enabled using a table of contents on a separate page.

Presentation

The *presentation layer* of a digital resource consists of the fonts, layout, graphics, color schemes, sound clips, video clips, buttons, and other elements that are used to render the resource. Presentation is what gives a resource its look and feel.

Presentation has two effects on reuse. First, combining resources with different presentation styles produces a jarring and totally unsatisfactory effect. Second, presentation elements may contain contextual information that makes a resource unsuitable for reuse in many settings. Examples include organizational logos or fonts and styles that are appropriate for only one age group.

A very basic way to improve reusability it is to use formats that completely separate content from presentation. HTML (or better, XHTML) does this through the use of cascading style sheets (Lie & Saarela, 1999). Ip, Radford, and Canale (2003) and others have used these techniques with SCORM content. Many other XML content formats do this as well. Using these formats allows presentation elements or "the skin" to be changed without touching the content.

Final Thoughts

Reusability is often considered the Shangri-La of digital learning content. Attaining reusability requires use of

---

[2] The notion of a learning objective derives from the work of Robert Frank Mager (1997), Robert Gagné (1985), Dick and Carey (1996), and others.

TABLE 29.1 Granularity and reuse

	Content Model (Adapted from the Learnativity Group)			
	Asset (Text, image, video, etc.)	**Information Object** (Fact, concept, principle, (process)	**Learning Object** (Self-contained learning resource with a single learning objective)	**Learning Component** (Course, unit, e-book)
	General Reusability Characteristics from Different Perspectives			
Author	Highly reusable. Authors frequently create libraries of assets for reuse.	Easily reused. Authors often "cut and paste" information objects.	Sometimes reusable—saves significant effort when it is.	Usually too big to reuse (unless it can be broken up into reusable learning objects).
Instructor	Easily reused but often of limited value.	Sometimes hard to reuse because of lack of context or presence of extraneous material.	Often reusable and very useful. Can fit into many instructional designs.	Reusable only in parts or when it happens to cover exactly what is needed.
Learner	Assets generally need more context to be useful learning resources.	May be just what is needed but often is not useful out of context.	Very useful for a learner who has a specific need. Can be used in self-directed, blended, or mentored settings.	Learners are more likely to use parts than entire learning components.

Source: Used with permission of Robby Robson.

metadata, management of rights, technical interoperability, and an understanding of reusable design. Although techniques involving the application of standards may be considered to be narrowly focused on reuse, most of the recommended practices and techniques involve are just good information management and design practices.

Techniques may be basic, but that does not mean that it is easy to make them into habits. Fortunately, as multimedia content (not just learning content) becomes more structured and lives in increasingly distributed networks, authoring tools and repository software will likely become more attuned to reusability issues. This will result in reusable design becoming easier if not automatic, as has happened with accessible design.

What does this mean for instructional designers? Over time, a premium will be placed on resources that have self-contained components with clear learning objectives and good reusability characteristics. Designers study reusability techniques and apply them in their work. At the same time, instructional designers take a good look at the tools they use, preferring those that make it easy to separate presentation from content, that conform to standards, and that automatically generate as much metadata as possible. Designers should demand repositories that can be searched using instructionally relevant metadata and that do a decent job of exposing rights information. But most importantly, instructional designers should develop a discerning eye for reuse opportunities and a practiced hand at finding and reusing resources rather than building them from scratch. As reusable content becomes more prevalent and easier to find, the benefits to be gained by honing these skills will serve future designers well.

More information, references, and examples of reusable design are available at the Reusable Learning Website (Robson et al., 2005) and in the References for this chapter.

Application Questions

1. You are asked to design a training module on building a box out of lumber. The module is to include a demonstration. How would you structure the course to be as reusable as possible?
2. Search for a course with poor reusability characteristics. Explain how the course could be redesigned to improve its reusability without changing the underlying content.
3. You are asked to design a search interface for a learning object repository for high school teachers. You can include 10 (and only 10) search fields. Which ones would you include, and why? What if the learning object repository were for a corporate HR department?
4. Read and discuss Boskic (2003) and Chang (2004) in light of the issues raised in this chapter.

References

Advanced Distributed Learning. (2004). SCORM homepage. Retrieved May 1, 2005 from **http://www.adlnet.org/index.cfm?fuseaction=DownFile&libid=648&bc=false**

Aviation Industry CBT Committee. (2005). Homepage. Retrieved May 1, 2005 from **http://www.aicc.org**

Barritt, C., & Lewis, D. (2000). *Reusable learning object strategy: Definition, creation process, and guidelines for building, Version 3.1*. San Jose, CA: Cisco Systems.

Boskic, N. (2003). Learning objects design: What do educators think about the quality and reusability of learning objects? In *Proceedings of the third IEEE International Conference on Advanced Learning Technologies* (pp. 306–307). Piscataway, NJ: IEEE.

Cardinaels, K., Meire, M., & Duval, E. (2005). *Automating metadata generation: The simple indexing interface.* Paper accepted for publication by the International World Wide Web Conference Committee, WWW 2005, May 10–14, 2005, Chiba, Japan.

Chang, V. (2004, June). Reusable e-learning development: Case studies, practices and issues of awareness for knowledge-based organizations. In V. Chang (Ed.), *Proceedings of the second International Conference on Information Technology: Research and Education* (pp. 145–149). London: London Metropolitan University.

Collier, G., Piccariello, H., & Robson, R. (2004a). *Digital rights management: An ecosystem model for the education community.* Research Bulletin, Vol. 21. Boulder, CO: Educause Center for Applied Research.

Collier, G., Piccariello, H., & Robson, R. (2004b). *Digital rights management: Tools and applications for implementing DRM in a digital ecosystem.* Research Bulletin, Vol. 22. Boulder, CO: Educause Center for Applied Research.

Colin, S., & Simon, J. (2004, July). A digital licensing model for the exchange of learning objects in a federated environment. In S. Colin & J. Simon (Eds.), *Proceedings of the first IEEE International Workshop on Electronic Contracting* (pp. 46–53). Piscataway, NJ: IEEE.

Coyle, K. (2004). *Rights expression languages: A report for the Library of Congress.* Washington, DC: Library of Congress.

Creative Commons. (2005). Homepage, Retrieved May 1, 2005 from **http://creativecommons.org/**

Dalziel, J. (2002, December). Reflections on the COLIS demonstrator project and the learning object lifecycle. In A. Williamson, G. Gun, A. Young, & T. Clieari (Eds.) *Proceedings of ASCILIT 2002* (pp. 159–166). Auckland, NZ: UNITECH Institute of Technology.

Dick, W., & Carey, L. (1996). *The systematic design of instruction* (4th ed.). New York: Harpercollins.

Dodds, P., & Thropp, S. (2004). *SCORM content aggregation model Vresion 1.3.1. Alexandria, VA: Advanced Distributed Learning.*

Dublin Core Metadata Initiative (DCMI). (2005). Frequently asked questions (FAQ). Retrieved May 1, 2005 from **http://dublincore.org/resources/faq/**

Duncan, C., Barker, E., Douglas, P., Morrey, M., & Waelde, C. (2004). *Digital rights management.* Joint Information Systems Committee. Linlithgow, UK: Intrallect, Ltd.

Gagné, R. (1985). *The conditions of learning and theory of instruction.* New York: Holt, Rinehart & Winston.

Green, M., & Baulch, L. (2005). *Australian Copyright Council's online information center.* Retrieved May 1, 2005 from **http://www.copyright.org au/**

Greenberg, J., Spurgin, K., & Crystal, A. (2005). Final report for the AmeGA (Automatic Metadata Generation Applications) Projects. Submitted to the Library of Congress, February 17.

Hodgins, H. W. (2002a). Are we asking the right questions? In *Transforming culture: An executive briefing on the power of learning* (pp. 1–4). University of Virginia, Batten Institute.

Hodgins, H. W. (2002b). The future of learning objects. In J. R. Lohmann & M. L, Corradini (Eds.), *E-technologies in engineering education: Learning outcomes providing future possibilities.* Engineering Conferences International Symposium Series, Vol. P1 (pp. 61–64). Berkeley, CA: Berkeley Electronic Press.

Horn, R. (1933, February). Structured writing at twenty-five. *Performance and Instruction, 32*, 11–17.

IMS Global Learning Consortium. (2005). Homepage. Retrieved May 1, 2004 from **http:// www. imsglobal. org**

International Organization for Standardization & International Electrotechnical Commission (ISO/IEC). (2004). *Information technology—Multimedia framework (MPEG-21): Part 5, Rights expression language.* Geneva, Switzerland: ISO.

Institute of Electrical & Electronics Engineers (IEEE). (2002). IEEE standard for learning object metadata. Piscataway, NJ: IEEE.

Institute of Electrical & Electronics Engineers (IEEE). (2005). IEEE Learning Technology Standards Committee homepage. Retrieved May 1, 2004 from **http:// ltsc.ieee.org**

Ip, A., Radford, A., & Canale, E. (2003). *Overcoming the presentation mosaic effect of multi-use sharable content objects.* In G. Crisp et al. (Eds.), *Proceedings of ASCILITE 2003* (pp. 256–262). Adelaide, AU: University of Adelaide.

JISC Legal Information Service. (2005). *Intellectual property rights.* Retrieved May 1, 2005 from **http://www.jisclegal.ac.uk/ipr/IntellectualProperty.htm**

Lagoze, C., Van de Sompel, H., Nelson, M., & Warner, S. (2002). *The open archives initiative protocol for metadata harvesting: Protocol version 2.0.* Retrieved May 1,2005 from **http://www.openarchives.org/OAI/openarchivesprotocol.html**

Library of Congress. (2002). *Building a national strategy for digital preservation: Issues in digital media archiving.* Washington, DC: Council on Library and Information Resources & Library of Congress.

Library of Congress. (2004). *SRW—Search/retrieve Web service, version 1.1.* Washington, DC: Library of Congress. Retrieved February 13, 2006 from **http://www.loc.gov/standards/sru/srw/**

Lie, H. W., & Saarela, J. (1999). Multipurpose Web publishing using HTML, XML, and CSS. *Communications of the ACM, 42*(10), 95–101.

Mager, R. F. (1997). *Preparing instructional objectives* (3rd ed.). Atlanta, GA: Center for Effective Performance.

Nantel, R. (2004). *Authoring tools 2004: A buyer's guide to the best e-learning content development applications.* Atlanta, GA: Brandon-Hall.

Online Computer Library Center. (2001, January). *Preservation metadata for digital objects: A review of the state of the art.* Whitepaper by the OCLC/RLG Working Group on Preservation Metadata. Dublin, OH: OCLC.

Online Computer Library Center. (2002, June). *A metadata framework to support the preservation of digital objects.* Report by the OCLC/RLG Working Group on Preservation Metadata. Dublin, OH: OCLC.

Open Digital Rights Language Initiative (ODRL). (2005). Homepage. Retrieved May 1, 2005 from **http://www.odrl.net**

Ranger, S. (2005). *Firefox market share rockets.* Retrieved March 1,2005 from **http://www/vnunet.com/vnunet/news/2126862/firefox-market-share-rockets**

Robson, R., Collier, C., & Muramatsu, M. (2005). *The reusable learning project.* Retrieved May 1, 2005 from **http://www.reusablelearning.org**

Simon, B., Massart, D., Ternier, S., Duval, E., Brantner, S., Olmedilla, D., et al. (2005). *A simple query interface for interoperable learning repositories.* Paper accepted for publication be the International World Wide Web Conference Committee, WWW 2005, May 10–14, 2005, Chiba, Japan.

Stanford University. (2005). Intellectual property rights. In *JGuide: Stanford guide to Japan information resources* (n.p.). Retrieved May 1, 2005 from **http://jguide.stanford.edu/site/intellectual_property_rights_245.html**

Stanford University Libraries. (2005). *Copyright and fair use center.* Retrieved May 1, 2005 from **http://fairuse.stanford.edu/**

University of Texas System. (2005). *Intellectual Property*. Retrived May 1, 2005 from **http://www.utsystem.edu/ogc/intellectualproperty/**

Wagner, E. (2002, October 29). Steps to creating a content strategy for your organization. *eLearning Developers' Journal*, n.p.

Wiley, D. A. (2000). Connecting learning objects to instructional design theory: A definition, a metaphor, and a taxonomy. In D. A. Wiley (Ed.), *The instructional use of learning objects: Online version* (n.p.). Retrieved May 1, 2005 from **http://reusability.org/read/chapters/wiley.doc**

World Wide Web Consortium (W3C). (2005). *Web accessibility initiative: WAI guidelines and techniques*. Retrieved February 13, 2006 from **http://www.w3.org/WAI/guid-tech./html**

CHAPTER 30

Using Rich Media Wisely

Ruth Colvin Clark
Clark Training and Consulting

Richard E. Mayer
University of California, Santa Barbara

Editors' Introduction

Ruth Clark and Richard Mayer contend in this chapter that rich media can improve learning if they are used in ways that promote effective cognitive processes in learners. The authors define *rich media* as learning products that incorporate high-end media such as video, animation, sound, and simulation. As in a number of their books, Clark and Mayer's chapter focuses on specific guidelines that help designers look at rich media as a tool, which can used well or poorly. Based on research conducted over a number of years, the authors concentrate on how humans learn and under what conditions rich media can enable effective instructional methods that promote learning.

Knowledge and Comprehension Questions

1. Define the *modality principle*. Summarize the evidence for it and its psychological rationale.
2. What kinds of audio will generally aid learning and what kinds will depress learning? Give examples of each.
3. Discuss the use of rich media to present themes or games in e-learning in order to enhance motivation.
4. What is the expertise reversal effect? How does it influence instructional design decisions.
5. Describe some of the features of simulations that will promote learning.

How can you use rich media—such as video, animation, audio, and simulations—to help people learn in computer-based training environments? Consider the three approaches to a computer-delivered technical training lesson shown in Figures 30.1, 30.2, and 30.3. All three are taken from e-training tutorials designed to teach similar skills—namely, how to use a computer application. Figures 30.1 and 30.2 use rich media extensively, whereas Figure 30.3 uses static screen captures rather than animation, and onscreen text rather than audio. Which version is more effective for learning? Which features of rich media promote learning and which features either detract from learning or do not add cost benefit? These are the questions that we explore in this chapter.

American businesses annually invest between 50 and 60 billion dollars in worker training, of which 16% is delivered via computer (Galvin, 2003). Therefore, instructional program designers need evidence-based guidelines to build multimedia training products in ways that will generate organizational payback. Most organizations evaluate the quality of training courses by way of learner feedback, usually provided on rating forms. Unfortunately, those learner ratings often do not correlate with actual learning (Dixon, 1990), so they are of limited use in assessing instructional effectiveness. Our goal in this chapter is to summarize guidelines about how to use the features available in rich media in ways that best accommodate human learning processes. We also provide references to additional sources for more detailed descriptions.

The Paradox of Rich Media

We define *rich media* as learning products that incorporate high-end media such as video, animation, sound, and simulation. Often Internet or intranet learning programs that incorporate rich media make use of special players such as Flash™ or Shockwave™. Alternatively, rich media are commonly seen in the production of CD-delivered training. In fact, current technology has greater capacity to deliver information to learners than learners have psychological capacity to assimilate that information. This is what we call "the paradox of rich media." Rich media will only benefit learners to the extent that its capabilities are harnessed in ways that support human cognitive learning processes.

We have all participated in both computer and classroom training events that were ineffective. They may present plenty of information, but not in a way that fosters learning. Conversely, we know of many courses delivered via computer or classroom that effectively support the learning objectives. The quality of the instruction is not

FIGURE 30.1 A thematic treatment used to motivate learners in a computer training course.
Source: Reprinted from *Graphics for Learning* (p. 175), by R. C. Clark and C. Lyons, 2004, San Francisco: Jossey Bass Pfeiffer. Copyright ©2004 by John Wiley & Sons. Reprinted by permission.

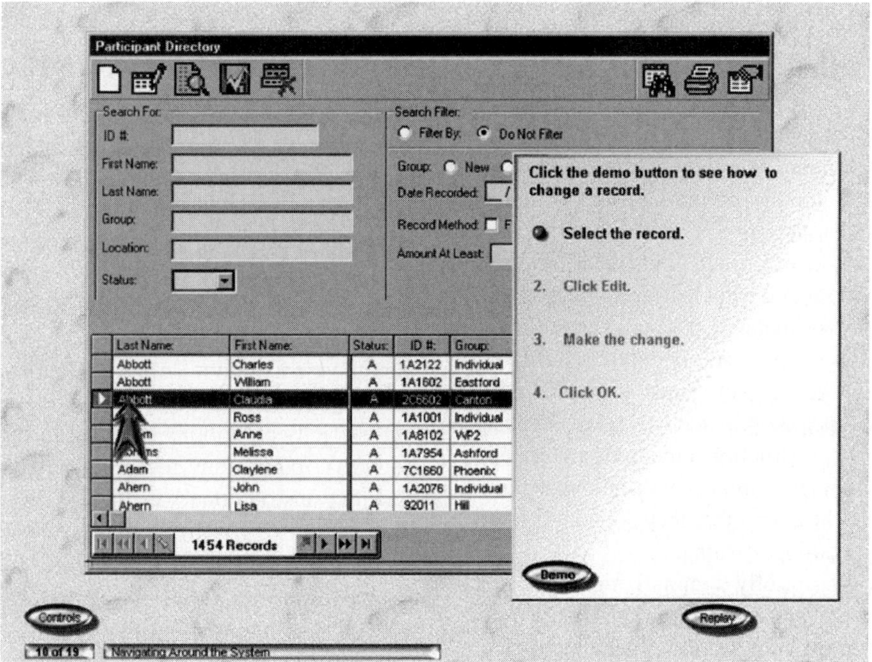

FIGURE 30.2 One screen from an animated software demonstration.
Source: Reprinted from *Graphics for Learning* (p. 115), by R. C. Clark and C. Lyons, 2004, San Francisco: Jossey Bass Pfeiffer. Copyright ©2004 by John Wiley & Sons. Reprinted by permission.

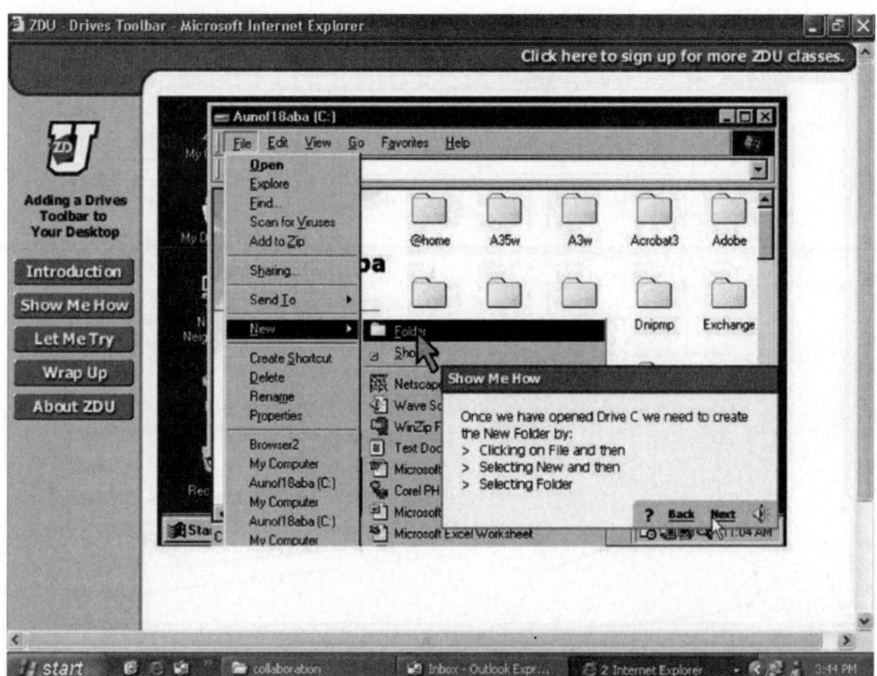

FIGURE 30.3 Screen from a software demonstration.
Source: Reprinted from *Graphics for Learning* (p. 236), by R. C. Clark and C. Lyons, 2004, San Francisco: Jossey Bass Pfeiffer. Copyright ©2004 by John Wiley & Sons. Reprinted by permission.

a function of the delivery medium. Many reviews of media comparison research have consistently shown that what causes learning is not the delivery media per se but the instructional methods that are used to build the lessons (R. E. Clark, 1994; Mayer, 2001).

We define *instructional methods* as the elements included in instruction for the purpose of supporting the achievement of the learning objective. Thus, instructional methods are intended to encourage learners to use appropriate cognitive processing during learning—such as paying attention to relevant material, mentally organizing it into a coherent representation, and mentally relating it to prior knowledge (Mayer, 2001). Some examples of instructional methods include practice exercises, feedback, analogies, and visuals. Instructional methods are effective to the extent that they are aligned with human learning processes; that is, to the extent that they support learners' cognitive processing during learning.

In this chapter, after briefly summarizing how people learn, we review research and the psychological basis underlying ways to maximize learning with rich media through the following:

1. Visuals—still and moving
2. Audio
3. Games and thematic treatments
4. Accommodation of the learner's characteristics
5. Simulations

How Humans Learn

The Cognitive Components of Learning

Figure 30.4 is a model of cognitive learning processes. Two memory systems, working memory and long-term memory, shape human learning. Working memory is the center of all conscious thinking, including deliberate learning. However, it is limited in memory capacity. The well-known limit of *seven plus or minus two chunks* of information first articulated by Miller (1956) applies to working memory. Therefore, effective instructional strategies must accommodate the limited capacity of working memory. The amount of mental work imposed on the limited capacity of working memory during learning is called *cognitive load*. Many recent studies have examined how specific instructional methods affect cognitive load (Sweller, 1999; Sweller, van Merriënboer, & Paas, 1998). In contrast, long-term memory is a permanent, large-capacity repository of information consisting of organized structures called schemata. However, it has no processing capabilities. There is an interaction between working memory and long-term memory in that, the more related knowledge that is stored in long-term memory, the larger chunks working memory can absorb. Therefore, novice learners with little related knowledge in long-term memory are much more susceptible to cognitive overload than are more experienced learners. This is why prior knowledge of

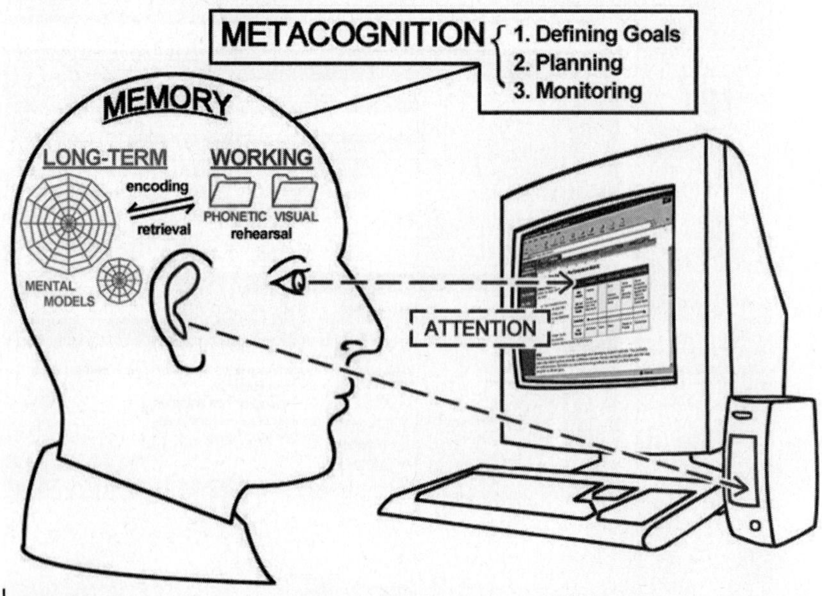

FIGURE 30.4 Human psychological learning processes.
Source: Reprinted from *Graphics for Learning* (p. 57), by R. C. Clark and C. Lyons, 2004. San Francisco: Jossey Bass Pfeiffer. (Source: Clark Training & Consulting.) Copyright © 2004 by John Wiley & Sons. Reprinted by permission.

the learner is an important individual difference characteristic that must be considered when designing instruction.

Another aspect of the memory system is that there are separate channels for processing visual/pictorial information and for processing auditory/verbal information, each with its own cognitive load limits. Graphics are processed in the visual/pictorial channel. Spoken words are processed in the auditory/verbal channel. Printed words are processed initially in the visual/pictorial channel and then may be converted for processing in the auditory/verbal channel.

The Cognitive Processes of Learning

Here we briefly summarize the major psychological events that lead to learning. To be effective, instructional methods must support one or more of these. For more details on these events, refer to R. C. Clark (2003).

Attention. Because working memory has limited capacity, instructional methods can help the learner to focus that capacity by helping direct attention to what is relevant.

Activation of prior knowledge. Learning requires the integration of new lesson content with existing prior knowledge stored in long-term memory. Therefore, this related prior knowledge must be activated to make it available in working memory for learning.

Encoding. Learning involves the integration of new content from the lesson with existing prior knowledge in long-term memory. This integration takes place through a process called *encoding*, which occurs in working memory.

Transfer of learning. New knowledge acquired in long-term memory during training must be accessible later when needed. During the process of learning, new knowledge must be indexed for future reference. The successful retrieval and use of relevant knowledge and skills from long-term memory to working memory after initial learning is called *positive transfer*.

Management of learning. An executive function referred to as *metacognition* is responsible for setting learning goals, selecting good learning techniques, monitoring progress, and adjusting learning activities as needed.

Motivation. We define *motivation* as any factor that leads learners to initiate and persist to achieve educational or training goals. Often rich media are used in ways that are designed to motivate learners by engaging them in intense, game like, sensory experiences. Using an approach called *edutainment,* these multimedia experiences attempt to motivate learners through additions to the instruction that are designed to add emotional appeal. For example, Figure 30.1 shows a fantasy theme added to a technical training course in order to motivate the learners. We will address the effectiveness of these motivational adjuncts later in this chapter.

In the remainder of this chapter we consider how to harness the capabilities of rich media in ways that support one or more of the previous processes and that avoid disrupting them. We begin with a summary of research on how best to use visuals in rich media.

How to Use Visuals Effectively in Rich Media

Note that our opening examples incorporate various types of visuals. The example in Figure 30.1 uses high-end art and music to project a fantasy theme designed to engage learners in the technical content to follow. Figure 30.2 shows an animation that illustrates how the learner should enter data into the screen. The example in Figure 30.3 uses static images described by text to illustrate how to access a menu item. Which is more effective? To address these issues, we offer the following evidence-based visual design principles: (1) *Improve learning by using relevant visuals to illustrate content.* (2) *Design relevant visuals based on their functional properties rather than on their surface features.*

Evidence That Visuals Can Improve Learning

Mayer and his colleagues have conducted numerous studies that compared lessons that presented content with words to lessons that presented content with words and relevant visuals (R. C. Clark & Mayer, 2003; Mayer, 2001). The results have consistently favored the use of visuals. For example, one lesson focused on teaching how bicycle tire pumps work. When comparing a text version with a version that included text and relevant pictures such as that shown in Figure 30.5, they found that learners scored 79% higher on transfer tests after studying the version with pictures. A positive effect for relevant visuals was found in 9 out of 9 studies, an average effect size of 1.5, which is considered a strong effect. Based on this research, Mayer (2001) proposes a *Multimedia Principle*: "Students learn better from words and pictures than from words alone" (p. 63). However, not all visuals are effective. Later in this chapter, we review research that shows that irrelevant visuals can actually depress learning.

Surface Features vs. Functional Features of Visuals

Rich media are much touted for their ability to incorporate motion visuals in the form of animation or video. Does animation or video enhance learning? A number of studies have compared learning from an animation with learning

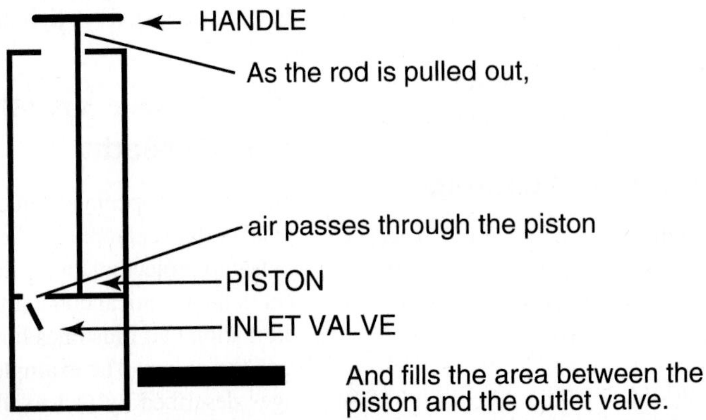

FIGURE 30.5 Words and pictures used to explain how a bicycle pump works.
Source: Reprinted from *Multimedia Learning* (Figure 5), by R. E. Mayer, 2001, New York: Cambridge University Press. (Source: Clark Training & Consulting.) Reprinted by permission of Cambridge University Press.

from a series of still visuals. These studies have found that there is no significant difference between the two. Hegarty, Narayanan, and Freitas (2002) developed a lesson on how a toilet tank flushes. One version used animation. The other version showed the movements through a series of still drawings that illustrated the mechanical state changes during flushing. Similarly, Micas and Berry (2000) compared several lesson versions designed to teach a simple bandaging procedure. One lesson used text alone. Alternative versions included line drawings alone, line drawings described by text, line drawings with arrows to show movement, and video. They found that any of the versions that communicated movement, whether by visual or textual additions to the graphics, was more effective than those that did not. Thus, the line drawing with arrows was as effective as the video version.

The research to date suggests that it is not the surface features of a visual—such as whether it is a line drawing or an animation—that determine its effectiveness. Rather, it is the functional features of the visual; that is, how well it conveys the intended message. R. C. Clark and Lyons (2004) recently have summarized functional taxonomies of visuals based on their communication properties and on their psychological support features. Table 30.1 summarizes the major communication functions of graphics and some ways to use each type most effectively. Table 30.2 summarizes the major psychological functions of graphics corresponding to the instructional events we summarized previously. For example, *transformational graphics* are defined as visuals that illustrate change or motion in time or over space. Transformational graphics may take the form of line drawings with arrows, animation, or video. Based on the research cited previously, any form of transformational visual can effectively communicate state changes. Therefore, in applying this guideline to our samples, it is likely that the example shown in Figure 30.3 that illustrates the procedure with a series of screen captures will support learning as effectively as the animated version shown in Figure 30.2. Importantly, the example shown in Figure 30.3 may be less costly to produce, requires less bandwidth, and imposes less mental load because learners can study each step at their own pace. Research on the role of animation and static graphics is continuing, but there is no strong evidence to date that presenting animation is inherently superior to presenting static frames (Tversky, Morrison, & Betrancourt, 2002).

How to Use Audio Effectively in Rich Media

One of the defining features of rich media is the incorporation of sound into lessons. Audio is most commonly used in one of three ways: to present words in the form of narration; to add background music to the instruction; or to add environmental sounds such as mechanical noises in a lesson on equipment. For example, in Figure 30.2, the animated demonstration is narrated by audio that describes

TABLE 30.1 Communication functions of graphics

Function	A Graphic Used to	Examples
Decorative	Add aesthetic appeal or humor	• Art on the cover of a book • Visual of a general in a military lesson on ammunition
Representational	Depict an object in a realistic fashion	• A screen capture of a software screen • A photograph of equipment
Mnemonic	Provide retrieval cues for factual information	• A picture of a stamped letter in a shopping cart to recall the meaning of the Spanish word, Carta (letter)
Organizational	Show qualitative relationships among content	• A two-dimensional course map • A concept map
Relational	Show quantitative relationships among two or more variables	• A line graph • A pie chart
Transformational	Show changes in objects over time or space	• An animation of the weather cycle • A video showing how to operate equipment
Interpretive	Illustrate a theory, principle, or cause-and-effect relationships	• A schematic diagram of equipment • An animation of molecular movement

Source: Reprinted from Graphics for Learning (p. 15), by R. C. Clark and C. Lyons, 2004, San Francisco: Jossey Bass Pfeiffer. Copyright © 2004 by John Wiley & Sons. Reprinted by permission.

the steps that the user should take to enter data into the application fields. In Figure 30.1, the futurist theme is dramatized with background music suggestive of space adventures. Which of these uses of audio has proven most effective? Fortunately, we have some research to guide your use of audio to best promote multimedia learning.

Explain Visuals with Audio Narration

Many research studies have compared learning from visuals that are described by words presented in text to learning from visuals that are described by words presented in audio narration. The results have been consistent: Audio narration is more effective. For example, lessons on how lightning storms develop, how car brakes work, and how to interpret a technical diagram have all resulted in better learning when the visuals were explained by words presented in audio (Kalyuga, Chandler, & Sweller 2000; Mayer, 2001). Mayer, Dow, and Mayer (2003) have shown that animated pedagogical agents, which are onscreen characters designed to promote learning, are most effective when they present guidance via audio rather than via text. Mayer (2001) reports an average gain of 30% with an effect size of 1.17, which is considered high, in 4 of 4 studies in which words were presented via audio rather than as onscreen text. Based on this research, Mayer (2001) proposes a *Modality Principle*: "Students learn better from animation and narration than from animation and onscreen text" (p. 184).

The limits of working memory are the basis for the modality principle. As we described previously, working memory has a limited capacity, commonly referred to as "seven plus or minus two chunks" of information. Working memory has at least two separate subsystems for storage of data: a visual/pictorial storage area, and an auditory/verbal storage area, represented as folders in Figure 30.4. When instructional materials include complex visuals such as animations, presenting words in the form of text

TABLE 30.2 Psychological functions of graphics

Instructional Event	Definition	Example
Support Attention	Graphics and graphic design that draw attention to important elements in an instructional display and that minimize divided attention	• An arrow to point out the relevant part of a computer screen • Placement of graphic close to text that describes it
Activate or Build Prior Knowledge	Graphics that engage existing mental models or provide high-level content overview to support acquisition of new information	• Visual analogy between new content and familiar knowledge • Graphic overview of new content
Minimize Cognitive Load	Graphics and graphic design that minimize extraneous mental work imposed on working memory during learning	• Line art versus photograph • Relevant graphic versus decorative graphic
Build Mental Models	Graphics that help learners construct new memories in long-term memory that support deeper understanding of content	• A schematic diagram to illustrate how equipment works • A visual simulation of how genes are transmitted from parents to offspring
Support Transfer of Learning	Graphics that incorporate key features of the work environment; graphics that promote deeper understanding	• Use of software screen simulation that looks and acts like actual software • Use of a visual simulation to build a cause-and-effect mental model
Support Motivation	Graphics that make material interesting and at the same time do not depress learning	• A graphic that makes the relevance of the skills to the job obvious • An organizing visual that clarifies the structure of the material

Source: Reprinted from Graphics for Learning (p. 16), by R. C. Clark and C. Lyons, 2004, San Francisco: Jossey Bass Pfeiffer. Copyright © 2004 by John Wiley & Sons. Reprinted by permission.

can overload the visual/pictorial channel. In contrast, presenting words in audio offloads the words onto the auditory/verbal channel. Note that the modality principle applies to situations in which a complex visual such as an animation is on the screen.

There are some caveats you should consider when applying the modality principle. Information that is presented in an auditory mode is transient. In some situations, onscreen text is more appropriate for memory support. For example, when giving onscreen directions for a training exercise, text is more effective because learners can refer to it over time as they work the exercise. In Figure 30.2, directions to complete a procedure are presented with auditory narration but are also recapped with summary onscreen text, which remains visible for learner reference. In addition, whenever audio narration is used to describe visuals, the opportunity to review it should be provided via a replay button.

Minimize Irrelevant Audio

If presenting words in audio results in better learning, what about incorporating environmental sounds or background music? Moreno and Mayer (2000) describe research using two separate multimedia lesson topics that compared learning from versions that did and did not include background sounds or music. One version taught how lightning works and the other focused on how car braking systems work. Both lessons used animated visuals with audio narration. In both cases, learning was better from lessons that omitted music and environmental sounds. In the two studies, a median gain of 69% was realized from the lessons that did not include the extraneous auditory information. Since working memory capacity is highly limited, including three sources of sounds—narration, environmental sounds, and music—overloaded the limited capacity of the auditory/verbal channel. Based on these results Mayer (2001) proposes a *Coherence Principle*: "Students learn better when extraneous words, pictures, and sounds are excluded rather than included" (p. 184).

However, before discarding all environmental sounds from multimedia lessons, consider the role of sound in achieving the instructional goal. For example, medical students learning patient diagnosis use sound as an important sensory cue. Sounds from the heart, lungs, and speech of a patient are among many important cues. Kamin, O'Sullivan, Deterding, and Younger (2003) found that medical students involved in problem-based learning discussions had deeper discussions when the patient case was presented by video than when the same case was presented in text. Some of the discussion centered around the visual and auditory features of the patient, which were more salient in the video then in the text case. In this instructional situation, rich media paid off by communicating sensory data that were relevant to the skills to be learned.

How to Engage Learners Effectively with Rich Media

Rich media have been used effectively as entertainment in the form of films and interactive games. Some have proposed to harness the appeal of these environments to increase the motivational features of multimedia instruction (Prensky, 2001). Various forms of edutainment have incorporated features of electronic games in the service of achieving educational goals. For example, a course with the goal of teaching a new computer application was spiced up by embedding the exercises in a "Tomb Raider" theme, in which learners help heroine Laura Croft by answering questions correctly. Learners experience Laura's adventure through visually and auditorially rich multimedia materials that surround the technical training lessons. Okan (2003), however, cautions against embracing edutainment materials that

> lead the students to a promised land of animations, audio clips, simulations, etc. [because] they teach them that learning does not have to be a process in which they persevere. Activating prior knowledge, reading critically, making connections between what is learned and what is already known, discussing with peers and teachers are activities that are old-fashioned, requiring effort on the part of students. (p. 258)

What research do we have on the learning value of edutainment approaches? How can learners be motivated to initiate and persist to complete an instructional goal?

Minimize Unnecessary Visuals and Text

In the early 1990s, Garner and her colleagues (Garner, Alexander, Gillingham, Kulikowich, & Grown, 1991; Garner, Brown, Sanders, & Menke, 1992) identified the negative effects of what they termed *seductive details*. In their studies, seductive details consisted of textual information inserted into instructional materials that were intended to arouse interest. Seductive details in lessons are typically related to the general topic but are irrelevant to the main instructional goal. Harp and Mayer (1997) evaluated the learning effects of adding both seductive text as well as seductive visuals to multimedia lessons. For example, throughout a lesson on how lightning forms, they incorporated brief discussions such as what happens when lightning strikes a golfer and the effect of lightning on airplanes. Learners rated the lesson versions that contained the seductive vignettes as more interesting than the lessons that omitted these details. However, these spiced-up lessons depressed learning dramatically. In six different studies, lessons that omitted seductive information showed a median learning gain of 105% with an effect size of 1.66, which is high, as compared to lessons with seductive information.

Harp and Mayer (1998) postulated that seductive details could exert their negative effects by distracting the learner (negative impact on focus of attention), by disrupting the building of a mental model (negative impact on rehearsal and encoding) or by activating inappropriate prior knowledge (negative impact on activation of prior knowledge). They created several lesson versions in which a countermeasure was added to overcome the possible negative effects of the seductive details. For example, to overcome potential distraction effects, they added attention-focusing techniques in the form of cues that pointed out the critical information. They found that only the countermeasures that overcame activation of irrelevant prior knowledge reduced the negative effects of seductive details. Thus they concluded that extraneous information added to spice up a multimedia presentation depressed learning by activating inappropriate prior knowledge.

Use Cognitive Sources of Motivation

If edutainment is not a productive road to motivate learning, what is a better alternative? Harp and Mayer (1998) distinguish between emotional sources of motivation, such as the seductive details described, and cognitive sources of motivation. *Cognitive* sources of motivation include any instructional strategy that helps learners more readily achieve the instructional goal. Some examples include the addition of an advance organizer, the use of an analogy, or the signaling of content through headers and subheaders. Harp and Mayer (1997) recommend that "the best way to help learners enjoy a passage is to help them understand it" (p. 100).

How to Accommodate the Learner's Characteristics with Rich Media

For whom does multimedia work best? In this section, we explore the idea that well-designed multimedia training—with corresponding words and pictures presented together—can be most beneficial for learners who lack appropriate prior knowledge.

Employ Design Principles Particularly for Inexperienced Learners

The learner's level of prior knowledge is the single most important individual difference variable involved in learning, and is the most important characteristic to know to help you design appropriate training. Well-designed multimedia training appears to be more helpful for low-knowledge learners than for high-knowledge learners. For example, in a series of studies, well-designed multimedia instruction (using words and pictures rather than words alone) improved the learning of low-knowledge learners, whereas high-knowledge learners learned well under all conditions (Mayer, 2001). Apparently, high-knowledge learners are able to compensate for poor presentation methods whereas low-knowledge learners are not. Similarly, inexperienced trainees learned better when text explanations were integrated into diagrams of electrical circuits, whereas experienced people learned better from the diagram without text (Kalyuga, Chandler, & Sweller, 1998). Integrating text and diagrams—which is considered a principle of good instructional design (Mayer, 2001)—helped low-knowledge learners but not high-knowledge learners. Kalyuga, Ayres, Chandler, and Sweller (2003) refer this pattern as the *expertise reversal effect*. Instructional guidance helps low-knowledge learners by substituting for missing schemata, whereas it might interfere with high-knowledge learners by increasing unneeded cognitive load. Based on such findings, Mayer (2001) offers an *Individual Differences Principle*: "When working with low-knowledge learners . . . be particularly careful to employ relevant principles of multimedia design" (p. 181).

How to Use Simulations Effectively with Rich Media

Simulations—ranging from flight simulators to simulations of a salesman trying to close a sale—hold the potential to improve learning. For example, Schank (1997, p. 15) argues that "the computer has made learning-by-doing a realistic option in many situations" so "computer simulations open up myriad possibilities." How can you take advantage of these possibilities? In this section we explore the conditions in which interacting with a realistic simulation can help people learn.

Simulations Can Add Value to an Instructional Program

Can simulations help students learn? The answer from a number of studies is affirmative (Clark & Mayer, 2003). For example, Moreno and Mayer (1999) designed a computer-based program to teach students how to add and subtract signed numbers, such as $3 - -2 =$ ______. Students were given problems, generated answers, and then were told the correct answer. However, some students could also interact with a simulation; by moving a joystick they could make a bunny face the right or left side of the screen and could make the bunny jump forward or backward any number of steps along a number line. For the problem $3 - -2 =$ ______, the correct simulation is to start the bunny on the $+3$ position in the number line, face left, and jump backwards 2 steps, ending on $+5$. Students who could use the simulation learned better than those who did not. In another example, Moreno, Mayer, Spires, and Lester (2001) report that students learned better from a computer-based simulation game designed to teach environmental science than when the identical material was presented as a tutorial with onscreen text and illustrations. Mayer et al. (2003) asked students to learn how an electric motor works by interacting with an onscreen simulation, with an explanation given by an onscreen agent named Dr. Phyz. Students who learned by interacting with the simulation performed better on subsequent transfer tests than did students who received identical information in an onscreen narrated animation. Similarly, White and her colleagues (White, 1993; White & Frederiksen, 1998) have shown that interacting with simple simulations—such as balls moving through a maze—can help students learn physics principles.

Extreme Realism May Not Be Cost Effective

Should the simulation environment be extremely realistic—with characters looking very lifelike and scenes creating a sense of physical presence? Preliminary research indicates that the high costs associated with producing extremely realistic simulations may not be justified because such simulations may not yield any better results than do less realistic simulations costing much less money. For example, Moreno and Mayer (2002) took a science education simulation designed to run on a desktop computer and converted it into a virtual reality (VR) simulation delivered via a head-mounted display. Although students rated a higher sense of physical presence in the VR simulation, they did not learn the content any better than students who learned via a desktop computer. We recommend that simulations aimed at teaching basic cognitive skills be psychologically realistic—in the sense that the situation makes sense—but that they need not have extreme physical realism. Of course, when the goal is learning a precise motor skill such as how to land an aircraft or how to dock an oil tanker, more realistic simulations may be warranted.

Learners May Need Scaffolding in Making Sense of a Simulation

How much guidance should students get in using simulations? In general, research on discovery learning shows that people learn better with guided discovery methods in which the instructor imposes some structure on the task than with pure discovery methods in which they are free to interact as they please (Mayer, 2004). This conclusion seems to apply to computer-based simulations as well. For example, Mayer, Mautone, and Prothero (2002) examined a geology simulation in which people learn to survey an area of a planet's surface to identify geological formations such as a trench, basin, ridge, island, or seamount. Students performed much better on learning this task if they received pretraining in what the various geological formations looked like. In a related study, students learned better from interacting with a simulation of an electric motor when they were given specific questions to answer rather than when they were allowed to explore freely (Mayer et al., 2003). Similarly, students who were given simulations related to the physics of motion learned more deeply when they were required to discuss their experiences in the simulation (White & Frederiksen, 1998). Overall, we recommend providing appropriate scaffolding to guide learners in their interactions with simulations.

Conclusion

Rich media can improve learning if they are used in ways that promote effective cognitive processes in learners. Visuals such as illustrations and animation can improve learning, but animation is not necessarily more effective than illustrations. Audio can improve learning such as when narration accompanies animation, but background music and environmental sounds can distract learners. Adding interesting but irrelevant words and graphics does not necessarily motivate deeper learning, and often detracts from learning. Using good design principles is more important for low-knowledge learners than for high-knowledge learners. Simulations can improve learning, but generally they do not need to be extremely realistic and they should be accompanied with some guidance. In summary, rich media per se do not create learning, but rich media can enable effective instructional methods that promote learning.

Application Questions

1. What do the authors mean by "the paradox of rich media"? Provide 2 or 3 examples to illustrate.
2. Describe the differences between surface and functional features of graphics. Find or create an instructional visual and describe its surface and functional features.
3. Illustrate the expertise reversal effect with a specific example.

References

Clark, R. C. (2003). *Building expertise: Cognitive methods for training and performance improvement* (2nd ed.). Silver Spring, MD: International Society for Performance Improvement.

Clark R. C., & Lyons, C. (2004). *Graphics for learning*. San Francisco, CA: Jossey Bass Pfeiffer.

Clark, R. C., & Mayer, R. E. (2003). *E-learning and the science of instruction.* San Francisco, CA: Jossey Bass Pfeiffer.

Clark, R. E. (1994). Media will never influence learning. *Educational Technology, Research & Development, 42*(2) 21–30.

Dixon, N. M. (1990). *Evaluation: A tool for improving HRD quality.* San Diego, CA: University Associates.

Galvin, T. (2003). 2003 Industry report. *Training Magazine, 40*(9), 21–45.

Garner, R., Alexander, P., Gillingham, M., Kulikowich, J., & Grown, R. (1991). Interest and learning from text. *American Educational Research Journal*, *28*(3), 643–659.

Garner, R., Brown, R., Sanders, S., & Menke, D. (1992). Seductive details and learning from text. In K. A. Renninger, S. Hidi, & A. Krapp (Eds.), *The role of interest in learning and development* (pp. 239–254). Hillsdale, NJ: Lawrence Erlbaum Associates.

Harp, S. F., & Mayer, R. E. (1997). The role of interest in learning from scientific text and illustrations: On the distinction between emotional interest and cognitive interest. *Journal of Educational Psychology*, *89*, 92–102.

Harp, S. F., & Mayer, R. E. (1998). How seductive details do their damage: A theory of cognitive interest in science learning. *Journal of Educational Psychology*, *90*, 414–434.

Hegarty, M., Narayanan, N. H., & Freitas, P. (2002). Understanding machines from multimedia and hypermedia presentations. In J. Otero, J. A. Leon, & A. C. Graesser (Eds.), *The psychology of science text comprehension* (pp. 357–384). Mahwah, NJ: Lawrence Erlbaum Associates.

Kalyuga, S., Ayres, P., Chandler, P., & Sweller, J. (2003). The expertise reversal effect. *Educational Psychologist, 38*(1), 21–31.

Kalyuga, S., Chandler, P., & Sweller, J. (1998). Levels of expertise and instructional design. *Human Factors, 40*, 1–17.

Kalyuga, S., Chandler, P., & Sweller, J. (2000). Incorporating learner experience into the design of multimedia instruction. *Journal of Educational Psychology*, *92*(1), 126–136.

Kamin, C., O'Sullivan, P., Deterding, R., & Younger, M. (2003). A comparison of critical thinking in groups of third-year medical students in text, video, and virtual PBL case modalities. *Academic Medicine, 78*(2), 204–211.

Mayer, R. E. (2001). *Multimedia learning*. New York: Cambridge University Press.

Mayer, R. E. (2004). Should there be a three-strikes rule against pure discovery learning? The case for guided methods of instruction. *American Psychologist, 59*(1), 14–19.

Mayer, R. E., Dow, G. T., & Mayer, S. (2003). Multimedia learning in an interactive self-explaining environment: What works in the design of agent-based micro worlds? *Journal of Educational Psychology*, *95*(4), 806–813.

Mayer, R. E., Mautone, P., & Prothero, W. (2002). Pictorial aids for learning by doing in a multimedia geology simulation game. *Journal of Educational Psychology, 94*(1), 171–185.

Micas, I. C., & Berry, D. C. (2000). Learning a procedural task: Effectiveness of multimedia presentations. *Applied Cognitive Psychology*, *14*(6), 555–575.

Miller, G. A. (1956). The magical number seven plus or minus two: Some limits on our capacity for processing information. *Psychological Review*, *63*, 81–97.

Moreno, R., & Mayer, R. E. (1999). Multimedia supported metaphors for meaning making in mathematics. *Cognition and Instruction*, *17*(3), 215–575.

Moreno, R., & Mayer, R. E. (2000). A coherence effect in multimedia learning: The case for minimizing irrelevant sounds in the design of multimedia messages. *Journal of Educational Psychology, 92*(1), 117–125.

Moreno, R., & Mayer, R. E. (2002). Learning science in virtual reality multimedia environments: Role of media and methods. *Journal of Educational Psychology, 94*(3), 598–610.

Moreno, R., Mayer, R. E., Spires, H., & Lester, J. (2001). The case for social agency in computer-based teaching: Do students learn more deeply when they interact with animated pedagogical agents? *Cognition and Instruction, 19*(2), 177–213.

Okan, Z. (2003, June). Edutainment: Is learning at risk? *British Journal of Educational Technology*, *34*, 255–264.

Prensky, M. (2001). *Digital game-based learning.* New York: McGraw-Hill.

Schank, R. (1997). *Virtual learning*. New York: McGraw-Hill.

Sweller, J. (1999). *Instructional design in technical areas.* Camberwell, Australia: ACER.

Sweller, J., van Merriënboer, J. J. G., & Paas, F. G. (1998). Cognitive architecture and instructional design. *Educational Psychology Review*, *10*(3), 251–296.

Tversky, B., Morrison, J. B., & Betrancourt, M. (2002). Animation: Can it facilitate? *International Journal of Human Computer Studies, 57*(4), 247–262.

White, B. (1993). ThinkerTools: Causal models, conceptual change, and science education. *Cognition and Instruction, 10*(1), 1–100.

White, B., & Frederiksen, J. R. (1998). Inquiry, modeling, and metacognition: Making science accessible to all students. *Cognition and Instruction, 16*(1), 3–118.

CHAPTER 31

Emerging Instructional Technologies: The Near Future

John W. Jacobs
Alion Science and Technology

John V. Dempsey
University of South Alabama

What is the use of a book, thought Alice, without pictures or conversations?

—Lewis Carroll

Editors' Introduction

Twenty years ago, it would have been hard to imagine that computer networking would have such a profound influence on the field of instructional design and technology (IDT) and throughout society as a whole. The quest to build a better mousetrap is now guided by emerging technologies that continually strive toward being faster, smaller, more intelligent, and distributed. Predicting the future of IDT in this blur of technological innovation is at best a risky endeavor. In this chapter, John Jacobs and Jack Dempsey review a broad spectrum of emergent technologies and select those they think will have a growing impact on the IDT field over the foreseeable future. Even within this limited scope, they present evidence of a technology-induced paradigm shift currently underway. The authors also describe ethical issues that may soon overtake the research community as it reaches out to incorporate advances within the related fields of cognitive science and neuroscience. We hope this chapter will spark an interest in the research of scientific fields that are on a convergent path with that of our field.

Knowledge and Comprehension Questions

1. What three technology areas are considered by the authors to have a meaningful influence on the field of instructional design?
2. What benefits are derived from development of distributed learning environments using an open architecture approach specified by advance distributed learning (ADL)?
3. According to the authors, what central element is required to make the course management system of a distributed learning system functional? Why do you think this element is considered so important?
4. What types of instructional systems are characteristic of what the authors have described as information pull (I-PULL) and information push (I-PUSH) learning environments?
5. Why is it important to discuss ethical ramifications when contemplating the use of neural stimulation to enhance learning processes?

In most professions, better tools make for better products. This also applies to the design of instructional systems. The past 15 years have witnessed the development and continual upgrading of sophisticated computer-based programs that have revolutionized the way instruction is developed and implemented. Embedding any of a variety of media into the instructional environment can be done almost effortlessly. Similarly, course management functions at the individual and group levels can be implemented quickly and efficiently as can sophisticated assessment, feedback, and branching capabilities. All in all it has never been easier to design, develop, and implement effective instructional courseware. And yet a core element of developing effective instructional systems continues to involve activities completed before the development process begins, including requirements analysis, task/skill analysis, matching learning demands to instructional technologies, and so on. Technology-enhanced tools continue to pave the way for improvements in how instructional courseware is developed and implemented. It is the adherence to sound instructional theory throughout the entire design and development process, however, that will ensure the achievement of high-impact learning outcomes.

This chapter reviews and discusses three emerging instructionally relevant technology areas that we believe will have a profound influence on the field of instructional systems, at least within the foreseeable future. The chapter also provides a glimpse of tools and trends that are likely to affect learning and instruction during the next 10 to 20 years and forge an enduring relationship between distributed cognition and the craft of instructional design.

The three technology influences or forces that we believe will make a conspicuous contribution to the field are (1) the proliferation of object-oriented distributed learning environments, (2) the use of artificial intelligence applications, and (3) the expanded effect of cognitive science and neuroscience.

Object-Oriented Distributed Learning Environments

Object-oriented programming languages, such as C++ and Java™, have been in use for several years, and SmallTalk, the precursor to these languages, has been in use since 1970. Object-oriented programming currently has a dominant role in guiding the future of software application development, including that for designing and delivering instruction. Among the primary benefits of using an object-oriented programming language is the ability to separate programming functions from associated data elements. This separation, in conjunction with a hierarchical layering of functional attributes, allows programmers to more easily reuse programming code and in many cases reduces the time and resources needed during software verification and validation (debugging). Object-oriented programming is being used increasingly to develop Internet applications because of its potential integration with HTML and XML. In the parlance of object-oriented programming language, program elements are linked rather than embedded. Conceptually and in practice, the notion of "linked objects" is creating a revolution in the way instruction is designed, developed, and delivered.

Linked Objects

The conceptual underpinnings of distributed learning environments are relatively straightforward. The devil, as always, is in the details. For starters, take a typical standalone, technology-based training (TBT) program that can be generated using one of the many commercially available software applications. Now engineer it so that instructional materials (including text passages, graphic images, video, and audio files) are integrated into the program as linked objects. Increasingly, organizations are developing a repository of instructional content materials (i.e., learning objects), to include specific elements (text passages, photos, etc.) as well as more complex instructional chunks, that can be reused via programming links as needed by one or more instructional platforms. Information content can be easily updated as needed to ensure that the information is accurate, up to date, and tailored to the specific needs of individual learners.

For example, say your organization developed instructional courseware using an off-the-shelf TBT development platform. The courseware involved training newly hired employees to operate an existing piece of equipment. One module of the instruction involved completing maintenance-tracking paperwork used to schedule ongoing preventive maintenance activities. Suppose also that the equipment is scheduled to be upgraded with new operating capabilities and that this will affect, among other things, the way equipment usage is reported. Using an object-oriented architecture, changes to the instructional modules involving the new equipment capabilities can be completed using resources developed by one group, while changes to the maintenance-tracking module can be completed by a separate group. The distributed nature of the instructional environment allows changes to be made to the central TBT program, which is then accessed by individual employees using a personal computer (PC) via a local or wide area network communication link.

You can now begin to see the potential for such a centralized control, decentralized application instructional environment. To enhance learning effectiveness, a TBT program needs to measure and keep track of key learning events and activities at both the individual and group levels. This is where a distributed instructional environment can have a significant advantage over a standalone system. Within a distributed instructional environment, learning activities and events can be tracked within and across lessons or entire courses of instruction, making it possible to detect and address specific learning trends. It will be possible for distributed learning systems to integrate information about an individual's aptitude, learning preferences, goal orientation, and so forth within a tailored instructional program that matches learning needs to instructional technologies and activities.

Electronic Training Jackets

Storing information pertaining to individual learners is a key component of any TBT program. However, storing such information in a central location is problematic due to privacy issues and the need to establish secure data transmission channels. An electronic training jacket (ETJ) is currently being implemented by the Navy as part of the Navy Training Management and Planning System (NTMPS). The ETJ combines a variety of personal, administrative, and educational/training data sources within a secure, centralized online data warehouse (see **https://ntmpsweb.ntmps.navy.mil/etjclient/login.aspx**). Over time, the Navy ETJ is expected to expand to incorporate a host of information related to the five "W" questions illustrated in Table 31.1, including different categories of job-related information (e.g., previous job assignments, licenses/qualifications, and awards).

The electronic training jacket is considered a key component within a comprehensive integrated personnel management system (IMPS). For the ETJ concept to work, it needs to be transportable and to have an embedded capability for positively identifying individual trainees. One security-related application currently being implemented by the military, as well as industry and higher education, for accomplishing this task involves what is referred to as *smartcard* technology. These identification cards/units contain embedded microchips that provide positive identification using one or more of the following: thumbprint, voiceprint, retinal scan, DNA scan, or some other as-yet-developed identification technique. If needed, the smartcard also can hold in its local memory the individual's ETJ information, making it readily transportable. Once the smartcard is activated using the positive identification technique, it has the capability to be inserted into a PC via a card scanner or other mobile computing device, thereby allowing the trainee to access the IMPS and initiate a training session. Interestingly, some relatively inexpensive and commonplace technologies such as Microsoft's MSN TV, which provides Internet access via television, have smartcard capabilities.

TABLE 31.1 Five W's applied to a training jacket

Query	Examples of Data
Who is the trainee?	Key biographical information such as name, identification number, position, aptitude, and learning styles
What is the trainee's personal history?	Key work experiences to include formal and informal education and training history
Where is the trainee headed?	Types of operational assignments the trainee is likely to encounter; overall career path goals/options
When will the trainee be expected to apply the training?	Immediately versus sometime in the future, operate with or without job aids, work independently or with others
Why is this training being completed?	Initial, remedial, or maintenance training; expected level of competence as a result of training (expert, journeyman, basic)

The Advanced Distributed Learning (ADL) initiative (U.S. Department of Defense, 1999; see also **http://www.adlnet.org**) has been a major source of funding for over five years in the development of a comprehensive object-based distributed instructional courseware standard. This standard, referred to as Sharable Content Object Reference Model (SCORM), has now emerged from the prototype development phase into what developers hope becomes an implementation phase (Wisher, 2003). This initiative involves developing electronic "data tags" that will facilitate the development of an object-oriented distributed training architecture to support military, industry, and academia (Graves, 1994; Wagner, 2002). Such an instructional development environment, when fully developed and implemented, would establish an open architecture within which individual (proprietary) solutions could be implemented, but would allow information and resources to pass between proprietary instructional development and delivery platforms.

Metadata Tags

Metadata tags (also called simply *metatags*) refer to "data about data" (see **http://www.imsglobal.org/metadata/index.cfm**) and are used to label the variety of learning resources needed to manage and deliver instruction within a distributed learning environment. Metadata tags can index an individual learning resource (object) using multiple attributes. According to the Institute of Electrical and Electronics Engineers (IEEE) standard used at the time of this writing (IEEE, 2002), metadata tags cover the following five areas:

- General—Information describing the learning object as whole.
- Lifecycle—Historical and current state information about the object.
- Metadata—Information related to features of the description as opposed to the resource (e.g., identifying label, who contributed what, etc.).
- Technical—Information about format, size, location, platform requirements, etc.
- Educational—Information about the educational or pedagogical nature of the object.

The metadata tag and associated sublevel attributes facilitate reuse of a given learning object across various courseware boundaries and within certain levels of granularity (e.g., course, unit, lesson, procedure, illustration). As an example, an animated graphic depicting the integration of various systems (hydraulic, electrical, mechanical, etc.) within an aircraft landing gear can be used in several lessons within the same curriculum that deal with aircraft maintenance, troubleshooting, system integration, hydraulic systems, electrical systems, mechanical systems, and so on. Similarly, other course developers involved in supporting an entirely new curriculum can use this same learning object. The IMS standards are aggressively promoting an open, distributed learning architecture that supports a variety of instructional development platforms. Due in part to the rapid and sometimes unpredictable advances driving the information technology fields, the ongoing IMS standards development process is slowly growing into market share acceptance. One can participate in or simply become a spectator in the ongoing SCORM development process by participating in IMS-sponsored "plugfests" that bring together vendors, content developers, and tool creators for the primary purpose of conducting cross-platform interoperability tests.

From an educational research perspective, acceptance and widespread use of a standard set of metadata tags may allow the field of instructional systems to develop theoretically based, empirically validated courseware design principles at a level of specificity as yet unimagined. For example, by collecting data across various instructional platforms and information content areas, it will be possible to determine what instructional features (e.g., media type, level of interactivity, etc.) interact with specific learning styles or preferences to produce above-average gains in learning and knowledge transfer. The key to making this a reality is to establish research-reporting guidelines to ensure that individual study results can be integrated within a larger body of knowledge and that support analysis using meta-analytic or other useful quantitative and qualitative review procedures (Hays, Jacobs, Prince, & Salas, 1992).

It may even be worthwhile to consider setting up a central data repository for the field of instructional design and technology. Why not? Such an effort is not unprecedented. Researchers in the area of neuroimaging are currently attempting to archive brain scan images from selected resources (i.e., peer reviewed studies) within a centralized database in an attempt to assist the research community's ability to answer longstanding questions related to brain function and associated behavior in humans and certain animals (Van Dorn & Gazzaniga, 2002). A similar effort to archive selected instructional data using a systematic approach could facilitate answering longstanding questions concerning the nature of human learning and performance as they relate to cognitive processing and instructional technologies.

The Application of Artificial Intelligence

Instructional systems of the future will be able to perform a number of high-level activities involved in monitoring and regulating the instructional environment at individual and group levels. At the individual level, future instructional systems will diagnose learning needs, learning aptitudes, and styles; develop instruction tailored to identified needs and aptitudes; modify the level and type of feedback and instructional strategy based on learner responses and progress; and implement best practices guidelines based on up-to-date research findings. At the group level, future instructional systems will monitor and allocate instructional resources (e.g., schedule team activities or computer simulator time); collect and analyze data across individuals, tasks, and settings; and generate lessons learned, best practices guidelines, and so forth for use by instructional systems researchers and practitioners.

These high-level functions can only be accomplished by integrating some form of artificial intelligence (AI) within the course management component of instructional systems architecture. Several approaches have been used by AI researchers to embed "intelligence" within computers (Gardner, 1985; Pew & Mavor, 1998). What follows is a brief description of two basic instructional approaches that we believe will integrate AI functionality and in so doing open up new vistas in development of future instructional systems. Several examples are included within this discussion that exemplify AI-based instructional applications and associated research currently underway related to these two approaches.

Instructional systems of the future will combine information content with automated teaching and learning principles (i.e., pedagogy) to create combination information push-pull learning environments. Information push (I-PUSH) learning environments will be based on an expanded use of intelligent tutoring system (ITS) applications. Information pull (I-PULL) learning environments will be based on intelligent interfaces allowing learners to construct their own learning experiences using integrated tool sets. These tool sets will include the capability to conduct concurrent information search and analysis operations and to rapidly develop simulated environments for testing ideas or fostering knowledge transfer to real-world settings.

Recent advances in the expanding fields related to AI provide a provocative view of technologies that will support such I-PULL tool sets. For example, data mining technologies are currently being developed that allow atmospheric scientists to scan large visually complex data sets (Hsu, Welge, Redman, & Clutter, 2002) and assist executives when making critical business decisions by mining complex, and often incomplete and mismatched (i.e., dirty) data sets (Kim, Choi, Hong, Kim, & Lee, 2003; Macedo, Cook, & Brown, 2000). Research in other AI fields, such as expert systems and intelligent autonomous agents, provide evidence of capabilities that may lead to tool sets that can aid in locating and translating knowledge, as well as enhancing creativity (Liane, 2002) by using single and multiagent systems (Williams, 2004).

ITS applications have been effectively employed in a variety of content areas (Zachary, Ryder, Santarelli, & Weiland, 2000) and have been shown to produce results approaching those attributed to one-on-one tutoring (Merrill, Reiser, Ranney, & Tafton, 1992). At their heart, ITS frameworks are viewed as highly interactive, computer-based instructional environments whose goal is to actively guide (i.e., push) learners toward achieving expertise within a given content area. Within an ITS framework, interrelated models are generated and used to guide the instructional process: one depicting how an expert would perform, another depicting how a novice would perform, and a pedagogy model for guiding instructional/learning processes (McCarthur, Lewis, & Bishay, 1993; Ohlsson, 1986). The expert model reflects an ideal solution path typically in the form of goals and subgoals that are generated by conducting an in-depth analysis of the cognitive process steps a typical subject matter expert performs when faced with the same problem or problem type. Similarly, the novice model may encompass several submodels, each of which depicts an erroneous solution path that a novice learner may explore when faced with a given problem or problem type. The pedagogy model is used to guide instructional/learning activities, such as the amount and type of feedback, as well as the use of branching. The key elements of ITS that set it apart from conventional computer-based instruction are its ability to accurately diagnose learning errors by matching error patterns to predefined models of novice performance and to tailor subsequent instructional activities (e.g., via feedback, branching, etc.) so that learner performance more closely matches that of the expert model.

In their paper describing applications related to executable cognitive models, Zachary, Ryder, Santarelli, & Weiland (2000) discuss progress made using a cognitive modeling system called the COGNET/BATON framework. The COGNET system models human decision processes in complex real-time, multitasking environments, such as decisions made by an air traffic controller. BATON is an executable cognitive architecture that represents three human information processing subsystems that work in parallel: sensory/perception, cognition, and action/motor. The paper describes several successful COGNET/BATON applications related to (1) integrating multiple telephone operator job functions, (2) developing a performance support system (i.e., intelligent agent) for assisting fire support operations aboard a new class of Navy destroyer, and (3) providing intelligent embedded training for Combat Information Center teams aboard Navy Aegis cruisers. Interestingly, these researchers note that the highly complex and time-consuming work needed to develop a given cognitive model can produce multiple applications, including intelligent tutors/embedded instructors, decision and performance support systems, autonomous agents, and design/interface guidance advisors. Thus, these researchers contend that ITS and related AI (cognitive modeling) applications have matured significantly over the past 10 years and are now poised to successfully tackle a range of content areas.

Within a typical ITS framework the tutor provides information, examples, feedback, and so forth necessary for learning to take place. McArthur et al. (1993) contrast instruction-led approaches engendered by the ITS framework with learner-centered approaches (in their words, "interactive learning environments" or ILEs), that in our view can be characterized as an I-PULL learning environment. Within ILEs, the learner takes on the primary responsibility of managing the learning process, typically by employing tools that allow information to be collected, manipulated, and represented.

Our vision of I-PULL learning environments expands the concept of ILEs on several fronts. For example, I-PULL intelligent interfaces will be off-the-shelf platforms that can be trained to work closely with an individual user/learner. Initially, an intelligent interface will gather information about an individual's learning style and information processing strengths and weaknesses based on the results of an extensive questionnaire coupled with the results from a series of preprogrammed learning assessment exercises. As individuals interact with the software tools to locate, store, and use information for ongoing work and leisure pursuits, the intelligent interface will provide suggestions on how to improve learning efficiency and effectiveness based on validated learning-to-learn principles and personal usage characteristics.

The following two examples provide a glimpse of adaptive learning environments that integrate what can be considered I-PULL functionality. Woods (2001) describes a math tutor system called the QUADRATIC tutor that uses scaffolding and contingent tutor design principles. These instructional design principles are based on research involving the amount and type of help that learners seek when they are provided tutoring assistance, to include self-regulation of time on task. For these researchers, one interesting and potentially useful instructional characterization that can be made comes from assessing the extent to which learners are likely to perform self-corrections and whether they refuse or overly rely on help (in his words, "help refusers" versus "help abusers"; see Woods, p. 285).

Another instructional system that includes adaptive elements that appear to support individual user needs through I-PULL type functionality is described by Weber and Brusilovsky (2001). Their instructional system, referred to as ELM-ART, is a Web-based adaptive interactive textbook. The authors suggest that the system provides intelligent adaptive functionality for the primary purpose of enhancing system versatility. Versatility, they contend, is a key instructional design characteristic because it offers the opportunity to collect information about a given learner's knowledge, preferences, and interests. In so doing, the system can provide more effective adaptive (and intelligent) tools for assisting learner performance when navigating within the instructional environment; for example, tools that help the learner choose what to learn next or what problem/assignment will promote knowledge transfer, when and how best to engage in a discussion forum, what hyperlinks to explore, or when to attempt a quiz or test. One important component of the ELM-ART system that helps promote versatility and thus adaptive intelligent functionality is its reliance on what is called collaborative student modeling. As described previously, ITS applications typically involve a "novice" model the system uses to determine the learner's current performance level. *Collaborative student modeling* refers to the ability of learners to inspect, and in some cases modify, their respective student (novice) model employed by the system at any given time. The system does, however, collect performance data in the form of time spent accessing one or more pages, embedded questions or problems answered correctly, quiz/test items answered correctly, and so on in order to validate the accuracy of the model.

Among the more valuable tools increasingly available to instructional designers are simulations and simulation games (Aldrich, 2004; Dempsey, Lucassen, Gilley, & Rasmussen, 1993; Jacobs & Dempsey, 1993). Simulations and simulation games may be used within both I-PUSH and I-PULL learning environments. A variety of simulation techniques, such as 2-D and 3-D modeling, role playing, video, and case studies, will increasingly be used to create realistic environments for developing and testing new ideas or practicing specific tasks and associated skill sets. Once created, simulation environments will be capable of being exported so others can use them for individual training or as part of a distributed simulation activity involving two or more participants. Intelligent computer-generated agents will also be included within the simulation environment to allow realistic collaborative interaction. Any Internet search will identify a number of companies offering instructional simulation-based products and services as well as several industry reports and articles suggesting that simulation tools are a rapidly growing niche within the instructional technology sector. Whenever artificial intelligence learning systems are discussed one question invariably materializes: When will AI systems truly demonstrate humanlike "intelligence" in the form of learning (i.e., the ability to change behavior based on past experience) and flexible problem solving? It is our belief these momentous achievements will occur at a modest level within the next decade due to developments in related fields. First, AI researchers have used a variety of cognitive modeling approaches that more closely mimic the functioning of human information processing to investigate such critical performance issues as situational awareness, decision making, and knowledge acquisition (Pew & Mavor, 1998). Second, recent advances in parallel processing offer a possible breakthrough in raw computing power, which has impeded the ability of AI researchers to write programs performing relatively simple cognitive tasks (e.g., object recognition) under real-time constraints. In addition, there are alternative technologies offering great promise. One such technology is field-programmable gate array (FPGA), a relatively new type of integrated circuit that can be thought of as intelligent hardware (Faggin, 1999). Using FPGA, future computing systems can not only be the size of the current microchip, they can have inherent hardware architectures incorporating properties currently found only in biological neural networks. Learning systems using FPGA technology may be capable of displaying such key intelligent functions as real-time learning and self-repairing. When used in combination with increasingly sophisticated and powerful cognitive processing software approaches, these hardware advances will usher in the beginning of a revolutionary era in intelligent computing that will greatly influence the field of instructional systems.

Cognitive Science and Neuroscience Contributions

Advances in the related fields of cognitive science and neuroscience have been based, in part, on the ability of researchers to monitor electrochemical activity within the brain and to more accurately match brain structure and associated neural activity to overt actions, such as psychomotor behavior, recall of information, and decision making (Davidson & Irwin, 1999; Tononi, Edelman, & Sporns, 1998). Technology improvements in this area, for example, combining standard imaging techniques such as positron emission tomography (PET) with other promising magnetoencephalography (MEG) or magnetic-source magnetic resonance imaging (msMRI) methods, continue to enhance the level of precision with which neural activity can be monitored. Innovations in this area will likely include the ability to influence brain activities affecting learning, and these innovations will be incorporated into advanced instructional systems. One promising technique, called transcranial magnetic stimulation (TMS), is being used as both a "brain mapping" tool, as well as a potential therapy (Hallett, 2000). Brain mapping tools such as these will open up a new vista for instructional technology research that will have direct application to the design of instructional systems. For example, researchers are studying brain regions that appear to give rise to memory and retrieval processes (Buckner & Wheeler, 2001; Simons & Spiers, 2003), thereby making it possible to monitor the level of knowledge acquisition and retention by measuring the relative amount of brain activity as well as the specific neural pathways being activated. This may even give rise to a new class of learning objectives that describe this unique learning activity, for instance, "The learner will demonstrate understanding of the concept of 'network interoperability' by exhibiting neural activity in .04% of his or her superior temporal gyrus mass and by exhibiting cross-modal activation starting in the temporal lobe and moving to the prefrontal lobe."

In the area of interdependent learning, where two or more individuals must collaborate their efforts to enhance team or group performance, much has been written about the need for establishing a shared mental model across team members (Stout, Cannon-Bowers, Salas, & Milanovich, 1999). By monitoring the timing and extent of neural activities across the various team members, it may be possible to determine what activities enhance team collaboration, cohesiveness, and overall performance effectiveness.

What if a learner is having difficulty assimilating new information? Can a gentle electrical impulse focused on a specific brain region spur acquisition and recall of to-be-learned information? If a learner is temporarily unable to focus on the task at hand or is experiencing a more general sense of low motivation, can focused neural stimulation assist the learner to refocus her attention or generate a more general sense of purpose and self-efficacy? These questions focus attention on much bigger issues that need to be addressed as research in this area expands. Indeed, researchers are actively studying neurobiological activities related to reward and expected reward (Jones, 2003; Schultz, 2000). Certainly, as one crosses the line between passive monitoring of neural activities into active manipulation of these activities, there is the need to pay heed to ethical and legal issues related to free will and mind control.

For researchers and practitioners in the area of instructional technology, monitoring neural activity associated with learning is intriguing because of the opportunity for obtaining direct feedback related to mental processes. Tracking internal activities at the neural level is important, but provides only a partial solution for advancing the field of instructional technology. Another important component involves the ability to track learner performance and provide effective feedback. The following section discusses advances in these two key areas.

Advanced Performance Tracking

Imagine your goal is to improve your serve in tennis. Now imagine slipping into a tight-fitting leotard-type outfit that fully covers your body from head to foot. This "body glove" incorporates an intricate electrical grid that transmits precise body position and relative movement information to a personal computer (PC) located several feet away.

The PC has attached to it a large, flat panel display system that visually simulates your movements in real-time using a realistic 3-D model that matches your body type, weight, and so on. You begin practicing your serve. After three or four tries, the system provides a verbal and visual (using the flat panel display) critique of key elements that make up an effective serve, such as initial stance, ball toss, and arm and racket motion. Your 3-D image is superimposed on an ideal image modeled after a highly proficient service motion of someone your age and with your ability level. The program then provides you with verbal and visual instructions on each service element individually, and then gradually combines two or more elements until you are now practicing the entire serve as one fluid motion.

After several much-improved practice serves, you check your progress on the computer by reviewing your three most recent service motions superimposed on the ideal image. In addition, you request an analysis and progress report from the program. Alas, your forward arm motion and wrist snap just prior to striking the ball needs additional work because it produces a slower-than-expected serve that has too much side spin. After several more attempts at self-correction (with verbal and visual prompts and feedback generated by the program), you decide you need more direct help. You now slip your arm into a device that looks like a long glove that reaches to your shoulder. This device is slightly thicker than your body glove performance tracking system and has embedded into it what the manufacturer refers to as "microhydraulic capabilities." Responding to the verbal directions from the program, you set your body position to a point where your forward arm motion is to begin. You now feel a warm sensation in your arm, wrist, and hand as the microhydraulic arm gently shows you the correct arm and wrist motion. During the next 20 or so practice swings you feel less and less influence from the microhydraulic device and, in fact, the program confirms that your muscle memory has now been altered slightly to incorporate the newly corrected arm motion and wrist snap. This result is confirmed by the program's analysis indicating key elements of your service motion more closely match that of the ideal model and your serve is now 5–10 miles per hour faster than before.

This example provides a vision of what an advanced performance tracking and feedback system can offer in the way of enhanced training processes and outcomes. Note also the system's ability to diagnose training needs prior to prescribing remedial training. Future instructional systems will have embedded in them the ability to conduct performance assessment at the whole-task or part-task level. Real-time body position and motion capture is now a reality. A search of "body tracking" on the Internet will produce numerous academic institutions and commercial enterprises actively involved in developing and marketing systems of this nature.

A Little Farther Down The Road: Cybernetics and Nanotechnology

For nine days in August 1998, Kevin Warwick, a professor of cybernetics at the University of Reading, U.K., wore a tiny capsule measuring 23mm by 3mm surgically implanted in his left arm. The capsule contained a power source and microprocessors. Warwick, an expert on intelligent buildings, programmed the implant to open doors, have his computer speak to him about his e-mail, run baths, and chill wine (Witt, 1999; Warwick, 2002). A number of authors consider activities like Warwick's either self-aggrandizing and idiotic (Horgan, 2005) or right on track (Kurtzweil, 1999). Although it may be a while before we can control computers directly from our nervous system (Brooks, 2002), it is something that even the middle-aged authors of this chapter are likely to see in their lifetime. Highly miniaturized, powerful computer implants will be available (at least for those who can afford it) and will likely be a more common elective operation than cosmetic surgery.

There are many implications of Professor Warwick's implant. For instructional designers, the question is an old one: Would a job aid be more practical or effective than an instructional program? Many well-known performance-technology authors (e.g., Mager & Pipe, 1970) have been asking that question for decades. If there is something too cumbersome to remember, why shouldn't we cart the knowledge as an external memory source, perhaps even one that can be inserted and removed as we now do with removable storage on a personal computer? Recall that 10 years ago the idea of 1GB of data on something the size of SD (secure digital) memory media was incredible! Just as Moore's Law, which originally stated that the amount of data storage that a microchip can hold doubles every 18 months (Raymond, 1994) is now outdated, looking at computer-based electronic performance support systems (EPSS) as static is unrealistic. We will learn more and more, yes. But we will also carry our knowledge with us. Although less invasive "wearable technology" will be more commonplace than implants, humans and technology will interact in ways that we are just beginning to envision.

Just as H. G. Wells was a leading visionary for many of the inventions that took place in the mid twentieth century, Neal Stephenson (1992, 1995) is emerging as a prophet for the future of learning technologies. Stephenson's novels contain many plausible future technologies that impact learning. In 1995's *The Diamond Age, or a Young Lady's Illustrated Primer,* for example, hundreds of new technologies are made available through nanotechnology, based on the manipulation of individual atoms and molecules to build structures to complex, atomic specifications (Drexler, 1986). In Stephenson's future, the age of "could" be done is replaced with the age of what "should" be done much more so than the twentieth century when, at times, we had initiated irreversible error. Regardless of how we attain them, we will unquestionably have available to us many new technology-generated tools in the very near future. For instance, in *The Diamond Age*, the "primer" from which the protagonist learns is made of "smart paper," which is very thin sheets consisting of infinitesimal computers sandwiched between "mediatrons" that project necessary images. Far into the future? Not necessarily; Xerox Parc and MIT, for example, have independently developed commercially viable electronic paper technologies that are lightweight and as flexible as newsprint. This electronic paper stores images viewable in reflective light, has a wide viewing angle, is relatively inexpensive, and is electrically writable and erasable. Like many of the newer innovations, electronic paper is fast on its way to becoming a commonplace fact of life.

Distributed Cognition and Instructional Design

The last decade has brought some dissatisfaction and, in certain cases, caustic criticism of the traditional ADDIE (analyze–design–develop–implement–evaluate) approach to instructional design (e.g., Gordon & Zemke, 2000). These critics charge that ISD is too slow and clumsy to meet today's challenges and (ironically) is too process driven, especially for use by less experienced designers who look at the instructional design models more linearly. Related criticisms contend that ISD is not a real "science." Although, as with most arguments, there are contrasting views (e.g., Merrill, Drake, & Pratt, 1996), these criticisms attract notice to the changing nature of instructional design. The exciting developments in learning technologies that we have discussed will no doubt shape the way future instructional programs are developed and implemented. Even so, advanced technology applications will not make up for a lack of sound instructional theory and educated instructional design professionals.

What is needed in our view are instructional design strategies and research aimed at identifying how best to implement emerging instructional technologies so that they increase learning outcomes while ensuring individual privacy and promoting the highest possible ethical standards. We are not advocating letting the technology drive the instructional design process. Rather, to aid learners in their attempts to "construct" meaning from information/knowledge, instructional designers will rely more and more on emerging educational technology. This not-so-subtle shift toward a learner-centered instructional environment will, in our view, usher in a new instructional systems paradigm that has an increased emphasis on developing new technology-based tools for aiding learning processes.

Much of what we have discussed in this chapter has been centered in instructional technologies that we believe to be viable in the foreseeable future. Many of these technologies employ what Salomon (1996) and others refer to as distributed cognition. In essence, *distributed cognition* recognizes that a person solves a problem or performs a task with the aid of other resources. The knowledge brought to bear on the task is distributed among the individual and other resources (e.g., computers or other people). Perkins (1996) refers to this as "person-plus." The theory of distributed cognition hypothesizes that information is processed between individuals and the tools and artifacts provided by the environment or culture. A primary force causing us to move toward distributed cognition is the limitation of the individual, unaided human mind. Professionals in most fields have jobs that are increasingly more complex, more specialized, and that require access to exponentially increasing domain knowledge. Distributed cognition is a compelling response to this limitation (Norman, 1988).

During the next few years, we will see the accelerated effect of distributed cognition affecting both learning and the field of instructional design. Distributed cognition and efficacious instructional design approaches (and cybernetics, for that matter) are all about humans and technology interacting as complementary infrastructures. Things (often sophisticated computer technologies) that can store, retrieve, and analyze information are becoming an integral part of our learning opportunities. Humans (teachers, coaches, other specialized professionals) have shared understandings and experiences that are unavailable in things. Even in the near future, instructional design certainly must become more facilitative in creating environments in which learners interact smoothly with these two infrastructures. The traditional instructional systems approach that seeks to engineer learning through a more or less linear approach is giving way to a new instructional paradigm that places a premium on learner control and the emergence of educational technologies that facilitate the learner's ability to construct meaning out of a rich pool of available information.

Summing Up

An acquaintance of ours shared a story of a vacation trip that she took with her young daughter to an historical settlement such as Williamsburg, Virginia, or Plymouth, Massachusetts, where past technologies are actively recreated. The mother spent the day explaining to the child the different functions of the various tools and furnishings within the aged buildings. We imagine the conversation went something like this:

"What's this place, Mother?"

"Well, this is a bakery, dear. Where they made bread."

Entering another building, the girl asked, "What did they do here, Mother?"

"Well here is where they used this big spinning wheel to make clothes."

Their tour progressed in a similar fashion until they came to a place where the technology seemed very familiar to the suddenly excited child. "I know what this is, Mother," she cried out with absolute assurance. "This is a school! It's set up just like my classroom!"

As the story suggests, education (and training) has for years been the most conservative of fields. Our use of technology has largely been pedestrian, isolated, and uninspired. In this chapter we discussed learning tools and technologies that we believe are likely to make a conspicuous impact. At least two implicit themes emerge. First, it is clear that learning in many environments will take place in much different ways in the future than it has in the past. Research is sorely needed in the effective use of these new technologies of learning.

Second, the accelerated rate of technological change is forcing instructional design, comfortable in its traditional models, to move to address these astounding changes. Our impact as a professional field will increasingly be linked with our ability to do so.

Application Questions

1. Using the example from the chapter as a model, write a new learning objective that would reflect the possible influence cognitive science research, such as brain mapping, might have on the instructional design process. Compare your response to others in your learning group.
2. Describe how nanotechnology could be used to improve a specific job or task with which you are familiar.
3. Working with a group, brainstorm ways that education and training are likely to change in the next 30 years. List these changes. Next to each change, list the impact that change could have on the processes of learning.

References

Aldrich, C. (2004). *Simulations and the future of learning: An innovative (and perhaps revolutionary) approach to e-learning.* San Francisco: Jossey-Bass Pfeiffer.

Brooks, R. A. (2002). *Flesh and machines: How robots will change us.* New York: Pantheon.

Buckner, R. L., & Wheeler, M. E. (2001). The cognitive neuroscience of remembering. *Nature Reviews Neuroscience*, *2*(9), 624–634.

Davidson, R. J., & Irwin, W. (1999). The functional neuroanatomy of emotion and affective style. *Trends in Cognitive Sciences*, *3*(1), 11–21.

Dempsey, J. V., Lucassen, B., Gilley, W., & Rasmussen, K. (1993). Since Malone's theory of intrinsically motivating instruction: What's the score in gaming literature? *Journal of Educational Technology Systems, 22*(2), 173–183.

Drexler, K. E. (1986). *Engines of creation.* New York: Doubleday.

Faggin, F. (1999, October). Hardware/SoftWhere? *Forbes ASAP*, 61–62.

Gardner, H. (1985). *The mind's new science: A history of the cognitive revolution.* New York: Basic Books.

Gordon, J., & Zemke, R. (2000, April). The attack on ISD. *Training*, *47*, 42–53.

Graves, W. H. (1994). Toward a national learning infrastructure. *Educom Review*, *29*(2) (Electronic version). Retrieved April 26, 2005, from **http://www.educause.edu/pub/er/review/reviewArticles/29232.html**

Hallett, M. (2000). Transcranial magnetic stimulation and the human brain. *Nature*, 406, 147–150.

Hays, R. T., Jacobs, J. W., Prince, C., & Salas, E. (1992). Requirements for future research in flight simulation training: Guidance based on a meta-analytic review. *International Journal of Aviation Psychology*, *2*(2), 143–158.

Horgan, J. (2005). Brain chips and other dreams of the cyber-Evange lists. *Chronicle of Higher Education, 51*(39), B12.

Hsu, W. H., Welge, M., Redman, T., & Clutter, D. (2002). High performance commercial data mining:

A multistrategy machine learning application. *Data Mining and Discovery*, *6*(4), 361–391. Retrieved January 30, 2004, from **http://www.kluweronline.com/issn/1384–5810/current**

Institute of Electrical and Electronics Engineers. (2002). *Draft Standard for learning object metadata*. Piscataway, NJ: IEEE.

Jacobs, J. W., & Dempsey, J. V. (1993). Simulation and gaming: Fidelity, feedback, and motivation. In J. V. Dempsey & G. Sales (Eds.), *Interactive instruction and feedback*, (pp. 197–227). New York: Educational Technology Publications.

Johnston, R. (1995). The effectiveness of instructional technology: A review of research. *Proceedings of the Virtual Reality in Medicine Developer's Exposition, Cambridge, MA* (n.p.). Retrieved January 30, 2004, from **http://www.vetl.uh.edu/surgery/effect.html**

Jones, R. (2003). Neurobiology of reward: Gambling on dopamine. *Nature Reviews Neuroscience*, *4*(5), 332.

Kim, W., Choi, B., Hong, E., Kim, S., & Lee, D. (2003). Taxonomy of dirty data. *Data Mining and Discovery*, *7*(1), 81–99. Retrieved April 26, 2005, from **http://www.kluweronline.com/issn/1384–5810/current**

Kurtzweil, R. (1999). *The age of spiritual machines*. New York: Viking.

Liane, G. (2002). Cognitive mechanisms underlying the creative process. In H. Thomas & T. Kavanagh (Eds.), *Proceedings of the Fourth International Conference on Creativity and Cognition* (pp. 126–133). Loughborough, UK, Loughborough University. Retrieved April 26, 2005, from **http://cogprints.ecs.soton.ac.uk/archive/00002546/01/CandC.htm**

Macedo, M., Cook, D., Brown, T. J. (2000). Visual data mining in atmospheric science data. *Data Mining and Discovery*, *4*(1), 69–80. Retrieved April 26, 2005, from **http://www.kluweronline.com/issn/1384-5810/current**

Mager, R. F., & Pipe, P. (1970). *Analyzing performance problems, or, You really oughta wanna*. Belmont, CA: Fearon.

McArthur, D., Lewis, M., & Bishay, M. (1993, November). *The roles of artificial intelligence in education: Current progress and future prospects*. Santa Monica, CA: Rand Corporation (MDR-8751515 & MDR-9055573). Retrieved January 30, 2005, from **http://www.rand.org/hot/mcarthur/Papers/role.html**

Merrill, M. D., Drake, M. J., Pratt, J. (1996). Reclaiming instructional design. *Educational Technology*, *36*(5), 5–7.

Merrill, D. C., Reiser, B. J., Ranney, M., & Tafton, J. G. (1992). Effective tutoring techniques: A comparison of human tutors and intelligent tutoring systems. *Journal of the Learning Sciences 2*, 277–305.

Norman, D. A. (1988). *The psychology of everyday things*. New York: Basic Books.

Ohlsson, S. (1986). Some principles of intelligent tutoring. *Instructional Science, 14*(3–4), 293–326.

Perkins, D. N. (1996). Person-plus: A distributed view of thinking and learning. In G. Salomon (Ed.), *Distributed cognition: Psychological and educational considerations* (pp. 89–110). New York: Cambridge University Press.

Pew, R. W., & Mavor, A. S. (1998). *Modeling human and organizational behavior: Applications to military simulations. National Research Council, Panel on Modeling Human Behavior and Command Decision Making: Representations for military simulations*. Washington, DC: National Academy Press.

Raymond, E. S. (1994). *The new hacker's dictionary*. (2nd ed.). Cambridge, MA: MIT Press.

Salomon, G. (1996*). Distributed cognition: Psychological and educational considerations*. New York: Cambridge University Press.

Schultz, W. (2000). Multiple reward signals in the brain. *Nature Reviews Neuroscience*, *1*(3), 199–207.

Simons, J. S., & Spiers, H. J. (2003). Prefrontal and medial temporal lobe interactions in long-term memory. *Nature Reviews Neuroscience*, *4*(8), 637–648.

Stephenson, N. (1992). *Snow crash*. New York: Bantam.

Stephenson, N. (1995). *The diamond age, or a young lady's illustrated primer*. New York: Bantam.

Stout, R. J., Cannon-Bowers, J. A., Salas, E., & Milanovich, D. M. (1999). Planning, shared mental models, and coordinated performance: An empirical link is established. *Human Factors*, *41*(1), 61–71.

Tononi, G., Edelman, G. M., & Sporns, O. (1998). Complexity and coherency: Integrating information in the brain. *Trends in Cognitive Sciences*, *2*(12), 474–484.

U.S. Department of Defense. (1999). *Strategic plan for advanced distributed learning*. Report to the 106th Congress by the Office of the Under Secretary of Defense for Personnel and Readiness. Retrieved January 30, 2004, from **http://www.maxwell.af.mil/au/afiadl/plans&policy/pdfs/dodstratplan.pdf**

Van Dorn, J. D., & Gazzaniga, M. S. (2002). Databasing FMRI studies: Towards a "discovery science" of brain function. *Nature Reviews Neuroscience, 3*(4), 314–318.

Wagner, E. D. (2002). The new frontier of learning object design. *The eLearning Developers Journal.* Retrieved January 30, 2005, from **http://student.philau.edu/GREEN3/mc76/learning%20object%20design.pdf**

Warwick, K. (2002). *I Cyborg*. Urbana, IL: University of Illinois Press.

Weber, G., & Brusilovsky, P. (2001). ELM-ART: An adaptive versatile system for Web-based instruction. *International Journal of Artificial Intelligence* [Special Issue], *Education, 12,* 310–324.

Williams, A. B. (2004). Learning to share meaning in a multi-agent system. *Data Mining and Discovery*, 8(2), 165–193. Retrieved April 26, 2005, from **http://www.kluweronline.com/issn/1384–5810/current**

Wisher, R. A. (2003, April–May). Reaching out after 5 years: Advanced distributed learning moves beyond developing standards. *Training & Simulation Journal*, 12–13.

Witt, S. (1999). *Is human chip implant wave of the future?* Retrieved April 26, 2005, from **http://cnn.com/TECH/computing/9901/14/chipman.idg/index.html**

Woods, D. (2001). Scaffolding, contingent tutoring and computer-supported learning. *International Journal of Artificial Intelligence in Education, 12,* 280–292.

Zachary, W., Ryder, J., Santarelli, T., & Weiland, M. Z. (2000). *Applications for executable cognitive modes: A case-study approach.* Paper presented at the International Ergonomics Association, 14th Triennial Congress and Human Factors and Ergonomics Society 44th Annual Meeting, San Diego, CA. Retrieved April 26, 2005, from **http://www.manningaffordability.com/s&tweb/PUBS/AppsExecCognModels/AppsExecCognModels.pdf**

CHAPTER 32

The Future of Instructional Design (Point/Counterpoint)

M. David Merrill
Brigham Young University

Brent Wilson
University of Colorado at Denver

Editors' Introduction

This final chapter is a delightful and friendly debate between Dave Merrill and Brent Wilson. The authors were asked to present a "point/counterpoint" perspective on the future of instructional design and technology. In writing the chapter, each author separately presented his perspective on the future of our field. When these were complete, each separately responded to their counterpart's perspective and tried to indicate commonalities and as well as differences. This resulting chapter is an example of the diversity of perspectives and philosophical approaches we can expect among academics and parishioners in the field, now and in the future.

Knowledge and Comprehension Questions

1. In what ways do nonprofessional "designers-by-assignment" pose a threat for the IDT field? How do Merrill and Wilson each respond to this threat? How do their responses differ?
2. In the chapter, Merrill's conception of ID is described as "narrow" and Wilson's as "broad." What is narrow about Merrill's approach? What is broad about Wilson's?
3. According to Merrill, what advantage does experimental research hold as a method of inquiry in the field? According to Wilson, why should we encourage additional forms of inquiry?

The Proper Study of Instructional Design (M. David Merrill)

For almost four decades I have been associated with academic programs preparing instructional designers. During this time there have been numerous projects examining the field of instructional technology and attempting to define the "field." Each of these attempts has caused me to reflect on our activities and the students who graduate from our programs. On the 20th anniversary of the publication of *Educational Technology* magazine I asked, "Can the adjective instructional modify the noun science?" (Merrill, 1980). In this paper I suggested that students of instructional design should be involved in both science and technology. Science activities involve theory development and experimental research to substantiate the theory. Technology activities involve the development of design procedures, instructional development, and evaluation (field research). I advocated a science-based approach in which the development of actual instructional materials should be done by the use of principle-based procedures derived from theory that has been empirically verified via experimental research. It is my observation that my hope for a technology of instructional design grounded in empirically verified theory is still the exception rather than the rule. So after a quarter of a century I return to this theme.

Everyone is a teacher (designer) and they always will be.

In a dinner conversation with my brother-in-law, who was a nuclear physicist, I listened carefully and without interruption while he explained some complicated mathematical derivation that had to do with particles in the nucleus of an atom. After he finished I began to describe my own work in developing instructional design theory. He interrupted me to disagree with my ideas. I said, "Wait a minute, I didn't interrupt you when you were describing your theory." His response was very typical, "Yes, but everyone is a teacher."

And of course he is right. Everyone feels that they are a designer. Most of us have been in school for a good portion of our lives. We have witnessed hundreds of hours of instruction, good and bad. There is probably no other human professional activity shared by almost all members of civilized societies. Why shouldn't we feel that we know a good deal about teaching or about designing instruction?

I work at a university. The university certainly subscribes to the proposition that everyone is a teacher. When the university hires a chemistry professor do they ask about his teaching experience, the classes he has had in pedagogy, or the training he has experienced in instructional design? Of course not! If professionals have published in their field they obviously know how to teach and design their courses.

Industry subscribes to this proposition that everyone is a designer. When a company needs someone in the training department, where do they go? Usually to the folks who have knowledge about the content to be taught. Only rarely does a company seek a professionally trained instructional designer. Of course, with the rise of the Internet and e-learning, companies are seeking professional help in putting training online because their folks lack the technical skills required. But it is the technical skills they feel they need, not help with instructional design.

95% of all instructional design is done by designers-by-assignment.

Data shows that most instructional design is done by designers-by-assignment. This percentage is increasing as the number of instructional designers in key companies decreased by 27% in 2002 (American Society for Training & Development, 2003). Today you are an engineer but your company needs a course in their latest product, so tomorrow you are an instructional designer. You are assigned to be an instructional designer, you were not trained as an instructional designer. You are a designer-by-assignment.

If everyone is an instructional designer, what is the unique role for our students?

Most of our instructional design programs in higher education, especially at the master's level, are preparing instructional designers. But if everyone is a designer, what is the unique role for these students? If companies are actually decreasing the number of instructional designers on their staffs and increasing the number of designers-by-assignment, then what is the unique role for these students?

More and more application programs are appearing that make it easy for almost everyone to put up a website or create e-learning. Can companies afford to hire professional designers when it is so easy for designers-by-assignment to create technology-based learning materials?

Perhaps we are in the same situation that was true of computer science a couple of decades ago. I remember being on a committee to approve every computer that was purchased on campus. Now we can go to any of a number of discount retailers and purchase computers with many times the capability of the computers in those days. We had long discussions about computer literacy; now almost every college freshman owns their own computer and already knows how to use dozens of application programs.

Companies perceive those who know instructional technology as those who know how to *use* the technology. As the technology becomes easier to use and as the number of experienced computer users increases, companies are seeing less need to hire professional instructional technologists. Computer science as a field soon realized that almost everyone would soon be able to acquire the skills necessary to use application programs. They realized that their focus needed to change from training computer users to studying computing. Computer scientists began to create tools that would allow everyone to be a more effective computer user. Computer literacy as an issue went away. The focus shifted to more and more user-friendly computer applications.

Is instructional technology facing a similar situation? Do we need to acknowledge that instructional design is and will continue to be done by designers-by-assignment? Do we need to shift our focus from training instructional designers to the study of instruction? Do we need to shift our activities from training instructional designers to creating instructional design tools that allow everyone, designers-by-assignment, to be more effective designers of instruction? Instructional systems design (ISD) is being seriously challenged as an effective technology (Gordon & Zemke, 2000). Most training is being created without using a systematic process. Many organizations do not see a need for professional instructional designers. If organizations are decreasing the number of instructional designers in their organizations and if the tools for creating e-learning are easier and easier to use, then is the primary role of instructional technology as a field to train instructional designers? Will instructional technology as a field survive if we continue to see this as our primary role? And if training instructional designers is not our primary role, what is? To use Hodgins's (2004) analogy, ice delivery companies saw their mission as delivering ice, and even though they had sophisticated refrigeration equipment they failed to see their mission as keeping things cold and went out of business when domestic refrigeration replaced iceboxes. What is the mission of instructional technology? If it is not training instructional designers, then what is it?

Most college-trained instructional designers become managers who train and direct the work of designers-by-assignment.

If you obtain a masters degree in instructional technology and go to work in the training department or business university of a large company, what is your role most likely to be? It most likely won't be developing instruction. It is far more likely, because of your education, that you will be a training manager. What does a training manager do? You are likely to hire designers-by-assignment to actually develop the training products your company will use. Is learning how to develop courses sufficient to be a training manager? Will you be equipped with the management skills you will need? Will you have had experience in helping subject matter experts (SMEs) develop instruction themselves? Will you have tools and materials designed to assist you in training your designers-by-assignment to create the necessary training materials for your company? The answer to all of these questions, if you graduated from one of the many instructional technology master's degree or Ph.D. programs in the United States, is most likely no. Your time in school concentrated on learning to design instruction. Your time on the job will most likely be spent in management and in training *others* to design instruction.

Unfortunately, many instructional products currently designed for corporate America fall far short of their potential. They are inefficient and often ineffective. Many of these products just plain don't teach. Of what use is a training course that fails to help the learners acquire the desired knowledge and skills? Many of our students suffer significant frustration when they realize that the products produced by their training department, especially if they are in charge, fall far short of the quality instruction they learned to design in school. How can you be better equipped to assist lay designers to create more effective and efficient training products? What is the proper study of instructional design?

The Proper Study of Instructional Design

Figure 32.1 suggests that the discipline of instructional design involves both science and technology. *Science* is the pursuit of understanding; *technology* is the creation of

SCIENCE		TECHNOLOGY		
RESEARCH	THEORY	TOOLS	DEVELOPMENT	EVALUATION
Experimental Research	Outcomes	Technology-Based Tools	Instructional Products	Field Research
	Concepts			
Product or Research Review		Conceptual Tools		
	Propositions, models, theories			

FIGURE 32.1 The science and technology of instructional design.

artifacts. The goal of science is knowledge about the physical world. Scientists are interested in understanding and predicting. The goal of the engineer or designer is the design of useful artifacts and predicting the performance of the products they design (Vincenti, 1990).

The science of instructional design involves both theory and research. *Theory* is about describing phenomena and predicting (hypotheses) consequences from given conditions. *Research* is applying appropriate methodology to test these predictions. Instructional design theory is about understanding what conditions are necessary for a learner to acquire specific instructional goals, specific knowledge and skill, or specific learning outcomes. Research is the method by which these predictions are empirically tested and verified. A major role for instructional technology should be the study of instruction and instructional design. Instructional design theory involves the careful specification of the instructional conditions necessary for a student to acquire the desired learning outcomes. Instructional design research involves the application of empirical quantitative and qualitative research methods to test these predictions or prescriptions.

The technology of instructional design involves using empirically verified instructional design theory to develop instructional products designed to enable students to efficiently and effectively acquire desired instructional outcomes. Instructional products can be, and often are, designed without sufficient consideration of the applicable verified instructional design theory. Such an approach is not a technology of instructional design but the art of instructional design. Although an artistic approach sometimes results in effective and appealing instructional products, it is often not possible to understand why such products are effective and too often it is not possible to replicate the success of a given product in a subsequent product.

The technology of instruction involves three distinct activities. Since most instruction is developed by designers-by-assignment, rather than by technologists, it is necessary that the principles of effective and efficient instruction (instructional design theory) be captured in tools that provide intellectual leverage to designers who may not know the required instructional design theory. Most of our current tools provide this kind of leverage for the technology skills required such as computer programming, but fail to provide equivalent intellectual leverage for the required instructional design theory. These tools too often assume that everyone is a designer and that the difficult skills to provide within the tool are technical skills such as computer programming.

Having developed the necessary design tools, the remaining activities of a technology of instructional design are to demonstrate the use of these tools in designing and/or developing an instructional product. The final step is to predict the performance of this product and then test this performance in a trial with students from the target population. The instructional scientist attempts to discover and test principles for instruction.

The instructional technologist, using the principles discovered by the scientist, develops and tests conceptual tools (procedures) and technology-based tools (design systems) that can be used by instructional designers (either professional or lay) for the production of instructional products.

Theory

The central activity of any scientific approach always involves theory construction. Thus, any generalization constitutes a form of theory, and any investigation requires some level of theory construction. Instructional design theory is prescriptive theory rather than descriptive theory. That is, the theory identifies instructional conditions required for particular instructional consequences or outcomes. We say that instructional design theory is goal driven. The instructional consequences or learning outcomes constitute the goal. The theory then specifies learning conditions thought necessary for learners to be able to acquire the learning goal in an efficient and effective manner.

It is important to distinguish learning outcomes from instructional outcomes. Learning always occurs. Human beings learn from every situation. Instructional goals are attained when the learning outcomes correspond with the specified instructional outcomes or instructional objectives.

How does instructional design theory arise? What is required to specify an instructional design theory?

"The cutting edge of science is reductionism, the breaking apart of nature into its natural components" (E. O. Wilson, 1998, p. 54). But what are these natural components? Where do these natural components come from? All science begins with the invention of concepts, that is, the operational definition of what in the real world will be observed. How does a scientist determine what to observe? Usually by paying careful attention in a qualitative way to the phenomenon under consideration. For instructional design theory the instructional design scientist observes many instructional and teaching situations. The scientist tries to abstract from these situations those events, those conditions that seem to be present when learning of a particular kind occurs. The scientist then carefully defines the event or characteristic of the teaching situation believed to contribute to the learning performance. The scientist quantifies this condition using some appropriate metric as simple as present or absent or as complex as numerical amounts on a ratio scale of measurement.

The next step in science is to enter the defined concept (condition) into a proposition, an if-then statement. *If* a given amount of some condition is present *then* there will be a corresponding improvement in the learning that occurs. This set of propositions constitutes an instructional design theory.

Often the instructional design theory is linked to an underlying learning theory. The learning theory explains why the predicted relationship may occur. It should be noted that the instructional design theory is the set of if-condition then-consequence prescriptions. The learning theory is a linking of these conditions to underlying learning constructs that explain why a given instructional proposition or set of propositions results in more efficient or effective learning.

An effective instructional design theory also specifies the relationships among the propositions of the theory so that the theory is not merely a set of conditions that stand in isolation but rather a set of interrelated principles that act together to produce the desired learning outcome or consequence.

Why are there so many different instructional design theories?

The answer lies in the nature of science. Different investigators may not feel that the concepts previously defined are the right things to observe. Or, they may feel that the terminology used to identify a given event or condition is not sufficiently descriptive so they use a different term. Instructional design theory is sufficiently immature that there has not yet been a general agreement on the conditions that have been found to be most useful nor has there been a general agreement on the terminology used to identify these instructional events or conditions. There have been several attempts at providing definitions of terminology in the field but to date the majority of the field has generally accepted none of these. Eventually, as more theory is defined and more research conducted to verify this theory, there will be a gradual coming together of the accepted terms and conditions that are thought to be important. The author has attempted to provide one such synthesis in an earlier chapter in this volume (see, Chapter 7).

Instructional Design Research

Instructional design research is the testing of the instructional design prescriptions (if-conditions then-consequence or learning outcome) in a carefully controlled situation where the logic of the methodology allows one to attribute a given consequence to the conditions manipulated in the instruction rather than to some other causes.

Effective instructional design research also comprises two distinct activities: first, finding out what has already been done; and second, conducting original investigations. It is often a challenge to find existing research investigations of a given instructional prescription because of the variety of vocabulary that is used in the field. One major activity of students of instructional design should be careful research. Another approach to research review is product review. A careful study of instructional products that have been evaluated can also provide useful data for the conditions or strategies involved in these products.

This chapter is not the place to provide a detailed description of empirical research. Most academic programs provide several courses in statistical analysis and research design. Nevertheless, there is a paucity of research conducted in instructional design. Too often instructional technologists are distracted by the plethora of new applications that constantly flood the market. Many instructional technologists find that their fascination with the technology overrides their discipline in conducting carefully designed research studies. There is also disenchantment with the slow progress of empirical research. This impatience has too often led to the abandonment of careful empirical investigations. Surveys, case studies, ethnographic studies, and other qualitative approaches all have their place but are not a sufficient substitute for carefully conceived and conducted empirical investigations. Far too much of the instructional theory available has not received sufficient empirical verification. If you cannot find empirical verification for the instructional prescriptions, then they deserve your careful attention and should be submitted to such verification.

Effective instructional design research starts with a prescription that if certain conditions (strategies) are present then certain learning outcomes will be achieved. There are many research studies that do not provide the required data and are of questionable value in the verification of instructional design theory. Several notable types of research that are unlikely to yield useful findings are technology-use surveys, media comparisons, when-to-teach (e.g., synchronous vs. asynchronous), and where-to-teach (e.g., classroom vs. e-learning vs. blended).

We continue to see dissertations that conduct surveys about the use of technology. How many classrooms have computers? How many computers are in each classroom? How many companies have e-learning? What percent of their training is e-learning versus instructor led? The answers to these questions may be useful for management purposes but do little to verify instructional design theory or to direct the creation of instructional artifacts that really teach.

Media comparisons are equally without value to answer these questions. Clark suggests that the delivery system is merely the truck, but it is what's on the truck that counts (Clark, 1983, 1994a, 1994b; Kozma, 1991, 1994). Choice of delivery system is a matter of economics and convenience, not a matter of instructional effectiveness.

Effective instruction can be asynchronous or synchronous. It is the nature of the interaction with the materials, the type of practice provided, the kind of learner guidance and coaching available, the type of feedback provided that will contribute to effective and efficient learning far more than whether the instructor is online in real time. Effective instruction can be conducted in a classroom and over the Internet. It is the effectiveness, the use of verified instructional theory, that will determine the effectiveness of the instruction, not the environment where it is delivered. The proper study of instructional design would leave these questions of convenience to others and concentrate research efforts on the verification of instructional theory that can be used to guide the development of effective and efficient instructional products that work.

There are a large number of instructional design theory questions that still do not have sufficient research support. The proper study of instructional design would investigate some of these questions. The two primary questions for instructional design are (1) what to teach and (2) how to teach. There are still unresolved questions about knowledge (subject matter content) selection. From all there is to teach, what should be included and what should be excluded from the instruction? Considering knowledge sequence, what should be taught first? What second? Does order matter? From the viewpoint of knowledge organization, how should the content be structured? What kinds of structure should we provide to students to help them internally organize new knowledge? In terms of knowledge segmentation, what is a knowledge object? How should knowledge objects be combined?

There are an equally large number of unresolved questions about how to teach. These questions involve effective demonstration for different types of learning, for whole tasks, for unstructured tasks; effective practice for different types of learning, for whole tasks, for unstructured tasks; effective guidance during demonstration; effective coaching during application; how to effectively activate prior learning; how to integrate the learning with subsequent activities in the students' real world; how to effectively use media. We have some answers to some of these questions, but there remain many unresolved issues.

The proper study of instructional design would get students involved in multiple research studies on these and related issues about effective and efficient instructional conditions.

Instructional Design Tools

Designers-by-assignment seldom read the research and theory literature. Formulating and verifying effective design theory is merely an academic exercise unless this theory is transformed into tools that provide intellectual leverage. In a previous paper the author (Merrill, 1997) described several levels of ID tools including information containers, authoring systems, templates and widgets, learning-oriented tools, and adaptive learning-oriented tools. To date most of the ID tools available fall into the first three categories. Information containers merely enable the presentation of information and media but usually enable only the most rudimentary of instructional functions. Unfortunately, most authoring systems have concentrated on making programming skills easier but have failed to provide sufficient support for important instructional design decisions. The inclusion of templates, widgets, and other preprogrammed instructional algorithms is structure oriented rather than learning oriented; that is, the focus is on how the interaction works not on what learning outcome the interaction enables.

What are needed are learning-oriented tools, tools that have built-in instructional strategies that are based on scientifically verified principles of instruction; tools that enable designers-by-assignment to not only easily use the technology but that provide them with extensive guidance in effective instructional design or provide them with verified, effective, predesigned instructional strategies.

Who should do what in the proper study of instructional design?

Designers-by-Assignment. How would the availability of learning-oriented instructional design tools facilitate the work of designers-by-assignment? How would their role differ? We suggest that rather than a haphazard or artistic approach, the effectiveness of the resulting instructional products would be dramatically improved if these folks were provided and taught to use learning-oriented design tools. These tools should also provide guidance, templates, and prebuilt strategies that would allow comparison of existing products, data assessing usability, and most importantly, data assessing student learning and performance. The training role of our graduates would be to provide training in the use of these learning-oriented tools and to monitor and quality control the resulting products.

Master's Degree Students in Instructional Design. For starters, we should significantly increase the amount of project management provided to our master's degree students in instructional technology. In addition, they should still learn to use existing theory and research to design instruction. But the emphasis should shift from our students as designers to our students as trainers of designers-by-assignment. As learning-oriented instructional design tools become available they should have experience first in using these tools but more importantly in helping novice designers to use these tools. The emphasis for our students should move to a detailed study of empirically verified theory and a challenge to develop technology-based or conceptual learning-oriented ID tools that they can use to help train the designers they will encounter in their organizations.

Ph.D. and Specialist Students in Instructional Design. What constitutes a proper dissertation or project? In our institution too many projects consist of a single empirical study or survey. Is this an adequate scholarly contribution for a doctorate in instructional design? I suggest that a proper dissertation would consist of all five of the parts identified in this paper. Ph.D. students should first identify, modify, or develop instructional design theory. They should then do extensive product and research literature review related to the theory. In addition, students should conduct additional original empirical research related to their theory development. But is this adequate for a dissertation in our area? I would suggest that students should go further. They should then develop tools that implement the theory in a technology-based or conceptual learning-oriented instructional design tool designed for designers-by-assignment. They should demonstrate the use of these tools for the design of instruction preferably by training novices to use them. Finally, Ph.D. students should evaluate or supervise the evaluation of the instructional product developed by the use of the tool in a field setting. Dissertations would consist of a collection of reports: A theory paper, a product/research review paper, a report of one or more original empirical investigations, a technology-based or conceptual tool together with a user's manual, an instructional product developed using the tool, and an evaluation report of the effectiveness of the instructional product in a real-world setting.

Conclusion

Will instructional design as a field survive or will design continue to become so commonplace that everyone feels that there is no special skill required? Can we increase the quantity and quality of our empirically verified theory development? Can we develop empirically based, learning-oriented instructional design tools that will significantly improve the quality of the instructional products developed by designers-by-assignment? Can we transform our master's degrees from the training of instructional designers to the training of instructional design trainers and managers? What will happen if we fail to rise to this challenge? If we don't, will instructional design still be recognized as a field of study in the year 2025?

Choosing Our Future (Brent Wilson)

Recent years have seen significant growth in the field of instructional design and technology (IDT), but at the same time a loss of control over research and professional agendas. Everyone, it seems, is doing research and development related to technology and learning, across:

- Settings—K–12, higher education, work, home, entertainment.
- Players—IDT specialists, educational specialists, researchers in other fields, and untrained enthusiasts.

This surge of interest is indicated by the proliferation of professional organizations and journals devoted to the study of technology and learning.

Growth, even with the accompanying pains, is generally welcome because it provides energy, new ideas, and attention to innovations. Often, however, a snazzy new technology becomes the sole focus, not the ideas or innovative uses that lead to improved learning. After many hard lessons, we have learned this much wisdom in the field: Uses of technology must be considered within the context of learning effectiveness; otherwise, the technological innovation becomes a kind of fetish with near-magical powers of its own. And even learning outcomes need to fit within the values of a larger society.

In the midst of ongoing change, it can be difficult to gauge where we are now and where we are headed as a field of study and as a professional community. The purpose of this contribution is to reflect on possible futures for IDT, considering lessons from our history, current needs of practice, and trends inside and outside the field.

Historical Influences

Historically, instructional design grew out of educational psychology and became integrated with instructional technology (Dick, 1987; Reiser, 2001). Key to this merger between designers and technologists was a broad view of technology that included "soft" or process technologies such as procedures, models, and strategies intended to achieve defined educational outcomes. This allowed instructional designers who saw their efforts largely as an implementation of learning principles to bring their work into line with instructional technology, and use technology-based environments as laboratories for their designs. Today, many academic programs in IDT continue an affiliation with educational psychology programs within a college or school of education. It's good to have the focus on learning and the scientific grounding that educational psychology provides. Over a period of a generation, however, IDT has become more focused on training and adult-learning settings, with a greater concern for human performance in work environments. Some tension between K–12 and adult-learning orientations will likely continue into coming years, but a defining feature of IDT as a field has been its intentionally broad focus across learning settings.

Also over the past 10 years, the learning sciences have become an alternative to traditional IDT research agendas (see, e.g., the May–June 2004 issue of *Educational Technology*). The small but growing numbers of learning-sciences graduate programs are marked by:

- A stronger cognitive-science focus.
- More attention to prototype development of tools and online environments.
- More attention to basic theory and research.

Compared to the learning sciences, IDT programs give more attention to:

- Practitioner concerns of management, use, and diffusion.
- Design principles and practices.
- Alternative, nonpsychological bases for theory development.

In the eyes of many IDT leaders, learning sciences researchers enjoy higher status because of their closer access to fundamental cognitive science. This may be good or bad, depending on one's point of view. My preference is to value the diversity and practical focus of IDT and forego the sole dependence on psychology as a foundational discipline. In any case, the growth of learning sciences programs demonstrates the continuing core importance of educational psychology and learning theory principles to learning technologies.

Where We Stand Now

In many respects the IDT community now stands at a crossroads as we choose to respond to outside influences. Early-generation leaders such as Robert Gagné are gone, although some theorists continue as bridging figures, notably David Merrill and Don Ely. A number of threats to coherence in the field persist, briefly summarized in the following paragraphs.

Loss of control due to growth. The splintering of professional organizations and journals is part of a success story, but makes it difficult to track general trends and theory developments.

Encroachment from related fields. More researchers with roots in other fields are engaged in IDT-related work, obviously those from the learning sciences but also from any field with a stake in education and training.

Constantly evolving technologies. Emerging technologies, notably such blockbuster technologies as the Web, inevitably spawn devotees and new conceptual models, leading in turn to new clusters of specialization and community.

Setting-specific focus. Researchers interested in specific settings and populations (e.g., K–12 vs. corporate) typically set research agendas specific to those settings. Eventually this can lead to a pulling away from general principles of IDT.

Expanded concerns about human performance. Studies of informal learning and workplace performance have pushed the boundaries beyond instruction and opened the door to myriad relevant influences, from organizational development to ergonomics.

Competing paradigms. Education's fragmenting is mirrored within IDT, most clearly in the ideological split between IDT's "instructivist" and "constructivist" camps, sometimes exaggerated but recurring in different forms.

"Difficult" knowledge base. IDT knowledge is hard to capture into specific rules and theories. Education generally is the "hardest science" (Berliner, 2002) because the systems under study are so contingent and dynamic—the knowledge and skills required for effective practice tend to be extremely sensitive to local conditions. This is surely true for IDT professionals seeking to design and use learning technologies and resources.

Two Roads Diverging

I can imagine two responses to the many threats to the field. One would call for a focusing and sharpening of our ambitions, our beliefs, our accepted methods and practices. A second response would encourage a continued openness in ideology and method, while striving toward a set of common goals and ambitions. Trying to avoid a caricature (because I fully support the second response), the two responses or "roads" are summarized in Table 32.1. (Professor Merrill, as a noted advocate for the first road, can correct me if I'm wrong about this portrayal.)

Note that both roads share a common goal of understanding and supporting effective instruction and appropriate use of learning technologies. This level of common purpose is needed to maintain a level of coherence in both roads.

Either road carries some risk for the future. Intransigent insistence on a tightened view of the field, as illustrated in the Narrow Road, could lead to hardening of the arteries and, over time, an increasing irrelevance to problems of practice. Likewise a broadly tolerant, anything-goes future could weaken the center and reduce any specific advantage to belonging. The upside potential is also different for the

TABLE 32.1 **Two roads toward the future of instructional design and technology (IDT)**

	The Strait and Narrow Road*	The Broad and Inclusive Road
Goals	Designing and using technologies/ resources to improve learning and performance	Pretty much the same as Narrow Road
Core Models and Ideas	Such as: • ISD • learning theory • instructional theory • technology-mediated learning	Value a similar core as Narrow Road, but maintain flexibility and a commitment to pluralism in ideology and theory base Always be open to change in the canon and entry of new ideas and models
Source of New Ideas	Science (primarily educational psychology and the cognitive sciences) Original thinking on instructional problems Professional practice New technologies	Same items as Narrow Road, with greater attention to professional practice and: • Other sciences such as sociology and anthropology • Other professional practices (e.g., management, leadership, commerce, communications, information systems) • Humanities (e.g., philosophy, cultural studies, politics)
Methods of Inquiry	Established research methods, particularly experimental designs	Full range of reasoned inquiry, including: • Qualitative and quantitative methods • Design/developmental research • Action research • Documentation of best practices • Local and applied research (e.g., program evaluations; product evaluations; performance and needs assessments; usability studies; policy studies; cost-benefit and resource analyses; strategic planning; case descriptions of professional practice)
Methods of Sharing	Emphasis on established refereed outlets	Established refereed outlets plus: • Web-style self-publishing and sharing • Conference-style forums online and face to face • Water-cooler meetings and communities of practice
Methods of Work	Apply methods and technologies known to work through research and validation studies Validate local solutions via systematic tryout and revision	Plus: • Locally developed solutions, both quick and dirty and validated • Local methods reflecting a value consensus of workers, clients, and sponsors • Going beyond established rules with professional commitment and craftlike attention to detail
Language	Use precise language with technical, theoretical meanings	More fluid meanings: use technical and theoretical terms, but be open to multiple meanings, figurative uses, and new, ill-defined terms and descriptions
Membership	Tighten up the boundaries to ensure expertise Encourage strong credentialing, certification requirements	Maintain semiopen boundaries to encourage cross-field dialogue and provide a quality check on expertise
Risks	Resistance to positive change Increasing lack of fit with real problems of practice Lack of resilience to changing external conditions	Loss of core constructs needed to establish identity Inefficient, redundant overlap in agendas and models Lack of common metric for establishing value among competing descriptions Internal disputes that threaten coherence
Potential Benefit	Substantial progress on a narrower agenda	Good chance at finding innovations to adapt and move forward

*In fun I am continuing the biblical allusion begun by David Merrill and his colleagues in "Reclaiming Instructional Design," *Educational Technology, 36*(5), 1996, pp. 5–7.

two roads. The Narrow Road would likely lead to substantial progress in certain key areas such as development of automated design tools, effective procedures for replicable designs, and validated learning control for targeted objectives. These are extremely valuable outcomes and, in the case of tools particularly, could change the way we work. The Broad Road could also see progress along these same lines, but it would have to share the limelight with other advances. These are harder to forecast but could include improved methods of documenting and sharing practitioner expertise, assimilation of ideas and methods from related fields, and better attention to the learning needs of the whole person. The Broad Road would result in a more diverse array of research accomplishments and a similarly diverse set of tools and models useful in field settings.

Overall, I support efforts to define the field in fairly eclectic, inclusive terms. This may be partly because I so often find myself at the margins of conventional thinking, but the stance is not altogether self-serving. In general, open systems are able to adapt and survive better than closed systems. Out of this "free market" of ideas and methods, positive innovations are more likely to be noticed and nurtured, which will in turn assure our relevance in the future. In short, we need to be open, inclusive, and innovative, while at the same time grounded in core ideas and pursuits to preserve a common identity. There will always be some measure of discomfort—as well as belonging—within a professional community, but room should be made for a variety of perspectives and infusions of new ideas.

Foundations of a Broad-Road IDT

I have been arguing for a broader conception of an IDT knowledge base, but what exactly does that mean? This section outlines a sample of foundational ideas we can and should draw on when addressing challenging problems of practice. These foundational items are presented as a reminder of the breadth and extent of our current knowledge base.

Media studies. What impact do various media have on learning? What mechanisms and processes are at play? IDT includes a long tradition of comparing media, examining media literacy, critiquing media impact, and using media integration as a means of reforming teaching practices.

Systems thinking. Systems thinking is evidenced in a variety of ways. Instructional systems design (ISD) has long been a driving metaphor that has helped keep the field together. The underlying idea is that changes in instruction need to be carefully planned out and developed—and moreover, tested and validated through careful assessment of outcomes. The very process of instruction has been defined in terms of systemic interaction between teacher and learner subsystems (Merrill, 1968). Reigeluth (1995) and others have helped reveal the series of nested systems within which instruction happens. Complexity theory continues to contribute to our understanding of adoption and change processes and of networked learning communities.

Technical/efficiency stance toward curriculum development. Tyler's (1949) objectives-driven approach to curriculum design is known as a "technical" or "efficiency" way to think about curriculum (Kliebard, 1987). This curriculum stance is deeply entrenched in IDT thinking. ISD models are closely related to alignment principles among objectives, activities, and assessment; and to rational-planning models of problem solving and curriculum development. It feels somewhat strange to observe, after years of resistance, a resurgence of these ideas in American public education through the standards movement. Workplace environments are seeing similar attention to these principles through learning management systems (LMS), which aid in the tracking of learning goals, objectives, activities, and assessments.

Design thinking. Near the core of IDT is a prescriptive stance, a valuing of design principles to help solve learning and performance problems. Seeing practitioners as designers of solutions adds to this prescriptive stance with greater emphasis on stories and shared experiences over formal design models. A design stance also binds IDT to other professional areas such as architecture, computer- and information-systems design, and industrial design. These connections lead us to consider a broader set of variables in the design process, including emotional and motivational influences (Norman, 2004), and aesthetic principles for improving the immediate experience of instruction (Parrish, 2004, in press).

Appropriate use. Technology has ascended in prominence not just in education, but in nearly all endeavors. Philosophers and historians of technology urge caution and care in determining appropriate use. Careful analysis can reveal the various affordances and constraints that affect how people receive new tools and innovations. Systemic impacts of an intervention inevitably lead to unintended side effects (Tenner, 1997), suggesting a general stance of caution, humility, and vigilant attention to outcomes. Assessing the true outcomes, intended and unintended, requires designers to look beyond targeted objectives, beyond effectiveness, to consider the "goodness" or appropriateness of an intervention.

Learning theories. Theories of learning help us understand what's happening at a deeper, descriptive level when we look at instructional interactions. The variety of metaphors and theories available can provide insight into why instructional interventions are working the way they do. Learning theories range widely in scope, from information-based theories of content and structure to activity-based theories to those stressing qualitative cognitive change. An overview of the last 40 years will show a significant number of innovations in IDT coming directly from new developments in learning theory.

Tech-mediated instruction. The acronyms have evolved from CAI to CBT, to WBL to DL and e-learning, but the basic idea has remained fairly constant: using technology as a vehicle for delivering instruction. A substantial knowledge base has developed around these efforts, including research on feedback, learner control, lesson structure and sequencing, and interactivity within lessons.

Technology as a means of change and reform. Implementing technology can prompt people to take a fresh look at teaching practices. Technology has taken on increasing roles in all phases of instruction, from planning to delivery to assessment. Each point affords opportunities for deeper change in thinking and processes. Reform is what brought many people to an interest in learning technologies, and change processes go hand in hand with technology use.

Technologies for performance support. As mentioned, a variety of hard and soft technologies have been designed to help people perform their jobs better. These include models and theories about performance causes and interventions, as well as various support systems such as information-help systems, procedural support systems, incentive and tracking systems, and better designed work tools.

Looking Forward: Trends That Could Affect Our Future

Futurecasting is a notoriously unreliable enterprise, but the following trends are posed to grow in their impact on the field.

Gaming and virtual worlds. Computer games have been big business for more than 20 years, and a growing body of literature relates to game design and larger issues surrounding "new media theory" (MIT Press, 2004). Some of this work has already been applied to education (e.g., Aldrich, 2004; Gee, 2003), but much more could be done to apply gaming and simulation principles to instructional design. We face a great need for theory development and empirical research to validate the promising notions currently available in the literature.

Tools for e-learning design and development. A number of theories, including those of David Merrill, Jeroen van Merriënboer, Richard Mayer, and John Sweller, approach instruction from an information-processing perspective that considers optimal strategies for managing cognitive load and effectively teaching well-defined content such as rules, concepts, and procedures. Because these theories are themselves fairly rule based, they are promising candidates for conversion to automated tools that specialists and nonspecialists alike could use in designing lessons. One journal issue was devoted to instructional design tools (van Merriënboer & Martens, 2002), energized in particular by projects originating in the Netherlands. Successful development tools will apply sound instructional theories in a practically usable and accessible way. Although on ideological grounds, some constructivists may have concerns about these kinds of instructional strategies, I am very hopeful that research in this area will lead to powerful tools and substantial learning outcomes, which is the bottom line for instructional design.

Expanding role for assessment and alternative credentialing. Students build a case for a credential in three main ways: seat time, formal assessment, and informal field assessment. Anyone hoping to avoid seat time must find a valid, accurate assessment they can pass. In a market economy, more students (and employers) are choosing assessments as an alternative to seat time. This is only one reason why assessment is growing in importance. Another is to hold educational and training systems more accountable for the investment made in them. In a society that has found a way to measure almost everything of marketable value, education is one of the late responders to the call for accountability. In both education and training settings, the importance of assessment can be expected to grow, along with alternative methods for credentialing expertise.

Tools for data management and learning support. Computers are particularly good at keeping track of information and guiding the use of that information for real-time use in solving problems. Learning management systems (LMS) in corporate settings and K–12's increased use of data mining for data-driven decision making are indications that data surrounding learning and instruction will be more routinely available to learners, instructors, and managers.

Changing economies. Education tends to be a very labor intensive, expensive activity, with expert designers and teachers crafting and delivering courses over extended periods of time. Network and presentation technologies have led to renewed emphasis on resource-based learning (Hill & Hannafin, 2001). That is, more attention is given to resource development for e-learning than is true of a typical face-to-face course. Several trends affect the economies in emerging e-learning environments (cf. B. G. Wilson, 2002):

- *Incremental accumulation of resources.* Class members (including the instructor) devote time to developing resources that are then adopted by a next generation of learners.
- *Global exchange of services.* The instructor who is so knowledgeable and attentive of student needs may be working from India and making $7–10 per hour.
- *Disaggregation of product.* Offerings and services may be unbundled, with students paying for what they need and value; e.g., community networking, information access, assessment and diagnostics, credentialing. Individual markets may be identified with different pricing structures for different products.
- *Large-scale learning technologies.* Learners may lessen their dependence on the instructor through large-scale, self-sustaining learning forums inhabited by hundreds or thousands of learners (Wiley & Edwards, 2002).

Communities of practice. Learning happens to individuals, but everyone belongs to some kind of community, and those communities play a large role in shaping expectations for behavior. When instruction breaks down, people turn to support communities for help in filling learning gaps and adapting to performance requirements. Consider knowledge workers, such as engineers. Off-the-shelf training may be unavailable for a new technical standard or product specification. A working group may end up researching and sharing knowledge among themselves, in effect coopting the "instructional" role through their own self-directed and collaborative learning activities. Other times the same group may find a suitable course or tutorial and send a member off to master the material. In both cases, learning happens within the context of a support group, with members contributing and reporting back to the group. We have only begun to understand how individuals relate to various groups and communities, and how both individuals and communities make use of these learning resources, including formal instruction, to address individual and group learning needs.

Conclusion

IDT has successfully established a fairly broad knowledge base, with foundations in psychology and other sciences, cultural studies, and professional practice. Of course the knowledge base is in sore need of further development, but the foundation is there. IDT's challenge in coming years will be in maintaining strong, broad-based grounding for professional practice, with a focus on a select few cohering principles and purposes to keep the field together. To a large extent, we can choose the future we want for ourselves.

Judging Roots by Their Fruits: A Response to David Merrill (Brent Wilson)

To some extent both initial contributions, Merrill's and mine, reflect a concern about the knowledge base of instructional design and technology (IDT). The future of IDT depends on what it is we have to offer the world. The world is full of problems that need addressing—for learning guidance, for designing and improving instruction, for using technology to support teaching and learning processes. What really constitutes expertise in these areas, and where does it lie? I have emphasized the embodiment of expertise within the professional community—in its practices, its artifact and tools, and its professional standards and literature. Merrill has emphasized, I believe, the storehousing of expertise within the field's disciplinary methods, rules, and theory—and within the tools and technologies derived from these core constructs. The community and its conceptual tools are two sides of the same coin, of course, but they reflect ideological differences currently existing within the field.

Designer Roles and Needed Forms of Expertise

I found compelling Merrill's critique of design practices in the corporate sector, particularly the persistent use of designers-by-assignment. I have simplified somewhat and extended Merrill's discussion of professional roles in Table 32.2. This framework outlines three basic roles for IDT professionals as Merrill suggests: designers-by-assignment, master designers, and design researchers. I have not considered additional roles of managers and instructors, although I accept Merrill's point about the need to train managers.

Designers-by-assignment are untutored in formal IDT knowledge, but that can be misleading. Designers-by-assignment typically have extensive practical and content knowledge that empowers them to understand local cultures and processes and to anticipate how IDT technologies will likely impact learners. For this reason we encourage design teams that include multiple perspectives and different forms of expertise. Designers-by-assignment stand peripherally as outsiders to the IDT professional community, but over time may be acculturated and come to see themselves as designers themselves. Likewise master designers begin with very low knowledge of the local culture, but over time absorb its rhythms and values.

Master designers are expert tool users; design researchers are expert tool designers (tools including theories and methods). Yet, even that distinction can be exaggerated. Master designers often develop concepts and tools to solve challenging problems of practice. This is

TABLE 32.2 A comparison of needed skills and expertise for three instructional design roles

Activity	Designer-by-Assignment	Master Designer	Design Researcher
Science			
Research	No particular research skills Appreciates value of empirical testing and validation	Applied research skills: • Evaluation • Change analysis • Policy analysis • Cost analysis • Budget, planning, and decision making	Competent at various forms of disciplined inquiry: • Problem-based action research, including program and product evaluation • Knowledge- or theory-driven research, including, but not limited to, experimental designs
Theory	Minimally familiar with basic ID theory No formal theory development skills	Familiar with foundational theories Knows how to find/study theories specific to problems Competent to develop quick-and-dirty theories of practice	Competent in theory development and validation Competent in theory critique, comparisons Competent in applying/combining different theories to practical problems
Technology			
Technology-based tools	Relying heavily on tools, designs and develops instruction	Applies technology-based tools to design and develop instruction Link tools to ID-theory origins Apply when-and-where knowledge concerning appropriate use; adapt to constraints of tools	Designs new tools with tech teams, uses teams Tests and validates tools for specific uses Studies tools in use
Conceptual tools	Relying on forms and performance supports, applys conceptual models and procedures	Applies conceptual models to problems of practice Sees links to established ID theories Develops and uses quick-and-dirty conceptual tools	Develops and validates new conceptual tools Studies tools in use
Critical Review	Draws on content expertise and experience as an insider to design fair and equitable experiences for learners	Reads or interprets layers of meaning and value Designs to convey positive meanings and respectful, equitable values Tests and evaluates for positive meanings and values	Provides expert critical review Conducts formal evaluations
Artful Design	Uses knowledge of content and local environment to create meaningful experiences for learners	Careful attention to design of the immediate experience Designs for peak experiences Critiques and revises materials to improve aesthetic response	Develops models and design methods for aesthetic response

because a professional knowledge base, no matter how advanced, is necessarily incomplete—otherwise the practice would shift from professional to technical. Professionals, by definition, make judgments about local situations based on extensive, eclectic knowledge of appropriate practice. Likewise, design researchers are often tasked with routine aspects of quality control, involving installing and monitoring tools and systems and requiring technical levels of expertise. I note in Table 32.2 that researchers need to be skilled at various forms of inquiry, including action-type inquiry such as program and product evaluation, as well as more theory-driven inquiry that we expect to see in refereed journals.

The bottom two rows of Table 32.2 are my extensions of the kinds of skills and knowledge designers need to apply in order to address the full range of instructional problems encountered in practice. In addition to research, theory, and technologies, designers need to analyze and critique their work based on a grounded value perspective (Thomas, 2003; B. G. Wilson, in press) and give careful attention to the aesthetics of the learning experience (Parrish, in press). ID professionals need more explicit training in these areas, but they also can be helped by collaboration with designers-by-assignment, who, as noted, are more attuned to local values and sensibilities.

Broad or Narrow? Back to the Future

I construe the two perspectives offered by Merrill and myself as a choice between narrow and broad conceptions of the field. As I noted earlier, risks attend either road. As a way of exploring the relative merits of these differing perspectives, consider a thought exercise. Think of the last time you spent a full hour distracted from your immediate task at the office, absorbed in browsing the Web for professional resources, pursuing link to link, compelled by the hunt for high-quality material relating to an interest or problem. More precisely, you are drawn to the Web in pursuit of an initial goal, but the browsing leads to new goals and modified pursuits. So what is it that you find sufficiently rewarding to keep you going?

When out browsing for resources, I get excited when I find resources such as the following:

> *Up-to-date links reflecting an informed perspective.* Collections of links often reflect the consensus of a community (an academic department or professional group) but also can take on the personality of a single professional, e.g., Martin Ryder's IT Connections (**http://carbon.cudenver.edu/~mryder/itcon.html**). Less often they would be maintained by a commercial interest. A link to this kind of site then becomes a portal into a whole area of potential value.
>
> *Well-designed information resources.* These resources (e.g., articles, research reports, databases, syllabi, lecture slides) are in contrast to "fluff" pages, that is, good-looking pages that link to shallow or low-quality information. These resources may come from single or multiple perspectives. You may find yourself agreeing or disagreeing with positions taken. But the information must be substantive, challenging, and relevant to your needs.
>
> *Tools relevant to your work that can be accessed and downloaded cheaply.* These might also include forms and job aids for doing tasks you're charged with doing or teaching.
>
> *"Real" instruction with defined goals, activities, feedback, and learning assessment.* Most "tutorials" on the Web present information and step-by-step procedures, but lack critical elements that would more directly guide and support learning. When you find real, full-featured instruction that relates to your learning needs, it's a treasure.

I want to draw a few parallels to the present discussion. Instruction (the last resource I mentioned) is valuable, but it's only one kind of find that gets you excited. The value of information or resources (including full-featured instructional resources) can only be determined within a larger context of use—whether for learning or performance. We as learning professionals have both concerns (our own learning and our own performance, and that of those we serve), and a number of resource types could help us in our work.

Straight-ahead information, if it's the right information, can be tremendously helpful for both learning and performance. I don't usually need fancy formatting, just lean and clear presentation. Again, it depends on the larger context of use and need, but once I get access to the truly relevant information, the right information, "minimally" designed without flourishes, points to its own use. It's exciting when information is so closely coupled with a context of use that the action becomes obvious.

What is distinctly valuable in many Web resources is the informed perspective of the site. Disembodied, depersonalized information can at times be useful, but I tend to get excited when someone I know and respect endorses a particular item. The credibility and authority I attach to that respected person then get transferred to the information, and I decide it's worth my time to pay attention to it. I am, in essence, drawing on a community of practice (loosely construed) to help me manage the glut of resources that I don't have time to filter myself. Likewise learners in classes ask their instructors to evaluate information in the same way, relying heavily on respected perspectives and on personalized, embodied forms of knowledge derived from those perspectives.

So how do these points relate to the future of IDT? I want to stress the eclectic grounding for practice of instructional design and the need to maintain a fairly broad conception of the field. Just as individual users find value in eclectic resources on the Web, IDT professionals can benefit from an array of tools and resources based on sometimes competing perspectives. A community of professionals needs some measure of shared vision and framing of problems and goals. We also need to accommodate diverse perspectives about problems and solutions. This is especially true of educational knowledge, which is more context dependent than many domains. Vibrant professional communities can make room for a number of theoretical stances and research agendas. In the end, we need a level of freedom and autonomy sufficient to notice and reward the promising lines of thinking, while maintaining enough coherence to keep us moving forward together. In a healthy community, promising and innovative "fruits" will be acknowledged and nurtured, while not threatening the "roots" that hold us together.

Response to Brent G. Wilson, "Choosing our Future" (M. David Merrill)

The future of instructional technology clearly has at least two roads, as indicated by Brent Wilson in his excellent review of some trends for the future. The many paths he identified will very likely continue to play an important role in education and technology. Many interesting approaches and techniques will likely come from the broad and inclusive way. However, I doubt that these will lead to a rigorous empirical base for the future of instructional design. I will come back to the biblical metaphor used by Brent:

> Enter ye in at the strait gate; for wide is the gate, and broad is the way, which leadeth to destruction [the demise of instructional technology as a formal field of study.]
>
> Because strait is the gate and narrow is the way, which leadeth unto life [the continued vitality of instructional technology as a field of study], and few there be that find it. (Matthew 7:13–14)

Instructional technology as a field has already diversified to the point that it is hard to distinguish yourself by claiming to be an instructional designer. As the instructional technology continues to diversify, as more and more folks from all professions clamor down the broad and inclusive road, it will become more and more difficult to determine if indeed there is an academic field of instructional design. On the other hand, there is so much that remains unknown on the strait and narrow path. There are so many answers that are unlikely to come unless more scholars find the strait gate and pursue a narrow, more rigorous way toward instructional design knowledge. The many are welcome to follow the broad road, but my appeal is to the few that are committed to the preservation of instructional design as a rigorous field of study.

> *Two roads diverged in a yellow wood*
> *And sorry I could not travel both . . .*
> *I took the one less traveled by*
> *And that has made all the difference.*
>
> Robert Frost

I hope to meet you on the strait and narrow path and on the road less traveled.

Application Questions

1. Do other design fields (architecture, urban planning, industrial design, graphic design, software engineering, etc.) experience the same sorts of threats to professional practice? What is there about the practice of IDT that makes it particularly vulnerable to practice by nonprofessionals?
2. Wilson lists a number of influences and ideas relating to IDT expertise, but few are based on experimental research. What advantage is there to drawing on eclectic sources in establishing a professional knowledge base? How does one confirm or validate knowledge coming from disparate sources?
3. In spite of their cordial tone, Merrill and Wilson appear to draw very different "lines in the sand" concerning their views of the field. What is the relationship of their two lines? Are they truly incommensurable, or can they be seen as complementary?
4. What position do you take about how the field should be viewed, and what implications for the future does your view hold?

References

Aldrich, C. (2004). *Simulations and the future of learning: An innovative (and perhaps revolutionary) approach to e-learning*. San Francisco: Jossey-Bass Pfeiffer.

American Society for Training & Development. (2003). *ASTD 2003 State of the Industry Report*. Retrieved February 22, 2005, from **http://www1.astd.org/news_letter/December03/links/SOIR_2003_Executive_Summary.pdf**

Berliner, D. C. (2002). Educational research: The hardest science of all. *Educational Researcher, 31*(8), 18–20.

Clark, R. E. (1983). Reconsidering research on learning from media. *Review of Educational Research, 53*(4), 445–459.

Clark, R. E. (1994a). Media and method. *Educational Technology, Research & Development, 42*(3), 7–10.

Clark, R. E. (1994b). Media will never influence learning. *Educational Technology, Research & Development, 42*(2), 21–29.

Dick, W. (1987). A history of instructional design and its impact on educational psychology. In J. A. Glover & R. R. Ronning (Eds.), *Historical foundations of educational psychology* (pp. 183–200). New York: Plenum.

Gee, J. P. (2003). *What video games have to teach us about learning and literacy*. New York: Palgrave/MacMillan.

Gordon, J., & Zemke, R. (2000). The attack on ISD. *Training, 37*(4), 42. Retrieved February 24, 2001, from **http://www.trainingsupersite.com/publications/ archive/training/2000/004/004cv.htm**

Hill, J. R., & Hanaffin, M. J. (2001). Teaching and learning in digital environments: The resurgence of resource-based learning. *Educational Technology, Research & Development, 49*(3), 37–52.

Hodgins W. (2004). Off course, on target: Why great companies are on a path to failure and how they can change, by Wayne Hodgins as visualized by Eileen Clegg. Retrieved March 18, 2006, from **http://opencourse.org/Collaboratories/ocot/ocot/wiki/FrontPage**

Kliebard, H. M. (1987). *The struggle for the American curriculum 1893–1958*. New York: Routledge.

Kozma, R. B. (1991). Learning with media. *Review of Educational Research, 61*(2), 179–211.

Kozma, R. B. (1994). Will media influence learning? Reframing the debate. *Educational Technology, Research & Development, 42*(2), 7–19.

Merrill, M. D. (1968, April). Components of a cybernetic instructional system. *Educational Technology*, 5–10.

Merrill, M. D. (1980, February). Can the adjective instructional modify the noun science? *Educational Technology*, 37–44.

Merrill, M. D. (1997). Learning oriented instructional development tools. *Performance Improvement, 36*(3), 51–55.

MIT Press. (2004). *New media*. Retrieved April 7, 2004, from **http://mitpress.mit.edu/catalog/browse/default. asp?sid=8B381990–B371-4DF9-BCFE-D1B68023530F&cid=12**

Norman, D. A. (2004). *Emotional design: Why we love (or hate) everyday things*. New York: Basic Books. Excerpts retrieved April 7, 2004, from **http://www.jnd.org/books.html**

Parrish, P. E. (2004, April). *Investigating the aesthetic decisions of instructional designers.* Paper presented at the meeting of the American Educational Research Association, San Diego, CA.

Parrish, P. E. (in press). Embracing the aesthetic of instructional design. *Educational Technology* [Special issue].

Reigeluth, C. M. (1995). Educational systems development and its relationship to ISD. In G. Anglin (Ed.), *Instructional technology: Past, present, and future* (2nd ed., pp. 84–93). Englewood CO: Libraries Unlimited.

Reiser, R. A. (2001). A history of instructional design and technology—Part 2: A history of instructional design. *Educational Technology, Research & Development, 49*(2), 57–67.

Tenner, E. (1997). *Why things bite back: Technology and the revenge of unintended consequences*. New York: Knopf.

Thomas, M. K. (2003). Designers' dilemmas: The tripartheid responsibility of the instructional designer. *TechTrends, 47*(6), 34–39.

Tyler, R. W. (1949). *Basic principles of curriculum and instruction.* Chicago: University of Chicago Press.

Van Merriënboer, J. J. G., & Martens, R. L. (2002). Computer-based tools for instructional design: An introduction to the special issue. *Educational Technology, Research & Development, 50*(4), 5–9.

Vincenti, W. G. (1990). *What engineers know and how they know it: Analytical studies from aeronautical history.* Baltimore, MD: John Hopkins University Press.

Wiley, D. A., & Edwards, E. K. (2002). Online self-organizing social systems: The decentralized future of online learning. *Quarterly Review of Distance Education*, *3*(1). Retrieved February 22, 2005, from **http://wiley.ed.usu.edu/docs/ososs.pdf**

Wilson, B. G. (2002). Trends and futures of education: Implications for distance education. *Quarterly Review of Distance Education, 3*(1), 65–77.

Wilson, B. G. (in press). Broadening ID's foundations: Four pillars for practice. *Educational Technology* [Special issue].

Wilson, E. O. (1998). *Consilience: The unity of knowledge*. New York: Knopf.

Epilogue

Robert A. Reiser

John V. Dempsey

In the Introduction to this book, we suggested that by the time you finished reading, you might be able to provide your parents (or anyone else who is really interested) with a clear picture of the field of instructional design and technology. Now that you have completed the book, what do you think? What is your view of the field?

Don't be afraid to answer the questions we just posed. As you must know by now, there are many different facets to the field, and there have been many ways in which it has been defined, so there is no "right" answer to the question. IDT professionals, including those who wrote chapters for this book, hold a wide range of views about the nature of the field, and as far as we know, none has been designated as the "correct" one. Now that you have studied this book and, hopefully, learned a lot about the nature of our field, you should be well prepared to join the debate. Of course, your views are likely to change over time, but we think that now is a good time to reflect on what you have learned and express your point of view to others.

So, go ahead. Call your folks and tell them what our field is all about. Perhaps they will finally understand exactly what it is that you are studying. But even if they don't understand what you are talking about, they will enjoy hearing from you!

Author Biographies

Peter Albion is Associate Professor of Education at the University of Southern Queensland in Australia. Prior to joining USQ he taught science, mathematics, and computing in secondary schools and was a secondary school principal for several years. He holds a master's degree in organic chemistry and graduate qualifications in education. He completed his doctorate at USQ in the areas of multimedia development and technology integration. His teaching and research are in technology integration in education and online education. He has been active in the Society for Information Technology in Teacher Education for several years and has served as Vice President for Graduate Education and Faculty Development, and as chair of the Information Technology Council of SITE. He was formerly department chair and currently coordinates the doctoral program in the Faculty of Education at USQ.

Robert Maribe Branch is a Professor in the Department of Educational Psychology and Instructional Technology at the University of Georgia. He earned a bachelor's degree from Elizabeth City State University, a master's degree from Ball State University, and a doctoral degree from Virginia Tech. Branch taught high school and college in Botswana over a five-year period. He taught graduate courses and conducted research at Syracuse University in Instructional Design, Development, and Evaluation, and earned tenure during his seven years there. Dr. Branch is a former Fulbright Lecturer/Researcher to the University of Natal in South Africa. He has co-edited the *Educational Media and Technology Yearbook* since 1997, and coauthored the popular *Survey of Instructional Development Models*. Branch emphasizes student-centered instruction and teaches courses related to instructional systems design. His research focuses on diagramming complex conceptual relationships.

Robert K. Branson is Professor Emeritus in the Department of Educational Psychology and Learning Systems at Florida State University. He was one of the original founders of the Instructional Systems program in that department. His work focused on three major programs. First, with collaborators, he redesigned the official training doctrine for military training that was published by the Army and Navy in 1976 as the Interservice Procedures for Instructional Systems Development. Second, he developed the Job Skills Education Program in collaboration with the Army Research Institute. That program was the largest basic skills program yet developed for computer-based training and is still in use. His third major program, called the Florida School Year 2000 Initiative, set out to redesign public education in Florida. Its focus was to implement systems thinking and design into public educational thought; a formidable and as yet unsuccessful undertaking. His teaching focuses on applying systems thinking to change management through online classes.

Mary F. Bratton-Jeffery serves on the headquarters staff of the U.S. Naval Education and Training Command. Her academic credentials include a B.A. and M.A. in Secondary Education from the University of Kentucky and a Ph.D. in Instructional Design and Development from the University of South Alabama. Dr. Bratton-Jeffery is an Instructional Systems Specialist for the Navy. Her area of expertise lies in the practical application of cognitive learning theories, adult learning and motivation, performance improvement, and large-scale systems design. Dr. Bratton-Jeffery is an experienced educator and teaches undergraduate and graduate courses for the University of South Alabama as adjunct faculty.

Richard D. Busby is a Human Resources Solution Planner for Accenture, a global management consulting, technology services, and outsourcing company. In this role he works closely with business executives to define the training strategy for a large offshore workforce in several regions across the globe. Rich's past experience spans the training lifecycle. His work has included project management, needs assessment, design, development, and delivery. Rich received a master of science degree from the University of South Alabama in 1993. Rich published *Carson's Book*, a story of adoption from China, in 2005. His current priority is raising a daughter.

Daniel Cernusca is a doctoral candidate in the School of Information Science and Learning Technologies at the University of Missouri. He is currently working on his dissertation focusing on the impact of an online constructivist learning environment on students' conceptual understanding of biblical criticism methods. Prior to starting his current doctoral program at the University of Missouri, he taught in the School of Engineering at Lucian Blaga University of Sibiu, Romania, where he completed a doctorate in mechanical engineering. His current research focuses on design research, impact of cognitive tools for knowledge representation on learners' conceptual understanding of complex topics, and problem solving.

Ruth Colvin Clark has focused her professional efforts on bridging the gap between academic research on instructional methods and practitioner application of that research. To that end she has developed a number of seminars and has written five books, including *e-Learning and the Science of Instruction,* that translate and illustrate important research programs for organizational training specialists. A science undergraduate, Ruth completed her doctorate in Instructional Psychology/Educational Technology in 1988 at University of Southern California. Ruth is a past president of the International Society of Performance Improvement and a member of the American Educational Research Association. Ruth is currently a dual resident of southwest Colorado and Phoenix, Arizona, and divides her professional time among consulting, teaching, and writing.

Gayle V. Davidson-Shivers is Instructional Design and Development professor at the University of South Alabama. Her master's and doctoral degrees are in Curricular and Instructional Systems from the University of Minnesota; her undergraduate degree in education is from Western Oregon University. She teaches online and on-campus courses on developing online instruction, psychology of learning, instructional models, and trends and issues in IDT. Her recent research focuses on gender and communication patterns in online discussions, technology integration, and the professional status of the IDT field. She serves on review boards of several major journals. Additionally, her service includes past president of the SIG–Instructional Technology of AERA, board member of the AECT Research and Theory Division, and faculty advisor to the IDD Student Group. She worked as an instructional systems specialist for a major lending institution and taught in Oregon and Minnesota public schools. Her consulting work has extended to business entities, governmental agencies, and educational institutions.

John V. Dempsey is Professor and Chair of the Department of Professional Studies, a member of the Instructional Design and Development faculty, and Director of the Online Learning Lab at the University of South Alabama. He received an M.S. and Ph.D in Instructional Systems from

Florida State University and a B.S. in Graphic Arts Technology from Florida A&M. He has taught a "Trends and Issues" course for most of his academic career. Dr. Dempsey has written numerous journal articles and book chapters, and coedited *Interactive Instruction and Feedback* as well as the first edition of the present text. A practicing instructional designer, he has working experience developing educational websites and CBT for the National Oceanic and Atmospheric Administration and the U.S. Army. Currently, he is developing a series of multimedia CD-ROMs for middle school children involving environmental education topics. His research interests are concerned with the balance between embodiment and embellishment of learning in technologically rich areas such as educational gaming, graphical displays, and pedagogical agents.

Walter Dick, a graduate of Penn State in educational psychology, is Professor Emeritus of Instructional Systems at Florida State University, where he taught courses on instructional design and performance systems analysis. He is the coauthor of two textbooks in the field of instructional design, *The Systematic Design of Instruction* (6th ed., 2005) and *Instructional Planning* (2nd ed., 1996). Dr. Dick has served as a short-term instructional design consultant on a number of international projects in South America, Europe, and Africa. During 1989 and 1990, he was a consultant to Motorola, Inc. and to the National Productivity Board of Singapore.

Marcy P. Driscoll is Leslie J. Briggs Professor of Educational Research and Dean of the College of Education at Florida State University. She is past president of the Association for Educational Communications and Technology (AECT) and the author or coauthor of six textbooks in learning and instruction, including *Psychology of Learning for Instruction*, which won the 1995 Outstanding Book Award in Instructional Development from AECT, and, with Robert M. Gagné, *Essentials of Learning for Instruction*. She has also published numerous articles in professional journals on learning, instructional theory, and educational semiotics. Professor Driscoll has been the recipient of teaching awards at the department, college, and university levels, earned for excellence in undergraduate and graduate teaching. Professor Driscoll received her B.A. magna cum laude from Mt. Holyoke College and her M.S. and Ph.D. degrees in Educational Psychology from the University of Massachusetts at Amherst.

Francis (Frank) M. Duffy is Professor of Change-Leadership in Education at Gallaudet University in Washington, DC. He held an honorary faculty position in the Harvard Graduate School of Education, sponsored by Chris Argyris. He is the founder and president of The F. M. Duffy Group and founder of the Alliance for Systemic School Improvement through Systems Thinking (ASSIST)—a small community of practice for educators in Maryland who are interested in whole-system change. Dr. Duffy has also published seven books on whole-system change in school districts, including *Moving Upward Together: Creating Strategic Alignment to Sustain Systemic School Improvement*. He is also the editor of Rowman & Littlefield Education's *Leading Systemic School Improvement* Series. He was a 2002–2003 Education Policy Fellow with the Institute for Educational Leadership (IEL).

Donald P. Ely is Professor Emeritus of Instructional Design, Development and Evaluation at the Syracuse University School of Education. He was the Founding Director of the ERIC Clearinghouse on Information Resources. He earned his B.A. from State University of New York at Albany, and his M.A. and Ph.D. from Syracuse University. He conducts research, writes, lectures, and is a consultant in the field of instructional design and technology. Recent consultations have been in Chile, Indonesia, South Africa, and The Netherlands. Recent edited books are the *International Encyclopedia of Educational Technology* and *Classic Writings on Instructional Technology*, volumes 1 and 2. He has served as a visiting professor of education at Florida State University and the University of Twente in the Netherlands.

Marguerite J. Foxon is Principal Performance Technologist with Motorola and has extensive experience in evaluation, performance improvement, and the design of leadership development programs. She has global responsibility for the core leadership and management development curriculum, and also undertakes evaluation research within Motorola to assess transfer and organizational impact. Previously she was National Director of Education with Price Waterhouse Coopers for Australia, Indonesia, and Papua New Guinea. Marguerite was a director with the International Board of Standards for Training, Performance and Instruction **(http://www.ibstpi.org)**, is on the Board of ASTD's Certification Institute, on the Board of LearnShare, and active in AHRD. She is on the Advisory Board of *Educational Media International* and a reviewer for *Human Resource Development Review*. Marguerite received her Ph.D. in Instructional Systems from Florida State University. Honors include twice winning the Outstanding Instructional Designer award from the Australian Institute of Training and Development, and the Association for Educational Communication & Technology's Robert de Keiffer International Fellowship for forging professional ties between the United States and Australia & New Zealand.

Donna Gabrielle is Professor of Education at Redding College and owner/CEO of Gabrielle Consulting, specializing in human performance technology, instructional systems design, and distance learning. Previously she taught and was Associate Director of the Center for Teaching Excellence at the U.S. Military Academy at West Point, NY. Other positions held include head of Training and Development at the Florida Department of Agriculture and Consumer Services and Instructional Technologies Administrator for the Justice Distance Learning Consortium, funded by a $10 million STAR Schools grant to bring educational opportunities to incarcerated youth. She holds a B.A. in Communication with an emphasis in journalism from Florida A&M University. She earned her M.A. in Mass Communication, Media Communication, and Marketing Research and her doctorate in Educational Psychology and Learning Systems, Instructional Systems from Florida State University. She has written many articles and presented numerous papers on motivation and technology-mediated learning. Dr. Gabrielle teaches computer science, education, and communications courses and her passion is to bring educational opportunities to people who could not otherwise be reached.

James J. Goldsmith is a Development Manager at Accenture, based in St. Charles, Illinois. His primary responsibility is to leverage design and technology to support critical education and performance initiatives. A training developer and project manager since 1982, he has directly created or managed the development of more than 1,500 hours of instructor-led and online training. He received an M.B.A. from the University of Connecticut, is a Pericles and multiple APEX reward recipient, and was named one of *Multimedia Producer* magazine's Top 100 multimedia producers. His clients include several Fortune 500 companies such as BP America Inc., Aetna, Wyeth Pharmaceuticals, Caterpillar, MassMutual, Accenture, and others. He speaks frequently on training and performance issues at industry gatherings and is currently writing a book on Project Management with Richard Busby.

Kent L. Gustafson is Professor Emeritus of Instructional Technology at the University of Georgia. His areas of scholarly interest include electronic performance support, computer-based curriculum development tools, professional education of instructional technologists, and examining trends and issues facing the field. He formerly taught courses in instructional design, change management, and research in instructional technology.

Michael Hannafin is the Charles H. Wheatley-Georgia Research Alliance Eminent Scholar in Technology-Enhanced Learning, and professor in the Department of Educational Psychology and Instructional Technology at the University of Georgia (UGA). In addition, he directs the Learning and Performance Support Laboratory—an R&D organization that studies the potential for and impact of emerging technologies for teaching and learning. LPSL R&D has been funded by the National Science Foundation, the U.S. Department of Education, the Department of Defense, and several private foundations. Prior to arriving at UGA and since completing his doctorate from

Arizona State University in 1981, he has worked at several universities, including the University of Colorado, Penn State University, and Florida State University. His research focuses on the study of technology-enhanced teaching and learning environments, especially those that are open and student centered in nature.

Byron Havard's interest in education began at a very early age growing up in a family of educators. He earned his B.S. at Auburn University and his M.S. in Instructional Design and Development from the University of South Alabama. Continuing his interest in education, he earned his Ph.D. in Instructional Technology from Georgia State University. Byron has roughly nine years of corporate experience in instructional design, needs assessment, and evaluation. At the time this brief bio was written he was serving as assistant professor in the Department of Instructional Systems and Workforce Development at Mississippi State University. His research interests include collaborative learning, online discussion, social and cultural dimensions in instructional technology, and instructional strategies.

Janette R. Hill is Associate Professor of Instructional Technology in the College of Education, University of Georgia. Dr. Hill holds a B.A. in Communications from the University of North Florida in Jacksonville (1988), and an M.S.L.S. in Library and Information Science from The Florida State University (1990), where she also completed a Ph.D. in Instructional Systems Design in 1995. Her research areas include community building in virtual environments, resource-based learning, and the use of information technologies for purposes of learning. Dr. Hill teaches undergraduate and graduate level courses in the Instructional Technology program at UGA in the areas of instructional design, research, and technology integration.

Robert Hoffman is an associate professor at San Diego State University's Department of Educational Technology, where he explores design and development with up and coming e-learning professionals of many stripes. He's served time in secondary school classrooms and educational television studios, and pioneered the first online courses the department offered in the mid 1990s. He's particularly engaged with the many phases of the museum experience, from exhibitry to educational programming and assessment. His Web-based inquiry learning experiments help graduate students turn theory into practice in his popular on-campus and online courses.

Suzanne Hoffman is an independent consultant. She has a B.A. in Spanish from the University of Florida, an M.A. in German from the University of Illinois, and a Ph.D. in Instructional Design and Development from the University of South Alabama. She has worked in higher education as an administrator, a program developer/coordinator, and adjunct faculty, and in industry as an instructional designer with emphasis on training needs analysis. Dr. Hoffman's areas of specialization include second language acquisition, English as a Second Language, and nontraditional adult learners.

Ioan Gelu Ionas began teaching in a Romanian university over 10 years ago with a bachelor's degree in mechanical engineering. Since then he has earned an M.B.A. degree from the University of Missouri–Columbia, and a Ph.D. in Management from a Romanian university. As the author of several books and research papers in Romania, he became interested in using technology in teaching and began the doctoral program of study in the Information Science and Learning Technologies (SISLT) program at the University of Missouri–Columbia. Currently, Gelu's research interests include implementing the precepts of design research for development and use of cognitive tools in the context of supporting causal reasoning and group decision making in business. In addition to this, Gelu is interested in using a contextual approach to technical training to improve information technology use in organizations.

John Jacobs is Science Advisor for the Modeling & Simulation (M&S) University Division of Alion Science and Technology, a leading research and development company. John has over

15 years experience as an industrial/organizational and instructional systems consultant, and has worked with numerous Fortune 500 companies and state and federal agencies, including the FBI, Defense Security Service, Defense Modeling and Simulation Office, Army Modeling and Simulation Office, National Defense University, Ford, Learning International, GTE, State of Alaska, and Eckerd College. Prior to Alion, John worked for 9 years as a faculty member and Senior Research Psychologist at the University of Central Florida's Institute for Simulation and Training (IST), where he was awarded Researcher of the Year in 2000. He is a principal and cofounder of Applied Simulation Corporation, a company that develops and validates simulation-based teaching skill assessment and training tools for use by teachers, schools/districts, colleges of education, and alternative certification providers.

Arthur Jeffery is assistant professor in the Mitchell College of Business, University of South Alabama. He holds a M.S. in Systems Management from University of Southern California, an M.B.A. from Kansas University, and a Ph.D. in Instructional Design and Development from the University of South Alabama. Dr. Jeffery has taught at the university level in the area of quantitative methods, quality improvement, and management for 15 years. He also has 20 years of experience as an Army officer, including several command assignments and work as an operations research systems analyst. He is a partner for RDIS, LLC, a small consulting firm providing services in instruction systems and human performance.

Burke Johnson is a professor in the Instructional Design and Development program at the University of South Alabama. He is a research methodologist. He received his Ph.D. in Evaluation from the University of Georgia in 1993, and also has graduate degrees in Psychology, Public Policy, and Sociology. He is author (with Larry Christensen) of *Educational Research: Quantitative, Qualitative, and Mixed Approaches* (Allyn & Bacon, 2004), and has published in journals such a *Educational Researcher*, the *Journal of Educational Psychology*, *Evaluation Review*, and *Evaluation and Program Planning*. His primary interests currently surround the philosophy and design of mixed methods research.

David Jonassen is Distinguished Professor in the School of Information Science and Learning Technologies at the University of Missouri. Since completing his doctorate in educational media and experimental educational psychology at Temple University, he has taught at the University of North Carolina at Greensboro, the University of Colorado, Twente University in the Netherlands, Syracuse University, Nanyang Technological University in Singapore, Pennsylvania State University, and the University of Bergen in Norway. Dr. Jonassen is working on his 30th book and has published numerous articles, book chapters, and technical reports. His current research focuses on problem solving, cognitive tools for knowledge representation, and computer-supported collaborative argumentation.

John M. Keller is a Professor of Instructional Systems and Educational Psychology at Florida State University. He received his Ph.D. in Instructional Systems Technology and Organizational Behavior from Indiana University. During his career, he has made major contributions to the development of approaches to designing motivational systems and he has contributed to the design of performance improvement and systematic training design processes for several school districts, major corporations, military organizations, and government agencies. He has delivered addresses, participated in conferences, conducted workshops, and completed consultancies in approximately 20 countries, and he recently completed a teaching assignment at the University of Salzburg, Austria. He is best known for the motivational design process he created that is called the "ARCS model." He is a coauthor with W. Wager, K. Golas, and R. Gagné of the fifth edition of *Principles of Instructional Design* (2005).

James D. Klein is a professor and program leader in the Educational Technology program at Arizona State University, Tempe, where he teaches courses on instructional design, research, and performance improvement. His most recent scholarly works include the book, *Instructor Competencies: Standards for Face-to-face, Online, and Blended Settings* (with Spector, Grabowski, & de la Teja) and a chapter on conducting instructional design and development research in the *Handbook of Research for Educational Communications and Technology* (with Richey & Nelson). Dr. Klein serves on the International Board of Standards for Training, Performance and Instruction (ibstpi) and previously served as the development editor of *Educational Technology Research & Development*. He has been recognized as an outstanding alumnus of the Instructional Systems program at Florida State University and for his service to the Design and Development Division of the Association for Educational Communications and Technology.

Brenda C. Litchfield is Professor in the Instructional Design and Development program at the University of South Alabama. Dr. Litchfield taught science and grades K–12 for 11 years and currently teaches educational psychology, project coordination, instructional learning theories, and design and development of training courseware at the graduate level. She received her B.S. in Elementary Education from The University of Florida, her Master's in Science Education from the University of North Florida, and her Ph.D. in Instructional Systems from Florida State University. She is active in environmental education and has directed the development of several activity books for the Environmental Protection Agency, the U.S. Fish and Wildlife Service, and state environmental organizations. She is currently designing and developing her second CD-ROM in environmental education. She teaches online courses in Instructional Design and Development and is developing a faculty training program at the University of South Alabama. Her areas of interest and research are self-regulated learning, motivation, and environmental education.

Craig Locatis has been an educational research specialist in the Lister Hill National Center for Biomedical Communications of the National Library of Medicine at the National Institutes of Health. He is currently with the Library's Office of High Performance Computing and Communications, where he manages external research projects and conducts internal research related to the use of advanced networks in health care. While at the Library, he has managed and conducted research and development on educational technology involving the Internet, hypermedia programs, videodisc, and authoring software, and has managed its Collaboratory Program's use of database, streaming, and videoconferencing applications. Other work at NLM has involved designing information interfaces and connecting the national medical libraries of eight newly independent states of the former Soviet Union to the Internet. Prior to joining the NLM, he was on the faculty of Rutgers University and has been a visiting or adjunct professor at other domestic and foreign universities.

Richard E. Mayer is Professor of Psychology at the University of California, Santa Barbara (UCSB), where he has served since 1975. He received a Ph.D. in Psychology from the University of Michigan in 1973, and served as a Visiting Assistant Professor of Psychology at Indiana University from 1973 to 1975. His research interests are in educational and cognitive psychology, and his current research involves the intersection of cognition, instruction, and technology with a special focus on multimedia learning. He is past president of the Division of Educational Psychology of the American Psychological Association, former editor of *Educational Psychologist*, and former coeditor of *Instructional Science*, former chair of the UCSB Department of Psychology, and the year 2000 recipient of the E. L. Thorndike Award for career achievement in educational psychology. He was ranked #1 as the most productive educational psychologist for 1991–2001 (*Contemporary Educational Psychology*, vol. 28, pp. 422–430). He is on the editorial boards of 10 journals, mainly in educational psychology. He is the author of 18 books and more than 250 articles and chapters, including *Multimedia Learning* (2001), *E-Learning and the Science of Instruction* (2003) with Ruth Clark, and *Learning and Instruction* (2003).

Jacquelin McDonald is a Senior Lecturer in the Distance and e-Learning Centre at the University of Southern Queensland (USQ), Australia. She has worked in education for over 25 years, and during the past 15 years as an instructional designer in tertiary and training environments. She is a practicing ID, and has designed traditional training and distance education and blended learning materials for on-campus, national, and international learners. She has taught ID courses in online programs. Her research interests include instructional design, hybrid/blended learning, communities of practice, grounded theory, and interaction and engagement in online learning. She has written a number of journal articles on hybrid and online learning and has presented at several international and national conferences. She holds a master's degree in flexible learning and is researching online interaction as a doctoral student at USQ.

Jan McKay is an Associate in Research at the Learning Systems Institute at Florida State University. She holds master's degrees in both Instructional Systems Design and Elementary Education. Ms. McKay has an extensive background in curriculum development, training, and staff development, as well as a range of experience in technical and professional writing. She has been involved in designing, developing, and disseminating electronic performance support tools for many years, including an electronic curriculum-planning tool for educators currently distributed through the Florida Department of Education.

M. David Merrill, professor emeritus at Utah State University, is serving as an education missionary and Professor of Instructional Technology at the Center for Instructional Technology and Outreach at Brigham Young University-Hawaii. Since receiving his Ph.D. in 1964 his primary interest has been and still is investigating what makes for effective, efficient, and engaging instruction. In the pursuit of this goal he has made several major contributions to the field of instructional technology. In the 1970s he was a primary designer of the authoring system for TICCIT, an early CBT system. In the 1980s he developed Component Display Theory and Elaboration Theory, which are still widely used as guides for effective instructional development. In the 1990s his work included knowledge objects and instructional transaction theory primarily aimed at facilitating the automation of instructional design. His recent work is an attempt to identify those first principles of instruction that are common to most theories and models of instruction. He is widely published in instructional technology journals. He has lectured throughout the world on effective instructional design. He was awarded the 2001 Distinguished Service Award by AECT "for advancing the field of Instructional Technology through scholarship, teaching, and leadership."

Gary R. Morrison is professor in the Department of Educational Curriculum and Instruction in Old Dominion University's College of Education, where he teaches courses in instructional design. After receiving his doctorate in Instructional Systems Technology from Indiana University, he worked as instructional designer for three Fortune 500 companies and the University of Mid-America. Previously, he was a professor in the Instructional Design and Technology programs at the University of Memphis and Wayne State University. His research focuses on cognitive load theory, instructional strategies, K–12 technology integration, and distance education. He is the associate editor of the Research section of *Educational Technology, Research & Development* and is on the editorial boards of *Computers in Human Behavior*, *Quarterly Review of Distance Education*, and Libraries Unlimited's *Instructional Technology Series*. Gary is the senior author of *Designing Effective Instruction* (4th ed.) and *Integrating Computer Technology into the Classroom* (3rd ed). Gary is also author of over 20 book chapters, over 50 articles, and over 100 conference presentations on topics in instructional technology.

Karen L. Rasmussen is Associate Professor and Chair of the Division of Engineering and Computer Technology at the University of West Florida. She has worked with teachers, business and industry, and the military on a variety of topics, ranging from standards-based education to e-learning solutions. Her research interests include professional standards and competencies for IT and HPT and design, online professional development, and development and implementation of Web-based and alternative learning environments. She is the codeveloper of the first online masters program at UWF and coauthor of a textbook on designing, developing, and implementing Web-based instruction.

Charles M. Reigeluth has a B.A. in Economics from Harvard University and a Ph.D. in Instructional Psychology from Brigham Young University. He taught science at the secondary level for 3 years and spent 10 years on the faculty of the Instructional Design program at Syracuse University, culminating as chair of the program. He has been a professor in the Instructional Systems Technology Department at Indiana University since 1988, and served as chairman of the department from 1990 to 1992. Dr. Reigeluth's interests include transforming public education and designing high-quality instruction. He has published eight books and over a hundred articles and book chapters on those subjects. He is the major developer of several instructional design theories, including Elaboration Theory and Simulation Theory. Two of his books received "outstanding book of the year" awards from the Association for Educational Communications and Technology.

Robert A. Reiser is a Distinguished Teaching Professor and the Robert M. Morgan Professor of Instructional Systems at Florida State University, and program leader of the Instructional Systems program. Reiser is the author of four books, including *Selecting Media for Instruction* (with Robert Gagné), *Instructional Planning: A Guide for Teachers* (with Walter Dick), and *Trends and Issues in Instructional Design and Technology* (with John Dempsey), which has won book awards from the Association for Educational Communications and Technology and the Division of Design and Development. Dr. Reiser has written over 50 journal articles on instructional design and technology. During his tenure at Florida State, Reiser has received a Professorial Excellence Award, a Developing Scholar Award, and a University Teaching Award. In April 2000, Reiser received the University Distinguished Teacher Award, the highest teaching award at Florida State, given annually to one professor at the university. Reiser received his doctorate from Arizona State University.

Rita C. Richey is Professor and Program Coordinator of Instructional Technology in the College of Education at Wayne State University. She has been at Wayne State for over 30 years and has extensive experience in program design and development, teaching, and in education and training research. She is widely published in the area of instructional design and technology. She has written or edited 10 books, including *The Theoretical and Conceptual Bases of Instructional Design, Designing Instruction for the Adult Learner,* and *The Legacy of Robert M. Gagné*. She is also coauthor of the third edition of *Instructional Design Competencies: The Standards*, the third edition of *Training Manager Competencies: The Standards,* and *Instructional Technology: The Definition and Domains of the Field*. The latter book received the 1995 Outstanding Book Award and the 1996 Brown Publication Award, both from the Association of Educational Communications & Technology (AECT), and has been translated into three additional languages. She has published over 30 articles and book chapters. She is a past ibstpi vice president for Research and Development and a past president of AERA's Special Interest Group on Instructional Technology. In recognition of her career's work, in 2000 she received the AECT Distinguished Service Award.

Robby Robson is president of Eduworks Corporation, principal investigator of the National Science Digital Library Reusable Learning Project, and chair of the IEEE Learning Technology Standards Committee. He holds a doctorate in mathematics from Stanford University and spent a large part of his career as a research mathematician on the faculty of Oregon State University. Dr. Robson started designing online learning technology and content in academic settings in the mid 1990s. In 2000 he took a position with Saba, Inc., where he architected commercial systems, served as a director of product management, and had the role of "standards evangelist." In 2001 he cofounded Eduworks, an e-learning research and consulting company that has done work for dozens of foundations, agencies, universities, and private companies. His current projects include the Reusable Learning Project, on which his chapter in this book is based; a project that is creating personal digital library technology for capturing, organizing, and preserving research and educational materials in a metadata-rich environment; and a project that is creating technology for disaggregating, converting, and reaggregating multimedia courseware (of the training variety) into instructionally meaningful SCORM content. Dr. Robson is involved in a variety of standards projects and test beds and has a personal interest in the areas of intellectual property rights, information organization, and emerging learning environments.

Marc J. Rosenberg is a management consultant, educator, and leading figure in the world of training, organizational learning, e-learning, knowledge management, and performance improvement. He is the author of two best-selling books, *E-Learning: Strategies for Delivering Knowledge in the Digital Age* and *Beyond E-Learning: Approaches and Technologies to Enhance Organizational Learning, Knowledge and Performance*. A highly regarded and much sought-after presenter, Dr. Rosenberg has spoken at the White House and keynoted more than 100 professional and business conferences. He has authored more than 40 articles and book chapters in the field, and is a frequently quoted expert in major business and trade publications. Dr. Rosenberg is a past president of the International Society for Performance Improvement (ISPI), and holds a Ph.D. in instructional design, plus degrees in communications and marketing. He also holds the CPT (Certified Performance Technologist) designation from ISPI.

Allison Rossett, a longtime Professor of Educational Technology at San Diego State University, is also a consultant in performance and training systems. Rossett was selected by ASTD for its Workplace Learning and Performance award in 2002; in 2001 ISPI honored her with its highest award, Member-for-Life. A graduate of the University of Massachusetts, a native New Yorker, a ping-pong champion in her youth, and an aspiring yo yo-er, Allison offers keynote speeches, seminars, and workshops in this country and abroad. Her most recent book is *The ASTD E-Learning Handbook*. Prior award-winning books are *Beyond the Podium: Delivering Training and Performance to a Digital World*, *First Things Fast: A Handbook for Performance Analysis, Training Needs Assessment*, and *A Handbook of Job Aids*.

Nick Rushby has been working in the area of educational and training technology for over 30 years. Following a first degree in Electronic Engineering, he gained his postgraduate Diploma from Imperial College, London, in Computer Science, specializing in artificial intelligence applications in computer-assisted learning. During his career he has coordinated projects for the National Development Programme in Computer Assisted Learning, directed an international information centre for the use of computers in education and training, led multimedia training activities for PA Consulting Group, and headed the engineering team developing a novel multimedia advertising system for airports and subway environments. He has worked with a variety of clients in most business sectors and at all levels of their organizations, including consulting at board level. Nick is a Director of Conation Technologies, which carried out strategic consulting in training technologies, is the author and editor of a number of books and papers in the field, and is the editor of the *British Journal of Educational Technology*.

Harold D. Stolovitch is Professor Emeritus of Instructional and Performance Technology, Université de Montréal, and Clinical Professor of Human Performance at Work, University of Southern California. He is also a principal of HSA Learning & Performance Solutions LLC, an international firm that specializes in the application of instructional technology and human performance technology to business, industry, government, and the military. He is a former editor of *Performance Improvement Journal*, editorial board member of several professional journals, coeditor of both award-winning editions of the *Handbook of Human Performance Technology* and coauthor of the award-winning bestseller, *Telling Ain't Training*. He is coeditor and author of the new Wiley/Pfeiffer *Learning & Performance Toolkit* series. His latest book, *Training Ain't Performance*, published by ASTD, was released in May 2004. Dr. Stolovitch completed a Ph.D. and postdoctoral studies in Instructional Systems Technology at Indiana University.

Daniel Surry is an associate professor at the University of South Alabama in Mobile. He teaches in the Instructional Design & Development program, conducts and disseminates research, advises master's and Ph.D. students, and provides service to the university, the profession, and the community. He holds a Doctor of Education degree in Instructional Technology from the University of Georgia and a Master of Science in Instructional Design from the University of South Alabama. Prior to coming to USA, he was on the faculty at the University of Southern Mississippi and the University of Alabama. From 1993 to 1995 he was Instructional Technologist at California State University, Fresno. His research and consulting interests relate to change, specifically how organizations can facilitate the implementation process, and technology innovations.

Katsuaki Suzuki is Professor of the Faculty of Software and Information Science at Iwate Prefectural University, Japan. He received a M.S. and Ph.D. in Instructional Systems from Florida State University and a B.A. in Educational Technology from International Christian University, Tokyo, Japan. Dr. Suzuki serves boards of directors for Japan Society for Educational Technology (JSET) and Japan Association for Educational Media Study, and boards of editors for *JSET* and *Japan Society for Information and Systems in Education*. He is an honorary member of e-Learning Consortium Japan, and has been directing projects for Japan Broadcasting Corporation (NHK) and the Japanese Ministry of Education, among others. His research interests include instructional design models, research methodologies, and curriculum design for informatics.

Richard Van Eck is Associate Professor and Graduate Director of the Instructional Design & Technology program at the University of North Dakota (UND). He received his M.A. in English from UND, and his Ph.D. in instructional design and development from the University of South Alabama. He was on the instructional design faculty at the University of Memphis for five years, where he was also a member of the Institute for Intelligent Systems and the committee chair for the Center for Multimedia Arts in the FedEx Institute of Technology. His scholarly work includes dozens of publications and presentations focused primarily on games for learning, authoring tools, and pedagogical agent research. He has developed several multimedia learning products and games independently and as a consultant, has created nine new courses as part of the redesign of the IDT graduate program at UND, is currently developing an IDT certificate program, and is moving both online. His research interests in K–12 and corporate settings also include intelligent tutoring systems and gender and technology.

Jeroen J. G. van Merriënboer is Professor of Educational Technology and Research Program Director at the Educational Technology Expertise Center of the Open University of the Netherlands. He holds a master's degree in Psychophysiology from the Free University of Amsterdam (1984) and a Ph.D. in Instructional Technology from the University of Twente (1990). van Merriënboer specializes in cognitive architectures and instruction, instructional design for complex learning, holistic approaches to instructional design, and adaptive e-learning applications. He has published more than 100 journal articles and book chapters in the area of learning and instruction and has coedited several books on computer-based instructional design models, the design of powerful learning environments, and integrated e-learning. His prizewinning monograph *Training Complex Cognitive Skills* (1997) describes his four-component instructional design model, which offers a systematic approach to designing task environments for complex learning.

Jan Visser is president and senior researcher at the Learning Development Institute, where he has prime responsibility for the Meaning of Learning and The Scientific Mind focus areas. In addition, he is one of the directors at the International Board of Standards for Training, Performance and Instruction. He is also UNESCO's former Director for Learning Without Frontiers, a global transsectoral program of which he was the principal architect. A theoretical physicist by original vocation and training, who graduated from the Delft University of Technology in the Netherlands, he strayed into many other areas, including filmmaking and instructional design. In the latter area, he obtained his degrees from Florida State University. While broadening his interests and activities beyond the study of nature, his original passion, he developed a career that lasted more than three decades in international development, working around the globe. Dr. Visser is also a musician (who builds his own instruments) and an avid walker.

Brent G. Wilson is Professor of Information and Learning Technologies at the University of Colorado at Denver, where he coordinates the master's program and leads a doctoral lab in instructional design. Over a career spanning nearly three decades, Brent has worked to strengthen the conceptual underpinnings of instructional design practice. His work has ranged from instructional theory to human performance technology to technology adoption. Guiding questions include: What is good instruction; and, How can we promote its design and use of valuable instructional resources and learning technologies? Much of his work is informed by cognitive theories of learning, but Brent has recently focused on broadening IDT foundations to give more prominence to issues of practice, value, and the aesthetic.

Index